Swanberg, W. A.

Pulitzer

DATE DUE

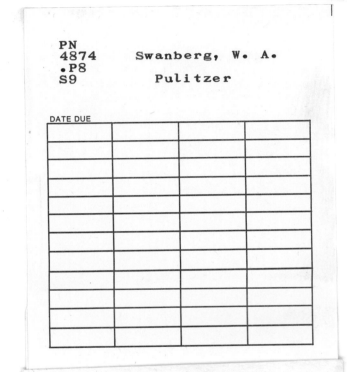

PULITZER

PICTURE CREDITS

Brown Brothers: 1, 7, 15, 17, 38, 39, 40, 42, 43, 44, 45
The Museum of the Confederacy, Richmond, Va.: 31
Culver Pictures, Inc.: 11, 12, 13, 22, 26, 41
Library of Congress: 9, 20, 27
National Archives: 6 (U. S. Signal Corps Photo, Brady Collection)
The New-York Historical Society: 8
The New York Public Library: 10 (Picture Collection), 18, 21 (From *The Empire State in Three Centuries* edited by General D. H. Bruce. Century History Co., N. Y. 1901), *Judge*, 1900, 23
Courtesy, Mrs. William Scoville Moore: 3
Courtesy, Mrs. Ralph Pulitzer: 28
Courtesy, Mrs. E. R. Quesada: 5
St. Louis Post-Dispatch: 2, 33, 46, 48
Scribner Art Files: 16, 24, 25
Courtesy, the daughters of Don C. Seitz: 37
Courtesy, Standard Oil Company (N. J.): 14
Courtesy, Mrs. William C. Weir: 4, 19, 29, 30, 32, 34, 35, 47
United Press International Photos: 36

PULITZER

by W. A. Swanberg

CHARLES SCRIBNER'S SONS

NEW YORK

PERMISSIONS

The author thanks the following for kind permission to quote extracts from the copyrighted works listed.

E. P. Dutton & Co., Inc.: *An Adventure with a Genius* by Alleyne Ireland (1914); Princeton University Press: *Pulitzer's Post-Dispatch, 1878-1883* by Julian Rammelkamp (1967); Harper & Row, Inc.: *The Story of a Page* by John L. Heaton (1913); The Bobbs-Merrill Co., Inc.: *Exit Laughing* by Irvin C. Cobb (1941); Alfred A. Knopf, Inc.: *This Is the Life!* by Walt McDougall (1926); J. B. Lippincott Co.: *The Gentleman and the Tiger: The Autobiography of George B. McClellan Jr.*, edited by Harold C. Syrett (1956); The Meredith Press: *From Then Till Now* by James Barnes (1934); Macdonald & Co., Ltd.: *Velvet and Vinegar* by Norman Thwaites (Grayson & Grayson, 1932); and Vanguard Press, Inc.: *Joseph Pulitzer and His World* by James W. Barrett (1941).

A-1.72[C]

Printed in the United States of America
Library of Congress Catalog Card Number 67-23695
SBN 684-10587-X (Trade cloth)
SBN 684-12818-7 (Trade paper, SL)

For Sara and John

Contents

II. SENSATIONALIST

III. TRIUMPH

Contents

V. WAR WITH HEARST

VI. THE SCHOOLMASTER

Illustrations

Key to the *World* Code

The Pulitzer code used for secrecy in communication filled a volume of some 250 pages containing at least 20,000 coded names and terms. This brief digest gives only those encountered in this book.

NAMES

ANDES: Joseph Pulitzer
CYBIRA: Ralph Pulitzer
VANDALIA: Joseph Pulitzer Jr.
ANFRACTO: John Norris
CANTABO: William H. Merrill
COIN: Dumont Clarke
DART: Ernest Chamberlin
DESTINY: Mrs. Ralph Pulitzer
GADROON: J. Pierpont Morgan
GAITER: James Gordon Bennett
GAMMA: Horatio W. Seymour
GAMMON: Boss Charles F. Murphy
GEORGE: Bradford Merrill
GLUTINOUS: Theodore Roosevelt
GORGON: Boss Richard Croker
GOSLING: Democratic party
GRAMERCY: Admiral George Dewey
GRAMMARITE: Frank I. Cobb
GRASP: Foster Coates
GRAVING: Grover Cleveland
GREGORY: Judge Alton B. Parker
GRENADE: John H. Tennant
GREYHOUND: Tammany Hall
GRINDING: Nelson Hersh
GUESS: John A. Dillon
GUIDANCE: George Cary Eggleston
GUIDELESS: Morrill Goddard
GUILDER: William Jennings Bryan
GUINEA: William McKinley
GULCH: Don C. Seitz
GUMBO: Pomeroy Burton
GUMBOIL: David Graham Phillips
GUSH: William Randolph Hearst
GYRATE: Caleb Van Hamm

HORACE: Arthur Brisbane

LASSO: Alfred Butes

LOS: Solomon S. Carvalho (also named GRANDEE)

MACAROON: William B. Hornblower

MACERATE: Whitelaw Reid

MALARIA: Republican party

MEDIOCRITY: Levi P. Morton

MELON: Woodrow Wilson

MOHICAN: Charles M. Lincoln

PINCH: Charles S. Chapin

PROMULGATE: James M. Tuohy

RAKE: Charles Evans Hughes

ROTUND: William Howard Taft

SAWPIT: George B. M. Harvey

SOLID: J. Angus Shaw

VALUATION: William Van Benthuysen

VOLEMA: Florence D. White

BUSINESS TERMS

SENIOR: The Morning World

JUNIOR: The Evening World

SENIORITY: The Sunday World

GENUINE: All three Worlds

GRASPING: St. Louis Post-Dispatch

CURATE: Circulation

GEOGRAPHY: New York Times

GEOLOGIST: New York Herald

GERANIUM: New York Journal

GESTURE: New York Tribune

GLOAT: Cash

GRANDAM: City Editor

GRUESOME: Managing Editor

NAPIER: Deficit

NAPOLEON: Expenses

NELSON: Net Earnings

NERO: Gross Earnings

POTASH: Advertising

PIGEON: Loss

PIGGERY: Gain

RAT: Combination of six advertisers

SOCIABLE: Your right Ear was good

SOCRATIC: Your left Ear was good

SODIUM: Your right Ear was bad

SOJOURN: Your left Ear was bad

I

Angry Young Man

Chapter 1

Westward Ho!

I. THE GOAT OF COMPANY L

As one of the many bands played "When This Cruel War Is Over," and the Army of the Potomac began the close-ranked procession that would take it seven full hours to pass the White House, there was universal relief that it *was* over. The sky was blue, new roses stirred in a gentle breeze, and spectators thronged the avenue and hung from bunting-bedecked windows, from lampposts and trees. The grand review was a noisy symbol of the end of slaughter and the beginning of a peace no one could foreknow but which must assuredly be wonderful. Drums rattling fit to shiver windowpanes . . . bugles pealing with a volume menacing to eardrums . . . a multitude of school children, free for the day, pressing the curb in excited rows, shouting, tossing flowers at the heroes. How lucky they were not to have been born ten years earlier!

When Sheridan's troopers clattered up the avenue, Joseph Pulitzer was one of the riders far back in the First New York Lincoln Cavalry—probably the unlikeliest-looking soldier in that vast sea of blue. Recently turned 18, he was six feet two and one-half inches tall, a scrawny beanpole with a hooked blade of a nose, an up-jutting chin that seemed determined to meet the nose, an enormous Adam's apple, and weak eyes peering through cheap spectacles. Although he spoke Hungarian, German and French, he had picked up only a smattering of English, his regiment being largely German. He had lied about his age to get in, and had bitterly regretted it. During his eight months of service he had easily been one of Sheridan's least dashing men. Perhaps he had shared in the skirmish at Antioch and one or two others—he seldom talked about it later—but most of his time was spent as goat of Company L. Pulitzer was one of those odd-looking, peculiar individuals soldiers instinctively seize on as a butt of hazing and practical jokes. Brilliant, haughty, emotional, eccentric, he had none of the patience and flexible humor required to withstand such treatment and ultimately win acceptance. For him, war had been precisely what Sherman called it. Enraged, he had eventually struck a non-com tormentor and might have been in trouble had not one Captain Ramsey, who admired Pulitzer's chess game and needed a partner, interceded for him. In the later months of the war, when Sheridan began circling around Lee, Pulitzer's company stayed in the Shenandoah and he had finished his time quietly as orderly for Major Richard Hinton.

It was over now. The riders were so close that he gave full attention to his horse and did not even see the official reviewing stand. "[All I saw was] the man and the horse on either side of me," he said later. "Not another thing. But how sore my knees became riding in close formation and pressed against the others in line." [1] The avenue had been sprinkled overnight, but the pounding of feet and of horses' hoofs raised a fine dust that stung the nostrils and the eyes. He did not see the incident at 15th Street when a pretty girl tossed a nosegay at the long-locked General Custer, so frightening his horse that the general was almost unseated, careering for two blocks before he got the animal under control. He did not see the huge sign on the Capitol: THE ONLY NATIONAL DEBT WE CAN NEVER PAY IS THE DEBT WE OWE TO THE VICTORIOUS UNION SOLDIERS.

Nor did he see Lincoln, of course. Only a few weeks earlier the President's body in its coffin had been borne down this same avenue, and it was Andrew Johnson up there in the flag-festooned reviewing stand with Stanton, Grant, Meade and the rest.

So Pulitzer passed by, and as that 23rd day of May ended he began to discover that it was not over after all. The army had red tape to unwind. Not until June 26 did his command leave Washington, and it was July 7 when he was paid his final $13 a month in New York and freed.

II. UNBURIED CORPSES

Peace also had its problems. New York swarmed with returned soldiers, many of them unable to find work. Pulitzer, still wearing his uniform as did hundreds of others, was at a disadvantage in job-hunting because of his rudimentary English. As his army savings dwindled, he haunted City Hall Park, often sprawling on a bench and gazing across at busy Park Row, where Horace Greeley, James Gordon Bennett and Manton Marble were mighty names and where the name of Joseph Pulitzer would ultimately surpass them.

Already New Yorkers were weary of the unemployed soldiers. Pulitzer, who had a taste for luxury even when pinched, occasionally went into

French's Hotel at Park Row and Frankfort Street to have his shoes shined. One day the porter asked him to leave because frayed blue uniforms sullied the hotel's refinement and annoyed fashionable guests. Pulitzer would one day have the pleasure of buying French's Hotel, tearing it down piece by piece and erecting there a $2,000,000 skyscraper. Even now he could have written his mother in Budapest for help, but pride forbade this. Instead, he went to New Bedford in the hope of finding work on a whaler, learned that whaling was moribund, and returned to New York with very little cash left. He was flat broke around October 1, sleeping in wagons on cobblestoned side streets, when he decided to journey by side-door Pullman to St. Louis, a city where there were plenty of Germans. He got 75 cents for his one prized possession, a fine silk handkerchief, and was off.

And so the young Joseph Pulitzer crossed a part of the broad land he had helped to save—New Jersey, Pennsylvania, Ohio, Indiana, Illinois—only a third of the way across this unfamiliar nation and yet as far as if he had traveled from Budapest to Vienna, Munich and Paris to reach London. Someone had stolen his army overcoat, and he shivered as the boxcars rattled through cornfields. In Budapest he could live in comparative luxury, but he had turned his back on that security, for he hated his stepfather. However, he carried a miniature of his mother's beautiful face with him always. The lonely locomotive whistle ahead, the limitless fields stretching off in the moonlight, the occasional sleepy villages—all must have been reminders of the break, the renunciation of the Old World and the casting of his lot with the New, unfriendly though it was.[2]

He had a half-humorous fancy that the number 10 was lucky for him, perhaps because he was born on April 10. The spell seemed broken when he arrived in East St. Louis on October 10 in a chill rain, penniless, hungry and soaked to the skin, to discover that he had the broad Mississippi to cross before he could reach St. Louis. "The lights of St. Louis looked like a promised land to me," he recalled. The operator of the Wiggins ferry spoke German, and Pulitzer worked out his fare by firing the boiler for several round trips, roasting in front and freezing in back. In St. Louis, German seemed as serviceable as in Munich. He found the office of the weekly Westliche Post, the leading German newspaper, where he saw an advertisement for a mule hostler at Benton Barracks. Next day he walked four miles to the barracks, got the job and held it for just two days, being revolted by the food but more particularly by the whims of the mules, saying afterward, "The man who has not cared for sixteen mules does not know what work and troubles are." [3]

Thereafter he subsisted on a succession of jobs of such uncertain tenure as to suggest that he was not highly employable, being indeed too skinny for heavy work and too proud and temperamental to take orders not issued with some degree of kindness. Far from being hurt by the war, St.

Louis had profited from the $180,000,000 spent by the federal quartermaster there and by an influx of new industries that made the city thrive. Often with intervals of unemployment, Pulitzer worked as gate-operator at the ferry slip, deckhand on a packet to Memphis, construction laborer, stevedore on the river docks, and hack-driver. For a time he was a waiter at Tony Faust's famous restaurant on Fifth Street, a place frequented by the erudite Scotch pedagogue Thomas Davidson and fellow members of the St. Louis Philosophical Society including the German-born Henry C. Brokmeyer, a nephew of Bismarck, and the Yale-educated William Torrey Harris. Under Brokmeyer's shabbiness and profanity lurked the philosopher who had translated Hegel. His companions were equally learned, and the fascinated Pulitzer "would hang on Brokmeyer's thunderous words, even as he served them their pretzels and beer." [4] This privilege ended when a tray slipped from his hand to deluge a patron, sending him job-hunting again. Thrifty, he saved money to tide him over the lean periods and spent his free time at the Mercantile Library at Fifth and Locust, studying English and reading omnivorously.

On one sad occasion he and several dozen other men paid five dollars each to a fast-talking promoter who promised them well-paying jobs on a Louisiana sugar plantation. They boarded a malodorous little steamboat, which let them off through a ruse some 30 miles south of the city. When the boat churned away without them, it dawned on them that they had been swindled. They walked back to St. Louis, where Pulitzer wrote an account of the fraud and was delighted when it was accepted by the Westliche Post—apparently his first published news story.[5]

His favorite haunt was the four-story building at Fifth and Market Streets housing the German newspaper edited by the kindly Dr. Emil Preetorius. There his halting English was no handicap. Now and then he was permitted to write minor squibs for the paper. The building also contained the offices of the attorneys William Patrick and Charles Philip Johnson, and the surgeon Joseph Nash McDowell, the latter recently returned after administering to Confederate wounded during the war. Patrick and Johnson, who called Pulitzer "Shakespeare" because of his remarkable profile, tided him over one workless stretch by giving him errands to run and legal papers to serve, while his acquaintance with Dr. McDowell proved dangerously helpful when cholera struck St. Louis in 1866. First noticed in August, it spread so swiftly that there were 768 deaths in the second week of the month and 918 in the third. Out of a population of some 260,000, at least 70,000 fled the city, while those who stayed fought panic and relied on illusory preventives. ". . . A gentleman who has travelled in the West Indies recommends six drops of oil of vitriol (sulphuric acid) in a tumbler full of water twice a day," the Missouri Republican reported, and suggested other safeguards: "half a teaspoonful of flour of sulphur put into each stocking," and "A teaspoonful of finely pulverized charcoal taken three times a day is also a very good preventive." [6]

Chicago, untouched by the plague, scattered handbills on all railroad lines warning immigrants against the Missouri rival. An English traveler, William Hepworth Dixon, who arrived at this unpropitious moment, noted, ". . . the council had ceased to make daily returns of the dead, the number of which could only be guessed from the march of funerals through the streets. . . . Fires were burning in every street; lime was being forced into every gutter; no one dared to enter a public conveyance; horrible tales . . . were whispered in your ears at table, where you heard that every officer had flown from the cemeteries, even the felons and murderers who had been promised their pardon on condition of interring the victims of cholera; that the unburied corpses were heaped together in the island. . . . The death-bells were tolling day and night." [7]

Through Dr. McDowell's influence Pulitzer was made warden of Arsenal Island, where many of the dead were buried—a post even freed criminals fled. He helped in the burials as well as the bookwork until the plague, after killing 3,527 St. Louisans, passed in October and his undelectable job ended. Now his attorney friends aided him again, steering him into a position with the projected Atlantic & Pacific Railroad (later the St. Louis & San Francisco), one of the land-grabbers of that opportunistic era.

With a Negro aide he rode south into wild Ozark country where many surly settlers refused to believe that the Civil War had ended, charged with the duty of recording the railroad's charter in the 12 counties it would pass through. Here one of his astonishing gifts came into play—a prodigious memory that marked him throughout his life. He learned the complicated articles of incorporation by heart and inscribed them in the county records from memory. Once, while fording the flood-swollen Gasconade River, Pulitzer and the Negro were swept from their horses, the Negro drowning, while Pulitzer, an excellent swimmer, barely made it to shore.[8]

His successful completion of these duties so impressed Johnson and Patrick that they gave him desk space and he made use of their library while he studied law. Bursting with ambition, he read law books as if he were renting them by the hour. On March 6, 1867, he renounced his allegiance to Austria and became an American citizen. He became a fixture at the Mercantile Library, forming a friendship with one of the librarians, Udo Brachvogel, that would last out his life. Often he visited the chess room in the library, where his remarkably aggressive game attracted the attention of another player, Carl Schurz, who would exert a lasting influence over his career.

The 38-year-old Schurz had already survived adventures that would have filled a dozen ordinary lifetimes. Educated at Bonn, he fought in the

German revolution of 1849, was captured and imprisoned, staged a hair-raising escape, fled to England and then America, where his conspicuous abilities soon led him into politics. His support of Lincoln in 1860 was rewarded by his appointment as Minister to Spain. Unhappy in Madrid because he felt it his duty to join the war against slavery, he resigned his comfortable post, returned and fought through the Civil War to emerge as a major general. After service as Washington correspondent for the New York Tribune, he arrived in St. Louis in April 1867 to become co-editor with Dr. Preetorius of the prosperous Republican Westliche Post. To Pulitzer the tall, slim, professorial Schurz was an inspiring emblem of American democracy, of the success attainable by a foreign-born citizen through his own energies and skills.

With Preetorius, also a veteran of the German revolution, Schurz formed the *Deutsche Gesellschaft,* devoted to aiding the flood of Germans arriving in St. Louis. They gave Pulitzer the secretaryship of the society, a part-time post at a small stipend that nevertheless aided him in his law studies. He was admitted to the bar, apparently in 1868, but his youth, his imperfect English and odd appearance kept important clients at a distance. He struggled along with the execution of minor papers and the collecting of debts. After almost three years in St. Louis, the new-world promise had failed of fulfillment and he was still poor and shabby—an annoyance rather than a sorrow, for his belief in himself was boundless. He was delighted when, later in 1868, the Westliche Post needed a reporter and he was offered the job. "I could not believe it," he said later. "I, the unknown, the luckless, almost a boy of the streets, selected for such a responsibility—it all seemed like a dream." [9]

The Post, under the vigorous Radical Republican editorship of Schurz and Preetorius, had become the most influential German-language paper west of New York. The 21-year-old Pulitzer, fortune's flounderer, had at last found the medium that would make him famous.

III. SEARCH FOR INDEPENDENCE

Far from being a part of the horde of poverty-stricken immigrants who came to America for a better life, Pulitzer had come for a worse one, solely to find independence. He was born April 10, 1847, in Mako, Hungary, a thriving market town near the Rumanian border, 125 miles southeast of Budapest. His father, Philip Pulitzer, was a cultivated Magyar-Jew grain dealer; his mother, born Louise Berger, an Austro-German beauty and a Catholic. She had three brothers who were officers in the Austrian army, infallibly a sign of "good family." There were four children, of whom the eldest, Louis, died early, leaving Joseph and his brother Albert, four years younger, and the still younger sister Irma. By

1853 Philip Pulitzer was prosperous enough to retire and move his family to Budapest, where the children were educated by private tutors and were expected to learn French and German. Evidently the mother's Catholic influence was strong, for Albert was intended for the priesthood.

But both sons were headstrong individualists, and Joseph in particular seethed with impulses and enthusiasms too powerful for any parent to curb. They would remain so. Nervous, excitable, he grew so fast that his gauntness was a worry and, as he later said humorously, he had to stoop over when his mother wished to box his ears. He was still a schoolboy when his father died of a heart ailment. His mother's remarriage to Max Blau, a Budapest merchant, made him unhappy. So little is known of these early years that one is tempted to guess at the influences that shaped in him a personality amazing both in its flaws and splendors, its most prominent characteristic being an ambition of such Napoleonic dimensions that it would ultimately wreck his health even as it sharpened his mind. Did the death of brother Louis, the death of his father, the trouble with his stepfather, leave psychic scars? Was there some atavistic explosive in his mixed ancestry—the ferocity of the old Magyar tribes, the intellect and energy of the Jews, the orderliness of the Germans?

Before he was 17 he struck out for independence, a quality that would always be strong in him. Early in 1864, excited by Bismarck's subtle moves against Schleswig-Holstein, he applied for a commission in the Austrian army, doubtless hoping for help from his officer uncles. He was rejected on three grounds—his age, his poor eyesight and fragile physique. Undeterred, he traveled to Paris and sought enrollment in the French foreign legion in Mexico, where Louis Napoleon was supporting the Archduke Maximilian on his uneasy throne. Again he was barred, for the same reasons. His next stop was London, where his hope to enlist in the British army in India was similarly crushed. Joseph Pulitzer, the boy who would not take No for an answer, moved on to Hamburg and tried to ship out as a sailor, only to meet another firm refusal.

In Hamburg, however, were agents seeking recruits for the Union army in America's Civil War, so anxious for federal bounties that they would accept anything that could walk. Here at last was an army that would take him. Soon Joseph was packed with a swarm of emigrants aboard a grubby ship that made the Atlantic crossing and reached Boston sometime in August or September, 1864. He wanted to collect his own bounty rather than have it benefit the recruiting agent. In Boston harbor he dived overboard at night, swam to shore, took a train to New York and was enrolled in the Lincoln Cavalry September 30, to undergo an experience that forever cured him of soldierly inclinations.

His younger brother Albert at 16 showed the same Pulitzer independence by following him to America and joining him in St. Louis in 1867.

Their sister Irma had died recently in Budapest—a sorrow Joseph would remember in naming one of his own daughters. Albert too was brilliant and ambitious, "writing tragedies at thirteen." He had found Hungary "too slow for him, and besides an illiberal sentiment made either social or political progress impossible to a Jew." [10] He was a true Pulitzer on another score, for he had spent 12 hours a day mastering English. Evidently through Joseph's intercession with Thomas Davidson, who taught Greek at the high school, Albert became a German instructor, teaching students hardly younger than himself. He stayed only a year, and by 1868, when Joseph began work with the Westliche Post, Albert was teaching German to "a class of young ladies" at the high school at Leavenworth, Kansas.

Joseph hurled himself into his reporting duties with an attitude of impetuous attack, working 16 hours a day—from 10 A.M. to 2 A.M.—as if the time were too short. His rampant nose, scarecrow frame, guttural English, shabby clothing and excitability made him a laughingstock in the St. Louis news fraternity somewhat as he had been in the army. One colleague wrote of his "singular appearance and peculiar garb," but also of his "unquenchable thirst for news," and said he "had to run the gauntlet of many a quip and jibe." Wiseacres called him "pull-it-sir," with special attention to his nose, and he was also known as Joey the German or Joey the Jew.[11] But the Post was ardently promoting the candidacy of General Grant for President, and Pulitzer's new post opened doors for him. He came to know Schurz and Preetorius intimately, becoming a special favorite of Mrs. Preetorius. He joined the Philosophical Society, which met at Brokmeyer's law office, and frequented the German bookstore of Fritz Roeslein on Fourth Street, the haunt of many intellectual spirits. Among his new friends was the Vienna-born Joseph Keppler, the actor and caricaturist who was even then planning a German humor magazine, *Die Vehme*. Most important of all was the red-headed, Aberdeen-born Professor Thomas Davidson, seven years older than Pulitzer, a truth-seeking heathen and rationalist. Davidson took a liking for the young man with the enormous hunger for education, and the two exchanged regular visits devoted to philosophy and learning.

This was one of the fruitful friendships of Pulitzer's life. Davidson glowed with such a radiance of good will that at least one perfect stranger who met him on the street "was compelled . . . to doff his cap and bow to him." A linguist commanding five languages, he conversed with Pulitzer in German, French and English. Once a pious Presbyterian, he had become so opposed to formal religion that his fiancée in Scotland, May McCombie, finally heeded the warnings of her clergyman father and rejected him. Venerating Aristotle, logical thinking and clear expression, he preached his belief that the highest good for man is the complete and habitual exercise of his full potentialities, the constant effort for usefulness. He pitied and scorned the "respectables" who felt their duty performed and their lives fulfilled through mere passive honesty and legality. He praised the doers, the fighters, the reformers—admirable even if mistaken, perfect if in the right. Pulitzer, a born reformer, had found an inspiring counselor. Though chary of extending intimate friendship, he would remain devoted to Davidson as long as he lived.

In this era of ferocious materialism he was lucky to sit at the feet of the idealistic Davidson, Schurz and Preetorius. Who could match the gifted Schurz, with his love for true democracy, his passion for public service, his effective literary style, his ability to grip a crowd with an oration either in German or English? Who but Schurz could tell of libertarian battles in Germany, farming in Wisconsin, talks with Lincoln, Civil War campaigns—then sit down at the piano and play Schumann or Mozart with almost professional finish? Kindly, benevolent, he had attributes of political greatness but was cursed by what party hacks would call excessive purity, a rejection of expediency. In the fall of '68 he had stumped for Grant in Illinois, Indiana and Ohio, and with the general's election he became one of the leading Republicans in Missouri, a hero to the Germans. In January 1869 he was elected United States Senator from Missouri although he had been in the state less than two years—a development that gave Pulitzer an example of quick attainment of political power and also moved him up one notch in the hierarchy at the Westliche Post.

Representing the Post at the small state capitol in Jefferson City, he saw for the first time the workings of the state legislature, the compromises, the deals, the ever-present lobbyists with money to spend. "Mr. Pulitzer's chief ambition," a colleague wrote, ". . . seemed to be to root out public abuses and expose evildoers." Reformist activity on the part of this callow beanpole who had the nerve to question hoary legislative procedures naturally aroused ire, and he suffered the ridicule that had become part of his life. Yet some recognized his talents, among them the respected Henry Brokmeyer, who said, ". . . They think because he trundles about with himself a big cobnose . . . and bullfrog eyes that he has no sense; but I tell you he possesses greater dialectical ability than all of them put together . . . mark me, he is now engaged in the making of a greater man than . . . Editor Preetorius, or even Schurz." [12]

On December 14, 1869, Pulitzer attended the Republican meeting at the St. Louis *Turnhalle* on Tenth Street, where party leaders sought a candidate to fill the legislative vacancy caused by the resignation of the Democrat John Terry. Their choice was the rising young attorney Chester H. Krum. When Krum declined, they settled on Pulitzer, nominating him unanimously, forgetting that he was only 22, three years under the required age. The Post said the nomination was greeted with "loud applause" and that Pulitzer responded with "a few obviously heartfelt words," explaining that he did not seek the honor but would campaign in earnest. The Missouri Democrat commented approvingly:

"We suppose that Mr. Joseph Pulitzer was greatly surprised by the nomination, since he is one of those people who never seek nor expect office, although he is certainly not the last to have earned one. He has an impetuous temperament and certain characteristics which can make those who do not know him blind to his good qualities." Without listing those "certain characteristics" the Democrat added that he was "very familiar with city affairs," had served in the Union army, was a solid Radical and was "a thoroughly upright young man with spirit, education, and definite talent." [13]

It must be borne in mind that political shifts had played semantic havoc with the names of the two leading English-language newspapers, and that the Missouri Democrat was a Republican paper whereas the Missouri Republican upheld the Democrats. Pulitzer's Democratic opponent was Samuel A. Grantham, a tobacconist whom the Post attacked as of doubtful eligibility because he had served in the Confederate army. The older Grantham had a clear edge in everything except energy. Pulitzer harangued street meetings, called personally on the voters, and exhibited such sincerity along with his oddities that he pumped a half-amused excitement into a campaign that was normally lethargic. The Democrat as well as his own Westliche Post gave him fatherly support. A snowstorm on December 21 kept the vote down, and it was a total surprise when he defeated Grantham by 209 to 147. It never occurred to him that he was under age, nor did it become known to the legislature, and he was seated as a state representative in Jefferson City at the session beginning January 5, 1870.

He later recalled this as the proudest day of his life. To men such as Schurz, Preetorius, Davidson and Pulitzer, who remembered vividly the autocracies of Europe, American democracy was not merely another form of government. It was something unique and precious, a huge stride in civilization, a hope for the oppressed not only in America but all over the world, a gift to be treasured and fought for, a blessing never to be taken for granted. To the emotional Pulitzer, for all his vein of materialism, the search for democracy already served as a substitute for the religious devotion that had no place in his life. He had no hostility toward religion. Like Davidson, he was an enlightened heretic, declining to ally with any individual creed, and there seems no record that he attended either the mass or the synagogue.

Chapter 2

Bitten by Politics

I. MURDEROUS INTENT

In sleepy Jefferson City, whose main activities were politics and the supervision of the convicts in the state prison, Pulitzer drew the five dollars a day paid legislators and saved money by rooming with a fellow St. Louis member, the German-born Anthony Ittner, on High Street. He wore two hats, still representing the Westliche Post as well as his constituents—a duality some members frowned on, but he was too interested in newspaper work to drop it. Now he had his chance to put in practice Davidson's doctrine of the useful life, the dedication to betterment which came naturally to him and had only been put into clear definition by the Scotchman.

It could seldom be said that he merely supported or opposed legislation, since to his ardent nature each measure had to be weighed in all its ramifications and then either assailed as one attacks a thug or upheld as if for salvation. Like his political mentor, Senator Schurz, he was disgusted with the bloody-shirt prolongation of Civil War hatred exploited by his own Republican party in order to trample the prostrate Democrats. Abolish all disqualifications for voting—color or past disloyalty! Let every citizen cast his ballot! His initial important vote favored the adoption of the Fifteenth Amendment, which gave the franchise to Negroes and was ratified by the legislature January 10. Soon thereafter he struck his first official blow against his lifelong enemy, corruption. St. Louis had a dual government in which the seven-judge County Court held sweeping powers untouched by the mayor and city council, with authority to appoint all county officials and through them enjoying control over taxes and disbursements. Notoriously venal, the court winked at wealthy tax-dodgers, manipulated city-county funds and arranged for its own judges to make illicit profits on public construction. One of the judges had furnished materials for the recently completed county poorhouse, and as chairman of the project had been in the pleasant position of sending himself bills which he approved promptly and rendered himself payment out of the public treasury.

Pulitzer, who had earlier assailed these practices in the Post, sought as a legislator to stop them. Now a new insane asylum estimated at $500,000 was planned for St. Louis County, another plum for the judges, with the contract slated to go to one of their favorites, Captain Edward Augustine of St. Louis. Augustine was also Superintendent of Registration for the county. It was quite apart from the issue that Pulitzer disliked the very existence of such an office as Superintendent of Registration, which had been established throughout the state by the vengefully Radical Missouri postwar constitution. The original duty of these officials had been to disfranchise anyone connected with the rebellion, and now, five years after the war, they still contrived to keep power in Republican hands by denying the vote to thousands of white Democrats. Although Pulitzer was a Republican, he deplored the Radicals' ruthless abuse of power. This was a factor in his disapproval of Captain Augustine, but his basic aim was to prevent the plundering of the treasury. By mid-January he was drafting a bill to reform the County Court.

His measure, calculated to destroy long-established political prerogatives, aroused the powerful opposition of all beneficiaries of the system. Augustine and several other lobbyists hurried to Jefferson City to exert influence against it. Meanwhile Pulitzer advocated his bill in dispatches to the Post, noting that Augustine was in town in the interest of the County Court and suggesting that his motives were worthy of scrutiny. "I would gladly raise the question: Who pays the expenses?" he wrote.[1] Augustine, interpreting this as a reflection of his honor, told Pulitzer's friend Theodore Welge that he intended to insult the young jackanapes to his face. Welge passed the word to Pulitzer, who perhaps reflected on Augustine's bull neck and powerful physique as contrasted with his own muscular negligibility.

At about 7:00 on the evening of January 27, Pulitzer entered Schmidt's Hotel, a rendezvous of legislators, to attend a meeting of the St. Louis delegation. Already gathered in the parlor was a sizable group of assemblymen along with others including Captain Augustine and Wallace Gruelle, a reporter for the St. Louis Dispatch and a friend of Pulitzer's.

Augustine advanced on Pulitzer, pointed a finger at his great nose, shouted that his statements in the Post were falsehoods and called him a "damned liar."

"Mr. Pulitzer," says one account, "cautioned Mr. Augustine against using such strong language." He walked away, whereupon Gruelle said,

"Pulitzer, why didn't you knock that man down when he called you a damned liar? You must keep up the *esprit de corps,* man."

"Oh, it's all about the County Court," Pulitzer muttered, and left the hotel. He headed for his room a few blocks away. His roommate Ittner was there when he arrived, highly excited, saying that Augustine had insulted him and that he intended to "return the compliment with interest." Ittner saw him ransacking his suitcase but did not notice that he took out his four-barreled Sharp's pistol. Pulitzer hurried out. As he reached the hotel he met Gruelle, who was on his way to the telegraph office.

"If you'll wait a little while, you'll have an item," he said.

Gruelle replied that he would be back shortly. There seems no doubt that Pulitzer, in blind rage, intended to kill Augustine. According to the Missouri Democrat, a paper friendly to Pulitzer, he strode into the parlor, "again approached Augustine and commenced anew his conversation in an insulting manner. Augustine called him a puppy, when Pulitzer called him a liar." Augustine started toward him as if to break his bones. Pulitzer suddenly drew the pistol and aimed it at his midriff. Startled bystanders shouted in warning, but Augustine threw himself at the younger man. The pistol exploded twice as the burly lobbyist bore Pulitzer to the floor with a crash. Luckily, he had deflected the weapon so that one bullet struck him below the knee and the second ripped into the floor.[2]

Schmidt's Hotel had never seen such excitement. Legislators dived into the scramble, snatched Pulitzer's pistol, pulled away the bleeding, cursing Augustine and called a doctor. Despite some muttering against Pulitzer, who had cut his head in the mêlée, no one detained him as he left to return to his room. A policeman soon arrived, arrested him and escorted him along with Ittner to the city magistrate, with whom Ittner posted bond, and Pulitzer was released. In police court next morning he was fined five dollars and costs of $11.50 for breach of the peace, but he was also arraigned on the far more serious state charge of assault with intent to kill.

Although Augustine's flesh wound was minor, that was sheer luck. Pistols were common personal accessories at the time, but it was felt that Pulitzer had violated the code governing their use, and the usually friendly Missouri Democrat said, "the act is generally declared one of shameless and murderous intent." Even Gruelle, who admired Pulitzer and tried to make light of the affair in the Dispatch, admitted, "His case may be bad enough in its best aspects, but I cannot see the necessity of making it worse than it really is." His case was truly a bad one unless Augustine had produced a pistol in the second hotel encounter. Here the contemporary accounts are vague, most of them failing to mention any gun in the captain's hand and suggesting that Pulitzer cut his head on striking the floor, and yet one of them saying that "Augustine struck

Pulitzer on the head with a Derringer, or some other kind of pistol . . ." Pulitzer himself years later insisted that his adversary whipped out a pistol and crashed it on his head.

Sentiment was so clearly against him that he published a statement "To the Public" in the Westliche Post saying, "All I want is the establishment of the truth . . ."

Immediately after he introduced his bill, he wrote, Augustine had stopped him in the capitol and uttered "highly inflammatory remarks." Knowing that Augustine would be at the Schmidt's Hotel meeting, that he invariably carried not only a revolver but brass knuckles and that he had "the temperament of a bear" [*"Bären-Natur"*] as well as enormous strength, Pulitzer explained, he naturally took along his pistol for self-defense. When the two men met in the hotel, Augustine shouted, "I want to tell you in clear and simple English that you are a damned liar and a puppy." He then raised his arm, holding a "yellow, gleaming instrument," whereupon Pulitzer shot him. The statement ended, "I desire only that each one put himself for a moment in a similar circumstance and in my place, and then ask, who will throw the first stone." [3]

Pulitzer's account is obviously evasive, the effort of a humiliated young man to put the best light on actions of which he was ashamed. It dodges the ten-minute interval during which he rushed back to his room to get his weapon—an interval which, as a lawyer, he knew to be highly significant, refuting any argument of self-defense. Had the "yellow, gleaming instrument" which Augustine held in his hand indeed been a gun, Pulitzer surely would have said so, and when one takes into account the general disapproval of his conduct one must surmise that the captain held nothing more lethal than brass knuckles or possibly even a heavy gold Masonic ring.

The affair demonstrated more clearly than his wartime striking of a sergeant that injured pride could make Pulitzer explode emotionally. Yet there were extenuations. Augustine may well have been the maddening climax of frustrations that had tormented Pulitzer since he came to America—the indignities in the army that had continued in some measure in St. Louis, the failures and poverty, the taunts about his spindling frame, his accent, his nose. Above all, Augustine represented political corruption, the robbery of the people.

Next day in the legislature, a resolution asked the appointment of a committee to investigate the affray. Cooler assemblymen pointed out that such a step might set a dangerous precedent and result in the investigation of legislators who indulged in a bottle of wine or fondled a pretty woman, but the resolution was defeated only by 58 to 42. Yet Pulitzer had firm friends. His old benefactor Charles Philip Johnson volunteered to defend him in the assault charge, and Johnson succeeded in postponing the case for months while feelings calmed. Best of all, Pulitzer's bill passed, reducing the powers of the County Court and depriving Augustine of his contract. His embarrassment over the affair did not inhibit his work for reform. In March he supported a group of liberal Republicans in a strong though futile effort to extend the voting franchise to former Confederates, and on March 24 his lone term in the legislature ended.

II. BREAKING WITH GRANT

Meanwhile the man of Appomattox, whom Schurz, Preetorius and Pulitzer had supported so ardently, had shown alarming ineptitude. At his vast inaugural ball in 1869, the cloakroom was so disorganized that hundreds had to leave without their wraps—a sorry harbinger of government under Grant. Some of his Cabinet appointments had incensed even friendly senators, including his naming of the millionaire A. T. Stewart, a principal donor of Grant's $65,000 house, as Secretary of the Treasury. Discomfited when informed that Stewart was legally ineligible, the President had given the post to George Boutwell. He had hobnobbed with the likes of Jim Fisk and Jay Gould and had seen these opportunists come close to wrecking Wall Street on Black Friday. He had put a pack of his relatives, some of them intriguers, on the public payroll. He had permitted Radical repression of the South. He had shown an innocent willingness to accept expensive gifts without inquiring into the motives of the givers. Ignoring sage congressional leaders, he had instituted government by crony, surrounding himself with appointive officers of dubious qualifications, some of whom attained great power. Easily the most sinister of these was the debonair, auburn-moustached young West Pointer from Vermont, General Orville Babcock, who had served with Grant in the war and often seemed to have the President in his pocket. As private secretary, Babcock had an office next to Grant's, opened all his mail, answered all but the most important letters, constantly gave advice which Grant was inclined to accept, and was felt by insiders to be in some degree the unacknowledged President of the United States.

Schurz, in the Senate, viewed these developments with growing concern. He was not yet ready to break with Grant, but when he returned to St. Louis in the summer of 1870 he was determined to fight for reforms in his own state—a movement heartily favored by Pulitzer. By now, with Schurz immersed in politics and Preetorius suffering from a nervous ailment, Pulitzer had become the moving spirit of the Westliche Post. His journalistic talents and growing political experience had made him a valued lieutenant of Schurz, the most powerful man in Missouri. In St. Louis, Schurz's antipathy to Grant was shared by William McKee, the influential chief proprietor of the (Republican) Missouri Democrat, for reasons Schurz would not have approved: McKee, a spoilsman, had supported Grant but had been angered when the President failed to heed his advice in making Missouri appointments and had given no plum to McKee's brother Henry. Under McKee as editor of the Democrat was the honest, brachycephalic William M. Grosvenor, a stout Schurz ally who wore a size 9½ hat, played chess expertly and sometimes had rousing games with Pulitzer. These four, along with other resentful Missouri leaders, formed the nucleus of a Liberal movement that would split the Republican party in the state and would have bizarre national repercussions.

Their deepest protest was aimed at the Grant-favored Radical Republicans' manipulation of the franchise. The national ratification of the Fifteenth Amendment gave the suffrage to 16,000 Missouri Negroes with the blessing of the Radicals, who could count on the Negro vote. But the Radical-controlled Superintendents of Registration foxily excluded unconfirmed whites, often for capricious reasons. Had a white man had a cousin or friend in the Confederate army? Had he once expressed sympathy with the Confederacy? Was he known to have kissed a lady from Arkansas? Or, more to the point, if he were given the vote would he vote against the Radicals? Enough! He was forbidden the franchise. In one of Missouri's 34 districts only 1,500 of 10,000 free white citizens were allowed to vote and the rest might as well have been natives of Van Diemen's Land.

On August 31, 1870, Schurz, along with McKee, Grosvenor, Pulitzer and a group of Liberal friends, attended the Republican state convention in the steaming statehouse at "Jeff." Feeling ran high as Schurz led his forces in support of amendments that would sweep away the voting disqualifications and end this sorry aftermath of war. When his bid was narrowly defeated, Schurz and some 200 Liberal delegates bolted the meeting, moved to the adjoining senate chamber, held their own convention and nominated the Yale-educated former United States Senator Benjamin Gratz Brown for governor. The Radicals in the next room were livid, accusing the Liberals of plotting with "rebels" to end Republican rule, and there was danger of fisticuffs. The Radicals went ahead to nominate the incumbent Governor Joseph W. McClurg for another term. The whole nation, north and south, watched the struggle—the first real challenge to Grantism in any major state Republican organization.

The Liberals had an able candidate with a solid background, for the charming Brown, a St. Louis lawyer, had helped form the Republican party in Missouri, had fought secession, and was fed up with bloody-shirt politics. The Radicals, in angry messages to Washington, assailed the Liberals as traitors to the party. Grant threw the full power of the administration into the fray, dismissing postmasters and other officeholders of Liberal sympathies, levying five per cent of the salaries of government functionaries for the Radical cause, and trying hard to woo McKee and his Democrat back to the fold.

Pulitzer, appointed secretary of the Liberal organization, had grown a reddish beard to conceal his somewhat unimpressive chin, and with his thick mass of jet-black hair swept back long over his neck, he resembled an excitable musician or schoolmaster. In November the voters were so disillusioned with the Radical regime that they brought about a Liberal landslide, approving the amendments abolishing disfranchisement and giving Brown a 41,000 plurality over McClurg. Yet the victory was not without worries for Schurz. Distrusting both old parties, hoping to build a new and reformist Republican organization, he found instead—just as the Radicals had predicted—that it was Democratic voters whose help had swept the Liberals into power and that he had in fact revived the long-suppressed Democratic Party which had ruled Missouri before the war.[4]

The shocked Grant administration made prompt efforts to retrieve the state for the 1872 presidential election. New federal concessions were offered William McKee to win him back along with his powerful Missouri Democrat and his able editor, Grosvenor. McKee's friend, the charlatan John A. McDonald, was named Supervisor of Internal Revenue over the protests of Schurz and many others. McDonald, obviously encouraged by Grant's secretary, General Babcock, soon organized a cabal for the diversion of the 70 cents per gallon federal tax on whiskey and its use for "party purposes" in Missouri. Some distillers agreed to the larceny on being offered a percentage of it while others were blackmailed into agreement by threats of trumped-up government prosecution. The plot ultimately worked so well that it defrauded the government of $2,000,000 a year in revenue, some of it used to seduce venal newspaper owners, some to build a campaign fund for Grant, some disappearing in kickbacks to distillers and a good deal of it furnishing McDonald and his cronies with diamonds, champagne dinners and fast horses.

A thousand dollars a week from this slush fund was enough to make McKee reconsider his enmity toward Grant. In January 1871 he discharged Grosvenor, who refused to change his mind about Grant, and replaced him with the then little-known Joseph B. McCullagh, an all-out Grant man who knew nothing of the subsidy. The Democrat, which had been the Schurz group's strongest editorial supporter, was now its enemy.

At the Westliche Post office, Pulitzer studied the out-of-town newspapers that streamed in, particularly those from New York. While he admired the Herald, he was most enthusiastic about Charles Anderson Dana's Sun, already attaining nationwide fame as the most fiendishly clever of papers. A master of the half-hidden barb, the deadly understatement, the parody, the pointed doggerel, Dana could skewer a victim in the most gentlemanly language—as he was skewering Grant now, making plain his opinion that the President was a dunce, a nepotist, a drunken corruptionist. The Sun made the Westliche Post seem as staid as a seed catalog. Pulitzer could not forbear writing Dana:

"I read the *Sun* regularly. *In my opinion it is the most piquant, entertaining, and, without exception, the best newspaper in the world.*" [5]

Dana published the accolade—Pulitzer's first appearance in a New York newspaper. Meanwhile he came to trial in Jefferson City for the Augustine shooting, defended by Johnson. On November 20, 1871, he was fined $100 and court costs that raised the total to $400. Not having that much, he borrowed from friends.

Chapter 3

The Right Hand of Schurz

I. A DREAM OF REFORM

St. Louis was the nation's fourth city, topped only by New York, Brooklyn and Philadelphia—bigger than Boston, bigger than Washington and Chicago, having almost doubled its 1860 population and feeling cocky about the 1870 figure of 310,864. It had a southern atmosphere of languor, shaded verandas, bourbon, Negroes on the levee, and side-wheelers plying the river. The race between the *Robert E. Lee* and the *Natchez* from New Orleans to St. Louis in 1870 had commanded national attention. The accent was soft, the state being called Mizzoura. The massive stone stairway of St. Louis' grimy old courthouse had once served as a slave market and was still used for sheriff's sales. Yet the American-born were equaled in numbers by the foreign-born, led overwhelmingly by the Germans, who were as prominent in business and politics as at the concerts and beer gardens.

Its hotels were the focus of some civic vanity, particularly the huge new Lindell, said to have enough plate glass to cover an acre, and the older but ornate Southern Hotel and Planter's House. The city was feeling its oats, full of boosters who pointed to its astonishing growth as proof that it was destined to be the nation's greatest metropolis. Henry Brokmeyer was sinking every available dollar in city land, certain it would make him rich. One local publicist, L. U. Reavis, struck the keynote in his widely read book, *St. Louis, the Future Great City of the World,* predicting that it would outstrip New York, London and Paris: "Henceforth St. Louis must be viewed in the light of her future, her mightiness in the empire of the world . . . Her destiny is fixed. . . . The city that she now is is only the germ of the city . . . that she will be, with her ten million souls occupying the vast area of her dominion. Her strength will be that of a nation."[1]

Chicago was doomed to minor importance, Reavis said, not only lacking St. Louis' central location and the priceless artery of the river but being unable even to furnish its citizens water fit to drink. He did not mention that St. Louis had erected handsome piles hard by slums and rat-infested warehouses, nor that most of the streets were unpaved and filthy. The Negro section along the river was a shambles of rickety hovels, whereas the area around exclusive Vandeventer Place on the west was reserved for tree-shaded mansions with spacious lawns, glittering chandeliers and solid silver services. Downtown Lucas Avenue had lost its refinement, many of the old residences now housing expensive bordellos where champagne was served to customers who arrived in shiny carriages. The cheaper ones lined Chestnut and Market Streets, along with all-night variety shows, faro and lottery joints and parading prostitutes. The frontier was not far distant. St. Louis' sinful attractions were so famous that booted cowboys and occasional Indians drifted in to mingle uproariously with hard-fisted men from the riverboats, and shootings were common. Pulitzer, reared in a sedate European culture but violent by nature, was spending impressionable years in an environment where violence was accepted along with Beethoven and *Hamlet*.

On January 19, 1872, Governor Brown, at Charles Johnson's urging, appointed Pulitzer a member of the board of three police commissioners in St. Louis—a two-year term at a salary of $1,000. Pulitzer, at first anxious for the appointment, now had second thoughts about accepting it. "He is one of the most unreasonable men I ever met withall," Johnson wrote in vexation. But Pulitzer reversed himself and took the post, a nominal one requiring little of his time. He had other fish to fry. Missouri's Liberal Republicans, chesty over their defeat of the state Grant machine—a feat that had won wide prominence for Schurz and Brown—were moving to spread their influence nationally, to purify the party by forcing the nomination of someone other than Grant that summer. Brown, in fact, had dreams of the nomination himself. Pulitzer was among those who signed a call for a Liberal convention to meet at Jefferson City January 24, and was elected a delegate.

This democratic gathering was preceded by a salute to royalty. Grand Duke Alexis, younger son of Alexander II of Russia, had been touring the United States, a trip described as a gesture of international friendliness but actually ordered by the czar with the idea of making Alexis forget a disapproved infatuation. He spent two days in St. Louis and on January 23 arrived with his entourage in "Jeff" in a special train of palace cars leased at $3,500 per day. He was greeted by an awe-stricken crowd of whites and Negroes, some of whom glued their faces to the car windows to see if the duke wore a crown. Cannon roared as the crownless Alexis was drawn by four white steeds to a reception at the capitol, then escorted to the new $100,000 executive mansion where, as the Jefferson City People's Tribune put it, "our Chief Magistrate had made arrangements to lunch him." All state officials and judges were on hand to greet him, as were others who stood well with Governor Brown, among them William Hyde, the crusty editor of the (Democratic) Missouri Republican, and "Joseph Pulitzer and ladies"—a vague phrase giving a picture of the young man surrounded by excited females anxious for their first glimpse of royalty. Alexis left for Kansas City that afternoon after giving $25 to a beggar. Next day the Liberals began their deliberations.[2]

Senator Schurz, in Washington, was behind the movement and in close touch with it. The delegates passed resolutions demanding that the Republican party stand for amnesty for southerners, tariff reform and civil service reform, and all sympathetic Republicans were invited to meet in a national convention at Cincinnati May 1. The hope was to pressure the national Republican party into a reform program in which all could join; but clearly in the background was the threat that if this were not done the Liberals would bolt and enter a third party in the national campaign.

By April it was obvious that the Republicans were not intimidated, that Grant would be the candidate, that heroic measures were necessary. Disaffection was growing among Republicans of principle everywhere who could not stomach another term for the General. Even Horace Greeley in his powerful New York Tribune had broken with Grant. Schurz had been in communication with other estranged Republicans, among them Charles Francis Adams, Samuel Bowles, General Jacob D. Cox and Horace White, all of them hopeful that the May convention would stir up a great Republican groundswell against Grant and that a coalition with the Democrats would result in the nomination of a reformist candidate who could win. Schurz, despite his distrust of the Democrats, was quite willing to solicit their support so long as the Liberal Republicans furnished the principles and the leaders, and he had done diligent spadework among the Democrats. The Democrats, on their part, largely southern and suffering from their rebel background, knew that their only chance to end Grant's suppression of the South lay in union with northern liberals.

Pulitzer, long since known as Schurz's shadow, left St. Louis with Grosvenor, the Missouri deputation and a brass band to join his mentor as a delegate. Grosvenor and Pulitzer, the political strategists of the group, were tagged as the team of "Bill and Joe." The Missouri men were strong for Governor Brown, but here swirled dangerous, unseen eddies of disunity. Schurz, feeling that Brown had been amply rewarded by the governorship and had a reputation too local to command nationwide support, opposed his candidacy without saying so openly because of the need to prevent a party rupture in Missouri. Brown, on the contrary, saw himself as the leader of the reform movement in the only state where it had resoundingly beaten Grant. He stayed home, counting on ardent Missouri support. Certainly Pulitzer knew of Schurz's secret plan to jettison Brown, for this sensitive young man would have been irreparably hurt by anything less than full confidence.

II. CINCINNATI FIASCO

It was a throng of unbuttoned dissidents who met at Cincinnati's huge, gingerbread Exposition Hall, recently erected for the National Saengerfest. The Republican New York Times called it the Sorehead Movement and commented on the machinations of Bill and Joe. To Schurz, the convention was the fruit of long labor and the hope of the future. "The first day of May is moving day," he said meaningly as he began his speech as permanent chairman, but there was some doubt as to the direction of motion. Schurz himself strongly favored the nomination of Charles Francis Adams, and had received assurances from August Belmont and other leading Democrats that if Adams were named the Democrats would throw him their support. But there were noisy champions of other hopefuls including Lincoln's old friend, Supreme Court Justice David Davis, General Cox, Governor Brown, Lyman Trumbull—even Greeley, whom Schurz abhorred because of his instability and his protectionist beliefs. There was a crowd of malcontents who shouted, "Anybody to beat Grant!"—an attitude repugnant to Schurz, who demanded a spirit of highest idealism. There were starry-eyed delegates innocent of political experience, and there were hacks and intriguers galore who had carefully avoided the Liberal bandwagon until it gave evidence of going somewhere. To the one-eyed, 32-year-old Henry Watterson, present both as a Democratic politician and as editor of the Louisville Courier-Journal, this "variegated omnium gatherum" began to look like a parcel of cranks.

Greeley's Tribune speculated "whether the chief managers (Bill and Joe) have offered to trade off Gov. Brown . . ."[3] There was no telling where these quarrelsome delegates, entirely lacking in the comparative discipline of regular party conventions, might turn. Schurz himself contributed to the dissension because of his cooling toward Gratz Brown. Brown had shown some jealousy of Schurz's power, and worst of all he had aided his double cousin (and Schurz's political enemy), the Democrat Frank Blair, in Blair's winning bid for the other Missouri Senate seat. Yet Schurz, the leading spirit of Liberal Republicanism, was confident that he had organized a solid bloc of true reformers who would thwart the machinations of the greasy politicians scrambling for power. Gathering with him Samuel Bowles of the Springfield Republican, Murat

Halstead of the Cincinnati Commercial and Horace White of the Chicago Tribune—three powerful journalists all for Adams—he was able to quell the boom for fat Judge Davis. As the convention got under way, Adams seemed all but safely in harbor.

The selection of Pulitzer, just three weeks past his 25th birthday, as one of the convention secretaries demonstrated recognition of the political abilities of this stripling who was so close to the inner councils. For him, Cincinnati was the first grand adventure beyond provincial Missouri, an experience that enlarged his horizons and ambitions, a personal mingling with men he had read about, some of whom would figure in his later life. One can imagine the respect the young man from the Westliche Post held for such newspapermen as Bowles, Halstead, White and Alexander McClure—even the younger Watterson, already well known if not precisely famous, a perfectly charming man despite his violent manner of utterance and one who would cross Pulitzer's path often. Pulitzer met the 35-year-old Whitelaw Reid, Greeley's assistant on the Tribune, who was there to promote the candidacy of his boss and who would later be Pulitzer's journalistic adversary for decades. And he met a comparative unknown who would stick firmly in his mind—the debonair, six-foot John A. Cockerill, managing editor of the Democratic Cincinnati Enquirer.

Reid and his New York colleagues were the busiest men at the convention, working for Greeley. On the day before the balloting began, Grosvenor, who headed the 30-man Missouri delegation, told them that Governor Brown had no chance for the presidency, urging that they support Adams and settle for second place on the ticket for Brown. One loyal Brown man telegraphed the governor that the Schurz forces were betraying him. The angry Brown took the next train for Cincinnati in company with his cousin, Frank Blair, bent on revenge. Arriving that night, they worked industriously through the dark hours to foil Schurz and beat Adams by arranging a quiet deal with the Greeley men and advising friendly delegates to swing the Brown strength to Greeley.

On the first ballot next day, Adams led with 205 votes, Greeley was second with a surprising 147, and among the other candidates Brown had 95. Brown, a small man who seemed a midget when standing with the tall Schurz and Pulitzer, now made his move. Gaining the floor, he withdrew his candidacy and made a rousing speech for Greeley that won applause from an Eastern claque. Somehow Schurz, who regarded Greeley as a buffoon and could not conceive of any sizable shift to him, failed to counter the threat. "Carl Schurz," Pulitzer said later, "was the most industrious and the least energetic man I have ever worked with. A word from him at that crisis would have completely routed Blair and squelched Brown." [4]

Greeley pulled ahead of Adams on the second ballot. On the sixth, thanks to shrewd work by Brown, Blair and Whitelaw Reid, Greeley was nominated and Brown was later named as his running mate.

The convention which Schurz had envisioned as an expression of political idealism had been betrayed by what he construed as gross huckstering between his own enemies in Missouri and the Greeley leaders, and all his fine plans lay in ruins. He and Pulitzer slunk away to the home of a Cincinnati friend, Judge J. B. Stallo, where the senator flung himself at the piano and played Chopin's Funeral March.

The gifted editor Greeley was indeed a preposterous candidate for any administrative post, let alone the presidency. His inability to administer even his own clothing hinted at a deep inner failing, for his cravat was invariably off-center and his soup-stained waistcoat buttoned askew. Now nearing 62, he had so thirsted for office that he was not free from tainted political associations. His naively impulsive nature had led him to embrace a parade of contradictory causes—Whiggism, socialism, Republicanism, trade-unionism, pacifism, all-out war against the South—as well as spiritualism and vegetarianism. To many New York colleagues he was an object of derision, some even questioning his sanity. Edwin Godkin of the New York Evening Post, who would have supported Adams, wrote Schurz, "I do not know whether you are aware what a conceited, ignorant, half-cracked, obstinate old creature he is . . ." [5] His childlike face, white fringe of chin whiskers and myopic gaze made him resemble a rural parson and offered a rich subject for cartoonists.

With heavy misgivings Schurz brought the Westliche Post out tepidly for Greeley. For weeks he even contemplated organizing another convention and putting a suitable reform candidate in the field. In July the Democratic party, meeting in Baltimore, demonstrated its anyone-but-Grant desperation by nominating the Greeley-Brown ticket though Greeley had fought the Democrats for almost 40 years. It was, as almost everyone admitted but the white-hatted candidate himself, the weirdest campaign within long memory, and it had the side effect of making Pulitzer a publisher. So depressed were Schurz and Preetorius by the political outlook, so convinced that their German readers would abandon them, that they sold Pulitzer a controlling interest in the Westliche Post on "very liberal terms," certainly on credit. As Pulitzer himself put it, "They thought I was necessary to the paper. They probably would have done the same thing to any other man who worked sixteen hours a day, as I did . . ." [6] Since the Post had recently become a daily, there were six issues to prepare weekly instead of one.

III. STUMPING FOR GREELEY

The hall-bedroom days were over. Pulitzer moved to the splendid Lindell Hotel at Washington and Sixth, four blocks from the Post. His growing ambition for public office, added to his detestation of Grantism, made him reconcile himself to the Greeley ticket, impelling him to take the stump and make 60 speeches in German for the candidate in Missouri and Indiana. Doubting his own spontaneity, he carefully prepared his harangues in advance. This was the era of oratory in the grand tradition of Webster and Clay, a period when cold newsprint was the only alternative method of reaching the voter and was regarded as far inferior to the living, shouting man on the platform. Pulitzer, speaking in small-town opera houses and from torchlit wagon beds, was not above bombast, but his voice was loud and clear, his German excellent and his sincerity evident. He frankly enjoyed the sensation of power over a crowd even though the grueling round of meetings exhausted him and the cause was hopeless anyway. Governor Brown did not help it when he made an undiplomatic speech at a Yale reunion, belittling the importance of the East, and then got publicly drunk.

Greeley was ridiculed by the Republicans, brutally caricatured by Nast and other penmen. His wife died a week before the election, his mind was tottering, and the surprise was that on November 6 he polled 2,834,125 votes. Had he won, the nation would have had a madman for President-elect, for his sanity was gone and he died in a mental hospital November 29. Schurz's dream, the Liberal Republican crusade, had really died with Greeley's nomination. It left the senator and Pulitzer in a political no-man's-land, rejecting Grant Republicanism but refusing to embrace the Democrats. The country was in for four more years of Grant. The rapacity of the administration had its reflection in a sort of national amnesia of conscience, a spirit of plunder fit to convulse honest men with despair. In New York the public was finally rising against Tweed. In sleepy Harrisonville, Missouri, citizens were so enraged by a fraudulent issue of bonds for which Cass County Attorney James C. Cline and Judge J. C. Stephenson were indicted that they contrived a more Western style of justice. When Cline and Stephenson boarded an eastbound Katy train with one of their bondsmen, Thomas Detro, a band of some 75 masked men stopped the train at Gunn City by laying logs across the track. "Where's the bond robbers?" they shouted as they rushed into the train. They shot both Cline and Stephenson dead and dragged them out by their hair. They found Detro cowering in the mail car, riddled him with bullets and tossed him out to bleed to death—a crime that was never solved but was said to have had a purifying effect on public officials of surrounding counties.[7]

In this atmosphere Pulitzer ran the Post and served as a police commissioner. Although little is known of his conduct of this part-time office, he was always inclined to worry less about small offenders than about corrupt officials who shielded vice. Of evenings he often went to the Planter's House or the Southern Hotel to enjoy champagne with such friends as Johnson, Keppler and Stilson Hutchins, editor of the St. Louis

Times. Keppler, publishing the short-lived German satirical magazine called *Puck,* was sometimes pressed for a cartoon subject and would say, "Well, Joey, there's only one thing left to do. I'll go back to the office and draw your nose." [8]

Certainly Pulitzer knew the gamy Supervisor of Internal Revenue McDonald, who lived at the Planter's, corresponded regularly with Grant's secretary, General Babcock, bought a summer place in Wisconsin, frequently sent game birds for the President's table, and continued his systematic robbery of the whiskey revenue. In 1872 a corporate disagreement forced William McKee to sell his interest in the Missouri Democrat, which thereafter could not be relied on as a Grant organ. McDonald solved the problem by giving more distillery loot to McKee, who immediately launched a new morning paper, the Globe, which sprang ardently to the President's side and assailed Schurz as a renegade. ". . . One of the obligations of the Whiskey Combination," as McDonald later put it, "was to fight [Schurz] to the death if possible," adding, "we felt a mutual interest in extending the circulation of the *Globe*. To accomplish this speedily I sent a notice to the ten thousand revenue officials in my district asking them each to subscribe for at least one copy of the daily *Globe* . . ." [9]

Although the Westliche Post lacked such a handy circulation builder, it did not suffer so severely from the Greeley fiasco as Schurz had feared. Under Pulitzer it sacrificed a shade of dignity to achieve much more dash. The senator was now in a peculiar position, since he still owned a lesser interest and often wrote editorials, but with the difference that his former lieutenant was now in charge. Indeed Pulitzer had a tendency to boss any operation with which he was connected. Schurz later observed that if Pulitzer had remained a partner much longer, he would have owned the whole paper. In the winter of 1872–73 Schurz and Preetorius tranquilized their lives by buying back a majority interest for a surprising $30,000, probably representing in part a reward for Pulitzer's vigorous preservation of the journal's prosperity. Still retaining a minor interest in the paper, he packed up and went to Europe.

His brother Albert had long since given up pedagogy and, after two years with the Illinois Staats-Zeitung in Chicago, had moved to New York as a reporter for the Sun. Probably Joseph visited him before he sailed, although the two brothers were as unlike temperamentally as they were in appearance, Albert being a plump, earthy six-footer more interested in success than reform. Certainly Pulitzer called on his friend Keppler, recently moved to New York and now a leading cartoonist for Frank Leslie's Illustrated Newspaper. In Europe he visited his old home in Budapest, where his mother greeted the son she had last seen as a 17-year-old. He had in astonishing repletion two qualities seldom intermixed—the capacity for hard work and for enjoyment. He traveled the continent, luxuriated on the Riviera, but all the while studied Europe with the eye of a political analyst, comparing conditions with those in America under a free constitutional republic.

In Paris, by accident or design, he met that seasoned globe-trotter Henry Watterson, wandering with him through Montmartre. The humiliating Franco-Prussian war was only a year past, and in a hole-in-the-wall playhouse they saw a melodrama in which the lovely Gallic heroine gave a German brigand his comeuppance, to great applause from the partisan audience.

"We are all 'brigands,'" Pulitzer said, as Watterson recalled it, "differing according to individual character, to race and pursuit. Now, if I were writing that play, I should represent the villain as a tyrannous City Editor, meanly executing the orders of a niggardly proprietor."

Watterson asked how he would portray the heroine.

"She should be a beautiful and rich young lady who buys the newspaper and marries the cub—rescuing genius from poverty and persecution." [10]

IV. THE REPUBLICAN TURNS DEMOCRAT

Although he had few doubts about his own genius, he returned to St. Louis in a strange mood of indecision. Incredibly, this young fire-eater who delighted in journalism, thrived on hard work and was trained for the law had no really steady occupation for the next five years and was uncertain what to do with himself. Pulitzer, who would later act as if every minute were his last, rather allowed his career to wait his leisure—this at a time when the Credit Mobilier scandals and the deepening panic of 1873 heaped further discredit on the Grant administration. The obvious explanation is that he was prosperous, choosy, and would make no move until certain it was the right move. He took an office in the Temple building and practiced a little law, although Johnson told him that journalism and not the bar was his true calling. He had backed himself into something of a corner, for he had no regular journalistic outlet, his reputation for bossing the show probably barred him from any newspaper job, and he was in political difficulties, being neither a Republican nor a Democrat. But Pulitzer in indecision was more active than most men of aim, a visitor, talker, questioner, analyzer, concertgoer and playgoer, interested in people and ideas. He saw John McCullough in *Lear* and *Hamlet* when the handsome tragedian brought his troupe to St. Louis and became friendly with McCullough, who doubtless had to answer a hundred Pulitzer questions about the interpretation of Shakespeare.

His shrewdness was as good as a salary. His former political ally, McKee, was handicapped in expanding his Globe because of the lack of a press franchise. The Missouri Democrat, now controlled by George W.

Fishback, was a member of the Western Associated Press and thus had a decided advantage over the Globe—an advantage Fishback maintained by steadily blackballing McKee's efforts to secure a franchise. But it was Pulitzer, not McKee, who noted the possibilities in the forced sale of the bankrupt Missouri Staats-Zeitung, which *had* an AP franchise. And it was Pulitzer, not McKee, who was present at the sale on January 6, 1874. He bought the Staats-Zeitung for "a few thousand dollars" and ran it for exactly one day. Then he sold the press franchise to the Globe for a sum estimated variously as "about $27,000" and "a little in advance of $40,-000." [11] Ironically, some of this money may have come from McDonald's Whisky Ring. Pulitzer added to his profit by selling the Staats-Zeitung's machinery to a German group that started another short-lived daily. He was suddenly rich enough to retire for years if he wished.

He invested money (very profitably) in the Mississippi River projects of Captain James B. Eads, one of them the mighty triple-arched bridge now nearing completion, which St. Louisans regarded as final proof of their defeat of Chicago. He took rooms at 1547 Papin Street on the prosperous South Side where Germans predominated and the Schurzes were neighbors. He bought a smart saddle horse and rode daily in the suburbs with Colonel J. L. Torrey and Colonel J. C. Normile, both St. Louis attorneys and colonels by courtesy. Next door to him lived the Westphalian-born Charles Balmer, a composer who owned a music store downtown, had three daughters who all sang and played musical instruments, and held musicales on Sunday evenings at which sauerbraten was served and German musicians visiting the city were often honored guests. Pulitzer, who cherished good music, seldom missed these entertainments, and there met a jocular journalist three years younger than he, Eugene Field. He went so far as to call the Balmer girls "the Nightingales," and showed some interest in Bertha, the most intellectual of them. He also paid gallant attentions to Schurz's eldest daughter. He attended the *volksfest* and was seen pirouetting at Bessehl's Charity Ball, his head towering above all the rest. Highly sociable and articulate, he quoted Goethe and Shakespeare, loved to draw others out without revealing himself, and could be impatient with stupidity. As Watterson noted, "he never spoke much of himself."

With Thomas Davidson he attended the Aristotle Society to study Plato and Aristotle in the original Greek. The political firm of Bill and Joe was still in business. With Grosvenor, now editor of the Democrat, he was trying to aid Senator Schurz and draw the Republicans of Missouri away from Grant. Bill and Joe doubtless were aware of the visit to St. Louis of General Babcock in the spring of 1874 to confer with Revenue Supervisor McDonald, though not of McDonald's gift to Babcock of a four-carat diamond shirt stud costing $2,400. "There was a flaw in the stone, however," McDonald recalled, "and the General not being very well pleased on that account, I took the stone back and purchased another and finer one for him."[12]

To Schurz, Pulitzer wrote in German:

"A plan is afoot to honor you on your return from Washington with a great reception. Of course you will be expected to make a speech. Should this not be welcome to you . . . I should appreciate a hint before arrangements go too far." Although the Times and Globe had come out against Schurz, he wrote with excessive optimism, he felt that the senator could be reelected by careful maneuvering, adding, "I have given up my plan to spend the summer in Europe or the East because of an unexpected and favorable chance to make myself contemptible by making money."[13]

But he was a mercurial soul, a mind-changer. By July he had moved to the Southern Hotel and *had* decided to go east, writing Davidson, who was summering in Gloucester, "Address first letter care 5th Av. Hotel New York, second care Carl Schurz Washington," and adding, "If I can bring you any Greek or other books from N Y name them and I'll go for them." He went on, apparently about an infatuation of Davidson's, "I never had that familiar Grecian countenance in Scottish red [meaning Davidson's] in my mind's eye without another face close to it—softer still, prettier still, and fully as intelligent & gentle. How it is, old fellow?"

Ten days later he had changed his mind again, writing Davidson:

> Tom!!!!! The battles of Salamis, Sadowa or Sedan were nothing compared with the struggle that just closed in my breast. It is decided. I leave tomorrow evening and go directly to Denver City. . . . Well, there is hope yet. I'll be back in less than 14 days and if upon my return I find a less mysterious & more detailed epistle I'll go right on to Boston &c.[14]

Was the Denver trip in connection with legal work, or to learn if there might be a newspaper for sale, or just to see the country? Whatever it was, on his return he joined with Grosvenor in promoting a reform movement christened the People's Party, which united with the Grange and dissident Republicans in an attempt to beat the resurgent Democrats in the fall state election. Because the new party sought to divorce itself from the Grant administration, McKee's Globe assailed it and scornfully termed it the Tadpoles. But here Pulitzer encountered the same dilemma that had confounded him and Schurz at Cincinnati—the tendency of a new party to ride the fence, to compromise in trying to please all shades of opinion. For six years he had worked in harmony with Schurz and Grosvenor, but for a man of such strong independence it had only been a question of time before he would burst the ties and emerge on his own.

At the People's Party convention at Jeff, he was angered by what he regarded as its evasion of issues and its nomination of safely mediocre candidates, among them the prosperous gentleman farmer William Gentry of Sedalia for governor. He returned to St. Louis in such disgust that he broke with Schurz, broke with Grosvenor and decided to support the Democratic ticket. The Globe gleefully aired this schism in a purported interview:

> The only importance that could be attached to an interview with Hon. Joseph Pulitzer just now arises from the fact that he is the positive circulating radiator of the Schurz element and was Bill's [Grosvenor's] right-hand bower from the birth of the puny and deformed Tadpole baby until that miserable infant breathed its last at Jefferson City. Joseph mourns the loss of the baby, but would feel much better had Bill and the other nurses poisoned it long before, rather than let it die such a horrible death. [The Globe quoted Pulitzer as saying in part:]
>
> "Mr. Gentry is, I believe, a gentleman, but I am not aware of any fundamental law . . . which forbids a man to have ideas beyond the culture of hogs. . . . The man Gentry is an ass, and he was nominated by asses." [15]

While the sarcasm sounds Pulitzeresque, he could not let the Grant organ make capital of his views. He clarified his stand in a long statement in the (Democratic) Missouri Republican, saying the Globe "interview" was mostly fiction:

"I do not deny having exercised the great privilege . . . the inalienable right of bolting. The political firm of Joe and Bill is dissolved. . . . I bolt both the platform and the ticket. Not that I fail to recognize in the movement some excellent men and good intentions." The road to hell, he pointed out, was paved with good intentions. ". . . The result of the convention reminds me very much of that leg of mutton on which old Dr. Johnson dined on the way to Oxford, and which he declared to be as bad as could be: 'ill-fed, ill-kept, ill-killed and ill-dressed.' Platform and ticket are ill-born, ill-reared, ill-principled, and . . . deaf and dumb. . . . Selecting candidates on the whole very much inferior to those of the Democracy, the convention remained still further behind by failing to protest against the real causes of the prostrate condition of the country—the corruption, the lawlessness, the usurpation and the profligacy of the national administration. . . ." [16]

This denunciation of the party he had helped organize would not have been necessary had he been willing to sit out the election. Instead, he was determined to support the Democrats, to abandon Schurz, Grosvenor and the many Liberal Republicans he had aided so long. Indeed his own convictions were more in line with the Jeffersonian concept of personal liberty, the limitation of federal powers and a low tariff than they were with Republicanism, and he would surely have joined the Democrats sooner but for the lingering aroma of the party's connection with slavery and the rebellion. He would be a Democrat—an *independent* Democrat—for the rest of his life.

So Pulitzer, assailed by his former associates, left in October to stump the state for the Democratic gubernatorial candidate, Charles M. Hardin, and the rest of the ticket. At the same time the St. Louis fair opened and the President arrived with Mrs. Grant and the ubiquitous General Babcock to lend their prestige to the occasion and to bolster the Republican ticket. Revenue Supervisor McDonald, still dispensing largesse hardly compatible with his $3,000 salary, paid the presidential party's ten-day bill at the Lindell and gave Grant the use of his speedy pair of bays. The President was so delighted by them that McDonald not only shipped the horses to him in Washington as a gift, but threw in the best buggy and harness he could buy, a $25 buggy whip and "a gold breastplate made for each horse, on which the President's name was engraved." [17]

From George G. Vest of Sedalia, later a Democratic United States Senator, Pulitzer received an interesting note: "Dear Sir, The name of the colored woman who was sold by Gentry in 1863, and who is now in St. Louis, is Susan Williams. . . ." [18] Having sold a slave was politically hurtful. Pulitzer gave the letter to Stilson Hutchins, editor of the Dispatch, who saw that Susan Williams was located and made an exhibit against Gentry.

As Pulitzer delivered speeches for the Democrats in the back country, he was not in reality undermining the Senate seat of his friend and benefactor Schurz, who would soon be up for reelection in the state legislature. Now the legislature was certain to be Democratic anyway, the thankless Democrats were ready to shelve the man largely responsible for their regaining of the franchise, and his six-year term would be his last. Yet he was failing Schurz in the limited sense that he did not go down fighting for him, and there must have been a cooling between the two.

Chapter 4

Love on the Run

I. RESOLUTE PULITZER, IRRESOLUTE TILDEN

Pulitzer backed the winning horse. Hard times and Republican scandals helped elect Hardin governor, send Democrats to all of Missouri's 13 congressional seats and return a large Democratic majority to Congress. He yearned for public office, admitting, "I am passionately fond of politics . . . perhaps too much so for my own pleasure," [1] and he sought it through the traditional avenue of work for the party. He was elected one of the 68 state delegates to the constitutional convention at Jefferson City, charged with revising the violently Radical constitution of 1865. Here, in sessions from May to July, he distinguished himself in a fight for true home rule for St. Louis, which had always been hamstrung by county and state supervision. Arguing that the city had a quarter of the state's population and paid half the taxes, he opposed an amendment that would give the legislature authority over the city, saying:

"Tweed derived all his power and based his entire system of public plunder on such an amendment as is proposed. The power of Tweed and his coadjutors lay in making charters in Albany and in carrying out charters in New York." [2]

He won the fight—one that benefited St. Louis permanently. Meanwhile, Treasury Secretary Benjamin Bristow, one of the few honest men in Grant's Cabinet, got wind of the whiskey ring and began prosecuting it so vigorously that the embarrassed Grant ultimately asked his resignation. But the cat was out of the bag. McDonald, McKee and others even including General Babcock were indicted, and although Babcock was acquitted thanks to direct presidential help, McKee and McDonald were among those found guilty and imprisoned. Pulitzer, suffering from the heat, to which he was highly sensitive, finished off at the convention, went to New York and pressed negotiations to buy the Belletristische Journal, a

German weekly. When the deal fell through he went on to Europe for a stay of many months, including another sojourn on the Riviera, a place he loved and would frequent much in later life but would never again see clearly.

In so doing he missed the first national political convention held west of the Mississippi—the Democratic convention that opened at the huge Merchants' Exchange right in his own city on June 27, 1876. St. Louis was ablaze with bunting, its downtown streets decorated with colored lights, its hotels and beer gardens jammed, but there was trouble because of the huge Tammany delegation's bellicose opposition to "Old Usufruct," Samuel J. Tilden. "There were three genuine fights of the old-fashioned Democratic kind in the Lindell House," the New York Tribune reported. ". . . One of the Tammany roughs drew a pistol on a Tilden Missourian right in the great hall of the Lindell, and proposed to put an end to him and his Tildenism together." [3] But no one was shot, and Henry Watterson was temporary chairman at a convention that howled for reform and quickly solved the Democrats' money disagreements by nominating the hard-money Tilden with the greenbacker Thomas A. Hendricks as running mate.

Pulitzer hurried home from Europe to enter the fray with real indignation against Carl Schurz. Schurz had conferred with the Republican candidate, Governor Rutherford B. Hayes of Ohio, had become convinced of Hayes's integrity and had dropped his status as a political orphan by coming out for Hayes. To Pulitzer, the expectation of anything but more fraud from the "party of corruption" was worse than naive. He sold back his interest in the Westliche Post and, when Schurz left to stump the Midwest for Hayes, Pulitzer followed to challenge and answer him—a parting of old comrades that drew considerable attention. The St. Louis Times observed:

> Of course Mr. Schurz will not consent to a discussion of the issues of the campaign with Mr. Pulitzer, because he would be the last man to acknowledge the intellectual equality of his former lieutenant and associate, but there is nothing that would be more satisfying to the Democracy and we fancy nothing more gratifying to Mr. Pulitzer. With all the strength and analytical resources of Mr. Schurz, he is immeasurably the inferior of the other in nimbleness of intellect, in practical knowledge and available requirements.[4]

Pulitzer's forensic skill was now so well recognized that he no longer spoke from farm wagons but addressed large gatherings in good-sized towns and such cities as Indianapolis, Detroit and Buffalo. He attacked without obeisance to old friendship. At the Detroit Opera House, where he spoke first in English, then German, he called it "ludicrous" that "a certain gentleman, Carl Schurz, distinguished in the past and extinguished in the future, advocates the election of Hayes on a reform platform." By late

October he was almost exhausted, coughing and spitting blood but still fiery. On October 30 he was in New York to receive recognition unusual for a 29-year-old, being one of the elect who attended a Manhattan Club reception honoring Governor Tilden and mingling there with August Belmont, Abram S. Hewitt, William C. Whitney, Manton Marble of the *World*, and such Tweed-era warhorses as A. Oakey Hall and John T. Hoffman. He met the 62-year-old Tilden, the bachelor millionaire attorney whose wealth had been accumulated in railroad deals not above question but whose record as governor was excellent—a stooped, secretive little man with a drooping left eyelid. For a man of his means, Tilden had contributed rather meagerly to his own campaign. No money had gone to aid the Dixie Democrats, which everyone would soon regret. Next evening Pulitzer addressed a "huge crowd" at Cooper Union in English, countering the arguments of Schurz, who had spoken earlier in New York. Denouncing the Republican party as "the shame of the country," he called for the burial of the bloody shirt:

"The Southern people belong to us, and we belong to them. Their interests are our interests. . . . We are one people, one country and one government; and whoever endeavors to array one section against another . . . is a traitor to his country." [5]

He visited Charles A. Dana and urged a Pulitzer-edited German edition of the New York *Sun*. Edward P. Mitchell, Dana's young aide, noted, "He was very earnest, very confident of success, very intelligent in his exhibit of the particulars he had worked out in advance." [6] Although Dana was interested, his publisher was not. A few days later, on November 7, came the election that would cause years of bitterness. Tilden, leading heavily in the early returns, said, "My election was due to the issues" and gave a victory dinner for 40. By November 10 new developments placed the result in doubt, Tilden having 184 certain electoral votes but with South Carolina, Louisiana and Florida (all three still under carpetbag rule backed by bayonets) claimed by both sides. Victory in any one of the three states would elect Tilden, whereas Hayes needed them all to win by one slim electoral vote.

Both Republican and Democratic emissaries hurried south with bags of currency, believing correctly that money in the right places could change close election arithmetic. J. M. Wells, head of the Louisiana election returning board, realizing how favorable was his position, shopped for the best price, playing one party against the other. A messenger from Louisiana told Abram Hewitt, chairman of the Democratic National Committee, that Louisiana would make Tilden President for $1,000,000—an offer the upright Hewitt refused even when the price was cut to $200,000. During weeks of intrigue and bribery the quarrel continued while the indecisive Tilden, to Pulitzer's disgust, said and did nothing and the anger on both sides rose to such a pitch that another Civil War seemed possible.

Dana had been impressed by the intense young man with the German-Hungarian accent. By December Pulitzer was in Washington as a special correspondent for the Sun, sending dispatches about the electoral controversy. The three southern states, by dint of judicious rejection of "illegal" Democratic votes by their returning boards, had "gone for Hayes," but the whole affair was so redolent of fraud that the decision was placed in the hands of Congress. In Washington, at Ford's Theater of fateful memory, Henry Watterson made a fiery speech urging that 100,000 Democrats hold a mass meeting in the capital to influence Congress by their numbers. Pulitzer, still apt to lose his head when excited, followed him to the platform and demanded that the 100,000 Democrats "come fully armed and ready for business." There was danger that he would lose his head in another direction when, through his friend the Missouri Congressman John E. Clarke, he met Kate Davis, the positively beautiful 23-year-old daughter of Judge William Worthington Davis of Georgetown.

But politics came first. Pulitzer's dispatches to the Sun were marked by his intensely partisan interest, his attitude of the dramatic critic witnessing a great national spectacle, and his liking for the bold and even purple stroke. He mixed his reports on the electoral question with occasional columns of Washington gossip, at which he was adept. There was more than a tinge of melodrama in his dispatch about Supreme Court Justice Joseph P. Bradley of the Special Electoral Commission whose vote, as it turned out, decided the election for Hayes: "His face is dark as if the shadow of his soul hangs over it and on his forehead could plainly be read, 'Guilty.' " [7]

So R. B. Hayes, whom the Democrats called "Returning Board Hayes," was pronounced President by one electoral vote despite Tilden's quarter-million popular plurality, and it was noted that Wells, the Louisiana election official, was later appointed Surveyor of the Port of New Orleans.

II. NOT WORTHY OF SUCH LOVE

Pulitzer's rage and despair were almost enough to make him ill. To him, the corruption of the Grant administration had been approved by fraud and perpetuated for another four years by fraud. To his disgust on the score of plain honesty must have been added the knowledge that had Tilden won he could have expected the reward of a government post of importance, and that now Schurz was going into Hayes's Cabinet as Secretary of the Interior. Pulitzer had satisfied New York's most demanding editor, but his temporary job was over. He stayed unhappily for Hayes's inaugural, then returned to St. Louis and took not one room but a suite of two at the six-story Southern Hotel on Walnut Street, famous for its Grand Corridor and Grand Staircase. Here he became friendly with other guests including George Frank Gouley, secretary of the Missouri Masonic fraternity, and Dr. Gerlact, the German consul.

He resumed the sporadic practice of law and wrote occasional pieces for Stilson Hutchins' Democratic St. Louis Times. His closest friend, Davidson, had quit St. Louis to join the Concord school of philosophers, and Grosvenor had become an editorialist for the New York Tribune. He was still uncertain about his career, annoyed at his own uncertainty, pulled by ambition in three directions—politics, journalism and the law.

On his 30th birthday, April 10, 1877, he attended a party at the home of Dan Morrison with Hutchins, Senator Lewis Bogy, the horse-car entrepreneur Erastus Wells and others. He seemed to have a luckless affinity for violence and tragedy that would pursue him throughout his life. He returned around midnight to the hotel, where his birthday had an ominous commemoration two hours later when the building caught fire. Several people jumped from upper windows as flames surrounded them, one of them Dr. Gerlact, who broke his leg, another a woman who leaped from the fifth floor, "turning over twice in her downward flight and alighting on her feet, with fatal effect." Pulitzer, clad only in trousers, escaped after being "nearly choked to death," but 11 persons lost their lives, among them his friend Gouley, who left a young widow. Another guest, the actress Kate Claxton, appearing as Louise in *The Two Orphans* at the Olympia across the street, was experienced, having earlier escaped a hotel fire in Brooklyn. She saved her life by wrapping herself in wetted blankets and rolling down the Grand Staircase. Pulitzer must have lost his personal belongings and papers, for the building was gutted.[8]

In June he went to New York, probably again looking for a newspaper, then visited that most fashionable of resorts, White Sulphur Springs, moving next to the almost equally fashionable Long Branch, where he was joined by Johnson and Hutchins. Back in St. Louis by early fall, he saw Edwin Booth in *Hamlet,* and near the end of October he went east again. The records are vague and his incessant wanderings hard to follow, but evidently it was then that he settled in Washington for a time with the idea of practicing law in the pleasant proximity of the dark-haired, laughing-eyed Kate Davis.

Until then he had escaped serious romantic involvement because of his dedication to politics and his impatience with female frivolity. Miss Davis, as she would prove during her long life, had intelligence, spirit, warmth, common sense, humor. Her father, Judge Davis, was in comfortable circumstances and socially impeccable, a distant cousin of Jefferson Davis, late president of the Confederacy. Her mother, a cousin of her father, was the former Catherine Louise Worthington, of an esteemed Maryland family.

The Episcopalian parents were not drawn to the lank "foreigner" who spoke gutturally and had no settled career. Pultizer had experienced anti-Semitism in Hungary, in the army and in St. Louis. General Grant's ord-

accusing Jewish speculators of causing army shortages and expelling them from the battle area had been one of the sensations of the war. As yet it was virtually impossible for a Jew to attain any standing in the eyes of such narrow and socially conscious families as the Davises. Doubtless fearing that he would be rejected out of hand, Pulitzer did not tell Miss Davis of his part-Jewish ancestry.

He lived at the Willard and practiced law in Washington. Yet he could not really settle down. For one thing, the best opportunities for lawyers here lay in lobbying, which he despised, and for another, he was on the *qui vive* for a newspaper to buy. When he and Kate were affianced it did not guarantee calm, for Pulitzer could not conduct even a romance without turbulence. He must have been vexing at times to her—a man determined to be rich and great and yet still, at 30, uncertain how to achieve his aims; a man with captivating qualities, flashing brilliance, but unstable, temperamental. When he went to St. Louis on some unstated business, he admitted to a friend that he still feared that Kate might throw him over and "he was in misery." From St. Louis he wrote her, sharply revealing his state of mind:

> My dearest Kate: What better answer can I make than this, that I shall return tomorrow evening? Have *you* not conquered, No? Yes. . . . If nothing happens to prevent my departure, I shall be in Washington 24 hours after you read this. Need I say that there will not be many hours after my arrival before I hope to have the pleasure of seeing you? Need I say that I long for that moment? If you knew how much I thought of you these last days and how the thought of you creeps in and connects with every contemplation and plan about the present and future, you would believe it. I have really felt miserable here in spite of the most cordial signs of friendship, the most gratifying flatteries to vanity, the most absorbing pressure of business. Why? I don't know. But I suspect there is a woman in it. I have an idea that you had a good deal to do with it. I have an ideal of home and love and work—the yearning growing greater in proportion to the glimpse of its approaching realization. I am almost tired of this life—aimless, homeless, loveless, I would have said, but for you. I am impatient to turn over a new leaf and start a new life—one of which home must be the foundation, affection, ambition and occupation the corner stones, and you my dear, my inseparable companion. Would I were not so stupid always to be serious and speculative! Would I had your absolute faith and confidence instead of my philosophy! I could not help thinking, I could not help feeling, how utterly selfish men are in love compared with women, when I read your letter and feel its warmth. I cannot help saying that I am not worthy of such love, I am too cold and selfish, I know. Still I am not without honor, and that alone would compel me to strive to become worthy of you, worthy of your faith and love, worthy of a better and finer future.
>
> There, now you have my first love letter. I hope it will be read in a less serious spirit than the one in which it is written. Don't of course, show my letters to anybody. I can't bear that thought. Confidential correspondence,

much more even than conversation, depends upon strict privacy. Men would certainly not make certain declarations in the hearing of others. But I must stop. Have kept a friend waiting all this time, and now another arrived.

Good-bye till Wednesday,

J. P.[9]

Possibly she was irked by his excessive adjuration to secrecy, but secrecy would always be important to him. And he would always convey the impression of a man in a hurry, running for a train with coattails flying. He was not long back in Washington before he left for New York on a new mission. His friend Keppler had founded another German-language *Puck* in New York in 1876, so successfully that he had brought out an English edition the next year. Pulitzer tried to buy a partnership but could not agree on terms with Keppler, who, one might guess, knew Pulitzer well enough to realize that he would boss any partnership.

III. UNCERTAIN AND INCONSTANT

Pulitzer and Kate planned to marry in June, with the possibility—depending on his business developments—of a European honeymoon. Returning to Washington, he encountered his friend, the actor John McCullough. The insatiably curious Pulitzer could not meet an interesting person without pumping him for his history and opinions. McCullough, born near Londonderry in 1837, had come to America at 16 and worked as an apprentice in a Philadelphia chair factory. An older worker named Burke who revered Shakespeare would, when enlivened by wine, slay young McCullough with a paintbrush and recite over him Marc Antony's oration over the dead Caesar. "I became perfectly enraptured with the man," McCullough said, "and made such a patient accommodating corpse for him that he finally made me a present of a copy of Shakespeare." [10] From then on he thought only of the stage, reading and practicing constantly. He worked up from small parts in Philadelphia and became so friendly with John Wilkes Booth that he thought it advisable to flee to Canada when Lincoln was murdered. After serving as Edwin Forrest's "leading support" for a half-dozen years, he came into his own and was regarded as a magnificent Lear and Othello.

Pulitzer admired people who started with nothing and achieved success through their own efforts, and the thought of the poorly educated McCullough's becoming a leading Shakespearian was an inspiring one. He was in a chaotic state of indecision, considering newspaper propositions both in New York and St. Louis and also entertaining the possibility of going to Europe not only for a honeymoon but to establish himself permanently in business there. Learning that McCullough planned to go to Europe, he arranged, in contravention of nuptial custom, that the actor should take ship along with the honeymooners. His letter to Kate reveals the irresolution of a man anxious not to make the wrong move:

My dearest Kate: Yesterday, at this hour, my friend McCullough (the actor) sat at the table and in this chair and we agreed to arrange it so as to cross the ocean together—he to put off his departure until after the 15th inst.—I to put off mine on the 6th of July—to go earlier. Two hours afterward I sent a telegram to New York insisting upon an answer. This morning I received a brief reply that a letter had been mailed without the remotest allusion to its contents. Also, a letter from St. Louis with a definite and rather advantageous looking proposition about my purchasing an interest in a newspaper there. Also, your note, my dear, which impressed me Europeanward.

I give you this brief outline of my day's doing, and you can now see yourself what an utterly inconsistent, uncertain and inconstant chap I am. Here I am within, perhaps, less than a fortnight, of our possible or probable departure for Europe, and for the life of me I cannot venture a positive opinion, whether, after all, we will go at all, nor whither we will go, where we will settle down. Funny situation, isn't it? As if to give you a foretaste of the future, you are met by difficulties even before you start on that lifelong journey which philosophers call so perilous; whatever may be thought of your discretion, my child, your pluck is really splendid.

I do not expect that letter from N.Y. until tomorrow morning, and doubt whether it will contain anything definite. If it should I'll telegraph. But, once more, don't wait for it or any other further information from me. Get ready. With my very much growing inclinations to go to Europe, I feel as if, after all, the chances are in that direction. Still, my dear child, while you may regard that as the probability, think also of the possibility of our not going abroad and like a sensible girl be ready for that contingency too. And do all you can to be ready by the 17th or 18th. I have an idea that, after all, you would care more about the presence of some of my friends than I.

I will probably come over to-morrow (Thursday) and telegraph you before I do. I said probably, so don't rely upon it and by no means let it interfere with your great mission. That takes precedence over everything now. I never dreamt how much interest I myself could take in—dresses. But I do, I assure you.

Write me every day, my child, and not so briefly.

J. P.[11]

There must have been some question in Kate's mind as to whether he would interrupt his journeys long enough for a side trip to the altar. Soon thereafter he was at the Gilsey House in New York, almost certain that he could make a deal for an unnamed newspaper, writing "My dearest Kate":

I write this downtown in the greatest haste, hoping that you are well, that you received my letter written before I left Washington, and that perhaps I shall find a letter from you at the hotel when I return this evening. Have been downtown since a very early hour, busy as a bee in the negotiations about the matter known to you. Prospects look quite favorable for a consummation of a bargain, though there is by no means any certainty of it whatever. I know and feel that you regret my absence, dear Kate, but I also know that your good head will not let your impatient heart run away with it. It is an important opportunity, perhaps a fortune, and you ought not expect me to neglect it. I must have business to occupy my mind and heart. You do the latter. Occupation will do the former, and unless all indications are grossly deceptive, the paper which I expect to purchase will turn out to be a great fortune both pecuniarily and politically. But then I am a sceptic, and leave you to be sanguine.

The worst of it is that I see no hope of getting away from here before Saturday or Sunday. I beg you, my dear child, to believe me that I am all the same with you in spirit. Make all arrangements, complete every preparation upon the assumption that I will certainly be with you on Monday for that important ceremony, thereafter to stay with you forever. What you think best, do. I'll accept cheerfully any arrangement you may make, hoping only that there will be so little ceremony, so much quiet, that there will be but little need of arrangement and few preparations necessary. Of course, I shall endeavor to return sooner. . . . You may depend upon that. But as I said it looks as if I absolutely had to stay here all of this week.

Don't fail to write me every day, dear.[12]

Again he sped back to Washington to tell of difficulties that thwarted the newspaper deal. He was in time for the wedding. And on June 19, 1878, he remained still long enough to be joined in marriage with Kate by the Rev. J. H. Chew at Washington's Episcopal Church of the Epiphany, where her parents had been married 30 years earlier. Kate's choice of a husband was said to have been a "great shock" to her family. Pulitzer, who had no religious affiliation but was tolerant of all religions, knelt at the altar with the devout daughter of Anglo-Saxon Protestants who thought she was marrying an unalloyed Hungarian. He had the large feet of a tall man. The soles of his shoes had been marked with his hotel room number, 17, by the porter who shined them. As he knelt there, turning his soles toward the audience, he later said, "I thought with dismay that the people back of me would think that I wore No. 17 shoes." [13]

IV. POLITICIAN'S HONEYMOON

The young couple spent ten weeks in Europe during which Pulitzer studied Victorian England, France under Marshal MacMahon and Germany under Bismarck for a series of articles for Dana's Sun. He had something more than even the strong prevailing conviction that the husband should rule the family. He regarded Kate as a lovely child, he adored her, he showered gifts and affection on her, scolded, praised and bossed her. Aware of his weakness for taking every remark in dead seriousness, she pulled his leg in Paris as she would continue to do for 33 years. She told him that she had bought a cookstove, provoking his wrath at the idea that his bride should soil her hands at such menial work. "Do you remember the awful temper you got into . . . ?" she later wrote him.[14]

A believer in individual effort, in private property, he disliked both monarchism and socialism. The German jumble of gaudy dukes and princes offended him, as did the clear threat of another war between France and Germany and the spectacle of 400,000 men drilling in uniform, supported by the toiling masses. Europe's established churches he regarded as tools of autocracy, and in England he was outraged by the nobility's display of splendor at the expense of the people. He had an enormous hatred for human exploitation, a powerful identification with "the people," and Kate doubtless listened to discourses on social justice as well as to words of love.

They reached New York September 5, after which his signed letters appeared in the Sun. His ruminations on the subject of liberty at times made him didactic, as when he wrote:

> Extremes meet. People without liberty have despots. People with too much have demagogues. . . . Both abuse liberty. The despot thinks there is too much liberty, the demagogue thinks there is not enough. When demagogism becomes socialism it is a danger to society. . . . Society means liberty and property. Socialism means the destruction of the latter. Imperialism to save it would trample over the dead body of [liberty].[15]

His description of England gave a better example of his alliterative journalistic style:

> We catch gilded and glittering glimpses of English life, we admire its traditions, love its literature, worship at the shrine of Westminster Abbey and forget the unspeakable misery of millions. . . . The aristocratic hold is so strong that probably the middle class would vote to retain it. I haven't time or space to tell of the injustices that came to my attention.[16]

Even for the Sun, such writing paid modestly, and by the time he and his wife reached St. Louis his nest-egg was small. Yet they stayed at the Lindell. Schurz and Preetorius perhaps still felt some resentment at his abandonment of Republicanism, for the Westliche Post had given only one line of 19 words to announce his marriage. Perhaps it was in St. Louis that Kate first learned of her husband's part-Jewish ancestry, and although it was said that she was greatly upset, she survived the shock. Nevertheless, anti-Semitism was a factor that both of them would have to cope with for the rest of their lives.

Pulitzer had learned of the coming forced sale of the bankrupt evening St. Louis Dispatch, which had lost money continuously under a succession of owners. He went for advice to his friend Daniel M. Houser, part owner of the prosperous combined Globe-Democrat, telling Houser he had only $5,200. Houser, who knew his mettle, encouraged him enough so that Pulitzer sent an emissary (secrecy again!), Simon J. Arnold, to bid for him at the sale on the courthouse steps at noon December 9. He was there himself, clad in a New-York-tailored chinchilla overcoat and soft hat, greeted by old friends, but he seemed merely a spectator as the auctioneer began his spiel. Bidding was sparse, starting at $1,000, and Arnold's bid of $2,500 eventually drew down the hammer.

At 31, Pulitzer finally had his own newspaper. A thing of ruin, it had a dilapidated office at 111 North Fifth Street, its ancient flatbed press broke down at critical moments, it had been reduced to stealing local news from morning newspapers, and its circulation was under 2,000. Its history of failure seemed ominous. It did, however, have a Western Associated Press franchise, which Pulitzer knew very well had a value of its own; and there were only two English-language evening competitors, the Post and the Star, both shaky.

The Post, only 11 months old, was published by the Harvard-educated, 35-year-old John A. Dillon, who had previously been a Globe-Democrat writer. Pulitzer and Dillon must have known each other well, not only through the newspaper fraternity but because Dillon was related to Pulitzer's good friend Captain James B. Eads and for five years had worked for Eads's bridge company. Amiable, accomplished, heir to a substantial real estate fortune which had dwindled, the socially prominent Dillon had made the Post a rather bookish sheet catering to the prosperous, and it had attained a circulation of about 2,000. A worrier, lacking Pulitzer's aggressive self-confidence and with a wholesome respect for him, Dillon foresaw trouble in battling his new rival. He called at once on Pulitzer and suggested a merger on equal terms.

Probably this was what Pulitzer had hoped for. Dillon was a modest liberal reformer, a hard-money man, and his Post's circulation would double that of the dying Dispatch. The two men called in William Patrick—the same attorney who had aided Pulitzer in his study of the law—and the two newspapers were combined as the Post and Dispatch, moving into the Post's decayed office at 321 Pine Street. Pulitzer and Dillon were co-proprietors, an arrangement that would grow increasingly uncomfortable for Dillon.[17]

II

Sensationalist

Chapter 1

How to Win Circulation

I. COLOSSAL NERVE

Pulitzer announced that the new paper would have a mind of its own: "The Post and Dispatch will serve no party but the people . . . will oppose all frauds and shams wherever and whatever they are; will advocate principles and ideas rather than prejudices and partisanship." [1] It would be nominally Democratic but strictly hard-money—would fight not only Grantism but also Democratic corruption.

The young David of the Post and Dispatch showed colossal nerve by his immediate challenging of the Goliath of Missouri journalism, the morning Republican, organ of the Bourbon Democratic moneyed clique which had taken control of the city and the state. Published by George and Charles Knapp and edited by the aggressive William Hyde, the powerful Republican had a huge five-story building at Third and Chestnut, the biggest staff in town and a circulation kept a close secret but which was somewhere near 20,000. The Knapps and Hyde, a trifle more interested in political maneuvering than in journalism per se, stood high in Bourbon councils which hand-picked candidates and elected them by steamroller methods.

While Pulitzer's specialty was attack, and he did not spare the morning (Republican) Globe-Democrat, in the main he got along well with McCullagh of the G-D, while his relations with the fellow Democrat Hyde would soon develop into mutual hatred. He always had a short-term and a long-term objective. Now his immediate goal was to rise above his present insignificance by winning quick circulation that would give him influence. His long-term intention was nothing less than to displace the Republican as the state's leading Democratic paper and to exert his power for party reform. The Republican was behind the St. Louis Bourbon

Samuel Glover for United States Senator, whereas the Post and Dispatch came out fighting for George G. Vest, the Sedalia ex-Confederate. Pulitzer assailed the Republican with gashouse vehemence, but he also expounded a principle that would remain with him through life:

> What is the great demoralizer of our public life? Of course, corruption. And what causes corruption? Of course, the greed for money. And who offer the greatest temptation to that greed? Corporations. . . .
>
> Money is the great power of today. Men sell their souls for it. Women sell their bodies for it. . . . Others worship it. . . . It is the growing dark cloud to our free institutions. . . . It is the irresistible great conflict of the future.[2]

The Bourbons were divided, and Vest won the election, to stay in the Senate 24 years. This victory of a new sheet with perhaps 3,000 circulation over the old and austere Republican was as pleasant to Pulitzer as it was galling to Hyde. "They live high around at the *Republican* office now," jeered the Post and Dispatch; "mostly crow." A month later it once more defeated the Republican in a battle over the city's monopolistic gas franchise. Again, it galvanized St. Louis by bombarding a tax-collection system that squeezed almost as much out of poor artisans in Kerry Patch as from the rich of the West Side, and by publishing in cold print the returns of some of the wealthy. The richest man in town, J. C. B. Lucas, swore to property totaling only $2,735. The Post and Dispatch headlined it "WEALTHY PAUPERS" and "WHOLESALE PERJURY AS A FINE ART," commenting: "When persons like Charles B. Chouteau, the Lucases, or Gerard B. Allen, swear that they do not have one cent in cash, or in bank, don't own one cent's worth of bonds or stocks or notes or other securities, they commit . . . a falsehood . . . And a much stronger term could be used without danger of libel suits."[3]

The paper even had the impudence to attack what amounted to a local religion—the conviction that the city was further outstripping Chicago as the metropolis of the Midwest. It presented figures to show that St. Louis was complacent, lazy, lagging both culturally and economically: ". . . It is 'playing baby' to console ourselves with dreams of future greatness. . . . No natural advantage can atone for the natural disadvantage of not having any sense. In the . . . fierce competition for business, not to advance is to recede."[4]

The sporadic crusade was a well-known journalistic device. But no journalist ever used it with such persistence, skill and effect as Pulitzer. The crusade would remain a foundation stone of his editorial policy for the rest of his life, always with two aims: to build circulation and to promote reforms. He used it not once a year but every week or every day. The lazy or uninformed editor was not equal to such a task. The crusade was something beyond and above mere newsgathering, placing the editor in the position of civic and political critic, saddling him with work and worry outside of the reporting function, thrusting on him a double responsibility—the strategic need for broad intelligence underlying accurate information about abuses to be attacked, and the tactical necessity to make the attack sharp, sure and effective. It was the Page 3 editorial function transferred to the Page 1 headlines. It took courage, for it was a sure enemy-maker. The fake campaign to "stir up interest" would be seen for what it was and would alienate the reader. Any campaign founded on mistaken premises would be punctured by rival journals and political enemies. Thus the constant crusader not only burdened himself with extra cares but risked his reputation with every crusade—reason enough why the device was used sparingly by other editors.

Pulitzer was the most effective of crusaders because no editor could match him either in background knowledge or the critical faculty. Criticism, fundamental dissatisfaction, the urge for something better, was his deepest instinct. Criticism was a characteristic so strong that he could not help applying it to journalism even if he tried. Throughout his years he would criticize everything with which he came in contact, from books and actors to houses and horses and down to his own wife and children. The crusade was simply the Pulitzer personality expressed in print. His crusades were effective not only because they reflected the intelligent protests of a born reformer who saw everywhere a need for reform, but also because he mounted them with the skill of the practical psychologist, the stump speaker who knew his audience. They were exciting—no one else dared to embarrass the Chouteaus, Lucases and Allens. They were informative, digging out facts unplumbed by other editors. They made the paper "talked about." They hammered insistently with the repetitiveness that advertisers years later would discover to be the basis of sales—what Pulitzer himself liked to call "the red thread of continuous policy." They persuaded readers that the Post and Dispatch was a watchdog against privilege, a friend of "the people." They sold newspapers.

If Pulitzer had had no other qualification, he would have gone far on his wonderful discovery that he could advance his own interests by defending the public's, and that he could do this with the sincerity of a preacher expounding the scriptures. There were dangers, for his three-week campaign against influential tax-dodgers made them pressure merchant friends to withdraw advertising from the paper—a temporary loss that hurt, but it did not stop the crusade.

". . . Mr. Pulitzer was performing every service on the paper," noted a St. Louis newspaperman, O. O. Stealey. "I remember one day he rushed into the editorial rooms, just as excited as a cub reporter, with an account of a runaway which he had written himself. The runaway horse had only damaged a cheap buggy, but the Pulitzer account obscured that fact for the last line."[5] He worked long hours—often far into the night, by gaslight—to make his paper bright, sharp, irreverent, surprising, a trifle shocking. It pricked the complacent. It assailed lethargy. It abounded in amusing paragraphs. It catered to the businessman, the workman, the housewife. It breathed a quality so newly animated by Pulitzer that one might say he invented it—*sensationalism.*

Of course the elder Bennett had conceived journalistic sensationalism in 1836, and others had essayed it—few liked a juicy story better than stocky Joseph B. McCullagh of the Globe-Democrat—but no one had exploited it with the virtuosity of Pulitzer. Innately excitable and dramatic, he saw the world as a sensational place whose sensational news must be reported sensationally. He disliked the euphemism, the prudish evasion. He agreed with Dana's *mot:* "I have always felt that whatever the Divine Providence permitted to occur I was not too proud to report." He believed that evil lay in the evasion, not the dissemination, of the truth. With his exaggerated emotional reactions, the truth was always exciting to him and this excitement pervaded the paper. Well aware that a journal losing its reputation for veracity would also lose its readers—aware also of his own tendency to see events in startling blacks and whites—he tried all his life to reconcile the two and never quite succeeded.

A Post and Dispatch reporter looked into a year-old grand jury report on prostitution, passed over by other journals, and produced a shocker. The paper printed a list of the owners—many of them substantial citizens—of houses leased knowingly or not to prostitutes, giving names and addresses. St. Louis' bordellos and their landlords had never been so well-publicized, and it was the landlords who complained bitterly of smutty journalism. When a local salesman died of apoplexy in a hotel room with a woman not his wife, the Post and Dispatch headlined it "A WELL KNOWN CITIZEN STRICKEN DOWN IN THE ARMS OF HIS MISTRESS" and front-paged an interview with the unhappy woman. It got the goods on its only evening competitor, the thieving Star, by publishing a fake report of a revolt in Afghanistan, which the Star promptly copied, to its humiliation when the Post and Dispatch exposed the theft. When Dolly Liggett, daughter of the rich tobacco manufacturer, outraged her parents by marrying a poor bookkeeper, a male Post and Dispatch reporter burdened with the name of Florence D. White actually gained entrance to the Liggett mansion, talked with the indignant mother, and the exclusive interview appeared under the headline "A ST. LOUIS HEIRESS CHOOSES A HUSBAND AGAINST HER FATHER'S WILL." When a young army officer killed himself in the Planter's House, the Post and Dispatch printed in full a personal letter found on the body telling of the hopeless love that caused his act. The singer Carlotta Patti sued the paper for asserting that she was drunk at her performance in Leavenworth, Kansas, but Pulitzer was so sure of his ground that he ran another story headed "FULL AS A TICK" which gave further evidence of her tipsiness and disparaged her attorney:

> Mr. Hermann is not so well provided with character himself that he can afford to be dancing in front of newspaper offices in war paint and

feathers, and we may take a notion one of these days to set him up where the public can admire his beautiful moral proportions.[6]

The Globe-Democrat attacked the Post and Dispatch for "mendacious fabrications of unscrupulous sensationalism," and the German Anzeiger des Westens and others followed suit. Pulitzer's attitude was clear in one of his replies:

> The press may be licentious, but it is the most magnificently repressive moral agent in the world today. More crime, immorality and rascality is prevented by the fear of exposure in the newspapers than by all the laws, moral and statute ever devised.[7]

This was a cardinal belief, logically impeccable, and the coincidence that it also tended to build circulation was most fortunate. One would have to be credulous indeed to think that Pulitzer did not know this, that he did not exploit it, that he did not play on sensationalism with the fond twang of a Hungarian with a zither. With his taste for the classics, he probably had not read the novels of Horatio Alger, which were spreading a philosophy of virtue and success over the land, but success was a passion with him. His St. Louis editorial contemporaries, nettled by the enterprise and independence that affronted wheelhorse Democrats and Republicans alike, would be happy to crush him. The most competitive of men, he saw journalism for what it was, a fierce struggle for supremacy, and as his cash dwindled it became a struggle for mere survival. Yet he seldom offended good taste as he interpreted it. Under the sensationalism was a journal that gave all the news conscientiously, that trumpeted its mission of reform with salutary effect as well as considerable noise.[8]

II. PISTOL-PACKING EDITOR

The Pulitzers were now living at 2920 Washington Avenue, west of the business district in the "best residential section." Kate was pregnant and the financial reserve was dwindling. Yet the Post and Dispatch's printing and office facilities were so poor that in February it moved back to the refurbished Dispatch building on Fifth Street and the proprietors pressed their luck by ordering a small new Hoe press and new type. The outlook was so dubious that Pulitzer said, "I drew out . . . $300 and put it in a trunk at home, against the coming expense of the birth of my first child." But after three months the income increased enough to encourage a precarious optimism, and by the end of the summer the Post-Dispatch (as it was now renamed) was a certain success.

Pulitzer generally carried a pistol, having accumulated new enemies by crusades against the gas company, a lottery racket, a horse-car monopoly and an insurance fraud. Kate, in pregnancy, had a yearning for tomatoes, and one evening, as Pulitzer carried a bag of them home, he saw a well-known thug crossing the street toward him with an expression of menace. According to a family story, Pulitzer "threw a tomato at him and dashed into the house." [9]

The birth of the first child, Ralph, on June 11, 1879, made the father ecstatic. John Dillon, however, was hardly ecstatic about the partnership in which he was less a partner than a highly regarded editorial writer. Although most of the staff came from Dillon's old Post, it was Pulitzer who evolved many of the ideas, supervised the counting room and dominated the small shop with a crackling enthusiasm that left his conservative colleague somewhat neglected under his green eyeshade. In fact Dillon had been deeply embarrassed during Pulitzer's tax-dodger crusade when journalistic enemies pointed out triumphantly that Dillon's own tax return had been judiciously shaved. In November he sold his half-interest to Pulitzer for an astonishing $40,000, remaining nevertheless a lifelong friend.

Pulitzer reached across the country to hire Ohio-born Colonel John A. Cockerill, the newspaperman he had met at the Cincinnati convention. Cockerill had since aided Pulitzer's old friend Hutchins in founding the Washington Post, and now was editor of the Baltimore Gazette. Now 34, two years older than Pulitzer, the big, handsome Cockerill had been stained by printer's ink ever since his return from drummer-boy service in the Civil War. The "Colonel" was a courtesy title freely handed out to men of note—even applied at times to Pulitzer. If Cockerill had never read the *Iliad,* he was yet an able writer familiar with every phase of newspapering including the mechanical, a workhorse, a man of humor, dash and authority. He was also a lover of the theater, a sometime stage-door Johnny who had been engaged to the actress Clara Morris and was still on affectionate terms with her. Certainly Pulitzer, who insisted on knowing a man's soul before hiring him, had learned something about Cockerill's soul from Hutchins and had offered a substantial salary. With the 1880 presidential year in the offing, he contemplated increased political activity and speechmaking tours, and in Cockerill he had an editor who could run the show while he was away. It is a safe guess that he went outside his staff, outside St. Louis, because he wanted a man with no friendships, enmities or local prejudices to impair his independence.[10]

The Post-Dispatch shop was a paternalistic chaos presided over by a Pulitzer who could be enthusiastic, eloquent, indignant or profane but never quiescent. He had a rare ability to communicate his fervor and sense of mission, so that something like a college loyalty pervaded the place, a sentiment far removed from normal journalistic cynicism. If he drove his staff hard, it had to be admitted that he worked harder than anyone else. He mingled with the crew in his shirt sleeves. Stealey recalled, "If a new reporter wrote a good story, Pulitzer, in his intensely enthusiastic way, would compliment the young fellow. He was just as free to point out mistakes." He was indeed the eternal instructor. He paid his men well, took a sincere interest in them, and gave special attention to his youngest cub, Florence White, who would remain with him for life. After three o'clock he would go out to the counter where the newsboys picked up their papers and josh with them: "He called them street merchants, and said they should favor sound business methods." A woman employee later recalled, "Mr. Pulitzer was a fine man and very considerate of all of us, just like a father."

This was the warmth of a happy husband and parent, a knight who had a new dragon to slay every day, a success hunter who was finding success after some years of floundering. Only on Sundays would he relax and spend hours playing with baby Ralph. The Pulitzers enjoyed a domestic harmony alloyed chiefly by Kate's fear that some enemy might shoot Joseph dead. As Stealey noted, "Mrs. Pulitzer, a remarkable beauty, called at the office with her first-born nearly every evening. Although having done the work of seven men, he would freshen up at seeing his wife and child and be as joyous as if they had just returned from a trip to Europe. He would . . . have as many compliments for Mrs. Pulitzer as would a young lover. In such an atmosphere, those were happy days for everyone." [11]

With the collapse of the Star, the Post-Dispatch was for a time the only English-language evening paper in St. Louis, and by the end of 1879 claimed a circulation of 4,984. Advertising came in so well that Pulitzer doubled the size to eight pages, hired servants and bought a handsome carriage. No paper could match his in injecting erotic allure even into a drama review:

> [Kisses] are the oases in the desert, the coral islands in the waste of waters, strawberries in cream in December. . . . Just imagine a divine girl with real warm blood glowing in every vein of her body, and a flush of health on her beautiful, up-turned face, her red lips protruding in the slightest possible pout, and her whole attitude meaning expectancy and waiting, and then fancy how that ripe, tender mouth would taste when you begin to feed on it, young man. . . . How would it strike you to play Romeo to Miss [Emma] Abbott's Juliet? [12]

Chapter 2

The Road to Power

I. ELECTIONITIS

Pulitzer was subject to a cyclical malady always coinciding with elections. The rolling drums of partisanship implanted a wild gleam into his kindly blue eyes. The disorder did not impair his reason—indeed it inspired some of his most brilliant feats—but it was injurious to his own tranquility and that of those around him. The symptoms were apparent to Kate and to his friends. Mild at first, they became aggravated as the campaign approached and were marked by a study of the issues and the men, discussions with politicians, the planning of strategy and the preparation of editorials and speeches, accompanied by increasing excitement. While the inflammation was common among politicians, even amusing in its normal manifestations, in him the *electionitis Pulitzerium* could reach an almost ruinous stage of distraction. At its worst it caused insomnia and extreme irritability, and it was followed by some mental depression when his candidate lost.

It would reappear again and again throughout his life, usually most pernicious during presidential elections but at times very painful in lesser canvasses. Since he always began to think about the next President two years in advance, the symptoms were noticeable in some form at least half the time. The science of politics was seldom out of his thoughts. Kate ultimately came to dread elections because they upset him and his family so. The comic overtones vanished when she beheld consequences harmful to his health and her own happiness. She must have realized that fond though he was of her and his son, winning elections was in a sense more important and that the quest for power was deep in his bones.

Pulitzer once told a friend, "I can never be president because I am a foreigner, but some day I am going to elect a president." [1] This was no mere small talk. It was a visceral yearning that would possess him as long as he breathed. It was the most driving ambition of his life, one over which he seemed to have no control, and his election malady was progressive as well as recurrent, as later events would show.

II. BEATEN BY THE BOURBONS

Now his ambition to make himself Democratic leader of Missouri was evident in the impetuosity with which he flung himself and his paper into the 1880 local and national campaigns. He searched for a Democratic presidential candidate as if for salvation, writing Tilden off as hopeless: "He was nominated as a bold leader. When the emergency arrived he led no more than a mouse." [2] He was steering a collision course with William Hyde of the Republican, a Tilden man. Hyde regarded his paper's position as Democratic spokesman for Missouri as unimpeachable. Pulitzer impeached it constantly. The enormous ambition of this aggressive "foreigner" with a small newspaper only a year old was infuriating to Hyde. The Post-Dispatch not only dismissed the mousy Tilden but put forward tentative candidates to replace him—Senator Thurman of Ohio, Senator Bayard of Delaware—and poured ridicule on the Republican. In March, when Hyde passed his rival on Olive Street, he suddenly swung and knocked Pulitzer down. According to Pulitzer's version in the Post-Dispatch, both men fell in the scuffle and he lost his glasses:

> Unfortunately, I wore a heavy overcoat and my revolver was not in it, but in my hip pocket. I had just got it out and was on the point of using it, when someone wrested it from me. The crowd separated us. . . . Hyde and everyone knows that I am extremely near-sighted and can't see at all without [my glasses].[3]

One suspects that he was hardly as trigger-itchy as he made out—that this public advertisement of his hip-pocket pistol was a calculated effort to discourage further attacks on him. Hyde's choler must have risen when Pulitzer, with considerable cheek for a youthful politician, rode the train to Utica, New York, to urge 70-year-old Horatio Seymour to make the race. "I have always said that you were too good a patriot and too good a Democrat to decline the leadership," he told Seymour according to his own account in the Post-Dispatch.[4] Seymour, perhaps dubious that this young man had the leadership to offer, and uncertain how it would affect older party helmsmen if he exchanged political confidences with the Missourian, was polite but noncommittal.

Hyde and his allies were ready when Pulitzer won a seat at the state Democratic convention at Moberly, where Hyde was the Tilden leader. "The Tilden managers had the galleries packed with St. Louis toughs, in order to howl Mr. Pulitzer down," wrote one observer. ". . . For nearly an hour Pulitzer defiantly held his place on the platform. . . . Finally, the toughs exhausted themselves, and Mr. Pulitzer made his speech." [5] He completed a remarkable victory over Hyde by finding enough sympathetic sentiment to secure an anti-Tilden delegation to the national convention at Cincinnati, and by being chosen a delegate to Cincinnati himself.

Here again, on June 22, the political firehorse from St. Louis met the spirited prancer from Louisville. Henry Watterson was chairman of the resolutions committee, and with Pulitzer, Manton Marble and others wrote the Democratic platform. The ailing Tilden finally bowed out, as did Seymour, and General Winfield Scott Hancock was the nominee against the Republicans' Garfield. Pulitzer hurried back to St. Louis to work for the candidacy of Thomas T. Crittenden for governor of Missouri. Crittenden won the nomination. Next the firehorse galloped into St. Louis politics, seeking the Democratic nomination for Congress from the city's second district, usually tantamount to election. Here it is not impossible that he felt forced to sacrifice ideals for expediency.

Edward Butler—for years thereafter the notoriously corrupt boss of St. Louis—was then gaining ascendancy over a group of local politicians known as the Dark Lantern. Butler, who started as a blacksmith, now employed blacksmiths and had the contract to shoe all the city's horses thanks to his ability to deliver votes. The Village Blacksmith and the Dark Lantern felt it no more than polite that a candidate should contribute liberally to the party's coffers in return for their support, and it was rumored, though never established, that Pulitzer did so contribute. Since nomination would mean election anyway, the Post-Dispatch said little about Pulitzer's candidacy.

Now at last the Missouri Republican, which so long had kept a rod in pickle for Pulitzer, had its revenge. Hyde and his allies persuaded Thomas Allen, wealthy president of the Iron Mountain Railroad, to enter the primary against Pulitzer. By quick work they mustered such strong Bourbon support that Butler and the Dark Lantern betrayed Pulitzer and went over to Allen on the day before the primary. In a shriek of protest, the Post-Dispatch assailed the "sordid, malevolent and domineering managers of the Republican" and described Allen as a monopolist who would represent the corporations, not the people: "As a railroad man Mr. Allen is the foe of the Mississippi River, and the day that sand-bars and snags made our levee a waste . . . would be a day of pleasurable emotion for him." [6]

Sandbars and snags it was, for Pulitzer was humiliated at the polls, receiving only 709 votes to 4,254 for Allen. It was his first and only defeat for public office, a staggering blow that must have made him a difficult husband for a time. The Republican rejoiced. "I am out of public life," Pulitzer told a meeting. "The only suffrage I solicit you can extend to me by purchasing my newspaper daily." [7]

At the same time he was warning St. Louis against Jay Gould, who had swallowed up the Missouri Pacific, Katy, Iron Mountain and Frisco railroads—even controlled the Eads Bridge—and was saddling the city with rates that favored Chicago. The very name of Chicago was bitter, for the decennial census had punctured the great illusion, the dream of the future world metropolis. Chicago had soared to a population of 503,000, while St. Louis was relegated to sixth city with only 350,000—a fact the Windy City newspapers rubbed in with salt. Pulitzer was as shocked as anyone, but he had the nerve to blame it on local lethargy and Bourbonism: "And now, after all her brag and blow, St. Louis sits in sackcloth and ashes, gnashing her teeth as the sixth instead of the fourth city of the Union." [8]

On September 30 Lucille Irma Pulitzer was born, but although Pulitzer was the most philoprogenitive of men, this great event stopped him only briefly. Kate long since had become aware that she was married to a galloper. Indiana being a pivotal state, as usual, he was off to speak for Hancock in Indianapolis, where on October 9 he repeated his theme of corporation-dominated Republicanism:

"We want prosperity but not at the expense of liberty. Poverty is not as great a danger to liberty as wealth, with all its corrupting, demoralizing influences. Suppose all the [corporate] influences I have just reviewed were to take their hands off instead of supporting the Republican party, would it have a ghost of a chance of success?

"Let us have prosperity, but never at the expense of . . . real self-government, and let us never have a government at Washington owing its retention to the power of the millionaires rather than to the will of the millions." [9]

The Republicans not only sent Roscoe Conkling to Indianapolis to answer Pulitzer, but a fortune in greenbacks that bought so many votes that the G.O.P. won the state election in October. Although Pulitzer went on another stumping tour ending in New York, he made what would become a habit with him, a skillful canvass of the election outlook, and admitted in the Post-Dispatch that Garfield seemed likely to win. He was right, as the P-D announced the day after the election under the headline "A DAY OF DISASTER." Garfield won with a plurality of 59 electoral votes although his popular plurality was less than 10,000. At any rate, Crittenden was elected governor. The St. Louis firehorse, exhausted, retired to pasture for a time.

III. THE LOUDEST VOICE ON THE MISSISSIPPI

After shouting himself hoarse in three national elections in eight years, Pulitzer had nothing to show for it—politically—but some deterioration in health. Journalistically he was in clover. By the end of 1880 the Post-Dispatch claimed a daily average circulation of 8,740. It was nearing the rival Republican in city sales (though not in the country), it was gaining on the big Globe-Democrat, and it had returned Pulitzer at least $40,000 in profits for the year. In St. Louis he was counted a rich man. Toward this early success he had precisely the same attitude as such contemporaries as Andrew Carnegie, John D. Rockefeller and F. W. Woolworth: it was not enough. A gain was encouraging, but really, when one considered the factors, it should have been bigger. A good income pointed only to a better one, and success was never here but ahead. He could look at a ledger showing gratifying profits and point out, in the most courteous and convincing way, how they could have been made larger. This was the line he took toward Cockerill, Business Manager John B. McGuffin, Advertising Manager William C. Steigers, City Editor Henry W. Moore and down the row to the newsboys.

Marriage and success so agreed with him that his uncertain health was not apparent. He had put on a few pounds, his face was a trifle fuller and the reddish beard and moustache now were ample enough to rescue the mouth from utter dominance by that formidable nose. The blue eyes that gazed through the thick pince-nez were keen, decisive, paternal. Possibly the doubts Kate's parents had held about him had whetted his resolution for mastery, but the powerful ambition had always been there and would always be there, driving him like a locomotive. There was much of the cheerleader in him, entirely spontaneous. Everyone on the staff sensed a peculiar electric force that emanated from him so strongly that the sparks seemed almost visible. Perhaps there was nothing more mysterious in this than his rare combination of intensity, enthusiasm, brilliance, sense of righteousness and skill in handling people. He analyzed each employee, knew his abilities, interests, weaknesses and vanities and took them into careful account. He shunned the chain of command, often dealing personally with everyone from Cockerill down to the typesetters, showing a sincere interest in them, infecting them all with his own sense of the importance of the Post-Dispatch. He liked to tell about his arrival as a poor immigrant boy, his tribulations as a hack-driver and waiter, his feeling of the boundless opportunities existing only in America, and to say, "You can do just as I did—start at the bottom of the ladder and go up."

He often lunched—very hurriedly—with friends at Faust's, where he had once waited on tables. The comfortable three-story Pulitzer home on Washington Avenue was the scene of parties and card games attended by journalists and by such members of the legal fraternity as Johnson, Patrick, Charles Gibson and Colonel Alonzo Slayback. The Pulitzers wintered at Aiken to relieve Ralph's asthma, and visited New York and Washington occasionally. Multilingual, familiar with plays and music, with the East and with Europe, they could instill into a gathering the flavor of an international salon, bringing to a sleepy provincial city echoes of far places and thoughts well removed from the Mississippi. Pulitzer himself could discourse intelligently about the arts, and his pride in his two children was immense, but inevitably his talk came around to politics and journalism.

After the political debacle of 1880, he turned the Post-Dispatch even more strongly into his twin specialties, reform and sensation. He took sweet revenge in a series of searching exposures of the Dark Lantern Democratic cabal. He showed his independence (and perhaps some spite) by opposing the Democrats in the 1881 city election, unveiling their corruption so effectively that the Post-Dispatch was the biggest factor in bringing about a miracle, the landslide election of the Republican mayoral candidate, William L. Ewing. He turned angrily against Governor Crittenden, who indeed became rather friendly with the Dark Lantern. On New Year's Eve he sent every last P-D reporter out to visit the gambling houses and filled his front page with their discoveries, embarrassing the police by listing the names and addresses of 17 places so wide open that "the gamblers themselves are beginning to think they are conducting a legitimate business." The Post-Dispatch went on: "We do not say that gamblers pay for immunity here, but it will be interesting to note the policy that will be pursued by the authorities now. . . . What will the police do about it?" [10]

These incessant exposures forced the police to arrest the politically powerful boss gambler, Robert Pate, who was ultimately convicted, given a six-month jail sentence, and then pardoned by Governor Crittenden. The Post-Dispatch thereafter referred to Crittenden as "Pate's Governor." Pulitzer was sued repeatedly but vainly for libel. He was attacked on the street by a burly hoodlum, but broke free and reached the safety of his office. There he was later visited by Jake Usher, the angry owner of an iniquitous den. A reporter who was present noted, "[Usher's] indignation was as a summer breeze competing with a Kansas cyclone. Mr. Pulitzer had the loudest voice on the Mississippi, and his flow of words came like Niagara. After describing the disgrace Usher was to St. Louis, he started for Usher, who . . . lost no time in getting away . . ." [11]

In the fond disclosure of public turpitude, he gave his paper free rein. If no eyebrow-raiser came to hand, his men went out and created one. Thus, a campaign against the variety shows, which had long existed and indeed were unsavory enough, gave opportunity for literary enlargement on loose women parading their charms before young men of the town and leading them into debauchery. Prose of dime-novel intensity blossomed out in new attacks on protected prostitution, on abortionists, on opium dens. The Post-Dispatch developed an inordinate interest in the sins of the respectable and prosperous, with spicy headlines: "AN ADULTEROUS PAIR," "DUPED AND DESERTED," "KISSING IN CHURCH," "LOVED THE COOK," "A WILY WIDOW." When the ailing Reverend George Lofton took an alcoholic stimulant prescribed by his physician, it made a two-column shocker suggesting that the parson was drunk. The paper kept a sharp eye on beauteous Nellie Hazeltine, the high-flying 24-year-old daughter of a rich St. Louis merchant, who frequented the Eastern watering places. Its interest was whetted by the fact that old Samuel Tilden, the luckless bachelor near-President, had once been smitten by the "belle of St. Louis." Nellie's flirtation with John Amweg, a singer at the city's popular entertainment garden Uhrig's Cave, received as much prominence as the shooting of President Garfield. When Nellie settled down by marrying Frederick Paramore, son of a railroad president, it was a loss to journalism but she was succeeded by such sensations as the case of the St. Louis priest suspected of fathering a child.[12]

While Cockerill had had experience with the excitement-loving Cincinnati Enquirer and knew precisely how to titillate readers, the policy was Pulitzer's and the paper became noted for its sensational creativity, its facility in manufacture, its skill at studying phenomena always present and making something new and galvanizing out of it. Pulitzer would have described this as editorial vision—the ability to find human drama in events overlooked by others in the mistaken belief that they were commonplace, the boldness to throw light on aspects of the news sidestepped by the prudish, the morally hypocritical. He had an irrepressible twist of logic in such matters, as he did in another argument that he used persistently through the years—his insistence that when he criticized an employee it was proof of his confidence and hope. If he did not criticize a man, the man was obviously hopeless.

By March, 1881, the Post-Dispatch's circulation had risen to 12,000, and in another 18 months it would soar to 22,300. Profits for 1881 were $85,000.

Side by side with the sensations was "legitimate" news, well reported if sometimes a trifle excited. Pulitzer himself hurried to Long Branch to send signed dispatches about the sinking President Garfield, one of them attacking the doctors' excessive optimism: "There is no doubt about it. The President has chronic blood poisoning. Unless his blood can be cured he can not be saved. I said this over a week ago and I repeat it. . . . The best sign this morning is the absence of Dr. Bliss [the chief physician], who has gone to New York. . . . The official bulletins are entirely untrustworthy, Dr. Bliss' particularly. Everybody here knows that he is a reckless liar." [13]

Obviously the paper's leading correspondent was a bit reckless himself. He also went to Washington to report the Star Route postal frauds, and to New York to send dispatches about Roscoe Conkling's humiliating failure to win reelection to the Senate. But the Post-Dispatch was frank about its discoveries concerning the pulling power of various types of news, saying in an editorial:

As a rule political events do not affect our sales favorably. Next to the assassination of President Garfield our greatest increase has been by a local hanging. Our people are not easily worked up by a sporting event, but they take considerable interest in a "social sensation." [14]

As success piled on success, Pulitzer spread its benefits among his staff, the best-paid in St. Louis, with top reporters earning as much as $35 a week. Cockerill was given a stock interest that paid him $2,500 a year over his salary. Each employee received a two-week annual vacation with pay—utter altruism at the time—and his salary continued when he was ill. Especially industrious newsboys were given such prizes as gold or silver watches, suits of clothes and pocketknives, and all of them enjoyed an annual Christmas dinner with all the trimmings. The proprietor understood the advantages of a loyal personnel and was sympathetic in general with union labor's efforts for fair treatment, but when the printers' union tried to organize his shop, he swiftly showed them who was boss. He sent them packing and fired a group of his own compositors siding with the union, showing his annoyance in an editorial:

> The Post-Dispatch believes in the right of trained artisans and skilled mechanics to organize for their own good, but the right to manage the internal affairs of this office, employ and discharge and to direct when and how labor shall be performed, is one that the proprietor reserves to himself. . . . [The union policy] is simply one form of mob law . . . It practically amounts to this, that a newspaper is expected to take out a license, not from the established authorities as is the case in despotic Russia, but from an irresponsible lot of unknown men who assume no risks and share no losses.[15]

There were, however, no current losses. The Post-Dispatch moved into bigger quarters on Market Street near Fifth. Pulitzer bought two new $25,000 Hoe presses and announced that he did not owe a nickel. In three and a half years he had built a ruin into a thriving newspaper, the most independent and constructive in town as well as the raciest. His "SHOCKING DISCLOSURE" and "GIRL IN RED TIGHTS" stories brought in more readers for his political instruction—the "hula dancer performing in front of a cathedral in order to attract the crowds." To be sure, he used sensationalism for circulation and money, but cynicism was not the mainspring. Wealth alone would have left him frustrated and unhappy. He later said, "You may write the most sublime philosophy, but if nobody reads it, where are you? You must go for your million circulation, and, when you have got it, turn the minds and the votes of your readers one way or the other at critical moments." [16]

Whether the editor protested too much would be told by his long-run achievements; but he considered his audience not only as readers but as thinkers and voters. Journalism was his road to instruction and power,

Missouri was not big enough for him, and wealth was essential for the huge capital investment he had in mind. Early in 1882, with his friend Daniel Houser of the Globe-Democrat, he went on another fruitless newspaper shopping trip in New York, where his brother Albert was now a valued writer for the Herald. He moved on to Boston, impelled by his habit of visiting extraordinarily successful newspapermen to learn what made them so. He called on the minikin Charles H. Taylor, who had brought the Boston Globe from debt to affluence by slanting it for the masses. "Pulitzer and I went off to luncheon," Taylor recalled. "Then I went up to his room, and we stayed together every minute from that Friday until Monday morning, talking all the while about building up newspapers. From that time on we kept in very close touch . . ." [17]

Chapter 3

Unwelcome in St. Louis

I. THE KILLING AT THE POST-DISPATCH

The third Pulitzer child, Katherine Ethel, was born June 30, 1882. That fall, the family left to spend the entire winter at Aiken to aid the health of both Ralph and his father. An election was in the offing to fill the seat of the deceased Congressman Thomas Allen, the man who had swamped Pulitzer in 1880. The local Bourbon Democrats, supported as always by the machine-bound Missouri Republican, picked James O. Broadhead as their candidate. Although Broadhead was one of the city's most eminent attorneys, a politician of standing ever since his efforts for the Union during the war, and one who had served with Pulitzer at the constitutional convention of 1875, he had connections which John Cockerill, now running the Post-Dispatch, could not endure. Nine years earlier he had represented the city in making a franchise agreement with the gas company that saddled St. Louis with exorbitant rates. Later he had switched to represent the gas company when the city tried to revoke the franchise. Now he was Jay Gould's attorney in St. Louis. Even without all this, his support by the Republican was enough to stamp him as an enemy of the people in the eyes of Pulitzer and Cockerill.

The Post-Dispatch's affection for Broadhead's primary opponent, John M. Glover, was less warm than its aversion to Broadhead. Cockerill assailed Broadhead for double-dealing in the gas dispute and branded him as a tool of the Village Blacksmith. When Broadhead's law partner, Colonel Alonzo W. Slayback, took to the hustings for his associate, the Post-Dispatch flung barbs at Slayback as well although he and Cockerill were brother Elks. Slayback, a convivial, hot-tempered Confederate veteran who composed poetry in his spare time, replied by calling the Post-Dispatch a "blackmailing sheet" in a public speech. Cockerill, who had a temper of his own, took revenge by digging out a "card" which John Glover had sent the Post-Dispatch a year earlier while quarreling with Slayback over a lawsuit. In it, Glover said in part, "so far from being a brave man, the Colonel, notwithstanding his military title, is a coward." [1] Pulitzer had wisely refused to publish it at the time. Now Cockerill not only published it but called attention to it in an editorial paragraph.

At five that afternoon, October 13, Slayback and a lawyer friend, William Clopton, strode into Cockerill's office on the second floor of the Post-Dispatch building "with blood in their eyes." Cockerill was chatting with McGuffin and Victor Cole, foreman of the composing room. Precisely what happened was known only to the survivors, who told conflicting stories. In any case, Slayback threatened Cockerill, who seized a pistol from his desk drawer and fired. Slayback sank to the floor with blood gushing from his mouth, dying almost instantly.

Reporters rushed into the office, getting details of a story that required no legwork. Cockerill went to his room at the Lindell, changed his bloody clothes, then surrendered to the police at the Four Courts building and was lodged in a cell. To friends who called on him, he said, "Too bad, but it couldn't be helped." [2]

The killing made headlines even in New York. The popular Cockerill had many supporters, including his former fiancée Clara Morris, who telegraphed him assurance of her belief in his innocence. But the thoroughly vindictive Missouri Republican vented its spleen in a story deliberately calculated to arouse public feeling against Cockerill and the Post-Dispatch, with headlines describing Cockerill as "WITH A REVOLVER READY AT HAND" and charging that he had murdered Slayback in cold blood. Slayback, whose brother was president of the Merchant's Exchange, was well-liked and there was great sympathy for his widow and family. The Republican continued its attacks with such virulence that a mob collected in front of the Post-Dispatch and made threats of lynching the owner and burning the building before it was dispersed.

At the inquest next day, Clopton swore that Slayback was unarmed, that he was merely removing his coat to prepare for a fistfight when Cockerill shot him dead. Cockerill, on the other hand, backed by McGuffin and Cole, testified that Slayback was aiming a pistol at him and that he fired in self-defense. The fact that a pistol was found in the dead man's hand seemed to bear this out, though there were the inevitable charges that the gun had been placed there afterward by Post-Dispatch men.

Pulitzer cut short his vacation and reached St. Louis on the 15th to stand solidly behind his editor. His position was made more difficult by his acquaintance with the Slaybacks, who had been his guests. But if he had doubts about Cockerill's wisdom in publishing Glover's card, he gave no public hint of it. He visited Cockerill at the Four Courts, assured him of his support, and in the Post-Dispatch asked the public to let the law settle the question. Two days later he published a statement that must have warmed Cockerill's heart:

> The charge of blackmail is the worst that can be preferred against any honest paper or editor. If Mr. Cockerill had remained silent under it, he would, by his silence, have confessed its truth. . . . The publication of the Glover card under the circumstances was purely in self-defense, justified, invited, made inevitable by Col. Slayback's own provocation.
>
> Mr. Pulitzer is willing to go further. If Mr. Cockerill had allowed the public stigma and brand of blackmailing to go unresented he would have been unfit for his position, and would have ceased to be managing editor of the paper.[3]

The Republican continued to attack Cockerill—and Pulitzer—and to give instructions to the grand jury investigating the case as well as to browbeat witnesses and attorneys. It persuaded the bar association to pass a resolution condemning the Post-Dispatch. Seven weeks later the jurors found that Slayback had been armed when he invaded Cockerill's office, a fact fully justifying them in refusing to return an indictment. The Republican assailed the grand jurors, then persuaded Mrs. Slayback to sue Cockerill for depriving her of her husband. Cockerill's reaction was understandable:

"I desire to say to the public that from the commencement of this regretful affair, I have been pursued with almost inhuman malignancy by the proprietors of the St. Louis Republican . . . These men have a deep-seated business hostility against The Post-Dispatch. . . . A more unwarranted abuse of journalistic power certainly was never manifested in this country."[4]

Indeed the Republican, still poised for the kill, continued a propaganda campaign aimed at destroying the Post-Dispatch and making St. Louis uninhabitable for Cockerill and the Pulitzers. It unified Pulitzer's host of enemies, the Bourbons, the "big people" in town, all of whom turned on him now. Cockerill resumed the editorship, but the Republican's incessant blackening of his name made him an embarrassment. The Post-Dispatch, after its unbroken record of gain, lost important advertisers as well as 1,300 subscribers in a few weeks. There was nothing for it but to drop Cockerill, which Pulitzer did with the greatest reluctance and, one may be sure, with assurances for the future that would not be long in fruition.

In a shrewd move to restore the paper's wounded reputation, he offered the editorship to his former partner, John Dillon, who by now must have been sorry that he let his half-interest go for $40,000. Dillon meanwhile had served as secretary of the American legation in Mexico, but recently had returned to St. Louis as editor of the weekly Spectator at a modest salary. He was a wise choice on two counts. He had a quiet conservatism that the paper needed in this crisis; and instead of being an outsider, as both Cockerill and Pulitzer were, he was a native of St. Louis and a member of one of the "best families" whose enmity was most hurtful. Under Dillon the hula dancer donned crinolines. The Post-Dispatch muffled its sensationalism somewhat like a naughty child forced to stand for a time quietly in a corner. Broadhead was elected in a close race, and soon thereafter Pulitzer rejoined his family, now in the East.

The whole affair had been a humiliation and a sharp business reverse. It had shorn him for a time of his precious journalistic freedom and had made it clear that he and his family were no longer welcome in St. Louis. To him, losing circulation was as losing blood, and the Post-Dispatch dropped another thousand readers that winter before it leveled out. It was on this Eastern trip that he discovered that the New York World was for sale. He was at any rate delighted by an editorial defense of the Post-Dispatch appearing in the Kansas City Star, owned by William Rockhill Nelson, a crusader who understood Pulitzer's language:

> Every bribe-taking official, every public plunderer, every greedy monopolist—in short every rascal in the land—deprecates "personal journalism". . . . [The Post-Dispatch] has antagonized all the evil elements in the city, and has not hesitated to attack wrong, however securely entrenched. . . . There isn't a rogue in St. Louis who does not hate the *Post-Dispatch*, and all the rascally elements would have been delighted to have seen its building razed to the ground and its editor lynched after the recent tragedy. But this was not to be. A powerful public journal cannot be wiped out in this manner by a howling mob, even when it is led by so-called "prominent citizens." [5]

II. GENTLEMEN, A CHANGE HAS TAKEN PLACE

On November 16, 1882, Pulitzer's brother Albert had scraped together $25,000 in capital—to which Joseph made a small contribution—and had founded the one-cent New York Morning Journal, renting space on the sixth floor of Whitelaw Reid's Tribune building on Park Row. Albert earlier had married an Englishwoman, Fanny Bannard, from whom he had separated. He had made a considerable reputation as Washington correspondent for the Herald, which later sent him to Europe to report the Russo-Turkish war. Yet in his new Journal he shunned politics and devoted such clever attention to entertainment and gossip, to the theater and sporting events, that it was immediately successful though it had no press franchise. Starting with a pressrun of 22,000, in six months it had attained a claimed circulation of 50,000,[6] which one need not take too literally. To the Journal, whose sole purpose was to make money, every woman was beautiful, the world was a romantic, spicy and humorous place, and any interest in civic affairs or reform was incidental. The brown-moustached Albert was tall, plump, cheery, an enormous eater who often topped off a heavy lunch with a whole apple pie and then sent out for sandwiches and wine in the afternoon.

In April, Joseph Pulitzer, his nerves badly frayed, arrived in New York with his family and took rooms at the luxurious Fifth Avenue Hotel. Their announced intention was a European vacation, but Pulitzer's first purpose was to buy the morning World if he could. He visited Albert, and once again ran into Henry Watterson, who was making one of his periodic sojourns in the city. Others who surely saw him were Schurz, now for a brief time editor of the New York Evening Post; Keppler, whose *Puck* was a money-maker; and Dana at the Sun. But the man he most wanted to see was Jay Gould, owner of the World.

Founded as a religious daily in 1860, the World had soon sunk into receivership and then had been strongly revived as a Democratic paper by the able Manton Marble. Marble, in disgust after the Tilden election disaster in 1876, sold it to a group headed by Thomas A. Scott, president of the Pennsylvania Railroad. Thereafter, still nominally Democratic, it became a pawn of capitalists. Scott, who bought it as a propaganda vehicle for his own stock enterprises, tired of meeting its growing deficits and in 1879 unloaded it on Gould in an odd transaction in which the paper figured as a throw-in. Scott sold Gould control of the Texas & Pacific Railroad and persuaded him to buy the World along with it. Gould always claimed that his ownership of the paper was unintended—a sort of railroad accident—but he was not prone to such accidents and he saw an advantage in using the World to promote his own designs. Its inspired editorials and "news" stories, for example, soon aided him in seizing control of Western Union. But in an era when many rapacious financiers had won disfavor, Gould was the unchallenged leader as an object of public loathing, a sort of national effigy of corporate chicanery. His ownership of the World was known, a stigma not even a good paper could survive. Not only had the World's usefulness to him dwindled but it was losing about $40,000 a year.

Pulitzer called on Gould at his office in the Western Union building at 195 Broadway. Gould, with his many Missouri interests, knew of Pulitzer and of his Post-Dispatch's bitter opposition to everything he stood for—knew of the killing of Slayback, partner of the Gould lawyer Broadhead. The slight, black-bearded robber baron and the tall journalist who dickered across a mahogany desk were natural enemies but both masters of elaborate courtesy. It was not to be expected that Gould, however badly he wanted to sell, would make attractive terms to a man he knew would transform the World from an "organ" to an implacable foe. The price Gould named was well over a half-million dollars.

This was a high valuation for a losing sheet with a circulation barely over 15,000. The fact that Pulitzer did not say good-day showed his enormous yearning for a foothold in New York and his knowledge that at least one other—the wealthy John R. McLean of the Cincinnati Enquirer—was interested in the World. New York already seemed oversupplied with newspapers, especially in the morning, with Dana's two-cent Sun leading the pack with an amazing 140,000 circulation, Bennett's three-cent Herald trailing it slightly in numbers but exceeding it in prestige and profits, Reid's Tribune and George Jones's Times both solidly successful at four cents. Not to be classed with these titans but still vying for morning readers were others including the Star, Truth and the Journal. In the face of all this, surely the two men in the Western Union office were both insane, Gould for asking a fortune for his moribund paper, Pulitzer for countenancing the proposition.

But Pulitzer, reflecting on how his brother and Keppler had succeeded in New York with little more than brains and skill, was thinking in terms of politics and reader-exploitation that were his alone. He was conscious, as he always was, of possessing abilities beyond those of the existing editorial establishment. The World had that invaluable asset, an Associated Press franchise, itself worth a huge sum. Politically the outlook was favorable, for the city, though preponderantly Democratic, had no such powerful Democratic paper as he envisioned. The Tribune and Times were both Republican, the Sun and Herald capriciously independent. With the Republicans still riven in the quarrel between Roscoe Conkling's Stalwarts and James Blaine's Half-Breeds, and the amazing landslide that had made Grover Cleveland governor of New York and swept in a Democratic House in 1882, the party's national prospects for 1884 looked rosy. A dynamic new editorial voice in the metropolis might not only propel the Democrats to victory but gather its own garlands along the way. Pulitzer, yearning to elect a President, felt it highly likely that New York State's electoral votes would decide the 1884 election. He wanted to help decide those electoral votes.

Was the city saturated with newspapers? He did not think so. The existing papers of consequence were dignified, literary, edited for educated people, uninspired by thoughts of reform, unread by the great mass of workers. Solid citizens, on the other hand, disdained such penny gazettes as Albert's Journal, the delight of apprentices and chambermaids. Pulitzer's ideal was a newspaper so astonishingly liberal, reformist and newsy that it would charm the workmen and still appeal to a segment of the white-collar class.

When Joseph broached the plan to Albert, "a violent discussion arose between them as to whether New York could stand two Pulitzers." Joseph's opinion of his earthy brother was not high, and some said that he treated him cavalierly. It is not impossible that Joseph, who had tried and failed for years to establish himself in New York, was exasperated at Albert's quick success as well as contemptuous of his newspaper. The real difficulty was in coming to terms with Gould, who wanted Pulitzer to retain part of the staff and to buy not only the newspaper but the two-year-old World building at 31–32 Park Row, which would add about $200,000 to the price. One day, Pulitzer, nervously unstrung, returned to his hotel, told Kate he had given up the idea and they would sail next day.

Here was where the charming Mrs. Pulitzer unwittingly saved Grover Cleveland and the Democratic party, at the same time striking a fatal blow at Blaine and the Republicans. Seldom would a domestic conversation in a hotel suite have such sweeping national implications. Always optimistic, Kate felt that her husband was defeated by nerves, not by reason. Her words were so persuasive that he renewed the bargaining and on April 28 closed the deal with Gould. He got the paper for $346,000, to be paid in instalments ending in 1886, and succeeded in leasing the building rather than buying it, and in preserving his full freedom in selection of staff.

"By the way, Mr. Pulitzer," Gould said, "I had quite forgotten that some time ago I gave a small block of this newspaper stock to my son George. I would like to have him retain his interest. I assume you will have no objections to the boy's keeping this little holding."

Pulitzer wanted no Gould foot in the door. "Not if you do not object to seeing it stated each morning in the year that the Gould family has no control or influence in the property," he replied.

Gould pondered the thought of such a daily invidious reminder and dropped the idea.[7]

Pulitzer had paid $346,000 for a press franchise and a bad name. Emerging on Broadway, he was oppressed by the huge debt he had incurred as well as the formidable journalistic retooling job that threatened his mental equipoise, and was instantly looking for someone to help him with both burdens. He ran into 35-year-old Melville Stone, the remarkably successful co-owner of the Chicago Daily News who was also on a New York visit, and steered him into the Astor House. "He invited me to share in the purchase," Stone recalled, "taking either the editorial or the business department." Being already well-entrenched, and realizing that working in harness with the tumultuous Pulitzer might be an ordeal, he declined with thanks.[8] Pulitzer sought out Watterson, who was usually to be found at that haunt of Democrats, the Manhattan Club, enjoying a julep. ". . . You are wasting your time about the clubs and watering places," he told Watterson. "I must first devote myself to the business end of it. Here is a blank check. Fill it out for whatever amount you please and it will be honored. I want you to go upstairs and organize my editorial force for me." Watterson, who was devoted to his Courier-Journal even though often absent, indignantly refused.[9]

The World's three-story building housed creaky press equipment and a staff headed by the handsome, cynical William Henry Hurlbert, who had made the paper a model of dignity if not of sincerity or interest. As one of the assistant editors, young Walter Hines Page, put it, "the *World* was preeminently the 'gentleman's' newspaper of New York," known for "the restraint that dignified its every department." These academicians must have experienced the despair of the Trojans at the wrath of Achilles when Pulitzer, clad in a Prince Albert with stiff collar and black Ascot tie, called them together and made a brief speech in language that was very clear despite its slight guttural accent.

"Gentlemen," he said, "you realize that a change has taken place in the *World*. Heretofore you have all been living in the parlour and taking baths every day. Now I wish you to understand that, in future, you are all walking down the Bowery." [10]

Several of them, including Editor Hurlbert, resigned then and there. Pulitzer added to his brother's resentment by raiding the Journal staff of Managing Editor E. C. Hancock and a few others. Precisely what else happened between the two brothers is unknown, but thereafter they were unfriendly. In the May 11 World, the first officially under his ownership, Pulitzer published the fondly alliterative manifesto that announced a totally new force in New York:

> The entire World newspaper property has been purchased by the undersigned, and will from this day on, be under different management—different in men, measures and methods—different in purpose, policy and principle—different in objects and interests—different in sympathies and convictions—different in head and heart.
>
> Performance is better than promise. Exuberant assurances are cheap. I make none. I simply refer the public to the new World itself, which henceforth shall be the daily evidence of its own growing improvement, with forty-eight daily witnesses in its forty-eight columns.
>
> There is room in this great and growing city for a journal that is not only cheap but bright, not only bright but large, not only large but truly democratic—dedicated to the cause of the people rather than that of purse-potentates—devoted more to the news of the New than the Old World—that will expose all fraud and sham, fight all public evils and abuses—that will serve and battle for the people with earnest sincerity.
>
> In that cause and for that end solely the new World is hereby enlisted and committed to the attention of the intelligent public.
>
> Joseph Pulitzer

III

Triumph

Chapter 1

Reformer and Salesman

1. A NEW SOCIAL CONSCIENCE

The Pulitzers forgot about Europe and leased the handsome residence of James W. Gerard at 17 Gramercy Park, installing there several servants brought from St. Louis including the Negro coachman Eugene Stewart, who would remain with them throughout his life. A next-door neighbor was the partially paralyzed Samuel J. Tilden, symbol of a wronged Democracy, whose great wine-cellar Pulitzer envied. If Pulitzer was a connoisseur of luxury, a lover of parlors and baths who preferred to stay aloof from the Bowery he ordered his men to cultivate, this did not mean that his manifesto was a humbug. He had served his time in St. Louis' equivalent of the Bowery, he had risen above it and he earnestly wanted others to do the same. His statement that the World was dedicated "solely" to reform contained pardonable poetic license. He wanted to sell millions of newspapers. He wanted to elect a President. He aimed for wealth and power—not an uncommon impulse—but to his great credit he wanted to help everyone to prosperity.

These two warring individuals within one man—Pulitzer the reformer and Pulitzer the salesman—were now locked in a struggle that would convulse him for the rest of his life, too evenly matched for clear-cut victory or defeat. This was as he willed it, in firm belief that the reformer was helpless without the salesman. Much as he admired the small-circulation Evening Post, edited intellectually by Schurz, Edwin Godkin and Horace White, it was like a fine sermon to empty pews. ". . . I want to talk to a nation, not to a select committee," he said.[1] If he, like his brother Albert, had been interested only in profits, he could have made his World a money-maker with ease instead of travail.

Deeply in debt, faced by what some of his contemporaries thought was certain ruin, he brought out the hula dancer on Page 1. Under Hurlbert the paper had selected news stories of uniform sedateness and preferred the somnolent-noun headline: "AFFAIRS AT ALBANY," "THE LAND LEAGUE," "MR. VANDERBILT'S TRIP," "OUR CABLE LETTER," "BENCH SHOW OF DOGS." Pulitzer's first front page, before he had really taken firm hold with a renovated staff, concerned events more earthy, violent or entertaining. A story about the condemned killer Angelo Cornetti was headed "CORNETTI'S LAST NIGHT," with the subhead "Shaking His Cell-Door and Demanding Release." Another slayer's fate appeared under the headline "WARD MCCONKEY HANGED," subheaded "Shouting from Under the Black Cap that his Executioners are Murderers." "THE DEADLY LIGHTNING" concerned a disastrous Jersey fire that killed six and destroyed 100,000 barrels of oil, while the misfortunes of a burglar discovered by police on his wedding day was celebrated under "MARRIED AND TAKEN TO JAIL: A Ceremony Where Congratulations Were Rather Too Previous." "IN LOVE WITH HER MONEY" dealt with a bride-to-be whose betrothed robbed her, and smaller stories were headed "A FORTUNE SQUANDERED IN DRINK," "WAS HE A SUICIDE?" and "IN PRISON FOR HIS BROTHER'S CRIME." Most of these were stories that Hurlbert would have relegated to back pages or would have excluded entirely—he had given only small back-page attention to Cornetti. All were handled with zest. Pulitzer's great passion, politics, was ignored on this first front page as he drew on his sure sense of psychology and his mastery of the come-on to win new readers.[2]

He fumigated his paper of its recent contagion by making it doubly clear through an interview with Gould that Gould no longer had any interest in it—a point he would drive home with frequent repetitions for more than a year. A man on springs, he popped out of his office to commune with the staff, striding among them, bushy hair flying, pince-nez glittering. He insisted on provocative headlines, short sentences, violent verbs, tight writing. "Condense, condense!" he shouted. His men must be suggestive, by which he did not mean obscene but prolific in ideas for headlines, stories and slants. Young James B. Townsend of Hurlbert's staff, away during the changeover to attend a funeral in Vermont, returned to find Pulitzer in charge and noted, "It seemed as if a cyclone had entered the building." He met Pulitzer, who said swiftly, "Good, I like you, get to work," and he remained ten years.[3]

He was an exception, for the Hurlbert era of dry tabulation of news was gone, and most of Hurlbert's gentlemen would soon be gone. Hancock, just over from Albert's Journal, found himself dazed by the demands of the new boss and lacking in suggestiveness, and was on the way out. Within three days Pulitzer sent telegrams to Cockerill and McGuffin in St. Louis, who arrived to take over as managing editor and business manager respectively. Pulitzer, amazed at the old World's apathetic announcement of the soon-to-be-opened Brooklyn Bridge—a historic event as important to the metropolis as the Eads Bridge was to St. Louis—spread the opening all over his front page, with a four-column drawing of the bridge. The World bristled with lively headlines, many of them alliterative: "MADDENED BY MARRIAGE," "WHILE THE HUSBANDS WERE AWAY," "MISS MITTING MISSING," "GOING TO THE BOW-WOWS," "BACHELOR BANG'S BRIDAL," "SCREAMING FOR MERCY." The Sunday World, reaching the reader on his only free day of the week, regaled him with feature stories about human sacrifice among religious sects, life in Sing Sing, odd instruments of murder, and cannibalism at sea.

Pulitzer was at heart a fond husband and father bound by Victorian conventions. Despite the seductive promise of some of his World's headlines and the minute descriptions of a bungled hanging or an atrocious murder, he carefully avoided impropriety in stories involving sex. He was studiously setting his bait for the masses he must first hook, then educate, as always with a short-term and a long-term objective in mind. He was in a race against time, the immediate necessity being circulation, success, the payment of his debts. The long-term aim did not give him as much time as he needed—only a year, 1884, until the next presidential election. The symptoms of his political malady were marked. His World could not have a decisive national voice in '84, could not help elect a Democratic President with 15,000 circulation. He needed a fantastically rapid rise—gains every month, every week, every day.

So the salesman was in the saddle. He was reaching for people who normally never read newspapers, who were uninterested in the gray dullness of Hurlbert or the polished periods of Dana—the city's teeming settlements of Irish, Germans, Jews and Italians whom the existing editorial establishment virtually ignored. More than five million immigrants had entered the country since 1870, and the city had grown by almost a half-million in a decade. Blind to sophistication, even rudimentary in the ability to read, the newcomers could be lured only by the most basic human interest presented in the simplest way. The new World gave it to them, and beneath the brummagem it had a heart totally absent in the old, reflecting the social warmth of Pulitzer as against the rapacity of Gould. It was earnestly interested in the metropolis whose handsome facade concealed a sink-hole of selfishness, corruption and despair. The robber-baron era was at its height. America was expanding so fast that it had no time to indulge in the luxury of social concern, which was left to such eccentrics as Pulitzer, Schurz and Abram Hewitt. Pulitzer's scorn for the irresponsible rich oozed in an editorial describing them as having "the odor of codfish and not the mustiness of age," and adding, "The new World believes that such an aristocracy ought to have no place in the republic . . ." He listed what he thought the country needed to bring about some approach to social justice:

1. Tax Luxuries.
2. Tax Inheritances.
3. Tax Large Incomes.
4. Tax Monopolies.
5. Tax the Privileged Corporation.
6. A Tariff for Revenue.
7. Reform the Civil Service.
8. Punish Corrupt Officers.
9. Punish Vote Buying.
10. Punish Employers who Coerce their Employees in Elections.

This is a popular platform of ten lines. We recommend it to the politicians in place of long-winded resolutions.[4]

Now that all but No. 6 of these planks have become law, readers accustomed to social reform—accustomed also to newspapers demanding more of it—can scarcely catch even a whiff of the radical smell some of these words had in 1883.

There has been some argument about Pulitzer's precise contributions to New York journalism. True, he produced a paper cheap enough in its externals to offend the decorous, and he brought to New York a bundle of nerves that occasionally made him unstable. But along with the tricks and the nerves he brought a quality exclusively his own, one that the city badly needed. It was the most earnest, powerful and efficient social conscience yet seen in journalism, not as pure and undefiled as that of Carl Schurz, but equipped with abilities Schurz lacked and which would spread its benefits to millions across the land.

II. DEMOCRATS, UNITE!

"Dear Pulitzer," wrote his friend Charles Gibson from St. Louis, "Your purchase of the World is the town talk. The comments are favorable to the enterprise & complimentary to you—a great change in the last six months toward you. The misfortune of last fall [the Slayback killing] is never mentioned and seems to be altogether forgotten. . . . There is only one thing about which I am concerned about you & that is with your tender feelings & well grounded affections your family may absorb much of the time & brain power, which your national position (for that is what it is) demands."[5]

On the contrary, he worked so hard that his family saw little of him. He later defined the proper attitude of mind of an editor: "He must . . . never go home to dinner without feeling sick, if the paper is beaten, if it is dull or poor; feeling elated and happy if the paper is victorious, strong . . . That is how I used to feel, both in St. Louis and New York."[6]

A fortnight after he took over the World he attended his first political dinner party at the sumptuous home of Congressman Roswell P. Flower, the Watertown man who had made his million in Wall Street and was fashioning a boom which he hoped would lead him to the White House. Although he had some Tammany support, Flower had at least one impediment to his presidential plans—a painful lisp that listeners sometimes unkindly linked with his name. He always called himself "a plain bithnethman." Among the Democrats Pulitzer met there was his friend William C. Whitney, six years his senior, the perfect Galahad of politics, handsome, able, charming, an intimate of Governor Cleveland, whose election was largely due to his support. Perhaps it was in one way tragic that Whitney had married the lovely Flora Payne, daughter of rich Henry B. Payne of Cleveland and sister of the Standard Oil millionaire Oliver Hazard Payne. The latter had spent $700,000 for a Romanesque mansion at Fifth Avenue and 57th Street and presented it to the Whitneys as one might present a poodle. Such in-law affluence was impossible for the comparatively impecunious Whitney to match, and he was even then launching into city traction adventures more profitable than public-spirited. To his wife in Europe, Whitney wrote of the gathering: "Pulitzer, six feet two or three inches, sharp faced with bushy hair and scraggy whiskers . . . antagonizing people at dinner, however, a sharp fellow, hard working and probably keen as a briar. . . . I knew him well in Seventy Six and we talked over the old campaign, and he expressed himself pleased with his first dinner party in New York." [7]

He did not antagonize Whitney, for the two became fast friends. Whitney was eyeing Cleveland as the possible Democratic nominee in '84, and Pulitzer, watching the governor with approval, as familiar with New York politics as if he had lived there for years, was intent on bringing the state's dissident Democrats into unity. There was Tammany, well below its usual level of corruption under "Honest John" Kelly, but angry at Cleveland; the reformist County Democrats who had fought Tammany under Whitney and Hewitt; the Brooklyn Democrats under Hugh McLaughlin; and the "haystack-and-cheesepress" Democrats of upstate New York who were not entirely trustful of the city gentlemen. In the World Pulitzer was insisting that unless the knives were put away there was no hope for '84. "In the sacred name of Andrew Jackson, let us have harmony," implored the World. Certainly this was one of the political problems Pulitzer and Whitney discussed at Gramercy Park or 57th Street.

The intersection of Fifth and 57th, with a palace on each corner, was one of those exhibits of the Gilded Age that Pulitzer, for all his love of luxury, viewed with scorn. Catercorner from Whitney was the enormous, turreted pile owned by Cornelius Vanderbilt II, whose New York Central Railroad Pulitzer would soon attack; across was the many-chimneyed castle of Collis P. Huntington, whose Union Pacific Railroad activities Pulitzer would also excoriate; and on the fourth corner was the only slightly less impressive edifice of Mrs. Herman Oelrichs, who seems to have escaped his attention. Whitney himself was collecting Bouchers and

Gobelins and was deeply involved in the new Metropolitan Opera House, so that the art- and music-loving Pulitzer enjoyed cultural discussions with him as well as the inevitable politics. Kate Pulitzer and Flora Whitney became good friends, and it was not until several years later that Pulitzer or anyone else began to suspect that Whitney's wealth was gained more after the manner of Tammany than of a reformist.

The speed with which the westerner was accepted into membership and indeed some leadership of the New York Democrats was proof of his own immense energy and the startling success of his World, which gained some 6,000 readers in its first two weeks. On June 19 he was elected a member of the Manhattan Club, a league of wealthy Democrats including Whitney, August Belmont, Watterson, Tilden, Hewitt and Manton Marble. Pulitzer paid a $135 entrance fee and joined in informal party councils at the clubhouse at Fifth Avenue and 15th Street, where Republicans were rigidly excluded except for one—the tall, proud Roscoe Conkling, who had been all but read out of the Republican party, had given up politics for the law and was felt to be practically a Democrat. Again the World had rejected the aging Tilden as a "fine intellectuality" but a man who had muffed his opportunity when "[a] good round oath might have saved him the Presidency in 1876." Already Pulitzer had cunningly encouraged the Cleveland boomlet without committing himself by his editorial saying that the Democrats needed "another Cleveland" for 1884:

> It may not be Governor Cleveland, who is doing fairly well in Albany. But it will be another Cleveland. He need not be great—he may not have distinguished himself in politics, but he will sweep the country as effectively as Cleveland did when he carried New York by a 200,000 majority.[8]

At the World, Pulitzer held a daily editorial council at 11 A.M. with Cockerill and City Editor David Sutton, also imported from the Post-Dispatch. He pinched pennies in small ways that did not include salaries, a habit he never shook off. He used cheap newsprint and ink and got along on worn type. A McGuffin order eliminated soap in the washroom and ice in the water-cooler, the latter economy being abandoned when Pulitzer himself took an unpleasantly warm drink. He advertised on the front-page ears that the World was the only eight-page paper in the country at two cents, and indeed he boasted constantly about its "amazing advance." In exchanges from newspapers in Chicago, Denver, San Francisco and other cities came editorial comments on the remarkable new flavor of the World, one even arriving from the Owen Sound Advertiser far up on Georgian Bay. John H. Holmes of the Boston Herald sent Pulitzer congratulations, writing, "I see you are putting your whole nature into the paper and making it wonderfully peppery and noticeable. . . . The present situation is not unlike that which the elder Bennett found when he moved to attack the established dailies." Holmes, who knew Albert

Pulitzer, added a line that surely made Joseph scowl: "Cleverness seems to run in the family." [9]

Circulation improvement was considered a glacial process requiring many months. What startled the newspaper establishment was the World's immediate gains. The sale began to improve after the first week, and on August 11, after only three months under the new regime, the pressrun was 39,000 a day, double that of the Gould era. Almost none of this increase came at the expense of the other morning papers, indicating that Pulitzer was finding readers among a class who previously had not read newspapers at all. His rivals treated him with silence until at last Dana gave him an equivocal welcome:

> We notice without surprise that the journals of this city have not paid much attention to Mr. Joseph Pulitzer. . . . There is a natural disposition against gratuitous advertising, but this need not prevent our welcoming a clever man . . . especially when he has once been a correspondent for the Sun, which shines for all.
>
> Mr. Pulitzer possesses a quick and fluent mind with a good share of originality and brightness; but he has always seemed to us rather deficient in judgment and in staying power. . . . Anyway, we tender all sorts of friendly wishes. . . .[10]

Dana was the dean of New York editors, 64 to Pulitzer's 36 and thus entitled to patriarchal criticism, so capable of acerbity that this appraisal was comparatively benevolent. His disparagement of Pulitzer's judgment and staying power of course referred to his years of flitting between St. Louis, New York, Washington and Europe and his alliance with reformers whom Dana held in cynical contempt. Pulitzer, not at all offended, replied, "If the editor of the World has shown deficiency of judgment heretofore, it has been because he has tried not only to imitate, but even to excel the *Sun* in its truthfulness, fearlessness, independence and vigor." [11]

In August, with Dana, Jay Gould and William Dorsheimer, Pulitzer had a friendly luncheon cruise on the Hudson aboard Gould's 250-foot *Atalanta,* which boasted rare Oriental rugs and a crew uniformed smartly in the Gould blue and white colors—a yacht that cost him almost $1,000 a week to maintain. Pulitzer, who disapproved of the source of this splendor, nevertheless began to want a yacht himself.

III. BUCKING THE ESTABLISHMENT

Although the World was not yet hurting its competitors, there was a general apprehension that it soon would, and a feeling in the Establishment similar to that of a group of comfortable club members of long standing whose quiet enjoyment of their leather chairs is suddenly interrupted by the entrance of a young new member exploding firecrackers. Who let him in? There was disapproval of the confidence and skill with which Pulitzer took New York politics as his domain and moved with equal assurance into the national scene—a tendency to forget that he had more practical political experience than any New York editor excepting Schurz. There was, in fact, a powerful inclination to whip the upstart westerner and send him packing back to St. Louis.

George Jones's Times started the onslaught on September 18 by dropping from four to two cents. A week later James Gordon Bennett reduced his Herald from three to two cents, followed by the conservative Whitelaw Reid, who cut his four-cent Tribune to three. The four-page Sun, already two cents, stayed put.

None of this hurt the World in the least, nor did it do the others any good. On the contrary, at this time when advertising was only a modest source of revenue, newspapers were expected to make a small profit over the cost of paper and printing and the reduction of the selling price by a cent or two was a momentous and hurtful step. The World greeted the Herald's drop as "Another victim, another victory for the World!" and added, ". . . the World is still booming. Brother Bennett, like Brother Jones, now believes in Western journalism. Owing to the pressure of advertisements, the World will enlarge its size to at least eight columns more than the *Herald*." [12] The Herald, in reducing its price, cut newsdealers' profits from one-half to one-third of a cent per copy, a move that caused the angry dealers to organize and refuse to sell the paper, forcing Bennett for a time to establish his own agencies at high cost and some loss of circulation.

The utter failure of the Establishment's pincer operation, and Pulitzer's amused capitalization of it, did not improve his standing at the club, nor did his firm belief in self-advertising. "[The World] had no infancy," said the World. "At once it sprang into full vigor. Its wonderful advance in circulation, in advertising, in influence, in popularity, worked a revolution in metropolitan journalism. Its older brothers of the New York press paid the tribute of imitating its features and reducing their prices. But the new World merrily rolls on to yet greater victory . . ." [13]

Grover Cleveland seemed almost as rare a specimen as a man with feathers, an honest politician. In October the World suggested him as the best candidate—an idea that affronted Henry Watterson, who was not alone in thinking the governor too inexperienced for the presidency. Another whom it affronted was Dana, who was disillusioned by an odd circumstance.

He had vigorously supported Cleveland for governor, and after the election had written to ask the appointment of his friend Franklin Bartlett, a stockholder in the Sun, as adjutant general. A further Dana purpose was to secure a job on the adjutant general's staff for his son Paul. Cleveland, who received thousands of such letters and was indeed deficient in a sense of public relations, not only appointed another man to the post but failed even to answer Dana. Dana's enthusiasm for the governor shriveled. Pulitzer himself, in his anxiety to unify the Democrats, criticized Cleveland sharply for his occasional rebuffs to Tammany. He was busy in many backstage Democratic parleys at the Manhattan Club and elsewhere, receiving notes such as one from August Belmont: "Can I see you for a moment this morning [*sic*] at about two o'clock at your office?" [14]

Now more than ever his reluctance to delegate authority began to hound him. This trait arose from his perfectionism, his unblushing and quite justified knowledge that he was a better newspaperman and politician than any of his employees and that therefore his papers gained in proportion to the amount of time and work he was able to give them, and suffered to the extent that others were in control. Even his best men were unable to match his swift brilliance. He was eternally overworked, trying to keep an eye on everything. What he needed was another Joseph Pulitzer as managing editor, still another as business manager, and others as city editor, editorial writer, plus several dozen as reporters. Although this was an extension of himself that he was never able to perfect, and with which he would have been dissatisfied even had it been possible, he never stopped trying. In St. Louis he had John Dillon, Ignaz Kappner and Henry Moore as publisher, business manager and managing editor of the Post-Dispatch—all men of ability—and yet he demanded weekly reports from them complete down to minor details. This mistrust naturally curbed initiative, and Kappner, for example, was afraid to replace a worn-out swivel chair without the boss's permission. This was true despite his insistence that his subordinates make their own decisions. John Dillon wrote him from St. Louis:

> You have a right to ask why I have sat here like a dummy . . . and blindly followed your orders. . . . In all cases in which my judgment has dissented from yours you have been so invariably right and I so invariably wrong that you have relieved me of the necessity of thinking for myself. . . . I can say with truth that I have done for you what I have never done for anyone else in my life, in surrendering my judgment to yours without question.[15]

In December Pulitzer was distressed when Kate suffered a brief illness. And he was truly shattered when little Katherine Ethel died of pneumonia on May 9, 1884, six weeks short of her second birthday. He took refuge in the creation of journalistic ideas, one of them a series on America's "snobocracy," a lampoon on pretensions to ancient family and noble lineage. Typically, he worked at this himself rather than handing it over to Cockerill, and had asked his Washington correspondent, Theron C. Crawford, for snob material from the capital. Crawford wrote him, "I have sent you crests & coats of arms of the following people. . . . Gen.

Van Vliet U.S.A. . . . U.S. Senators Pendleton and Armstrong and the crest of Blaine." [16]

When the Republicans in June nominated the tarnished Blaine, the Democrats had an issue and a target. "Grover Cleveland is available, not assailable," trumpeted the World, and after his nomination at Chicago gave four reasons for supporting him: "(1) He is an honest man. (2) He is an honest man. (3) He is an honest man. (4) He is an honest man." [17]

Along the way, Pulitzer, whose prodigious memory contained instant dossiers on literally thousands of politicians, had become aware of an infant prodigy, a dapper state assemblyman with beribboned pince-nez, blond side-whiskers and a strident voice. Wealthy, Harvard-bred Theodore Roosevelt had represented a New York City silk-stocking district since he was 23. He had made sharp and sometimes successful efforts to thwart machine jobbery and had become a political *wunderkind* viewed by the press with mingled amusement and respect. After denouncing Blaine as morally reprehensible, he had gone to the Republican convention and had been appalled when Blaine was nominated. Roosevelt refused to commit himself and left in a rage for his Dakota ranch where, after lonely self-searching, he made up his mind: "I intend to vote the Republican Presidential ticket. . . . I did my best and got beaten, and I propose to stand by the result." [18]

Pulitzer pounced on him in the World: ". . . Young Mr. Roosevelt [is] a reform fraud and a Jack-in-the-box politician who disappears whenever his boss applies a gentle pressure to his aspiring head. . . . What an exhibition he makes of his reform professions . . . when he signifies his intention to seek by his vote to elect as President of the United States a man he admits to be venal and corrupt, and for whom he blushes to speak!" [19]

It was the first brush between two formidable fighters whose relationship would shiver over intermittent snags before it ended a quarter-century later in a furious quarrel that had to be settled by the United States Supreme Court.

Chapter 2

Electing a President

1. THE DEFECTION OF DANA

By the time Cleveland was nominated it was evident that he and the party had suffered a terrible blow in New York, though it was not then generally known that the candidate's own gaucherie was responsible. Cleveland, hearing of Dana's resentment, had sought to make amends by letting him know through an intermediary that he would invite Dana to dine at the executive mansion if he would accept. Dana agreed. Then Cleveland became so involved with the legislature that he found no time either to extend the invitation or to send an explanation—a blunder that Dana understandably regarded as a deliberate affront.[1] Dana ran a gentlemanly newspaper shop compared with the World madhouse, and although he was a stickler for syntax and could fire a man for a violated adverb, he was generous and kindly enough so that he was revered by scores of newspapermen who had learned their trade from him. Yet this one-time idealist who had labored five years at Brook Farm had aged into a cynic whose convictions depended on his mood. In a bitter mood now, he turned against Cleveland and made the greatest mistake of his political and journalistic life. He could not support Blaine, whom he had long excoriated. He brought his nominally Democratic Sun out for that egregious political adventurer Ben Butler, the presidential candidate of the Greenbackers.

Since New York State was invariably close in national elections, and its 36 electoral votes were felt essential for a Cleveland victory (as they proved to be), the defection of the powerful Sun could well be fatal to the Democrats. It could be said that the next occupant of the White House might be decided by Cleveland's failure to dictate a courteous note of perhaps a hundred words. At the same time, Dana's move gave a new responsibility and opportunity to the World. While it was true that neither the Times nor the Herald could stomach Blaine and came out for Cleveland, the Times was normally Republican and no man could say what the whimsical Bennett was. The result of the realignment was a Dana gift to the World that would make it—if Pulitzer could carry the load—a paper of enormous importance to the Democrats.

He did not lighten the load by allowing himself to be nominated for Congress in the city's ninth district even though it was safely Democratic and little campaigning was required. Ever afterward he insisted that he did not want the post and was only persuaded by the argument of Whitney and others that it would strengthen the ticket; but he had long yearned for a seat in the House, and he would not have been Pulitzer had he not reflected on the triumph it would represent not only in New York but over the St. Louis Bourbons who had cheated him in the local election and later had urged that his building be burned and that he be tarred and feathered. He contributed $1,000 to the Democratic campaign fund, a sizable sum for a man in debt, while Whitney made the grand gesture with $20,000. Pulitzer and Dana had exchanged friendly notes in December. Now, aching to elect the first Democratic President since Buchanan, he was so disillusioned by Dana's treason that a coolness grew between them as they entered the most gutter-raking campaign in the nation's history.

"You will be a leader in the House," Gibson wrote him. "But how can one man attend to two great news papers and act a great part on the national stage? It is difficult, however, to fix a limit of your power to labor —arrange, and execute important affairs." [2]

Unlike Cleveland, James G. Blaine *was* so brilliant and magnetic as to be irresistible, never forgetting a name or a face, possessor of a smile and handclasp that made not only friends but worshipers, brimming with abilities and yet "all flawed and specked" by his love of luxury and looseness of principle. As congressman and Speaker in the seventies he had been investigated for his involvement with Warren Fisher, a Boston speculator, in the affairs of the government-aided Little Rock & Fort Smith Railroad. It was charged that he had worked secretly for rascally railroad promotions and had received $64,000 from the malodorous Union Pacific Railroad for worthless bonds of the largely fictitious Little Rock & Fort Smith, this being interpreted as a bribe from the Union Pacific. One witness was James Mulligan of Boston, who had been Fisher's clerk and had letters from Blaine regarding the transactions. Blaine's escape from this crisis has been the wonder of historians ever since.

He went to Mulligan, persuaded him by some legerdemain to hand over the letters, and later read them to the assembled House so disarmingly that they appeared quite innocent. It was a tribute to his artistry that few seemed to reflect that Blaine might not have read *all* of the letters, or read them exactly, or in the order in which they were written, or to notice that Mulligan feebly insisted that Blaine's reading was entirely incorrect, or that Blaine had long lived beyond his means, or even—strangest of all—that Blaine himself refused to hand over the letters for examination. His performance must stand with the greatest of Booth's, or more strictly with those of the late Mesmer, for the hypnotized House failed to inquire more deeply. The Plumed Knight squeaked out of it and actually was a strong contender for the presidential nomination in 1876 and 1880.

Now in '84 his hour had struck, except that the Mulligan business would not down. It looked worse from this distance than it had when his own great personality neutralized it. The name of Mulligan became as prominent in the campaign as those of the candidates, and indeed Dana protested that Mulligan should have been Blaine's running mate rather than John A. Logan. The eastern Mugwumps, led by Schurz and encouraged by Pulitzer, bolted Blaine and campaigned for Cleveland—a cheering omen that was countered by Dana's apostasy and by the coolness of Tammany toward the governor who had tossed them few plums, so that no one knew how the state would go.

There was, as Schurz and Pulitzer well knew, an issue in this election that overrode either the parties or personalities involved and might leave a permanent stamp for good or evil on the nation. The issue was whether the electorate had grown so cynical as to abandon the fight for honesty and accept corruption as a legitimate and established part of government by rewarding with the presidency a candidate who was clearly tainted. Every politician, every thinking voter, knew that Blaine at the very least had dipped for several years into undercover politico-financial operations clearly improper for a public official. Could his warm handshake, his wonderful smile, his admitted abilities, outweigh this at the polls? If so, then the national virtue was gone and the republic was drifting into the torpid political climate of Latin America.[3]

II. MA! MA! WHERE'S MY PA?

Pulitzer meanwhile had embarked on a surprising friendship with Blaine's most implacable enemy, Roscoe Conkling. Eleven years had passed since Blaine had convulsed the House with his classic lampoon of Conkling and his "turkey gobbler strut," but the hatred between them had been livid ever since. Now the tall, haughty, brilliant Conkling, estranged from his wife because of disagreement over their daughter's marriage, had lodgings on 29th Street and a rich law practice in Wall Street. How could the reformist Democrat Pulitzer feel warmth for the man who in the Senate had been the tutor of Grant, a roughshod Republican spoilsman who jeered at reformers as "the men-milliners of politics"? How could Pulitzer employ as attorney for the World the man who had also done legal work for Jay Gould and Collis P. Huntington? Certainly they had met at the Manhattan Club, and Pulitzer, always fascinated by rare abilities, found them in Conkling. Yet the friendship between these two opposites, which soon became truly warm, is so astonishing that one might suspect a Pulitzer undermotive.

Although he had fallen with the crash of an oak, Conkling was still the embodiment of the Stalwart-Halfbreed feud, of Republican disunity, still championed by admiring Stalwart Republican followers who resented his exclusion. These admirers were voters. It was the Republican strategy to win them by placating Conkling, to heal the feud once for all by persuading him to come out for Blaine. It was the Democratic strategy to keep his disgruntlement alive, to inflame it if possible and to coax him to join the Mugwumps. Pulitzer, to whom Democratic victory was more important than the millennium, had taken shrewd action to preserve his disgruntlement a year earlier, long before he knew Conkling intimately, with paragraphs such as this one in the World:

> Will not the people remember that Roscoe Conkling—in intellect a giant among pygmies, in public life an honest man in the midst of corruption and rascality—has been retired by his own party to private life? [4]

This was the perfect line to follow with a man of such hurt vanity. In the summer of 1884 Pulitzer and Conkling rode companionably together in Central Park. Blaine, desperately wanting Conkling's endorsement even if lukewarm, sent obsequious emissaries to entreat him for peace and support. His reply—a delight to Pulitzer—was deadly: "Gentlemen . . . I have given up criminal law." Although he would not go so far as to endorse Cleveland publicly, his silence was hurtful to Blaine and at Pulitzer's urging he did consent to become an effective, if anonymous, assailant of Blaine. Conkling's asperity was not tempered by the publication early in 1884 of the first volume of Blaine's *Twenty Years of Congress,* a lucid and masterly history, generous even toward Conkling—a spirit which, however, might have been motivated by a foreglimpse of the very predicament Blaine now found himself in.

Indeed, with the new nationwide fame of Mulligan, the Republicans badly needed something to destroy Cleveland's image of purity. They found it in July when the Buffalo Telegraph broke a story that made all further Democratic efforts seem as futile as if their candidate had suddenly died—an account of the bachelor Cleveland's affair ten years earlier with the free-living Buffalo widow, Maria Halpin. Cleveland, then a practicing attorney, had been one of those enjoying Mrs. Halpin's favors. When she bore a child she named it Oscar Cleveland, insisting that he was the father. Although skeptical, Cleveland had not only made provision for the child but had done his best to aid the erratic Mrs. Halpin, who sometimes drank and became irresponsible.

This was a time when "respectable" newspapers evaded specific descriptions of immorality. The more daring sheets throughout the country, however, picked up the Telegraph story in full, Republican workers spread it by handbills and enthusiastic retelling, and even the staider party papers whipped up the scandal by cunning indirection. Reid's New York Tribune referred to it incessantly as something it would rather not refer to, mentioning unspecified "revolting details" about Cleveland's "private life" and adding, "*The Tribune* finds quite enough in his official career to make his supporters contemptible when they call him a 'Reformer.'" [5] This vague treatment had the effect of adding odious overtones of suspicion worse than the actual case justified. There was so much talk about Cleveland as a drunken immoralist that the pro-Cleveland New York Herald threatened that Democrats incensed by "the infamously dirty warfare against Governor Cleveland, have determined to retaliate by exposing the private life of Mr. Blaine . . ." [6]

To Dana, Mrs. Halpin was a blessing. When Cleveland was running for governor the Sun had said warmly, "he possesses those highest qualities of a public man, sound principles of administrative duty, luminous intelligence, and courage to do what is right, no matter who may be pleased or displeased thereby." Now the Sun speculated wickedly about the "coarse debauchee who might bring his harlots to Washington and hire lodgings for them convenient to the White House"; and about a man revealed as "low in his associations, leprous with immorality, perfidious, whose name was loathsome in the nostrils of every virtuous woman and upright man who knew him." [7] Republican torchlight paraders in New York and elsewhere took up the chant:

> Ma! Ma! Where's my Pa?
> Where's my Pa, Ma?
> Where's my Pa?

Cleveland's courageous reply to dismayed party leaders asking what to do—"Tell the truth"—was of no help. There was despair in the party councils, imprecations against the Buffalo baggage who had risen like a ghost after ten years to play into the hands of Blaine and wreck the best candidate the Democrats had had since Tilden. Few could take the pragmatic attitude of the Chicago Democrat who pointed out that since Blaine was delinquent in office and unblemished in private life, whereas Cleveland had a record of official honesty though his personal affairs were censorable, "we should elect Mr. Cleveland to the public office which he is so admirably qualified to fill, and remand Mr. Blaine to the private station which he is so eminently fitted to adorn."

Pulitzer at first seemed either to disbelieve the Buffalo scandal or to hope that the Republicans would decently give it small space. The July 27 World said, "The pretended charges against Cleveland . . . are baseless rumor, so transparently false and libelous that no reputable Blaine journal even will father them." On August 6 it grew warmer: "A villainous libel was fastened upon [Cleveland] by a vicious, dirty journal in Buffalo, and all the respectable Republican journals have indirectly given it their endorsement." On August 8, with the story spreading all over the nation, the World came out in the open, printed a candid account of the Halpin affair on its front page, and gave Cleveland credit for his warmth of heart in making provision for a child not known to be his own. An editorial in the same issue assailed the Sun's "filthy record," adding, "It is true that Gov. Cleveland once had a sporadic association with a middle-aged female. Is such an offense unpardonable? . . . If Grover Cleveland had a whole family of illegitimate children . . . he would be more worthy of the Presidential office than Blaine, the beggar at the feet of railroad jobbers, the prostitute in the Speaker's chair . . ."

Pulitzer tried to dispose of Mrs. Halpin as an irrelevancy, but he knew she was not an irrelevancy at a time when some proper people still separated books by men from books by women in their libraries, and now could read Dana and others speculating about presidential harlots. His despair must have been profound. The Democrats in '76 had been defeated by fraud, in '80 by an uninspiring candidate, and now in '84 by an illegitimate child.

Still he gained stature and circulation as he all but appropriated Cleveland as a World property and published a stream of the most effective editorials of the contest. In the World also appeared a series of pungent letters exposing Blaine's unsavory record in office, remarkable for their inside knowledge and signed only, "Stalwart." The writer's identity was a close secret, one that so intrigued a World proofreader that he sneaked a sheet of Stalwart's copy, had a handwriting expert compare it with Roscoe Conkling's known script and found it identical. At the office one day a young artist, Walt McDougall, left a cartoon of Blaine and went on elsewhere. "At noon," he recalled, "I received a telegram from Joseph Pulitzer . . . asking me to come to the World office at once." Cartoons then had to be very simply drawn or the engraving would quickly fill up with ink. When McDougall arrived, Pulitzer shook his hand warmly and ushered him into Cockerill's office.

"We have found the fellow who can make pictures for newspapers!" he exclaimed. "Young man, we printed the entire edition . . . of the *World* without stopping the press to clean the cut, and that has never happened in this country before!" [8]

McDougall was hired at $50 a week, an enormous salary. The World's reputation was so low that his mother grieved as if he had gone into crime—an infamy caused less by its sensationalism than by its candid appeal to the working class, its "revolutionary" social program and the contempt of such "respectable" papers as the Sun. If Pulitzer was enraged by the barbs flung at Cleveland by Dana, he could congratulate himself that some of his rising circulation now was coming at the expense of the Sun. That paper's support of Butler so angered many readers that they trampled the Sun underfoot. Dana was losing hundreds of them daily—in one week his circulation dropped almost 7,000—but the snowy-bearded editor stuck to his grudge.

On August 10 an earthquake rattled dishes from Maryland to Maine and derailed a New York horse-car—an event some clergymen interpreted as a divine reproof to the sinful Cleveland. Democratic muckrakers, seeking to counter the Halpin unpleasantness, spread rumors that Blaine many years earlier had been brought to the altar in a shotgun wedding with his wife six months pregnant. The World said with acid virtue, "No matter how much nor how disgracefully the Republicans should lie about the Democratic candidate, we have determined not to touch any of the Blaine scandals at our disposal" [9]—certainly a loaded rejection of talebearing. Pulitzer was so infuriated by the Republican exaggerations about Cleveland that he was not solicitous of the feelings of the Plumed Knight and his wife, and other backhanded mention of the rumors appeared in the World. It happened that the new trade paper *The Journalist* was edited by Leander Richardson, a burly writer famous for his pothouse affrays who had worked several months for the World and had left after a quarrel. Richardson conducted a bitter vendetta against his former boss, invariably calling him "Jewseph Pulitzer." "I should like to point out to Jewseph Pulitzer," he wrote, "that the man who casts nameless slurs at another is a thousand times dirtier a coward than he who boldly makes public his charges and places himself in a position to be punished under the law . . ." [10]

When the Indianapolis Sentinel printed the allegations about the seduction, Blaine made the mistake of bringing suit, thereby making it safe for everybody to publish. The World (and other Democratic papers) thereupon felt compelled to front-page the tale that Blaine, when a young Kentucky school teacher, had decamped to Pittsburgh and had been brought back unwillingly to marry the young lady. There was much journalistic speculation about the exact dates of the wedding and the birth of the first child, who had since died. The speculation was heightened when it was discovered that some vandal had chiseled at the tombstone of the dead son, removing the date of his birth.

Thus the question of who would be the next President seemed to bear somewhat on whether it was more iniquitous to have a child unwillingly sanctified by marriage or to have one not sanctified at all. Here there could be little argument, since the public at large had more sympathy with a hasty marriage than with a case of outright adultery and illegitimacy which the Republicans heaped high with overtones of sordidness. Cleveland's chances had vanished somewhere in Buffalo and he seemed fated to subside into the comparative obscurity of a Roswell P. Flower.

III. BURN THIS LETTER!

Yet the campaign kept turning on a series of incredible mischances which were not yet finished. The Democrats were overjoyed in September to learn that James Mulligan in Boston had *more* Blaine-Fisher letters, a score of them. They had been ticking like a time bomb in dusty files for eight years, ever since Blaine's congressional tour de force of 1876, and now at last they exploded. These letters did not introduce any new element. What they did do was to amplify the old one with vivid new hints of jobbery that justified another Democratic press assault, and above all to expose a disastrous Blaine three-word sentence.

In some of the letters Congressman Blaine asked Fisher for more money for services rendered—always money—and in one the desperate politician from Maine revealed his shiftiness to anyone who could read. It was addressed to Fisher from Washington April 16, 1876, shortly before Blaine was investigated and when he was the favorite for the Republican presidential nomination. But although Blaine knew that Fisher was at the Commonwealth Hotel in Boston, he cautiously sent the letter to the Parker House and wired Fisher to pick it up there. In it he enclosed a draft of a letter he had written, as if written by Fisher to Blaine, clearing him of any impropriety in the railroad deals and describing his conduct as "in the highest degree honorable and straightforward." The letter read in part:

> Certain newspapers are trying to throw mud at me and injure my candidacy . . . and you may observe they are trying it in connection with the Little Rock & Fort Smith matter.
>
> I want you to send me a letter such as the enclosed draft. You will receive this tomorrow (Monday) evening, and it will be a favor I shall never forget if you will at once write the letter and mail it the same evening.
>
> The letter is strictly true, is honorable to you and to me, and will stop the mouths of slanderers at once.
>
> Regard this letter as strictly confidential. Do not show it to any one. The draft is in the hands of my clerk who is as trustworthy as any man can be. If you can't get the letter written in season for the nine o'clock mail to New York, please be sure to mail it during the night, so that it will start first mail Tuesday morning; but, if possible, I pray you to get it in the nine o'clock mail Monday evening. . . .
>
> (Burn this letter) [11]

That postscript was understandable to millions who might be confused by railroad bonds. Now the Republicans in their turn heaped quiet maledictions on a candidate-wrecker, this time the enigmatic Mulligan. Blaine could do nothing but brazen it out, declaring, "There is not a word in the letters which is not entirely consistent with the most scrupulous integrity and honor." The Mulligan disclosures were published from coast to coast, though with far more display in the Democratic press. Indeed, Blaine's firmest supporter in New York, the Tribune, at first hesitated to publish or comment on the letters, waited a full day in unhappy pondering, then printed the letters in part on page 2. It insisted that they exhibited "the language of a thoroughly honest and upright man," but failed to explain why such upright language required burning.[12]

The World gave the letters the front-page attention they deserved, pilloried the Plumed Knight as he deserved to be pilloried, and said, "All other issues sink into insignificance beside the crying necessity for reform . . ." Democratic paraders now had a marching song of their own:

Blaine, Blaine, James G. Blaine,
The continental liar from the State of Maine,
Burn this letter!

Pulitzer, watching his circulation figures, was winning his race against time with the fastest gain in following yet seen in journalism. By midsummer the World had passed 60,000 and on Sundays neared 100,000. Yet to the voters it remained a choice between a charming grafter and a stolid immoralist. As this dirtiest of all campaigns entered its closing days the advantage was still with Blaine. With his Irish ancestry and several Roman Catholic relatives, along with his occasional shrewd attacks on the English, he could count on the Catholic vote by a wide margin over the Presbyterian Cleveland. The presidency was Blaine's until this suave politician, so remarkable for his tendency to mix inspired abilities with downright follies, committed two blunders in one day.

On the morning of October 29, weary after a speech-making tour, he greeted a group of Protestant New York clergymen who called on him at the Fifth Avenue Hotel—one of those platitudinous affairs a candidate had to live through. Their elderly spokesman, the Rev. Samuel D. Burchard of the Murray Hill Presbyterian Church, said in part, "We are Republicans and don't propose to . . . identify ourselves with the [Democratic] party whose antecedents have been rum, Romanism and rebellion."

The tired Blaine was not listening. The remark escaped him and he did not contradict it. That night, although party colleagues tried to dissuade him because times were hard and the common people might misunderstand, he attended a thoroughly capitalistic dinner at Delmonico's. It was arranged in his honor by Cyrus Field and Jay Gould, the latter not long since a "Democratic" newspaper owner. It was attended by 180 financiers including such synonyms for wealth as William H. Vanderbilt, Russell Sage, John Jacob Astor, Andrew Carnegie, Whitelaw Reid, Henry Clews,

Chauncey Depew and Levi P. Morton. Blaine, fronted by an elaborate floral piece lettered "J.G.B.," addressed the group about "Republican prosperity" despite the economic hardship in many parts of the country. Later his campaign manager, Stephen B. Elkins, spoke on another subject, the Republican need for money for the last-minute vote drive. Reporters were excluded except for one Associated Press man friendly to Gould, and even he was shown the door before the fund-raising began. Reid's Tribune, of course, could be relied on for sympathetic coverage.

Characteristically, the World learned of the proceedings from start to finish. One can imagine Pulitzer striding into his office that night with a triumphant smile on his somewhat diabolical face. The front page of the World next morning was devoted entirely to Blaine, his implied "insult" to Catholics and his love-and-money banquet with the plutocrats. A seven-column streamer opened the show:

THE ROYAL FEAST OF BELSHAZZAR
BLAINE AND THE MONEY KINGS

Under this was a half-page McDougall cartoon showing Blaine surrounded at the table by bejeweled nabobs, Gould at one shoulder, Vanderbilt at the other. All were partaking of "Monopoly Soup," "Lobby Pudding" and "Gould Pie," heedless of the pleas of a passing unemployed worker, his emaciated wife and ragged child for a crust from the groaning board.

The flash of inspiration showed in the item that headed the story below. It was a bulletin from Lewiston, Maine—the candidate's home state—reporting the closing of textile mills that threw hundreds out of work and swamped the Overseer of the Poor with appeals for aid. From stark Lewiston the World shifted the scene to the banquet:

"Delmonico's was filled with millionaires last night. The object of the banquet was two-fold—nominally to honor Mr. James G. Blaine but really to raise a corruption fund of $500,000 with which to defeat the will of the people. . . . Every gentleman was expected to bring with him a check to be used for the guest of the evening." (Pulitzer of course had a clear conscience about the $1,000 he had given the Democrats.)

There was display of Dr. Burchard's remark, Blaine's silent "assent," and relentless stress on this affront to all Catholic voters—a theme the World pounded at incessantly in ensuing days. The banquet was described with emphasis on the splendor of the surroundings, the diamonds which the World insisted were worn by all present, the champagnes and brandies, and the menu, which included dishes unfamiliar to Lewiston textile workers: *Huitres, Timbales à la Reynière,* Kingfish *à la Richelieu,* Canvasback Duck, Filet of Beef, Terrapin *à la* Maryland, *Gelée à la Prunelle,* and *Soufflés aux Marrons.* There was a list of the diners, with pejorative comment on the source of their wealth, and particular mention of Gould, whose public detestation would damage any candidate with whom he was friendly. There was devilish emphasis on the fund-raising finale, at which Gould and his colleagues pledged a half million "to aid Mr. Blaine in buying up the votes in Maryland, New York and Connecticut." There was much, much more in this journalistic enfilade that rattled on into succeeding pages and into a World editorial that impugned the motives of the banqueters and demanded, "Are they friends of the workingman?"[13]

A comparison with other morning newspapers is instructive. There was of course no such thing as journalistic objectivity in political matters. The Tribune covered the event as a Blaine triumph, with no mention of Dr. Burchard's rum-Romanism statement or of fund-raising. Even the pro-Cleveland Herald and Times let slip their opportunity, evidently construing the banquet as Blaine publicity it was best not to feature overmuch, relegating the story to inside pages and also missing Dr. Burchard and the fund-raising. Only the World recognized the full political potential of Blaine's day of error and squeezed every partisan drop out of it. The rum-Romanism remark went out over the wires, and the Democratic National Committee was so impressed by McDougall's cartoon that it struck off thousands of copies for use as placards and in parades.

There were some 500,000 Irish-Americans residing in New York State. No pollster counted the Irish, German and Italian Catholics who discussed Blaine's failure to resent the insult given them, nor the workmen who pondered that Lucullan dinner, but it was obvious that he had lost thousands of votes in New York City alone.

On November 5, the day after the election, the World printed 223,680 copies, a hot-press day and about double its daily average—itself an incredible gain over the 15,000 Pulitzer had bought 18 months before. For three days the issue was in doubt, though it was soon apparent that New York was the decisive state and the candidate who won it would be President. On November 7 the closest of all presidential counts was in, and New York's Union League Club lowered its flag to half-mast. Cleveland, whose popular vote was only 25,000 more than Blaine's in a national total of almost ten million, had taken New York State by a mere 1,149 votes, thereby winning with 219 electoral votes to Blaine's 182. Five hundred and seventy-five votes the other way in New York would have elected Blaine. Those interested in the amusing game of ascribing credit for pluralities might say that James Mulligan put Cleveland in the White House, or that the Reverend Burchard did, or the Mugwumps did, or that the "Democratic rains" that swept upstate New York on election day were responsible, or give the palm to Roscoe Conkling, whose undercover work against Blaine bore heavy fruit in his home county of Oneida, formerly a Republican stronghold but for Cleveland this time. Cleveland would have lost had any one of these factors been missing. And he would have lost had Pulitzer been missing. Could anyone say that Pulitzer, in four months of vigorous campaigning topped by his smashing exploitation of Blaine's errors—not to mention his rides in Central Park with Conkling—had not influenced many times 575 voters and satisfied his gnawing ambition to elect a President?

"My dear Mr. Pulitzer," Conkling wrote, "Thanks for your note with check $1,000 [*sic*] . . ." [14]

Almost forgotten in the excitement was the fact that Pulitzer had put himself in Congress, beating the Republican Herman W. Thum by 15,518 votes to 8,510. But the sensation of Park Row was the disaster visited on the Sun, which latterly had stressed Cleveland's official role in two hangings when he was sheriff at Buffalo and insisted that hangmen made poor Presidents, then had wound up (along with the Tribune) by publishing an affidavit describing Cleveland's affair with Mrs. Halpin. When the campaign was over its circulation had dropped from its all-time high of 158,000 to 78,000. The World had passed the Sun, passed the Tribune and Times and was pressing hard on the Herald's claimed (but misleading) 138,500. Suddenly the World was the biggest Democratic newspaper in the country. *The Journalist* commented, "As a business manager of a clothing establishment somewhere in the direct vicinity of Chatham Street, Jewseph Pulitzer would be an honor to his race and a glory to his surroundings." [15]

Chapter 3

Disenchantment

1. WALKING THE BOWERY

To his rivals, Pulitzer must have brought a reminder of the jocular definition of a Hungarian—a man who follows you into a revolving door and emerges ahead of you. The success of his World was not due to luck or to a feverish political campaign, but to his perceptive appraisal of social conditions to which others were indifferent and his evolution of a hard-driving journalistic technique and policy perfectly tailored to exploit them. He won the masses with three qualities he labored to instill daily into his paper—readability, excitement and education.

Readability, almost extinct in the staid Tribune and Times, was often present in the Sun and Herald but of a kind appealing to the cultivated. Pulitzer perfected a terse, simple, colloquial style which the World itself described as "brief, breezy and briggity." For excitement he offered not only sensationalism but constant attack. Though aware of the basic human interest in struggle, of children leaving all other interests to watch a fistfight, he was driven to battle not out of expediency alone but by his own irrepressible combativeness. There was always a rousing fight on in the World.

The matter of education, which included endless publicity of social evils and strenuous instruction for reform, showed the real heart of the World and the authentic genius of its teacher-proprietor. In him the Davidson credo of contempt for passive legality, of worship of dynamic progressivism, blew up a gale.

The horror of the eighties lay in the quick industrialization of the nation and the ruthless exploitation of labor in a laissez-faire economy. With the unions still weak and divided, $1.25 was a good wage for a workday of ten or twelve hours. As almost 500,000 immigrants poured in annually, many of them staying in New York, ghetto conditions below Union Square became ghastly. Labor was cheapened, women and children toiled for 50 cents or less a day, and an average of more than a thousand hopeful Europeans arrived daily by steerage to aggravate the problem. New York City had the distinction of encompassing the most crowded and brutal squalor in the world, worse than London, worse than Bombay. Nowhere could there be found such a social contrast as between Fifth Avenue, where Richard Morris Hunt and other architects were erecting French châteaux and Italian palazzos for the new millionaires, and the abysmal filth and despair of Mulberry Bend. Expanding America, complacently believing in the McGuffey dogma of equal opportunity, was unaware that equality had vanished. The land of the free was too busy scrambling for success to realize that freedom had got out of hand, and Fifth Avenue was so segregated from the slums as to be virtually unaware of them.

Fifth Avenue had its voices in the Tribune, Times, Sun and Herald. The poor had no effective voice at all until Pulitzer, to his everlasting honor, gave them one. To his instinctive feeling for their deprivations, needs and interests—astonishing in itself for a man with such perfectly manicured nails and such a taste for vintages—he added a spirit of practical, intelligent reform which journalism had not yet seen. His activist doctrine shone in his criticism of Watterson's definition of a good newspaper as one that gave a faithful history of yesterday. Not enough, he said:

> The newspaper that is true to its highest mission will concern itself with the things that *ought to happen tomorrow,* or next month, or next year, and will seek to make what ought to be come to pass. . . . The highest mission of the press is to *render public service.*[1]

Pulitzer was the first to exploit, to publicize, to attack the shameful incongruity between Murray Hill and the Lower East Side and to demand corrective social and political action. He was indeed the first of the muckrakers. The World habitually assailed the "low upper classes," the "vulgar wealthy," the "watered-stock aristocracy." It welcomed the immigrants who "bring us . . . strong blood and unlimited possibilities." It courted the Irish by devotion to Home Rule and scorn for the English, the Germans by news of Bismarck and of Liederkranz balls, the Jews by attention to Purim. It aided them with incessant skillful crusades against their greatest enemies—corruption, complacency, the robber-baron mentality, a wage scale insuring serfdom, a reprehensible tax system, and appalling housing and health standards.

It threw light into dark corners never illuminated before. It excoriated the assertions of such stand-pat papers as the Tribune that the worker was well-paid and content in the most glorious of democracies. To read the World was to be reminded *every day* that this was not true, that reform was not only urgently needed but was easily possible if a social conscience could be aroused, if laws could be remedied and enforced.

Its crusades for reform started the very day Pulitzer took over and never really ended. Thus it was an incident of continuous policy when the World supported the striking dollar-a-day workmen on Jay Gould's Missouri Pacific Railroad and pointed out, "One bottle of [Gould's] choice wine costs more than a Missouri Pacific laborer can spend for food for his family for two weeks"; [2] or when it solicited funds for working girls' vacations; or when it attacked Assemblyman Theodore Roosevelt's objection to a bill that would reduce the workday of horse-car drivers to 12 hours —a proposal he thought communistic. It was part of a constant exposure of tenement horrors when it gave statistics on infant mortality; when it pictured the poor at Christmas without bread, much less turkey and plum pudding; when it assailed the laggard sanitary inspectors for letting tenement conditions sink to savagery; or when it said, "Take a lot 25 feet front and 100 feet deep, and erect a building 25 by 80 on it, with accommodations for four families on each of its five or six floors, and you are simply making a trap to smother people." [3] One measure of the World's greatness was its insistence on treating the poor as human beings rather than ciphers. Other papers thought vulgar or unimportant the slum tragedies which the World featured as grist for reform, such as the death of Kate Sweeny:

> She had lay [*sic*] down in the cellar to sleep, and the sewer that runs under the house overflowed and suffocated her where she lay. No one will ever know who killed Kate Sweeny. No one will ever summon the sanitary inspectors. . . . Nobody seems to have thought it worth an investigation.[4]

Pulitzer had not been joking when he told his staff, "You are all walking down the Bowery." It was time that someone of sympathy and influence walked down the Bowery and showed interest in the Kate Sweenys. Pulitzer, who gave deep thought to civic improvement, was contemptuous of those who felt they had fulfilled their duty by voting the Republican ticket. Intending to become an honest millionaire as soon as possible, he disliked those who made fortunes out of watered stock and underfed labor. He despised the bogus coats-of-arms, the fierce competition for glitter, the rush for Newport palaces, the pet dogs with jeweled collars, the yearning to marry foreign titles. "Take it altogether," the World said with delicate understatement, "some of our good society, when measured by the demands of the community in which it lives, is a very selfish and barren society." He had supported the new Metropolitan Opera House enthusiastically and often had a box there with Kate, but he regarded the opera as a cultural feast for all the people, not as a vehicle for social ostentation:

There is no doubt about it, the Valet as an opera accompaniment must go. He is objectionable for more than one reason. He is apt to be mistaken for a stockholder as he stands at the door of his master's box; he is impertinent and drops his h's; and he doesn't fit into the amusement machinery of New York. . . .

If the musical public are to be depended on to help support the opera-house, then do not aggravate and insult American freemen by a show of shoddy aristocracy that is made nowhere else in the world.

We understand that the people who introduced this business at the opera intend to introduce it at their churches, where the enlivening spectacle will be presented of a row of valets and footmen in the aisles standing at their "masters'" pew doors. Still, as these churches are run entirely in the interest of the rich members and not for the public the impropriety is perhaps not so great.

But in an opera-house. Bah! [5]

If the World's indignation often impaired the Molière touch it sought, it recognized the scope for satire in the often lubberly parvenues of Wall Street and trade. It ridiculed their absurdities. It campaigned steadily for a graduated tax on incomes over $10,000. It showed that the existing tax structure, which derived most of its revenue from real property, loaded the tax on the poor in the form of high rents. "The laborer pays the same tax as the millionaire on the tea, coffee, sugar and tobacco he consumes and the blankets and clothing he buys," the World noted. It examined the tax rolls (an old Pulitzer habit) and disclosed that William H. Vanderbilt, whose fortune it estimated at $200,000,000, until recently had avoided taxation altogether by swearing that his debts exceeded his income. The telegraph and transit magnate Cyrus Field had done the same. "Wealth escapes taxation," said the World. Vanderbilt, whose granddaughter ultimately would become Pulitzer's daughter-in-law, took further World punishment in the estimate (exaggerated) that his fortune would make a gold ingot of 350 tons requiring 25 freight cars to haul. Vanderbilt's New York Central Railroad caught it steadily for rigging rates, as did Vanderbilt's viceroy, Chauncey Depew, when he lectured on the threat of communism and anarchism to America's "splendid" society. The World commented:

> Mr. Depew would have done much . . . if he had pointed out to the greedy corporations and monopolies of which he is so brilliant a representative that there is no Communism in the country and can be none except through the insane folly of corrupt wealth.[6]

The World courted revenge when, in demonstrating the favoritism and influence-peddling in taxation, it hired real-estate experts who affirmed that the buildings of the Sun, Herald, Tribune and Times were all taxed at from one-third to one-half of their real value. This took money-courage, since Pulitzer knew he was on the way to great wealth and knew that his rivals would see that he was taxed to the hilt. But he could give even Vanderbilt grudging praise on the ground that his ostentation was a shade less vulgar than that shown by others and that his offspring did not go title-hunting: "We do not believe that the coat-of-arms on his carriage is as big as a full-sized hand. His servants do not wear yellow tags and cockades. We never saw Mrs. Vanderbilt nursing a poodle. . . . The young Vanderbilts, male and female, have all married plain Americans." [7]

At the same time that the World's editorial page pilloried both the robber-baron methods of accumulating wealth and the bandwagon display of it, its news columns covered the balls and entertainments of these same plutocrats without satire and with careful attention to pomp. The poor, with their dreams, wanted to read about them. But the lesson was never far behind: "Does Fifth Avenue forget that it is flanked by the tenements of Eleventh Avenue and Avenue B, and outnumbered 1,000 to 1 in point of mere numbers? . . . Our bankers and brokers . . . cannot too speedily recognize the peril of teaching the people to despise all law, by showing them that its grip is only firm on the threat of the poor . . ." [8]

Never a revolutionist, Pulitzer rejected socialism and anarchism and saw in enlightened capitalism the great hope of democracy. He sought to enlighten it by exposure and ridicule. His fierce attacks on the excesses of wealth reflected his fear that they might cause disastrous class warfare: "We respect wealth when it is made the instrument of good. . . . We despise wealth when it . . . is prostituted to shoddy display and to the gratification of coarse and vulgar tastes." [9]

New York City had become the hussy of the Gilded Age, the resort of the most shameful corruption and social injustice the nation had ever seen. Joseph Pulitzer, fresh from St. Louis, had instantly recognized, exposed, lampooned, protested and fought them. Naturally he and his World were detested by those who profited by these injustices. Naturally it was fashionable to regard the World as cheap, lying, proletarian and revolutionary. Naturally its envious rivals, the mouthpieces of the status quo, heaped dirt on it. The courage and vision of Pulitzer, who really loved Fifth Avenue, wanted to be accepted, and knew that all these unpleasant things would happen when his World strode the Bowery, has perhaps been underestimated. But if he was cursed at the Union League Club, he was blessed in the rookeries. Workmen who could not spell his name thought him one of the greatest of men. He was performing the great service of educating ignorant people in the issues that confronted them, instructing them in the possibilities of democracy, showing them the importance of their votes, insisting that America could realize its promise. Pulitzer was the voice of the future, the herald of reforms that would come ten, 20 and 30 years later and which would have been still more laggard but for him.

If all this had been done by a thoroughly cynical opportunist who knew the right buttons to press to attain circulation, wealth and power, the accomplishment would have been none the less prodigious. But Pulitzer, who indeed knew how to press the buttons, would prove over the years that he pressed them not for power alone but also to promote ideals of justice so advanced that they were almost exclusive with him.

II. OFFICE SEEKERS

To Pulitzer, the election of Cleveland was not merely a reason for satisfaction but for rapture—the elevation of a plain "man of the people," a vindication of the democratic process, a triumph over the forces of evil. Though he badly needed rest, now came the office seekers who felt that his own election to Congress and his aid to Cleveland placed almost any government post at his disposal. A St. Louis friend, J. F. Conroy, wrote that he had found the climate of New Mexico Territory beneficial to his wife's health, adding, "The election of Governor Cleveland to the Presidency and your share in that good work and our long continued friendship leads me to hope that, through your influence, I can become Governor of New Mexico. Your personal and political influence ought to be all powerful with Governor Cleveland and I am confident you will exert it in my behalf." [10]

Pleas flooded in for offices big and small. J. A. Beard begged Pulitzer to make him postmaster at Jefferson, Oregon. G. S. Chilton of West Virginia sought appointment as doorkeeper of the House. Jasper L. Harben of Illinois wrote that he spoke French quite well and "My desire is to obtain a Diplomatic position." Scores of young men pleaded for appointments to Annapolis or West Point, one of them Cockerill's nephew, strongly recommended by Cockerill. There were utter strangers who sought office and who might or might not have some claim on the party, and there were the inevitable friends whose requests must get kindly attention if friendship was to be preserved. Among the latter were James W. Gerard, Pulitzer's landlord, interested in a European mission; Dr. Montrose A. Pallen of New York, a cultivated but impecunious physician who was in poor health and wished to be United States Consul-General in London; the kindly Charles Gibson of St. Louis, long a Pulitzer ally and a devoted party worker, who wanted to be Minister at Berlin; and M. H. Keevil, father-in-law of Pulitzer's old St. Louis friend William Patrick, who had set his heart on the consulship at Bristol, England, and wrote, "May I take the liberty to ask if you can consistently bring any influence to bear at Washington in my behalf?" [11]

Because of the long lame-duck interval, Pulitzer would not take his seat in Congress for more than a year, but the vexations began at once. A cheering factor was the growing profits of the World, which once skeptical advertisers were now accepting in steadily greater numbers. He was forced to think of easing his financial and mental burden by selling the Post-Dispatch, which was now circulating 30,500 copies a day but which disappointed him, despite the general business slump, because it had not yet quite turned a $100,000 annual net profit. Gibson was representing him in strict confidence in St. Louis, looking guardedly for a buyer at $500,000, a price that would pay off the remaining debt to Jay Gould and leave Pulitzer a handsome fortune besides. If the Post-Dispatch was valued at $500,000, the World was now easily worth $2,000,000. In less than six years Pulitzer had ballooned his original investment of a few thousand dollars into two newspaper properties worth some $2,500,000—an achievement that did not win him universal praise. "Dear sir," wrote his friend James B. Eads, "I read with surprise that your enemies [in this case Dana's Sun], evidently jealous of your exceptional success as a journalist, have started the ridiculous lie that you were once employed by me as a coachman some fifteen years ago in St. Louis." [12]

For all his theoretical riches he was somewhat pinched because of the luxurious scale of his family life and his debt to Gould, a man he hated to owe. "If you need money I will endorse your paper to any amount," Gibson wrote him.[13] The Pulitzers were active socially, which stole time from days never long enough and required the best vintages. August Belmont aided him on this score, querying his Frankfort agent and writing Pulitzer, ". . . None of the Johannisberg Cabinet (blue seal) wines of 1862 or 1868 are to be had and . . . the next best quality is the white seal wine of 1880 costing, as per price list attached . . ." [14] Kate was pregnant again. Pulitzer lavished affection on his wife and children, and now that Ralph was over five and still sickly he put earnest thought on the boy's health and education. Rushing from home to office to political meetings, he was under continuous pressure that Kate, in her worry about him, succeeded in breaking only with an occasional outing. One man who had an appointment with him wrote angrily, "I have made three attempts . . . and am each time told that you are not in. . . . I have no doubt your time is very valuable but so is mine." [15]

He was stricken briefly at the year's end by exhaustion and illness. A fortnight later he was a snappish guest at a Lotos Club reception for George Augustus Sala, whom the glacial Whitelaw Reid introduced to the gathering with remarks about the late election. "We've not only forgiven our countrymen, whom our guest used to sympathize with," Reid said, "but we've put . . . the most of them into office."

"A good deal better for the country," Pulitzer sang out from across the table.

"We are now considering how much they are going to forgive us," Reid went on.

"We have a good deal to forgive," Pulitzer remarked, after which he allowed the successor of Greeley to continue.[16]

III. RESCUING THE GODDESS

Before he could rest he must first put the World in order with new personnel—particularly a business manager to succeed the ailing McGuffin, who had been moved to circulation. Finding a new man was itself a nerve-racking chore. He expected qualities closer to perfection than were available terrestrially, and any candidate's qualifications must be examined under the microscope. Furthermore, he wanted a top executive—a man of heroic proportions—to fill his own place at least a part of the time, one so accomplished that Pulitzer could take his seat in Congress without undue torment.

Few such men lived. He went to Boston and put a proposition to Charles H. Taylor of the thriving Globe. "He told me," Taylor recalled, "if I would come over [to New York] for three days a week he would give me one hundred thousand dollars a year." [17]

Taylor was too busy in Boston. Probably he did not mention a young Harvard student who had made a success of the *Lampoon*, had come into the Globe building frequently to study its operations, and had an overpowering admiration for Pulitzer's World. The collegian, a strong Cleveland man, was named William Randolph Hearst. Pulitzer went on a similar mission to Philadelphia, where he sought the help of George W. Childs, who had made the Public Ledger a rich property paying more than $400,000 profit in 1884. Childs, who like Taylor would remain a lifelong friend, sent rather frightening advice in a subsequent note:

> . . . You must have a fully capable, and honest *business* manager. . . . Greeley, Forney, and other great *editors* were wrecked by bad *business managers*. You have the most promising newspaper property in the United States, and with tact, energy, and ability in the *business* department, "there are millions in it." [18]

Childs was appalled by the ruin visited on another man who needed a business manager, his friend General Grant. The nation was still buzzing over the ex-President's incredible naiveté in allowing himself to be taken in by the swindler Ferdinand Ward, in becoming the figurehead partner in the firm of Grant & Ward, losing every cent of his own and others when the bubble burst. Now it was known that Grant had cancer of the throat. A World reporter was among others posted in a death watch outside his home at 3 East 66th Street, where he was feebly writing his memoirs in an effort to recoup, now and then glancing out to see those waiting newspapermen, who must have reminded him of the buzzards at the Wilderness.

Meanwhile, Cleveland would be inaugurated March 4, 1885, William Whitney would be his Navy Secretary, and Pulitzer gave thought to the office-seekers. While he opposed a ruthless sweep of the thousands of appointive offices held since the Civil War by Republicans, he took it for granted that there would be a substantial reward for deserving Democrats who had come into their own at last after their long banishment. His own requests were nominal. He seems to have asked only for the appointment of Charles Gibson, an able lawyer of long Democratic loyalty who had stumped Indiana for Cleveland, as Minister to Berlin; and Dr. Pallen, a man of some cultivation, as consul general in London. His letter recommending Pallen was humble enough:

> Dear Mr. President: I hope you will appreciate my firm resolve not to trouble you about appointments.
>
> But a friend of mine labors under the lamentable illusion that a letter from me will aid him in his ambition. I cannot well refuse his request.
>
> I refer to Dr. Montrose A. Pallen of this city, who is anxious to get the position of Consul General at London. I can say with perfect truth that Dr. Pallen is a gentleman of high education, rare culture and varied accomplishments. Though an American by birth he speaks French like a Parisian and is thoroughly familiar with European society.
>
> I should like to see him realize his ambition.[19]

Before his inauguration, Cleveland, who had 100,000 jobs to dispense, came down from Albany to stay at New York's Victoria Hotel and face the patronage-seekers. He first dined at the Brevoort with a group including three newspapermen—Godkin of the Post, Jones of the Times and Oswald Ottendorfer of the Staats-Zeitung, all Cleveland men but none with such medals as Pulitzer. The charge of eager Democrats into the Victoria next morning was reminiscent of Balaklava. Among them were senators, congressmen and politicians from all parts of the country, one of them Pulitzer. Cleveland was barricaded in an upper-floor suite, with one usher outside the door and another in the vestibule. A squad of bellboys brought up the cards of the callers, handed them to the outer usher, who passed them to the usher inside, who gave them to Cleveland's secretary, who scanned them with the President-elect. The cards of those accepted for interviews were sent down one by one by bellboy and the names called out in the lobby. Pulitzer cooled his heels in growing irritation as others were summoned to the presence. At length, when his card was ignored, he left in a rage. While one card could easily be lost in such a maelstrom, and Cleveland later explained that this was what had happened, it was unfortunate that the mislaid card was that of the man who had performed the greatest journalistic service for the party.

On Taylor's recommendation, Pulitzer hired the Bostonian George Walter Turner as his business manager. As his own personal watchdog at the World he took in Kate's amiable brother, Colonel William H. Davis, a mining engineer whose chief qualification was his thorough trustworthiness. Pulitzer was off to Washington to attend the most joyous of inaugurations, an event the World celebrated with front-page hosannas under the headlines:

AT HOME
In the old Democratic
White House Again.
After Twenty-four Years Wander-
ing in the Wilderness
. . . . .
President Cleveland, by the
grace of God
And the Supreme Will of the
American People [20]

He planned a rest in Europe once Kate had had her child and once he had rescued the Goddess of Liberty. Kate did her part, for Joseph Pulitzer Jr. was born on March 21. France had done her part, for Auguste Bartholdi had long since completed the magnificent nine-foot model, and on July 4, 1884, the completed copper sheets that would compose the 152-foot colossus had been formally presented in Paris to United States Minister Levi Morton. Here rose an embarrassment—a gift goddess who had no place to go. A committee had raised $150,000 for the pedestal on Bedloe's Island, but this was far from enough, collections had lagged and the work would cease if money were not forthcoming. The 16-foot torch-bearing hand had been displayed at the Philadelphia Centennial in 1876, and the 17-foot head was shown at the Paris Exposition of 1878, but now the unassembled figure lay waiting in humiliation in France. Pulitzer, whose reverence for liberty was as powerful as his desire for circulation, combined the two in a crusade that could have been sponsored by any other New York newspaper had the imagination and the desire for public service been present. The World's opening editorial said in part:

> It would be an irrevocable disgrace to New York City and the American Republic to have France send us this splendid gift without our having provided even so much as a landing place for it. . . . There is but one thing that can be done. We must raise the money.
>
> The World is the people's paper, and it now appeals to the people to come forward and raise this money. The $250,000 that the . . . statue cost was paid in by the masses of the French people—by the workingmen, the tradesmen, the shop girls, the artisans—by all, irrespective of class or condition. Let us respond in like manner. Let us not wait for the millionaires to give this money. It is not a gift from the millionaires of France to the millionaires of America but a gift of the whole people of France to the whole people of America.
>
> Take this appeal to yourself personally. . . . Give something, however little. . . . Let us hear from the people.[21]

Pulitzer placed John R. Reavis, a reporter he had brought in from the Post-Dispatch, in charge of the fund drive, to which Pulitzer contributed

$250 of his own. His phenomenal ability to galvanize subordinates with zeal was a compound of his own deep earnestness and the stirring language born of a hundred stump speeches. "I have known no other boss who personally infected his employees with [such] fiery ardent energy," the cartoonist McDougall noted.[22] Reavis accepted the commission with sacerdotal devotion. The Post-Dispatch, which liked to call the World "the New York edition of the Post-Dispatch," campaigned for funds in St. Louis. The Pulitzers sailed in May, leaving the children in the care of servants, a physician and the general supervision of Colonel Davis. A recent letter from Childs in Philadelphia must have given Pulitzer satisfaction:

> I am lost in wonderment at the ability and tact shown in the management of the "World." You have done what all others failed to do. There has been no luck nor chance in the matter. Brains! [23]

IV. THE CREATIVE MENTAL POWER

In Paris the Pulitzers visited the offices of Figaro and other newspapers, paid a call on the beaming Auguste Bartholdi, attended art sales and purchased wines. Both were at ease in the French language, both thorough believers in the curative massages and waters at spas. They not only went on to take the cure at Aix-les-Bains but traveled from there to Bad Kissingen for further ministrations. But Pulitzer, unable to divorce himself either from journalism or politics, found his nerves still on edge and insomnia a problem. Henry Moore, his expenses undoubtedly paid by the boss, called on him in Paris to give a thorough report on the Post-Dispatch and to return with instructions for both papers. Pulitzer was scanning the World and other New York papers sent by mail, was receiving reports from several World men, sending frequent directives, and was almost as preoccupied with work as if he were on Park Row. He was giving anxious thought to his coming appearance in Congress and to the question of who would run the World while he was in Washington. But he was so delighted by the work of Reavis, who in four months had collected almost $75,000 of the World's $100,000 goal for the statue, that he cabled New York that Reavis must have an immediate bonus and salary increase. Reavis' lyrical acknowledgment bespoke the passionate loyalty Pulitzer was able to instill:

> I am glad of my success not alone for my sake but for your sake, the paper's sake and the sake of the country. . . . The heart of the people is with us and the people will stand by us and help us to the end. It is a grand thing to see a paper leading the sentiment of a nation. That is what The World is doing today. Never before did a journal have such a hold upon the people. I see new evidences every day of the confidence the

public has in The World and it is a very sacred trust The World has to guard.[24]

Customary journalistic cynicism was not to be found in Reavis or his colleagues. But the other papers took a cynical view of the World's campaign, which was accompanied by the usual vigorous self-advertisement. In June the French transport *Isere* arrived with the statue's sections in 210 packing cases, to be greeted in the harbor by United States vessels and the World-leased steamer *Emmons,* with Cockerill, Sutton, Reavis and many other World staffers and their families aboard. "The Herald," Cockerill wrote Pulitzer, "by its foolish treatment of Liberty, has driven another nail in its coffin. . . . Of course you will see by the papers how we received the Statue of Liberty. It was really a grand success, despite the indifference of the other newspapers. . . . The *Sun* is still falling. . . . Turner [the new business manager] is doing well but he is too nervous to have so much responsibility. He complains now that he doesn't sleep more than four or five hours a night. . . . I am sincerely sorry to hear that you have thus far derived no substantial benefit from your trip." He admitted that he was working 13 hours a day, that the World looked a little foggy because "the types are absolutely worn out," and thanked Pulitzer for "your kind and appreciative words."[25] He addressed his letters to "My dear Mr. P.," a middling familiarity allowable because of his years of association with the chief. Despite Pulitzer's great kindliness, there was that about him that forbade any employee to call him Joe.

From Dillon in St. Louis, who always addressed him as "My dear Mr. Pulitzer," came a letter which, after its redundant first sentence, conveyed a careful diagnosis of his condition:

> Mr. Moore's message to the effect that you did not wish to be bothered with details from this office leaves me little or nothing to report. . . . You are suffering from something more than mere overwork. Overwork in business . . . will break a man down but in your case the injury is greater because you have been overworking those powers and faculties which stand the highest. I mean simply the creative mental power, that faculty which in man is the type of the higher or divine creative power. Not one man in ten thousand has it at all. (Now please excuse the apparent flattery of all this. I mean it seriously and soberly, and I have been trying for a long time to make up my mind to say it. . . .)
>
> The faculty which creates, which out of nothing save its own potency, produces that which otherwise had not existed, is a faculty which you possess to a rare degree. You have overstrained it. . . . But if you can do as the rest of us do, go six months without creating an idea, and get cured thereby, the cure will be worth the sacrifice. . . . If you wish you can do the work of a lifetime in five years—and break down; or you can do the work of a century in a lifetime, and live while you do it, which is much better.[26]

Pulitzer understood all this perfectly but was helpless to stop the "creative mental power." His brain was a perpetual motion machine refusing to cease or even slow its motion. Subject to increasing nervousness whenever he stayed in one place too long, whenever novelty and interest flagged, he crossed with Kate to London and whirled into a busman's holiday of activities. He dropped in at the consulate which Dr. Pallen hoped soon to occupy. He visited many of the newspapers including the august Times and called on friends and Members of Parliament to whom Childs and others had given him letters of introduction. While he was there, Grant died at Mt. McGregor on July 23 and New York's Mayor William R. Grace, noting the World's financial deliverance of the Goddess, appointed Pulitzer to a committee to raise funds for a monument to the President he had regarded as disgraceful. By the time he reached home in August, the World's fund for the Statue of Liberty totaled $101,091, representing 120,000 contributions ranging from a nickel to $250—a felicitous public outpouring for the great figure that would become the world's most famous monument to democracy and freedom. The completion of the work, which would still take another year, was guaranteed.

V. *LOOKING FOR SUGGESTIVE MEN*

Pulitzer immediately hired two men in an effort to reduce his own pressures and Cockerill's. One was smart young Edwin A. Grozier, a former Boston Globe man he enlisted on Taylor's recommendation, who knew shorthand and became Pulitzer's private secretary. The other was tall, 36-year-old Ballard Smith, an Indiana-born Dartmouth graduate who had held increasingly important posts with Watterson's Courier-Journal, the old New York World, the Sun and Herald—dashing, arrogant, socially popular, a driver. He had about him, as Watterson noted, "the air of a baron of the Middle Ages who would brook no delay." [27]

Pulitzer, who admired the Herald's sophistication as much as he deplored its political irresponsibility, stole Smith from Bennett's paper, where he had been managing editor, at a salary not far from $10,000. In so doing he angered the haughty Bennett, a man too eccentric for plausible fiction. A drinker since boyhood, in 1877 he had committed the city's most celebrated gaffe when on New Year's Day he entered the crowded home of his betrothed, Caroline May, and urinated into the grand piano—some said into a rubber plant. That ended the engagement. Caroline's brother, Fred May, horsewhipped Bennett two days later in front of the Union Club, and the pair subsequently fought a bloodless duel. Angered by his ostracism from society, Bennett moved to Paris and ran his Herald from there, making only occasional trips to New York. On his first visit after Ballard Smith's departure, he shook his fist as he strode through the Herald office, threatening to make his stenographer managing editor, then shouting, "I'll have no managing editor. I'll abolish the job." There was never another managing editor on the Herald, though this merely meant a change in nomenclature.[28]

Smith, whose heiress wife would have preferred that he devote himself to a drawing-room career, was in journalism because he loved it. The Smiths often joined the Pulitzers in social affairs. Pulitzer's own brilliance and his wife's beauty and charm already opened great Fifth Avenue doors to them, though most of them were Democratic doors. Indeed, the aging connoisseur August Belmont remarked that Mrs. Pulitzer was "so much like Mrs. [William Waldorf] Astor when she was at her loveliest." [29] Another Pulitzer guest, the debonair Wall Streeter Leonard Jerome, had seen his own beauteous first daughter marry Lord Randolph Churchill and had rejoiced when she gave him a grandson named Winston.

Ballard Smith, with his flair for the big-splash story and the pungent interview, and his lordly tendency to run the show, clashed almost immediately with Cockerill. Until then supreme except for the chief himself, Cockerill now had high-level competition and suspected that Smith was gunning for his job—nor is it impossible that part of Smith's usefulness to Pulitzer was in furnishing a rival who might smarten Cockerill's pace and make him more suggestive. When young Charles Edward Russell, who had newspaper experience in the West, applied for a reporting job, Pulitzer said swiftly, "Are you suggestive? . . . I am looking for suggestive men." Russell affirmed that he was highly suggestive and he became a World reporter.[30]

A sad reality Pulitzer faced on his return was Cleveland's rejection of both of his suggestions for office. Dr. Pallen did not get the London consulship nor did Charles Gibson get the mission to Berlin. True, the President was so besieged by office seekers that he was working far into the night at the White House, and it was also true that the man to whom he gave the important German post—ex-Senator George Pendleton of Ohio—was even more qualified and deserving than Gibson. Yet Cleveland himself understood the World's decisive influence in electing him. During the summer Cockerill had written Navy Secretary Whitney in Pulitzer's behalf, asking him to speak to Cleveland about Dr. Pallen, pointing out that a member of the Times staff had received an appointment and a brother-in-law of James Gordon Bennett had been given a foreign mission, so that "an old Democratic paper like the *World* may be allowed to inquire as to the disposition of an application which its editor has endorsed." [31] It appears that the only favor given the World was the appointment of Cockerill's nephew to the Naval Academy. No record comes to light that the President wrote Pulitzer in apologetic explanation, and though there may have been explanations later when the two met personally in Washington, one feels that the overworked Cleveland handled the matter with his usual lack of finesse.

Now Pulitzer knew precisely how Dana had felt in 1883. Angered though he was, he did not succumb to the Dana vindictiveness. Soon after the election the World had denied the suggestion of other newspapers that it would be the "administration organ," saying, "The World . . . will gladly and zealously support all that is good in President Cleveland's administration. But it would oppose anything that should be clearly wrong or mistaken. We regard the editorship of The World as a great public trust, as Mr. Cleveland regards the Presidency." [32] Although the World's criticism of the President might have been gentler had Dr. Pallen been in London and Charles Gibson in Berlin, it would certainly have criticized nevertheless.

Hungry Democrats everywhere were aroused by Cleveland's slowness in spreading manna. The World was joined by many Democratic papers, including Watterson's Courier-Journal, in warning that if Democrats who had toiled in the barren vineyards for 24 years were not rewarded now with grapes from the first harvest, the vines would go untended forevermore. Pulitzer sent out reporters to interview leading Democrats, who agreed. The new Assistant Postmaster General, Adlai Stevenson, was bold enough to criticize the President by implication when he praised the World's stand and said, ". . . The six months which have elapsed since Cleveland's accession finds only between ten and twelve per cent of the offices [postmasters] occupied by Democrats." [33] Said the World: "Cleveland must remember the obligations which an Administration elected by a great historical party owes to that party." [34] At the same time the World campaigned successfully for the election of David Bennett Hill to the New York governorship, calling him "in State politics a disciple of President Cleveland," which he decidedly was not. Hill would soon prove himself a thoroughgoing machine spoilsman, but he had written to praise what an "excellent and reliable a Democratic paper . . . the World now is." [35]

Pulitzer, whose own manners were exemplary when he was not suffering from nerves or a headache, was highly susceptible to courtesy and praise. One evening he attended a Lotos Club dinner addressed by the ubiquitous Chauncey Depew, whom he had never met but had assailed unsparingly along with the New York Central Railroad. Depew, the most urbane of soft-soapers, announced to the gathering, "We have with us tonight a great journalist from the wild and woolly West," and added further graceful remarks. Pulitzer later shook his hand and said, "Chauncey Depew, you are a mighty good fellow. I have been misinformed about you. You will have friendly treatment hereafter in any newspaper which I control." [36]

Chapter 4

Nerves on Edge

I. PROFANE PHILANTHROPIST

In addition to his own emotional sympathies, Pulitzer had a deep conviction—most uncommon among the wealthy at the time—that any man's success must be matched by his philanthropies. When his benefactor Will Patrick died in St. Louis, he immediately contracted to pay for the education of Patrick's two sons, got Gibson to handle the details and received a letter in which Mrs. Patrick called him "a noble hearted true friend." He sent a $100 check to Gibson's son. When that wandering, impractical scholar Thomas Davidson (one of the few who called him Joe) came down from Concord to live in New York, he was welcomed at the Pulitzer hearth and given a $100 monthly retainer to write book reviews and articles for the World, though his writing was not the kind that lured circulation. Davidson, a good friend of Longfellow, Lowell, Howells and William James, a lecturer and translator of learned books, would often receive help from Pulitzer.

Pulitzer signed a $1,000 note for Charles P. Johnson. He was sending financial aid to Udo Brachvogel, the friendly librarian at the St. Louis Mercantile Library, and he sent a generous donation to the library. He gave $100 to the Parnell Fund, $100 to the New York Sanitary Aid Society, and $100 to Mother Mary Clare of a Catholic organization, adding words that must have astonished Mother Mary: ". . . You may call on me for a regular contribution every year if you need it." [1] He gave $5,000 to the New York Press Club to endow perpetually a bed at Roosevelt Hospital for ailing journalists—a bed that often would be occupied by men suffering from delirium tremens. He bought part of a Hoboken park to serve as a playground for the families of World men, and aided in founding the World Building and Loan Association to help them purchase homes.

Although he was the shrewdest of businessmen, well aware of the advantage of a loyal personnel, he went considerably further than mere expediency would require. He distributed turkeys to all employees at Thanksgiving and Christmas, paid better-than-average salaries, and the "stars" who offered him exceptional talents—Cockerill, Turner, Dillon, McGuffin and Smith—were rewarded with paychecks of a size then unknown anywhere in journalism. Cockerill received well over $10,000 a year, which put him in the bank-executive bracket in 1885, when the press was still regarded as not quite respectable. Pulitzer invariably paid a bonus, sometimes accompanied by a salary increase, for any especially meritorious work. He offered prizes for the best news ideas, news condensations, headlines and editorials. All this, when he still could not afford needed new presses, showed his belief in men—something not true, for example, of Bennett, who once said to a reporter asking for a raise, "All the brains I want can be picked up any day at twenty-five dollars per week." Pulitzer took a kindly personal interest in his men, especially the suggestive ones, McDougall noting, "he was very approachable, and even companionable . . ." [2]

In return, he expected them to give their life's blood to the World. Any indication that an employee did not place a World idea, headline or news story in the same category of importance as his wife, his children and his God aroused his instant indignation. The possibility of ruinous lawsuits for libel gave him nightmares. As his health deteriorated and he spent less time at the office, he was forced to demand impeccable reliability. One man he discharged for some enormous blunder was the city editor David Sutton, who wrote him in contrition, admitting his error and saying that Pulitzer had been like a father to him.[3]

While the quick-tempered Cockerill was held by some to be unsurpassed in his colorful use of profanity, connoisseurs generally gave Pulitzer the edge because of the deep sincerity and inventiveness of his swearing. "When J.P. was dictating an editorial upon some favorite topic," McDougall recalled, "such as Collis P. Huntington's extremely ill-gotten wealth, Jay Gould's infamous railroad-wrecking or Cyrus Field's income, his speech was so interlarded with sulphurous and searing phrases that the whole staff shuddered. He was the first man I ever heard who split a word to insert an oath. . . . His favorite was 'indegoddampendent.' . . . He apparently felt all the red-hot indignation he daily voiced." [4] It is not impossible that Pulitzer, whose language in polite society was so correct, was a victim of the syndrome described not long before by Dr. Gilles de la Tourette—the pathological need to curse found in some neurotics.

His nerves tended to grow more frazzled as the day wore on, impairing his usefulness. As Cockerill put it, "He was the damnedest best man in the world to have in a newspaper office for one hour in the morning. For the remainder of the day he was a damned nuisance." [5] Although he had visited St. Louis only once since invading New York, the Post-Dispatch newsboys chipped in to buy him a gold-headed cane, sending it along with an engrossed scroll reading: ". . . We wish you to interpret [it] as a token both of the high esteem in which we hold you personally, and of our full and perfect appreciation of the many kindnesses we have received at your hand. . . ." [6]

Perhaps no one but Kate realized that he was cracking under the strain. At home he became dictatorial, sometimes utterly unreasonable. In October the family left Gramercy Park, took a year's lease on the handsome John Hoey house at 616 Fifth Avenue—Millionaires' Row—and hired a new butler. Hardly were they installed than Pulitzer, who had been in a bad humor for weeks, precipitated a preposterous quarrel with Kate. Nothing was where it ought to be in the new quarters. He exploded when he could not immediately find a pair of drawers that would encompass his somewhat expanding middle. As Kate described the encounter in a diary:

> He said that he was uncomfortable, that I did not understand the proper relations between husband and wife. That all the little attentions [,] all the little things that go to make a man comfortable, that I failed in. I told him that . . . there was not a servant in his house who had worked harder than I had. That I had put him first, have sacrificed the children and myself to him . . . I lost my temper, and said I had made a slave of myself [,] that he was utterly spoilt, that with his disposition he must have something to criticize . . . [He said] I did not understand, had never been taught to understand the duties of a wife . . . He then ordered me out of the room saying that these scenes left a blot on me in his mind that he never forgave. . . . When will these scenes end or when will I be at rest? [7]

II. FOUR-MONTH CONGRESSMAN

In Washington, Speaker John Carlisle was cordial when approached by Pulitzer's correspondent, T. C. Crawford. "Mr. Carlisle is anxious to place you upon the committees which will be the most agreeable to you," Crawford wrote him. "If you will write us concerning your preference, I will give him the information . . ." He followed this with a letter showing that the congressman-elect was at heart a newspaperman: "The last thing you said to me when I saw you in New York was that you wanted a good sensation. I have sent you one by this night's mail." [8]

This was the case of Cleveland's Attorney General, August H. Garland, who was discovered to own stock in the Pan Electric Telephone Company, a corporation he seemed about to favor in a government lawsuit. The World immediately prepared a dossier on Garland and began an attack bolstered by information purchased by Crawford from a former bookkeeper of Pan. Yet Pulitzer seemed determined on a vigorous congressional career when he went to Washington in December. First he wanted his party to wipe out the high Republican tariff, replacing it with a low "tariff for revenue only." He was given a place on the important Interstate and Foreign Commerce Committee. He did not take with him his secretary, Grozier, who had proved too valuable to the World, and he did not seek a quiet suite at the Arlington or Willard. Wanting to be first to hear every rumor, political or personal, he took rooms at John Chamberlin's expensive hostelry at 15th and I Streets, a clubby rendezvous of convivial, poker-playing politicians which Chamberlin had created by connecting three houses, one of them the former mansion of Blaine. A few squares away at 1731 I Street was the 26-room town house, complete with Washington's grandest ballroom, where William and Flora Whitney entertained an average of 15,000 guests a year, including the President, the Cabinet, John Hay, Henry Adams and the legation people. At 1719 Connecticut Avenue lived Kate Pulitzer's parents and her spinster sister, Clara Davis. In Congress were dozens of Pulitzer friends encountered in years of politicking, among them the New Yorkers Abram Hewitt and Bourke Cockran.

For the tactless Hewitt, Pulitzer held the high admiration he reserved for that rare bird, the captain of industry with an ideal of public service. Hewitt had built the first open-hearth furnace in the country, produced the first high-quality steel, become a director of many corporations, and as his fortune grew had devoted much of his time to civic projects and governmental reform, serving with distinction in Congress since 1875, fighting his heart out for the lost Tilden cause in 1876. Like Pulitzer, he had campaigned for Cleveland, then become disillusioned with the President over his failure to make effective use of the patronage. Now, like Pulitzer, he hoped that Cleveland would take aggressive leadership in the tariff reform promised in the Democratic platform.

The President disappointed them both. In his annual message he dealt only casually with the tariff and resigned his initiative by declaring that he would not try to influence Congress. He permitted the lackluster William Morrison of Illinois to be made head of the Ways and Means Committee, and though Morrison did his best in framing a new tariff bill, its chances were nil without vigorous support from the White House. Pulitzer, who indeed gave deep study to governmental problems, would have denied hotly that he was cocksure, but it had to be admitted that he invariably knew exactly what the President should do in any given circumstance. Besides, debt always weighed on him like a curse, he was concerned about clearing up the final payment to Gould, and he worried that the feud between Cockerill and Smith might get out of hand. He could take little interest in such congressional debates as that over a bill to regulate the manufacture and sale of oleomargarine when he felt that the most important issue facing the country was leaking away in committee. It was common to see members intoxicated on the floor of Congress, and Pulitzer himself at times forgot his frayed nerves in conviviality. On one occasion he brought his cartoonist Walt McDougall to Washington with him. ". . . One or two man's-sized drinks had the effect of bringing out in him a boyish, noisy boisterousness," McDougall observed. "[One] night, when we were leaving the Capitol grounds, he was lit up to the seventh magnitude by a few cocktails . . ." [9]

"Dear Sir," wrote the New York prohibitionist Harriet Goff, advocating a bill for school instruction in temperance, "Surely you will not deny the mothers of our City, when they urge that you remember the children whom they wish should receive the fore-warnings . . . that shall save ours from becoming a Nation of drunkards." [10]

Still came the incessant pleas for office, one of them from H. A. Brachvogel, brother of Udo, soliciting a clerkship at the Southern Ute Indian Agency for his son Max, adding, "I know that you have great influence . . ." [11]

Had he, Joseph Pulitzer, donated $1,000 to the party, created the Cleveland boom, worked himself to exhaustion to elect him, and gone to Washington from New York's ninth district for the purpose of landing Max Brachvogel at the Southern Ute Agency while his own World went to ruin?

He could ask himself such plausible questions and forget others equally logical. Did he, Joseph Pulitzer, a freshman congressman in his first session, expect the Senate and the President to dance to his tune?

One feels that he did, with the weight of his World behind him. At 38 he had become accustomed to quick mastery of anything he essayed and was devoid of the patience required in the slow-moving Washington legislative mill. His dream of national power had dwindled in terrible disappointment. Years later he would write Cleveland, "I remember our last long talk at the White House and your wonderful patience and good nature," [12] but now his feelings were less sympathetic.

The congressman began to spend less time in Washington and more in New York. There was a huge Christmas tree in the Pulitzer sitting room for the holidays, when he poured gifts and affection on Kate (pregnant again) and on Ralph, Lucille and the baby Joseph. In the Sun Dana snapped that the congressman was nonexistent, seldom present at roll call. When Pulitzer was in Washington he spent much of his time with his capital correspondents, Crawford and his assistant, George G. Bain, perfecting newspaper campaigns. The World's attack on Attorney General Garland, whose resignation Cleveland had unwisely failed to ask, was so ferocious that Garland offered fearfully to transfer his stock in Pan Electric to the World, which could dispose of it for charitable purposes. Pulitzer telegraphed Crawford:

> Garland's offer to transfer stock to World is against my inflexible rule never to touch any speculative stock whatever. I must adhere to that principle but if he positively wants to transfer the unclean thing to you not as representative of World but as trustee for sole purpose of getting rid of his embarrassment and publicly disposing of stock for some charity [,] that might be considered.[13]

Crawford produced a different kind of shocker—the case of a Cabinet member's son who was said to have seduced a hotel chambermaid before removing to Arizona. "If he has since married the young woman," Crawford pointed out, "why the story would be romantic instead of scandalous." [14] Crawford was also digging into an affair more scandalous than romantic, the case of a New York Democratic politician lured into a tryst at New York's Hoffman House by a woman who proved to be employed by his political enemies, who promptly blackmailed him. He was investigating Collis P. Huntington's corrupt lobbying activities for the Union Pacific. He was looking for fraud in government agencies, writing Pulitzer, "My idea is to employ some veteran clerk in any one of the department bureaux which you desire taken in hand. This clerk can be employed to do the work confidentially." [15]

Pulitzer kept his two Washington men so busy that George Bain wrote in some despair, "My office hours are 8:30 a.m. to 10:30 p.m.," and asked for a raise in pay. The boss himself became almost a stranger in Congress. "It is . . . impossible to be both in Washington and New York at the same time," he observed. He did what he could for the languishing tariff bill. He offered a resolution for a pension for the family of the late General Hancock. His nerves were running wild again. By late winter he saw that he had made the error Dillon had warned him about, believing that he could spread his "creative mental power" everywhere—believing also that he could serve in Congress while he operated two newspapers devoted to reforming the government. He resigned his seat effective on his 39th birthday, a lucky ten, April 10, 1886.

"I will clean up your desk tomorrow," Crawford wrote him. "I am glad you have resigned . . . I am sure you have a much better position as editor of The World than any official in Washington." [16]

He received $1,762.83 for his Congressional salary, $96 for mileage and $118.79 for stationery. He donated the latter sum to a newsboys' industrial school and washed his hands of his last public post. Roscoe Conkling wrote him:

> But what an outcome of all the plans you and your confreres wrought out in the summer days and nights when sometimes you carried me into

the cool breathings of the Central Park! I sometimes wonder what our common friend W. C. W. [Whitney] thinks.[17]

III. BOODLING ALDERMEN

Pulitzer, whose seat later went to the ebullient S. S. "Sunset" Cox in a special election, looked to his own fiefdom. His World had gained 48,000 circulation over the previous year and was now averaging 170,000, while the Sunday World was booming at 230,000. He had paid off Gould. The Post-Dispatch held to its 30,000, and he was wounded to learn from Kappner that a young advertising clerk recently raised from eight to ten dollars a week "has defrauded the Post Dispatch of about 5 to 700 dollars. . . ." He let the young man go without prosecution and heightened the World's crusade against Jacob Sharp and the Boodle Aldermen in New York.

Sharp, a traction magnate, had followed customary city business procedure in offering a $20,000 cash bribe to each alderman who would support his bid for a 999-year transit franchise on Broadway. The board had met under the gavel of the immaculate Alderman Henry W. Jaehne, who represented himself as a real estate operator, and chose to accept Sharp's bribe over that of another traction combine, whose slightly higher offer had the disadvantage of being partly in stock. Two of the 22 aldermen who had no part in the bribe-taking found their honesty unavailing as the rest overrode them. The idea of streetcars on Broadway was bitterly opposed by merchants and civic groups, so that very night Sharp had his workmen tear up the street and start laying tracks.

The facts came to light when detectives discovered that Jaehne, far from being a real estate man, was one of the city's most prosperous fences, doing a thriving business in buying stolen goods at a discount from the underworld and selling them at profit. Caught with stolen gems and silverware in his home, Jaehne confessed not only his private but his aldermanic misdoings. The news sent another alderman, Charles Waite, hurrying to the district attorney's office to lighten his punishment by turning state's evidence. Two others who confessed were Aldermen Michael Duffy and L. A. Fullgraff, the latter a name in which the World took saturnine pleasure.

Six other aldermen hurried to Grand Central Station and left for Montreal, where they read of their indictment and that of Jacob Sharp. Their performance prompted an inspired passage in one of the low-life comedies of Harrigan and Hart—a scene in which a group of aldermen dozed off in the Mulligan living room after dining very well:

CORDELIA MULLIGAN: Whatever will I do? The aldermen are all sound asleep.

DAN MULLIGAN: Lave them be. While they sleep, the city's safe.[18]

Pulitzer, the nonpracticing lawyer, was delighted by the work of Assistant District Attorney De Lancey Nicoll, who had cheered him previously by his conviction of Grant's evil genius, Ferdinand Ward. The 32-year-old, Columbia-educated Nicoll sent Jaehne to Sing Sing for nine years and began the prosecution of the others with a vigor that marked him in Pulitzer's mind as a coming man. His knowledge that powerful efforts were being made to reach Nicoll and that the prosecutor was resisting financial and political pressure in his efforts to convict all the boodlers made him prize Nicoll as that most unusual of creatures, an incorruptible public servant. To Pulitzer, the professional burglar and the emotional killer could not approach the infamy of the dishonorable official, the worst criminal of all since his crimes involved calculated betrayal of the people, the looting of public property he was sworn to protect. The World was an avenging angel, cheering Nicoll's efforts to visit retribution on the remaining delinquent aldermen. It heaped expert sarcasm on the aldermen's attorneys. One of them, Ira Shafer, became so upset at being lampooned in McDougall cartoons and in deadly paragraphs that he unwisely uttered a public challenge to Pulitzer. Next day he wrote Pulitzer:

> Sir, I am just out of [court and] I received a note: . . .
> "I. M. Shafer Esq Sir You blathering Irish Catholic I will meet you at any designated place you like, the sooner the better. —Joseph Pulitzer"
> This brutal note I ought to treat with silent contempt. . . .[19]

He should have indeed, for the World, along with other New York papers, leaped on him with such fury that he collapsed and wrote the World piteously:

> I was and am now ill in bed . . . I felt justified in telegraphing you as I did but now deeply regret [.] The New York papers have injured me beyond measure . . . I will not sue them nor will I indict them and can only ask them to let me alone to pursue my profession is all I ask. . . . I have asked the Star to publish my regrets that I employed toward . . . Mr. Pulitzer the language I did [;] again I beg of you to let me alone.[20]

To Kate's occasional illnesses of pregnancy was added worry over the uncertain health of seven-year-old Ralph and the strange malady of six-year-old Lucille, who seemed to have the symptoms of typhoid. Pulitzer, believing that faulty plumbing was filling the house with noxious vapors, ordered heroic measures including the sealing off of some of the piping.

There was labor trouble at the World, George Murray of the Knights of Labor demanding that "the press room be made a Union office, none but Union men to be employed hereafter."

Escape was essential. To Governor Hill, Pulitzer wrote, "Can't go to Boston, as I am trying to take a trip abroad—a very short one though. I need rest and have not a moment to spare before I sail." [21] Since Kate could not go, he secured the bachelor Thomas Davidson as companion, doubtless paying his expenses, to sail June 20. On June 19 he became the father of Edith Pulitzer, a joyful event but not without its toll on the nerves. He sailed next day with Davidson nevertheless, calling Ballard Smith on shipboard for last-minute instructions to raise the pay of World correspondents throughout the country and to urge them to get news-beats. Kate must have been glad to see him go, for the master ran the household much as he did the World, like a hurricane.

Odder shipmates could hardly be found than Pulitzer and Davidson, each gripped by ambition to reform the world, one through politics, the other through God. Davidson's life had been one of such ardent pursuit of ennobling truth that he was seldom aware that poverty was pursuing *him.* From atheism he had moved successively to an embracing of Fichte, Comte, Boston transcendentalism, Schelling, and Aristotle, becoming disillusioned in turn with each. Feeling that the Greek church might satisfy him, he had spent a year in Greece with "monks and priests and archimandrites and bishops." The glory of the ruined Parthenon made him burst into tears, yet Greek theology left him cold. He had settled in Italy in 1881 to test Catholicism, gaining a private audience with the pope, mingling with cardinals and professors, telling a priest, "If you can prove to me that your church is the organ of the Divine, and the pope its mouthpiece, I will go tomorrow to the Vatican and kiss his slipper." Orthodox Catholic dogma proved a disappointment, but in the late Catholic theologian Antonio Rosmini (who had been assailed by the Jesuits and his works placed on the Index) he found "the greatest thinker of modern times." He spent two years in Italy, living as a hermit as he translated some of Rosmini's works. Then he went to England to hold meetings that inspired the founding of the Fellowship of the New Life, a group that had a less spiritual offshoot, the Fabian Society, which would become much more famous.[22] Now he was preaching the New Life in New York to working-class audiences. That Pulitzer chose him as companion showed a breadth of interest and a liking for spirited mental inquiry found in few practical politicians.

Though he was gone only a month, he sent anxious cables to the World and Post-Dispatch. A year earlier the World had laughed at the rumor that Cleveland was contemplating marriage: ". . . The World correspondent is permitted to state, upon the best authority, that matrimony is not included among the President's intentions." Now the correspondent had to eat his words when Cleveland's engagement to the lovely young Frances Folsom became known. The World covered the wedding on June 2 with praise for both bride and groom but made a lamentable typographical error in an editorial hailing the event: "President Cleveland marries under suspicious [*sic*] circumstances."[23]

Soon afterward, Pulitzer hired William H. Merrill away from the Boston Herald, Merrill writing, "I will come to you on the 1st of September for $7,500 for one year's service as editorial writer on the World

. . ." [24] The salary was enormous for the time, but Merrill had one year to prove himself.

IV. ELECTING A MAYOR

Pulitzer, terribly sensitive to heat, fled with his family to Lenox, came down August 7 for the funeral at Yonkers of Samuel Tilden, returned briefly to Lenox, then dashed off to St. Louis late in August to look to his Post-Dispatch. The heat there was worse. He stayed in the rebuilt Southern Hotel, and although this was his first visit to the city of his youth in three years, he finished off his business with Dillon and the others swiftly and left town without seeing Gibson, ex-Senator J. B. Henderson and other friends who later wrote him reproachfully.

He received complaints from Professor Davidson, who was giving the World two columns of copy a week and finding that the editors threw most of it away: ". . . I have no relations with your editors, to enable me to see or discover the cause of this." A word from Pulitzer and Davidson received a $100 check from the World—too much, he protested. "My good friend Henry George is likely to be nominated for Mayor of New York," he went on, "and I want you, *if you conscientiously can,* to give him your (the *World's*) support. He is one of the best & most honest men I have ever known." [25] Pulitzer replied:

> I will be glad to see Mr. George whenever you can bring him round. I had made up my mind weeks ago . . . that he should be treated fairly, but what I shall do in the way of *support,* I cannot, and should not, know myself until all the entries are made, and all the candidates are in the field—Then I shall do whatever I think is best for the City.[26]

Another complaint came from Dr. Pallen, the eccentric would-be consul, who evidently was playing the stock market and had received a $250 Pulitzer loan intended to keep him afloat. Pallen tartly returned the money:

> Very many thanks for the enclosed, but it came too late. Had you accommodated me when I first asked you, I would have been a rich man today—as it was I lost *two hundred and thirty seven thousand* ($237,000) dollars because I couldn't raise enough to pay my assessment.[27]

Pulitzer was asked to sit for a portrait for *Judge,* invited to dinners at the Manhattan Club, Philadelphia's Clover Club and many others. He and Kate were disgusted with the Hoey house and looked madly for another, while Hoey himself was angry at the violence done the plumbing and asked compensation. The World had passed the long-leading Herald in advertising as well as circulation and was coining money, but was so overcrowded that reporters fell over each other. Pulitzer was examining

Park Row property valued at $500,000 on which to erect a new building. On top of all this loomed the 1886 mayoral election, a matter of desperate importance.

What with the peculations of the aldermen, many of them still to be tried, the World had public opinion behind it in its demands for reform. It seemed inspired on October 10 when it suggested Congressman Abram S. Hewitt as the best candidate. Although Tammany Boss Richard Croker could scarcely be called a reformer, the powerful support of Henry George by united labor groups frightened him by its clear warning that the Wigwam must put forward an honest man or lose all. The thought of losing was so loathsome that Croker, on the day after the World's suggestion, achieved a miracle of self-renunciation and swung Tammany for Hewitt. Hewitt, although he had once kindly supplied funds to defend Croker in a murder charge arising out of a partisan quarrel, did not live in the same political realm as the boss. Stunned by the nomination, he would not accept until Croker promised a hands-off policy in city affairs.

During the campaign there were three days of receptions and banquets preceding the dedication of the Statue of Liberty, completed at long last. The World's great services were not forgotten—indeed the paper had not allowed them to be forgotten—and Pulitzer dined at Delmonico's, the Hoffman House, even at the Union League Club with Bartholdi himself and such committee members as William Waldorf Astor, Levi Morton, Theodore Roosevelt, J. Pierpont Morgan, Navy Secretary Whitney and Joseph W. Drexel. Although Whitney, like Pulitzer, had contributed $250 to the pedestal fund, many of the other nabobs now so prominent in the celebration had been indifferent when money was badly needed. The World had commented on the close-grained granite cornerstone of the pedestal: "If it is half as 'close-grained' as the churlish millionaires of New York who manifested their contempt for Liberty and buttoned up their pockets when solicited for a subscription . . . it must be a wonderful specimen." [28]

Rancor was forgotten now. On the third and culminating day, October 28, a great military parade marched downtown and passed under the World's triumphal arch spanning the street in front of its Park Row building and bearing the motto *Vive L'Entente Fraternelle des Deux Republiques.* Pulitzer had hired two steamers to take hundreds of World employees and their families to Liberty Island, while the Pulitzer family itself rode out in the steam yacht *Hinda.* No civic affair was complete without Chauncey Depew, who gave one of his facile speeches on the island. The oration of the day, however, was made by Senator William Maxwell Evarts, famous for rhetorical stamina. When Evarts had only well begun, he paused for breath after an impressive period. The functionary at the lanyard, thinking him finished, pulled hard. The huge tricolor that covered the Goddess' face was swept away, Bartholdi's great work was revealed, bedlam convulsed the throng below, and Evarts' speech went forever unfinished. The ceremony closed with a brief address by President Cleveland, who said, "We shall not forget that Liberty has here made her home . . ."

Pulitzer, who could be quite sentimental about liberty, took justifiable pride in his paper's role in the event, and the World would remind readers about it for years in anniversary issues. He had already put a likeness of the Goddess on the World's nameplate—a proprietary gesture annoying to other editors. Now he used the $1,000 surplus in the subscription fund for a Tiffany-executed silver-and-gold globe with Bartholdi's head in *repoussé* and an inscription acclaiming his work, which he presented to the sculptor. M. Bartholdi dined with the Pulitzers, who had just moved to a brownstone mansion at 9 East 36th Street, a block from J. P. Morgan. When Bartholdi inquired about the famous Falls of Niagara, the host did not merely describe them but applied to Depew (whom the World often attacked) for a private car on the New York Central (which the World constantly excoriated) that would take Bartholdi and the whole Pulitzer family to the falls. The Republican Depew—one captain of industry who had decided that Pulitzer had come to stay and that good humor might be the best strategy—replied:

> The car will be attached to the "Limited Express" leaving the Grand Central at 9:50 . . . I have uniformly refused to attach the cars of any of the allied sovereigns to it on account of the additional weight . . . This statement is only to show, that in this free and glorious country a Democrat who is earnest and consistent attains results denied to Sovereigns.

Bartholdi would never forget the Falls, nor would he forget Pulitzer, who seemed a natural phenomenon of equal force, although Depew on the party's return took a different view:

> I am more than delighted that you had a happy trip and a safe return. It reinforces my opinion that the two most remarkable things in this Country, in nature and art, are Niagara Falls and the New York Central Railroad. [Your bill will be] in figures strong enough to pulverize the most enlightened anti monopolist.[29]

Astonishingly, the 1886 city election offered the voters not a choice between party hacks but three men of ability and integrity—Hewitt for the Democrats, Theodore Roosevelt for the Republicans and Henry George for the workers' "Anti-Poverty" party. The nomination of Roosevelt, not yet 28, was a blow to Hewitt, for whose election Roosevelt had earlier promised to work, since he would make inroads on Hewitt's vote and none at all on George's. "It is too good a chance for a young man to advertise himself!" he explained to Hewitt. The World disposed of Roosevelt as "a young man of wealth . . . who is something of a reformer, a very good lecturer and a first-class bear hunter," suggesting that the city needed something more than a bear hunter.

Although the World aimed at the working classes, which supported George almost to a man, Pulitzer's journalistic courage as well as his essentially conservative political thinking was shown by his powerful advocacy of Hewitt. Yet he did not join the city's respectables in regarding the small, red-headed George as an incendiary agitator fomenting class warfare. The efforts of labor for decent wages and working conditions had been swelling, the Knights of Labor were attaining some power, there had been strikes in New York and all over the nation, and the recent Haymarket Riot in Chicago had raised among the sedate the specter of proletarian revolt and bomb-throwing. Pulitzer himself, as a capitalist, had had difficulties with the Knights both in St. Louis and New York. Yet he merely felt that George's theories were fallacious. In Hewitt he had an outstanding candidate, able, honest and liberal, whose administrative experience George could not match. The World did not pummel the single-taxer with fearful charges of anarchy as did the Tribune, and indeed it was fair enough so that Davidson wrote Pulitzer, "You are doing excellently well by George, better than if you openly supported him." [30]

As the race neared its end amid torchlit oratory, the realization that George might win although he had not a single newspaper on his side aroused something like terror among the timid. The praise heaped on him by revolutionaries such as Johann Most, serving a jail term at Blackwell's Island, was frightening, and there were pleas that Roosevelt withdraw so that his following would swing to Hewitt and rescue the city from "anarchist" rule. The bear hunter refused to quit, but in the end many Republican leaders and voters abandoned him for Hewitt and saved the day for the ironmaster. The vote was Hewitt, 90,552; George, 68,110; Roosevelt, 60,435.

In the space of two years the World had helped elect the President, the governor of New York and the mayor of New York City. Dr. Pallen, regretting his acerbity about the $250, immediately wrote Mrs. Pulitzer asking that she request her husband to intercede with Hewitt for a post for Pallen on the Board of Health: ". . . It would not only be *bread and butter for me*, but it would be something that would make me famous . . ." [31]

Chapter 5

Spinning Like a Top

1. A DEMOCRAT IN BABYLON

Pulitzer, as he approached the great crisis and tragedy of his life, was driven by inner and outer forces too strong for his emotional and physical structure to contain. The very qualities which contributed to his brilliance—his nerves and overpowering drive—were wearing him down. He had attained quick wealth, which alone has demoralized many a man, and at the same time had achieved great power, which never comes unaccompanied by the sly voices of corruption. To adjust himself to simultaneous power and wealth which revolutionized every aspect of his life, to maintain balance and poise when his whole existence was on a new plane of grandeur, would take more than ordinary character. He was as aware of the temptations as he was confident of his ability to resist them. The World had spoken of the capitalistic prejudices of New York's rich newspaper owners, meaning chiefly Bennett, Dana, Reid and Jones:

> They cannot help it. It is only human nature. Man is greatly controlled by his environment. . . . There is one [newspaper] not controlled nor in any way swayed or influenced by the side of capital. . . . That is the World.[1]

Thus Pulitzer, with some truth, declared that the "human nature" and "environment" that influenced other men were inoperative on him. The rich World held to precisely the same principles proclaimed by the struggling World of 1883, smiting the corruptionists and monopolists hip and thigh. This was true although Pulitzer, who seldom saw a miracle he felt incapable of performing, sought now to do the impossible, to become friendly with the very "purse-potentates" he belabored. The social aspirations of this tribune of the lowly are paradoxical enough to merit some examination.

They must be weighed against the background of the painful hostility that had darkened his family's last year in St. Louis. He wanted no more of that. Now the newspapers of the respectables, the Sun, Tribune, Herald and Times, made frequent attacks on him which in their combined vindictiveness could make life as difficult as the Missouri Republican had done. It was natural that Pulitzer and Kate sought to forestall such unpleasantness, that they made every effort to prevent their exclusion from the fashionable society which had eyed them askance because the World had treated that society so roughly.

Both were innately sociable in any case. Pulitzer's nature contained a strong streak of the patrician, a love of luxury and fine living which he regarded as the realization of the American dream to which everyone aspired. The man who so perfectly identified himself with the city's Sweenys frankly loved diamonds and old masters. It was disagreeable to take Kate to the opera and to be snubbed by neighboring box-holders—depressing to summer at fashionable Lenox and to find no friends there. Kate wished to continue the sociability in which she was reared, refused to be blacklisted because of her husband's politics and refused also to let her children grow up under such a cloud. Pulitzer liked good company, enjoyed making speeches and saw no reason why he should not meet in drawing-room cordiality with monopolists whom he flayed in his newspapers, nor did he see any conflict in this so long as it did not affect his principles. Always aware of power, he knew that his own and the World's influence would be impaired if he were a pariah, and that conversely they would be strengthened if he were accepted socially by leaders of the political and worldly opposition. He could have smoothed the way, now that the World was an assured success, by moderating its criticism of the wealthy. He did not do so, and one of his bitterest reflections over the years was that his duty to criticize destroyed friendships that he valued. He would have been a happier man had he been a thoroughgoing unwashed proletarian. The discord between his social and political life must have added to the factors that ultimately struck him down.

Thus the Pulitzers essayed a maneuver hardly less improbable than the camel passing through the needle's eye. They would never have succeeded had they not offered between them a combination of brilliance, beauty and warmth rarely found in any married couple. The many fashionable events surrounding the Statue of Liberty triumph had somewhat broken ice long intact, and thereafter the Pulitzers entered into a social life not restricted to Democrats but including Republicans who made and spent their millions in ways unapproved by the World.

Fiscally Pulitzer was ambivalent, at once a spendthrift and a scrimper. Though his profits were huge, he was contemplating heavy expenditures for land and buildings that worried him enough to make him haggle over a five-dollar engraver's bill; yet he was unable to curb his taste for luxury.

His family was no sooner in the 36th Street house than he was looking for something better. He considered buying the 125-foot yacht *Orienta* belonging to the millionaire J. A. Bostwick of Standard Oil (a frequent World target), and took Conkling, the Childses and other friends on a tryout cruise on the Hudson. He made inquiries about buying the late Samuel Tilden's wonderful wines. He spent $538 for art objects at the William Schaus gallery, $1,000 for etchings and engravings at Knoedler's, and at Blakeslee's offered $4,000 for one Stevens, one Homer and one Millet for which they asked $4,800 but finally gave him for $4,500 if he would keep it quiet. Having an enormous admiration for Napoleon—indeed, Childs had called him "the Napoleon of journalists"—he spent $150 for a bronze bust of Bonaparte. He had agents looking for a summer place for his family, listing for him a dozen including the 21-acre De Lancy estate in Westchester at $110,000 and the 168-acre Henry Havemeyer property on Great South Bay that would run around $250,000. He bought two shares in the projected private club at Jekyll Island, Georgia, planned as a place where men of wealth could meet on a democratic basis.

In the fall he presided at a Delmonico dinner sponsored by New York Hungarians and honoring Mihály Munkácsy (born Michael Lieb), the Hungarian painter of storytelling canvases such as *Milton Dictating to his Daughters* and *Christ Before Pilate*. Pulitzer was flanked by Mayor-elect Hewitt and Munkácsy, and the many non-Hungarian guests included Cyrus Field, Henry Ward Beecher, Whitelaw Reid, Carl Schurz, Leonard Jerome, George Jones, Levi P. Morton, John Bigelow, Chauncey Depew, and Ballard Smith of the World. It is likely that Pulitzer, less seasoned at the dinner table than on the stump and believing firmly in learning from experts in all fields, had studied the postprandial speeches of Depew. He began with the light touch: "Gentlemen, we have met tonight to honor M. Mihály Munkácsy because he is a great artist and also because he is a stranger in this great Republic and needs a hospitable welcome." But he worked in the democratic line so prominent in the World: "We welcome you, sir, because true Americans, having no aristocracy, are ready to worship the aristocracy of virtue and the royalty of genius." He finished gracefully by linking Munkácsy with Kossuth and Liszt, saying, "Tonight we are all Hungarians—we are all Americans." Depew, who liked Pulitzer and perhaps also hoped to get the World off his back, was seldom known to attend a gathering without making a speech. He paid tribute not only to the painter but to the editor, saying, "Without the contribution which Hungary gave in Mr. Joseph Pulitzer and the aid of the columns of the World the pedestal for the Statue of Liberty would never have been completed." [2]

Pulitzer commissioned Munkácsy to paint Kate's portrait. He was taken ill soon after the dinner, but recovered quickly enough so that a month later he and Kate inaugurated a series of entertainments at their home by giving a pre-Christmas dinner in honor of Munkácsy. It was their most ambitious social effort thus far, engraved invitations going out to dozens including Hewitt, Edward Cooper, August Belmont, Carl Schurz, Leonard Jerome, S. S. Cox, Levi P. Morton, Governor Hill, Depew, William Maxwell Evarts, St. Clair McKelway and Ward McAllister. There was no Bowery flavor here. Indeed the affair was more reminiscent of the unforgettable Belshazzar's Feast, for gems were in evidence, the menu and wines were choice and at least three of the guests—Depew, Evarts and Morton—had also sat at Delmonico's and applauded Blaine.

Perhaps Leonard Jerome, whose three daughters had married into the British peerage or gentry, was not aware that the World frequently assailed "the sordid aristocracy of the ambitious matchmakers, who are ready to sell their daughters for barren titles to worthless foreign paupers." But a few months later, when the World announced domestic disagreements between Lord and Lady Randolph Churchill (the latter the former Jennie Jerome), Jerome wrote very plainly to Pulitzer:

> It is not the first time the World has published similar dispatches & not the first time you have sent me your regrets.
>
> Of course I know you would not willingly publish scandalous articles about me & my children even if true, but when it turns out that they are manufactured . . . I think you will agree with me that something more than "regrets" is in order. . . . Imagine a perfect stranger calling on you a half a dozen times & finally getting in states his business to be to ascertain *how you were getting on with Mrs. Pulitzer!* That's your London correspondent. I should like you to ask Mrs. Pulitzer what she thinks of him.[3]

A cable went from Pulitzer to Theron Crawford, now his London correspondent: "Jerome-Churchill story very wrong. Let them alone. Be careful avoid scandal gossip."[4] He not only wrote Jerome in apology but had Ballard Smith do the same. A retraction was published in the World. Truly, there were difficulties in publishing a newspaper for the masses. But another letter, from one F. B. Conner, was an unmitigated pleasure. Conner, a Newark compositor, declared that "*The World* is beyond comparison with any," noted that his wife had recently presented him with a baby boy, and went on:

> I proposed the child bear the name of one whose opinions are welcomed by millions each week; the successful, enterprising man who wields with his pen an influence never before exercised by any man on earth. My wife "unanimously" coincided, and our best hope is that
>
> *Joseph Pulitzer Conner*
>
> may grapple the rungs of fame's ladder with a fraction of the success of his illustrious namesake, the Saviour and Redeemer of *The World*.[5]

Pulitzer had his Jersey representative, George Harvey, make inquiries about Conner. Harvey found him a substantial citizen, and Joseph Pulitzer Conner received a sizable check along with a kindly letter from his namesake.

But it was Pulitzer's mingling with the upper crust that annoyed Dana of the Sun. The Sun frequently tossed nosegays at its rival, once reprinting a "social note" from Town Topics, published by the notorious blackmailer Colonel William D'Alton Mann, which was headed "JUDAS IN SOCIETY" and suggested that Pulitzer had hired the socially eminent Ballard Smith in order to gain entry into society:

> Mr. Smith's career in this city has been an extraordinary success. Coming from one of the most aristocratic families of Kentucky—the same which produced the handsome Nicholas Smith who married Horace Greeley's daughter—his entrée into the highest social circles here was assured from the moment he first appeared. . . . With Mr. and Mrs. Pulitzer, Mr. Smith's success has been . . . great . . . and under his wing Mr. and Mrs. Pulitzer are now welcomed anywhere that Mr. Smith introduces them as "my friends." . . . [He] has, I hear, opened the way for Mrs. Pulitzer to be some time during the coming winter both the guest and the hostess of the President's wife.[6]

11. WHAT IS FORTUNE WITHOUT HEALTH?

The World, constantly accused by its rivals of lying as a matter of policy, was indeed guilty of occasional error or exaggeration. The general level of press accuracy was low at this time when objectivity was virtually unknown and political bias appeared on the front pages as well as in the editorials. The other New York papers, having their own quota of moonshine, were motivated by jealousy rather than purity in their charges and the likelihood is that the World was as reliable in its news as any of them. In point of editorial conscience it was unmatched. The Democrat Pulitzer could assail Tammany corruption and even support an honest Republican if need be, whereas to Reid's thick-and-thin Tribune all Republicans were paragons and if the Tribune ever backed a Democrat the heavens would fall.

Pulitzer, aware of his own love for a slam-bang story and the weakness of the press for exaggeration, worked conscientiously to drill his staff in reverence for fact. On his order the city-room walls were plastered with big placards reading, "ACCURACY! TERSENESS! ACCURACY!" and he was fond of repeating, "Accuracy is to a newspaper what virtue is to a woman." The reporter who said 10,000 appeared at a rally only attended by 5,000, or gave a $200,000 loss to a $75,000 fire, received a rebuke and sometimes a fine. It must be admitted that this placed a heavy burden on his editors, who knew that the boss detested a dry factual account, delighted in a scoop or thriller, and would explode in anguish at any slump in the World's gains in circulation and profits. The editors could always feel him looking over their shoulders in their effort to walk that careful line and yet to make the cold news appear a trifle hotter than it really was.

He let light into that darkest and most guarded closet of journalism, the matter of circulation—a joyful exercise since he was first. Until he arrived, only the Sun among morning papers (then being first) published its circulation figures. The Herald followed a disingenuous practice of publishing its "high water mark" figure, which remained the same for months and was totally misleading since it referred to some murder or election issue that might have sold double the average. The Tribune and Times, far behind, breathed no word about their circulation, and on June 7, 1886, the Sun lagged badly enough so that it joined them in secrecy, claiming a weekday average of 84,000 before the curtain dropped. If there is anything as inflammatory as to call public attention to the crow's-feet of a once reigning belle, it is to publicize the decline of a leading newspaper—an offense Pulitzer committed four times over. The World made fun of them all for their reticence, ridiculed the Herald's "High Water Mark Nonsense" and won their general detestation by publishing almost daily sworn statements of its own growing circulation. In reply to his rivals' frequent assertions that his figures were falsehoods, Pulitzer invited them to see for themselves: "The Editors, Proprietors and Publishers of all New York Newspapers can visit The World's Press-Room and verify The World's circulation . . ."[7]

His figures were accurate, as shown by later detailed office charts covering the sale for many years and disclosing losses as well as gains. A firm believer in ballyhoo backed by fact, he gave close attention to the wording of World self-puffery. The World got its Sunday edition to eight states before breakfast by fast train. Every new circulation milestone—100,000, 150,000, 200,000—was marked by a World celebration in which Pulitzer gave silk hats (a favorite gift) to the staff and bonuses to the deserving. When the World hit 250,000 early in 1887 (the Sunday World, that is, which was some 60,000 ahead of the daily), he had a handsome silver medal struck, precisely the size of a silver dollar. On one side it bore a relief of the Statue of Liberty, on the other the quarter-million circulation mark, the nation's largest. The medal was broadcast to advertisers and to newspapers all over the country, causing considerable awe and further annoying his New York contemporaries.

Politically the World mirrored its chief in what he liked to call his independence but which was also an aspect of his emotional instability, his swings from enthusiasm to disillusionment. To him, every reporter was a shining hope as a future editor, but every editor was a frustration; each honest candidate was a promise of enlightened public service, every elected official a disenchantment. He fidgeted endlessly. No one could fulfill his ideal of perfection since this consisted of making every move exactly as Pulitzer would have made it. Cleveland, the inspiring victor over Republican roguery, had become Cleveland the disappointment in the White House, and even sturdy Mayor Hewitt would occasionally feel the Pulitzer censure. After Cleveland's first year in office the World had given him somewhat impersonal praise:

> Has not the Government grown stronger in the proof that the people can elect and inaugurate a President of their own choice? Has not the declining bitterness of sectionalism . . . [made] the Union more perfect than ever? Do not the people feel safer now against the encroachments of monopolies than they did a year ago? [8]

But Cleveland's shortcomings—and possibly his seeming lack of appreciation for the World's support—had so disillusioned Pulitzer that by 1886 the World was reading him frequent lessons. He had conducted his administration "more with the idea of mollifying Republicans than of satisfying Democrats. His financial policy has been a continuation of that of the Republicans and adapted to please the 'business men' of Wall Street." What was the result? In the vital New York City election, the thankless Republicans refused to back Hewitt, an ideal candidate regardless of party lines, but did their best to beat him with the inexperienced Roosevelt. Cleveland had so antagonized New York Democrats that in his own district "no Democrat would stand, except one who proclaimed his hostility to the Administration." He had given an appointment to Gideon Tucker of New York immediately after Tucker had supported Henry George against Hewitt and had done his best to "overthrow the Democracy in New York City." But Democratic disappointment, said the World, was founded on things deeper than mere patronage. The administration had failed to reform the tariff or to take aggressive action against the trusts. "The taxes have not been reduced. Needed reforms have not been advanced. . . . The people hoped for better things when a Democratic Administration reinforced a Democratic House." [9]

These criticisms were measured and usually justified in view of the dissatisfaction in the New York Democracy, and were balanced by occasional praise for Cleveland's "plain, common sense." On one occasion the World seemed spiteful, when Cleveland's uncle, Joseph Neal, died in Baltimore and he failed to attend the funeral: "When it became positively known that the President would not attend the funeral, some of the friends were indignant that he should ignore such a worthy relative as Mr. Neal." [10] Actually, it was said, the Neals had asked the President not to come as he would have attracted a curious crowd.

In Pulitzer's view, Cleveland's ineptitude had divided the party, cooled the voters and endangered the bright Democratic hope for continued power and reform. He had virtually given up on the President as a candidate in 1888. While the World praised his speech at the unveiling of the Statue of Liberty, it added significantly, "At the same time we feel constrained to remark that, in our opinion, all bets that Mr. Cleveland will be nominated for a second term will be lost." [11]

The Tribune, delighted that the nation's most powerful Democratic editor was "not on speaking terms" with the Democratic President, waggishly predicted warfare when it was rumored that both Pulitzer and Cleveland thought of spending the summer of 1886 at the onion-growing resort town of Litchfield, Connecticut: "There will be mutual recriminations. . . . Pulitzer will reply by shying a casual onion contemptuously in the direction of Cleveland's hotel. The next day the women and children will be removed for safety outside the Litchfield walls . . ." [12]

The public was still accustomed to the slavish party loyalty that newspapers usually observed. Some Democratic readers of the World misunderstood its comparative political independence and felt it a betrayal. Not a few canceled their subscriptions, one of them, E. A. Richards, declaring that the paper was no longer Democratic. The Whitehall, New York, Times said the World had ceased to be "the national organ of the great Democratic party" since it had abandoned the party's "men and principles." It believed Pulitzer to be envenomed by his failure to get the legation for Charles Gibson:

> President Cleveland thought that this country should be represented at Prussia by Hon. George H. Pendleton and thus Mr. Pulitzer was ignored, and thereby opened the vials of his wrath upon the President. . . . The World's success has evidently turned the head of its proprietor, but the proprietor will find that the Democrats will not be his patrons if he persists in his crusade against the President whom they elected.[13]

Pulitzer's motivation was hardly that simple. He had supported the President warmly for a time after the Gibson-Pallen disaster. Like Hewitt, Belmont and other Democrats, he was sincerely disappointed in Cleveland—so much so that it probably was a factor in the illness and exhaustion that beset him after the fall elections. Though one may doubt romantic tales of disappointment in love proving fatal, one should never doubt that Pulitzer's health could be shattered by the failure of his political plans. But he was unable to slow down unless flat on his back. No sooner was he on his feet after a collapse than he spun like a top again. George Childs, to whom he sent a morocco-bound book (and an armload of orchids to Mrs. Childs), wrote Mrs. Pulitzer in concern about his recurrent illnesses. He was too valuable a man, Childs warned, to drain his energies as he had been doing, and repeated the familiar advice: "Throw more of the responsibility on others, keep the reins in his own hands, but let others do the work and details, do nothing himself that he can employ others to do, even if it is not so well done. What is fame, fortune &c without health [?] You must back me up in all I write and then we can see him enjoy the results of his wonderful brain and energy." [14]

III. STAR-SPANGLED TIGHTS

The feud between John Cockerill and Ballard Smith was bitter, and Business Manager Turner did not get on with either of them. A $60-a-week sub-editor, John Greene, was so offended by Smith's imperiousness that he resigned, writing Pulitzer, "I decline to permit myself to be governed by such a man." Perhaps Pulitzer did not know that one of his youngest reporters for a brief period was William Randolph Hearst, recently expelled from Harvard, who so admired Smith's abilities that he tried vainly to lure him away to his father's newspaper, the San Francisco Examiner, before Hearst left to run the Examiner himself. Pulitzer found a new worry in the 42-year-old Cockerill's infatuation with Leonora Barner, an actress who had minor roles in such melodramas as *The White Slave,* in which the heroine made the show-stopping speech, "Rags are royal raiment when worn for virtue's sake." A World man should really have no love other than the paper. Could Cockerill be trusted when his thoughts were centered on a lovely young creature half his age?

From Fred May, who had fought the bloodless duel with Bennett after the celebrated incident, came an interesting note. The Herald's best newsman was one Sadley, he wrote. If Pulitzer would hire Sadley away, he would at once bolster the World and hurt the Herald, especially since Bennett was in Burma and could not repair the damage.[15]

From that seasoned political warhorse Manton Marble, friend of President Cleveland and of Treasury Secretary Daniel Manning, came another. There were rumors that Manning, a banker and owner of the Albany Argus, would resign because of ill health. The World had declared that Manning was leaving not on the score of health but to "[ally] himself in business with what is regarded as the Wall Street class of this city." Marble scored a palpable hit:

> Is it fair to reproach a friend for not sacrificing the hope of restored good health and repaired fortune when you yourself, most wisely as I think, would not sacrifice your newspaper business to the public place which you had accepted [?] . . . Really now is that a wise use of your enormous power . . . [?] [16]

From Dr. Pallen, that inveterate office-seeker:

> Many thanks for your visit to [Mayor] Hewitt, but, alas! it leaves me *now,* without even a hope, unless you are willing to try me as a writer on the "World?" [17]

And from Professor Davidson, after a visit with the Pulitzers:

I fear you were trying to think up some scheme that would allow you to pay me a salary without hurting my self-respect. . . . Now, you must not think of doing anything of the kind. . . . Though I am, & always shall be, a poor man, I am in no trouble of any sort . . .[18]

From J. P. Morgan, just coming into prominence as one of the nation's leading financiers, came a different sort of request. He had met Pulitzer but was scarcely a friend. He was accustomed to the World's assaults on Wall Street, but he was sensitive about the *acne rosacea* that made his nose resemble a gigantic ripe strawberry and he inquired if Walt McDougall could not put less stress on the nose in his frequent cartoons. Pulitzer could sympathize, since his own nose was a frequent object of caricature. ". . . To my surprise," McDougall recalled, ". . . [he] advised me to moderate my zeal." [19]

That was also the winter of Pulitzer's last fistic encounter. It came about when Joseph Howard, a World writer of impressive bulk and arrogance, was scheduled to cover the Montreal winter carnival and the chief decided to send him on another assignment. Howard insisted on going to Montreal. When Pulitzer pointed his finger at him, his reply was so hot that the Herald recorded it, probably with exaggeration, as, "You ____ ____ ____ ____, don't you point that at me." By the time a few blows were struck, each man lost his glasses. Since Howard was as helpless without them as Pulitzer, the two men were groping blindly on the floor for their spectacles when newsmen came between them.

The Herald made a rousing two-column lampoon of it, treating it round by round as a prizefight would be handled on the sporting page. It supplied a "Sketch of the Field of Gore," a diagram of the World office showing (A) where the quarrel began, (B) where words changed to blows, and going on to G. "Mr. Howard wore a Prince Albert coat, dark trousers and rubber shoes," the Herald said. "His colors, red and black, were shown in the scarf around his neck. . . . Mr. Joseph Pulitzer . . . seemed too finely drawn. The overexertion of swearing to the circulation of the gift enterprise sheet, which is his pride, had evidently worn on him. Mr. Pulitzer had on the star-spangled tights now so familiar through exhibitions in his great feat of jumping from one side of the fence to the other." In a deft allusion to the famous nose, it declared that when Howard swung, "as the room is small, [the blow] necessarily landed on Mr. Pulitzer's smeller." In the second round, "Howard led out and Mr. Pulitzer dodged—he learned the trick during the few weeks he served in the war in the rear ranks of the Lincoln cavalry." The real reason for the encounter, it hinted, was that Pulitzer had reduced Howard's salary "because he had refused to fill a vast area of vacant space in the journal of 'brag, swagger, inflation and mendacity.'" The Herald even parodied Byron:

The editor came down like a wolf on the scribe,
And his language was seething with sneer and with jibe;
And the snap of his eyes was quite lovely to view,
Till a well-planted blow turned them black and then blue.[20]

Howard left to make a good living thereafter as a syndicated writer. This was one of the ripples in a season that saw the World mount an admirably sustained and effective exposure of Collis P. Huntington, who swore that the $6,000,000 he spent in Washington for the Union Pacific had never been intended for use in bribing Congressmen. The World was unmatched in a crusade of this kind, with the boss demanding an array of hard facts from Washington representatives who became detectives as well as correspondents, pounding away day after day until the public understood the issues. This crusade resulted in solid achievement, for it was instrumental in forcing an investigation of government relations with the railroads and the passing of the first regulatory interstate commerce law. In another crusade to raise a fund to honor Gladstone, the British premier whose efforts for Irish Home Rule had overthrown him, Pulitzer had that most satisfying of causes, one that stirred his passion for self-government and also appealed to Irish-American readers of the World.

He seemed as intent on appropriating Gladstone as he had the Statue of Liberty. In April, soon after his 40th birthday, he sailed with Kate for England, where he ordered a bronze bust, ornamented by an Irish harp, executed by Tiffany and was careful that the efforts of the World were mentioned on the inscription. Enthusiastic Irish sympathizers elected him an honorary member of the National Liberal Club in Whitehall Place. He and Kate crossed to Paris to buy paintings from S. P. Daniell, wines from C. Vasseur, and to enter a social whirl that included a charity ball given by the Society Ladies of Paris and a "grand fête" for the benefit of the *Ambulances Urbaines.* Pulitzer, a compulsive buyer of bijoux, found at Tiffany's establishment on the Avenue de l'Opera a diamond necklace for Kate and gems for Lucille Pulitzer and Mrs. Childs. Later he had another jewelry inspiration, Tiffany writing him, ". . . We have not any small piece having belonged to the crown jewels left on hand," but assuring him that they had fine pieces of their own design priced up to £5,000.[21] In Paris the Pulitzers enjoyed the companionship of the Joseph W. Drexels (Drexel had been on a Statue of Liberty committee and was a friend of Childs), unprejudiced by Drexel's position as the partner of J. P. Morgan. After going on to Aix for a fortnight's cure, they returned to London in June. Here they made a tour of England with Dr. and Mrs. James W. McLane of New York, the doctor (Yale '61) having become a family friend after ministering to the frequent illnesses of Pulitzer and his family.

"I am so anxious for you to retain your health and vigor. . . ." Childs wrote Pulitzer. "You must hold your ground," adding later, "I want to see your income from the 'World' a round million a year . . ." [22]

But Pulitzer in euphoria was no more able to limit his energies than an overbred terrier. One of his missions must have distressed Kate, as it would have shocked his physicians and his friend Childs. He was contemplating a transatlantic journalistic combine, seeking to purchase a London newspaper, considering the Recorder, Daily News and Morning Post. There was perhaps significance in the fact that Bennett's Herald had a Paris edition, and Bennett was a man Pulitzer conscientiously sought to outdo. His London correspondent Crawford wrote him, "I am told *The Morning Post* can be bought for £40,000. . . . It has a good office and respectable plant." [23]

Doubtless the negotiations would have continued had not fate intervened a few months later. In London the Pulitzers attended art sales, saw the young American actress Cora Potter at the Haymarket in *Man and Wife*, and attended a succession of dinners, one of them at the home of the brilliant Liberal J. P. Morley, late editor of that superior journalistic voice, the Pall Mall Gazette. With Morley, Pulitzer could discuss not only London journalism, with which he had become almost as familiar as with its New York counterpart, but English politics, for Morley had been a powerful Home Rule ally of Gladstone in his toppled cabinet.

On July 9, Kate and Crawford were among the guests as Pulitzer was the testimonial speaker at the presentation of the bust in the formal gardens at the 78-year-old statesman's borrowed suburban home, Dollis Hill. The voice that had spoken for Greeley, Hancock and Tilden came through clearly with its noticeable guttural accent, speaking words that outraged every Tory:

> Mr. Gladstone, 10,689 people of the first city of America ask the first citizen of England to accept this gift. They ask you to accept it as an offering of their sincerest sympathy . . . as a tribute to your great public service in the cause of civil and religious freedom. . . . It will never be possible to convince true Americans that your demand for an Irish Parliament for Irish affairs is not right and just. . . .[24]

Gladstone replied with a twinkle that while some Englishmen resented such American interference, they really should not since England had long interfered in affairs throughout the world. Pulitzer, anxious for a good press, cabled Ballard Smith: "Were Gladstone's speeches and mine sent verbatim did you have a good report and how much [?]" The World gave it two solid columns on the front page.

Early in August the Pulitzers were back at 36th Street, where they soon had as their guest 22-year-old Varina Anne Davis, known as Winnie, youngest child of the ex-president of the Confederacy. Although the kinship between Kate Davis Pulitzer and Jefferson Davis was remote, a correspondence had grown between the two families and the Pulitzers were sympathetic with the impoverished leader of the lost cause. On a previous visit with friends in Syracuse (where the Pulitzers sent her orchids), Winnie had fallen in love with Alfred Wilkinson, a Syracuse attorney against whom there was one vehement objection: his grandfather had been an Abolitionist. Winnie, who often represented her ailing father at Confederate gatherings and was known as "the Daughter of the Confederacy," was so sensible of the still vigorous ghost of sectionalism that she had not yet dared to tell her parents. The Pulitzers (who were also trying to reconcile Roscoe Conkling and his estranged wife) applauded the match. To Pulitzer himself, so impatient with the smoldering animosities of a war 22 years past, the marriage of Winnie and the Yankee Wilkinson could serve as a romantic proclamation of an end to all that, a symbol of the unification of the nation's infernally stiff-necked Montagues and Capulets. It would also make a grand story for the World—very possibly a scoop.

Another young lady who entered his life was petite, 21-year-old Elizabeth Cochrane of Pennsylvania, who called herself Nellie Bly and concealed her own powerful ambition behind an innocent exterior. The Pittsburgh Dispatch, where she worked, was not big enough for her. She burst into Cockerill's office to plead for a job, impressing him with her nerve—impressing Pulitzer too, who hired her and gave her $25 when he learned that she had lost her purse. Soon Miss Bly was performing stunts for the World, one of them being to feign insanity and get herself committed to the asylum on Blackwell's Island. Her discoveries of abominable conditions there not only made vivid reading in the World but caused a grand jury investigation resulting in improvements at the asylum.

At the same time Pulitzer was entertaining a proposition from William Henry Smith, director of the Associated Press, that he spend $300,000 for a controlling interest in the Chicago Times. Obviously, had his health permitted, he would have founded a newspaper empire stretching across two continents.[25]

Chapter 6

The Feud with Dana

I. "RENEGADE JEW"

On March 17, 1887, Dana brought out the Evening Sun, a four-page paper for a penny that quickly reached a 40,000 circulation. He had sneered at Pulitzer's military record, made inquiries at the War Department in a vain effort to discover unchivalric conduct, and had lampooned his lowly early years in St. Louis. His rival's failure to attend the synagogue or to take part in any Jewish activities furnished another Dana weapon. Pulitzer, nominally a member of St. George's Episcopal Church, shepherded by the liberal Reverend William S. Rainsford, seldom if ever attended, though Kate was a communicant and the children were baptized there. The Sun took note of this with polished venom:

> Mr. Pulitzer never enlists in anything unless there is a good big bounty offered. He came to this country, not to promote the cause of his race or his native land, but to push the fortunes of that part of Jewry which is situated over the soles of his boots and under the hat that covers his head.[1]

As the cartoonist McDougall noted, "the sting of that human wasp, Dana of the *Sun*, drove [Pulitzer] almost frantic." Certainly revenge played a part in his next move. He hired the talented Solomon S. Carvalho away from the Sun, teamed him with E. Tracy Greaves and a small staff, and on October 10 inaugurated the Evening World, a four-page penny paper aimed at whipping the Evening Sun. October 10 was the 20th anniversary of Pulitzer's arrival in St. Louis, a combination of lucky tens.

When the new paper got off to a slow start, Pulitzer had a word with Carvalho and Greaves. "You are making a three-cent newspaper for a one-cent constituency," he said. "I want you to make it a one-cent newspaper." [2] The Evening World was immediately shorn of dignity and converted into a frank sensation merchant. Soon it passed the Evening Sun and by the end of the year was selling 75,000 copies daily. The Sun commented:

> How odd it was for that truck load of unsaleable *Evening Worlds* to break down in front of Newspaper row! The news of it set the whole town roaring with laughter yesterday. The bluster and brag of our contemporary mystified a great many persons who see how tame and tedious the *Evening World* is and could not understand what gave it the circulation its owner boasted it possessed.[3]

The morning World remained Pulitzer's "personal" newspaper, the one on which he lavished his attention and in which he drove incessantly for public service and reform. When anyone spoke of the "World," he meant the morning edition, but to simplify matters at the office the World was called Senior, the Sunday World Seniority and the Evening World Junior. Was Junior, the black sheep of the family, designed solely to make money or to wreak vengeance on Dana? One wonders whether Pulitzer would have fathered it at all had it not been for the Evening Sun—wonders also whether his order to make it flashy was not inspired by his overpowering need to punish Dana. In any case, Junior's success was a factor in the growing fusillade between the two editors that reached astonishing heights of abuse.

Another factor was the election for district attorney that fall. Pulitzer, who had cheered De Lancey Nicoll's conviction of three of the franchise boodlers and of the briber Jake Sharp himself, was among those urging the Democrat Nicoll for the post. To him, there could be nothing so salutary as the conviction of every last one of the accused aldermen and nothing so shameful as the escape of any of them. To him, Nicoll was the man to continue the work he had so brilliantly started. When Pulitzer made a decision for the public good, it was no longer mere opinion but a universal truth which every decent citizen should sustain. He knew there were powerful political objections to Nicoll, who was too upright for Tammany leaders seeking a finger in the pie. There were, moreover, those sly, corrupt pressures aiming to end the stream of prosecutions so embarrassing to the politicians and so disturbing to the voters. This was already evident in the trial of Alderman Thomas J. Cleary, which ended in a jury disagreement and a suspicion that someone in the panel had been reached. Several of the aldermen who had fled to Montreal were so emboldened as to return to New York with stories that they simply feared political persecution. This sort of thing provoked in Pulitzer the kind of rage that was injurious for a man whose wife, friends and physicians warned him to avoid excitement.

Tammany rejected Nicoll, who was then nominated by the Republicans and supported also by many independents. Tammany's man was another assistant district attorney, John R. Fellows, no corruptionist but no crusader either, an able man who had worked loyally for President Cleveland and Mayor Hewitt. Cleveland and Hewitt promptly came out for Fellows, bringing them instant reproof from the World. The Sun, which originally had supported Nicoll, turned against him—interestingly, only six days after Pulitzer's new Junior emerged to compete with the Evening Sun. When the World demanded the reason for Dana's change of front, the Sun replied:

> The *World* has taken up the cause of Mr. Nicoll after the fashion of a highwayman with a pistol . . . The *World* breaks into the affairs of the city as train robbers enter an express car. [Nicoll is a promising young man but] we deplore his association with the *World* . . . We have withdrawn from our support of Mr. Nicoll because we distrust the *World* and its motives, and because more than suspicion exists to indicate what these motives are.
>
> Col. John R. [*sic*] Slayback was shot and killed, under shocking circumstances, in the editorial rooms of Mr. Pulitzer's newspaper, by Col. John R. [*sic*] Cockerill, then as now Mr. Pulitzer's managing editor. It has been charged that the reason why the St. Louis Grand Jury failed to indict Col. Cockerill for murder, was that such was the degree of Mr. Pulitzer's hold upon the District-Attorney of St. Louis and his administration that the indictment was frustrated. . . . It is our manifest duty to take account of [these facts] in the light of the unprecedented, frantic and astounding effort which the same men are now making to obtain what is virtually the control of the District-Attorney's office. . . .
>
> We submit the case to the whole public of New York and to the young man who is on the verge of a shipwreck of his fame. We call upon him for his own sake to recede if he be not implicated beyond recall.
>
> . . . We look with horror upon the contingency that an enmeshed captive of the *World* should fill an office which could give it any peculiar power over the criminal prosecutions of New York county.[4]

The World replied in part:

> The statements . . . [are] about what might be expected from Charles Ananias Dana. A mendacious blackguard who, not content with four months of virulent lying about a candidate for the Presidency, has insidiously attacked his wife and sister; who has sought to annoy the widow of General Grant, and who has polluted the grave of Henry Ward Beecher to satisfy his personal hatred, is capable of any distortion. . . .
>
> The revival of the St. Louis affair . . . is worthy of an assaulter of women and a mortgaged, broken-down calumniator in the last agonies of humiliation. . . . Two grand juries thoroughly investigated the case of Mr. Cockerill and refused even to return a bill. . . .[5]

Said the Sun:

> The candidate who stands for boss dictation is Nicoll, and the boss behind Nicoll is Judas Pulitzer, who exudes the venom of a snake and wields the bludgeon of a bully. . . . he has accepted the candidacy of Nicoll from the Republicans with as much thankfulness as in the days when he cringed for a nickel on the barroom floor . . .[6]

As the days wore on, the epithets the Sun applied to Pulitzer included "this Dick Turpin of journalism," "Judas Iscariot," "that political road agent," "a renegade Jew who has denied his breed," and "Choe Bulitzer." The World in turn described Dana as "a tool of Jim Fisk and Gould," "a betrayer of Hancock, a bolter against Tilden," "a poltroon in an hour of danger," and "poor, despised, disgraced, old Ananias!"

II. MOVE ON, PULITZER!

In the midst of it Pulitzer purchased for $200,000 the four-story C. T. Barney mansion at 10 East 55th Street, built by McKim, Mead & White four years earlier. The address included a ten and two fives, which should have been lucky, but Lucille Irma was ill again and Kate packed her off to a Lenox cottage, where two physicians examined the plumbing to make sure it was safe. A week before the election Pulitzer appeared at a Cooper Union rally, joining others including Carl Schurz, Joseph Choate and Elihu Root in speaking for Nicoll. It was to be his last political speech. He scoffed at the claim that Democrats would refuse to vote for Nicoll because he was on the Republican ticket, saying, according to his own World:

"The crime of seeking Republican votes any Democrat can bear. Who elected Cleveland? (Long applause, voice: 'the World')." [7]

Roscoe Conkling took Nicoll aside and said, "Nicoll, I have known all the prominent men of my generation in America and many abroad. Who do you think is the ablest man I have ever met?" Nicoll made several guesses, at which Conkling shook his head and said, "Joseph Pulitzer." [8]

The symptoms of Pulitzer's electionitis—the mounting excitement, incessant labor and explosive nerves—became even more acute in this campaign for a municipal office than in a presidential canvass. It was as if the fate of the nation hung on Nicoll. Certainly the fever was heightened by the struggle with Dana. The World made capital of the Sun's loss of circulation and prestige, while Dana, aware of New York's large Jewish vote, returned to the "renegade Jew" theme.

Pulitzer indeed seemed unable to adjust himself comfortably to his fractional Jewish ancestry. He was so abnormally sensitive that any slur struck him like a whiplash. Quite possibly the "Joey the Jew" taunts in St. Louis and the jests about his nose had left permanent wounds. His withholding of his pedigree from Kate, if comprehensible on the ground of his fear of losing her, had placed him under the impossible obligation of guaranteeing her against the anti-Semitism which she had never bargained for. Her own staunch Episcopalianism in turn had made it possible for Jews to misinterpret his religious skepticism as a denial of his race. The savage Jew-baiting Richardson had practiced in *The Journalist* had rubbed in salt. He was so relieved when Allan Forman replaced Richardson in charge of the paper and published an article flattering to Pulitzer and the World that he promptly acceded to Forman's request for a $200 loan.

Pulitzer swarmed with neuroses and anxieties, the gnawing inner fears that accompany pride and ambition. Above all he could not stand ridicule or indignity and had no defenses against them—no more now than when he had struck a sergeant during the war or when he had shot Captain Augustine—a thinness of skin particularly painful for him since he specialized in journalistic attack that was bound to draw return fire. Though he was never anti-Semitic, and numbered Jews among his friends and employees, he tended to recoil from racial or religious discussions, to escape them, push them away. Perhaps because of his own accent, he forbade his editors to use comic dialect of any kind, be it German or Italian, in his newspapers. Later in life he sent money for the relief of victims of pogroms, but it was said that he asked his companions never to discuss Jews or Jewishness. Dana could have hit on no tactic more brutal or mortifying. Pulitzer's heterodoxy annoyed some Jews—especially Democratic Jews angered by his "desertion" of the party. On election morning Dana reprinted an attack from the Fellows-supporting Hebrew Standard saying in part:

> We Jews have a special interest in this would-be "Sahib" of the Bohemian tribe. He happens to be of Jewish extraction, which he denies, however, for some reason or another, probably as an impediment to certain ambitious designs of his. He is a Jew who does not want to be a Jew. And the peculiarity of it is that this unholy ambition of the said editor to lord it over the people and dictate to them who they should elect and who not, will probably be laid at the door of the Jews, who [*sic*] he has denied, and who have never been anxious to count him as their own.
>
> . . . The man who will deny his race and religion for the sake of ambition, social standing, or whatever motive, will betray his political friends, will betray his party, if his aspiration is served thereby.

To which Dana added his own comment:

> The Jews of New York have no reason to be ashamed of Judas Pulitzer if he has denied his race and religion . . . the shame rests exclusively upon himself. The insuperable obstacle in the way of his social progress is

> not the fact that he is a Jew, but in certain offensive personal qualities. . . . His face is repulsive, not because the physiognomy is Hebraic, but because it is Pulitzeresque. . . cunning, malice, falsehood, treachery, dishonesty, greed, and venal self-abasement have stamped their unmistakable traits . . . no art can eradicate them.
>
> Jewish citizens have the same interest as all other intelligent, self-respecting, and law-abiding people in the defeat of Pulitzer and his young dupe, Nicoll. The Jewish vote will contribute very largely to that effect.[9]

Doubtless it did. While Pulitzer believed in religious freedom and in the irrelevance of race or religion in the matter, the question of his heterodoxy was not one that the World felt it should discuss. Fellows defeated Nicoll by a 22,000 plurality. Dana blazoned his triumph with a crowing rooster on his front page and ascended a new summit of scurrility:

> And now, Pulitzer, a word with you!
>
> You stand before this community in the same startling light that you stood in some years ago in St. Louis when your career of scandal and blackmail culminated in murder. You have reached your apogee of remunerative infamy here without having had to resort to any form of homicide. In fact, your path here has been easier than it was there. . . .
>
> Now, however congenial to you may be the contempt of mankind, and however you may prize the testimony of general aversion, it cannot be denied that such an attitude on the part of the public has for you its practical disadvantages. We could wish with all our heart, Pulitzer, that St. Louis had possessed a stronger stomach. You might have stayed there, Pulitzer, and then we should have been spared the infliction of your presence here. Today you are a fugitive from the unexecuted justice of that town . . . a fugitive from the scorn, the ridicule, and the contumely of its people. . . . We wish, Pulitzer, that you had never come.
>
> But that you are here is indisputable, and that the public has found you out is obvious. In this experimental stage of universal sentiment it is not possible to state definitely what your fate will be. We can only see clearly that it will be something unpleasant.
>
> Perhaps your lot will be like that of the mythical unfortunate of the same race you belong to and deny, that weird creation of medieval legend, a creation, by the way, far more prepossessing than you are—we mean, The Wandering Jew! In that case it may shortly please the inscrutable Providence, which has chastened us with your presence, to give you that stern and dreadful signal—
>
> Move on, Pulitzer, move on! [10]

Dana's witch's curse seemed leveled with all the authority of a Merlin, for Pulitzer would soon be traversing the world in restless flight. After a measured editorial on the election result, he answered under the heading "YES, HERE FOR GOOD!" with considerable truth:

The editor of the *Sun* . . . seems to think that by helping to elect a man whom The World opposed on public grounds, he could boast of a triumph and thereby affect the prestige of a newspaper which he long ago ceased to compete with.

The editor of The World accepts the hatred of Mr. Dana as a compliment. He is only one of a vast number of people who have been favored with the creature's malice and have prospered under it. He especially appreciates the agonized heart-cry of Mr. Dana, which appears in yesterday's issue of the *Sun* . . .

"We wish, Pulitzer, that you had never come."

Nothing could be truer than this. From his innermost soul the broken and humiliated editor of the *Sun* wishes that the regeneration of The World had never taken place. In four years' time he has seen the circulation of his paper dwindle until it has fallen into the third rank; he has seen his dividends vanish; his income swept away. He has seen a mortgage for $175,000 placed upon a property which once yielded monthly dividends of 10 per cent. . . . With the hatred of a felon on the way to prison or worse, he has sought to hold The World responsible for the damage which he has mainly inflicted upon himself by his total lack of principle and honor. That the discriminating public should prefer The World to his vile sheet he has held as a cause for a quarrel with the editor of The World—such a quarrel as only the jealous bankrupt can make with the successful rival around the corner.

Sad, no doubt, Mr. Dana is, that somebody came who could provide the New York public with the newspaper which it wanted. But the man is here, and he will remain. The World is stronger and better today than it ever was. It has never advocated a bad cause nor proved recreant to a good one. Its circulation is *three times that of the* Sun and its influence is in proportion. It will continue to war against corruption with renewed vigor. It rests upon a solid foundation of Honesty and Public Service and against it the disappointed, malice-cankered sons of darkness cannot prevail.[11]

IV

Disaster

Chapter 1

The Breakdown

I. TORTURED NERVES, FAILING EYESIGHT

To Pulitzer, the defeat of Nicoll—and probably even more, his own defeat by Dana—was nothing less than a disaster. A fortnight after this unpleasantness he walked into his third-floor office and called for the editorials. "I was astonished to find," he said later, "that I could hardly see the writing, let alone read it." [1] Undoubtedly he swore. Without a word to his colleagues he took a carriage to his new home and put himself under the care of his good friend Dr. McLane and New York's most noted oculist, Dr. Herman Knapp. Knapp, finding a broken blood vessel in one eye and deterioration in the other, sternly counseled six weeks' confinement in a darkened room if he was to save his eyesight at all. McLane had other worries, for the patient was troubled with asthma, weak lungs, a protesting stomach, insomnia, exhaustion and fits of depression. He was not only threatened with blindness but racked by severe physical ills, and behind all this—perhaps responsible in part for it—was suffering from a serious, if undiagnosed, psychosis.

While psychiatry was then in its infancy, there seems no doubt that Pulitzer was what would now be called a manic-depressive. His symptoms would scarcely allow any other deduction. His extremes of mood and conduct, his changes of mind, his swings from warmest kindness to something near ruthlessness, from optimism to pessimism, from joy to rage, from prodigal spending to penny-pinching, his cultivated tastes and his searing profanity, his great hope in politicians and quick disillusionment with them, his vaulting ambitions, and above all his periods of euphoric confidence and torrential physical and mental energy for which he paid in descents to despair—all these are characteristic of the cyclothymic.

"Dear Mrs. Pulitzer," wrote Navy Secretary Whitney from Washington,

"Is it true that Mr. Pulitzer is seriously ill? I heard from a mutual friend in strictest confidence. I sincerely hope not. I am aware that my friends here have not always seemed to him to be his friends & that my silence upon many subjects has separated us somewhat. . . ." [2]

"I am not quite dead yet," Pulitzer himself replied through his secretary, adding, "It is simply a bad case of overwork. You had better take heed yourself and take things easy . . ." And after some pale words of commendation for Cleveland, he went on, "Politically, I cannot see that we [Pulitzer and Whitney] can be separated next year [in the presidential campaign]. It certainly looks as if we would again fight together as we did in 1884." [3]

What with his vehement need for action, his six weeks in quiet darkness, added to his worry over his eyesight, must have been torture for him and hardly less difficult for Kate. They were relieved by the visits of Dr. McLane, who held him in deepest affection, took the time for long conversations and received the inevitable gift—an expensive striking clock as a memento of those endless hours. From Manton Marble, who had an apt nickname for him—"Samson Agonistes"—came a note combining his sympathy and his hope to win Pulitzer back to Cleveland for the election:

> My judgment is . . . that *your* critical moment has come, and will not wait if it is to be the World that strikes decisive strokes and recovers an unchallenged lead in the Democratic party. . . .
>
> My God! What a calamity for the party that you are ill now. . . .[4]

Just as his six weeks were over, an officer sought to arrest him on the complaint of an immigration official, Edmund Stephenson. The World had libeled him, Stephenson said, in charging that he "unlawfully detained and imprisoned immigrants and abused and insulted helpless women, inhumanely treated mothers and children, and plundered immigrants, and that he shielded employees . . . who had been guilty of lecherous practices." [5] The officer was turned away because of Pulitzer's illness, and Roscoe Conkling had another lawsuit to defend.

Meanwhile Dana stepped up a campaign of vilification aimed at driving Pulitzer from New York. Obviously he was as incensed by Pulitzer's social acceptance as by his flourishing business enterprise. In the "Jew who does not want to be a Jew" editorial from the Hebrew Standard the older editor saw a weapon that might hurt his rival both socially and journalistically, a means of exploiting devious anti-Semitism from concealment behind the Standard. The Sun reprinted the Standard editorial again and again, usually three times a week, always on Saturdays and Mondays, always double-leaded for greater prominence, always headed, "MOVE ON, PULITZER!—REPUDIATED BY HIS RACE." Certainly they were read to Pulitzer in his darkened room. They visited great distress on Kate, who was kindly disposed toward everyone and could see no reason for this bitterness.

The World replied by publishing a copy of the Sun's $175,000 mortgage—a sally hurtful enough to bring a Sun explanation that it had indeed borrowed the money, a common business practice, to buy new equipment and "to erect a new building." New presses were bought, it was true, but no new Sun building would be erected for years. The Sun varied its "Jew who does not want to be a Jew" line with editorials accusing Pulitzer of lying about circulation, publishing fraudulent news, betraying the Democratic party (an odd posture considering the Sun's venom in 1884) and insulting Catholic nuns, and pinned on him such epithets as "incorrigible liar" and "impostor and swindler." Dana published "letters from subscribers" attacking Pulitzer which had a flavor of being composed in the Sun office. Few issues of the Sun appeared without an assault on the World's owner, one issue containing three on the same editorial page. Invariably they contained the line "Move On, Pulitzer, Move On."

Pulitzer moved on. On Dr. McLane's advice he left for California on January 14 in the private car "Newport" with Kate, Ralph, Lucille and a male secretary. They traveled by way of New Orleans, making a side trip to Beauvoir to visit the Jefferson Davises and to ask if Winnie Davis might accompany them to California. Beauvoir, a mansion in slow decay, was a mournful memorial to the late Confederacy, but Varina Howell Davis was a vivid conversationalist and the 80-year-old Davis, himself blind in one eye, could sympathize with Pulitzer. Since Winnie had not yet dared to tell her parents about Wilkinson, the Pulitzers were unable to urge the felicitous national implications of the match. She was unwilling to leave her ailing father, so they rode on to California, taking a suite at the Hotel Del Monte in Monterey.

Pulitzer immediately sent crates of prime oranges to Conkling, the Childses, the McLanes, Davidson, the Drexels, the Davises and others. Forbidden to read or write, able to function only through his secretary, he was thoroughly miserable and "made every one else so." From one Marshall Gates came a note: "I see by the papers that you are liable to go blind. I have an *eye salve* which I believe will cure you. . . . Don't think me a *Crank* or *Fanatic*, because I write to you, a stranger. I work on the square." From Dr. McLane, enjoying his oranges, came a long, chatty letter: "I cannot tell you how much I miss you & my frequent visits to you. . . . I am grieved not to get better accounts of your eye. . . . I wish I was where I could cheer you up." The striking of Pulitzer's gift clock, he added, "reminds me of your generous loving-kindness to me." Turner, the World's business manager, wrote, "I . . . beg of you to cease worrying about the paper and if a sea voyage is possible to take a long one when it will be impossible to get reports or issue directions." [6]

The advice to stop worrying came from doctors, family, friends and staff, but Pulitzer's whole career was founded on worry, or what he would have called the ceaseless and intelligent attention to details. He was the personification of worry, and now, as always, there seemed plenty to worry about. While Junior, the Evening World, was pushing near 100,000 circulation, Senior had actually dropped a few thousand from its 1887 figure—the first time it had done anything but gain. Were resentful Democrats quitting the paper? Could Cockerill, who had married Leonora Barner and installed her at the Astor House, be a bridegroom and a good editor simultaneously? An angry Pulitzer cable from Monterey incontinently fired Tracy Greaves, recently arrived in London to replace Crawford as World correspondent there, because Greaves had spent too much on cables and had sent a man to Berlin without authorization. Greaves wrote a long explanation, saying, "your conduct towards me, when I could talk with you personally, has always been kind and considerate . . ." [7] A second Pulitzer cable reinstated him.

There was worry about one of the biggest of news stories, the Blizzard of 1888, which began March 11 and paralyzed New York for three days under 21 inches of snow, stopped all transportation and raised a threat of famine. World men slept on the office floor, unable to get home. Thousands of marooned citizens slept at Grand Central Station, Macy's, in elevated railroad cars and other unlikely places. Telegraphic communication was dead for a time, the only outside news coming over Cyrus Field's Atlantic cable. The determined Roscoe Conkling fought gales and drifts in a three-mile walk from his office to his lodgings, then collapsed. Dr. McLane wrote Pulitzer of the desperate shortage of milk for babies and invalids: "Here it is Wednesday evng. & there has not been a train out of, or into the Grand Central Depot since early Monday morning—and 'Chauncey' says he don't know when there will be."

Pulitzer got a telegram through to Conkling, who had recovered enough to reply with typical reproof, "Would gladly face greater storms to make your eyes strong enough to be squandered reading newspapers." [8]

There was worry about the confoundedly independent Mayor Hewitt, who was guilty of the most impolitic utterance of all time when he was visited by a group of Irish leaders who thought they were merely fulfilling a formality in requesting him to review the St. Patrick's Day parade. "We all know that the Irish vote is strong enough to elect any candidate in this City . . ." Hewitt told the delegation, which included men named Mullins, Reilly, McGuire and Finnegan. "But, for the purpose of getting that vote, I shall not consent to review any parade, be it Irish, or Dutch, or Scotch, or German, or English." He showed the stunned Irishmen the door. This was madness. He compounded it later by pointing out that the number of Irish on the Board of Aldermen and the police department was far over their percentage of the city's population, then twisted the knife by adding, "But when we come to examine the nationality of the inmates of the institutions under the care of the Commissioners of Charities and Correction we find that a larger [Irish] ratio appears." [9]

Obviously he did not want another term. Pulitzer, getting word that Conkling had suffered a serious relapse, received daily bulletins about his condition. ". . . I fear that long before this reaches you, he may have passed from us," wrote their mutual friend, S. L. M. Barlow.[10] The affection between Pulitzer and Conkling had been warm, and the Stalwart's death at 59 on April 17 was a desolation to the ailing man in California, forbidden to attend the funeral, able only to follow the oranges with a huge floral piece and a stirring obituary in the World.

11. REVENGE ON DANA

From Monterey Pulitzer consummated one of New York's largest real-estate transactions. He had tried for more than a year to buy Park Row property immediately across from James Gordon Bennett's Herald building at Ann Street so that he could erect an edifice that would dwarf the four-story Herald structure. He envisioned this not only as a personal victory over the lone New York newspaper publisher who still offered the World any challenge, but as a stroke of architectural publicity impressive to everyone. Unable to secure enough land there, he paid $630,000 *cash* for the old French's Hotel property three blocks north on Park Row—the place where he had been requested not to come for a shoeshine in 1865. The deal was completed on April 10, 1888, a lucky ten and his 41st birthday.

He had an implacable talent for paying off old scores. If the location spared Bennett, it enabled him to wreak a calculated vengeance on Dana. The property was directly across Frankfort Street from the Sun. Every rising girder and stone in the new World building would be a noisy and visible humiliation to Dana, day after day and month after month. Dana had tried vainly to block the deal, beseeching the city to buy the land for a courtroom building. The World commented maliciously on his efforts, noting that the new building would increase the value of adjacent property:

> Even the shabby little building of the *Sun* will be benefited by the splendor of its near neighbor. . . . [Yet the Sun] dreads being overshadowed architecturally by The World, as it already has been overshadowed by us in circulation, influence, character, enterprise and all that makes a newspaper successful and powerful.[11]

By now the Pulitzer-Dana feud was such a nationwide journalistic sensation that Eugene Field could not forbear romancing about it in his "Sharps and Flats" column in the Chicago Daily News:

> During his recent trip to Europe Colonel Charles A. Dana met Joe Pulitzer, proprietor of the *World,* in Paris. Colonel Dana was exceedingly cordial and shook Pulitzer's lean, clammy hand very heartily. "I'm glad to see you looking so well," said Dana. "What paper are you working for now?" [12]

Pulitzer, who could never take a joke or indeed understand one, was so offended that he had Cockerill write a protesting letter to Victor Lawson of the News. By mid-May he was back in New York after a stopover in St. Louis—his final visit there. He was still so nervous that visitors were barred, even his good friend Childs. On June 9 he sailed for England with Dr. McLane in attendance, to consult the best neurologists of Europe. In London he visited the Harley Street specialist Sir Andrew Clark, who had treated the late George Eliot. Sir Andrew rekindled his interest in the novelist whose nervous afflictions were not unlike his own, but his prescription was the same old inanity offered by Dr. McLane—rest, with complete separation from work. This was like forbidding meat to a Bengal tiger. Pulitzer fought the advice no matter who gave it to him. His newspapers, the instruments of his genius and ambition, had become almost as much a part of him as any limb or organ of his body. The creation of ideas, the manipulation of men and measures, the development and exercise of power in politics—these things gripped him beyond his own control, much less the control of any physician. He was not manufacturing steel, like Abram Hewitt, or operating a railroad like Depew. He was running the World, a daily newspaper, unlike any other enterprise, a new product each day that yet reflected and advanced abiding principles—each day a crisis, an onslaught of problems to be met with judgment and speed, each day a battle against time and events and against competitors who hated him and his success. Quit the battle indeed!

He and Dr. McLane went on to Paris, where they were joined by Kate. Here Pulitzer consulted a galaxy of French specialists including Drs. Bouchard, Dupuy, De Wecker, Meyer, Brown-Sequard, Lamboldt—even the renowned Jean Charcot, whose insight into the nature of hysteria would later be praised by Freud. Pulitzer's hope was to find a physician who would tell him what he *could* do, not what he could not, but the doctors' unanimity was expensive and appalling: rest, a banishment of business cares, of worry and excitement.

The advice was wasted on this most unruly of patients. He returned to New York in September to do precisely what he was warned not to do—direct the World personally in the city, state and national elections. His eyes were only slightly improved, his nerves in terrible shape. Twenty-three-year-old George Brinton McClellan Jr., only son of the general and later to become mayor of New York, was a cub World writer at the time. "I never once set eyes on him [Pulitzer] . . ." McClellan recalled. "But we heard him frequently. When anything went wrong, and things seemed to go wrong with him very often, there would come from his office . . . a stream of profanity and filth that almost overwhelmed even that expert blasphemist . . . John A. Cockerill."[13] With Kate pregnant again, the Pulitzers retreated to a Lenox country house where the plumbing had been duly inspected and Mr. Edison's electric lights had been installed. The Whitneys were also at Lenox, the impulsive Flora Whitney in outrage at the rumors some Republicans were spreading about Cleveland and his young wife. It was said that Henry Watterson took Mrs. Cleveland to the opera, so angering the President that he called her vile names and slapped her—a report Watterson heatedly denied; that Cleveland drank heavily and beat his wife on one occasion so that she fled and the Whitneys took her in; that his savagery had forced her mother to leave Washington; and that the Clevelands would be divorced after the election (they remained happily married until his death).

To read the World one would have been scarcely aware that a President was being elected. It punished Cleveland by virtually ignoring him, giving him a frigid line or two before the election: "President Cleveland represents the principle of Tax Reduction through Tariff Reform. As such . . . he merits the support of all voters who believe in this principle and policy."[14] It beat its biggest drums for the Tammany-allied Governor Hill, running for reelection with his eye on the White House. In the city, Mayor Hewitt, whose term had been one of the most constructive in years, was ditched by Tammany but allowed himself to be persuaded to run again on a fusion ticket.

Pulitzer had had enough of Hewitt too. He could not forgive Hewitt's support of Fellows, nor could he forgive his characterization of Pulitzer (though not by name) as a "newspaper boss." "The political boss is responsible to his party," Hewitt had said, "the newspaper boss is responsible only to his own pocketbook. He is as dangerous as he is despotic." These words, plus his remarks about the Irish, assured his retirement from public life. The World did not really crusade for the winning Tammany candidate, Sheriff Hugh J. Grant, chiefly famous as one of the two honest aldermen who had voted against the boodle franchise. But it might as well have, for it hammered vengefully at Hewitt as a "boss-backed candidate," a "Know-Nothing," a "common scold" and a "demonstrated humbug."[15] Hewitt was drubbed. Cleveland lost New York State by 13,000 votes and lost the presidency to Benjamin Harrison although he had a 98,000 popular plurality. Hill, on the other hand, was reelected governor by 19,000 votes.

Pulitzer, the present-giver, sent a gold-and-diamond pin in the shape of a crowing rooster to the governor, who had invariably been deferent and had inquired kindly about his health. His ambition to "make Presidents" would continue as strongly as ever despite the Cleveland disenchantment, and his eye was on Hill for 1892 just as surely as the diamond rooster was on Hill's lapel.

III. DEFYING THE DOCTORS

If Pulitzer's desertion of Cleveland was understandable, his pummeling of Hewitt seemed a lapse from the patient, far-sighted policy of the reformer he claimed to be. As a political realist he foresaw that Hewitt had no chance. Yet Tammany's victory, to which he contributed, handed the city over to Boss Croker and corruption that would erupt in inevitable scandal. Indeed, 1888 marked the defeat of Pulitzer the idealist by Pulitzer the intemperate victim of disappointment and rage, and Hewitt's charge of "newspaper bossism" seemed not far from the mark. He had become more and more the authoritarian, the dispenser, the man of command who expected almost the same obedience from politicians that he exacted in his own home and his own newspaper. He was of course a sick man. For two years he had been ailing, irascible, not his normal self, and it is reasonable to believe that he would have been less capricious and vindictive had he been well. From this point on in his life he would be so torn by disaster and on occasion so emotionally unstrung that all his acts must be judged as those of a man fighting for survival.

On December 13 Constance Pulitzer was born. By January her father was in such nervous torment that he could not go on. One can imagine Kate's pleas that he must put all work aside for many months, but it was only because he was forced to that he agreed to a long sojourn in Europe. Who would run the World and watch over construction of the great new building while he was gone?

His decision reflected his innate inability to place his faith in any one person. He passed over Ballard Smith and vested a divided control in Cockerill and Business Manager Turner. But since the two were at open war, he made Kate's brother Colonel Davis—known as Uncle Willie by the Pulitzer children—a vice president and triumvir to arbitrate between them. He then sailed with Kate, Ralph and Lucille, taking a hotel suite on the Rue de Courcelles in Paris. He was beginning 22 years of wandering precisely as if he were following Dana's editorial anathema.

He hired as his secretary young Claude A. F. Ponsonby, nephew of the last Marquis of Huntly, one of whose ancestors had been a favorite of Mary Stuart. What with his dim eyesight and illness, he had need of a secretary-companion, but the incorrigible doctor-defier at once began to stretch the rules and use the secretary for communications with the

World, from which he was supposed to have shut himself off. With Ponsonby and a couple of servants he moved on to St. Moritz to take the cure and to dictate messages, one of his efforts being to snare the editor Julius Chambers away from the Herald. "See Chambers again, renew offer of $250 per week and three years' contract," he cabled the World.[16] Chambers entered the World family. Pulitzer, driven by nervousness to frequent movement, soon rejoined Kate and the children in Paris, where they had attended the great exposition dominated by the amazing new tower of Alexandre Eiffel. He was in such depression that Kate took Ponsonby aside and warned him to change the subject whenever her husband got on the topic of his health.[17]

Like an alcoholic returning to hidden bottles, Pulitzer kept his hand in at the World. By remote control he hired the editorialist George Cary Eggleston away from the sedate Commercial Advertiser. He was having the World read to him by Ponsonby, and dictating a flood of careful letters. He was receiving reports from several executives and was writing Chambers that he was "delighted" with his work, adding, "Never fear of troubling me with any suggestion concerning either the welfare of the paper or your own; and nothing, looking to the elevation and improvement of the paper, is too small to mention." He was so pleased with Bill Nye's letters to the World about the Paris Exposition that he presented Nye with a scarf pin, "a cornucopia in design, surrounded by five diamonds." [18]

In June he left his family in Paris and went with Ponsonby to Wiesbaden, where he took another cure and also consulted Dr. Hermann Pagenstecher, the foremost oculist of the day. He was now forced to dictate even intimate messages, and his letter to Kate was informative rather than ardent. "I am really much better—at least compared with a week ago," he wrote in part. "But remember again all my statements of improvement are *comparative*." He defied the doctor's orders enough to write his real feelings at the top in his own bold hand, "*My Dearest*," and to sign the letter, "With sincere love, ever your devoted husband, J. P." [19] Ponsonby himself reported to Kate ten days later:

> The nerves are in a better state, and the sleeplessness is not quite so great, though there is much left to be desired upon that point. He is able to walk at least an hour a day; and, what is more, seems to enjoy it. He does not complain of dullness, & in fact is quite different from what he was . . . in Paris. . . . I am sure you will be glad to hear that he *scarcely ever* alludes to his health . . .[20]

But he fumed at the World's "inept" handling of the great Johnstown flood in July. He put his deepest thought on the new building which would bear his name, be a proud monument to his own efforts, but which he hoped would be more than that. It must be grand but not gaudy. It must clothe newspaper efficiency in beauty. It must be an inspiration to every World man. It must be a permanent advertisement of World supremacy, telling New York and the nation plainly but not quite insolently of its triumph over the Sun, the Herald and the rest. Its construction must be marked by ceremonies striking a note of dignity combined with homely touches appealing to the masses—ceremonies that would themselves make news, create publicity, overshadow his rivals, increase circulation, but all in the best of taste. His rivals—among them James Gordon Bennett in his Champs Élysées apartment—already showed signs of jaundice.

"Poor, misguided, selfish vulgarian," Bennett said. "Can't last. He is going to put up a skyscraper of fourteen or fifteen storeys." [21]

Pulitzer was still in Wiesbaden when on October 10 (that propitious ten again) the cornerstone was laid with ceremonies as directed by the absent chief. Among the dignitaries present were Governor Hill (who made a speech), Chauncey Depew (who gave the official oration), William C. Whitney, Thomas A. Edison and many others, including four-year-old Joseph Pulitzer Jr. Young Joseph supplied the homely touch for the masses. Clad in a blue-and-white sailor suit, he advanced to the cornerstone, smote it with a silver trowel and piped three times, "It is well done!" In a recess in the stone were placed papers and documents reflecting Pulitzer's conviction that the building would stand at least a century, along with $36.75 in gold and silver coins dated 1889 and a picture of mother and father Pulitzer with the five children, ranging from ten-year-old Ralph to ten-months-old Constance. From Wiesbaden Pulitzer cabled a message couched in prayerful idealism which his enemies were apt to label as cynical but which was entirely sincere:

> God grant that this structure be the enduring home of a newspaper forever unsatisfied with merely printing news—forever fighting every form of Wrong—forever Independent—forever advancing in Enlightenment and Progress—forever wedded to truly Democratic ideas—forever aspiring to be a Moral Force—forever rising to a higher plane of perfection as a Public Institution.
>
> God grant that The World may forever strive toward the highest ideals—be both a daily schoolhouse and a daily forum—both a daily teacher and a daily tribune—an instrument of Justice, a terror to crime, an aid to education, an exponent of true Americanism.
>
> Let it ever be remembered that this edifice owes its existence to the public; that its architect is popular favor; that its moral cornerstone is love of Liberty and Justice; that its every stone comes from the people and represents public approval for public services rendered.
>
> God forbid that the vast army following the standard of The World should in this or in future generations ever find it faithless to those ideas and moral principles to which alone it owes its life and without which I would rather have it perish.
>
> Joseph Pulitzer [22]

In November Pulitzer rejoined his wife and two children in Paris, where they had the ailing Winnie Davis as their guest. The intelligent, neurotic, oval-faced Winnie seemed shadowed by the curse of sectionalism. Jefferson and Varina Davis had blanched at the thought of her marrying the Yankee Wilkinson. Although they had come around grudgingly, friends of the Davises had been so shocked by the romance that Winnie was despondent—a mood she hid in a letter to her father: "The other night Kate and I took Ralph to the opera, and you should have seen the grandeur of that little fellow with his miniature beaver and dress suit!" [23] Jefferson Davis never read the letter, for he died the day after it was written, receiving a contemptuous obituary in the New York Tribune but understanding (without approbation) in the World. Winnie, who could not return in time for the funeral and was too ill in any case, remained with the Pulitzers, who gave her what comfort they could. Another guest in Paris was the new World editorialist, George Cary Eggleston—all expenses paid.

"I have invited you here with the primary purpose that you shall have a good time," Pulitzer told Eggleston, as though he had no intention of giving him careful instruction. "But secondly, I want to see you as often as I can. We have luncheon at one o'clock, and dinner at seven-thirty. I wish you'd take luncheon and dinner with me as often as you can, consistently with my primary purpose that you shall have a good time. If you've anything else on hand that interests you more, you are not to come to luncheon or dinner, and I will understand. But if you haven't anything else on hand, I sincerely wish you'd come."

Eggleston later reflected, "In all my experience . . . I think I never knew a hospitality superior to this . . ." [24]

Both Pulitzer and Winnie were in such poor health that Kate soon took them south to the Grand Hotel in Naples. The solicitous Wilkinson visited them there; yet despite the Pulitzers' encouragement of the match, Winnie was in a state of depression almost matching her host's, unable to forget the disapproval of the Confederacy. Ultimately she gave up the romance and never married. To Kate, the sojourn in Naples with two despondent companions must have been burdensome indeed.

Thereafter, for the rest of Pulitzer's life, he and Kate would be separated most of the time, though this meant no loss of affection. The separation was made inevitable by his ceaseless travels in search of relief, but certainly the reason was deeper than that. The two were of antithetic temperaments, in his condition he could endure only deferential and compliant attendants, and her own health could not stand constant exposure to the gloom and occasional tyranny that accompanied his illness.

Chapter 2

Searching for Health

1. TWO WORLD TRAVELERS

By spring Pulitzer was in such despair that he bowed to fate and planned a leisurely voyage that would get him around the world in a year or so. The physicians' theory was that this would shut him off from business. They did not know their patient. He wrote his brother-in-law Davis, who was driven to the wall in his efforts to mediate between Cockerill and Turner and to soothe the temper of Ballard Smith:

> Remember that the mail to India goes by way of England, allowing about four weeks from New York; and remember also that the Indian mail leaves London every week on Fridays. Don't therefore mail anything by the Saturday steamers, as that mail would simply stay over in England from Monday to Friday; but instruct everybody in the office to mail by the Wednesday steamers. . . .
>
> As to the amount of letters and correspondence to be sent, you may judge from this simple rule. As many pleasant and agreeable reports as possible. No unnecessary questions for my decision. Nothing disagreeable or annoying unless of REAL IMPORTANCE. . . . I do not want to have my trip spoilt by ordinary bothers, nor to pay a dollar or two per word for such things. But if an extraordinary thing of real importance [arises], you need not hesitate, and I want you to cable me fully whether I am in Singapore or in Yokohama, even if it costs four dollars a word or forty. . . .

He fussed about the new building, writing, "I want to be sure that no *false* economy or niggardliness will mar the building inside." He asked for sketches by MacMonnies of the figure of Atlas supporting the world—a piece of statuary planned for the lobby. He gave shrewd arguments for a low price from the Hoe Company for new presses:

> The big point to be made with Hoe . . . is that, in getting the new order for new-sized presses, he not only receives the most extraordinary order ever received by his firm but that it will lead to a quasi revolution in press machinery, forcing the other leading papers to imitate this change, as they have imitated every change introduced by the *World*. It will mean a great many presses to Hoe, besides those ordered by the *World*. This point ought to be very strongly used. . . .[1]

Few details are known of his unhappy voyage. He sailed with Ponsonby and the servants, apparently on a regular cruise ship. His aides, aware of his condition and well paid, had to be ready for any mood ranging from warmest amiability to petulance and to downright unreasonable rage. Ponsonby, who endured occasional tongue-lashings, was so understanding of the kindly man underneath the quivering nerves that he remained a lifelong friend. To Pulitzer, the publication of 365 daily issues of the World without his personal supervision was an invitation to disaster, and at this time—with the building that proclaimed the greatest journalistic success in American history rising into the sky—it was as if Cheops had been denied a view of the construction of his pyramid. One comforting thought was the humiliation of Dana. It was said that Dana, gazing out at the new structure that already blocked his view of Brooklyn Bridge, remarked to his colleague, William M. Laffan, "Laffan, that begins to look serious."

Another round-the-world traveler, a few months ahead of Pulitzer and emphasizing speed instead of leisure, was the hard-headed little Nellie Bly. She had left New York on November 14 in a highly publicized and of course preposterous effort to best the 80-day circumnavigation of Jules Verne's fictional Phileas Fogg—a prime example of the World's "invented news." She had stopped briefly at Amiens to interview Monsieur Verne, who smiled indulgently and said she would never make it. It was a typical World promotion, a race against time, the creation of a continuous story and continuous headlines eschewed by the incensed journalistic opposition, the World whipping up excitement with stories of her progress and with "Your Nellie Bly Guessing Match," urging readers to estimate the number of days and hours it would take her. The exploit was also designed to draw even more attention to the skyscraper rising on Park Row.

The young lady traveled like the wind. Brindisi . . . Port Said . . . Colombo . . . Hong Kong—it appeared that Verne and the whole world were wrong, that she actually *would* make it. She sailed from Yokohama January 7 and reached San Francisco on the 21st. When she arrived in New York January 25 after traveling 24,899 miles in 72 days, cannon were fired on the Battery and thousands cheered the intrepid girl in the checked suit. "FATHER TIME OUTDONE!" headlined the World, spreading the story all over the front page. The whole nation was talking about the female reporter who made travel seem easy and shrank the world to petty proportions. Although she made news in papers from coast to coast, the Sun, Herald, Tribune and Times showed their contempt by avoiding mention of her entirely.

At a Greek port, Pulitzer received a cable from Davis mentioning the dissension in the World office. It threw him into the kind of passion a dozen doctors had warned him to avoid, and he was still seething a few days later when the ship reached Constantinople. Standing on deck with Ponsonby, he said in sudden puzzlement, "How dark it is getting!" Ponsonby stared, for the Levantine sunlight was bright. Pulitzer had lost much of his remaining vision and could see only dimly.[2]

Constantinople physicians urged a return to Europe for expert appraisal. Pulitzer's world cruise was ended. One can scarcely conceive the ferocity of the shock he suffered, calamitous to a normal man but catastrophic to one whose nerves were already throbbing near the danger point, a man whose whole being demanded action and whose eyes were his primary avenue to the world of action. He took ship to Naples, where it was discovered that the retina of one eye had become detached.

Again he was placed in a darkened room for days—days which must have been almost as harrowing for Ponsonby, trying to keep him cheerful. As he lay there in deepest depression, Italian soldiers began daily artillery practice in the harbor, with thunderous reverberations that made him cringe. It was the beginning of his extreme sensitivity to unexpected sound that would eventually make him wince at the scratching of a match. A plea to the Italian authorities caused the cannoneers to desist, and he was soon moved to the bracing climate of St. Moritz. Here the air from the glaciers brought on an attack of bronchitis. Pulitzer, who was not certain of the existence of God, must have felt that if there was one He had deserted him. He was taken down to a sanitarium in milder Lucerne, where he lay in August 1890 when Mrs. Pulitzer arrived with Dr. George Washington Hosmer.

The professorial, 59-year-old Dr. Hosmer, a colorful personage in his own right, came as much as companion as physician. Mrs. Pulitzer knew that her husband's greatest long-run ailment was neuropathic, that his condition was somewhat worse than he had been told, and that every effort must be made to help him avoid his frightening pits of melancholia. Since he could not read, and indeed was allowed to do nothing but talk or be read to, he soon exhausted the conversational and mental repertoire even of brilliant companions, became bored and sank into depression. His threshold of boredom was almost nonexistent. He needed the stimulation of new voices, new minds, new personalities to ward off despair.

Hosmer, a graduate of New York's College of Physicians and Surgeons and also a member of the bar, had practiced medicine and law only briefly because he had fallen in love with journalism. For years a Herald man under both Bennetts, he had reported many Civil War engagements including Gettysburg, later become head of the Herald's London bureau, covered the Franco-Prussian War and for a time was immured in Paris during the terrors of the Commune. Falling out with the demonic younger Bennett, he had joined the World and had immediately impressed Pulitzer with his tact, learning and intelligence. He would need all of it now, for although Ponsonby stayed on, Hosmer for 19 years would see little of his family as he became Number One man in an elaborately organized effort to save Pulitzer from utter frenzy. There was a confidential agreement with Kate that he would keep her informed of her husband's condition wherever he was. It would also be his duty to sit in at talks with the stream of specialists Pulitzer consulted, translate their medicalese, decide on the best course when they disagreed, and persuade the master to follow the prescribed regimen and diet. Hosmer, who kept a diary, wrote of the invalid:

> He was very ill—in a state so feeble that he could scarcely get around on foot. He passed days on a sofa . . . it was a physical strain for him to cross the room and sit at the table. . . . Physical collapse had assumed the form of nervous prostration . . . directly due to his intense efforts in building up *The World*. He had previously compromised his health by his labors on the *St. Louis Post-Dispatch*, which he had also raised from the dead.[3]

Hosmer's calm ministrations were probably more beneficial than those of any specialist. Widely traveled, well-read, the author of two books, with a background of adventure as well as learning, familiar with New York newspaper problems and able to describe minutely the progress of the new Pulitzer Building, he seemed the ideal companion for a man who found flaws even in perfection. By early September Pulitzer was well enough to move to Paris, where he visited more specialists, some of whom, ironically, recommended Dr. S. Weir Mitchell, the great Philadelphia neurologist. Despite Hosmer's disapproval he began to have Ponsonby read him the World and to resume correspondence with the office. "With this small recovery," as Hosmer put it, ". . . he listened to the telegrams from home which urged him to new activities. . . . In steering through the depths and shoals of politics, with Tammany always dominant, evil to the public welfare might be done with a feeble hand on the tiller [of the World]."[4]

Not only that. He planned a visit home, which would plunge him into the very worries he had been warned at all cost to avoid. True, he had the excuse that he must consult Dr. Mitchell, and no one could blame him for wanting to see his family—particularly little Constance, whom he had seen only as an infant and was now nearing two. There was the ghastly thought that if his eyesight worsened he would never see any of them again. But Pulitzer, endlessly resourceful in taking a mile when given a millimeter, wanted to get his hand back on the tiller. He wanted also to attend the dedication of his new building, now nearing completion. And—with the 1890 congressional elections in the offing, the political fire-horse was eager for the gallop. From Paris he wrote Julius Chambers, "I am not well enough to say more than this—that your work on the last issues of the Sunday World has pleased me very much indeed. I shall see you very soon now—& hope that in the meantime you will keep on planning good things & will try to give me an especially big idea on my return." [5]

II. THE GOLDEN DOME

During Pulitzer's extreme illness, a veritable miracle in reform had come to pass for which the World had fought from the beginning and for which it deserved great credit. On July 2 the Sherman anti-trust act had become law—a social landmark, the first significant assault on laissez-faire, on the ingrained American tradition of business freedom that had in fact become business license.

Never had Pulitzer's "red thread of continuous policy" been more effective. He had exposed the trusts for years, centering much of his attack on Standard Oil, "the most cruel, impudent, pitiless, and grasping monopoly that ever fastened upon a country." He had heaped columns of obloquy on mousy John D. Rockefeller, "the father of trusts, the king of monopolists, the czar of the oil business . . . [who] relentlessly crushes all competitors . . ." [6] The World had campaigned steadily for state and federal action against the trusts. Its crusade had been largely responsible for an 1888 investigation of the trusts by the House Committee on Manufactures that developed into a highly illuminating probe of the sugar trust and Standard Oil, putting Rockefeller and many of his executives on the stand. These hearings supplied vivid evidence of railroad rebating and other cutthroat practices that solidified public demand for control and speeded the admonitory pen of Senator Sherman. It was the most important example thus far of Pulitzer the schoolmaster-propagandist-muckraker not only pointing the way to badly needed reform but actually hastening it.

Ironically, his own suspicion of "big government" as an encroachment on freedom still held, though this was one encroachment he applauded. True, the Sherman act, like the Interstate Commerce act before it, would fail of enforcement for years despite the World's incessant efforts. One could say also that the incandescent lamp was not practicable when

Edison began to study it, and had he not tinkered with it its usefulness would have been further delayed.

If Pulitzer won that battle, he lost another when the same Harrison administration passed the industry-minded tariff fathered by Congressman McKinley, which the World fought every step of the way. The Republican argument was that the new imposts would not only encourage industry but would bless labor with better pay. Pulitzer, after a brief holiday at Trouville, sailed with his aides, reaching New York in October to learn that the new tariff had become law while he was at sea. Prices, he discovered, had risen immediately with no corresponding rise in wages, and a new World crusade was forming in the brain that was ordered to be quiet, placid, at rest.

In Silas Weir Mitchell, Pulitzer found a physician of broad cultivation and commanding personality, the author of respectable poetry and several novels, but best known for his psychological approach toward nervous sufferers and his rest cure. In Pulitzer, Mitchell must have found his most interesting as well as most unfortunate patient, a man whose nervous ailments, grave enough in themselves, were complicated by his fear of total blindness. The doctor came to New York, dined with the Pulitzers, examined the patient and doubtless had conversations with Kate about her husband's long history of nervous disorder. He prescribed daily exercise, a rest after each meal, and evening massages to induce sleep. The rest of the regimen was the same as that Pulitzer had paid a fortune to hear in Europe: complete relaxation, utter divorcement from business—not a letter, telegram or even a rumor. He was impressed enough to order an announcement of his retirement to be published in the World:

> Yielding to the advice of his physicians Mr. Joseph Pulitzer has withdrawn entirely from the editorship of The World.
>
> For the past two years Mr. Pulitzer has been unable, by reason of a misfortune to his sight, to give a personal supervision to the conduct of his journal. . . . The change is . . . more nominal than otherwise. It involves no change of men, of methods, of principle or of policy. The World will continue to be guided by the ideas of the man who made it what it is. . . .[7]

Nothing was said of the nervous condition that was the primary cause of his incapacitation. He was delighted by the generous notice taken of the event by the Herald, which said in part: "What the Greeleys and the Raymonds and the Bennetts did for journalism thirty years ago, Pulitzer has done today. It is true his methods have been queer and peculiar, but after all they have suited the present American public. As for us of the Herald, we droop our colors to him. . . . *Le Roi est mort, vive le Roi!*" Pulitzer ever afterward held a certain affection for the eccentric Bennett.

Though he avoided the World office, he flouted the doctors in his own way. A stream of executives visited his 55th Street residence, receiving orders from the fount and in some cases gifts—the efficient young E. A. Grozier was given a "bag of gold," a purse containing $1,000 in $20 gold pieces. The World mounted a typical Pulitzer crusade aimed at the "Shopping Woman" who paid higher prices for everything because of the new tariff. The November returns showed an astonishing Democratic resurgence—victory in the New York legislature, a congressional upheaval that swept 235 Democrats into the House and left only 86 Republicans, and solid Democratic gains in many states including Ohio, where the voters rebuked the author of the McKinley tariff by turning him out of office. Certainly Pulitzer was justified in foreseeing the election of a Democratic President in 1892, and he was keeping his friend Hill in mind.

Yet he was resigned enough to look for a steam yacht that would theoretically take him into exile. Business Manager Turner, an enthusiastic yachtsman, recommended the *Katerina*, once owned by the Duke of Sutherland but now for sale in New York, and Pulitzer began negotiations for her. He spent time with his wife and children, to mark their figures and characteristics in his memory while there was yet time. Since he was able to distinguish only the largest headlines, the subtler facial lineaments and movements—a smile, a dimple, a frown—were already blurred.

"Father spoiled the children outrageously," his daughter Edith recalled, "but when they were 12 they were expected to be adults." [8] The eldest, Ralph, was still only 11, so indulgence was the rule. Pulitzer visited William Whitney (another presidential hopeful for '92), two blocks up Fifth Avenue, and was pleased when three-year-old Dorothy Whitney climbed into his lap and pulled his beard. Ever afterward he was interested in Dorothy's career, saying, "she stays in my memory as among the last of those whom I could see." His brother Albert, whom he had shut out of his life, was now in Vienna, running his New York Journal in absentia and already showing signs of the insanity that would eventually claim him—terrible insomnia and compulsive eating that made him fat as a Buddha.

On December 10, 1890 (the figure totaled 190 lucky tens and the date was the 12th anniversary of the acquisition of the St. Louis Dispatch), the new Pulitzer Building, at 309 feet the tallest structure in New York, was officially opened with ceremony and fanfare on which World men had worked for weeks. Governor Hill was there again, along with 11 other governors, ex-governors and governors-elect, Mayor Grant, a host of other celebrities, journalists from all over the country, and a throng of spectators so dense that any movement was difficult.

The first impression given by the handsome building was the exact impression intended—one of complete dominance of Park Row. It towered over City Hall, of course, but more important, it looked down on the runty Sun, Times and Herald—even on the slim 260-foot Tribune campanile, the marvel of 1875. The Pulitzer Building was Joseph Pulitzer's 20-story shout of triumph over his rivals, the structural equivalent of the World's steady self-advertisement. Designed by George B. Post, it was "of the Renaissance order with a tendency to Venetian detail." The World was now printed in the bowels of the building, its business offices occupied the first floor and mezzanine, it was renting out 149 office suites in floors Two to Ten, and above that—especially in the great gilded dome, the first thing seen from ships coming in from Europe—were its brains, its newsrooms, its editorial offices. Pulitzer's huge semicircular office in the Dome had three great windows giving him a sweep of vision (useless to him) from Governor's Island and Brooklyn to the upper East River and Long Island. Its ceilings were frescoed, its walls wainscoted with embossed leather, his desk equipped with telephone and with call buttons to every department, which he would never use. Next was the slightly smaller office of Colonel Davis, then a fine library, then a council chamber for editorial discussions. Not forgotten were "charming bedroom apartments" on the 11th floor for editors working overtime and unable to get home—a touch that made some of them nod meaningly. It was literally true, as they said, that they could "spit on the Sun." To Ballard Smith the new building brought uneasiness, for he suffered from acrophobia and dared not look out the Dome windows.

Representatives of the Times, Tribune and Herald who attended (the Sun stayed home) were inclined to envy. The Times' casual page 3 account made fun of the World photographer who stationed himself atop City Hall to make the pictorial effort of his career, used far too much flashlight compound and caused an explosion that "shook the very asphalt of the plaza," broke scores of windows, but luckily missed injuring anyone. The Times added, "It is understood that Mr. Pulitzer . . . issued strict orders that no brickbats should be dropped into Mr. Dana's chimneys, no matter how great the temptation." The World, of course, treated it as the achievement it really was, giving it the full front page both on December 10 and 11, calling it correctly "THE GREATEST NEWSPAPER BUILDING IN THE WORLD" and adding, "A People's Palace Without a Cent of Debt or Mortgage."

Without further mention of Dana's mortgage, Pulitzer took special pains to make it known that he owned his $2,000,000 building down to the last Hoe press and brass doorknob, having paid cash on the barrelhead for everything, incurring not a nickel of debt that could impair his independence. Debt was his horror, independence his fetish. Under the headline "NO MORTGAGE UPON IT" was a copy of a certificate from County Register Frank Fitzgerald verifying his untrammeled ownership—a notice of his refusal to be beholden to "the bankers." [9] It was truly an impressive achievement, astonishing to Wall Street and arousing awe in every sapient journalist in the country. It also impressed six-year-old Joseph Pulitzer Jr., who wrote his sister Lucille:

> We went up into that golden dome and into Papa's and Uncle Willie's rooms and went into the printing room and saw the large engines at work. One was called "Lucille" and one "Ralph." Papa says he will call the others "Joseph," "Edith" and "Constance," as they have no names.[10]

Where was the master of the feast while the governors and the public celebrated this greatest event of his career? He was not at the table. He had not entered his new building. His nerves could not stand it. Joseph Pulitzer sailed the day before on the *Teutonic* with his wife and aides.

He was an invalid at 43, his success turned to mockery. Extreme manic-depressives, when shackled for their own protection, often fight violently for freedom and have been known to die of sheer exertion. While Pulitzer was quite sane, he was full of revolt against his self-imposed restraints. The man who had always given the orders was now helpless in the grip of fate, and he would never stop railing at his fate, fighting against it. Blindness alone is a shock to a normal person, making the world a frightening place, magnifying the victim's sense of suspicion. As Pulitzer left for Europe, his friends and executives thought him through, totally incapacitated, a nervous wreck who would do well to cling to the raw shreds of his existence in distant retirement.

This would have been true of almost anyone but him. Indeed, he would never be the same again. Irritability would always lurk near the surface. At times he would be melancholy, suspicious, unreasonable, devious or cruel. The wonder is that his indomitable spirit fought back, that he had intervals of charm, gaiety, affection and generosity—that in the end he defeated the doctors, defeated his own nerves and got his hand back firmly on the tiller of his enterprises. He achieved this by a maneuver uniquely Pulitzeresque in its audacity, one that would take him years to perfect. He could not really cure himself. Therefore he undertook to cure his surroundings. What he did, with the determination of a convict scraping at stone prison walls with a spoon, was to encircle himself with an artificial world in which he could function with an efficiency unknown to most normal men.

III. EXIT COCKERILL

From Paris the party went to Menton, chartered the comfortable English steam yacht *Semiramis* and took it for a trial spin. As Hosmer wrote, "Mrs. Pulitzer had determined to accompany Mr. P. on this cruise but soon made the discovery that nature had not intended her for a sailor and she reluctantly withdrew." [11] Pulitzer embarked with guests including John Foord of *Harper's Weekly,* Lionel Earle, Charles Fearing and Dr. J. Madison Taylor of Philadelphia, with Hosmer and Ponsonby as secretaries.

For the first time he resolutely shut himself off from the World as they sailed to Barcelona, Gibraltar, thence eastward along the African coast. He devoted himself to conversation, cards (with huge markings), chess (with gigantic pieces) and fiction. When Hosmer read him George Eliot's *Romola,* he was so pleased with this Florentine romance that he went on with *The Mill on the Floss* and *Felix Holt* in quick succession. Since he could not abide ignorance or vagueness on any subject, the yacht's sizable reference library got heavy use, and a visit to the scattered ruins of Carthage precipitated a study of the Punic Wars and the career of Hannibal. By cable he closed the purchase of the *Katerina* in New York for $100,000. After Tripoli, Athens and Smyrna, the *Semiramis* turned westward again, Hosmer writing, "He had rigidly adhered to his purpose to keep out of his life all those sources of irritation that had induced his malady . . . but the old enemy, insomnia, was not conquered . . . other evils were mitigated but not cured." [12] In short, he was frustrated beyond endurance at his utter detachment from the World.

Returning to Paris early in May, he learned that Dr. Mitchell was sojourning in Rome. He made a quick trip there to uphold the proposition that since the World was his life's blood, cutting him off from it was more hurtful to his health than any activity would be. Dr. Mitchell took a firm negative. The doctor lost when Pulitzer got word through family channels that the World's management was slipping. There were rumors that Cockerill was not always at his desk and that Turner was often away on his yacht. It appears that both men believed that Pulitzer's separation from the paper was final, that their own responsibility was magnified and that they were now indispensable and deserving of greater rewards. Each felt that he had earned part ownership of the paper. Turner, in fact, made the mistake of demanding a substantial interest—an ultimatum that must have sent Pulitzer into a fury.

Cockerill's salary was now something over $15,000 a year, biggest of any nonshareholding editor in the land. Turner's could not have been far behind. The World had still not recovered from its slump since its week-day circulation mark of 188,000 in 1887 and was now averaging 157,000. It is not surprising that Pulitzer, feeling that his executives were taking advantage of his illness, took steps to show that no one was indispensable but the boss. In a flurry of communication with New York he dismissed Turner outright and ordered Cockerill back to the St. Louis Post-Dispatch. From St. Louis he brought John A. Dillon to replace Turner as business manager. Cockerill, whose post was unfilled for the moment, declined to return to Missouri, resigned in anger and became editor of the small Morning Advertiser, while Turner moved on to the New York Recorder, recently begun by James B. Duke. Pulitzer was so concerned by the upheaval that he sailed for New York June 3.

He arrived in the midst of a torrid spell that had him gasping. Although he did not visit his new building—had not yet been inside it—a parade of World officials again called at 55th Street. He plugged holes in his staff by making Ballard Smith acting editor in Cockerill's place and, *mirabile dictu,* moving Vermont-born George B. M. Harvey up to managing editor.

The persuasive, fun-loving Harvey was an able newsman, but he was only 27. Pulitzer, who always cross-examined his men with courtroom thoroughness, had taken a fancy to Harvey, who had three Pulitzer characteristics—a tendency to asthma, a genius for conversation and an infallible memory. After starting as a reporter at 20, Harvey had built up the Jersey edition and had gone on to such circulation-building exploits as the promotion of a Sunday World beauty contest among Connecticut factory girls, won by Katherine Rooney of Danbury with more than 20,000 votes. Pulitzer's regard for him had warmed into something near tenderness, as it would for other promising men who, in the end, usually disappointed him. Now Harvey was managing editor with almost autocratic power, since his contract read that he would not "be responsible to any person except Mr. Pulitzer." It was one of those arrangements whereby Pulitzer guaranteed a maximum of office intrigue and knife-throwing, for older hands such as Smith, Merrill and Dillon were not pleased by the sudden elevation of the stripling whose authority clashed with theirs and who could always go running to the boss.

Despite all the turmoil and the leveling off of the World, the lusty Evening World (now selling 152,000) and the Sunday World (234,000) made 1890 a year of record profits. Pulitzer began a lifelong series of benefits to education by giving five-year scholarships of $250 per annum to 12 deserving students at the City College of New York. With the aid of Whitney, the former Navy Secretary, he secured a crew for his yacht, which lay at a Hudson River pier and which he had rechristened *Romola* after his favorite novel. Alas—he went aboard to get the feel of her and almost swooned at the heat in the cabin. He abandoned the idea of voyaging to Europe in the *Romola,* called for the installation of ventilating blowers and ordered the crew to deadhead her to Leghorn, where he would take possession.

He sailed June 17, having spent exactly a week in New York—a week crowded with activity that would have dismayed Dr. Mitchell and which took its toll. "There was a partial loss of even the little eyesight that he possessed," Dr. Hosmer wrote.[13] Suffering from insomnia and spasms of asthma, he hurried to Wiesbaden to take the cure and consult Dr. Pagenstecher. Back in the Dome, by his order, every Monday at three the

World Council met in the persons of Messrs. Davis, Smith, Merrill, Dillon, Harvey and Carvalho, with Grozier as secretary. Complete reports were sent to the invalid in Germany covering their discussions of hundreds of subjects including the following:

Would it be advisable to send a World correspondent to Russia to report on the persecution of the Jews? . . . Should there be a story about Police Captain Brogan, who, it was felt, could be proved to be in the pay of brothel proprietors? . . . The World had published an analysis of James G. Blaine's urine to show him unfit for the Republican nomination in 1892, getting it in confidence from a physician. Now the Sun and other papers denounced the analysis as a fraud. How to prove its authenticity when the doctor's anonymity had to be protected? . . . A young man named Richard Harding Davis was writing such excellent fiction for the Herald that he ought to be secured by the World. . . . A playground for children should be included in the East River park project. . . . There was much discussion of New York press animosity against the World, hurtful in its endless slurs. It was decided to try to soothe the enemy with a series of flattering Sunday articles about competing newspapers and their editors.

From the invalid came a typical cablegram: "Special subject every Monday for Council. What public service, what popular agitation for World? Every councillor must think sharply." [14] Every councillor *did* think sharply, knowing that he was watching.

Ill as he was, he made the side trip to Leghorn, where the yacht awaited his pleasure. After spending one night aboard her, he doubtless uttered some of the more compound of his curses at his late Business Manager Turner. The *Romola,* blower and all, was as hot in Leghorn as she was in New York, and the dining quarters were inadequate. Indeed, in his unhappy condition probably no yacht in the world would have suited him. He gave up on the *Romola,* sending her back to New York, where she lay for several years in the Erie Basin before she was sold at a $75,000 loss to Venezuela for conversion as a gunboat.

He spent the summer under treatment at Wiesbaden, "always," as Hosmer noted, "in the shadow of the fear of absolute loss of sight." Yet he had the World and the council reports read to him. He sent a stream of messages of praise or reproof to New York. A vivid story about a train wreck so pleased him that he cabled Ballard Smith, who showed the cable to the writer, a new reporter named Charles E. Chapin. Chapin noted, ". . . The proprietor had directed him [Smith] to convey his personal compliments to me and to present in his name a substantial cash award." [15]

His increasing sensitivity to unexpected noise caused his entourage—Hosmer, Ponsonby and several servants—to shield him with all but their own bodies. He enjoyed the Wiesbaden concerts. He relished very mild cigars. He listened to readings of the novels of Thackeray, Trollope, the

Brontës and others, always impatient for the story to get on, bored by passages of exposition or description, consumed by his need for action, to "get to the point." Hosmer, familiar with most of the classics, skillfully edited them, passing over inert pages with brief transitions of his own. The aides had long since trained themselves to shut out annoyances that could throw Pulitzer into one of those tempests of frustration so hurtful to him and so certain to cause nights of fearful sleeplessness; but no man could anticipate them all, and there were times when he succumbed to rage or depression for no apparent reason other than the black fate that was seldom out of his mind.

He often felt that he was watching himself die. In October he sailed for New York to look to the World and start preparing his will.

IV. ESPIONAGE

There was building the legend of Pulitzer the monster who drank editors' blood, and another legend of Pulitzer the most generous if the most demanding of employers. Both had some truth, although he was increasing somewhat his intake of blood. Even before his worst illness, his Napoleonic certainty of his own genuis, along with the supreme importance he set on his World, made him fearful that his editors would commit errors or use their power for improper ends. To guard against this he invariably placed two jealous executives with overlapping authority in each top position so that one would watch and compete with the other and neither would feel indispensable. Now his mental torment and the swelling sense of suspicion that was part of his ailment had been increased by the Cockerill-Turner incident. He practiced efficient office espionage. He insisted on long, careful reports not only on developments at the World but on the capabilities and performance of individual members of the staff. When in Europe he called one executive after another to visit him, to discuss policy and also to pump each one for an exhaustive picture of doings in the Dome and for appraisals of his colleagues. One promising young sub-editor, Arthur Brisbane, who had come over from the Sun in 1890, sent regular reports on the usefulness of the staff, and of course there were others reporting on the usefulness of Brisbane.

"He adopted the Bennett system of espionage," observed the editor Julius Chambers, "which begets much falsehood and occasions some injustice. A reporter whom I saved from peremptory discharge . . . afterwards became a constant letter-writer to Mr. Pulitzer, and some of his messages, which . . . [were] repeated to me, were gorged with malicious misrepresentations and deliberate falsehoods."

The World man Charles Edward Russell, noting that professional backstabbing was common in metropolitan journalism, found it worst in the Dome: "What are called 'office politics' were in a state of highly irrational ferment. The news editor and the city editor were deadly enemies and engaged in a savage effort to ruin each other . . ." Because of Pulitzer's insistence on ideas from his men, Russell added, each of them kept a record of his suggestions "so that none might steal his credit."

"The office theory," observed Assistant Business Manager Don Carlos Seitz, "was that he liked competition and sought to gain advantage by the strivings of one man to outdo the other. If this was correct, it never worked; either hopeless deadlocks followed or the men divided their domain and lived peacefully."

"The plan was as unproductive as it was mean and clumsy," said the cartoonist McDougall. "It produced in time a condition of suspicion, jealousy and hatred, a maelstrom of office politics that drove at least two editors to drink, one into suicide, a fourth into insanity, and another into banking [*sic*]. Even those of his employees who were naturally kindly and of generous instincts were compelled in self-protection to resort to unseemly tricks." [16]

Behind it all was Pulitzer's conviction that calm destroys initiative, that competition begets inspiration. His ruthlessness arose from his demonic conception of the importance of the World (which of course was an extension of himself), to which the importance of any staff member was secondary. One pragmatic answer to the criticism of his methods is that they *did* work, that all three Worlds maintained their leadership. Another is that Chambers, Russell, McDougall and Seitz all admired him personally and stayed in his employ for years. His passion for absolute, unmortgaged ownership extended somewhat feudally to his men. He would have been surprised at any suggestion that there was intrigue or underhandedness in his efforts to learn all he could about his World and its staff from whatever source. On the contrary, in his enforced absence it was his *duty*.

His occasional savagery was balanced by his delight at good work. "In his search for talent Mr. Pulitzer was steadily driving up salaries," Russell observed. McDougall said, "J. P. never placed the least check upon my energies and he never uttered one word of . . . harsh criticism during the sixteen years I was with the *World* . . ." Once, when McDougall was tempted to accept a Herald offer of $75 weekly, Pulitzer regarded him with pain, then snapped, "I'll make it a hundred and ten dollars. You go away and be a good boy and don't bother about Bennett!"

The argument that Pulitzer's success came simply from luck in hiring good men is easily refuted since he found success for decades both in St. Louis and New York by employing a wide variety of good men. George Cary Eggleston, a devoted admirer, brushed away any such suggestion:

". . . The plans were his, just as the choice of lieutenants was, and the creative genius that revolutionized journalism . . . was exclusively that of Joseph Pulitzer."

John Cockerill wrote bitterly about the "absentee publisher" whose address nobody knew: "But the address of his bank is always known. Thither, on the first day of every month, large sums of money must be forwarded, and if they are not forthcoming, sharp criticism of the policy and management which have led to their diminution is sure to follow." Cockerill listened unmoved to a friend abusing Pulitzer, but when he suggested that the World's success was due to Cockerill, the editor raised a hand: "Say what you like about Pulitzer, but understand that he alone built up the New York *World*, as well as the St. Louis *Post-Dispatch*. He is the greatest journalist the world has ever known." And when Cockerill died in 1896 he had so far relented as to name his "faithful and sincere friend" Pulitzer as his executor.[17]

Chapter 3

Editor in Absentia

I. THE INTERROGATOR

In New York, Pulitzer worked at his will and also on an offer to President Seth Low of Columbia College to present money for the founding of a school of journalism—an offer the trustees eventually rejected. He felt, from his own reading of the World and also from office reports, that Ballard Smith was slipping. Another problem that plagued him as though the solution were his own responsiblity was the selection of the best possible Democratic nominee for President in 1892.

Two strong contenders were Whitney and Hill, both personal friends. Another friend, the crafty Manton Marble, was Hill's closest adviser in the White House sweepstakes. But in December at Elmira, Hill spoke in favor of free coinage of silver, and Pulitzer rebuked him severely for this heresy in the World. Hill was so alarmed that he sent Marble to conciliate the panjandrum of 55th Street. He did not get to see Pulitzer, who was choked with asthma, so he left a note, which did no good for the World continued to hammer at Hill's folly for days.

After Christmas with his family, Pulitzer went to Washington in January to cock an ear to the rising political overtures. When his asthma came near asphyxiating him, he fled in February to Jekyll Island, Georgia, the most exclusive of winter resorts, limited to 100 members, all of them millionaires, including J. P. Morgan, William Rockefeller, John Jacob Astor, E. H. Harriman and James J. Hill. This galaxy of plutocrats was said to represent the greatest concentration of wealth on the globe. Most of them favored Reid's mossy New York Tribune and would not be caught dead with a copy of the World. The fact that Pulitzer was a charter member showed his enormous strides in wealth and prestige in nine years. Jekyll Island offered him the quiet, privacy and benign climate that he needed to stay alive. Here he could mingle with robber barons whom he assailed relentlessly in his newspapers and whose infernal Republican tariff he abominated. Socially ambitious though he was, he sought companions on the score of ability and intelligence, shunned wealthy drones and in his illness had little to do with his neighbors. "During all this time," Hosmer wrote, "he was in constant communication with his staff in New York and suffered as much from labor and worry as though he had been in New York . . ."

Now Senator Hill committed his greatest political blunder, planning his famous "snap convention" of New York Democrats for February 22 at Saratoga—a convention traditionally held months later. His strategy was not only to win all of New York's delegates to the June Democratic convention in Chicago, but to do it so early as to kindle a Hill boom at other state conventions. The maneuver demonstrated his uncertainty of his real strength and also his weakness for intrigue. The wires were busy between Jekyll Island and the Pulitzer Building. A World editorial urged Hill to drop the idea, a later one warning him, "Don't overlook forty-three other States while seizing your own." Hill went ahead and bagged the state convention, and his political star waned thereafter.

Pulitzer headed north and on April 10 sailed for France where, after long thought in Paris, he made up his mind about the Democratic nominee. It had to be Cleveland, whatever his shortcomings. Hill, said the World, writing off the diamond rooster, was "an impossible candidate," adding, "If the Convention shall have the courage of its preference and nominate Mr. Cleveland, The World believes that he will have the largest vote ever cast for a Democratic candidate in this State." [1] Certainly a factor in Pulitzer's forgiveness of the presidential sinner was his stout insistence on the gold standard. The World's vigorous campaign was a telling factor in bringing the ex-President out of the shoals of political indifference and whipping up enough enthusiasm so that he was nominated.

Pulitzer simultaneously weighed Ballard Smith's complaint that some of his authority had been transferred to Carvalho. He replied that the reason was Smith's failure to carry out certain policy instructions: "Therefore . . . I was compelled to give somebody else power to execute them. Carvalho is instructed to show you utmost consideration—*and you can make the exercise of his power unnecessary*. . . . General supervision should mean the *initiative;* new ideas—suggestions and sleepless control and entire absorption in the paper." [2]

But Smith, earlier the recipient of salary increases and gifts, and who had written Pulitzer, "I thank you most sincerely for another proof of your constant and thoughtful generosity," was not sleepless enough for the master's taste. He was thinking of elevating George Harvey to the editorship and boosting Carvalho to top fiscal authority—something he would not do without probing each of them to the marrow. His standards, severe in any case, were raised to celestial perfection because of his own breakdown and possible death. To Harvey he wrote from Paris:

> Suppose [Smith] should take his favored trip around the world, or for any other reason should make both you and me unhappy by retiring from the paper; and suppose all his functions were to fall upon your young, delicate and inexperienced shoulders, and you had entire responsibility—
>
> What difference would such change make in your work, your hours, and the general progress of the paper? What changes, reforms, improvements, would you propose? What lines, ideas and faults would you alter? In short, would the paper be run differently if you had the chance? And how? What methods and men would you change?
>
> Please be as specific, suggestive and fearless as possible; and please remember that this is only a hypothetical case; that I do not wish to promise anything; and that I remain with kindest wishes, always your friend, J. P.[3]

Harvey's purely hypothetical reply was not sufficient to settle the matter, and Pulitzer ordered him to come to Europe as soon as he could tear himself away from the Cleveland campaign. In July he summoned Carvalho to Paris to study his brain. Carvalho's success with the Evening World was not proof enough, since Junior was a mere money-maker, not to be mentioned in the same breath with Senior. Pulitzer was a master interrogator who fired pointed questions at merciless speed, expected quick answers, searched for flaws, weaknesses and failures in logic. One can be sure that Carvalho was expected also to give a detailed picture of current operations at the World, and his studied opinions of its executives, including Harvey, as well as his own purely hypothetical plans for reform and improvement *if* he were elevated. Pulitzer always offered the best in wines, cigars and hospitality as he picked a man clean. He took his guest for a ride in the Bois as he grilled him, then asked how he liked the Bois. ". . . I answered that I had not seen it," Carvalho recalled, adding, "It is really an ordeal to put your brains against his," and summing up, ". . . His is the greatest mind by far I have ever known in my life." [4]

II. SACRIFICING PLEASURE

In June had come ominous rumblings from Andrew Carnegie's vast Homestead steel mill, where the Scotch ironmaster's cool deputy, Henry Clay Frick, proposed a wage reduction which his workers rejected. Frick thereupon locked them out, announced that he would reopen the plant July 6 with what labor he could get, and hired Pinkerton guards to protect the works. The infuriated workers charged the plant and took possession, driving out officials and guards.

Chief Editorialist William Henry Merrill had had his wrist slapped by Pulitzer for failing to pour enough acid on the McKinley tariff. Now he saw in the Homestead struggle a vivid example of the tariff that was supposed to raise wages, lowering them instead. "The only beneficiary of the tariff," said a Merrill editorial, "is the capitalist, Carnegie, who lives in a baronial castle in Scotland, his native land." The "foreigner" Carnegie had hired "Pinkerton Hessians," turned his plant into a fortress against American laborers, and this "is the kind of amity engendered by the tariff . . . in the most thoroughly protected State in the Union." The forcible seizure of the plant by the workers scarcely modified Merrill's stand. A platoon of Ballard Smith's reporters were in Homestead covering the conflict with news stories as favorable to the workers as the editorials:

> As Carnegie's millions have increased . . . so have the wages of his employes decreased. . . . Every year Carnegie has tried to reduce wages. . . . The man of millions acquired through the high tariff on steel is the foe of organized labor.[5]

Frick next hired 300 Pinkerton men to retake the captured plant. When they were towed up the Monongahela on a barge, the embattled workers, fighting from behind barricades, showered them with missiles, bullets and dynamite, sent out blazing rafts in an effort to burn the barge, and even brought an old cannon into play. The Pinkerton men fired back, but eventually were forced to retire after casualties on both sides mounted to ten killed and 65 wounded. The World covered the conflict with three pages of illustrated accounts sympathetic with the workers, one subhead describing the carnage as "The First Fruit of the Ironmaster's Resolve to Crush his Men." While Merrill's editorial deplored the violence, he blamed it largely on the steel company's importation of mercenaries.

Pulitzer, in Paris, was getting the World at least a week late. He learned of the violence on July 11 from the Paris papers and was horrified. To Carvalho, still with him, he said, "There have been as many killed and wounded in this labor war as in many a South American revolution."

How was the World handling it? He ordered an immediate cabled summary. When it was read to him he exploded. Angry though he was about the tariff, he saw instantly that the workers had overstepped in seizing the plant and holding it by violence. Pulitzer sent a careful cable tempering the World's stand, which changed overnight without embarrassing retractions. Its July 12 editorial incorporated much of his cable, saying in one cogent paragraph:

> There is but one thing for the locked-out men to do. They must submit to the law. They must keep the peace. Their quarrel is with their employers. They must not make it a quarrel with organized society. They must not resist the authority of the State. They must not make war upon the community.

When Carvalho sailed for America he was instructed to remove Smith as acting editor *without giving him another position*—a clear sign of imminent banishment—and Harvey was moved provisionally into the post.

In mid-July, Pulitzer, miserably ill and depressed, went to Wiesbaden for treatment. Harvey was still trying to break away and visit him, but with his expanded duties and the presidential campaign to worry about he was making use of one of those "charming bedroom suites" in the Pulitzer Building, and his wife had sailed with the plan of meeting him in Europe. On July 22 Pulitzer wrote to ask that Harvey bring full political information when he came, simultaneously repeating the invitation and subtly dismantling it:

> Please bring about 200 cigars, the very lightest that exist and, of course, the best, regardless of price. Have every box opened separately and examine them so as to make sure that each is the lightest shade existible.
>
> . . . Of course I assume that you will sail, but this is based upon the assumption that you would not sail if, by so doing, any great opportunity were neglected . . . I want to see you very much, but I must say frankly that it is not about "The Paper" half so much as because I think the trip will be a pleasure to you and its loss a disappointment. You are personally sympathetic to me, and I would enjoy your visit, you must know by this time. But I always sacrificed my pleasure for the paper, and I would like you to feel the same way. . . .[6]

Harvey chewed over that last paragraph, decided that it might be best to "sacrifice his pleasure," and his wife toured Europe alone. Pulitzer moved to Baden-Baden, where he was visited by Kate, Ralph and Joseph Jr., who found him tormented by insomnia. Whitney's 18-year-old daughter Pauline, touring the continent, stopped to see them at the spa, writing her parents that Pulitzer was "so very melancholy of late that they did not know what to do." Melancholy or not, he wrote Mrs. Harvey apologizing for her husband's failure to sail, putting her straight on her own importance as compared with the World: "My regard for you is so high that I cannot for a moment believe you would allow your private wishes to interfere with your husband's public duties . . ." He cabled Harvey urging that he spend a full 12 hours a day at his job, then followed this with a lenitive message through his secretary:

> Mr. Pulitzer particularly begs you to take care of your health and not to regard his twelve hour telegram strictly. He is not worrying as much as you seem to think, though he is very anxious that you should make a success in your present trial—as anxious, he says, as if his own boy Ralph were in your place.

Having expressed concern for Harvey's health, he began to undermine it with further instructions:

> After all, perhaps of fifty different essentials for improving the paper, none might be more immediately felt than if you were to be your own City Editor for a month—going into that department and through it and into every detail and minutia with the utmost vigor. If you could for a month or so arrange your work so as to have two or three hours every night to teach the different copy-readers, both at the City and the Telegraph desks, how to condense, how not to pad, how to eject all water, padding, rot, rubbish, etc., you would do the most necessary work.
>
> Every night you ought to go to bed feeling that you have cut down and condensed at least one page, if not two.
>
> Every night you ought to go to bed feeling that you have taught the other fellows something that will save you trouble in the future.
>
> Every night you ought to go to bed feeling that you are yourself developing as a great condenser.
>
> Every night you ought to go to bed feeling that the great work of an editor after all is not what he does himself, but what he teaches and trains others to do for him.[7]

Every night Harvey was going to bed (in the Pulitzer Building) feeling exhausted. For a sick man, Pulitzer was doing well at "teaching and training others."

Dr. Pagenstecher wrote Kate: "As to Mr. Pulitzer I should not advise to tell him the real character of the disease of the left eye, because it would take away every hope from him and would have a great and unfavorable impression on his total nervous system. In his present state of health every thing should be avoided that might affect his nervousness." [8]

For all that, he had flashes of humor. An English lady at the spa, a Miss Beere, observed his blindness and wrote, "Dear Mr. Pulitzer: . . . I hate to force myself in this way but honestly I should die if I couldn't get books and . . . I will, with the greatest delight, read whatever you like —on the terrace—in the reading room—anywhere. Tomorrow at three if you like an hour's reading command me." He sent the letter on to Kate, now in Paris, scribbling on it:

"My dear Kate: The enclosed shows the terrible danger I am exposed to. Save me! Come quick! So far still faithfully & devotedly J. P." [9]

III. NO CARDS, NO CHESS

Ballard Smith was given a farewell dinner at Delmonico's, at which a Pulitzer cable was read to him over the wine: "Grateful memories for loyal services, sorrow for parting and confident hopes for happy career. The *World* will always be a tender Alma Mater, proud of your talents, watchful of your fame and helpful of your high aspirations." [10]

It was at any rate a courteous way to swing the ax, and indeed it turned out that Smith was shifted rather than dismissed. After a vacation he became the World's chief correspondent in London. The shake-up in the Dome was completed when Carvalho was made assistant vice president with complete authority over expenses and flat orders to reduce them—a move that attenuated the power of Pulitzer's old colleague, Business Manager John Dillon, who was felt unsuited to the job. Dillon was transferred to the editorial page and replaced as business manager by John Norris, who came from a similar position at the Philadelphia Record. Supreme control of the World (under the supreme boss) was now vested in a triumvirate consisting of Carvalho, Harvey and chief editorialist Merrill, who were required to meet daily to decide policy and hatch ideas. To Harvey, Pulitzer proved with subtle logic that his criticisms, even when severe, were quite the opposite from derogatory and were in fact a flattering sign of confidence:

> . . . Right now, in the honeymoon, so to speak of your wonderful opportunity, I make a request of you. Don't be sensitive if I should in the future seem brusque, harsh, or even unjust in my criticism. I sincerely hope I never shall be; but if I should, remember that fault-finding is perhaps both my privilege and my weakness, that correction is the only road to improvement, and that my quick temper and illness are entitled to some consideration.
>
> As long as I find fault with you, I hope and believe in the use of trying to train, teach, and perpetuate you. When I find it hopeless to improve a man, I always quit the job and never criticize.[11]

By September he was in Paris, where he further defined for Harvey the qualities he expected: "You ought to realize that the originating, initiating, critical and suggestive functions make the real editor. . . . You ought to have six hours a day, if possible, to read the papers. These six hours' reading or skipping should give birth to suggestions, ideas and criticism, requiring again several hours of talk with the executive men of the staff, giving out ideas, instruction, criticisms, suggestions. Later you ought to have two or three hours a day for book reading to cultivate and equip your mind. . . ." [12]

Harvey found the honeymoon a difficult one, with all too few hours in the day. He worked so hard during the campaign that he was limp after Cleveland's victory, but more suggestions as to how he should improve each hour came from Pulitzer, who also showed his forgiveness of past errors in a cable to the President-elect:

> Cordial congratulations on glorious triumph it is the voice of the nations character and conscience for true Americanism [.] The next President is a democrat [.] [13]

He moved on to Monte Carlo for the winter. No longer able to play cards or chess, he relied heavily on Hosmer's readings and attended concerts given by the fine orchestra maintained by the Prince of Monaco. Hosmer wrote, "In going to the opera at Nice, he caught cold which kept him in bed two weeks and neutralized the advantages of the climate," adding disapprovingly, "Another detriment was the avalanche of reports from New York. No climate has any curative compensation for evils of that character." [14]

One effect of his failing eyesight was to stimulate a memory always prodigious, so that he carried in his mind an enormous mass of details little and big. He was annoyed at Cleveland for selecting the Bostonian Richard Olney (a corporation attorney!) as Attorney General. He was not forgetting that Zebulon R. Brockway, superintendent of the New York State Reformatory at Elmira, occasionally had inmates flogged. Brockway today is remembered as a pioneer penologist who introduced trade instruction for prisoners, but Pulitzer could not forgive those floggings and the World repeatedly demanded his removal, calling him "The Paddler." Nor was he forgetting that the World's tenth anniversary under his control was approaching, an event he wanted to mark with the biggest and greatest newspaper ever.

He sailed for New York (as always, with his entourage) on the *Majestic*, which gave him a soundproofed stateroom, arriving May 10 to be handed a copy of the anniversary issue, a record-breaking 100-pager dated May 7 which had sold 400,000 copies. It gave a good résumé of events of the past decade and did not fail to publicize the World and the new building, along with the information that the paper had spent $17,680,442.02 in the decennium. That very night Pulitzer gave a dinner for his top 20 men—among them Carvalho, Merrill, Harvey, Dillon, Norris, Brisbane and Eggleston—at Delmonico's. The precedence observed here was as significant as that at the White House. William Henry Merrill sat at Pulitzer's right, to show the importance of the editorial page, and S. S. Carvalho sat at his left to show the rising importance of Carvalho. Young Harvey had to make do with one remove from the throne. Many toasts were drunk, with the chief taking only an infrequent sip because liquor went quickly to his head. Boredom seized him as the affair dragged on past midnight in convivial gaiety he could not feel. At last Harvey teetered to his feet.

"Let us—ah—drink," he said, searching for someone who had not yet been toasted, ". . . to the—ah—King!"

Pulitzer's forbearance snapped. "Oh, damn it, Harvey," he growled. "No Kings! No Kings!" [15] The party broke up on this peevish note. Although he stayed in New York exactly three days, and there was the usual queue of World men calling at his home, he took note of the new edifice Bennett was building for his Herald at Broadway and 35th Street, a Stanford White copy of the Palazzo del Consiglio in Venice. It was two stories high—a calculated slap at Pulitzer's skyscraper. To his aide, Ralph

Blumenfeld, who protested that the location was too far uptown, Bennett replied, "Never mind about all that, Blumenfeld. Thirty years from now the *Herald* will be in Harlem and I'll be in hell; so what do we care?" [16]

Pulitzer also found time to improve his acquaintance with a promising young reporter, David Graham Phillips. The six-foot-three, Indiana-born Phillips, six years out of Princeton, had worked for the Sun until the World lured him away. The number of Sun men who went over to the World—Carvalho, Brisbane, Phillips and E. O. Chamberlin among them —showed Dana's high standing as a journalistic teacher and perhaps also reflected Pulitzer's pleasure in outbidding Dana, who still hurled editorial epithets at him. Phillips dressed perfectly, which Pulitzer could not see but which he certainly knew about, since he knew everything. Already dreaming of the novels that would later startle conformists, Phillips was well-read, intelligent and ambitious, a charming conversationalist. Invited to dinner at 55th Street, he impressed his host, who thought immediately of providing himself with a stimulating new companion.

"How would you like to go to London as correspondent of the *World*?" he asked.[17]

Phillips said that nothing could suit him better. When Pulitzer sailed on May 13, Phillips sailed with him in addition to the established caravan of Hosmer, Ponsonby and the servants. Pulitzer's obsessive search for interesting new companions reflected his need for conversation, the chief avenue of communication still open to him—reflected also his constant fight to avoid the resigned withdrawal of the invalid, his furious refusal to let slip the remnants of his own youth, his demand to be informed about what was going on in the world (especially *at* the World), his love for spirited discussion of these things, and his clear understanding that the way to achieve all this was to cultivate and challenge the young, the effective, the brilliant.

As they crossed the Atlantic, Phillips asked that his London dispatches be signed and was certain that Pulitzer, though usually adamant against any byline but his own, agreed.

Pulitzer was back late in June to lease the Louise Livingston estate, Chatwold, at Bar Harbor, Maine, for a four-month stay, during which the country sank into depression. Although the Chicago World Fair had opened in May, heralding a new world power confident of its destiny, the economy was slipping and the catastrophic panic of 1893 was on the way. To Democrats the trouble had its roots in the McKinley tariff and the silver purchase act of the Harrison administration, while the Republicans blamed it on Cleveland. When ill-paid workmen struck at Henry Havemeyer's sugar refineries in Brooklyn, a huge unit of the sugar trust which Attorney General Olney failed to prosecute, and Havemeyer called for police protection, the President learned that Pulitzer's forgiveness was a sometime thing. The World commented:

> But how admirable was Mr. Havemeyer's assurance in thus invoking the law quite as any law-abiding citizen might! He knows that this Sugar Trust of his is a lawless, criminal conspiracy . . . He knows that its very existence is a crime, and that the only reason those who maintain it were not long ago brought to trial . . . is that there has been an era of inefficiency in the Attorney-General's office during which only those criminals who wear shabby clothes and have no social position have been prosecuted.[18]

Editorialist Merrill, very cautious since his Homestead blunder, was getting almost daily instructions from the chief. A greater worry was young Harvey, who had been offered the consul-generalship in Berlin, a post he rejected after some hesitation which Pulitzer construed as an evidence of flagging World loyalty. Harvey had enemies in the feud-ridden Dome and there were rumors that he sometimes edited the paper by telephone from uptown clubs. Pulitzer pondered methods of inflaming his allegiance. He forbade any office-seeking in his staff, one of his memoranda reading:

> No man in The World office can ever run for public office, or be a candidate. The World must retain its independence. I do not want The World at any time ever to ask the appointment of any human being. . . . The character and integrity of the paper must be above suspicion.[19]

However, Zeus occasionally could not forbear breaking laws which plowboys must observe. At Bar Harbor lived a delightful couple, the Lawrence Townsends of Philadelphia. When Townsend mentioned his longing to be secretary of legation at Vienna, Pulitzer let the President know through Harvey that he would be pleased by the appointment, which was speedily made. In return, Cleveland's good friend Secretary of War Daniel Lamont said it would be appreciated if the World would accept the appointment of James J. Van Alen of Newport as Minister to Rome—a hint Harvey relayed to his chief.

Van Alen was a friend of Whitney's who had contributed $50,000 to Cleveland's campaign. Whitney had labored loyally for the President, who tendered him any Cabinet post he wished—an offer he declined because his wife was seriously ill, and indeed Flora Whitney had died in February. When he urged Van Alen as minister, Cleveland acceded. Van Alen, widower of the late Emily Astor, an Oxford graduate who had spent much of his life in England, was a notable eccentric whatever his qualifications, a monocle-wearing collector of antique English clocks and pewter, so charmed by the Tudor period that he laced his speech with locutions such as *'Zounds, egad, prithee, forsooth* and *varlet*.

The World editorially pointed out Van Alen's lack of "public service or prominence earned" and denounced the appointment as "an affront to all patriotic citizens." A World reporter came back from Newport with a scorcher, quoting a friend of Van Alen's as saying, "If Van Alen doesn't get that appointment, the Democratic party need expect no aid from gentlemen in the future. *He paid for the office like a gentleman . . .*" The story went on:

> Van Alen is short and fat. He prides himself on his resemblance to the Prince of Wales. . . . He wears a single eyeglass with a heavy string attached. He speaks with a weird bastard cockney, which fills Englishmen with wonder. It is the sort of English accent that a man with no talent for imitation might get from hansom-cab drivers and Strand barmaids. A prize-fighting gentleman of the Bowery was brought to Newport to train the fat off Van Alen. The fighting gentleman, called One-eyed Connelley, said he had never met a man who seemed less fit to be on earth than Van Alen. . . . His progress has been slow in spite of his wealth. The Ambassadorship for $50,000 is the greatest bargain of his life. . .

Whitney protested angrily in an interview in the Sun. Cleveland declared that Van Alen's contribution had nothing to do with the appointment and wrote a friend, "I think it would be a cowardly thing in me to disgrace a man because the New York *World* had doomed him to disgrace." [20] Van Alen waited until he was confirmed by the Senate, then resigned with dignity. Meanwhile Pulitzer perfected another educational benefaction, arranging to give free tuition plus $250 a year to deserving students at Horace Mann School and Columbia College. He also offered to pay the cost of bringing Oxford's crew to America to compete with Yale's—a proposition the Yale men, who perhaps disliked his politics, declined with thanks. And his World, along with every other newspaper but one, was missing an astonishing news event within a few hours of Park Row.

On June 18 a malignancy was discovered in President Cleveland's mouth. What with his loathing for the keyhole press, and with Wall Street already palpitating, he wanted no rumors to add to the economic uneasiness. With a small retinue sworn to silence, he boarded the yacht *Oneida,* owned by his friend E. C. Benedict, for what was taken to be a presidential pleasure cruise. On June 30 as the *Oneida* sailed up the Hudson, a delicate operation was performed. The yacht then steamed around Manhattan and up to Cape Cod, where Cleveland submitted to a second, smaller operation July 17. By September he had recovered. Not a word of these momentous doings appeared in the World or any other New York newspaper. Only the Philadelphia Press got hold of the story, and was denounced as a lying sensation-monger just as the World had been for its publication of Blaine's urinalysis.[21]

Chapter 4

The Jones Problem

I. CONFUSION IN THE DOME

Now Carvalho and Business Manager Norris were not speaking, communicating only through memoranda. Pulitzer straightened this out by reducing Norris' powers. He was still pondering plans to infuse more fire and labor into Harvey, who for a time was out with pneumonia. He looked for another editor to place next to Harvey in that uncomfortable status of divided control that he felt stimulated creative effort. He was adept at pushing a man to the very limit of his endurance without quite pushing too far, but here he committed a blunder that calls to mind a later liberal who admitted that he seldom pulled a boner, but when he did it was a beaut.

He lit on "Colonel" Charles H. Jones, a 45-year-old Floridian who had gone to St. Louis in 1888 to replace William Hyde (of evil memory) as editor of the lagging Missouri Republican. Jones had created a stir by his aggressive editorship, increasing circulation and attacking Governor David R. Francis of Missouri so bitterly that the two men came to blows in the street. Certainly these two factors—the circulation increase and the fisticuffs—were important to Pulitzer. Such a man must have a dash of the Cockerill in him. Jones had visited New York to see the Pulitzer Building open, and may have talked with the proprietor then. Pulitzer now summoned him to Bar Harbor and cross-examined him for a week.

If Pulitzer had weaknesses, they were for convincing talk and aggressiveness. Of Jones it was said, "His belief in himself was monumental and was matched by his ability to convince others. Else how . . . was he able to do what no other human being had done or did afterwards—hypnotize Joseph Pulitzer [?]" [1] A red-hot Democrat, he was a familiar in Washington and at the political conventions and assumed to speak for the party in the whole Southwest. The bad, the impossible thing about Jones was his leaning toward Populism and free silver. Pulitzer felt he had Jones straightened out on that. Another mistake was the owner's underestimation of the resentment of his staff at the elevation of an outsider, a man unfamiliar with New York, over the heads of faithful veterans. With his incurable suspicions that his "regulars" were growing lazy and might be dividing up the World domain among themselves, it is a safe guess that he wanted an outsider who had no staff connections or friendships and would be loyal to him only, at least for a time.

Late in July Jones traveled to the Pulitzer Building bearing a blue envelope containing his mandate to supreme power. Carvalho, until then top man, could scarcely believe his eyes. Harvey was as mortified. Jones, a small man with elaborate side-whiskers and pompous mannerisms, instantly became the target of a universal plot to make him look silly. He soon left for Washington, where Cleveland's forces were organizing to repeal the Sherman silver purchase act—an effort in which Pulitzer was heartily in accord with the administration. The World's Washington bureau head, John H. Tennant, who had sent frequent dispatches forecasting repeal, was amazed when Jones wrote a 4,000-word polemic *against* repeal and ordered him to file it, which Tennant did with great forebodings.

When this treason reached New York, Carvalho communicated with Bar Harbor and killed every line of the dispatch. Jones returned to New York breathing fire, but by now Pulitzer had clipped his wings and the World ardently supported repeal, which later became law. Jones's humiliation was celebrated by every loyal World man, and he became the butt of insults such as only aroused journalists can invent. In the Sunday World, for example, McDougall drew a cartoon of a boardwalk flirtation that included "a very accurate portrait of . . . Mrs. Jones." Pulitzer already regretted his choice, but Jones had an ironclad contract and he continued with reduced authority.

Where did all this leave Harvey? In August, Pulitzer summoned him to Bar Harbor, where he spoke of his plans for Harvey while the latter recovered the strength lost in his bout with pneumonia, one of them being that Harvey should remain with him and take at his dictation a book on journalism. But Harvey, disgruntled by the Jones appointment, appalled him by saying, "But, Mr. Pulitzer, I have resigned!" [2] Pulitzer always disliked to have anyone make plans that interfered with his own, and doubtless there was a tempest before Harvey left, later to attain riches as a lieutenant of William C. Whitney and then as president of Harper and Brothers. From London, where David Graham Phillips had scored a brilliant beat on the accidental sinking of the British battleship *Victoria*, came more treason, Phillips sending a cool note to "Dear Mr. Pulitzer":

> As the office still has no order from you to let my signature stand at the end of my letters, I have begun to think that I am laboring under some sort of misapprehension. I have it clearly in mind that . . . you gave an affirmative answer to my request that my letters should be signed.[3]

Pulitzer replied courteously that he was not yet quite satisfied with Phillips' dispatches, to which Phillips astonished him by responding, "the management of the *Sun* and the *Herald* have formed a rather more favorable opinion," and resigning. Yet Pulitzer so liked the young man that when he returned to New York he was persuaded to rejoin the local World staff and to push a crusade near the chief's heart.

The anti-trust act for which he had fought so long had fizzled and all but died. Rockefeller had made pious gestures toward dividing Standard Oil into 20 independent and nonmonopolistic segments but had been easily defeated. Holders of Standard's 972,500 shares liked their profitable stock just the way it was and refused to turn it in for conversion into proportionate shares in the constituent companies. Standard decided it could not force them to do so and quietly forgot about the Sherman act. In the end the trust remained intact, firmly under Rockefeller control from his office at 26 Broadway—scarcely a warning to other trusts. No federal action was taken against this clear illegality, and the prosecution of a few small trust offenders was feeble and unsuccessful. At the World, Phillips was soon writing a series exposing the misdeeds of one trust after another, calling Attorney General Olney's attention to them, ending each article, "Such, Mr. Olney, are the facts, and here, sir, is the law"—then quoting from the anti-trust act. The President twice wrote Pulitzer to argue that his interpretation of the law was erroneous. One of Pulitzer's continuing quarrels with the administration was this failure of any really aggressive prosecution of the trusts. He would have to gnaw his nails until the 20th century, when relief would come from an astonishing quarter.

Pulitzer sailed October 27, found the noise of Paris unbearable and soon fled to a villa at Nice facing the sea. By now the problem of arranging for his travels and finding suitable quarters for him was complex enough so that a new functionary was added to his personal staff, George H. Ledlie, who had come from the Post-Dispatch as Dillon's assistant. Ledlie became an expert on European rentals. When Pulitzer wanted a house in a given area, Ledlie would explore it, take the specifications of the best available, furnish photographs and minute descriptions of them and their surroundings, and see that necessary alterations (especially elaborate soundproofing) were made before the master took occupancy. He would be in difficulties if the plumbing gurgled or if there were barking dogs nearby. Another Ledlie chore was to be on the lookout for new secretary-companions, since Pulitzer always wanted more.

One candidate was the journalist Charles Whibley, Whistler's brother-in-law, who had gone to Pulitzer's Paris apartment for an interview and had been so unlucky as to upset and break a costly Persian jardiniere. This disqualified Whibley. Another Briton, young Alfred Butes, had better control of his feet and was admitted to membership in the retinue. Butes, who had seen service in Africa, was discreet, intelligent and a fine stenographer, and he speedily became a Pulitzer favorite. A Riviera companion for six weeks was chief editorialist Merrill, who called it "the longest and most delightful vacation of my life." Another temporary companion that winter was Arthur Brisbane, who also arrived at the boss's order and expense, eager and athletic at 29, hard-working, filled with some of his late father's radical idealism—bursting also with ideas for circulation. Pulitzer had given up riding because of his dim vision. Brisbane persuaded him to try a gentle horse, rode beside him as guide, and thereafter Pulitzer resumed riding for the rest of his life.

It need not be said that the two men discussed the World and the Jones problem. To Harvey, Pulitzer wrote reproachfully about the "apparently pangless severance of our relations," adding, "If you happen to have any use for money, I shall be glad to send you some," a few weeks later making the ultimate concession: "I am not afraid to go even a step further and to say that while the lamp still holds out to burn, my favorite Prodigal may return."[4] To this Brisbane added in his own letter to Harvey, "If you send him [Pulitzer] the right sort of cable, you can have your old job back, if you want it."[5] Harvey, cherishing his freedom, politely declined but remained a lifelong Pulitzer friend.

Perhaps the Jones problem added choler to one of Pulitzer's stormy spells. Dr. Hosmer, who was reporting regularly to Kate about her husband's condition, wrote of fits of anger in which he would turn on anyone at hand. Hosmer, apparently piqued at his chief's liking for Butes, observed, "when a little pet-secretary of the amusing variety gets absolute control of a great man's mind—the old serious donkey style of secretary must take a back seat & shut up. . . . It seems to me impossible to stand the winter in the difficult circumstances & I may have to get out. In that case I shall ask for a position on the paper. Will you support my application with your illimitable influence [?]" He added later, "J.P.'s mind is perfectly normal—as to his getting into a rage & being wrong—He has probably done that all his life. But his immeasurable fondness for his new friend is a symptom worth attention."[6]

Another disturbing factor was young Ralph's heart condition and a siege of pneumonia that threatened his lungs and sent him to Switzerland for a year's recuperation. Pulitzer joined him and Kate at St. Moritz only briefly, for long association with his family upset both his work schedule and nerves, and in April he moved to Ragatz to try the mineral waters of the Pfäfers-Bad. He invariably avoided Vienna, where his brother Albert spent much of his time—Albert, who like himself suffered from insomnia and added to this "an unbearable sensitiveness to the slightest changes in temperature and light." Pulitzer, who had relatives in Vienna and knew all about Albert's maladies, must have been chilled by their resemblance to his own. At Ragatz he received from Chauncey Depew a copy of his *Life and Later Speeches,* which embarrassed him because the World had been assailing Depew and the Central again. He sidestepped blame in writing Depew:

> It is like greeting an old friend to see, as I dimly can, the excellent portrait frontispiece. I thank you heartily for the remembrance, which gives me real pleasure. It is a splendid book. . . . It is, I hope, not necessary to say that I had nothing to do with some very stupid paragraphs relating to you which have appeared in my beloved *World.* I have knocked the perpetrators down with a little cable club, and hope that there will be no further lunacies in this line.[7]

Concerned about Ralph, he sent Dr. Hosmer first to Davos, then across the world to Colorado Springs to see whether their climate and altitude might be beneficial for the boy. Both were rejected and Ralph stayed in St. Moritz.

II. CONFUSION IN ST. LOUIS

Seldom did a week pass that the World was not favored with an assault by a less successful rival. The Times, in debt and dying with only 10,000 circulation, pronounced the World guilty when Julius Marcus and Juliette Fournier committed suicide by mutual consent in Central Park and a clipping from a Sunday World series on suicide was found in Marcus' pocket. The godless Robert Ingersoll was among those who had contributed, defending the individual's right to suicide. The World had misquoted Ingersoll, said the Times. When Ingersoll declared he had been correctly quoted, the Times grew even angrier at the correct quotation of such an infidel and resorted to the device of publishing a "subscriber's letter" laying the double death at the door of the World's "satanic journalism" and citing other crimes:

> It clamors for a Sabbath of "swimming, baseball, music, and beer for little and big." It . . . has made police spies of young women and sent girls to "investigate" social crimes. It . . . commanded a young woman of education to attend the cruel flagellation of a thief in Delaware in order that she might describe "piquantly" the spectacle of his agony and shame. [It] employed a young woman of education to simulate a thief, to be arrested on the charge, and to record, gloatingly, the indecencies and inhumanities of such an experience. . . .

Another "reader's letter" praised the Times's attack, demanding, without mentioning names, "Is there no law by which the leprous Jew can be punished?"[8]

Leprosy was one of the few ailments he could not claim. By June he was back in New York, retreating quickly to the leased estate at Bar Harbor. Chatwold faced Frenchman's Bay, its salt air soothed his asthma, and excursions on his launch provided the movement he needed. If there was incongruity in the spectacle of America's foremost journalistic spokesman for the common man joining the aristocratic Bar Harbor set, it did not bother him. However he might scoff at fashion, the Pulitzers were part and parcel of fashion, and it had to be said that Bar Harbor had little of the gaudy splendor of Newport. Among Pulitzer's friends who were regulars were the tweedy Dr. S. Weir Mitchell and the J. Madison Taylors. Others who lent intellect were three college presidents, Charles William Eliot of Harvard, Seth Low of Columbia and Daniel Coit Gilman of Johns Hopkins, as well as a covey of diplomats including Pulitzer's friend Baron Hengelmuller, minister from Austria-Hungary. From 1891 the Pulitzers were listed in the New York Social Register, which mentioned the master's membership in the Manhattan, Reform, Racquet and American Yacht clubs.

The nation was in terrible straits. There were foreclosures, bank failures, three million unemployed, and Coxey's army was on its erratic journey. Cleveland's efforts at tariff reform had been emasculated by 408 amendments, saving the sugar trust and other malefactors. With gold being hoarded, the administration had floated a $50,000,000 bond issue for popular subscription, and the sale lagged so badly that Treasury Secretary Carlisle had to plead with New York bankers, who bought the remainder and saved the government from humiliation. Near Chicago the Pullman Company lowered wages, and when most of its workers struck the company laid off the rest and shut up shop. Eugene Debs' American Railway Union asked arbitration—a request Pullman icily rejected.

The union countered by refusing to handle Pullman cars—a move that tied up 24 railroads centering in Chicago, began to paralyze transportation eastward and westward and caused serious delays in the mails and in vital freight shipments, with total stoppage a frightening possibility. It was the most menacing strike the nation had ever seen. As the tie-up spread to 27 states and territories with occasional violence despite Debs' stern order against it, the general reaction in the East was one of fear. Hindsight suggests that Cleveland's best immediate move would have been to bring every ounce of presidential prestige and pressure to persuade the employers to arbitrate, as Theodore Roosevelt did so brilliantly in the coal strike eight years later. Cleveland saw only his duty to maintain the mails and interstate commerce. He placed much faith in the tough Attorney General Olney, and on July 2 the government secured a blanket injunction prohibiting interference with trains.

Pulitzer, with his horror of outlaw violence, supported the President. Not so Colonel Jones, who freed himself from his shackles long enough to write (and publish) a World editorial attacking the injunction, embarrassing in its departure from policy.[9] Summoned to Bar Harbor, he stoutly defended his views. How to jettison Jones? An obvious solution would have been to strip him of all authority and let him clip exchanges until his contract expired, but Pulitzer was in one of his thrifty moods when he balked at throwing money away. Indeed his steps from beginning to end of the matter are inexplicable, entirely at variance with his usual swift dismissal of anyone questioning his authority. Hitting on the idea of shipping Jones to St. Louis, he offered him a half-interest in the Post-Dispatch for $300,000, for which he would pay only $80,000 down and the rest out of profits. Jones rejected the proposition and returned to the Dome, where he was worse than useless.

Meanwhile Cleveland sent troops to Chicago, the strikers countering by blocking tracks, burning hundreds of boxcars and six World Fair buildings. A World editorial reflecting the boss said in part:

> The World appeals to the reason of the working-men. It asks them what just cause of offense it is to them that the Federal and State troops are employed to sustain the law, to guard property against destruction, to protect commerce and the mails? [10]

After the arrest of Debs, the strike soon collapsed, an event that joined with hard times and the silver issue in turning many Western Democrats toward Populism. In New York, Superintendent Brockway at Elmira was charged with "brutal" punishment of inmates, and although a commission appointed by Governor Roswell P. Flower exonerated him, the World resumed its campaign for the removal of The Paddler. Senator Hill had decided to replace his man Flower and run for governor himself that fall. With Democratic support clearly waning he knew he had a hard fight on his hands. He summoned the rising young Democrat George B. McClellan, who was now president of the New York City Board of Aldermen, and sent him posthaste to Bar Harbor to solicit the World's support.

Reaching Chatwold October 20, McClellan was met by young Ponsonby. McClellan, whose memory of it may have been colored by bitter enmity toward Pulitzer, wrote, "Pulitzer always had as his private secretary some poverty-stricken gentleman whom he always treated abominably. He paid one hundred dollars a week, a large salary in those days, in return for which the secretary was required to take smiling the lashings of Pulitzer's very active tongue." Soon Pulitzer came in on Ponsonby's arm and, according to McClellan, "He began proceedings by telling Ponsonby to bring cigars, and on the latter bringing the wrong cigars cursed him up hill and down dale." When the two men were alone, McClellan gave Pulitzer Hill's promise that in return for World support, he would see that Governor Flower removed Brockway.

"I am surprised that Hill should make such a proposition," Pulitzer said. "He knows that I am not for sale, nor is the *World* for sale."

McClellan assured him that the senator was incapable of such a thought. Finally Pulitzer said, "I feel that Brockway must be got rid of at all costs, and I have always liked Hill. You can tell him that I never make a political bargain. At the same time if he agrees that Brockway shall go, I agree to support the Democratic ticket." [11]

The World *did* support Hill that November, but unenthusiastically, mostly out of opposition to the Republican candidate (and Pulitzer's friend), the millionaire banker Levi Morton. Disaster befell the Democrats, for Hill lost by 156,000 votes, the Democratic majority in the House was replaced by a huge Republican majority, and the Republicans ruled the Senate. A feeble ray of light was the election of the Republican-Fusion William L. Strong, whom the World had supported, as mayor of New York, but the signs were clear that the Democratic party was in deep trouble.

Although Governor Flower remained in office until the year's end, he did not remove The Paddler. Was Hill taking revenge for the World's lack of fire? Pulitzer waited, but Brockway clung to his post for another six years and Hill thereafter had to get along without World help.

Late in 1894 Albert Pulitzer arrived from Europe and sold his New York Journal for $1,000,000 to John R. McLean, wealthy publisher of the Cincinnati Enquirer. Since McLean was a staunch Democrat with silver inclinations, Joseph Pulitzer now had a New York rival he would have to watch. He bought the Chatwold estate and planned extensive renovations as he grappled with the Jones problem. In December, at his urging, Jones went to St. Louis to make a survey of the Post-Dispatch, returning with numerous suggestions. Pulitzer, now at home in New York for Christmas, wrote him to urge a longer stay in St. Louis. Jones visited him Christmas morning—a meeting at which they reached substantial accord, Jones resigning from the World as of January 1 and agreeing to take charge in St. Louis provided he could have "absolute control" backed up by a majority stock interest. Pulitzer left in relief for Jekyll Island December 26. A few days later he blew up when he received the contract drawn by Jones' lawyer, for by its terms Pulitzer would not only lose control but would supply the cash for most of Jones' purchase of 5,003 of the Post-Dispatch's 10,000 shares of stock—in effect paying for his own loss. Jones soon joined him at the island, where they hammered out a new agreement: Jones would buy only a one-sixth interest with his $80,000, gradually accumulating more, but from the start Jones would have *full editorial control.*

No sooner had he decamped than Pulitzer began to fret. Could Jones be trusted in full charge of the Post-Dispatch? In mid-February he sent Carvalho to St. Louis with a new plan and an amended contract cunningly devised to limit Jones' control. This was unwise, for Jones lost his temper, showed Carvalho the door and ran amuck. He discharged Editor George S. Johns, Advertising Manager Steigers, Managing Editor Florence D. White and several other Pulitzer veterans, brought in his brother as business manager and thereafter ran the Post-Dispatch as a strictly Jones newspaper, supporting free silver. Pulitzer, perhaps reflecting how much better and cheaper it would have been simply to let Jones warm a swivel chair until his contract expired, gave World jobs to the ousted men and brought suit to recover his control of the Post-Dispatch.[12]

Chapter 5

Loneliest Man in the World

1. PIGGERY NERO, PIGEON NELSON

In May, Pulitzer sailed for England, leasing Moray Lodge in Kensington for a short stay. The shrieking of the royal peacocks in Kensington Gardens upset him, and he tried vainly to have them silenced or removed. To save wordage and insure secrecy in his messages to the Dome, he devised an elaborate code, taking pleasure in indulging his fancy. Himself, with no false modesty, was "Andes." Carvalho was "Los," Merrill "Cantabo," Brisbane "Horace," Norris "Anfracto," Dillon "Guess," and Don Seitz "Gulch," while scores of other functionaries had names ranging from "Pinch" (Chapin) to "Grenade" (Tennant). The code ran to the G's and grew to include many non-World personages, President Cleveland becoming "Graving," William Jennings Bryan "Guilder," J. P. Morgan "Gadroon" and William McKinley "Guinea," Boss Croker being traduced with "Gorgon." Governor Levi Morton would have been wounded to learn that he was "Mediocrity." The Democratic party was a tender "Gosling," the Republican party properly "Malaria." The cipher further expanded to take in hundreds of much-used business terms, circulation being "Curate," advertising "Potash," advertising revenue "Navarre," gross earnings "Nero," net earnings "Nelson," gain "Piggery," and loss "Pigeon." [1] Thus Pulitzer could cable the World:

"SEND CURATE SENIOR JUNIOR SENIORITY. EXPLAIN PIGGERY NERO BUT PIGEON NELSON." In New York, where the code book grew to great thickness, it was known that he wanted circulation figures for the World, Evening World and Sunday World, and wished to know why gross earnings went up while net earnings sagged.

In London as elsewhere he continued his incessant "reading," not only of the World and other papers but of novels, plays, biographies and histories, steadily adding to his store of learning. Often he went to the theater, hearing Henry Irving, Beerbohm Tree and becoming friendly with the British comedian Charles Wyndham. But playgoing usually disappointed him since he could not see but heard acutely, being annoyed by coughs and rustling programs—annoyed most of all if the drama's action was slow and often leaving in disgust after the first act. His secretaries became accustomed to seeing only first acts. He could never understand why a drama or novel should not move with the Gatling-gun staccato of a World news story.

This was the London of the 76-year-old Queen Victoria, the 54-year-old Prince Edward (whom Pulitzer had met at Wiesbaden), the aging Whistler, the young Shaw, the crippled Henley who wrote, "I Am the Master of My Fate"—a verse that Pulitzer could ponder with sympathy. Oscar Wilde's shocking trial was still the town talk, and he had just gone to prison. Pulitzer became acquainted with the astonishing radical Henry Labouchere, who published the muckraking magazine *Truth,* sat in Commons and had the audacity to urge that the queen's allowance be cut. Indeed, "Labby" was something of an English Pulitzer without nerves. Pulitzer took tea with the dynamic, 30-year-old Alfred Harmsworth, who had run the obscure *Answers* up to a million circulation weekly and now was beginning to form the biggest newspaper-periodical combine yet seen. To Harmsworth he said sadly, "I am the loneliest man in the world. People who dine at my table one night might find themselves arraigned in my newspaper the next morning." [2]

True, he had at times felt forced to attack dozens of friends—Schurz, Whitney, Hewitt, Belmont, Morton, Depew, Hill, Morgan and many others. But the loneliness, though real, was instead the terrible isolation of the helpless megalomaniac and egocentric, the perfectionist who loved to criticize, an isolation he tried all the rest of his life to break and failed. He was known in London as he was known wherever he went—as the semiblind genius who surrounded himself with secretaries and kept looking for more, the invalid who worked like a horse and jumped at the creak of a hinge. D. S. MacColl, the art critic, was offered a Pulitzer secretaryship but recoiled at the slavery of it. Whistler himself, in one of his less tasteful sallies, said that one of a secretary's duties was "to pick up Pulitzer's eyes that had a way of falling out and getting lost on the floor." [3]

So the search for secretaries became an international joke, the foible of a wealthy eccentric. To Pulitzer, with his need for mental action and his abnormal curiosity, it was no joke but a necessity, something absolutely required if he was to ward off the horrors. Perhaps few of his paid companions understood that their function was largely therapeutic. The "regulars" such as Hosmer and Butes stayed on to keep his ever-moving household operating efficiently. The new ones came and went to supply him with different voices, emotions and mental challenges. The pathos of it is that he was starved for friendship and affection and kept searching for it in his companions, certainly aware that affection could not long survive his megalomania and compulsive criticism but seeking it nevertheless. To one of them he wrote, ". . . How much I would give if I could only deceive myself with the thought that my anxiety to attach you to me as my long lost and longed for friend is not entirely unappreciated" [4]—words themselves revealing the egocentricity that frustrated him.

He even tried dogs as companions, but they failed him in their inability to talk. He regarded conversation as a high art embodying sound logic and great learning, and since his own logic and learning were profound, the demands he made were immense. To converse with him was to submit to a drumfire of questions during which the companion felt his comprehension and knowledge being probed to lengths that could grow uncomfortable—this without any comparable unbosoming on the part of Pulitzer, who always showed flashing intelligence but seldom revealed himself deeply. Or it might take the form of a debate about politics or about Shakespeare—a debate in which the companion found his every word weighed instantly and often felt himself backed into a corner from which there was no escape. His brain-picking could be so intensive that only the most accomplished and emotionally stalwart secretaries could stand it. Even they wore out and had to have occasional vacations.

Since he was capable of sparkling wit, it was strange that his perception of the humor of others was obtuse. He could send with ease but receive only with difficulty. This defect took friends aback, for he loved an amusing story that he could understand, and often they would go to considerable effort to bring a jest to its triumphant conclusion only to find him still waiting in puzzlement for the denouement. His failing imposed a greater hardship on his secretaries, who were required to lighten the day occasionally with a joke. They gathered amusing stories from the journals with a strict eye for those in which the humor was easily apparent. Otherwise they took a sharp rebuke for wasting his time with a story that had no point at all.

Perhaps worst of all were those occasions when Pulitzer sank into depression and sat in wordless agony or hostility, saying nothing while the secretary vainly tried to keep the "conversation" going. He *had* to keep it going, had to continue speaking without response, for the master could not stand empty silence and would explode if he stopped. Joseph Pulitzer was indeed the "loneliest man in the world," but not only because of the independence of his newspapers.

II. THE ROOSEVELT SALOON CRISIS

In July "Andes" returned to spend the summer at Chatwold, where a $100,000 edifice had risen to supplement his artificial world. It was a four-story, 40-foot-square granite building, painstakingly soundproofed, immediately called the Tower of Silence by the secretaries. His magnificent living room took up most of the main floor, his bedroom and those of the secretaries were above, a huge veranda faced the sea, and the whole basement was a swimming pool where water was pumped in from the bay and steam-heated. In misty weather the foghorn at the lighthouse drove him frantic. His own tranquility being more important than the safety of ships, he tried vainly to have the government silence the horn.

In his illness and preoccupation he had lost touch with some of his friends, among them Thomas Davidson, who had not written since 1887 and indeed thought Pulitzer was living permanently in Europe. A note from Davidson brought a prompt invitation that he visit Chatwold not only for a rest but to advise on a college for Ralph:

> When I did not hear from you for eight years I did worry a good deal about your silence, thinking it most strange. I did suffer more during those eight years by loss of sight, sleep, health and activity than in all my previous existence. I do feel very much like seeing you and talking over those happy days of poverty.[5]

The panic was now so severe that it seemed to affect everybody but Pulitzer, who carried some World advertisers who were unable to pay cash. The remedy of course was to elect in 1896 a sound Democrat who would crack down on the tariff and the trusts—not one of those Populist simpletons who shouted about silver. The widowed William C. Whitney steamed up to Bar Harbor on his yacht *Columbia*, and although he said he was not a candidate one can be certain that he was a guest at Chatwold and that Pulitzer urged him to get into the race. The World boosted him, canvassing 30 important New York editors and announcing that 26 of them were Whitney men. At the same time, Pulitzer experienced his second encounter with Theodore Roosevelt—"Glutinous" in the World code.

Roosevelt, after six able years on the Civil Service Commission, had joined the four-member New York City Police Board under the reformist Mayor Strong and had promptly run away with the board. Now almost 37, he was clean-shaven but for an aggressive mustache, as impulsive and dynamic as ever. "His teeth are big and white," noted the World, "his eyes are small and piercing, his voice is rasping. . . . His heart is full of reform."[6]

He stopped the political sale of police appointments, demanded merit, prowled the streets at night and hauled in on departmental charges every bluecoat he found dozing or drinking forbidden beer. The effect was salutary, but he stirred up a hornet's nest when he dried up the town on Sundays.

A traditional source of graft lay in the old excise law decreeing the closing of saloons on the Sabbath—a law whose practical effect was to close only the front doors. The great brewers, who owned most of the big saloons, paid the party bosses handsomely for winking at side-door Sunday trade, while owner-operated pothouses paid the beat men directly. Although Roosevelt had no liking for this law, he was incensed by its subversion into police corruption. He decided that the only way to stop it was to enforce the law rigidly—lock up every saloon on Sundays.

His program began Sunday, June 23—a day that saw the small steamer *Sarah* appear on the Harlem River with a huge sign: "No Whisky or Beer Aboard, but Plenty of Water. Try the Water." Groups of men who rowed out to try the water were followed by three uniformed policemen, but the *Sarah* steamed away from them, only to return later and be boarded by plainclothesmen who made arrests. By July a New York Sunday was insufferable to the convivial. Ferries to Hoboken and other Jersey oases were jammed. New York's many Germans, who liked lager with music on Sundays, were outraged, and the Staats-Zeitung assailed Roosevelt as a desecrator of the Sabbath. Politicians embarrassed Glutinous by resurrecting ancient blue laws requiring the Sunday closing of delicatessens, flower shops and icehouses. Would the commissioner enforce these laws as he was sworn to do? Roosevelt, though troubled, said he would. He closed ice-cream resorts, suppressed Sunday pinochle games, and one detective arrested a peddler who sold him five cents' worth of violets.

Although the World had applauded Roosevelt's first reforms, Pulitzer sided with the corrupt political machines and the liquor interests on the Sunday issue, though from different motives. He was anxious to see Mayor Strong's admirable administration defeat the bosses on the larger issues. He always opposed sumptuary legislation as an infringement of personal liberty, and his strictly secular attitude toward Sunday was that it was the one day in the week when the people were free to enjoy themselves. Mayor Hewitt had insulted the Irish; now Strong was offending the Germans and many others. The Sunday law was undemocratic and detested because it permitted clubs and hotels to serve liquor with meals—a luxury only the prosperous could afford—and as Roosevelt admitted, "[My enemies] are united in portraying me as spending my Sundays drinking heavily at the Union League Club." [7] For all his honesty, he was placing the administration in the posture of a snoop, playing into the hands of the machines by making reform hateful.

"Your course advertises yourself, Mr. Roosevelt," said the World, "as effectively as if you were a brand of soap. But does it . . . commend 'reform' to have the innocent annoyed in its name while crime runs riot and criminals go free?" [8]

But the World admitted that he had courage when he accepted the invitation of combined German societies that he attend their anti-blue law parade—an invitation tendered in purest irony. The commissioner laughed as the floats passed by—one depicting men in evening dress drinking champagne and labeled "Millionaires' Club," another representing a coffin placarded "Teddyism"—and large signs with such inscriptions as, "Liberty, Priceless Gem, Where Hast Thou Flown? To Hoboken!" Files of paraders brandished empty beer steins. One nearsighted Teuton marcher squinted at the reviewing stand and asked, *"Wo ist der Roosevelt?"* The commissioner bared his equine teeth in a smile and shrieked, *"Hier bin Ich!"* Even the Germans guffawed and had to agree that there was something fascinating about this destroyer of innocent pleasures.[9]

The World published a list of crimes unsolved because he was too busy watching saloons. He hit back with a report that some *had* been solved, others were robberies involving less than ten dollars and some were not on the records and must be fakes. He had a flair for the well-phrased insult. "It is always a question," he said, "how far it is necessary to go in answering a man who is a convicted liar. For the same reason it is a little difficult to decide whether it is necessary to take notice of any statement whatever appearing in Mr. Pulitzer's paper, The New-York World." [10]

In St. Louis, Pulitzer's case against Colonel Jones came to court September 30, but he had so clearly signed over control that Jones won and the problem persisted. There was an interval of joy when Mrs. Pulitzer presented him with his sixth living child, Herbert, on November 20—a joy alloyed by his inability to see the infant more than dimly. He solved this in part by hiring an artist, Charles Mortimer, to make strong black drawings on the whitest paper of Herbert in successive stages of infancy, and similar drawings of his other children.

He could not have been dejected to learn that John R. McLean, in trying to infuse politics into the giddy Journal and raising the price to two cents, had lost most of his chambermaid readers and seen his circulation sink to 77,000. In September he sold it for $180,000 to that odd young Democrat from California, William Randolph Hearst, who had done very well with the San Francisco Examiner. Hearst, the son of the late unlettered millionaire Senator, dropped the Journal to a penny and expanded it to 16 pages—a sure sign of fiscal madness.

III. SMASH THE RING!

Pulitzer's attention was not on Hearst but on an international crisis that arose, of all places, in Venezuela. The boundary between British Guiana and Venezuela existed dubiously on the basis of a rough provisional survey made by the British explorer Robert Schomburgk in 1841–43, a survey incomplete in the jungle interior and one which the Venezuelan government never either authorized or accepted. The discovery of gold in the disputed area heightened feeling. In 1895 President Joaquín Crespo of Venezuela cited the Monroe Doctrine in begging President Cleveland to aid him against "British aggression." Pulitzer's old bête noire, Richard Olney, had recently been named Secretary of State on the death of Walter Q. Gresham. Olney, an able lawyer but a man so domineering that he had refused his daughter admittance to his home after her marriage, sent a note to London that his daughter would have understood but which stunned Lord Salisbury, the Prime Minister. Invoking an extended interpretation of the Doctrine, it virtually demanded that England submit the boundary to arbitration, adding:

> Today the United States is practically sovereign on this continent, and its fiat is law. . . . Why? . . . It is because, in addition to all other grounds, its infinite resources combined with its isolated position render it master of the situation and practically invulnerable as against any or all other powers.[11]

There was a tone here that caused fury in Canada and other American nations. Lord Salisbury took his time about replying, and when he did he read Olney a little lesson in statecraft, denied that the Monroe Doctrine applied, and rebuffed him by offering to submit some of the area to arbitration but refusing to allow arbitration to extend to existing British settlements.

When Congress met, Cleveland gave his momentous special message, largely written by Olney. He denounced the British attitude, asked for a United States commission to "determine the true divisional line" and called the English stand a threat to the "peace and safety" of the United States. He added fighting words: "In making these recommendations I am fully alive to the responsibility incurred and keenly realize all the consequences that may follow." [12]

Suddenly the nation was gripped by a jingoism unknown since the *Virginius* affair. With few exceptions the press praised Cleveland's rash policy and talked of war. Dana's Sun described anyone not in accord as "an alien or traitor," urged alliances with France and Russia and spoke of coming "naval battles" in "the British Channel and the Irish Sea." Reid's Tribune said, "The message will not be welcome to the peace-at-any-price cuckoos who have been clamoring that the Monroe doctrine is a myth . . ." Cleveland's message was read in schoolhouses in the cities and out in the prairies. Gray-haired Civil War veterans offered their services to the country. Police Commissioner Roosevelt wrote a friend, "If there is a muss I shall try to have a hand in it myself!" and joyfully contemplated "the conquest of Canada." A drop in the stock market caused a few Wall Streeters to deprecate war. The Times snarled, "Under the teaching of these . . . patriots of the ticker, if they were heeded, American civilization would degenerate to the level of the Digger Indians, who eat dirt all their lives and appear to like it." [13] Congress, which fought Cleveland on almost every other issue, was behind him on this. The House passed unanimously the Hitt resolution authorizing a United States-sponsored boundary commission and appropriating $100,000 for its expenses—a measure also unanimously approved by the Senate. Few seemed to reflect that such a boundary commission appointed without consultation with the British was almost as preposterous as the sanctioning of the Schomburgk line without the consent of Venezuela.

In New York only three major newspapers counseled moderation: the Evening Post, guided by the judicious Godkin; the Herald, owned by the erratic but internationally-minded Bennett; and, of course, the World. Only Pulitzer, now at Lakewood, New Jersey, appropriated the dove of peace and sent it winging over the nation and across the sea in a master stroke of journalistic propaganda.

He had supported Cleveland in major issues—always strongly behind him in opposition to "imperialistic" designs such as the clamor to seize Hawaii. He had scoffed at the talk of war against Chile in 1892 when some free-wheeling United States sailors were handled roughly by the Valparaiso police. Now he took a stand that might be unpopular enough to cost him circulation and revenue. He dictated or outlined a stream of daily editorials mixing calm common sense with canny appeals to emotion:

> Is the integrity of Venezuela "essential to the integrity of our free institutions"? Does the determination of a boundary line in South America threaten "the tranquil maintenance of our distinctive form of government"?
>
> Merely to ask these questions is to expose the . . . preposterously inadequate basis of the war-threat which the President has fulminated. It is an insult to the understanding of an intelligent American school-child. . . . There is no menace to the boundary line. It is not our frontier. It is none of our business. . . .

He attacked Olney's interpretation of the Monroe Doctrine and the insolence of his note, adding:

> Before The Sunday World again appears we shall have taken down our wreaths; the holly and the mistletoe will have gone . . . but we shall retain our hopes. The white doves, unseen, will be fluttering somewhere. . . . Rancor and revenge have come and gone but they will not dampen the desire of men for peace on earth.[14]

The old stump-speaker knew how to tug the heartstrings. It was his aim to demonstrate not only American error but the fundamental friendliness of the British, and to convey the message with some homely sentiment that would appeal to the public. How better than to link it with the Christmas season now at hand? Hundreds of expensive cablegrams signed "Joseph Pulitzer" had gone out to British leaders—the Prime Minister, two former Prime Ministers, the Prince of Wales, the Duke of York, Members of Parliament and eminent clergymen—asking them to state their pacific views by cable collect. Replies poured in. The Christmas issue of the World was a journalistic hymn to international harmony, with the headline "PEACE AND GOOD WILL" spread over the portraits of the prince and duke and a facsimile of their joint reply:

> . . . The Prince of Wales and the Duke of York . . . thank Mr. Pulitzer for his cablegram. They earnestly trust and cannot but believe the present crisis will be arranged in a manner satisfactory to both countries, and will be succeeded by the same warm feeling of friendship which has existed between them for so many years.

Under this were cordial replies from Lord Salisbury, Lord Rosebery, Gladstone, Cardinal Vaughan, the archbishops of Wales, Dublin and Armagh, the bishop of Manchester and many others, all strongly for peace. The Christmas front page was a Pulitzer front page, one whose like had never been seen. It won attention from newspapers all over the country, spreading a feeling that the British after all were not unreasonable. Every day for more than a week the World plucked the harp of peace, gaining the support of Cardinal Gibbons, Bishop Henry C. Potter and American businessmen worried about the slump in trade—encouraging also the sober second thoughts of the early flag-wavers. In Washington, Secretary Olney scented treason in the World's commerce with the British. He dusted off a statute passed in 1799 which Henry Cabot Lodge quoted approvingly in the Senate:

> Any citizen of the United States who, without the permission or authority of the Government . . . carries on any verbal correspondence or intercourse with any foreign government, with the intent to influence the conduct of any foreign government in relation to any controversy with the United States . . . shall be punished by a fine of not more than $5,000 and by imprisonment during a term not less than six months, nor more than three years.[15]

The World pleaded guilty and dared reprisal:

> The statute cited is aged, obsolete, moldy, moth-eaten, dust-covered, and was forgotten until resuscitated by the zeal and watchfulness of Secretary Olney. It is true, furthermore, that the more modern laws, notably the anti-trust laws and anti-monopoly laws, are not enforced. . . . The World will not descend into the dungeon and put out its million-candle-power torch of liberty and intelligence without a struggle.[16]

Roosevelt wrote Lodge, "As for the Editors of the . . . *World,* it would give me great pleasure to have them put in prison the minute hostilities began."[17]

The crisis had been real. Possibly, though not certainly, common sense would have averted war in any case, but the World had seized leadership in a good cause and proclaimed it to both nations. The jingoes subsided and the air was cleared for negotiations that would settle the dispute with never a battle in the Irish Sea.[18] But the World peace crusade was only in mid-career when another crusade won space on its front page.

This concerned the matter of government borrowing. Pulitzer, with his fiery faith in "the people," was opposed on principle to quiet deals with private bankers. True, in 1894 Cleveland had announced a public sale of bonds, with demand so feeble that he had been forced to go hat in hand to the bankers to bail him out, but to Andes the fault here was a lack of publicity. He abhorred the aura of secrecy and special privilege in closed-door deals with financiers. The World had protested earlier bargains with Wall Street. Now, in the midst of the Venezuela crisis, its Washington chief, John Tennant, learned that another loan was in the offing. It was said that J. P. Morgan conferred with the President, and that James Stillman of the National City Bank and James T. Woodward of the Hanover Bank also were in Washington seeking a piece of the deal.

The World calculated that the Morgan group had bought an earlier government bond issue for $65,112,743, then sold them to the public for $73,418,575, making more than $8,000,000 in profits less expenses. Again it cautioned against "further costly dickers with a bond syndicate." The martinet at Lakewood was an occasional neighbor of Morgan at Jekyll Island, but Morgan had already learned, as had so many others, that there was no relationship between the cultivated Pulitzer with whom one had tea, and Pulitzer the editor. When it seemed apparent that the syndicate deal was all but made, Pulitzer summoned editorialist Eggleston and News Editor Ernest O. Chamberlin to Lakewood with a staff of aides.

"You think you're to stay here all night," he told Eggleston, "but you're mistaken. . . . You must be back in the office of the *World* at ten o'clock. I've ordered a special train to take you back. It will start at eight o'clock and run through in eighty minutes." He outlined the editorial:

"You are to write a double-leaded article to occupy the whole editorial space tomorrow morning. You are not to print a line of editorial on any other subject. You are to set forth, in compact form and in the most effective way possible, the facts of the case and the considerations that demand a popular . . . loan instead of this deal with a syndicate, suggestive as it is of the patent falsehood that the United States Treasury's credit needs 'financing.' . . . Then, as a guarantee of the sincerity of our convictions you are to say that the *World* offers in advance to take one million dollars of the new bonds at the highest market price. . . . It will *compel a public loan.*"[19]

Eggleston hurried back to New York. Chamberlin and his men had already sent out 10,370 telegrams to banks and financial houses throughout the country asking if they would support a public bond issue and prepaying their replies. Some 5,300 replies broke a Western Union record for telegrams sent in one day to a single addressee. Though many bankers favored the Morgan deal, there were enough pledges to buy $235,000,000 in bonds whereas only $100,000,000 would be put on sale. With this proof of a strong public market, Eggleston's editorial drove home the point:

> To you, Mr. Cleveland, The World appeals. It asks you to save the country from the mischief, the wrong and the scandal of the pending bond deal. . . .
>
> The needless waste of ten or fifteen millions in this transaction is not the only or even the chief objection to it. It involves something of immeasurably greater worth than any number of millions. It involves popular confidence in the integrity of the Government. . . . Secrecy of negotiation . . . awakens, unjustly, suspicions against the honor of the Government itself. . . . The most damaging thing that could happen to the Republic is the lodgment of conviction in the people's mind that ours has become a Government by Syndicates for Syndicates.
>
> Trust the people, Mr. Cleveland! You can get all the gold you need . . . without paying any premium at all.
>
> So sure are we of this that The World now offers to head the list with a subscription of *one million dollars* on its own account. . . . The whole country will respond with like alacrity. . . . Trust the people, Mr. Cleveland,
>
> And smash the Ring! [20]

The "ring" was further identified in a cartoon showing Pulitzer's clubmate Morgan (without undue exaggeration of the nose) as a pirate leading his mates in a demand for $12,000,000 ransom from Uncle Sam for his "sweetheart," the national credit.

Two days later, on January 6, 1896, Treasury Secretary Carlisle announced that the bond issue would be opened for public subscription, the angry President insisting that he had always intended this, the World on the contrary taking credit for forcing his hand. The issue was oversubscribed, the World's bid for $1,000,000 at 114 being the highest for any large amount.

The price of the new issue soon rose to give Pulitzer a quick gain of about $50,000—an embarrassment, since he did not wish to profit on the loan he had proclaimed as a patriotic duty. At his order a conference of executives was held in the Dome to decide the question of what to do with the $50,000. Brisbane suggested giving it to West Point, but it was learned that the military academy was forbidden to accept gifts, and there were objections to other proposals. Finally Business Manager Norris had a novel idea, saying, "Why not keep it?" This counsel was sent to Andes at Lakewood and was accepted.[21]

V

War with Hearst

Chapter 1

Persuasion by Checkbook

I. HOW TO CRUSH GUSH

It appeared that Pulitzer would need his $50,000 and more, for young Hearst ("Gush" in the World code) was now challenging him on a dollar basis. If Hearst did not have more millions at his disposal than Pulitzer, he was at any rate more reckless with those he had. His one-cent morning Journal had crept near 150,000 circulation and was losing big money—a loss he took imperturbably, certain he would recoup when advertisers came in. Pulitzer, though he was now selling about 200,000 Worlds each morning at twice the price (not to mention 340,000 Evening Worlds at a penny), could no longer laugh at the Californian.

Though reckless with money, Hearst bet on what seemed a sure thing by imitating every Pulitzer policy and carrying it a mile or two farther. His Journal appealed frankly to the working class, used the simplest language, lured the reader with entertainment, sensationalism and crusades, and indulged in self-advertisement so blatant as to make the World appear self-effacing. But it also had the same backbone of social protest as the World. It exposed corruption and fought the watered-stock-and-monopoly evils of the Gilded Age which the old editorial establishment had either winked at or beaten with a feather.

Hearst's admiration for Pulitzer's methods was evident also in his kidnaping of World talent. Bill Nye wrote a friend, "I am leaving the 'World,' at an advance of 50 per cent on salary, by cracky, and going to the 'Journal' . . ."[1] Hearst pecked away, taking the World cartoonist

T. F. Powers, the drama critic Alan Dale, and others. Now these sortie tactics changed to a bold mass attack that astonished all Park Row.

One of Andes' rockets was 30-year-old Morrill Goddard, a Dartmouth graduate nine years with the World. He had once distinguished himself by interviewing Blaine at his home in Maine, then bursting into the kitchen and interviewing the servants. Boosted to city editor and later to Sunday editor, he had evolved a lavishly illustrated supplement style providing unsophisticated excitement in pseudo-science, sex and crime. He had inaugurated the "funnies" in 1894 by bringing in young R. F. Outcault to draw the adventures of a smiling slum urchin known as "The Yellow Kid." The Sunday World had risen from 266,000 circulation in 1893 to pass 450,000 at the end of 1895, and was so fat with advertising that its 52 annual issues returned a revenue not far from that of the parent weekday World's 313. It need not be said that Pulitzer, despite his occasional warnings against oversensationalism, regarded Goddard with fondness.

In January 1896 Hearst hired away Goddard and the *whole Sunday staff,* including Outcault and his Yellow Kid. Only Emma Jane Hogg, Goddard's secretary, remained.

While Pulitzer had taken men away singly from other shops, this wholesale raid seemed an open declaration of war and raised the question of who would help Miss Hogg get out next Sunday's paper. On his order, Carvalho coaxed Goddard and his crew back with a higher salary offer—alas, only for a day, for Hearst opened his purse still wider and the company returned to the Journal for good. Pulitzer's detestation of Hearst, which would grow, dated from this moment. He came in from Lakewood for an all-night pow-wow with executives including Carvalho and Norris. Brisbane was hastily moved into Goddard's place as Sunday editor with a pickup staff including Harriet Hubbard Ayer, a young "beauty expert" not yet seasoned in the newspaper trade. The conference turned on measures to crush Gush.

Carvalho and Norris argued that the way to do it was to drop the two-cent World to a penny, a step they felt sure would raise its circulation to a million, bring in a wealth of new advertising and wipe out the Journal. Pulitzer was dubious enough so that the matter was not settled when he took a private car next day for Jekyll Island. Carvalho and Norris rode with him as far as Philadelphia, by which time the decision was made.

On February 10—with hope that the ten would bring luck—the World appeared at the one-cent price with results that confounded the experts. It affected the Journal not at all, nor did it harm the still mighty Herald, although it badly hurt the smaller Advertiser, Press and Recorder. For Pulitzer it was disastrous. The World's circulation rose a mere 88,000 per day, and a simultaneous rise in its space rates alienated many advertisers, who felt that the penny price meant readers without buying power and who boycotted the World until the rates were forced down again. "When I came to New York," Pulitzer reflected, "Mr. Bennett reduced the price of his paper and raised advertising rates—all to my advantage. When Mr. Hearst came to New York I did the same. I wonder why . . . ?" [2]

The loss of revenue, both Nero and Nelson, appalled him. From Jekyll Island came stern orders to cut costs. The World reduced its number of pages, curtailed its Wall Street reportage and eliminated book reviews entirely for a time—retrenchments that convinced Hearst that he had his rival staggering and caused him to step up his spendthrift poster-and-billboard campaign. Since the World had hired George Luks to continue the kid cartoon, both publishers featured Yellow Kids and the Pulitzer and Hearst papers were lumped under the opprobrious term "yellow press." Yet the distinctions between the two men were marked.

Each was a millionaire, but Pulitzer had won his own fortune while Hearst inherited his. The World always paid its own way, never failing to turn an annual profit, whereas Hearst would spend some $8,000,000 before he rounded the corner into profitable operations. Pulitzer was the originator of a newspaper style all his own, while Hearst was more the able imitator, the man who would outdo rather than originate. Each had an ideal of public service (however mixed with expediency) combined with enormous talents at attracting the masses. While each loved politics and power, Pulitzer was more successful in keeping his papers independent, and Hearst would later become so ambitious for office that he turned his newspapers into his own campaign organs. Andes had a clear advantage in experience and cultivation of mind, Gush in health. Each was well over six feet tall, but Hearst was strapping at 32, Pulitzer a gaunt, half-blind nervous wreck at 48. Hearst was at his office every night, personally in control. Pulitzer had only once been inside his building.

There was about Hearst the air of a precocious, unpredictable, slightly raffish adolescent taking the measure of an aging and ailing rival. The whole opposition newspaper fraternity watched this battle of titans with the unanimous hope that the combatants would kill each other off.

Pulitzer, always thoughtful in honoring valued men, arranged a birthday dinner for Richard A. Farrelly to mark his elevation to the managing editorship of the World. Farrelly received the Hearst summons and deserted to the enemy the day before the banquet, which was canceled. The World had to recruit Bradford Merrill (not related to editorialist William H. Merrill) from the New York Press to take Farrelly's place. In March, Pulitzer sent Carvalho to parley with Jones in St. Louis, then changed his mind and telegraphed Carvalho, suspending his mission. Carvalho, who had been contending with angry advertisers and indeed had suffered from Pulitzer's whims ever since the advent of Jones, returned in a rage, resigned and walked down Park Row to join Hearst. John Norris took over his duties, while Don Seitz replaced Norris as business manager, but there was a feeling of suspense in the Dome. Who would go next? It is a safe guess that Pulitzer quickly raised salaries in an effort to prevent more desertion. Just as he had driven up journalistic wages, now Hearst was increasing them still more.

II. RECRUITING

After a stay in Washington to sniff the political breezes, Pulitzer sailed for England in May with an expanded entourage—Hosmer, Butes, Ledlie, Ralph Pulitzer, David Graham Phillips and another young World man named Samuel M. Williams, plus the servants. In London they again engaged Moray Lodge, and Pulitzer hired a stocky, cheerful valet, Jabez Dunningham, who sometimes dropped his H's but was the soul of discretion and patience. Unlike previous valets who had fled the master's outbursts and sought easier employment, Dunningham would become invaluable and would remain for life.

Now looking in earnest for high-echelon newsmen, Pulitzer had his eye on Ralph Blumenfeld, who had left the Herald after incurring Bennett's wrath by buying him a $750 desk to match the grandeur of his building, and was now in business in London. Blumenfeld was invited to lunch, recording in his diary his impressions of the interview:

> "J. P." very petulant because Dr. Hosmer refused him permission to eat certain foods. I sat next to him, and he pelted me with questions. Talk ranged from metaphysics to spiritualism, murder trials, and police reporting. A man with a most astonishing range of conversation. Tall, cadaverous, reddish beard . . . piercing but dead eyes, long bony hands; a fascinating yet terrifying figure. He is not quite blind, but cannot see to read even with the most powerful glasses.

After lunch, Pulitzer took Blumenfeld for a drive, assuming that he would join the World and bombarding him with questions about the Herald, its operations, profits and office politics. "He was obviously bent on getting inside information," wrote Blumenfeld, who preferred not to tell tales about his old employer and evaded the questions in some annoyance as they drove into Chelsea.

"You are not very communicative," Pulitzer observed. "I expect when you've joined the *World* you will be more so. . . ."

"Excuse me, Mr. Pulitzer," Blumenfeld corrected. "I have never said I would join your staff. I do not want to do so."

The older man's rosy complexion became a vivid pink. "Why not, please?"

"Because I do not choose to be on the *World.* At least not at present."

Pulitzer sat bolt upright, poked the coachman with his stick and said,

1. For once seemingly relaxed, Pulitzer shows his warmth and kindliness in this rare photograph, taken a few years before both his health and eyesight failed.

2. At 21 the young man with the emphatic nose had a goal of wealth, power and reform.

3. Still under 40, he had realized every dream when fate produced a nightmare.

4. Kate Davis—her marriage to the ever-busy Pulitzer was performed almost "on the run."

5. Her portrait years later by Sargent caused her spouse a jealous twinge.

6. Carl Schurz for years was Pulitzer's mentor and ideal in journalism, politics and reform.

7. Thomas Davidson, a lifetime friend.

8. John A. Cockerill, the "perfect" editor.

9. Dana of the Sun vilified Pulitzer.

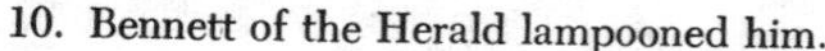

10. Bennett of the Herald lampooned him.

11. Reid of the Tribune, a polite enemy.

12. Only Hearst could shatter his poise.

13. Jay Gould was a frequent World target.

14. Rockefeller also took hard punishment.

15. J. P. Morgan was regularly pilloried.

16. —Depew too, though Pulitzer's friend.

17. The Pulitzer Building, wonder of 1890.

he World.

NEW YORK, SATURDAY, NOVEMBER 8, 1884—WITH SUPPLEMENT.

LIBERTY, EQUALITY, HONESTY!

The Government Again Belongs to the People and Not to Corrupt Monopolists.

18. McDougall cartoon hails Cleveland.

19. Pulitzer sits with Mrs. Gladstone, Gladstone with Kate Pulitzer, at London fête.

21. Roscoe Conkling gave Pulitzer expert aid in barring the White House to Blaine.

20. Blaine—President but for the World.

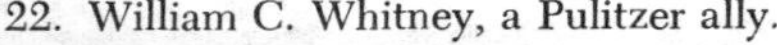

22. William C. Whitney, a Pulitzer ally.

A CHRISTMAS BATH.
"Mr. Croker, it will take something stronger than the waters of Carlsbad to remove those spots."

23. The World had much to do with sending Boss Croker of Tammany into European retirement.

24. Bryan, the quadrennial plague.

25. Admiral Dewey broke Pulitzer's hea

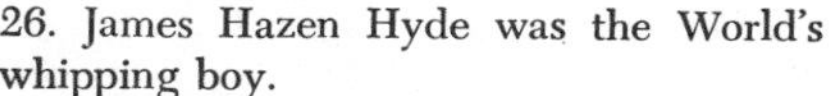

26. James Hazen Hyde was the World's whipping boy.

27. —But the paper pushed Hughes fame and the governorship.

8. Lucille Irma's death was a cruel blow.

29. Herbert Pulitzer, papa's favorite son.

0. Norman Thwaites (right) behind mas-
r in boat.

31. Winnie Davis, who was "adopted" by the Pulitzers.

32. Edith and Constance Pulitzer made a fetching pair in their stylish carriage.

33. Pulitzer rides in Central Park with Billing, coachman Stewart riding behind.

34. Ralph Pulitzer clowns with wife Frederica, who never got over her fear of her crusty father-in-law.

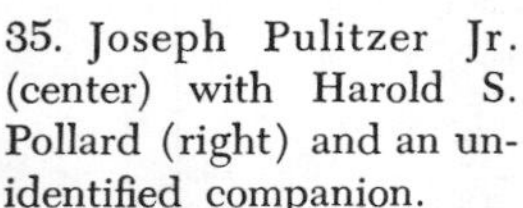

35. Joseph Pulitzer Jr. (center) with Harold S. Pollard (right) and an unidentified companion.

36. Frank Cobb, the boss's trusted editor.

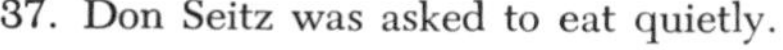

37. Don Seitz was asked to eat quietly.

38. The World-sponsored globe tour by Nellie Bly (above) got headlines in the World but was ignored by jealous contemporaries.

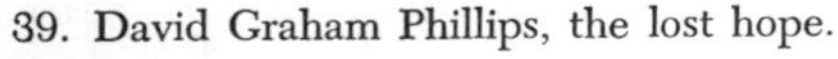

39. David Graham Phillips, the lost hope.

40. Henry Watterson, a friend for 40 years.

41. President Roosevelt invited Pulitzer to dinner, later tried to imprison him.

42. The Pulitzer 73rd Street mansion. Narrow front of Ralph's home is immediately adjacent.

43. The granite Tower of Silence is at far right in this photo of Chatwold, at Bar Harbor.

44. The baronial Villa Arethusa on the Riviera was one Pulitzer winter home. He also had a luxurious "cottage" in Georgia.

45. But the great yacht *Liberty* came nearest perfection as the invalid's "artificial world."

46. The aging Pulitzer's blindness is hardly apparent as he strolls Fifth Avenue with Ralph, who suffered much from his caprices.

47. Age only brought matronly perfect to the charm of Kate Pulitzer, seen he well after she had become a grandmother.

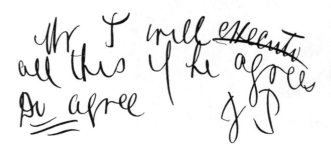

Mr S will ~~execute~~
all this if he agrees
Do agree JP

48. Pulitzer wrote in a huge bold scrawl long after his eyes had dimmed, as in this memo to Seitz: "Mr S will *execute* all this if he agrees *Do* agree JP." One can be sure Seitz agreed.

"Stop, please. This gentleman is getting out here." Blumenfeld was dropped off in Chelsea to get a hansom for himself.[3]

Moving on to Wiesbaden, Pulitzer sought to capture the 25-year-old Briton, Wickham Steed, an anti-bimetallist who had been contributing as a free-lancer some excellent letters to the World from Berlin about the German attitude toward the silver-gold controversy. Steed joined him in Wiesbaden to receive a handsome offer to become the World's regular Berlin correspondent. Steed, however, had just been offered a Berlin post for the London Times, and though the salary was only a third of what the World would pay—and though he especially admired Pulitzer's vigorous aid in averting war over Venezuela—his reverence for the intellectual Times won out over the noisy World. It was to Steed that Pulitzer pointed out that sublime philosophy was useless if nobody read it: "You must go for your million circulation, and, when you have got it, turn the minds, and the votes, of your readers one way or the other at critical moments."

But Steed was of the Godkin persuasion, preferring to influence a few enlightened minds than a million numbskulls. "Mr. Pulitzer bore with me," he recalled. "He let me see that he thought me a young fool, but he did it so kindly that he won my heart." [4]

After his cure, Pulitzer returned to London to meet one-eyed Henry Watterson, the master of flapdoodle who more than made up for his notorious unpunctuality with his zest for living and for criticism, his love of the table and his violence in language combined with the most perfect personal courtesy. These two, with long political memories, saw Democratic disaster ahead in 1896 unless the sound-money men could defeat the silver simpletons.

"Absolute authority made Pulitzer a tyrant," observed Watterson, unaware of the nature of his friend's ailment. ". . . He seriously lacked the sense of humor and even among familiars could never take a joke. His love of money was by no means inordinate. He spent it freely though not wastefully or joyously, for the possession of it flattered his vanity more than made occasion for pleasure. Ability of varying kinds and degrees he had, a veritable genius for journalism and a real capacity for affection." [5]

On June 5, Watterson and Phillips were among the witnesses when dozens of representatives of British peace societies—among them Cardinal Vaughan, Sir Lewis Morris and Sir Robert Head Cook—called at Moray Lodge to honor Pulitzer for his work during the dispute over Venezuela. Presented with an engrossed tribute on vellum, he heard the cardinal and others praise his efforts, then stepped forward amid applause.

"I am deeply touched," he said, "but am, unfortunately, an invalid, and under a doctor's orders, and I ask permission that my response be read by a young American friend—my son."

He could have spoken himself, but preferred in this way to improve his son's self-confidence. On his 12th birthday, Ralph had received from his father a splendid set of Plutarch's *Lives,* from which he was expected to pick a hero and to follow similar ideals—a practice Pulitzer would follow with his other two sons. Now 17, he read his father's appeal for the arbitration of international quarrels, which included the point that he did not believe in peace at any price:

"There are certain issues that are not arbitrable. War against a cruel despotism or slavery Americans regard as not only just, but as inevitable. [Pulitzer politely omitted mention of the American revolution.] . . . They naturally sympathize with the uprising of any people against despotism, whether in Greece or Hungary or Poland in the past, or in Cuba today." [6]

Chapter 2

The Plague of Bryan

1. HEARST'S BURNING MONEY

By July 1 Pulitzer was back in New York, then quickly to Chatwold, where the Tower of Silence had its noisiest season. The Republicans had nominated McKinley in June, and with Mark Hanna in the saddle they had disowned the silver Republicans and come out for gold. In July, Whitney and Hill went to Chicago in the forlorn hope of holding the Democratic convention to a gold plank and were buried under an avalanche of silver and the evangelism of 36-year-old William Jennings Bryan. To Mr. Dooley, ". . . [Bryan] come out in a black alpaca coat an' pushed into th' air th' finest wurruds ye ever heerd spoke in all ye'er born-rn days. 'Twas a balloon ascinsion an' th' las' days iv Pompey an' a blast on th' canal all in wan. I had to hold on to me chair to keep fr'm goin' up in th' air . . ." Ironically, if the Cleveland administration had been able to carry out four long-standing Pulitzer policies—an income tax, real tariff reform, control of the trusts and the enforcement of fair railroad rates—western discontent would have been mitigated and the silver rebels might have lacked the strength to capture the Democratic party.

Never had Pulitzer faced so serious a crisis in policy—one that threatened to destroy him both politically and financially no matter what course he took.

For all his independence in local politics and in specific issues, he had been an ardent Democrat nationally since 1876, supporting Tilden, Hancock and Cleveland (the latter three times, or at least two and a fraction), certain that the Democrats were closer to the people than the protectionist, monopolistic Republicans. True, he could not have any grassroots understanding of the terrible poverty and injustice that inspired the Populist revolt, but to him silver was a fraud. He was not free from the eastern fear that the populists attracted cranks and madmen, that they were linked with the Homestead and Pullman rioters and such fiascoes as Coxey's army. Now he had his choice between two candidates, both of whom appalled him. Bryan, who adopted silver as a religion and seemed dangerously ignorant of other important issues, was no Democrat as Pulitzer defined the term. McKinley—a confounded Republican, tarred by Hanna and the tariff and yet for sound money, law and order.

As for the wallet, how could Andes forget 1884, when Dana had abandoned the Democrats and damaged the powerful Sun to Pulitzer's advantage? Now the situation was reversed, for Hearst came out for Bryan. If Pulitzer bolted the Democrats, would he be repeating Dana's blunder, losing his own circulation and prestige, handing it all over to Gush?

Bryan promptly sent an emissary to Chatwold, where Eggleston, a guest at the time, saw him. He bore a personal message from Bryan, who said his election was a certainty and kindly called Mr. Pulitzer's attention to the damage the World would suffer should it fail to support the winner. When Eggleston relayed this to his chief, he laughed. While Eggleston jotted down the figures, Andes named the states Bryan would win, with the number of electoral votes for each. He then listed the states that would go against Bryan, with their electoral strength.

"I don't often predict—never unless I know," he said. "But you may embody that table in an editorial predicting that the result of the election four months hence will be very nearly, if not exactly, what those lists foreshadow. Let that be our answer to Mr. Bryan's audacious message."

Eggleston noted, "As we sat there on his little private porch at Bar Harbor, Mr. Pulitzer correctly named every state that would give its electoral vote to each candidate, and the returns of the election—four months later—varied from his prediction by only two electoral votes out of four hundred and forty-seven. And that infinitesimal variation resulted solely from the fact that by some confusion of ballots in California and Kentucky each of these states gave one vote to Bryan and the rest to his opponent. . . . I record it as phenomenal."

He also recorded as phenomenal Pulitzer's ability to work far into the night on editorial policy with Eggleston until suddenly he realized that his guest was exhausted and said, "You've been overworking. You are to go to bed now, and you are not to get up until you feel like getting up—even if it is two days hence. Go, I tell you. . . . You shall not be interrupted in your sleep." [1]

A stream of Pulitzer messages, a dozen or more a day, some highly detailed and representing careful thought, went to various World executives. Would Mr. Norris watch Horace (Brisbane) sharply, report on the hours he spent daily at his desk and whether he showed signs of flagging interest? . . . "Why such failure about colored potash [advertisements] everybody here agrees that last magazine disgracefully printed . . ." . . . Paper had to be saved, and yet there was at least three-quarters of a column of useless verbiage in the market section; condense, condense! ". . . Please pay pressman's funeral expenses and continue pay for present [;] find out what family left and make suggestion what is right to do." Norris, who had been working hard, was instructed to take an extra week's vacation. . . . Why did Geologist (the Herald), with much lower circulation, have as much Mustard (want ads) as Senior? More Mustard was requested. . . . The Journal, which was giving away newspapers by the thousands containing Bryan speeches, should not be mentioned by name, but as "the silver paper." . . . There were leaks in the World office; what was talked of there seemed to be known the same day at Geranium. . . . "If you could do anything quickly in the way of relieving suffering of the poor say by distributing ice or whatever it may be I should like it." . . . Eighty thousand returns on Seniority, he warned, was enormously wasteful and must be cut down. "Mr. Pulitzer is sorry to complain. . . ." [2]

During the campaign, the World accurately represented his views, supported neither candidate, made clear its reservations on both sides and lectured each of the nominees on his duty to the nation. It assailed Hanna and his "professional corruptionists," urged McKinley to take a more progressive stand on the trust problem, and ran an educational series on the fallacy of free silver, which it called "a craze, a species of hysteria." Pulitzer, determined to give the best in news coverage, sent the ablest political reporter of the day, James Creelman, around the country with Bryan, wiring him detailed assignments daily from Bar Harbor. He gave his frail physique its most violent mistreatment since his breakdown, working furiously for four months, "never for a waking moment out of touch with the telegraph, dictating, urging, informing."

The World gained an advantage in the general loathing for Bryan in sound-money New York, where such papers as the Tribune, Herald and Sun depicted the Commoner as a satanic disciple of riot and repudiation. A Bryanite in the East had to run his chances of social ostracism or worse. Young George B. McClellan, a Democrat but opposed to silver, was running for Congress and strictly avoiding any mention of Bryan or bimetallism. All the same, he found it "extremely unpleasant . . . to go to the Union Club during the campaign. The fact that I was on the Bryan ticket made my fellow members regard me as a social pariah and I stayed away." [3]

The only important Bryan paper in the city and for many miles around was the Journal, visiting on Hearst a strange combination of gain and loss. The Journal, appealing to people who had little understanding of currency and little to lose in any case, sucked them in like quicksand, sending papers as far away as Washington, Philadelphia and distant upstate New York. Homer Davenport's Journal cartoons showing Hanna as a gross monopolist covered with dollar signs, giving base instructions to the puppet-sized McKinley, became famous. The small son of Representative Champ Clark said in puzzlement, "Papa, I've just seen Mark Hanna and he hasn't any dollar marks on his clothes." Hearst was sacrificing everything for circulation, for now his Bryan-hating advertisers quit him and his losses swelled with his circulation. One of his editors, Willis Abbot, remarked, "It seemed to some of us who day after day inhaled the fumes of his burning money, that he was mad, but he was only . . . shrewd and daring." [4] Unruffled by the backs turned toward him at the Metropolitan Club, he raised $40,000 for Bryan among his readers and doubled it out of his own pocket. In September, as if determined to increase his deficits, he started his Evening Journal—a clear threat to the Evening World. He disregarded some of the niceties of Pulitzer, whose standing instructions were to keep politicians out of the Dome. With Tammany Hall unhappy about Bryan, the Journal diggings in the Tribune building virtually became eastern headquarters for the silver Democrats.

True, on the day after the election the Journal had to announce a McKinley victory. But the pain of it was diminished by its claim of a record pressrun for that day of 956,921 copies of the morning edition and 437,401 of the evening. While this of course was a big-press issue, and its figures were not audited and perhaps could not be taken too seriously, it was obvious that in 12 months in New York Hearst had wrought a miracle by his shrewd use of four factors: money, sensationalism, liberal sympathies and the Bryan campaign. In circulation he had vaulted over the waning Establishment—the Herald (about 140,000), Sun (75,000), Tribune (16,000) and Times (9,000)—and was breathing close behind the front-running World. In a chesty editorial so reminiscent of the World's self-puffery he explained how the Journal under its "present proprietor" had outstripped the mossbacks:

> No other journal in the United States includes in its staff a tenth of the number of writers of reputation and talent. It is the Journal's policy to engage brains as well as to get the news, for the public is even more fond of entertainment than it is of information. . . .[5]

11. DAMN YOUR IMPERTINENCE

Perhaps, as Pulitzer sailed with his old colleague Dillon for Genoa on the *Columbia* after the election, the Hearst problem had something to do with his increased nervousness and his irritation at the ship's band that belabored such tunes as "After the Ball." He intended to winter at Monte Carlo, but no sooner was established there than he found it impossible—

ships' bells were ringing constantly in the harbor. Butes and other assistants received their orders: *Find Andes a quiet place.* After testing many, they selected the Hotel Cap Martin on the picturesque peninsula between Menton and Monaco, where James Gordon Bennett called for a few minutes, as Pulitzer put it, "pretending to be friendly." He cabled Anfracto (John Norris), "Tell everybody stop all letters also papers." [6] He arranged by cable for the Christmas presentation to all his editors of luxurious Persian lamb-lined overcoats—all, that is, except Frederick Duneka, editor of the Evening World, who was for some obscure reason out of favor. Duneka, who had several times been a temporary secretary-companion of the chief, wrote him immediately. His coat had not yet arrived, he said, probably because it would be a handsomer one with a sable collar, and he thanked Mr. Pulitzer and sent cordial Christmas greetings. From the Riviera Andes replied:

"Damn your impertinence; coat will arrive by New Year's." [7]

Yet for a time depression lay on him like a curse. "I have never seen him so steadily and persistently gloomy," Alfred Butes wrote Kate Pulitzer, "or in so deep a gloom." [8] Most of the roster of eminent European physicians had been consulted earlier, but a new one was found—the bullying, satyr-bearded Dr. Ernst Schweininger, famous for his successful treatment of Bismarck, who traveled to Cap Martin for an enormous fee. Pulitzer, whose attitude toward doctors ranged from great interest to derision, soon decided that Schweininger was a humbug. Yet he followed his prescription of massage, diet, heroic exercise and baths out of sheer desperation and the necessity of trying anything that offered hope.

"I stopped smoking with the new year," he wrote Kate (to whom he sent $60 worth of orchids), "have stopped drinking claret; have never been more careful in eating, have never taken so much exercise . . . as during the last six weeks. . . . But I have never been so miserable yet in spite of, or perhaps on account of this I am more miserable in some respects (physical)—than I have been in years. Then I do not sleep as well as in America. I am counting not only the days but the hours, for the infernal ship which sails exactly two weeks from today from Genoa.

"I have thought of you every day. I have thought of you every hour of every day. I have thought of you many an hour of the night while awake. I have intended to write every day but could not because I was determined not to write more complaints and felt I could not write anything else." He had gone nowhere and done nothing, he added, and the Riviera was a "dreadful bore" to which he had no desire to return (he would return there almost annually). He had a firm rule that his older children must write him regularly, and they had not, so he sent his love to baby Herbert and Constance but not to Edith, Joseph, Lucille and Ralph: ". . . You can say I do not love them and that they ought to be ashamed of themselves for not writing—especially Lucille, about whom I must have sent at least half a dozen cables. However, I thank you, dearest, for your letters—all the more a balm." [9]

He allotted Kate $6,000 a month for family expenses, but warned insistently that she must economize. To Brisbane he sent $400, probably as a circulation bonus. Brisbane, whose chief aide on the Sunday World was the able Charles Edward Russell, was locked in a circulation struggle with Goddard of Hearst's Sunday Journal. Brisbane had doubled his color comics to eight pages, ascended new peaks of luridity and had pushed Seniority's Christmas 1896 issue to a record 623,000 sale. He was now drawing $15,000 a year. But when Pulitzer returned to New York he discovered that Seniority, like the Sunday Journal, was such a welter of freaks, crime and thinly clad girls that other newspapers assailed them both, clubs excluded them and church people demanded their suppression. Although this had no effect on their rising circulation, Don Seitz noted that "the effect on Mr. Pulitzer was severe"—probably meaning the purification drive rather than the sensationalism that caused it. He gave Brisbane stern orders to clean up, then left with Mrs. Pulitzer for a few weeks in Washington.

Here Bryan called at Pulitzer's invitation. There was a long, long discussion, the publisher remarking that Bryan had caused him "a great deal of trouble" and trying earnestly to show him his errors. Bryan did not budge an inch. Pulitzer made a request he often did to men who interested him: Could he feel of Bryan's face? The strapping Silver Knight reached for his hand and guided it over his prognathous jaw, remarking, "You see, Mr. Pulitzer, I am a fighter." Although Andes' jaw was less impressive under its beard, he insisted on drawing Bryan's hand over it, replying, "You see I am one too." It was their only meeting, and Pulitzer's impression was not of a demagogue but of a sincere, kindly man however misguided.[10]

By June he was at Bar Harbor, pushing the economy campaign which, rather than reflecting any real pinch, was a reaction to the shrinkage of his newspaper income. Seniority was booming, but Senior had suffered a grave reduction in profits and Junior was dropping off a trifle. Although his infallible selection of lucrative investments gave him an enormous income quite outside of his newspapers, the total was smaller. Always fluctuating between parsimony and extravagance, he often suspected creditors of padding their statements because of his known wealth, sometimes being greatly upset by minor bills. He complained bitterly about his coal bill at Bar Harbor. The charge for repairing his launch outraged him and he succeeded in getting it reduced. He had quarreled with several European doctors over their fees, and regarded Schweininger as a gross money-grubber. Now he put his foot down at a request of his wife for an extra allowance over her regular $6,000 monthly to clear bills partly arising from the care of baby Herbert. Kate, who indeed had little knack for thrift, wrote Butes in strenuous protest, insisting that she had observed stringent economies but that she was actually embarrassed by a number of outstanding bills:

> Will you bring this matter to Mr. Pulitzer's attention immediately, or the baby & I will be thrust into prison. Seriously, do get Mr. Pulitzer to attend to this *at once*, & send me a check *at once*.
>
> Don't let the paper, in this instance, come before his family, as I cannot leave [for Bar Harbor] before these bills are all settled. . . .
>
> Do make him careful in avoiding high winds, bright lights, glare, and sudden violent movements. As long as his eyes trouble him he should not go into the pool, nor ride horseback. These things, at least, he can do, even though it be impossible for him to stop worrying. . . . I wish there was no such thing as money in the world. . . .[11]

Pulitzer's total expenses for 1897, audited confidentially by the trusted J. Angus Shaw ("Solid"), cashier of the World, were $348,040.57. His newspaper income, which in pre-Hearst times had approached $1,000,000 a year, was dropping every month. His Sunday World, due to its disinfecting, had lost 48,000 from its 1896 circulation while the Sunday Journal, as wild as ever, kept gaining—a development that left Pulitzer (and editor Brisbane) in disgruntlement. *Economy! Economy!* was his constant order. While there was tension in the Dome, the boss himself could so far indulge his predilection for luxury as to look for a suburban mansion near New York—possibly in part a strategic move to show Hearst that he was not impoverishing his rival. He sent Seitz and Dillon to inspect William Rockefeller's magnificent estate near Tarrytown, Rockwood Hall, which Rockefeller vowed to sell for $350,000 because his tax assessment had been raised to $2,500,000. But Rockefeller had second thoughts about selling, and Pulitzer gave up the idea after some further search in the suburbs. If he was inconsistent about "economy," he nevertheless augmented rather than reduced his philanthropies, giving a new series of scholarships to 47 students at Teachers' College. He gave the widowed Mrs. Jefferson Davis writing work on the Sunday World, though much of her copy was thrown away. He sent a quarterly check of $1,250 to Kate's sister Clara Davis in Washington, sent occasional sums to relatives in Hungary and distributed the usual expensive gifts when the mood struck him.

He was pleased meanwhile when, after two and a half years, he recovered control of his St. Louis Post-Dispatch and got Colonel Jones off his back. The defeat of Bryan and financial considerations of his own persuaded Jones to relinquish his interest for the $80,000 he had paid plus $45,000 in profits. Pulitzer's luck was prodigious, for Jones, in supporting Bryan and silver where they were popular, had boosted circulation and left the shop in thriving condition.[12] The men he had discharged—Steigers, Johns and the rest—returned to their St. Louis posts, with Dillon also rejoining the Post-Dispatch briefly to steer its new course. Throughout the controversy, Jones, represented by Attorney Frederick N. Judson, had been the technical legal victor, a fact so clear to Pulitzer that he retained Judson as his St. Louis counsel for the rest of his life.

Strange things had been happening to Mayor Strong's reform administration. The legislature, in an effort to solve the Sunday liquor problem, had passed the Raines bill, permitting the Sunday sale of liquor at hotels and strictly defining a hotel as a building with at least ten bedrooms and restaurant facilities. Underworldlings quickly saw opportunity rather than control in the law. New ten-room hotels sprang into being—dives where liquor flowed, an occasional ham sandwich fulfilled the restaurant requirement, and where the spare rooms were used for prostitution. More than 2,000 "Raines hotels" were doing a roaring business. One department store advertised that it would furnish all ten rooms for $81.20. Commissioner Roosevelt, who at first praised the law, discovered that it raised an almost insoluble police problem. In the summer he resigned to become Assistant Secretary of the Navy. That fall, the World and the city took a beating at the polls. Many citizens were sick of reform, and the World-supported candidate for mayor, Seth Low, was roundly beaten by Croker's amiable errand boy, Robert Van Wyck.

III. BUSINESS AS USUAL

At Chatwold, 17-year-old Lucille Irma Pulitzer had a September coming-out party in an atmosphere of gladioli and violins. Educated by tutors and at a convent, she, more than any other of the children, had inherited her father's energy, curiosity and desire for achievement. A fortnight later she was stricken by typhoid, but she rallied so well that Pulitzer invited Professor Davidson for a visit, warning him, "only you must understand that I am just as absolutely crazy and absorbed in politics as I was before." Even when Lucille relapsed and lingered in serious illness for weeks, he could not quell his compulsive need for a change that might pacify his nerves. He wrote Davidson December 8:

> Poor Lucille is still very ill and I need not tell you that I have been worried almost to death. You never wrote me from Boston—never gave me your address—ran off like a bad boy. Yet here I am thinking of you and proposing to you a trip to Naples *if* I am able to get off (which is still very doubtful, depending not only on Lucille's condition but on other things.) I intend to sail for Naples on January 4th and return on same ship from Naples January 28th. Would you like to make the trip with me and my party? I do it simply for a change and break.[13]

In New York, his mortal enemy, Charles A. Dana, died at 78. The World ran a two-column cut of the great editor with a long obituary account of his "stirring life" and never a word about his unpleasantness. Business went on as usual at Chatwold despite the master's worry. W. H. Merrill, Norris, Brisbane and Seitz visited him separately to get his verbal instructions, and he sent the customary torrent of daily messages to the Dome covering every phase of operation—news, business, circulation, advertising, salaries, politics, the purchase of newsprint and mechanical equipment—with the sure hand of the expert. There was trouble with Horace (Brisbane), who badly wanted his own byline, who disobeyed orders by returning to freaks in the Sunday paper, and was suspected of inclinations toward Hearst. He reproved Horace and shifted him to the Evening World, which had lost $4,000 a month during the summer doldrums. The scope and intensity of his communications is only faintly indicated by a few quotations and summations from them:

"News head-line type should never be used in advertisements, and advertising type should never be used for head-lines." "Tammany advertisement on fourth page very bad I forbid any political advertisement . . . unless marked by the word advertisement fully spelled out."

"The best parts of the paper, for canvassing, are the two ears if used with originality and imagination. . . . The ablest man in the office is not able enough to write striking & strikingly effective ears." "The ears are the windows of the newspaper." "I judge a business manager largely by his ears."

Who, he asked, left out the temperature in yesterday's weather report? Surely the World's readers deserved to know how hot it was.

"I wish you [Norris] would think very, very acutely and make an estimate . . . of the present deficit of Geranium [the Journal] . . . without giving any reason whatever or any hint of your own basis of computation ask Bradford Merrill to make an estimate of his own, and ditto Seitz. Each ought to be separate and uninfluenced by the others."

"Grumbler [a paper dealer] will lose golden goose by trying to pluck a feather too much [i.e., ask too high a price]."

". . . Kindly give him [Pulitzer] your judgment about the character of the Evening [World] *generally* . . . how low, how unobjectionable has it been. Mr. P. does not see it & does not get any reports about it . . ."

Bradford Merrill, perhaps unaware of the chief's dislike for resounding titles, had caused the legend "Editorial Manager" to be lettered on his office door, inspiring this directive to Seitz: "Gently, softly, and early in the morning—say before eight o'clock,—before anybody is about—have that celebrated editorial manager sign wiped out. But really do it so early in the morning that nobody will notice it."

". . . Advise how Horace talks and acts whether disgruntled."

Real or imaginary Hearst offers to World men were a constant worry. He wrote: "[Let me know] the precise degree of accuracy in the statements recently sent me as to Geranium's [the Journal's] propositions to

George [Bradford Merrill] . . . and probably some other people. . . . And besides this you might give me your own personal impression as to what has been the effect of these offers on the gentlemen named—whether they are really to be depended upon or are to be regarded as insecure."

To Norris: "Recommend some investments for me."

"Will you [Seitz] have a copy of the 7th Edn Evening World mailed here to Joseph Pulitzer *Jun* every day."

". . . Will you [Norris] not immediately, without a moment's delay, sit down & tell me what you think of its [the Post-Dispatch's] character—that is, its tone and tendency, taste and temper rather than actual news. Is the character of the paper respectable? Good or bad, which? Pardon me for remarking that you have not uttered a single syllable on the subject."

In response to an editor's suggestion that the newspaper's attorney, John M. Bowers, should be consulted about the legal safety of a World crusade: "Thank you for your caution and prudence—but!—but!—the paper would never do anything brilliant if Bowers not boldness were in control."

"Apropos of Marshall, the hardest thing to treat is vanity. I fully appreciate your [Norris'] difficulty with Marshall . . . yet I wish you would strain every effort . . . not to lose the gentleman or even seriously disturb his brain & self-satisfaction; for imaginative mercurial impulsive faculties like his will be perfectly useless for work the very moment his enthusiasm is destroyed."

"Ding Dong Ding Dong Ding Dong Ding Dong the word economy into [E. O.] Chamberlin until he has nervous prostration . . ."

"I am particularly interested in knowing who wrote the Xmas advertisements—every line of them—and who furnished the ideas. I think it was *admirably done*."

"Mr. Pulitzer liked the appearance of the want section: but wants to call your attention to the Castoria ad which still hurts his eye!"

". . . Will you please . . . suggest the name of anybody entitled to reward recognition encouragement or a little Xmas present—I mean more particularly among the younger and small salaried men, whom I hardly know." [14]

His last message for a time was dated December 30, when Butes relayed his orders along with the word that Mr. Pulitzer "has a very bad headache." By that time the doctors had informed him that Lucille had only a short time to live. She died at Chatwold next day. William B. Fitts, a temporary secretary, wrote Davidson, "I hardly dare think how this loss will affect Mr. P., & doubt if there is anyone who appreciates or understands the depths of his nature. . . . Of course Mrs. Pulitzer is prostrated with her grief. . . . The funeral will be Tuesday." [15]

Lucille was buried at Woodlawn Cemetery in New York. A few days later Pulitzer left for Jekyll Island, and by February 3 the instructions from the chief erupted again:

". . . The new color [press] is all important and should receive the utmost attention and brain and advertising, to make a hit. Geranium will soon follow us anyway and we ought to use the little advance time to impress this novelty on the public mind as the greatest progress in Sunday journalism. . . ."[16]

Chapter 3

Cuba

I. WAITING FOR PHOEBE

The next two years would be the least creditable in Pulitzer's life, a period his admirers prefer to pass by, yet inevitable in the circumstances. During this time he violated most of the journalistic principles which he had upheld for years. Cynics who had already noted the commercial nature of his Evening and Sunday Worlds observed that it took Hearst to prove that Pulitzer's ideals were, after all, only window dressing and that money was his sole object. If Hearst did nothing else, it was said, he at least exposed his older rival as a liar and a fraud.

This simplistic theory ignored several underlying issues. Obviously money, expediency and pride were factors in Pulitzer's policies. It would be humiliating, ruinous for the Napoleon of journalism to be whipped on his own ground by a callow newcomer from the West. But for all his love of wealth and power, he never quite lost his hold on his ideals. Intrinsic in his thinking was his megalomaniac belief in himself as a force for public good, and his opinion of Hearst as a public menace. Intrinsic also was his hard appraisal of circulation and money as absolute essentials for independent journalism. Hearst threatened his survival in the only profession in which he cared to exist. If money were the sole consideration, Pulitzer's virtuosity in investments was such that he might have emerged a richer man had he confined his activities to that field; but he would have died on the vine without a public platform.

In the beginning he stood on visibly higher ground than the enigmatic Hearst. If he did run two junk shops, his third and most important establishment dealt in quality merchandise. If his Junior and Seniority existed chiefly to pay for mansions, horses and wines, they also paid for scholarships. The young Hearst lacked his rival's grasp of affairs, could not match his quarter-century of constructive political vigilance. To Pulitzer, who at first underestimated Hearst's abilities, he seemed a crude boy having fun with millions, a mere stunt specialist masquerading as a reformer.

There were mitigations even if one could not forgive Pulitzer's descent into irresponsible journalism. In the struggle between the two, politics was as important a factor as money. The Bryan campaign had rocketed Hearst to prominence, brought him close to the prevailing free-silver Democratic national leaders and had alienated them against Pulitzer. If the latter had a religion, it was his belief in the Democratic party, his hope to nurse it back to sound-money health. Now it appeared that Hearst might replace him as the nation's leading Democratic newspaperman and that the Journal would succeed the World as the party's watchdog and interpreter. The thought of Gush and his Journal guiding the party of Tilden and Cleveland was one to pluck at every one of Andes' tortured nerves. It was something he could not allow to happen, and it had a great deal to do with his resolution to fight Hearst on his own ground even if it meant scuffling in the gutter.

But money and circulation rather than principle would decide the victory, and here lay an error in his thinking. He was convinced, as were most observers, that Hearst was heading for such early bankruptcy that the alley battle would at any rate be short before the World could resume business as usual. Hearst's only income was some $100,000 a year in profits from his San Francisco Examiner. He was losing that much *every month* in New York, dropping more than a million dollars a year, operating at the most enormous deficit ever seen in journalism. The money to make good his losses came from the mining fortune of the late Senator Hearst and was doled out to the son by his fond mother, Phoebe Apperson Hearst, who thus became the key figure in the conundrum.

How long before Mrs. Hearst would close her purse? How long before she would send the ultimatum that would force her son to shut up shop?

No one but Hearst would have had the effrontery to fight on despite such losses, and the general opinion in Park Row was always that he would be lucky to last another month or two. It was Anaconda copper and South Dakota gold that was keeping the Journal alive. Pulitzer's strategy was based on the theory that he must hang on at almost any sacrifice until either Hearst or his mother gave up. There were incessant rumors that Phoebe Hearst was at the end of her patience and was about to end her financial support of her son's hare-brained venture. She had installed her cousin, Edward Hardy Clark, in New York to watch over her son's disbursement of her millions, and it was no secret that Clark was uneasy. One of the many likely-sounding rumors of the crackdown came in a message from Bradford Merrill to Pulitzer: "Mrs. Gush . . . is having expert accountants examine the [Journal] books in New York over the heads of Gush, Grandee [Carvalho], and Clark."[1] Who could have imagined that she would let her son pour $8,000,000 down the Journal drain before the money began to come back?

Pulitzer, who had a fortune of his own of at least $8,000,000, plus an income now around a half million a year from his three Worlds and almost $150,000 from the Post-Dispatch, plus enormous investment profits, was in the position of a well-armed general who believes his enemy running out of food and ammunition. Strenuous efforts were made to determine Hearst's losses and how much more he would be permitted to lose. Espionage was prevalent. A World memo disclosed that I. N. Stump, whom Clark had replaced as financial manager, said he believed that Mrs. Hearst would draw the line at $5,000,000, and much of this was already spent. Her total income was estimated at $450,000 a year. World accountants were studying all three Journals, trying to learn accurate circulation figures, counting the sparse advertisements and computing the revenue, calculating the cost of paper, printing, wages, rental and promotion to come up with an estimate of Hearst's monthly losses which Pulitzer studied sharply. Seitz, Bradford Merrill and other World executives often had lunch with former World men now with Hearst, subtly pumping them for information, at the same time uneasily aware that these renegades might have given World secrets to the Journal.

In each shop there was a mighty effort to impose stricter security, to narrow the number of executives who knew vital figures, to split them so that no one man knew them all, and to insure the loyalty of these few with high salaries and preferential treatment.

This was the situation as the nation's two largest newspaper publishers brought up their siege guns in an attempt to exterminate each other by the cunning use of news. By pure chance it happened that the first big, continuous news issue that came to hand was the revolution in Cuba.

II. POISONED QUAIL

It has been mistakenly believed that Pulitzer, the peace advocate, reversed his field and became a champion of the liberation of Cuba simply to beat Hearst in circulation. On the contrary, he spoke up for Cuba (as did Hearst) when Hearst was still a California newspaperman unknown in New York. His passionate belief in self-government and his hatred of imperialism were instantly aroused by the plight of the Cubans. Their latest revolution—really a resumption of earlier ones—broke out in February 1895. From the start the World gave it sympathetic attention. In an editorial seven months before Hearst invaded New York, Pulitzer's position was clear:

> It is not questionable at all that the people of Cuba would be much better off with a government of their own. Certainly they could not be worse than now when their industry is hampered by the dictation of ignorant foreigners in Madrid who know little about them and care only to make a profit out of them.[2]

He was perfectly sincere when he told the British peace advocates that he did not believe in peace at any price, that Americans "naturally sympathize with the uprising of any people against despotism . . . [as] in Cuba today." Had Hearst never been born, Pulitzer would have urged Cuban independence.

But the fact that Hearst indubitably was born and constituted a threat transformed Pulitzer from a judicial observer to a worried tycoon. Hearst was first to adopt the Cubans as his own, exploiting this popular cause for circulation. Although he swore he would spend all his mother's millions if necessary in defeating the World, his money was burning so fast that the smoke undoubtedly added recklessness to his already rash measures. Authentic news from Cuba was almost nonexistent. There were dispatches from Spanish authorities in Havana and Madrid invariably describing Spanish successes, and a flood of rumor from Cuban revolutionary sources recounting the triumphs of the rebels along with tales of Spanish treachery. From the beginning, Hearst's Journal renounced all faith in Spanish sources but placed confidence in rebel informants even though the rebels often contradicted each other. A dramatist in bold contrasts, he built in the Journal a daily scenario of the Cuban conflict which had little relation to fact but was exciting to the mass mind in much the same way as a cliff-hanging continued story, and in its stark delineation of a struggle between villain and hero, its depiction of the Spaniards as cowardly knaves and Cubans as noble, long-suffering victims of outrage. In the Hearst press the typical Spaniard emerged as a monster of cruelty who raped Cuban women, tortured and murdered their husbands and children, then burned their houses.

Hearst often described the Journal as Cuba's only friend, ridiculed his conservative journalistic rivals and gave the impression of being personally at war with Spain. A few months after he bought the Journal he sought to repair the news famine by sending Charles Michelson, Frederick Lawrence and C. B. Pendleton to Cuba. But the Spanish authorities there, irate at American distortion of their position, required the Journal men to register, restricted their movements severely and censored their dispatches. The trio spent most of their time at Havana's Hotel Inglaterra while obscure skirmishes took place hundreds of miles away. They had secret meetings with rebel sympathizers and "sworn eyewitnesses" who told blood-curdling yarns of Spanish atrocities—exciting copy but useless since the censors would eliminate it and there was no way to get the "news" out except by the uncertain method of smuggling it to places such as Key West. Indeed it was found that Key West, which swarmed with rebel adherents who said they had escaped from Cuba or had relatives there and were brimming with sworn eyewitness information, was the best source of thrilling Cuban rumor. Michelson was put in charge of a bureau there, and the Journal throbbed with electric dispatches from Key West. In January 1897 it began to feature its rumor with an innovation in journalism—streamer headlines in type that would grow from one inch to three inches and ultimately to five.

The World's Cuban coverage was at first measured and factual. In the months before Hearst arrived, Pulitzer's correspondent in Cuba was William Shaw Bowen, aided for a short time by the adventurous, 20-year-old Winston Churchill. Traveling over much of Cuba, Bowen discovered that the Spaniards were not all cutthroats nor were the Cubans invariably heroic, and he supplied responsible reportage that normally would have had Pulitzer's full support. But a kind of Gresham's Law of journalism took effect, with cheap correspondence driving out the good. Later it became evident that fewer readers followed Bowen's calm dispatches than the Hearst dramaturgy emanating from Key West. In January 1896, when General Valeriano Weyler was sent from Madrid with orders to suppress the rebellion (and when Hearst had just stolen Goddard and the Sunday World staff), a pale imitation of the Hearstian line began to appear in the World.

The stocky, 58-year-old Weyler had aided in quelling an earlier uprising and as military attaché at the Spanish legation during the Civil War had accompanied Sherman's forces as an observer. Even before he reached Havana, the Journal and the World, relying on rebel propaganda, denounced him. He was, said the World, "noted for his . . . extreme cruelty," adding later, "The crueler Weyler should prove, the better for the Cuban cause; the more barbarous his policy, the greater resistance will the Cubans make and the sooner will the United States be forced to consider their recognition." A few weeks later it told of the killing of "defenseless, harmless people hiding in their own homes," saying, "Weyler's butchery begins to reach its highest point." [3] But the World's prose could not match that of the Sunday Journal:

> [Weyler is] the prince of all cruel generals this century has seen. . . . [Spain's] most ferocious and bloody soldier . . . the fiendish despot whose hand Cuba well knows. . . . Hundreds of Cuban women, maids and matrons, shudder. . . .[4]

Two weeks later the Sunday World followed suit by unveiling a series of four weekly articles by Pulitzer's young favorite, David Graham Phillips, beginning with "The Hideous History of Old Spain" and bringing it up to date with luridly illustrated accounts of Spanish soldiers clubbing

Cuban men and women in the streets, the massacre of unarmed Cubans and the skill of the Spaniards with the garrote. The Sunday World solemnly ran an interview with its own impetuous female feature writer, Nellie Bly, who told of her plan to recruit volunteers for a special regiment, officered by women, to fight with the Cubans—a project heard of no more.

In the midst of the World's vilification of Weyler, some editor allowed a Bowen dispatch to get into print describing him as a good soldier whose reputation for cruelty was undeserved, "a man of extraordinary energy and great intelligence." Was there a hurried conference in the Dome about this inconsistency? One does not know, but at any rate Bowen was obviously too tame and the colorful, black-bearded James Creelman was sent to Cuba. Creelman soon managed to spirit out thoughts like the following:

> No man's life, no man's property is safe. American citizens are imprisoned or slain without cause. American property is destroyed on all sides. . . . The horrors of the barbarous struggle for the extermination of the native population are witnessed in all parts of the country. Blood on the roadsides, blood in the fields, blood on the doorsteps, blood, blood, blood! The old, the young, the weak, the crippled, all are butchered without mercy. . . . Not a word from Washington! Not a sign from the President! [5]

Creelman was joined in Cuba by other World correspondents including Sylvester Scovel, a young Wooster College graduate hot for Cuban freedom, and as techniques for smuggling dispatches through the censorship improved, these men played with fugal insistence on the theme of Spanish atrocities, joined by indignant editorialists in Manhattan. Madrid had ordered Weyler to "shoot or bury all those opposed to Spain," said the World, adding a daily string of sworn-eyewitness stories of Spanish poisoning of Cuban food and water, the Spanish butchering of 40 wounded prisoners, Spanish assaults on Cuban women, the fury of a drunken Spanish major who single-handed killed 50 Cubans ("old men and little boys were cut down and their bodies fed to the dogs"), the perverted nature of Spanish patriotism causing cruelty to become "almost a religion with the Spanish soldier," references to "the old Spanish habit of fusillading unarmed prisoners," and further bouquets to Weyler: "Genghis Khan and Timour, who made trophies of the skulls of their slaughtered enemies, were no more barbaric than is the Captain-General of Cuba, whose policies are outlined by the corpses of bound prisoners left lying along the march of his troops." [6] Reporter Scovel gave a minute description of some Cuban dead:

> The skulls of all were split to pieces down to the eyes. Some of these were gouged out. All the bodies had been stabbed by sword bayonets and

> hacked by sabers until I could not count the cuts; they were indistinguishable. The bodies had almost lost semblance of human form. The arms and legs of one had been dismembered and laced into a rude attempt at a Cuban five-pointed star . . . The tongue of one had been cut out, split open at the base and placed on the mangled forehead . . . Fingers and toes were missing. . . . The Spanish soldiers habitually cut off the ears of the Cuban dead and retain them as trophies.[7]

Bowen's dispatches could not compete with these, and he was eventually recalled to New York. After him came the deluge of dismemberment specialists who permanently alienated the Spanish authorities, had little opportunity to see actual combat and whose work consisted largely of trysts with rebel sympathizers who expected a fee for a good horror yarn, guaranteed to be true. The press, angered by Weyler's censorship, took heroic revenge on him, especially after he began to arrest or expel offending ink-slingers. One Herald correspondent in Cuba, George Bronson Rea, became so gorged at the ready acceptance of wild rumor and the outright manufacture of sensations by the New York press that he published a book, *Facts and Fakes About Cuba,* whose 300 pages exposed scores of frauds.

If the rebels were outmatched in the field, they were peerless in propaganda. In Washington they had their "Chargé d'Affaires," Gonzalo de Quesada, grinding out accounts of Spanish atrocities for the attention of sympathetic congressmen and aided by active Cuban cells in Florida and other states but particularly in New York City. Here the Cuban Junta was headed by the dedicated, silver-haired Tomás Estrada Palma, who had fought in an earlier rebellion and now was raising funds, encouraging filibusters and operating the most complaisant of news agencies. Hot-eyed Latins conferred sotto voce in his office at 66 Broadway, where news releases were manufactured daily. A flock of reporters called there every afternoon—a gathering called the Peanut Club because the host supplied a big box of peanuts which they crunched as he gave them sworn accounts of Spanish outrages in Cuba from his own private sources. The Spanish minister in Washington, Enrique Dupuy de Lome, tried vainly to counter the work of Estrada Palma and Quesada. Although he was able to disprove some of the more extravagant newspaper charges of Spanish bestiality, he found this of little use since new charges outran the old and he could never catch up. He said with great truth and moderation, ". . . The rebels . . . hope in some way to create bad blood, and, ultimately, war between Spain and the United States, with the idea of having their fighting done by American troops." [8]

Millions of words of error or pure fiction appeared in print. There were nasty little skirmishes never known or reported by the New York papers. There were other encounters, featured under headlines, which never took place. When the Cuban "government" was formed, the New York press disagreed as to its personnel, the date of the "convention" and its location, reporting variously that it took place at Camagüey and Timaguayu. Although rebel forces never threatened Havana, there were reports that they had captured the city, and equally erroneous dispatches about the capture of Pinar del Rio and Santa Clara. A lesson may be read in headlines about the same battle appearing in the Herald, which tried to maintain sanity, and the World, given in that order:

ANTONIO MACEO LOSES A BATTLE
Leaves Hundreds Dead on the Field, Being Compelled
to Retreat in Haste

MACEO CHASING SPANISH
Another Hot Fight With General Echague,
This Time Near North Coast [9]

The death, wounding or capture of Spanish General Martínez Campos and rebel General Máximo Gómez were regularly (and mistakenly) reported, while rebel General Maceo met a soldier's death at least a dozen times in as many places, once being reported a suicide. When Maceo *was* killed near Punta Brava in 1896, the New York press at first expressed doubt, then angrily gave ear to conflicting rebel charges of foul play. The Herald understood that Maceo was poisoned by his own perfidious physician, the Mail & Express said he was shot in a treacherous Spanish ambush, while the World and the Journal agreed that the Spaniards had killed him after asking him to confer under a flag of truce. Still another version, spread by the rebel publicity mill in Washington, ascended imaginative peaks, saying that Maceo and 40 of his men had been invited to a truce breakfast by the Spanish general, who served them poisoned roast quail, killing them all.

Few seemed to reflect that Maceo had been fighting with real bullets and might have been honorably shot, as indeed was later established. Minister De Lome was entitled to believe that no credence would be placed in this spectacularly contradictory rebel fake. On the contrary, legislators gave excited ear to the World and Journal charges, Senator William Chandler of New Hampshire being one of the many to express outrage, saying, "It has no parallel in the history of the world. The massacre of Gen. Maceo and his staff should cause Congress and President Cleveland to immediately recognize the absolute independence of the Cubans." [10]

The Rev. R. S. MacArthur, a Baptist clergyman, prepared a sermon for the Sunday World in which he urged immediate American intervention and affirmed that a regiment of preachers would willingly enlist for Cuba. The World-Journal treatment of the Maceo fiction, spread over the country by news services, influenced scores of inland editors, inspired hothead public speakers in many cities to demand intervention, helped decide the

American Federation of Labor convention to urge recognition of Cuban belligerency, and blew up such a storm in Congress that Minister De Lome was affrighted. The Spanish government was compelled to deny Spanish bestiality. General Weyler announced officially that Maceo was killed most punctiliously, a fate common in war, and from Madrid Minister of State Tetuán cabled the same intelligence to Washington. After some strenuous work by De Lome, cooler heads prevailed and it became a question of waiting for the next atrocity.

"The Cubans are fighting us openly," Weyler told the World's James Creelman. "The Americans are fighting us secretly . . . The American newspapers are responsible. They poison everything with falsehood." [11]

Shortly thereafter, a Hearst offer made Creelman leave the World and become a Journal man.

III. IMITATING IMITATIONS

Particularly galling to Pulitzer was the knowledge that Hearst had seized the journalistic initiative held by the World since 1883. He had done it by imitating time-tried World methods and ballooning them to circus extremes one might think the public would reject. Instead, the public loved it, and the World could do little but imitate the Journal's imitations. Hearst regularly dismissed his competitors as mossbacks, ran the motto "While Others Talk, the Journal Acts," and laughed at the World and Herald as "those eminent exponents of the old journalism." Badly needing an Associated Press franchise, he was blocked by Pulitzer, a charter member, and had to buy the Morning Advertiser (it cost him $500,000) to gain membership. For this he excoriated his enemy in pot-and-kettle terms:

> [Pulitzer is] a journalist who made his money by pandering to the worst tastes of the prurient and horror-loving, by dealing in bogus news, such as forged cablegrams from eminent personages, and by affecting a devotion to the interests of the people while never really hurting those of their enemies, and sedulously looking out for his own.[12]

Pulitzer had met his master in an art he felt his own—publicity. The Journal made more noise than all the other New York papers combined. It staged a "Yellow Fellow" bicycle relay from San Francisco to New York, a variation on an earlier World St. Louis-to-New York balloon voyage that failed of its destination. It opened a soup kitchen for the unemployed and gave sweaters to the needy. (The World had doled out coal in the winter and ice in the summer.) Hearst promotion men were constantly staging parades, hiring bands, exploding fireworks and sponsoring a series of benefit performances, one of them at the Metropolitan Opera House featuring such dazzlers as Anna Held and Mlle. Olitzka and raising $5,303.65 for the poor. Always the Journal gave headlines to its own philanthropies and spoke of "The New Journalism that Gets Things Done." Pulitzer wrote Norris:

> [Hearst] is welcome to spend another million or two if he wants to advertise himself still more as the man who could not, like Bennett and Greeley, create a paper with brains and ideas of his own, but who *did* have the distinction of sinking millions.[13]

Yet he had to revise his opinion about the enemy he had first considered a mere checkbook genius, as he wrote Seitz: "I personally think Geranium [the Journal] a wonderfully able & attractive and popular paper, perhaps the ablest in the one vital sense, of managing to be talked about; of attracting attention . . ." As usual he asked the impossible of his staff, demanding that expenses be cut and that new talent be found; insisting that the World guard its integrity and yet outdo the Journal. "I want a radical reduction of expenses from beginning to end of every department," he wrote Norris. He instructed Seitz, "Please find somebody in Geranium's office with whom you can connect, to discover exactly who furnishes their ideas, who is dissatisfied and obtainable or available even in the second class of executive rank. We are getting shorter and shorter . . ." From Norris he requested another estimate of "the present deficit of Geranium." Again, he insisted on a paper with "the respect and confidence of the public, the destruction of the notion that we are in the same class with the Journal, in recklessness and unreliability." From Cap Martin one of his semihumorous instructions was to "cable something pleasant." [14]

The most unpleasant news possible was that the World was losing and the Journal gaining. The editors were so well aware of this and so fired in the circulation battle that they were inclined to discount the warnings about recklessness and permit more colorful buncombe than the blind owner realized. The World was one of the few newspapers then scrupulously honest about its circulation. According to its own office figures, Senior had dropped from its all-time high average of 312,000 in 1896 to 289,000 in 1897; the Evening World had slipped from 360,000 to 341,000 and the Sunday World from 562,000 to 514,000. For all of 1896 the World claimed an average weekday circulation, morning and evening and tri-weekly combined, of 743,024. Two months later the Journal claimed a combined morning-evening circulation of 750,000, apparently including the German-language edition. Although the Journal had not yet established a reputation for strict honesty and was notorious for giving away copies by the thousands for promotion, it was evident that it was gaining on the World and was close behind.

Only one who has been involved in a circulation struggle can understand the pressures, the temptations, the pummeling of wit and imagination, the tendency to move by degrees away from reality into fantasy, the alternate triumph and panic, that were felt in the World and Journal offices. Costs soared for both of them, not only in covering the rebellion but in printing many competitive "extras" every day and getting back masses of unsold copies. At the World, the eternal question was, "How much longer can Hearst last?" By 1897 Hearst had three speedy dispatch boats operating between Florida and Cuba, while Pulitzer had only one. Hearst had twice as many correspondents in Key West and Cuba, men he cunningly dignified by calling them "Journal Commissioners" (a term the World had used earlier to designate the writers of more sober feature articles), which seemed to imply some official status and in any case placed them beyond the mere reporters of other papers.

In January 1897 there were nearly 40 "war correspondents" from all over the United States in Key West, some merely exploiting rebel rumor, others trying to slip into Cuba to join the insurgents. Eight of them were Journal Commissioners. One carried a $2,000 dress sword, purchased by Hearst from a Fifth Avenue jeweler, with gold-plated hilt glittering with diamonds and engraved: *"To Máximo Gómez, Commander-in-Chief of the Army of the Cuban Republic"*—and many vain attempts were made to deliver the gift to an officer whose men were without shoes. A Hearst physician was also there, with surgical instruments and medicines that stayed in their chests because he was unable to spirit them to the rebels.[15]

In January, 1897, Hearst snagged a prize—handsome Richard Harding Davis, already on his way to becoming a national idol because of his romantic fiction, who agreed to spend a month as a Journal Commissioner in Cuba for $3,000 and expenses. He was under careful Spanish surveillance and was unable to get near any fighting, but the Journal represented him as being "with the insurgents" and ran an enormous illustration of him, mounted and crisscrossed with cartridge belts. Although he sent out some well-written atrocity stories, his most famous dispatch concerned the three Cuban girls who boarded the American vessel *Olivette*, bound from Havana to Tampa, and were stripped and searched by the Spaniards as suspected spies. This story underwent a subtle change at the hands of some Journal editor in New York. As it appeared in print under the five-column headline "DOES OUR FLAG PROTECT WOMEN?", the humiliated girls were undressed by male detectives, and a half-page drawing by Fredric Remington showed one of the girls stark naked, with interested policemen examining her clothing.[16]

The account raised an uproar almost equal to that over the "assassination" of Maceo. Congressman Amos Cummings of New York (a former Sun editor who should have known better) introduced a resolution asking the Secretary of State to investigate. When the *Olivette* reached Tampa, the Cuban girls said it was all a great mistake. Undressed by men? Not at all. They had been searched by women matrons while the policemen waited outside. The World vengefully front-paged the story under the heading "THE UNCLOTHED WOMEN SEARCHED BY MEN WAS AN INVENTION OF A NEW YORK NEWSPAPER," but the Journal had no comment. The Journal editor Willis Abbot later observed, "It was characteristic of Hearst methods that no one suffered for what in most papers would have been an unforgivable offense. I never heard the owner . . . express the slightest regret for the scandalous 'fake.' "[17]

Pulitzer had no one in Cuba as famous and expensive as Davis, nor did he have any lawmakers reporting for him, as the Journal did when it sent the jingo Senator-elect Hernando Money of Mississippi as another Journal Commissioner to the island. The World countered by praising its own best-known Cuban man, Scovel, and belittling Money: "The World's correspondent [Scovel] reported what he saw and knew. The amateur visitor to Weyler and [United States Consul in Havana Fitzhugh] Lee tells only what he heard and believed." Scovel, said the World, "combines all the great and high qualities of the war correspondent—devotion to duty, accuracy, graphic descriptive power, absolute courage and skill." When Scovel was arrested in February for obtaining a false police pass under an assumed name, the World blew it into a Spanish outrage and an affront to the United States. Scovel was imprisoned in a "vile jail, in a filthy and small-pox infected town," was unable to get adequate counsel, and (most shameless of exaggerations), "He is in imminent danger of butchery by a decree of a drum-head court-martial." The World reported several "free Scovel" mass meetings and the requests of a dozen state legislatures for his release.[18]

Actually, Scovel's gravest danger came from roaches in his cell. Consul General Lee hastily interceded for him, and Spain was so anxious to avoid offending the powerful Yankee press that it was a foregone conclusion that he would be sent packing after a little discomfiture.

The Journal ignored Scovel as a World promotion and concentrated on its own, the death of Dr. Ricardo Ruiz in his cell at Guanabacoa. A dentist, Ruiz had fled Cuba after participating in a previous insurrection, become an American citizen, then returned to practice dentistry and become embroiled in the new rebellion. He was one of a large group particularly vexatious to Spain—Cubans who used their American citizenship as a protection for their rebellious activities. Arrested for alleged involvement in a rebel raid on a train, he spent a fortnight in jail and then committed suicide, the Spaniards said, by pounding his head against the cell wall.

A Hearst correspondent, George Eugene Bryson, was permitted to see Ruiz' body. He smuggled out a story saying there was "strong evidence to show that this man was murdered," which the Journal, as so often happened, converted to fact in its headline "AMERICAN SLAIN IN SPANISH JAIL."

The World also let suspicion become fact under a Ruiz headline, "THE UNITED STATES MAY FIGHT SPAIN YET," but showed a reluctance to let the case steal the limelight from its own Scovel sensation by saying, "The murder of Dr. Ruiz—an inoffensive American citizen in a Cuban cell, sharply illustrates the peril in which Sylvester Scovel is placed." [19]

The Journal seized Ruiz to its bosom and carried him away. Almost its entire February 22 front page, and many inside columns, were devoted to fortissimo variations on the theme of Ruiz. There was an "interview" with Senator John Sherman of Ohio, soon to become McKinley's Secretary of State, under the headline "SHERMAN FOR WAR WITH SPAIN FOR MURDERING AMERICANS," in which the senator was quoted as saying, "If the facts are true . . . and American citizens are being murdered in cold blood, the only way to put an end to the atrocities is to declare war with Spain." There were statements from dependably bellicose Congressmen—statements also from Creelman, now in Madrid for the Journal, and from a Journal Washington correspondent, Alfred Henry Lewis, assailing the administration for its craven failure to demand justice.

Consul General Lee, a very busy man, secured permission for an autopsy, which disclosed only that Ruiz had died of head injuries. Hearst telegraphed Mrs. Ruiz money to enable her (with her children) to visit the United States as a Journal special representative. The Journal took no heed when Senator Sherman testily disavowed the interview: "It is a lie from beginning to end. I am surprised that the *Journal* should make such a statement. I wish you would denounce it as emphatically as possible." The World happily publicized Sherman's denial.[20]

IV. DISAGREEABLY AGREEING

Joseph Pulitzer and William Randolph Hearst agreed so substantially on so many issues of the Cuban problem that—but for their quarrel about circulation—one might have expected World and Journal men to be enthusiastic allies cooperating in their joint crusade, mingling fraternally and exchanging scoops the better to serve the cause.

They agreed, of course, on the enormity of Spanish atrocities, the villainy of Weyler and the falsity of De Lome. Each became impatient with President Cleveland's patience with the Spaniards, and each hoped that McKinley would show more spunk. Each moved (with Hearst usually a trifle in advance) from a demand that the United States recognize Cuban belligerency, then Cuban independence, to downright incitement of war with Spain. Each denied that dollars had any bearing on the matter of Cuban liberation, yet said it was a shame that Spanish tyranny had cut the $100,000,000 United States trade with Cuba to one fifth of that. Each noted that the stock market broke with every war scare and promoted an interesting theory: that war was opposed by selfish Wall Streeters fearful of their profits, and supported by the liberty-loving masses. Each had a tendency to link his enemies with Spain, the World calling Secretary Olney "the strongest . . . supporter of Spanish Toryism," the Journal saying of Cleveland, "Spain's lone ally is in the White House," and referring to the anti-war Senator Eugene Hale of Maine as "the Spanish Senator." Each gave alarmed attention to the increase of yellow fever in the South, declaring it was spreading from Cuba because of the Spanish disregard for sanitation. Pulitzer and Hearst agreed on all these things—that war was needed on humanitarian, libertarian, economic and antiseptic grounds—and yet remained deadly foes.

Each gave close heed to McKinley's inaugural address, in which he spoke calmly about "a firm and dignified foreign policy" and added, "We wants no wars of conquest. We must avoid the temptation of territorial aggression." The Journal felt his speech "vague and sapless," Cleveland all over again, while the World expressed guarded approval that would soon change to criticism. Each dumped on the new administration its own well-publicized problem, the World demanding that Scovel be freed from his dungeon, the Journal stressing the Ruiz case.

The Journal sent Mrs. Ruiz to Washington and saw that she secured interviews with President McKinley, Secretary of State Sherman and Representative R. R. Hitt, chairman of the House Committee on Foreign Affairs—all lavishly publicized in the Journal. The paper again interviewed jingo Congressmen and published their indignant comments.

Hearst's strategy embodied an old Pulitzer device. He made the Ruiz case so loudly his own that other New York papers played it down rather than take the position of climbing on the Journal's bandwagon. The World neglected Mrs. Ruiz and hammered on the Scovel matter. That young man managed to smuggle out daily reports from his Cuban cell—so interesting that the World's circulation increased by 8,000 during his month of imprisonment. The Spaniards released him March 10 on condition that he leave Cuba, causing the World to cheer, "All honor to President McKinley and to the grand old Secretary of State, John Sherman!" [21] The Journal, after draining Mrs. Ruiz of news value, dropped her and looked for something new. It found its fondest ideal in a pretty, 18-year-old Cuban girl named Evangelina Cosio y Cisneros.

Chapter 4

Journalistic Dramaturgy

I. THE FLOWER OF CUBA

Senorita Cosio, who came to be known in the United States as Miss Cisneros, was the daughter of a Camagüey revolutionist condemned to execution for organizing a rebel cavalry unit. On her appeal, however, the Spaniards commuted the sentence to life imprisonment at the penal colony in Ceuta, Africa. A spirited girl, she later made another plea to General Weyler himself. The general so often pictured as a monster relaxed the sentence still further so that her father was given milder confinement at the Isle of Pines, south of Cuba, and Evangelina, whose mother was dead, was permitted to stay near him.

There she devised a plan to free him. She invited the Spanish commander on the island, Colonel José Berriz, to her cottage, where rebel sympathizers seized him, beat him, then were overpowered by soldiers coming to his aid. Miss Cisneros was sent to the Recojidas prison in Havana, charged with sedition.

America knew nothing about her until months later, in August 1897, when Bryson, the same Hearst correspondent who had exploited the Ruiz case, talked with her in the prison. In his dispatch to the Journal he passed over her attempted jail delivery, saying instead that she was imprisoned because of her brave defense of her person against the lustful advances of Colonel Berriz. James Creelman, back from Europe, was in the Journal office when Hearst read Bryson's dispatch, slapped his knee and said, "We've got Spain now!" [1]

The story was treated as a sex case, a woman's defense of her honor. Secretary of State Sherman was notified, as was the United States Minister to Spain, Stewart L. Woodford. A Journal telegram to the merciless General Weyler urged him to be merciful. Bryson was ordered to send more detail, much more, about Miss Cisneros. The Hearst sob sisters Annie Laurie (Winifred Black) and Beatrice Fairfax (Marie Manning, formerly of the World) were alerted to write emotionally about her. A Journal petition was composed, asking Queen Regent Maria Christina of Spain to intercede for the girl's pardon. More than 200 Hearst stringers throughout the United States were wired copies of the petition and ordered to call on local women—influential women first—and get their signatures.

Pulitzer must have been enraged that Hearst appropriated the publicity methods used by the World in its crusades against war with England over Venezuela, and for a popular sale of government bonds. It also must have irked him that one of the first signers of the Hearst petition was Mrs. Jefferson Davis, who was drawing a World salary. Among other famous signers were General Grant's widow, President McKinley's mother, Frances Hodgson Burnett, Julia Ward Howe and Clara Barton. The Journal was enlivening its front page daily with affecting stories about Miss Cisneros.

"This tenderly nurtured girl was imprisoned at eighteen among the most depraved Negresses of Havana, and now she is about to be sent in mockery to spend twenty years in a servitude that will kill her in a year."

"At last the ruffians who rule Cuba in the name of Spain have gone too far. They have roused America from its apathy . . . In Washington and Havana the excitement aroused by the Journal's recital of the infamy perpetrated against Senorita Cisneros is so great that the Spanish authorities are alarmed, and are appealing to the bestial commandant to withdraw his charge.

"For the sake of the poor girl it is to be hoped that these varied efforts may prove successful. But if they should fail the unnatural alliance between our government and the barbarians who are devastating Cuba would be ended, and the Cuban republic would date its independence from the martyrdom of Evangelina Cisneros." [2]

Weyler expelled Correspondent Bryson for his fictions. He telegraphed the facts in the case to the World, which jealously published them and commented, "The Spanish in Cuba have sins enough to answer for, as The World was first to show, but nothing is gained for the Cuban cause by inventions and exaggerations that are past belief." [3] Spanish Minister De Lome wrote an open letter to Mrs. Jefferson Davis which was widely published, pointing out that the women of America had been misled and that the Journal's accounts were entirely erroneous. Facts could not stay the avalanche. The Journal used 12 columns to print the names of women signers of its petition, listing them by states. It described Miss Cisneros as "in death's shadow," supplying sketches showing her in lovely bloom before her imprisonment but now pathetically emaciated. The Hearst drive for women's signatures extended to England, where some 200,000 women added their names, and a Hearst cable asked the intercession of Pope Leo XIII. In Spain, the Queen Regent, feeling that whatever the girl's guilt she was not worth offending His Holiness and the women of two sovereign nations, urged Weyler to remove her gently to a convent. Weyler, understandably angry, was in no hurry to accede.

On September 8, Consul General Lee, arriving in New York for a vacation, delivered his opinion of the Journal's crusade:

". . . I wish to correct a false and stupid impression which has been created by some newspapers. . . . [Miss Cisneros] has two clean rooms in the Casa Recojidas, and is well clothed and fed. It is all tommy-rot about her scrubbing floors and being subjected to cruelties and indignities. She would have been pardoned long ago if it had not been for the hubbub created by American newspapers. . . . That she was implicated in the insurrection on the Isle of Pines, there can be no question. She herself, in a note to me, acknowledged that fact, and stated she was betrayed by an accomplice named Arias." [4]

The World gave the Lee interview delighted prominence, whereas the Journal buried it and omitted his remarks about tommyrot. Indeed, after three weeks of drum-beating, public interest in the Cuban Joan of Arc (as the Hearst press called her) was inevitably subsiding and Hearst had already sent burly Karl Decker, formerly a Journal Washington correspondent, to Havana armed with plenty of money and orders to deliver the girl from jail. The work had to be done swiftly before the Spaniards pardoned her, which would be disastrous to Hearst's plans. Decker's bribing of Recojidas prison guards on October 6 and his departure from Cuba with Evangelina has long been accorded the prize in journalistic impudence.[5] When news of the jailbreak reached New York, Hearst's orders to his editor, Samuel Chamberlain, displayed not only his showmanship but his belief that he had performed a feat of political importance.

"Now is the time to consolidate public sentiment," he said. "Organize a great open-air reception in Madison Square. Have the two best military bands. Secure orators, have a procession, arrange for plenty of fireworks and searchlights. Announce that Miss Cisneros and her rescuer will appear side by side and thank the people. Send men to all the political leaders in the city, and ask them to work up the excitement. We must have 100,000 people together that night. It must be a whale of a demonstration—something that will make the President and Congress sit up and think." [6]

A comparison of this with Pulitzer's directive for an Eggleston editorial about the government bond issue is instructive—the vaudeville juggler as opposed to the talented impresario. "EVANGELINA CISNEROS RESCUED BY THE JOURNAL," was the Journal's headline. "An American Newspaper Accomplishes at a Single Stroke What the Best Efforts of Diplomacy Failed Utterly to Bring About in Many Months." The story omitted mention of bribery, too unglamorous a device, and had Decker performing the deed with the aid of disguises, ladders and hacksaws.[7] Later headlines read, "BAFFLED WEYLER RAGES AT THE JOURNAL," "INTERNATIONAL COMPLICATIONS MAY RESULT FROM THE CISNEROS RESCUE," and finally, "EVANGELINA CISNEROS REACHES THE LAND OF LIBERTY." She reached New York in rosy good health to become Hearst property.

The Sunday Journal began a fictionalized version of Evangelina's life which ran for three months. When her news interest was exhausted in New York, the Journal took her to Washington, where President McKinley so far succumbed to the power of the press as to greet her and congratulate her in the White House. There could have been no more studied affront to Spain than for the President to give this form of highly publicized approval to Hearst's violation of Spanish law and authority, and it was no wonder that Madrid newspapers assailed the "Yankee pigs." After that, except for her interminable life story, Miss Cisneros faded out of the Journal's pages, having been given 375 columns or about 230,000 words. The World gave her 12 columns, the Times ten, and other New York papers one column or less.

II. HEARST GOING BROKE?

Still Phoebe Hearst kept bailing her son out of debt. Would the cornucopia never empty? That gentle, charming lady who divided her time between California, Washington and Europe could hardly have been aware of the uproar her millions were causing not only in the World and Journal offices but in the capital, in Cuba, Spain, England, the Vatican and the Peanut Club, not to mention the worry she was bringing to Joseph Pulitzer.

Hearst, personally directing his newspapers, knew exactly the lengths to which they were going and believed them justified. Pulitzer, never in the office, insulated from Park Row talk, operating from Bar Harbor, Jekyll Island or Europe, was perhaps less aware of the extravagances of the World. Yet his "reading" of the papers was so exhaustive, his sources of information so numerous and his news instinct so acute that of course he knew that his papers were daily violating his ideal of "Accuracy!" and he condoned the practice. The short battle he had envisioned had dragged out interminably. He had a tiger by the tail, and if he was sorry he had seized the tail in the first place, he found it inadvisable to let go. In his hundreds of directives to World executives in 1897–98 there comes to light no criticism of exaggeration in dealing with Cuba. Indeed, he avoided the subject, and while he deplored Hearst's humbug, he was frank in his admiration for Hearst's ability to produce popular ideas. He wrote Seitz:

> That is the sort of brains the World needs. Pardon me for saying also, that with all [the Journal's] faults, which I should not like to copy—though they have been *exaggerated*—it *is a newspaper.*

Again he wrote Seitz through a secretary:

> [Mr. Pulitzer] would like to have you extend your relations . . . with men who know the inside workings of the Geranium and other establishments, with a view to ascertaining who is producing the good ideas. If it would be helpful, get some tactful and discreet man to assist you in getting information; and he authorizes you to expend $25 a week, or more if required as a "luncheon fund" to promote sociability!—a secret service, diplomatic fund, as it were.[8]

His hope of victory was inflated in November when Hearst sought an interview with him to discuss mutual problems. Kate's brother, "Uncle Willie" Davis, no longer with the World, was at the 55th Street house at the time, and Pulitzer from Bar Harbor authorized him to invite Gush there, listen closely and make no commitments. It turned out that Hearst wanted to establish a modus vivendi, his major suggestion being that both the Journal and World go up to two cents.

At last—the sign of weakness, the evidence that Mrs. Hearst had called a halt and the money was running out! Pulitzer, who earlier had debated the idea of returning to two cents on his own, quelled the thought. He gave instructions that everything Hearst said was to be repeated to him in as nearly his exact words as possible. He wrote Norris, "You may assume that I am determined to stick to the present price on the theory that *they* must go up to 2¢," later repeating, ". . . I do not entertain any idea of ever going up to 2¢," and adding, "Our motto is, *we can wait* . . . we are not anxious about the future . . ."[9] His feelings must have been similar to Napoleon's on seeing the "sun of Austerlitz." He waited with an assurance of triumph.

III. EXIT BRISBANE

He waited, but nothing happened. The Journal remained at a penny. Still, the crack in the Hearst armor seemed evident, and Pulitzer could feel his own cuirass stout and intact around him. But he was dissatisfied with his executives, his nerves were stretched taut, his doctors were warning him, and what he sought was the impossible—a second Pulitzer who could take over the top supervision, relieve him entirely of financial and business details and let him get the rest he needed. For months he had set lures before Melville E. Stone, who seemed to have the specifications of genius—great success as a Chicago editor and publisher, then as a banker, and now for four years as general manager of the Associated Press and the recent victor in a bitter battle with the United Press.

"I saw [Pulitzer] at Washington and at Bar Harbour," Stone recalled. ". . . To ensure my absolute control of the property, he said he would enter into a hard-and-fast contract for five years, go away . . . and leave me undisturbed." The salary "would be whatever I named it, provided it was not less than that of the President of the United States," who then got $50,000. Stone had heard enough about the World shop and Pulitzer's inability to leave anyone undisturbed so that, as he put it, "I feared the work would be more strenuous than I cared to engage in," and ultimately he declined, noting, "I do not think Joseph Pulitzer ever quite forgave me." [10]

Still the long shadow of Hearst reached into the Dome. In addition to lesser talent he kidnaped the feature specialist Rudolph Block, and in October the valued "Iron-Faced Charlie" Russell went over, although Brisbane tried to dissuade him from such folly. Brisbane himself was irked by the chief's criticism of his belief in smashing the reader in the eye. Pulitzer demanded more appeal to the brain, censuring "Brisbane's idea of making the [Sunday magazine] simply for five minutes, not for reading but for pictures and to be thrown away when glanced through," and asking for a magazine containing thoughtful text that "nobody could get through in five hours . . ." [11] In addition, Brisbane felt himself a man with a message and was provoked by the strict Pulitzer ban against any byline but his own—particularly now that Hearst was giving bylines to virtually everyone. In November he took the risk of signing his name to an Evening World editorial and was promptly suspended. Pulitzer telegraphed Norris, "Please make sure that Horace received a telegram sent yesterday . . . telegraph me whether he has been about the office today." [12] Brisbane, the recipient of fur coats and bonuses, was not about the office because without losing a day he joined Hearst in what would be a profitable 39-year association, with bylines.

Again Pulitzer had to recruit men from outside, capturing them in careful contracts which he knew were useless if a man wanted to leave, but offering salaries which a few years earlier were unheard of. One of them, William Van Benthuysen, was investigated like a candidate for a bishopric before he left the Chicago Tribune to take over the Sunday World on a two-year contract at $18,200 a year.

Adding to Pulitzer's disgruntlement was the inauguration of Greater New York on the last day of 1897. The World had campaigned for years for the incorporation of Brooklyn, Staten Island and parts of the Bronx and Queens into one vast city, and now that the event came to pass, it was Hearst who elbowed into the limelight. When city officials could not decide on a ceremony, the Journal's offer to put on a show at its own expense (more of that burning money) was accepted. The proprietor, with his faith in fireworks, hired Henry Pain, the impresario of rockets and whizbangs, organized a monster parade, called in scores of bands, singing societies and bicycle clubs, two batteries of artillery and many pretty actresses. The Journal offered prizes of from $10 to $1,000 for the best displays. Its seasoned production unit achieved a rousing celebration of the 234-year-old city's expansion, and despite bad weather and the refusal of some embittered Brooklynites to join, saloon doors swung merrily and Broadway was a mosaic of shimmering umbrellas. Fireworks near the Broadway Central Hotel caused alarmed horses to plunge into Fanciulli's 71st Regiment Band, injuring 15 and battering several brasses, but the injured were taken away and the festivities continued. At 12 o'clock, as the old year and Old New York faded out together, hundreds of Hearst magnesium lights illuminated a vast throng in City Hall Park, so noisy that they heard nothing of the choral singing of "Auld Lang Syne," not a word of what Mayor Strong said as he handed over the government to Boss Croker, in the person of Mayor Van Wyck.[13] Lucille Pulitzer had died that afternoon at Chatwold, but her father, who missed nothing, could not have been unaware of this Hearst coup.

As the World's huge profits shrank near the vanishing point, the orders for economy became insistent. Norris wrote Ernest Chamberlin of the Evening World, "Do you not think it absurd to pay $4.00 for the 2 column cut . . . printed on April 22nd?" and Chamberlin was required to explain.[14] Kate Pulitzer, who saw her husband for only a few weeks each year, and for only brief periods during that span, was told that she must cut her $72,000 annual allowance for family expenses. George Ledlie, directed to audit her accounts and find leaks, subtly informed the master that the biggest leaks arose from expenses he incurred or authorized at Chatwold. What with all the servants, secretaries and guests, the average number of people fed there daily was 53. The cost of food, mineral water and wine for August alone was $3,000. The cost of the stable and its 35 horses—one of them named Conkling—came to more than $15,000 a year. Pulitzer, surprised, continued Kate's $72,000 allowance.[15]

IV. CHECKING ON THE STAFF

For a half-blind man to essay to run a group of metropolitan newspapers from a distance, to keep abreast of news pouring in from all over the globe, to direct executives who were on the spot and aware of many details unknown to him, would seem preposterous. That the effort largely succeeded was due to his enormous labor and his insistence on equal labor by his men. The exhaustive reports he required them to send, often daily, rose to a mountain of paper that harassed them and took much of their time. It was his intent to fix responsibility for everything. Whenever he sent an order by telegraph or cable he ended it with the word "Sedentary," which meant that an immediate reply was expected. The reply was usually in one word, "Semaphore," meaning not only that the recipient understood the message but that his duty to act on it was on the record and he had better not forget it.

While his messages were sometimes humorous and invariably polite, there was no nonsense about them. Occasionally he would stipulate that his order must not be followed if conditions unknown to him so dictated, and sometimes in sending an idea he would add, "Humbly submitted—not even suggested." Humility, however, seldom troubled him. More often he would write, "Go ahead—but *be sure you are right,*" which laid a terrible onus if the man was not right. He insisted that he wanted to devote his energies to editorial matters and be relieved of all business problems except the most important basic decisions, and he often reproved Norris for bothering him with details, writing, "Management must manage." Yet this was a difficult line to draw, and at times a reproof would come because Norris had acted without consulting him.

His four top men (except for W. H. Merrill, who was devoted exclusively to editorials) were Norris, Seitz, Bradford Merrill and (a little later) Florence D. White. Each had long experience both in the news and business domains. Since none was really "boss" over the other but responsible directly to Pulitzer, they were essentially rivals whose areas of authority overlapped, causing bickering and intrigue. Each knew he was not indispensable but could instantly be replaced by one of the others—Pulitzer's deliberate method of protecting himself from holdups, insuring alertness and keeping final control strictly in his own hands. He would have justified this Machiavellian policy on the ground that it was the only way a blind, absent proprietor could safeguard the World, just as he justified his constant demand that each executive and editor watch and report on the others.

Each man, as he reported on his colleagues, knew that others were appraising him. Andes' insistence on such reports is illustrated by excerpts from a few of his messages.

To Seitz: "Report especially on the adaptability of the men now in charge of the evening [World]."

To Norris: "I would like to have on my pictorial imagination an outline of the value & character of every man in that paper [the Post-Dispatch] beginning with Anthony or the messenger boy. Mention particularly how [F. D.] White impressed you while out there [at St. Louis]—not in a *general* way but in detail. Apropos of this, this is the sort of news, knowledge and information I have frequently begged of you about the people on the World."

To Seitz: "Will you not be kind enough to tell me what, exactly, is Botsford's salary, and what it was a year ago, and more recently. Also please write me a little about his character temperament family, age &c. Where did he come from and when." (Botsford's salary was raised.)

To Seitz: "I wish you would watch Eakins' [Joseph J. Eakins, sporting editor] work particularly—most minutely. And let me know." (Eakins received a salary increase.)

To Seitz: "Please ascertain what hours Duneka was at the office in [Foster] Coates' absence—and whether he was there Sunday."

To Norris: "Want to know particularly what time Horace will spend at office every day this week."

To Norris: ". . . While [Mr. Pulitzer] does not want to get things submitted to him for decision he *does* like to know what is going on. While he does not want to *do* anything, he wants to hear everything!" This last conveyed the lighter touch of Alfred Butes, who handled most of the business correspondence, and with signal ability.

To Seitz three days after the *Maine* was sunk: "Please let me know how many hours, & which hours—Mr. Van Ben[thuysen] spent at the office Saturday, Sunday and Monday. Try to be as exact as possible. . . . Also be kind enough to tell me exactly who of the Big Four—the two Merrills, Norris, & yourself—was at the office Sunday and Monday—and at what hours— Another test of headship—and *heart*ship—I don't remember two days of greater importance. I never can catch Van B at the office on the telephone. . . . Also [Nelson] Hersh—what were his hours."

To Seitz: "Mr. P. notes that Mr. [Joseph] Altsheler has finished 2 or 3 novels in the last year, and is also contributing to magazines. He is glad to have so bright a man on the staff, *but* he thinks somebody ought to know how much time Mr. A. gives to his duties on The World?—what his *hours* are? . . . Mr. P. has a good opinion of Mr. A. and makes these inquiries in no unkindness, but as a matter of principle."

In regard to Pulitzer's strict order that World men should never become friendly with politicians—especially Tammany politicians—Seitz reported to him that Brooklyn Boss Pat McCarren had taken a fancy to Nelson Hersh of the Sunday staff, and went on: "The other night, Mr. Van Benthuysen was at Koster & Bials and met [Boss] Croker in his box in brotherly friendliness. Mr. Eakins has been connected with the Tammany fellows through Jack McDonald and Kelly, two of the ablest gamblers in town . . ." [16]

The Pulitzer system was indeed a matter of principle and was not precisely espionage since it was usually done openly. Often, if A criticized B, the chief would send A's report to B and ask him to comment—a practice that tended to make the critic think carefully and keep his judgment cool and honest as the boss wished it to be. He wrote Seitz after an especially indignant report on a colleague: "I wish I could make you believe that I mean no unkindness to you personally in suggesting the extreme importance to the paper of freeing your judgment about the editors from any personal feeling. Whatever basis you may have, however right you may be in some of your reflections . . ." [17]

The rest of the message is lost, but its meaning clear. He wanted no animus, no talebearing—merely wanted to know the facts. But of course there *was* some talebearing, some vindictiveness, some backbiting. Men of the World and Post-Dispatch realized this, had to bear up under it and had to learn to rely on the ultimate fairness and justice of the proprietor. He was, at any rate, so careful in his judgment that few instances come to light of men discharged unjustly.

Chapter 5

War and Peace

I. NEAREST APPROACH TO HELL

Meanwhile the Spanish government had fallen, to be succeeded by a cabinet under Práxedes Mateo Sagasta which accepted the inevitable. It promised the Cubans self-government under Spain, recalled Weyler, replaced him with General Ramón Blanco (who even let Sylvester Scovel return to Cuba) and was so conciliatory that President McKinley resolved to give it every opportunity for success.

The rebels (supported by the World and the Journal) rejected the self-government plan and continued the war, demanding full independence. On the recommendation of Consul General Lee, who had heard rumors of anti-American plots, the battleship *Maine*, under Captain Charles D. Sigsbee, arrived in Havana January 25, 1898, on what was described as a friendly visit. The Spaniards presented Sigsbee with a case of Jerez sherry and were most courteous, but to them the *Maine*'s 24 guns did not look friendly and they countered by readying the Spanish battle cruiser *Vizcaya* for a "friendly visit" to New York.

On the evening of February 15 the *Maine* exploded in Havana harbor, taking the lives of 260 of its 360 officers and men. Sailors from the Spanish cruiser *Alfonso XII* joined in rescue work made perilous by exploding ammunition on the burning ship. General Blanco burst into tears when he heard the news, realizing what it meant. Captain Sigsbee, shaken but unhurt, reported the facts by wire to Navy Secretary John D. Long, adding:

> Public opinion should be suspended until further report. . . . Many Spanish officers including representatives of General Blanco now with me to express sympathy.[1]

To Spain, which had swallowed its pride and made every concession possible to pacify the United States, the fate of the *Maine* was a disaster. To think that she plotted the explosion was preposterous, as all the New York papers—even the Journal and the World in their finer print—agreed. The Times, Tribune, Herald and Evening Post all sensibly counseled patience and deprecated any talk of war. There was the strong probability that the *Maine* had suffered an accidental internal explosion—a question that would have to be decided by the United States Navy's board of inquiry that would examine the sunken battleship.

Yet both the Journal and the World seized on the tragedy as a pretext for immediate war with Spain. The Journal burst out with American flags and a daily series of inflammatory headlines laying the blame on Spain. The World was not far behind, and although it admitted editorially that "Nobody outside of a lunatic asylum" believed that Spain officially plotted the explosion, it implied a moral guilt and in its headlines quite baldly entered the lunatic asylum by dark talk of plots and "Spanish treachery." It had the impudence to send a dispatch boat to Havana with "expert divers" intending to investigate the cause of the explosion and prove its contention of treachery—an idea the Spanish officials quite properly vetoed. On February 17, along with the Journal, it published what it called a "suppressed cable" from Sigsbee to Secretary Long saying the explosion was not an accident—a cable later discovered to be an outright fake. While the Spanish authorities in Havana gave the American dead a great state funeral with every mark of respect, the World and the Journal employed against Spain the rumor, the insinuation, the slant, the accusation, the fabrication. When the *Vizcaya* reached New York at this most unpropitious of moments, three days after the *Maine* sank, public feeling was so high that the Navy and the New York police wisely protected her with a flotilla of patrol boats. Her colors were at half-mast in honor of the American dead, but her commander, Captain Antonio Eulate, firmly refused to permit any Hearst reporters to board her. World men were not barred although the World was so incendiary as to suggest that the *Vizcaya* might shoot up New York, saying, "While lying off the Battery, her shells will explode on the Harlem River and in the suburbs of Brooklyn." [2]

The Times, now reviving under the shrewd ownership of young Adolph Ochs, said the law should forbid the "freak journalism" employed by the Pulitzer and Hearst papers. Edwin Godkin wrote, "Nothing so disgraceful as the behavior of these two newspapers in the past week has ever been known in the history of journalism," and assailed their "gross misrepresentation of facts, deliberate invention of tales calculated to excite the public, and wanton recklessness in the construction of headlines . . ." He added, "No one—absolutely no one—supposes a yellow journal cares five cents about the Cubans, the *Maine* victims, or any one else. A yellow journal is probably the nearest approach to hell, existing in any Christian state."[3]

During the week after the *Maine* disaster, the World sold five million copies, calling it "the largest circulation of any newspaper printed in any language in any country." Yet it would actually lose money that year because of its high expenses. Scovel was back in Havana, sending the Dome such vicious humbug as the report that "a Spanish general on the very day that the Maine was destroyed" had been heard to say, "We are going to blow her up mighty soon."[4] World headlines read, "World's Discoveries Prove the Mine Theory," and "War Spirit Rises from World's Evidence." It joined the Journal in impugning the courage and patriotism of anyone counseling delay, and in the suggestion that such advice came from money-grubbers, that Wall Street opposed war simply to safeguard investments and make more filthy profits. It could not quite match the imaginative flights of the Journal, which planned to organize a regiment of bull-necked athletes including Bob Fitzsimmons, Jim Corbett, Pop Anson, Jim Mitchell and William Muldoon, and commented, "Think of a regiment composed of magnificent men of this ilk! They would overawe any Spanish regiment by their mere appearance. They would scorn Krag-Jorgensen and Mauser bullets." The World on its part gave prominence to Buffalo Bill Cody's claim that 30,000 Indian fighters could chase the Spaniards out of Cuba in 60 days.

Ernest Chamberlin, the managing editor of Junior, stayed on the job almost without sleep during the crisis, sending out for crackers and milk as he pored over incoming news and devised bizarre interpretations and headlines. One night after the last edition was finished and his staff had gone home, he leaped from his desk and dashed up the stairs to the composing room. "War!" he cried. "We must get out an extra!" He telegraphed his staff to return. They found him excited but efficient, saying, "The war has begun, boys." He supervised the production of the extra, writing a single-word headline in mammoth type, "WAR." His men were unnerved by his increasingly distracted manner—also by the fact that nothing in the news stories under the headline bore out the claim of war, nor did the wire reports substantiate it. By now Chamberlin was discovered in his office, quite insane, mumbling, "War! War!" The presses were stopped and the editor, still talking wildly, was taken home by cab. As he recovered his sanity he contracted pneumonia and later died, his place being filled by the headline specialist Foster "Curser" Coates.[5]

Pulitzer, who had been at Jekyll Island, returned in great excitement to his 55th Street home late in February for about a ten-day stay during which he must have called in his editors and given them minute instructions on their treatment of the Cuban situation. Did he prefer to do this orally rather than leave any written record of his directives? One cannot be sure, for there is no proof that some of his written orders were not lost. Yet in those that remain after his return to Jekyll he avoided direct mention of the war and gave such routine instructions as one to Seitz: "It seems to [Mr. Pulitzer] also that your suggestion as to book notices could be made to the editors." [6]

When the United States naval board of inquiry finished its inspection of the sunken *Maine* and gave its opinion that it had been destroyed by a "submarine mine" but admitted its inability to fix the blame, the World fixed the blame at once and blasted McKinley for his confounded delay in getting at the war. Pulitzer, still skirting blunt mention of the issue, wrote, "Please tell Mr. Norris and Mr. White *privately* that I am going abroad in a few weeks and want to feel I have done all I could in the way of putting on more steam and fight for the summer in every edition . . ." [7]

He was back in New York early in April, his nerves frayed. Ralph, now at Harvard, needed special tutoring in algebra and physics, and Joseph at St. Mark's School was lagging in his grades. Pulitzer cheerfully furnished his sons with luxuries but expected brilliant academic work from them as his eventual successors in the responsibility of running his newspapers. He expected all his children to cater to his blindness and absence by reporting by mail virtually on their every move, thought, party, new necktie or gown. Although he lived his own life, coming and going as he pleased, and in consequence the spirited Kate had been forced to embark on a life of her own, there were times when he was irked by her absence. Now he was angry at her for sailing to England and deserting him, angry at Ralph for his poor grades and his failure to write, upset because both Butes and Jabez Dunningham were ill and unable to help him. George Ledlie wrote confidentially to Kate, who had sent lilies for her husband's 51st birthday:

> His father met [Ralph] cordially and so far there has been no outbreak and I begin to think there won't be any for the illness of Butes and Dunningham's slight breakdown have not been unmixed evils for Mr. P.'s family, for they have made him aware of the fact that if one quarrels with their family *who can they* turn to in an emergency like the present. . . . [Mr. Pulitzer] is wildly absorbed in the paper and war times just now and though I am forbidden to say so—looks and seems very well. . . . I am hoping the temper is over and that you will be greeted on the other side by a reasonable gentleman, who I think begins to be anxious to get over where you are. . . . It is possible this probable war may delay his departure. He has hoped it would be fought and ended before he started—but that now is impossible. I think unless he takes a new turn of some sort,—when he arrives in England, while he may take the attitude of a deserted husband etc., he will be quite ready to be urged to be amiable. . . .[8]

In Madrid, the American Minister Stewart Woodford found the Spanish government so anxious to avoid war that it was ready to bow to all the important United States demands, even offering to proclaim an immediate armistice in Cuba. Woodford took it for granted that these concessions meant peace and congratulated himself for his part in the peacemaking. He reckoned without American popular sentiment. On April 10, Pulitzer's birthday, his signed editorial demanding immediate attack appeared in the World. He was not guilty of the bad taste of connecting his birthday or the lucky number 10 with the question of war, but simply wanted to influence Congress, which would be addressed by President McKinley next day. His editorial read in part:

> Spain is a decaying, ignorant and well-nigh bankrupt nation. . . . No Spanish ship could stand an hour before the Americans. Havana is at our mercy. And this is the nation that talks of war with the United States. Now fifty-four days have passed since the *Maine* was destroyed by a stationary mine. . . .
>
> God forbid that The World should ever advocate an unnecessary war! That would be a serious crime against civilization. . . . The first duty of the President and Congress is to order the navy to proceed to Cuba and Porto Rico without delay. No declaration of war is necessary. Send the fleet to Havana as Jackson would do and demand the surrender of the miscreants who blew up the *Maine*. . . .
>
> It would hardly be a war but it would be magnificent.

McKinley, knowing he had already lost popularity because of his efforts for peace, quit the effort in his message to Congress next day. Rather than highlighting the Spanish concessions at the beginning of his speech where they belonged, he relegated them to two paragraphs at the very end, took no real stand and left the whole problem to Congress. On April 19 the Senate passed a war resolution by the close vote of 42 to 35. The shift of only four senatorial votes would have made it 39-38 against war—a result the President might conceivably have won by aggressive leadership. But the house's 310 to 6 vote for war made it clear that had McKinley won peace he might have failed of reelection in 1900. To say that the World and the Journal and their imitators had helped to inflame the public with untruth, to sway a peaceable President from his course and to bring on an unnecessary war is to say the obvious.

II. LOSING MONEY

While the World did not decorate its front pages with spread eagles and cannon, as the Journal did, nor descend to the vulgarity of Hearst's blurb, "HOW DO YOU LIKE THE JOURNAL'S WAR?", its coverage of the conflict was excited rather than factual. Both the World and Evening World were printing so many extra editions that the later editions of Senior were competing with early editions of Junior, and late editions of Junior were on the streets at the same time as early editions of Senior. Unsold copies by the thousands came back to both the Pulitzer and Hearst shops.

Hearst, whose advertising brought in far less revenue, was losing money heavily. Still he continued to act as if his mother had given him her whole fortune. He chartered the steamship *Sylvia* and set out for Santiago to cover the war himself along with Creelman and a staff of photographers, although the Journal already had at least a dozen Commissioners with the American forces. With Creelman (who caught a bullet in the shoulder) he watched the skirmish at El Caney, and he sent a series of dispatches to the Journal that won praise from the Times.

But no one praised him so fervently as did his own Journal, which ran his reports on the front page in large type under enormous headlines with insistent mention of his name, running also a headlined story about the admiration expressed for his exploits by Vice President Garret Hobart, Navy Secretary Long, General Nelson A. Miles and others. Hearst was on hand July 3 when Admiral Cervera slipped out of Santiago harbor only to have all six of his ships destroyed by Admiral Sampson's gunners. And Hearst and his party actually "captured" 29 Spanish seamen who swam to shore and gladly surrendered to the Yankees rather than be butchered by the Cubans. The Times commented, "This is the most genuine . . . increase of circulation, so to speak, which [Hearst] has of late achieved . . . We admit that we cannot imagine Mr. Pulitzer in the act of corraling shipwrecked Spaniards for the glory of his journal and the country. . . ." [9]

Mr. Pulitzer was so preoccupied with the war that he was unable to go abroad as he had hoped. Unwilling to arouse unhappy memories at Chatwold, he escaped the heat by leasing the W. A. Miles mansion at Narragansett Pier in June. It seemed perfectly clear to him that the best strategy was to take Havana at once, and the American failure to adopt this course annoyed him. He ordered the World to reduce the ruinous number of returned copies and showed his usual interest in Hearst's progress: "Please give me a very acute little analysis of Geranium's small ads in May—compared with both last May and two years ago. Do they grow [?]" [10]

The war, so successful in the field, was in some ways humiliating for the World. Since no newspaper could cover all the action, the World and the Journal were industriously cribbing news items from each other. Brisbane used an old journalistic dodge, the same as the fake report of the Afghan revolt with which the Post-Dispatch years earlier had trapped the St. Louis Star. In the Journal appeared this item:

> Colonel Reflipe W. Thenuz, an Austrian artillerist of European renown, who, with Colonel Ordonez, was defending the land batteries of Aguadores . . . was so badly wounded that he has since died.
>
> Col. Thenuz was foremost in the attempt to repulse the . . . advance and performed many acts of valor. . . .

The unwary World handled the death of Colonel Thenuz a trifle differently, with a formidable dateline:

On board the World dispatch boat *Three Friends*, off Santiago de Cuba, via Port Antonio, Jamaica.—Colonel R. W. Thenuz, an Austrian artillerist well known throughout Europe, who, with Colonel Ordonez, was defending the land batteries of Aguadores . . . was so badly wounded that he has since died.

Joy was unrestrained in the Hearst newsrooms. The Journal disclosed that Colonel Reflipe W. Thenuz was its own invention and rearranged the letters of his name into "We pilfer the news." For a time the World's encounter with Colonel Thenuz was given almost as much space in the Journal as the war news from Cuba. It published a poem, "In Memoriam," honoring the colonel. It ran a fanciful cartoon of him, captioned, "specially taken for the *World*, by the *World's* special photographer." It stressed the World's larcenous ingenuity in datelining the story. It urged the erection of a monument to Colonel Thenuz' memory, invited artists to compete in its design and suggested that the public would contribute enthusiastically to the Thenuz Memorial Fund. Artists sent in burlesque sketches for the design, while amused readers contributed Confederate currency, repudiated bonds and Chinese coins to the fund. The Journal kept it up for more than a month while the mortified World preserved a pained silence.[11]

Another harassment arose from a dispatch received from Stephen Crane as a World correspondent in Cuba, which mentioned the wavering of the 71st New York Volunteers at San Juan. Colonel Roosevelt was among those at the scene who verified the shaky conduct of the 71st, but the Journal blew it into a World slander. "SLURS ON THE BRAVERY OF THE BOYS OF THE 71ST," said the Journal headline. "The World Deliberately Accuses Them of Rank Cowardice at San Juan." It listed their casualties—14 killed and 59 wounded—saying the World had insulted men as valorous as the Spartans at Thermopylae. Hearst, on his return from Cuba, kept up the assault with the headline "EDITOR OF THE JOURNAL'S PERSONAL EXPERIENCE OF THE SPLENDID HEROISM OF THE SEVENTY-FIRST." Under this was Hearst's warm praise of the regiment along with that of the Journal correspondent Edward Marshall, though neither had been at San Juan and had no "personal experience."[12] Although Crane *had* been there, his dispatch caused such indignation that the World sought to purge itself by starting a subscription fund for a memorial to the 71st and the New York men of the Rough Riders.

It was an unwise move. The Journal lampooned it as the groveling of a traducer. A group of members of the 71st, egged on by the Journal, announced (in the Journal) their rejection of any favors from the libeling Pulitzer, while Roosevelt on his part angrily refused to let his Rough Rider heroes be lumped with the chicken-livered 71st. The deeply embarrassed World in the end was forced to return the money it had collected.

Pulitzer, heartily sick of the war, urged an early peace. Spain, after losing one fleet at Manila and another at Santiago, was prostrate and the two-month conflict was, in effect, over. Mrs. Jefferson Davis and her daughter Winnie arrived at the Rockingham Hotel in Narragansett and were frequently Kate's guests, but none of them saw much of Pulitzer who had an endless stream of World executives riding the rails to the Pier for lessons in economy. The World in 1898 had achieved an all-time record circulation and was *losing money*. Although he was making good its deficits out of his own pocket, he was not as complaisant as Phoebe Hearst. As always, he regarded a problem as something to be solved, and he asked blunt questions such as Why had the advertising declined?, pointing out, "If you can get hold of the cause you may find a remedy."

After the shooting was over, the sale of both the World and Journal plummeted toward the normal scale. Hearst was obviously hurting, for the Journal discharged more than 100 employees and Carvalho had occasional meetings with Seitz to discuss a truce and a proposal to cut expenses on both sides by reducing disastrously competitive practices in circulation and advertising. Pulitzer wrote Seitz, ". . . You can tell every night editor, city editor, managing editor & editorial writer, to *let the Journal alone* as long as they let us alone—and possibly even longer." [13]

III. A NORMAL NEWSPAPER

With the war over, Pulitzer urged the aggressive and popular Judge William Jay Gaynor on the Democrats as their gubernatorial nominee. But Boss Croker, long since finished with reformers, picked Judge Augustus Van Wyck, brother of the hapless mayor, while Thomas C. Platt, the Republicans' "Easy Boss," selected the dashing Colonel Roosevelt. Roosevelt called on Platt and said that if elected he would "on all matters of importance consult Senator Platt as leader of the party"—an announcement that drew Pulitzer's deepest scorn. The Rough Rider was covered with embarrassment when it was discovered that he had avoided New York taxes by swearing himself a resident of Washington, which would have made him ineligible for the governorship had not Elihu Root given plausible arguments that he was indeed a resident of Oyster Bay. Pulitzer was as disgruntled with the Tammany candidate, and the World showed no enthusiasm on either side.

Before the campaign got under way, Winnie Davis fell ill at the Rockingham Hotel. Kate called in two physicians to attend her, but the fragile Daughter of the Confederacy died September 18. The Pulitzers, who had held her in deep affection and for years had aided her and her mother, furnished flowers and paid the funeral expenses.

This reminder of Lucille's death brought pangs. In October Pulitzer sought his usual anodyne by making a brief trip to England, taking as one of his companions David Graham Phillips, by now elevated to editorial writer. Although Phillips' code name was Gumboil, he was known in the Dome as the chief's special pet. Being a pet placed a man in a difficult position with the staff even if he exercised diplomacy, and Gumboil, an aloof personality, had few friends at the World. Pulitzer, aware of the dangers of favoritism, tried to distribute free European trips to his top men equally, but his fondness for Phillips overbore the rule and besides he was grooming the young man for highest authority at the World, which meant that his brain and character had to be given special training. What he did not know was that Phillips planned to quit newspaper work as soon as he felt able to support himself by writing, and that he was irked by the daily chore of discussing journalism and politics with an "irascible semi-invalid" as well as by Pulitzer's refusal to permit him to smoke cigarettes in his presence.

In London, Pulitzer hired a new permanent secretary to aid Hosmer and Butes, tall Arthur Billing, son of a bishop. One of his continuing foibles was to buy hats for people he liked, and his approval of Billing was soon marked by the gift of an eight-dollar silk hat. The entourage returned to New York just in time to see Roosevelt win the governorship by a mere 18,000 votes over his weak opponent. It was clear that had Gaynor been the candidate he would in all probability have won, much history would have been changed and Roosevelt might never have become President—a thought that would recur to Pulitzer in later years.

Now, after two years of World immoderacy, Pulitzer made a cautious admission of his knowledge that matters had got out of hand and must be corrected. He did it gently, softly, and early in the morning. He did it verbally, by implication, keeping it off the record. He did it in such a way as to make his own confession of error negligible. But he did it.

He called his executives separately to his home and talked with them. A "Special Notice" appeared on the Pulitzer Building bulletin board calling all members of the news staff of the morning World to meet in the city room at 11 A.M. Monday, November 28. Scores of newsmen appeared there to be addressed by Don Seitz, Bradford Merrill, William Van Benthuysen and Nelson Hersh. All of them spoke in parables, finding it impossible to admit that the World had been a bit of a liar, which was a logical preliminary to talk of reform.

Van Benthuysen uttered heavy platitudes: "To begin with the cardinal principle, the basic idea which made it possible to rear this great modern contribution to modern journalism, the Pulitzer Building, is truthfulness and absolute accuracy. . . . We must heed it in every department, in every vocation that goes to make up this great newspaper. Absolute accuracy! Write it down! Have it ever before you! . . . Sensational? Yes, when the news is sensational. But the demand is this, that every story which is sensational in itself must also be truthful."

Hersh also made general remarks about accuracy, but Merrill came closer to the point:

"[Mr. Pulitzer] has very often said to me that it is right dealing and right thinking which is always at the very foundation of the success of a great newspaper as of a man. He holds that the foundation of everything in life which is worth having, the only success which can possibly endure is the success built on honesty to convictions and fidelity to truth. I think I may say that it is a familiar experience that in strenuous competition a man may do a thing for a newspaper which he would not do as an individual. I think I may say it is Mr. Pulitzer's desire that no man in any capacity, high or low, great or small, should ever do anything as a member of the staff of the World which he would not do or believe in doing as a man. The great mistakes which have been made—I speak with modesty, because I have made a number of them myself—have been caused by an excess of zeal. Be just as clever as you can. Be more energetic and enterprising than any other man if you can, but above all, be right."

Seitz echoed the theme with discreet euphemisms:

"There is and has been for two years, as you know, a fierce competition . . . This has developed a tendency to rush things. It has not been to the advantage of any newspaper so doing. The World feels that it is time for the staff to learn definitely and finally that it must be a normal newspaper. . . ."

Van Benthuysen closed: "On behalf of Mr. Pulitzer, who wished us all to get together, I want to thank you for being present." [14]

VI

The Schoolmaster

Chapter 1

Grooming the Admiral

I. GENTLEMAN WANTS COMPANION

Not without difficulty did the World staff, accustomed to a somewhat inebriate interpretation of the news, swear off and observe reasonable sobriety, and there was occasional backsliding before the paper walked the line. The elimination of the war costs, the endless extras with their ruinous returns and the prodigal spending to outdo Hearst, tightened the ship. By 1899 the paper's lone year of deficit was over, although the profits were still so slim that Andes remained chopfallen despite the fact that his stocks were sound and he had enough cash to ask his friend John G. Moore if he knew of any good investments for $500,000 he had lying around. He kept up the Pulitzer scholarships but refused Kate's request that he donate to a hospital, asking her only to think of his reverses.

His purification order applied only to the World, Senior, his heart and soul. Junior and Seniority, being mere money-makers without significant editorial influence, were allowed to continue their strident ways except that Pulitzer ordered Foster Coates, in charge of Junior, to melt up the three-inch type he favored for banner headlines. The order was observed for a time, but Arthur Brisbane was now using billboard type so successfully in the Evening Journal that it crept back into Junior and indeed has become routine in evening newspapers ever since. Hearst did not have any regrets. His morning Journal remained as feverish as ever, but it likewise dropped to its prewar circulation which—despite his claims—was only the merest shade above Senior's.

Pulitzer sought to improve his position and rid himself of a worry by selling the profitable Post-Dispatch to the St. Louis Republic, a deal that fell through. He fussed about Joseph's poor grades and Ralph's failures in filial solicitude, writing Kate:

I have never received a line of affection from him in my life. And even after I telegraphed, when you literally forced him to write, I never received even one kind word of inquiry or sympathy—nothing but shallow commonplaces—Considering his age & circumstances—cold and dull and unfeeling.[1]

But Ralph was with him, along with John Dillon and the entourage, when he sailed in May and leased Maitland House in Kensington, a place which in his prickly mood seemed possessed by devils, as he let Kate know:

But really this house is conceded by everybody to be the noisiest place imaginable—3 churches and 4 clocks, for the barracks next door has one, every stroke of which I hear by day & by night, with chimes thrown in, bugles from six in the morning till a quarter past ten at night, relieved only by drums and fifes and the bellowing tones of the drill sergeant. [Ralph is enjoying himself, fencing, boxing, riding in the park, and] has even unfolded as a talker a little and we have not had a row, which I am sure you will put to his credit and not mine, but which really was a possibility considering my watchfulness over his hours at night.[2]

His London bureau chief, James M. Tuohy, had earlier placed an advertisement in the Times:

Gentleman, with somewhat indifferent health, who travels a good deal, WANTS AS COMPANION, a cultivated, well-read gentleman of about 40, who is a bright, ready, well-informed talker, with literary tastes and knowledge. The principal desideratum being agreeable, intellectual companionship, exceptional conversational gifts essential. Musical accomplishments (not singing) and riding are both highly desirable also. Liberal salary. Unexceptionable references as to character and attainments required.[3]

One candidate was Walter Leyman, who spent a fortnight with Pulitzer, enjoyed the first few days, then encountered one of the master's moody-silent spells and resigned, writing him an explanation that contained a penetrating appraisal:

I want you to forgive me if I speak rather freely as it is only by so doing that I can explain to you why I and the situation would not have suited each other. You have passed the life of a very busy man, & have for many years been in a position of command with many dependant [*sic*] upon you. You have therefore become so used to command that any other position with regard to those always with you became impossible to you.

Friends and interesting acquaintances outside your daily life you like & possess, but an intimate friend always with you who could treat you as such & speak freely and intimately would be to you not only no necessity . . . but an annoyance and an irritation. That I felt very soon. It is not a question of your health and nerves but of temperament and disposition.

. . . I felt that I had on certain occasions to make conversation, so to speak . . . When the conversation became a monologue it would become irksome & then impossible to the most resolute, & even break his heart in the effort. . . .

You may find the man you want, but you are a man of remarkably strong will, & great individuality & self reliance. It is of course of these qualities that you have made your success in life, but such men have few if any intimate personal friends. The qualities which command great success militate against intimacy.

You must forgive me for a further observation. Like all very successful men you have to a degree a contempt for those whose lives have been to some extent failures, and . . . you cannot help letting them feel that you regard them, through being in the necessity of taking such a position, in an inferiority in life. I doubt if you perceive this, but it is so, and it makes close daily intercourse with you harder each day.[4]

Leyman added, "I also feel that I have learnt more of American life & politics, not to mention American Journalism, than I was likely to learn in any other way." This was a typical discovery of all those who could stand the strain. To converse with Pulitzer was to encounter the most stimulating and provocative of minds, an education in itself. When he returned to Bar Harbor in midsummer, he felt that young Phillips needed further education, writing him with devilish humor:

Let us make a bargain, apropos of your imperious sensibility . . . Promise me, upon oath, that when you come here you will insist upon my telling you the truth about your work, your development and your ambition during the last three years.

Promise me also to insist very emphatically, for I am so cowardly about criticising sensitive and delicate, likeable persons, that I am sure to run away from it unless you use a club. Promise me further that you will use that club, with the understanding that it is for your own good, and for the sake of your future. Mine is behind me, as you know.[5]

In addition to Phillips, Bradford Merrill, Don Seitz, John Norris and W. H. Merrill visited Chatwold for education. These sessions were not without strain for the lecturer. Seitz was distinctly audible in eating soup and particularly with toast—an offense to sensitive ears—while Bradford Merrill sometimes was so carried away by his own eloquence as to interrupt the lessons. As for W. H. Merrill, he had never even read Dickens, so that sometimes the chief's literary allusions were lost on him. Pulitzer's conversation as always ranged from the most exalted editorial idealism to the most rigorous examination of profits, one of his instructions to Seitz being to have lunch with Herald advertising men and discover how it was they secured such rich Mustard (want advertising).

To Kate, who was in Hot Springs, Virginia, he wrote rather wistfully about his efforts with the World, "which, with all its faults I think has done some things that will be remembered after I am gone—if anything is remembered that a daily newspaper does." [6] Another visitor was Thomas Davidson, not an unmixed pleasure because he was in failing health and talked of his ailments, something Pulitzer felt was his own province. Listening to Pulitzer praise the work of one World reporter, Davidson admitted puzzlement that he always spoke so highly of reporters and so severely of editors. "Well," the host admitted, "I suppose it is because every reporter is a hope, and every editor is a disappointment." After returning to New York, Davidson wrote him gratefully, "I was greatly touched when I found that a stateroom had been engaged for me on the sleeper. You do not know how much pain I was spared thereby." [7]

III. DEWEY SAYS NO

One of Kate's constant efforts was to dissuade her husband from the President-making mania that so aggravated his nervousness and insomnia. In 1899 her endeavors were less effectual than usual and the symptoms of his *electionitis Pulitzerium* became more pronounced than they had been since the Nicoll-Fellows disaster of 1887. To have been excluded from any influence on the Democratic convention of 1896 had been a mortification that he labored to redress in 1900. He was moved not only by his will to power but by the desperate need to find a candidate who would save the Democrats from the otherwise certain blight of Bryan. The obvious man was the hero of Manila, 61-year-old Admiral George Dewey, so popular that he could have the presidency for the asking although it was not even known whether he was a Democrat or a Republican.

Pulitzer determined to make him a Democrat and to make him President. But to a World man sent to the Orient to urge his candidacy, Dewey scouted the idea, saying he was too old, his health was uncertain, and adding, "I have no desire for any political office. I am unfitted for it, having neither the education nor the training." These words, so welcome to Bryan and McKinley, were galling to Pulitzer and all anti-Bryan Democrats. As the admiral sailed home, Pulitzer cabled the journalist Frederick Palmer to "report what Dewey ate and when, whether he took one or two cups of coffee for breakfast, how many hours he slept, whether in nightshirt or pyjamas, every sartorial detail." [8] The pudgy, white-whiskered admiral reached New York in September to encounter the most rhapsodic ovation ever given an American hero.

Pulitzer contributed $1,000 to a public subscription taken to buy him a mansion in Washington. Boss Croker gladly spent $175,000 in municipal funds to decorate the city, the *chef d'oeuvre* being the magnificent, 100-foot plaster Dewey Arch in Madison Square. Hundreds of babies were named for Dewey, as was a new brand of chewing gum, Dewey Chewies.

Girls wore the jaunty Dewey hat, men sported Dewey neckties, and the admiral's likeness appeared on dishes, watch charms, shaving mugs—even on a laxative bearing the blurb "The 'Salt' of Salts." Sheet music about him sold fast, one lyric reading:

Oh, dewy was the morning
Upon the first of May,
And Dewey was the Admiral
Down in Manila Bay. . . .
And dew we feel discouraged?
I dew not think we dew!

So many thousands swarmed into New York to see the hero glorified in two vast parades that hundreds were forced to sleep in Central Park and other chill places. But before he left for further adulation in Washington and other cities he still scoffed at mention of his candidacy, saying, "As for me, I know as much about politics as Bob here," pointing to the chow dog he had picked up in Hong Kong. Pulitzer must have ground his teeth at the pertinacity of the man the World was booming for President. Dewey (whose World code name was "Gramercy") did not know how to say "No" in such a way as to mean "Maybe." He not only gave a blunt refusal but disqualified himself so publicly on the grounds of age, health and capacity that his remarks would haunt him should he change his mind.

Nevertheless Pulitzer set out to change his mind for him. He was far from the only Democrat who eyed Dewey as the party's salvation, for Boss Croker, Hearst, Watterson and many others were courting him. But unlike the others, Pulitzer refused to be defeated by the sailor's intransigence. He saw Dewey, as he saw every dilemma, as a problem that could be solved by intelligent strategy. The World published a flattering colored supplement about him. It printed interviews with Watterson, Seth Low and others endorsing Dewey for President. It ran a series of ten editorials emphasizing that Dewey was the man who could heal the silver schism, the man on whom all Democrats could unite, the man who could sweep the country as he had swept through Admiral Montojo's fleet. His talk about his lack of qualifications, said the World, only endeared him to the public the more because it was so obviously untrue. His qualifications were unmatched. The World perhaps stretched a point here, declaring that at Annapolis he had learned history, government and a knowledge of democratic institutions, and his career ever since had proved his character and his ability to defend the right.

Pulitzer even had a man confer with Dewey's physician about his health, which was pronounced good. He called one of the most accomplished of World interviewers, James W. Clarke, to Chatwold and gave him careful instructions to seek an interview with Dewey in Washington through the aid of Pulitzer's old friend ex-Senator James B. Henderson, who was close to Gramercy.

By now Dewey had locked his door to newspapermen. The best Clarke could do was to get a second-hand interview, off the record, through Senator Henderson's son, who told the admiral that Pulitzer was warmly supporting him and therefore felt entitled to know his real intentions. Dewey reiterated his refusal in the most decided language. He was now 62, he said, had enough of honors, had no political ability, and he cited Grant as an example of a sad political ending to a fine military career. "Of course, Mr. Pulitzer has a right to know this," he said, "and I hope you will let him know it once for all. Tell him to drop it." [9]

To Andes, upset as always by any interference with his plans, the news brought sheer anguish, as did Dewey's published remark to President McKinley that the former would be a "failure" as President. His telegram next day to Kate, still in Virginia, reflected the Dewey tragedy without mentioning it: "Utterly alone here, weather blusteringly cold [,] nervous as a cat, everything going wrong, when do you get back." [10]

But it was still a year before election time and he reserved some hope. As Henderson left, Dewey had said, "Wouldn't I be foolish to refuse what has not been offered to me?"—which might be construed as a hint that he would not decline if given solid party backing. Meanwhile Pulitzer was irate at the British moves against the Boers. The World sent a parchment peace petition to Queen Victoria, Lord Salisbury, President McKinley, and to a thousand of the leading newspapers of the United States and a hundred of the leading newspapers of Europe. The World threw open its columns to President Paul Kruger of the Transvaal, and vainly urged the McKinley administration to extend its good offices for peace. When the war began, Pulitzer heaped such maledictions on the British that life became difficult for his two English secretaries, Butes and Billing. In a burst of anger he swore that he hoped that every English soldier in Africa would be killed. "Yes, killed . . . !"

When Butes pointed out that Billing's brother was among those soldiers, he recoiled. "My God!" he said. "The poor fellow may be dead now!" And indeed word came of his death not long after.[11]

III. DEWEY SAYS YES

Admiral Dewey, the least sophisticated of men, was being shadowed by Washington reporters but finding the public cooling toward him. There was criticism of his recent marriage to the widowed, 49-year-old Mrs. Mildred McLean Hazen. The new Mrs. Dewey was the sister of Pulitzer's friend John R. McLean, now publisher of the Washington Post as well as the Cincinnati Enquirer. She was an heiress to millions and, more than that, had become a Catholic after some years as a Presbyterian and then an Episcopalian—a course wounding to many American Protestants.

When Dewey deeded over to her his $50,000 gift house on Rhode Island Avenue, many citizens thought him ungrateful and some Protestants declared that the mansion bought by public subscription would now become the seat of the papacy in Washington. It was learned that he had filed suit for prize money, bolstering his case with a valuation of the Spanish fleet he had destroyed at $751,141.89, even listing such items as "40 galvanized rings, 2 cents each," and "one brad-awl, 4 cents." This came as a shock to those who felt that patriotism alone should have been enough to inspire his victory at Manila. Mrs. Dewey, it was noted, left no doubt of her opinion that her husband could handle the presidency or anything else, and there was speculation that he was in the hands of an ambitious woman.

Pulitzer sent David Graham Phillips on a tour of the country to write on the political outlook—another move to train him for leadership of the World. ". . . Let me have your address every day while you are swinging around the circle," he wrote Phillips. "I may be of some use to you in suggesting or be disagreeable and critical." [12] Still hopeful, he sent his man Clarke to interview William C. Whitney at Lenox, where Whitney came out strongly for Dewey for President. But Dewey himself remained silent, and by spring Pulitzer was confronted by the awful probability that McKinley and Bryan would be the candidates again. On April 3, the World wired its Washington bureau head, Samuel Blythe, to make one last query just for the record. Blythe shrugged and handed the telegram to an assistant, Horace Mock, who stopped at the Dewey home and in turn simply gave the typed message to the admiral.

Dewey read it and nodded. "Yes," he said, "I have decided to become a candidate."

Mock sank limply into a chair and asked him to go on. With the aid of Mrs. Dewey, he gave the following statement:

"I realize that the time has arrived when I must definitely state my position. . . . I have had the leisure and inclination to study the matter, and have reached a different conclusion. . . . If the American people want me for this high office I shall be only too willing to serve them. . . .

"Since studying the subject I am convinced that the office of the President is not such a very difficult one to fill, his duties being mainly to execute the laws of Congress. Should I be chosen for this exalted position I would execute the laws of Congress as faithfully as I have always executed the orders of my superiors."

He refused to say, however, whether he was a Democrat or a Republican. "But on what platform will you stand?" Mock asked.

Dewey shook his head. "I think I have said enough at this time, and possibly too much." [13]

He seemed unaware that to give one journal a scoop on such an announcement was an unforgivable political blunder. Other papers would have been incensed even had his statement been a wise one. Apparently he was also unaware that political movements took time and that it was now all but too late for him to throw his hat in the ring.

The World splashed its newsbeat under an unprecedented double banner headline with a three-column photograph of the admiral in a cocked hat—a story that startled the country. Dewey's brother Charles declared that the admiral was indubitably a Democrat, while his nephew was certain he was a Republican. To the World next day he refused to clear up this question, saying, "You may say, though, that I stand for the Constitution of the United States," and adding that his health was now excellent. Evidently regretting his earlier jokes about his political ignorance, he sought to mend matters by declaring that he had been reading the newspapers carefully all winter and felt quite well-informed politically.

Comment across the nation was acid. Many agreed with the New York Times that his words really represented the ambitions of Mrs. Dewey. "I don't believe Dewey is responsible for that fool interview," said Cordell Hull, then a congressman from Tennessee. "If he is, he does not realize the dignity of the position of President." The New York Tribune sneered, "No party. No platform. Just Dewey." The admiral's friend Captain Charles Sigsbee explained of the statement, "Its apparent inappropriateness is characteristic of a man whose life has been spent at sea." [14] Sigsbee intended no joke, but many observers agreed that Dewey was indeed at sea. When a World man cornered him yet again to ask his party affiliation, he said, "Mrs. Dewey will speak to you," which seemed to verify rumors as to who was the real skipper in the family.

"The admiral has a mind of his own," Mrs. Dewey corrected. "He does his own thinking."

"All right, I will answer that question," he said. "I am a Democrat." [15]

He refused to say more, but that was enough, or even too much. "If he had consented last fall," Henry Watterson said sadly, "he would have carried all before him. Now it is far too late." Bryan could not repress his joy as he told a reporter, "I would rather not comment on the Admiral's statement."

Pulitzer must have reflected bitterly that what Dewey needed was a few months of concentrated political instruction at his hands. Yet so powerful was his aversion to Bryan and his own yearning to sponsor a Democrat who could win, that the World for one day tried to rekindle a Dewey boom, saying, "Welcome to the nomination table, Admiral Dewey! Draw up a chair and unfold your napkin. The last comer is not always the worst served." [16] But there was no room for him at the table. Bryan had control of the party machinery, and the admiral's popularity had fled. A public subscription to perpetuate the handsome Dewey Arch in marble, already lagging, gave out entirely and the contributions were returned. When the dilapidated plaster arch was torn down a few months later, it symbolized the uncertain tenure of public acclaim.

"Whin a grateful raypublic . . . builds an ar-rch to its conquering hero," said Mr. Dooley, "it should be made of brick, so that we can have something convanyent to hurl after him when he has passed by."

Chapter 2

The Twentieth Century

1. STIR HIM UP, CLUB HIM UP

Early on the morning of January 9, 1900, while Pulitzer was at Lakewood with young Joseph and Ralph was at Harvard, his 55th Street home was destroyed by a fire so disastrous that Mrs. Pulitzer, Edith, Constance and four-year-old Herbert were lucky to escape, barefooted and in their nightclothes. As it was, the housekeeper, Mrs. Morgan Jellett, and Elizabeth Montgomery, a governess, lost their lives. That 17 other servants escaped indicates the amplitude of the household. Kate was praised for her bravery in forcing them all to descend a smoky and flaming stairway to safety.

Gone in the ruins were scores of paintings—a Hals, a Millet, some Bouguereau sketches, three portraits of Kate, a portrait of Pulitzer by Heinrich von Angell—along with Gobelin tapestries, bronzes, porcelains, silver, rugs. A pet dog that had belonged to the late Lucille Pulitzer died in the blaze. Gone also was a fortune in gems including Kate's diamond necklace, bought for $120,000 at a sale of the French crown jewels, and "Mrs. Pulitzer's famous pearl necklace, valued at $150,000." [1] Pulitzer's great library went with the rest, and the insurance coverage was only partial. Kate and the children removed temporarily to the Netherlands Hotel, where Carl Schurz and other friends called to extend their sympathy.

The death of the servants was at first kept from Pulitzer. But as often happened, his nerves, so inflamed by minor irritations, held steady in the face of heavy reverse. He sent fond messages to his family and dispatched Dunningham to New York to help. He donated $500 to the fire department pension fund in appreciation for their efforts, $250 to the police pension fund, and of course bore the funeral expenses. "Please take five o'clock train this evening," he wired Phillips. "I need you to cheer me up." [2] He leased the Henry T. Sloane mansion at 9 East 72nd Street as a temporary home for $17,000 a year.

From William Whitney he received a paragraph of polite commiseration followed by several paragraphs of cold anger. Promoting corporate affairs with a ruthlessness common at the time, but with uncommon finesse, Whitney had joined Thomas Fortune Ryan in the water-soaked Metropolitan Street Railway Company and other enterprises. The World had fought brilliantly for a tax on public franchises, pointing out that the Metropolitan paid 25 per cent dividends but not a penny in franchise taxes. The campaign resulted in a new tax measure unwelcome to Whitney. Now the World sailed into his and Ryan's use of the State Trust Company in their operations, causing the state banking department to investigate rumors that the institution's directors, Whitney included, illegally loaned themselves its assets for their private speculations. Governor Roosevelt refused to make the department's report public, saying only that State Trust had been found solvent. Whitney urgently tried to see Bradford Merrill, evidently to present his case, but on Pulitzer's order Merrill declined to see him. The World pointed particularly to State Trust's loan of $450,000 to the notorious corruptionist Louis F. Payn, state Superintendent of Insurance, and another loan of $2,000,000 to Daniel H. Shea, Ryan's young secretary. It referred to Shea as an "office boy," suggested that the money really went to Ryan, charged that Whitney's brokers received excessive fees and implied fast work on the part of the Whitney-Ryan group.

Whitney wrote that Shea, far from being an office boy, was 30, a college graduate and an able man. On top of that, the loan was guaranteed both by Whitney and Ryan, each of them worth more than $10,000,000. He accused the World of irresponsibility in making such charges against a financial institution. His relations with Pulitzer, he added, had begun long before when neither of them was wealthy, and he had appreciated Pulitzer's intellectuality perhaps more than any other man, but he felt quite able to defend himself against malice.[3]

It was the end of their cordiality. Pulitzer followed his usual code of never allowing friendship to influence his newspapers. The World, staging a bit of its not uncommon Albany witchcraft, secured a copy of the report withheld by Roosevelt, published it for all to see, noted that it called the Shea loan illegal, and again assailed the Whitney-Ryan operations, which would later come under greater fire.

In the echelon immediately below the World's top men were Van Benthuysen, Frederick Duneka, Foster Coates, Nelson Hersh, and John Tennant. Each wrote voluminous reports to Pulitzer covering not only their own work but appraising the work of others, thoroughly aware that the boss had them all under surveillance. To work efficiently under such circumstances required steady nerves, a sense of humor and some understanding of the talents as well as the peculiarities of the master. Early in 1900 Norris decided that life was too short and resigned, writing Pulitzer, "Temperamentally I am not equipped to get along with you." [4] Surprised, Andes tried to hold him and, failing, recommended him highly to his next employer, the Times. His old colleague John Dillon, who had fallen somewhat into the background as an editorialist because he was felt to be coasting, likewise resigned to join the Chicago Tribune and received a magnificent diamond pin on leaving. The chief was unhappier about the resignation of Duneka, who deserted to Harpers' and wrote him, "I thank you for the privilege of knowing you." [5] He tried vainly to get Duneka back. Still it was impossible for him to forgo the recurrent needling which he felt essential to stimulate the kind of work the World deserved. He wrote Seitz:

> Have a little talk with Mr. Van Ben as pleasantly as possible. Tell him frankly that I am disappointed in his record as Edit. Manager. . . . That I am extremely anxious to keep him. If I did not want to, I would not criticize him but would make up my mind that the case is hopeless & try to gain his good opinion & respect by flattery rather than make myself hated by being disagreeable.
>
> My object is to wake him up: to stir him up: to club him up. To show . . . more initiative more originality more real assertion of his powers. . . .[6]

He was astonished when Van Benthuysen, near the end of his contract period, said he must resign and take a rest. Pulitzer swiftly gave him a bonus, an extra vacation and paid all his expenses during a restful sojourn in California, thereby holding the man in whom he had been disappointed. He was of course disappointed in everybody, and the man who disappointed him only moderately was valuable indeed. He brought in F. D. White (Volema) from St. Louis to replace Norris and elevated Pomeroy Burton (Gumbo) to city editor of Senior, sending him a diamond-and-pearl pin but sternly warning both Seitz and Bradford Merrill to watch him.

He gathered James Creelman back in the World fold. When Sam Chamberlain, Hearst's top editor, quarreled with his boss and disappeared for some weeks, Pulitzer tried to pierce the mystery with the idea of hiring this remarkable newsman. Although Chamberlain was an occasional drinker who vanished at intervals, and his irresponsibility was at odds with the World staff's comparative steadiness, he had an unsurpassed dash in getting news and could do less harm to Pulitzer in the World shop than at the Journal. His young son, who was a World reporter, swore that he had no idea where his father was but felt that he must be on one of his recurrent alcoholic adventures. Chamberlain surprisingly turned up as editor of the Philadelphia North American. Pulitzer held out lures, but evidently Hearst bid higher for soon the prodigal was back with the Journal.

From Mrs. George Frank Gouley, widow of Pulitzer's good friend who had died in the disastrous Southern Hotel fire in St. Louis in 1877, came a pathetic letter. Mrs. Gouley, now in New York, was ill and about to be evicted from her 25th Street lodgings. "[I] entreat you in the name and memory of my kind husband to have compassion. . . ." she wrote. "God help me and send you as my Good Samaritan." [7] One can be sure that Pulitzer aided her instantly. From St. Mark's School came an ominous note: "Joseph has gone steadily down since the first of the year . . ." Joseph received an outraged letter from his father, who also wrote the school to stress the boy's need for more than an ordinary education:

> The position I hope he will hold is so exceptional that special training is indispensable—something like that given to boys intended for the Army and Navy. . . . I hope you will believe me when I say that the World is to me far more than a property. I regard it as a public institution, capable of exercising daily influence on public thought, watching and safeguarding public morals and the public interests. It is my fervent hope that, when this inheritance falls to my sons, they will fully realize their public responsibilities, and be so equipped as to exercise for the public good whatever influence may be theirs. But Joseph is as yet destitute even of the elementary knowledge he ought to have by this time. . . .[8]

On his graduation from Harvard in June, 21-year-old Ralph was the subject of a Pulitzer telegram to Seitz: "Oblige me by putting Ralph at your elbow teaching training explaining rudiments business like clerk at bottom ladder [;] pupil schoolboy ignorant [;] hours nine six strictly note infractions daily . . ." [9]

Seitz obliged: "Ralph [has] managed to be on time every morning except one . . . He is, I think, accumulating interest, although he still finds it difficult to remember when the editions go to press." And later, in response to an anxious query about Ralph's weight and health: "Ralph weighs one forty two net appearance excellent needs more sleep perhaps . . ." [10] Pulitzer's long-time banker and investment counselor, Dumont Clarke, whose code name was Coin, was aware of the excessive demands he made on his children. He wrote, "He is a good boy, my dear J.P. and only wants to be handled right, and you will be proud of him some day . . ." [11] Pulitzer had been corresponding with his learned cousin in Vienna, Professor Adam Politzer (a spelling used by some branches of the family), who also urged patience:

> What you tell me about Ralph and Joseph proves that you claim too much from these young men. Do not forget that they were born and brought up under quite different circumstances than we. Self-made men like you and myself come to maturity in the hot battle for existence—and who knows should we have been the sons of wealthy parents, if we were

> what we are now. . . . But I have seen more than once, that such young men, after having grown out a certain stage, and particularly when no pleasure was denied to them in their youth, the gravity of life suddenly takes hold of them, ambition awakes . . .[12]

Kate herself often essayed to smooth the relations between father and sons, once writing him about Joseph, "In thinking of him, dear, do remember that nature does not make us all alike and that Joe happens to be one of the undemonstrative kind but there never was a more loyal, honest nature than his." [13]

Both sons, doubtless spurred by their mother, wrote their father more frequently and carefully, describing their daily routine and including such expected details as their time of rising and retiring, where and with whom they dined, and any newspaper ideas that struck them. Indeed, Ralph could not refrain occasionally from pulling his father's leg a bit, once writing him in part, "I then went up to the house (it being 5.45) took a bath, changed my clothes, and joined Phillips at the Manhattan Club at 7." [14] He knew that his father would miss the humor of this and applaud the minutiae.

II. PURSUING WHITE MICE

In April Pulitzer sailed for Liverpool, his one-way passage as usual costing about $3,000 because he always had several servants, three or four secretaries and a guest or two with him. To this was added the cost of transporting his own horses and those of the guests. He used the White Star Line exclusively, for that line not only gave him a palatial stateroom but spread a rope drugget on the deck above so that footsteps would not bother him. Ledlie had arranged for him the three-month rental of the mansion of Sir John Poynder in Chesterfield Gardens, London, at £1,200. James Tuohy, the World London chief, had been alerted to look for new secretary-companions, a canvass that took much time and effort and which he referred to privately as "the pursuit of the White Mice."

The pursuit was deadly serious, however. The chief devoured White Mice and his peace of mind depended on a continuous supply. He once wrote Tuohy, "The man must be found, absolutely must," and he defended his fastidiousness in selection because a secretary's status was "almost equivalent to matrimony." Although Kate and Ralph Pulitzer, Ledlie and American friends of the family often looked for replacements, experience had shown that Americans generally were unsatisfactory because few of them could submit for long to the strict secretarial discipline or the occasional kingly explosions. Britons were far and away the best material—particularly Britons of good family and education but uncertain income—possessing a patience and tenacity most Yankees could not muster. Thus Tuohy remained for years the central functionary in recruitment, a duty at least as important as his alert reporting of British news. It was his custom to insert advertisements in the Times and the *Athenaeum* and to invite likely candidates to dinner so that he and Mrs. Tuohy could analyze their abilities. The pair, who had become expert interrogators and sharp judges of personality, took some chaffing from other World people because of their side duty of judging geniuses. Since an unpleasant voice, noisy breathing or eating, unpolished manners or inadequate conversational gifts automatically barred an applicant, probably less than one out of ten of those who called on the Tuohys ever saw Pulitzer for an actual tryout. The 41-year-old, Cork-born Tuohy had been an assistant at the London bureau for nine years before becoming its head, and was as intimate with Pulitzer as an employee could become. He had reported Queen Victoria's Jubilee for the World with distinction, but he admitted that the search for secretaries was often more difficult. He had written Butes earlier:

> I have been awaiting news of Mr. Pulitzer's coming over, which I suppose will be sometime next month. The uncertainty has interfered with my secretary researches, and it has caused some with whom I have been in communication to drop off or take other positions. Mr. Pulitzer will remember that I introduced to him last year a Mr. Montague Wood, a tall, gentlemanly young fellow, with whom he was rather, I think, impressed. I put an end to the negotiations with him under the misapprehension that he was the Mr. Wood who was mixed up in the Dunlo divorce case. I have since learned however that I confused Mr. Montague Wood with a Mr. Marmaduke Wood, and I think it would be worth while for Mr. Pulitzer to see him again when he comes to town. He does not sing or play, but he has a very good manner and is evidently of a good disposition. One thing against him is that he has a slight lisp.[15]

While in London, where his stand against the Boer War caused coolness among some of his acquaintances, Pulitzer interviewed Frank Harris for a post as roving European correspondent and rejected him. One of the advantages of being a World executive was shown by the arrival in London of four of them at intervals—Seitz, Bradford Merrill, Foster Coates and Nelson Hersh, better known in the World code as Gulch, George, Grasp and Grinding, respectively. All came at Pulitzer's expense, all to enjoy themselves but also to suffer somewhat as they drank journalistic instruction at the schoolmaster's unfailing fount. Seitz, now the top man in the hierarchy by a shade over Merrill, had received a $1,000 bonus three months earlier and his importance was signalized by the transatlantic passage of his horse at the chief's expense. But Pulitzer, always looking forward to change and then quickly wanting more change, grew impatient with the Poynder place. In turn he sent Ledlie, Dr. Hosmer and his invaluable major-domo, Jabez Dunningham, to investigate accommodations at Scheveningen, then decided against it after great research expense. This, too, after Kate, also in Europe, had visited Scheveningen and recommended it highly, adding:

> Darling, your telegram gave me great pleasure, as any word of tenderness from you always does. Dr. Hosmer must hide his blushes now—I slept with it under my pillow. I think I forget I am an old married woman with five great children. Never you *dare* say I can't go *any* where again. Acknowledge you are mistaken in what a woman can do, if she is as high headed as I am.[16]

From Alfred Harmsworth, later to become Lord Northcliffe, whose Daily Mail now had almost a million circulation, he received a breezy note:

> I am sorry to have been so faithless this year, but your visit synchronises with the height of the angling season, to which all other personal gratifications must of course go, but I will come with pleasure tomorrow . . .[17]

Late in June Pulitzer returned to America, leaving Ledlie to worry about adjusting the account with Lady Poynder for the unused month of the lease. Kate, who had been in Aix recuperating from sciatica and had expected to join him in London, was surprised at his sudden change of plan. The economy campaign was still in force, it was perilous for her to go over her $6,000 monthly allowance, and from Paris she had to cable him in no letter-under-the-pillow mood: "Steamer tickets and three hundred and fifty dollars absolutely necessary to leave . . ."[18]

The economy drive was also felt by a Bar Harbor coal dealer, who dunned Pulitzer repeatedly for a settlement of a $139 bill, and by Alexander Matier, a New York interior decorator who charged $1,400 to redo the rented Sloane house and wrote, "I am compelled once more to appeal to you for a settlement . . ." A World accountant finally sent him $1,350, writing, "[Mr. Pulitzer] seems to feel that your bill is very excessive and that the amount . . . is ample for the services rendered."[19] Pulitzer was preoccupied with plans for a new $250,000 house being drawn by McKim, Mead & White, straining his dim vision in scrutinizing drawings done in "the blackest black on the whitest white." He gave thought to a memorial to Thomas Davidson, who had died September 14, 1900. He was upset because David Graham Phillips had taken a trip to Europe which he said Pulitzer had insisted on paying for, Pulitzer saying he had not.

Bryan, on a visit to New York, fairly bowed and scraped before Bradford Merrill, adjuring him two times over to convey his respects to Mr. Pulitzer, who was unimpressed. The World, disavowing Bryan's silver theories, supported him with muted strings, leaving the brasses to Hearst, who spent $2,000 on bands and fireworks during the Commoner's stay. For the first time Pulitzer heeded Kate's advice and left the country before a presidential election in order to spare his nerves. He sailed in

October, stayed overnight in London, then started for Wiesbaden via Ostend. Near Brussels the train stopped because of a wreck ahead, and the passengers had to get out and stumble through damp fields to another train beyond the wreck. Dr. Hosmer reported his employer's reaction in a letter to Kate: ". . . Everything was wrong all the time & the world was full of damn fools." [20]

Pulitzer tried to coax the irrepressible journalist Charles Edward Jerningham, who wrote the amusing "Marmaduke" series in Labouchere's *Truth,* to come to Wiesbaden and furnish companionship. Failing this, he endeavored to lure Jerningham's friend, the British writer Ralph Nevill. Nevill, declining, wrote Jerningham, "[Pulitzer] appears quite unable to battle with the malady of the century—*unrest*—why can he not settle down peacefully to the soft music of Hungarian bands?" [21] The creature of unrest sent home 1,018 bottles of wine. From the Agence Daguerre of Nice he received a letter: "We have in the present time for a castle having cost 1,800,000 dollars to be sold for the sum of 100,000 dollars."

He rejected the castle and by November 7 was back in London, pondering the rout of Bryan and a message from the local Journal man: "I have received a cablegram from Mr. Hearst requesting the favor of an interview with you for the Journal upon 'What must Democrats do to bring all factions of the party together?' " [22] One good solution would be to stop nominating Bryan. But there was a different tone about Hearst these days, the ingratiating manner of the candidate. He had discarded his dudish attire in favor of senatorial broadcloth. He had become president of the National Association of Democratic Clubs, he had actually made a few speeches despite his stage fright, and he would bear watching. Two days later Pulitzer was in a leased house at Bournemouth, urging Jerningham to find him a companion to supplement Hosmer, Butes and Billing. Jerningham proposed two candidates, Ronald Scarlett and Lord Frederick Bruce, and although neither qualified, Pulitzer sent Jerningham a case of Liebfraumilch. His first secretary-companion of all, Claude Ponsonby, came over delightedly to visit him, proving that at least one of these hard-pressed men could retain affection.

Butes, also looking for companions, had six prospects in mind. Another man on the alert was Professor Politzer in Vienna, who recommended a fellow Viennese, Kurt Leitner. Leitner wrote Pulitzer that he spoke four languages, was accomplished in music, art and literature, and had been acquainted with Wagner, Liszt, Brahms and others. He had been secretary for Baron Anselm Rothschild for nine years, then for ten years with the Duke of Bielitz, "who is very eccentric and only goes to sleep in the early morning." Here was a man with battle experience. "I beg to tell you that I have not lost my energy and my good humour in spite of some unfortunate experiences," Leitner added, "and hope to say I am not a bad companion. I am not nervous. I am accustomed to accommodate myself to others." [23] He sounded so promising that Pulitzer wired him to come at once. He was in one of his more unreasonable spells, abandoning his diet, eating like a horse and suffering from dyspepsia. When he read that Beethoven placed great reliance on a good Viennese cook to promote digestive calm, he asked his aides to find one—even wrote Kate to solicit her help. "It seems very strange that I feel like apologizing for putting you to this trouble," he wrote pettishly. "Yet I presume it is the most natural thing in the world for nobody but wives to do this sort of thing and be happy when they look after the comfort of their husbands." [24]

From Seitz came bad news: "Mark Twain has refused to edit our comic supplement and we are looking for someone else . . ." From Seitz also came an explanatory "Memo on Failure to Get World Promptly at Wiesbaden," which supplemented his earlier "Memo on a Method of Keeping Track of Mr. Pulitzer's Messages." From Bradford Merrill, temporarily running the noisy Evening World, he received a journalistic aria:

> Yesterday was a splendid day for the Evening newspapers. At 7 o'clock, there was a jail delivery in the Essex Market Court; five burglars escaped and a keeper was shot dead. At 12 o'clock a wholesale drug house at Warren and Greenwich Sts. was blown up and about 30 people killed and 40 buildings partly, or wholly wrecked. At 5 o'clock Alvord (the $700,000 N. Y. bank thief) was caught in Boston. Of course the explosion was the great thing. . . .[25]

From Leitner, a plaintive, "Bad bronchitis since some days . . . very unhappy," and Leitner faded out of his life.[26] Pulitzer left Bournemouth on his own special train (£60, 5s. plus first-class fares for each member of the party), to sail from Liverpool December 19. Among his fellow trans-atlantic passengers were Mr. and Mrs. Alfred Harmsworth, and as he sailed westward with Harmsworth he devised a novel journalistic celebration of the dawn of the twentieth century.

On the night of December 31, at Pulitzer's invitation, the dynamic Harmsworth was in the golden Dome in complete charge of the January 1 World. The staff (all but Gumbo, who felt such feathers ridiculous in a newsroom) marked the occasion by appearing in evening dress, startled by Harmsworth's decision to issue the paper in diminutive tabloid form, nine by 18 inches. At the stroke of midnight, with Pulitzer home in bed, William H. Merrill, dean of the staff, raised a glass of champagne and proposed a toast to Harmsworth in behalf of the absent owner. The first copy off the press one second after midnight was given to a messenger, who caught the 12:15 train for Washington in an effort to beat the Journal in presenting the first twentieth-century New York newspaper to President McKinley. The Journal thought to win the palm by sending *its* newspaper by special train, which reached the capital well ahead. But it reckoned without the attitude of McKinley, who was being savagely attacked in the Journal whereas the World was impaling him with a fairly gentlemanly saber. The World was handed to the President as he went to breakfast, the messenger having the great delight, as he left, of seeing the Journal's man with his first copy (enclosed in a silver box) still waiting in the anteroom.

"I don't suppose," Harmsworth said, "any great newspaper proprietor in the world except Mr. Pulitzer would entrust his entire plant for one day to the discretion of a young man who has no other recommendation than some little success three thousand miles away." Although Harmsworth's napkin-sized newspaper sold almost 100,000 more than usual, this was regarded as curiosity sale and the World next day returned to its blanket size. There was fear that Harmsworth, who was not known for gentle business practices, might steal some of the World editors. On Pulitzer's order, strenuous efforts were made to keep him at a respectful distance, and indeed the precaution seemed justified. When he proposed giving a dinner for the staff, Bradford Merrill politely vetoed the idea. When he asked for a directory of the staff, Merrill wrote Pulitzer, "This I succeeded in not giving to him." [27] Pulitzer, however, sent cigars to Harmsworth and flowers to his wife at their hotel.

III. A BIRD IN A GILDED CAGE

The advent of the twentieth century marked Pulitzer's 33rd year as a newspaperman although he was still only 53. He had studied every national political issue (not to mention many local ones) of the seventies, eighties and nineties with the avidity of a seminarian, and had given the same exhaustive scrutiny to every important politician. He had commented on all of them, issues and men, with singular courage, frankness and freedom from fence-sitting. Politically he was probably the best-informed man in the nation. With few exceptions he had been steadfast to his credo of liberalism and reform, the most powerful progressive force in journalism, educating the people, dropping boulders rather than pebbles into the pool of public opinion. Most of his few errors could be laid to inability to control his nerves and his ambitions—failures perhaps blamable on illness—but now and for the rest of his life he would keep closer check on both nerves and ambitions as they related to public issues. Once the fond paterfamilias, he had fallen into his orbit of work and travel so firmly that his gatherings with his wife and children were special rather than daily occasions.

As he had long been a conversation piece among journalists, so he became one in society—the eccentric genius who fled from one place to another as if the devil were at his heels. Word had trickled across the sea that Albert Pulitzer had occasional delusions of persecution, and there was some speculation as to whether Joseph could long retain his sanity. That horrid fear must often have been in his own mind. He was not unaware that he had similar, if milder, delusions—fantasies that were at times psychopathic, suspicions that his editors were deceiving him, that his family and friends were deserting him—not to mention those periods of black depression. He was fighting a constant and conscious battle against derangement. Somewhat as a mother can forget illness and exhaustion to attend an ailing child, so he achieved a measure of self-therapy by his immersion in his newspapers. This salvation would have been impossible but for his protective cocoon, the artificial world in which he functioned, the soundproofed rooms, the private cars, the cordon of secretaries around him.

The World had bought for $2,000, as a tryout and for its advertising éclat, the first motor-driven delivery truck used by any New York newspaper. It would soon buy 20 more, retiring 70 horses. The talk of the town was the new electrically operated 12-passenger buses plying Fifth Avenue, and another revolution in transportation was promised by the awarding of a $35,000,000 contract for the city's first subway. Hearst and a few other adventurous spirits were actually driving automobiles of their own, and with more than 10,000 such horseless carriages in the country, there was apprehension about their dangers. Vermont passed a law requiring an automobile to be preceded by an adult on foot waving a red flag. Lillian Russell, who would have denied that she was 40, drew a staggering $1,250 a week, and Broadway was alive with dozens of productions including those of Weber and Fields, De Wolf Hopper and Julia Marlowe, but moving pictures were gaining in favor. People were humming the tunes of Victor Herbert, though he had nothing to do with one that swept the country—"Only a Bird in a Gilded Cage." There was a telephone for each 66 people, the wires now reaching beyond Omaha. The nation's population exceeded 76,000,000, and "McKinley prosperity" was a fact. If it was true that clerks got only four to eight dollars a week, and that an advertisement in Pulitzer's Post-Dispatch for a night watchman working 72 hours a week for a wage of $15 drew 725 applicants, it was also true that a man's suit cost ten dollars, eggs were 14 cents a dozen and bourbon two dollars a gallon.

Pulitzer, a bird in his own extraordinary gilded cage, could hear the sounds of the new century but was denied clear sight of it. He could not dispute the soothing effect of McKinley's reelection on the financial world, for his own investments soared, one of them, Jersey Central, rising from 116 to 146. He still shunned speculative stocks, investing heavily in substantial companies performing useful services, particularly railroads—Pennsylvania, Baltimore & Ohio, Louisville & Nashville and Northern

Pacific among them—buying shares in lots of 5,000 or more through the invaluable Coin, Dumont Clarke. He was so gratified by his gains that he gave Clarke a $1,000 organ for Christmas. It is likely that in some years his dividends approached or exceeded his newspaper profits, and indeed he considered the former in part as a protection for his newspapers, always his first consideration.

During the unhappy war period he had been forced to give the World a transfusion of $524,600 of his own money. By January 1901 it had repaid him $276,300.[28] But the Hearst competition was still hurting both circulation and profits. The morning Journal now, for a brief period, had an edge in circulation over the World, although so much of it was out of town that Senior still held leadership in the city. The two evening papers were in a close struggle, but under the gaudy Goddard the Sunday Journal had passed Seniority. The World code lumped Hearst's three New York papers under the term Geranium, while the three Worlds were Genuine and advertising was designated as Potash. As Hearst had anticipated, Potash was coming in despite the general scorn for his three papers (along with the Evening and Sunday World) as "yellows," and World auditors calculated that Geranium's Potash was now about 60 percent of Genuine's.[29] Since this meant that Gush was still slightly in the red, the question remained as to how long he (or his mother) could meet the deficit, and there was a stream of memos to Andes about this.

Although Hearst had recently started his Chicago American, there was a wishful rumor that he was so badly pinched that he was plunging in the stock market in an effort to recoup. On Pulitzer's instruction, however, Don Seitz had a long talk with Whitelaw Reid (Macerate), who was still renting space in his Tribune building to Hearst. Macerate said that about $7,000,000 was left in the Hearst estate following the sale of the Anaconda mine. ". . . Mrs. Gush had originally determined to leave him to his fate on the three and a half millions," Seitz reported to his chief, "[but] the investment had become so large that the estate could not afford to let it drop."[30] Hearst evidently had sufficient backing to carry him into the period—not long distant now—when he would be operating at a profit. The hope that Gush would go broke was exploded. He was in New York to stay, and he was raiding again.

He had snatched away the Evening World's genius of three-inch headlines, Foster Coates, who as a result was driving a new $1,700 automobile. He was trying to seduce Junior's city editor, Charles Chapin, and others. He called personally on the very important Bradford Merrill and offered him a three-year contract at $20,000. The usually kindly Seitz showed a bit of the World backbiting when he reported to Pulitzer that Merrill had declined but "without making any pretense of loyalty to Genuine." In retaliation, Seitz wrote that he was scanning Geranium's force "for someone to steal."[31] There were strong efforts to lure away Hearst's business manager, C. M. Palmer, and the invaluable Goddard, who unfortunately was under an ironclad contract. Seitz took Palmer to lunch and pumped him assiduously for information but found no leaks in him, a quality that made him more desirable than ever, and the attempt to win him over continued for months. Merrill was required to swear fealty, which he did by telegram to Pulitzer: "My whole heart and ambition are centered in Genuine and away from Geranium." [32] The Hearst threat again caused a Pulitzer defensive flurry as he raised the salaries of Merrill and others and gave two weeks' extra pay as a gift to valued men including Chapin, Tennant and Burton. His uneasiness was evident in a letter to F. D. White: ". . . You should make up your mind to shut that open [Hearst] door across the street, and shut it *tight,* shut it for your own good. . . ." [33]

He had gone to Aix and then to Wiesbaden in the spring, busily buying paintings and tapestries for his new home at 7–11½ East 73rd Street though it was far from completed. Stanford White wrote him, "I feel certain . . . the house will be as fine a one as we have ever built." [34] Pulitzer gave him sharp orders to eschew fanciness and display: ". . . No ballroom, music room, or picture gallery under any disguise. . . . There must be no French rooms, designed or decorated to require French furniture—least of all old furniture. The rooms to be designed to preclude, to make it impossible even to think of such a thing. . . . I want an American home for comfort & use not for show or entertainment." [35] Either he changed his mind or Kate changed it for him, for the house was designed to contain not only a ballroom and music room but also a pipe organ and swimming pool.

IV. GERANIUM AND GENUINE

Pulitzer was vexed by the continuing tendency to lump his papers (including the now redeemed Senior) with Hearst's as "the yellows," and for some clubs to exclude the World as well as the Journal. Both of course were reformist, antimonopolistic, defenders of "the people," and nominally but far from slavishly Democratic. Both spent great effort and huge sums to expose corruption.

The differences were as evident, reflecting the disparity between the two men. The Hearst press was more extravagant and sensational, exhibiting an increasing tone of vengefulness growing from its owner's as yet secret determination to make himself President. His papers were gradually becoming tools for his political ambitions, whereas Pulitzer had long since put that aside and become the editorial gadfly and schoolmaster. He sought to inform and guide his readers, whereas Hearst aimed to fill his with rage against social injustices which he would soon tell them that he could correct if elected to office. Pulitzer was constructive, full of suggestions for all parties, able to bestow warm praise for the progressive acts of Republicans like Roosevelt. The Hearst press by comparison was negative, narrow and violent. Pulitzer was content to strip public offenders bare, while Hearst beheaded them. The World, with the nation's most carefully edited editorial page, could handle with ridicule what the Journal sprayed with poison. There was the underlying, the all-important question of sincerity. While Hearst had more earnest progressivism than his enemies granted him, the editor in him was becoming ever more overpowered by the office-seeker.

Into the work of Hearst's ablest cartoonists, Homer Davenport and Frederick Opper, often crept a note of savagery. The radical Brisbane, who had chafed under Pulitzer's restrictions, now lived at Hearst's house, was privy to his ambitions and had virtually a free hand. His editorials at times were virulent, especially toward the national administration, one of them describing McKinley as "the most hated creature on the American continent." Another, unsigned, assailed the President and added the incendiary line, "If bad institutions and bad men can be got rid of only by killing, then the killing must be done." [36] Hearst himself had this incitement removed from later editions and even sent an emissary to apologize to McKinley for the Journal excesses, but the abuse continued. Another shocker was a quatrain Ambrose Bierce wrote for the Journal when Governor-elect William Goebel of Kentucky was shot dead in an election quarrel:

> The bullet that pierced Goebel's breast
> Can not be found in all the West;
> Good reason, it is speeding here
> To stretch McKinley in his bier.[37]

The watchdog World, whose own criticism of McKinley was sharp but decent, had uttered its most effective growls during the appalling Croker–Van Wyck administration. By constant attack it had helped defeat the notorious Ramapo water franchise grab, and had exposed the American Ice Company's monopolistic stratagem of giving large blocks of stock to Van Wyck, Croker and other politicians in return for exclusive use of city ice docks, allowing it to double the price of ice. In both crusades it was ably abetted by the Hearst press. The World made lavish use of its own attorneys in its continuous attacks on Croker, one of them, James W. Gerard (son of Pulitzer's first New York landlord), noting that Pulitzer "simply refused to tolerate the idea of failure," and "used the *World* consistently for the public good." [38] At his urging, Gerard found an obscure law under which any taxpayer could demand an investigation, and used it to bring the mayor and his dock commissioners before Judge Gaynor to admit ownership of ice trust stock. ". . . While [Van Wyck's] salary as Mayor was $41.09 a day," the World observed, "his dividends from his Ice stock were

$95 a day." [39] Croker so clearly recognized his enemy that during one investigation, when questioned about his vast increase in wealth, he said testily, "You have been reading the *World.* You are just catering for that paper now." [40]

Thanks largely to the World and the Journal, Croker and Van Wyck were through. The city, so like an alternately backsliding and repentant drunkard, was ready for reform again. In the fall, the World supported Pulitzer's friend Seth Low, nominated for mayor on a Republican-fusion ticket against Tammany's Edward Shepard. Before the campaign got under way, McKinley made his journey to the Pan-American Exposition at Buffalo and was shot September 6 by the half-mad Leon Czolgosz.

It was characteristic of Pulitzer, who was at Chatwold, that although he knew that several World men were speeding to Buffalo, he sent his own trusted Dr. Hosmer there to report to him directly. Hosmer's first telegram relayed the attending physicians' conviction that McKinley would recover. His second read: "President dying respiration said to be 40 does not respond to treatment cannot survive." [41] He died September 14, and "that damned cowboy," as Hanna termed Roosevelt, was sworn in as President.

There was an instant eruption among Hearst's journalistic enemies in New York. The Tribune and others republished the Bierce quatrain, the inflammatory editorials and cartoons, and suggested that Hearst was an accessory in the murder. There was a bogus report that a copy of the Journal was found in Czolgosz' pocket when he was arrested. Angry New Yorkers snatched bundles of Hearst papers from newsboys and burned them. Some of the Journal's hard-won advertisers immediately withdrew. Hearst was hanged in effigy in New York, New Brunswick, Chicago and other cities. The Grand Army of the Republic at its Cleveland convention passed a resolution urging every member to "exclude from his household 'The New York Journal,' a teacher of anarchism and a vile sheet." The New York Chamber of Commerce under the lead of former Mayor Abram Hewitt condemned the Hearst press and urged a boycott, which soon assumed sizable proportions.

Here was a rich opportunity for Andes to take revenge on Gush and Geranium. He did not do so. Perhaps remembering that he had not always been free from violence, he ordered Seitz and William H. Merrill to avoid Hearst-baiting and to limit coverage of the public revulsion against Hearst to strictly factual reporting. The World, so heavy a sufferer at Hearst's hands, did not kick him when he was down. In fact, the editors leaned so far backward in objectivity that Pulitzer complained, ". . . ignoring Geranium and personalities did not mean suppression of current legitimate news like Hewitt's speech chamber commerce meeting or even burning anybody in effigy if facts absolutely correct, true, and the thing is not displayed maliciously." [42]

Seitz, seeing in the uproar an opportunity to publicize the World's cleansing of its yellow stain, wrote him, "My notion is that for the first time in five years, we now have a chance to part company with Geranium in the public mind. . . . We have been coupled with them perpetually to the injury of our character and our business . . ." Pomeroy Burton urged it as the occasion to bring Junior back to the respectability to which Senior had already returned, writing the chief, "Is this not the time—the exact time—to effect the same change in the Evening World . . . ?" [43]

Pulitzer agreed to the extent of reducing the headline size and placing a firm rein on City Editor Chapin, a zealot who frankly gloated over news-making disasters. "Do not fear that I will . . . get back to The Evening Journal style or want to resume startling heads," Chapin promised him, in the same letter warning that these were the things that built circulation.[44] Junior, which had crept steadily back to return a $200,000 annual profit, remained a commercial enterprise. Senior alone was the master's voice. It showed a mettle rare for the day when the new President's luncheon with Booker T. Washington blew up a gale of criticism not only in the South, remarking editorially:

> An American named Washington, one of the most learned, most eloquent, most brilliant men of the day—the President of a college—is asked to dinner by President Roosevelt and because the pigment of his skin is some shades darker than that of others a large part of the United States is convulsed with shame and rage.
>
> The man is a negro. Therefore in eating with him the President is charged with having insulted the South. This man may cast a ballot but he may not break bread. He may represent us in the Senate Chamber, but he may not "join us at the breakfast-table." He may educate us, but not eat with us; preach our Gospel, but not be our guest . . . die for us but not dine with us.
>
> Truly Liberty must smile at such broad-minded logic, such enlightened tolerance. Or should she weep? [45]

V. NOISY EATING

For 16 years Dumont Clarke, who was president of the American Exchange Bank and a director of the World (he owned five token shares of the 5,000 total, Andes holding 4,990 firmly in his own hands) had advised Pulitzer in stock transactions amounting to many millions and was an occasional dinner guest. At long last he scaled a hurdle too high for most and changed his form of written address from "Dear Mr. Pulitzer" to "My dear J.P." But evidently he feared that too great an intimacy might be risky in view of Andes' unpredictability, for he gracefully dodged invitations for long stays at Chatwold or companionable trips to Europe. Pulitzer was ready to relax somewhat in his rigid refusal to speculate, writing Clarke, "I do not buy to sell but to lock up for my children. . . . I have enough real estate and so-called gilt-edged things to feel safe to make further investment less exacting and take some little chances." [46]

When Pulitzer directed him not to buy any Consolidated Gas stock because he was contemplating an attack on the company's political manipulation, Coin replied that he had never noticed the remotest connection between his stock holdings and his editorial line: "My experience has been that you have always led in attacks upon the coal combination, although the Lackawanna (in which you are largely interested) was the most important of all the companies affected." [47] Pulitzer nevertheless preferred to have no financial interest in any company which might draw either his praise or blame. His virtue intact, he sailed October 22 and was gone exactly a month, dining in London with Sir Thomas Lipton, telling him he was thinking of buying a steam yacht and picking the brain of the world's foremost authority on yachts. Although he dropped the idea, he would return to it later.

No sooner was he back in New York than a new threat to his personnel arose. The capricious Frank Munsey had bought the Tammany-slanted New York Daily News, known as the "hod-carriers' favorite," and was kidnaping talent, vainly offering Brisbane $50,000 a year to quit Hearst and take charge. "There are street rumors," Seitz reported anxiously, "that Munsey is after Gumbo [Burton], George [Bradford Merrill], Volema [F. D. White] and Phillips." [48] Although Munsey probably caused strategic World pay increases, he got no important man and soon proved his journalistic incompetence. He alienated his hod-carriers with a new silk-hat approach, lost readers in droves and sold out after three disastrous years, taking a $750,000 loss.

Pulitzer had the satisfaction of seeing Low elected mayor and reading Croker's bitter words: "The defeat of Tammany Hall is due to the newspapers, The World among them, and way up among them." [49] Meanwhile Ledlie and Butes each spent a night in Pulitzer's bedroom in the unfinished 73rd Street house to investigate the problem of noise from the New Haven Railroad to the east, the New York Central to the west, the Madison Avenue trolley a half-block away, and possible clamorous neighbors. "*I am certain* you cannot hear a sound . . . when the windows and doors are closed," Ledlie wrote with dangerous confidence.[50]

During his post-holiday stay at Jekyll Island, Pulitzer summoned W. H. Merrill (Cantabo) down and gave him instructions to pass on to many members of the staff, two of a personal nature. He had only about an hour a day of real brain freshness, he said, which he must utilize efficiently. Bradford Merrill, valuable though he was, was inclined to interrupt with rambling arguments, wasting his limited time of creativity. Would Cantabo kindly ask the other Merrill to be as terse in speech as he was in writing? As for Don Seitz, he had that unfortunate habit of eating audibly, crunching his toast, talking with food in his mouth. Cantabo was directed to approach Seitz very discreetly about this, which he did on his return, writing his chief, ". . . I stopped in on Seitz this morning, and after an interchange of general news brought in the subject you mentioned by telling him of your sensitiveness to *noise in eating*. . . . I suggested pleasantly that he keep a piece of crust by his plate as a reminder . . ." [51]

Chapter 3

Eccentricities of Andes

1. THE FAMILY CIRCLE

Judged by externals only, the Pulitzers were a comic-strip family combining elements of the Katzenjammers, Hairbreadth Harry, Everett True and other strips too implausible for successful syndication. There was the outrageous father, the charming but determined and somewhat flighty mother, and there were five remarkable children who displayed characteristics ranging from the rebelliousness of young Herbert and the occasional wildness of Joseph to Edith's high mettle and the sense of duty attained by Constance and Ralph. The keynote of their lives was feverish activity. They were surely the most widely traveled family extant, all of them exhibiting the sophistication bestowed by globe-trotting. Their travels were often individual rather than en famille, so that at a given moment Ralph might be shooting bear in Colorado, Joseph failing his courses at St. Mark's, Herbert defying his tutors in New York, Edith and Constance visiting their aunt in Washington, Pulitzer himself at Wiesbaden and Kate on the Atlantic going east or west.

Yet they had a strong familial attachment. Their separations inspired thousands of highly literate letters as well as telegrams and cables costing enough annually to support a less prodigal family. They sometimes communicated like secret agents, in preposterous codes. Gifts they sent each other were always riding the rails or burdening steamers. Now and again they would be drawn together for short stays at Bar Harbor, New York or Jekyll Island, or groups of them would meet in London or Paris, chattering in German or French, only to scatter to the winds again. Their conversations could range from discussions of the latest murder mystery to the virtuosity of Nordica and the sins of Roosevelt. There were frequent Pulitzerian explosions during their meetings, Dr. Hosmer being amused enough to record a very minor one between Pulitzer and Edith when Edith had been accused of injuring Constance's horse:

PULITZER: Oh—Edith—one thing I want to say to you—several things for that matter; but one just now—you must not ride Constance's horse.

EDITH: Now, father—

PULITZER: Never mind—never mind—I know all about it. I am tired of buying horses; and you must not ride Constance's horse.

EDITH: Father, you must listen—I must answer—

PULITZER: Well, answer.

EDITH: But will you listen to me—will you hear what I have to say or will you constantly interrupt me?

PULITZER (laughing): I shall probably interrupt you; but go on.

EDITH: The trouble with Constance's horse is not my fault. The veterinary says so. He says the horse either hurt itself in the stall or was kicked by another horse—and that the trouble was not caused by me.

PULITZER: But I want you not to ride Constance's horse.

EDITH (near tears): Oh, dear! If anything happens to any horse everybody comes to me about it—and everybody says I am to blame. It is not fair. I am tired of this. I will not have it.

PULITZER (his voice becoming stern): What do you say?

EDITH: I say I am tired of these accusations.

PULITZER: Please remember that you are talking to your father.

EDITH: Certainly, but I must defend myself. It is not fair—

PULITZER: Fair or not fair, don't forget that you are talking to your father. If you are going to talk in that way I wish you would leave the table.

EDITH: I was going to when you came; but I came back to talk to you.

PULITZER: I don't want you to talk to me in that way. I don't want you at the table if you intend to talk in that way. Don't come to the table. Don't come to my table at all.[1]

This was Pulitzer in a mood of lenient chiding. But there was nothing comic whatever in his illness nor in the demands and pressures it imposed on his family—particularly on Ralph and Joseph, the heirs apparent. Long before they became of age the children knew that their father was not like other fathers and that they must humor him and bow to his wishes or court disaster. One outgrowth of his depressed moods was an intense self-pity accompanied by irrational suspicions. He once wrote Joseph:

> But are you not a thousand times better off than I am? Just ask yourself that question every day, at least when you can sleep you can do anything you like, you can see, you enjoy perfect health, you have no cares to bother you, no sorrows, no suffering, no children to provide for, to give you anxiety as to the future, no business, no illness, no thought that life is a terrible failure and nothing left except a dark fragment.[2]

His mood could switch instantly from kindliness to bitterness, as in one letter to Ralph which began with words of warmest affection and then went on:

> I have no sympathy or encouragement from my family. Every time I go into the dining room day after day, week after week, month after month with only strangers about me, left with complete strangers, nobody at my table except paid employees, I ask was there ever a human being in this whole world so truly forsaken and deserted and shamefully treated by fate, destiny or family.[3]

On the contrary he had constant tenderness and commiseration from his family. Too much "family" overexcited him and his wife and children were allowed to be with him only at stated intervals. To such outcries his sons replied with long, careful letters, thoroughly adult except when touching his illnesses, when they took on the pitying tone one might use toward an ailing child, expressing their sympathy not in one sentence but many, ringing many changes on the theme of sympathy because they knew he demanded sympathy, commenting admiringly on his fortitude, suggesting another doctor or a cure at a spa, assuring him of their love and insisting that he was always in their thoughts. Their letters took much of their time and were sometimes inspired by downright fear, since he occasionally sank into almost suicidal despair. There had been at least one time at Bar Harbor when he rode out alone in desperation, unseeing, skirting cliffs that could have killed him, seemingly inviting death.

One sure way to please him was to write him in rich detail. He liked this not only because it was a proof of love and satisfied his insatiable curiosity but also because it improved his children's powers of thought and expression. As he once wrote Edith, "In your next letter you must rack your brain to describe every hair of Miss W's head and her nose, toes and feet, complexion, measurement of her waist and smallest details. Apropos of this I see no reason why you should not make a description of all the girls including their clothes, appearance, voice." [4]

He was alternately an ogre and a St. Nick, showering gifts on them all—an automobile for Ralph, a yacht for Joseph big enough to need a small crew, gems for the girls, $200 at a clip for young Herbert. When Edith had an appendectomy he ordered fresh flowers for her room every day. He incessantly sent the children books, urging them to read, learn, think, wake up their lazy minds. He delighted in surprise gifts. All of them received generous allowances plus occasional extra largesse. To them he was the great unpredictable, an almost mythical or supernatural creature who had the power to confer joy or sorrow. Only Herbert, still young enough to be spoiled, largely escaped his wrath. Ralph and Joseph, being not only the eldest but in training for a great public responsibility, were under his severest scrutiny by mail or cable wherever he was. Especially to Ralph his instructions bore the urgency and sternness of a general's orders for a military campaign, and his castigation could be withering if they were not followed to the letter. Joseph, six years younger and inclined to skylarking, escaped the extreme demands placed on Ralph but took expert dressings-down for his transgressions. Still, he had the courage to make a logical criticism:

> I'm sorry I haven't written, but kindly remember that though you haven't heard from me for two weeks I have not heard from you for nearly two months. And I like to receive letters just as much as you do.[5]

Joseph and Kate Pulitzer were deeply attached, his own affection becoming most articulate when she was ill. "My dearest Kate," he wrote her, "I wish you knew how much I have thought of you during the trip. If thinking and worrying and wishing and sympathizing and deploring could do any good or alleviate suffering you would be perfectly well. There was not an hour of the day you were not on my mind . . ."[6]

Yet they clashed frequently because of their antithetic attitudes toward money. Pulitzer never conquered his conviction that his money (except when spent for his own comfort) should be husbanded on a strict budgetary basis. He always signed his own checks even though he could not see them. To Kate, money was something to be enjoyed. Although her allowance had been boosted to $8,000 a month, she gaily refused to observe it and in at least one dreadful month ran over to a total of $23,000. Forced to lead a life of her own, she flitted between New York, Bar Harbor, Florida and Europe with her secretary-companion, Maud Macarow, and two servants, occasionally joining her husband (when he permitted it) on a bird-of-passage footing. Sociable, luxury-loving, she could not resist Tiffany's or Worth's. From Paris she wrote him:

> I must ask you to send me some money to Paris . . . I have been very economical, my only extravagance, if it would be possible to call it such, has been automobiling into Geneva and back. I have bought a few furs there for Edith—I am chuckling at your despair at this statement, I am sure I can hear you say she would find something to buy were she in a forest untrodden by civilized man, but you are quite mistaken I never buy anything save the strictly needful. You should consider yourself very fortunate that you have such an economical wife, in fact my own feeling is that you should be a little ashamed of my parsimony. Had I any spirit of enterprise I should collect things, pictures, objets d'arts, priceless fans, priceless snuff boxes, have a hobby, such as a self respecting wife of every rich man should have.[7]

She was of course pulling his leg, as she often did, but most jokes were lost on him, especially when they cost him money. He would grind his teeth, complain bitterly, make her wait but eventually pay up. Although there were times when she was actually embarrassed by importunate creditors, this had little effect on her spending. Probably she reasoned that since he spent enormous sums on himself it was unjust not to allow her similar freedom; and the years would bear her out in the sense that Pulitzer's millions never became seriously depleted. While she could be wonderfully warm and sympathetic, there were times when she felt that he used his illnesses as an unfair weapon over his family and that he occasionally dramatized them. She cabled him a few weeks later:

> Last cheque spent before receiving please cable money. . . .

And again:

> I hope a letter of credit will soon be forthcoming, if not, you might soon hear of us landed in debtor's prison.[8]

She sometimes forgot his strict order never to wire or cable him in the afternoon, his reason being that late-arriving messages excited him so that he could not sleep. He wrote Miss Macarow wrathfully:

> . . . Above all stop her cables to me. . . . Of course she is making me utterly miserable, destroying any chance of mental rest & cure and she should have put into her brain the idea that her sense of duty . . . might include her husband.[9]

Since he found his greatest satisfaction in maintaining complete authority and control over his environment, anything that impinged on his dominance vexed him. He saw no selfishness in this, being convinced that he was always right and that his orders were never other than just. He employed tyranny and money to enforce his control, a strategy always successful among his secretaries and editors, usually so among his children, but failing utterly with Kate. She was the one person around him who refused to come to heel. She represented a breakdown of his authority. As a result, the affection between them was punctuated by intermittent thunder and lightning. On one occasion, when he refused to see her before her departure for Europe, she telegraphed him from the harbor:

> Sorry not to have said good by you are a spoiled child take care of yourself and telegraph me that you are feeling better and brighter address Claridges Kate [10]

11. HIRE A MAN WHO GETS DRUNK

In 1902 Pulitzer, aided by Kate and George Ledlie, bought art in earnest for the new house—a Millet for $1,250, a Titian for $13,000, a Douw for $2,500—spending $36,000 for 21 canvases and paying more than $6,000 in duties on shipments of statuary and other art from Europe. He received W. R. Warren's portrait of the late Thomas Davidson, which he had commissioned. He was upset by the defection of two of his closest companions, Dr. George Hosmer and David Graham Phillips. For 12 years the aging Hosmer had been almost constantly at his side, a length of service that could produce a condition similar to shell shock. He badly needed a rest, he had seen his family only occasionally, his daughter was ill, and in his own state of agitation he spoke sharp words to the master in London, quit him flat and sailed home.

Hosmer, who was indispensable to his well-being, would return to front-line duty before the year was out, but the case of Gumboil was beyond healing. In 1901, since his World contract at $8,000 a year forbade outside writing under his own name, he had published his first novel, *The Great God Success,* under the pseudonym of John Graham. His authorship was known, and Pulitzer suffered real anguish when he got around to reading it. The story concerned a newspaperman named Howard, galvanized with ambition and a reformist instinct, who rises swiftly through sheer ability from reporter to ownership of a New York newspaper much like the World. "And his vigour, his enthusiasm pervaded the entire office. He went from one news department to another, suggesting, asking for suggestions, praising, criticising. . . . And he dictated every day telegrams to correspondents, thanking them for any conspicuously good stories . . . adding something to [their] compensation . . ." Howard, moreover, becomes a heavy investor, especially in railroads. A slave to work and ambition, sacrificing family life, he gradually becomes corrupted and makes his paper the servant of his investments, refusing to expose the thievery of railroads in which he holds shares. "Through all his scheming and shifting Howard had kept the [paper] in the main an 'organ of the people.' . . . His real reason was not his alleged principles but his cold judgment that the increases in circulation which produced increases in advertising patronage were dependent upon the paper's reputation of fearless democracy." In the end, rich and powerful but wretched, the man who had started out in such high sincerity realizes bitterly the depth of his own corruption and self-betrayal, realizing also that he is in the game too deeply to change.[11]

One can imagine Pulitzer's incredulity and shock as the book was read to him. The affection he had bestowed on Phillips, the high hopes he had built on him, must have crumbled chapter by chapter. The novel in a sense was Phillips' admission that he had accepted Pulitzer's bounty as long as it was useful, and now was publicly declaring his emancipation. Perhaps he was also paying off a score, for he had been annoyed about the quarrel concerning his trip to Europe. While he could claim that he had only used World atmosphere and that the leading character was imaginary, the parallel was too close in its externals for comfort. Pulitzer *had* become a slave to his work, a slave to wealth, a thinking machine at times verging on the inhuman. It was as if Phillips now proclaimed him a sham and a demagog. Pulitzer could rightly fancy himself one of the more enlightened and generous of capitalists in an era when capitalists were almost invariably brigands, but the question was, did Phillips think the opposite? There was a further consideration quite apart from what Gumboil did or did not believe. He was known as the author, the book had made quite a stir, and would of course be accepted as an insider's exposure of the utter venality of Joseph Pulitzer.

Pulitzer's letter to Phillips, written from Aix, showed the man of power's refusal to admit that he could be hurt: "Your . . . *Great God Success* I not only read but enjoyed very much with one single reservation [he did not specify the reservation, hardly needing to]. The book showed undoubted talent, imagination, and skill in constructing dialogue. . . . Talking about novels, have you ever read *Crime and Punishment* by Dostoyevsky? If not, don't let 24 hours pass before you do. . . . In point of skill, workmanship, constructive genius and perfect finish, it is the greatest novel I have ever read." [12] Dostoevsky aside, his hopes in Phillips withered and six months later the former favorite resigned to make his living as a writer. Pulitzer's magnanimity was also tested by the death of Edwin Godkin, whose Evening Post he read faithfully and regarded as the best paper aimed at intellectuals. He wrote the World:

> Mr. William H. Merrill must write an editorial, a tribute to Godkin's ability, all the more so because the man never failed in fifteen years to abuse the World, and no doubt hated me. I think the profession has lost the ablest mind since the death of Greeley. It is a great loss to the independent thought of the press.[13]

After a sojourn with Kate in London, he returned with her to Chatwold, where one of their guests that fall was John A. Dillon, the man so intimately connected with the stormy beginnings in St. Louis—the man who eventually had seemed to lack the initiative required by the World. Dillon had been unhappy at the Chicago Tribune and had returned to the World's bosom as editorialist, a modest position for one of his broad experience and abilities. While riding one of Pulitzer's horses, he took a fall, cracked a rib and came down with pneumonia. His hosts called in Dr. Weir Mitchell and the almost equally famous Dr. William Sydney Thayer, and for a month Chatwold again took on a hushed sickbed atmosphere, with Mrs. Dillon and relatives arriving, before the 59-year-old Dillon died October 15. Pulitzer was indeed too much surrounded by illness and death for a man cursed by melancholia. To the many payments he had made for doctors and funeral costs for dear friends and World employees of all degree he added $1,715 paid to nurses, physicians and an undertaker, including shipment of Dillon's body to St. Louis.[14]

In November, Hearst's drive for the presidency began with his election to Congress from New York's 11th district in the midst of a tragedy resulting from his reliance on Pain's fireworks. During a Madison Square election-night spectacular, a large pile of nine-inch bombs exploded accidentally, killing 18 onlookers, injuring more than 50 and saddling Hearst with lawsuits that would dog him for decades. Fireworks were standard election appurtenances, and the World laid no particle of blame on the sponsor. Andes, meanwhile, was nagged by a conviction that the World had lost its spark. During a stay at Lakewood he summoned Seitz and discussed the problem.

"I think it's because nobody on the staff gets drunk," he said. "Brad [Merrill] never gets drunk; Burton lives in Flatbush—he never gets drunk; Van Hamm [managing editor] sleeps out in New Jersey, he never gets drunk; Lyman [night managing editor], he's always sober. You live in Brooklyn and never get drunk. When I was there some one always got drunk, and we made a great paper. Take the next train back to the city, find a man who gets drunk, and hire him at once." [15]

Seitz dutifully returned, and in Park Row encountered Esdaile Cohen, a brilliant writer handicapped only by his inability to pass swinging doors. He had once worked for Albert Pulitzer's Journal and for almost every newspaper in town. He admitted that he had recently been fired by Hearst's American (the new name of the morning Journal), saying, "I can't let the hard stuff alone."

"I have a life job for you," Seitz said. Cohen went on the payroll and stayed, religiously fulfilling the specification under which he was hired and on one occasion, defending himself against a "blue dog" visible only to him, he struck out wildly, broke a glass door and cut his wrist so deeply that it took fast work to save him.[16]

III. JUDGE OF ALL THE EARTH

On his 56th birthday April 10, 1903, Pulitzer followed his usual custom by giving gifts to his family and friends and fine cigars to his executives. This reversal of the usual order was part of an elaborate scheme of bestowal to which he gave much thought. It made sure that he would be remembered on his birthday, that he would receive acknowledgments, and doubtless it reflected his great loneliness as well as his generosity. He loved to get thank-you letters from his staff—delighted in pleasant missives from anybody at any time. But when it came to disciplining any World man below the upper echelons, he preferred that his executives do it, a habit that sometimes irked them. When he ordered Bradford Merrill to punish reporter Emory Foster for exaggerating the numbers in a St. Patrick's Day parade, Merrill replied, "As rewards are invariably bestowed . . . in your name, might it not be well to let punishment come from you also?"[17]

But no one could gainsay his warm consideration for faithful employees, as when, this very spring, he sent the ailing James W. Clarke (Grumby) to England for two months with strict orders to rest. Still, he could not refrain from hoping that Clarke would improve his mind while resting, for he wrote that to escape boredom he might read up on the rising question of the day, socialism: "I deliberately say do not do this if it will interfere with your brain and mind but if you feel perfectly fresh and need some reading, the intellectual pleasure of learning something . . . then I submit this to you."[18] At the same time, John Tennant, who had been presented by the chief with a fine horse a year earlier, now was accused by some colleague of arriving at the office at 10. In a letter to Pulitzer he swore he was usually at his desk shortly after eight, adding, "I really feel much hurt by the malicious misrepresentation . . ."[19]

But it was Pomeroy Burton, the talented Gumbo, who fell deeply into the soup. One of Pulitzer's rising young men, the recipient of fatherly instruction and several lavish gifts, he was now managing editor of the World, supervising an investigation of the shockingly stock-watered Metropolitan Street Railway Company headed by William C. Whitney and Thomas Fortune Ryan. While this was in progress, it was said, he wrote a friend that Metropolitan stock was going down and he would like to have a part in any deal resulting from this information. The friend passed the letter on to Ryan. Ryan, delighted at this opportunity to smear his journalistic enemy, photostated the letter and used it in an attack accusing the World of deliberately manipulating stocks for its own pecuniary gain. He declared that the embarrassed World had sent James Creelman to beg for the letter's return.

Andes had an immediate headache and suspended Burton, who wrote him in contrition admitting an error but insisting that it would harm no one but himself.[20] Quite the contrary—the World *was* hurt in this demonstration of the chief's old saw that honesty is to a newspaper what virtue is to a woman. Although Burton was not discharged, Caleb Van Hamm was given his place, while he was demoted to the Sunday World and would go over to Hearst a year later. Pulitzer ordered Seitz to make a sharp investigation of possible speculation by World men. The incident was not lost on District Attorney William Travers Jerome, who would ultimately make use of it.

Pulitzer, annoyed because his attorneys gave him yes-and-no answers about the validity of a newsprint contract, was pleased when a 40-year-old lawyer named Charles Evans Hughes gave a straight reply. He invited Hughes to Lakewood, had lunch with him, asked permission to pass his hands over his face and thus apprised himself of the noblest set of whiskers then extant. Although it was their only meeting, he forgave Hughes's Republican affiliation and developed a life-long admiration for him. Hughes, on his part, saw his host surrounded by editors and secretaries, in touch with everything. "One would have supposed that Mr. Pulitzer was sitting as the judge of all the earth," he remarked, "and I was vastly entertained by the way in which this man, so physically dependent, dominated all by his intellectual power." [21]

When Pulitzer sailed in the spring of 1903, his 73rd Street home was still unfinished and a 26-room residence was being built for him on the river road at Jekyll Island, along with a 12-room cottage for servants. He went on to Bad Homburg, having long since primed his staff to get out an issue of the World celebrating his 20th year of ownership, one so big and splendid that it would constitute a great advertisement for the paper. They had worked at it for weeks, getting tributes from dozens of the eminent including Grover Cleveland, who admitted publicly for the first time that without the World he would not have been elected in 1884. Andes was so pleased when the anniversary issue appeared Sunday, May 10, that he cabled warm thanks, raised the salaries of those involved and distributed more gifts. Delighted at Cleveland's statement, he cabled Bradford Merrill, "Cantabo should also have short editorial on Cleveland's letter admitting World elected him in eight four thereby made history," and urged, "Remember continuing push for tributes congratulations months after issue out as recognition of press as whole as new power complimentary to every newspaper." [22] He cabled his thanks for publication in the World, letting his own handicaps be known (he rather liked to stress his illnesses) as well as his reservations:

> Disobeying the doctors, I obey the cabled request of the editors and my own instinct in gratefully acknowledging the astonishing expressions of kindness and appreciation . . . I say astonishing because personally I feel ashamed to see the virtues of The World exaggerated and its faults minimized. There is no man more conscious, more critical of his many shortcomings; none can be more disappointed by his failure to have attained his ideal of a newspaper. I assume the responsibility for both faults and failure, yet it may be pardonable to say that for sixteen of these twenty years I have been unable to read the paper or go to the office, having suffered the loss of sight, of health, of sleep, although continuing the burden of responsibility for the conduct and character of the paper to which I gave every moment of my waking time.
>
> I feel deeply grateful that this condition is understood and that however many are the faults, they are attributed to manner rather than motive . . . never to lack of integrity or principle. . . .[23]

Someone in the Dome recoiled at the Old Man's line, "I feel ashamed to see the virtues of The World exaggerated and its faults minimized." This was not good publicity. It was edited to read, "I say astonishing because personally I feel The World is undeserving of such overwhelming praise." Meanwhile Tuohy, after a visit with the chief at Homburg, returned to

London to resume his search for white mice. The need was critical because Arthur Billing, after five years of intrepid service under fire, had finally been felled by the same shell shock that had put Dr. Hosmer temporarily hors de combat. Pulitzer, appreciating his courage, granted his request that he be transferred to the World staff, where he ultimately became a valued editorial aid, subject to recall to duty with the chief only during occasional emergencies. Since Pulitzer expected a secretary to read a news or magazine article swiftly and give him its essence in very few words, the Tuohys put a new succession of candidates to this test as well as observing other qualifications. Tuohy wrote Pulitzer:

> Beaman did not pan out as well as I had expected . . . I found that like most other writers of fiction, he seems to read very little by any contemporary author. His knowledge of general affairs, current events and so forth, was rather deficient, and although he has points, and you might be able to develop him, I did not think that he was promising enough to send him to Homburg . . . I have never had my faith so much shaken of advertisements as a means of securing what you want as in these last few months. . . . Bashford is the best in point of literary taste, attainments, and adaptability—others I have seen were personally more agreeable but were deficient in knowledge of books. There is a man named Foggo, who was very pleasant, intelligent, and good-humored, plays the violin, has been all over the world, has excellent references, but he frankly admitted that reading has not occupied much of his time.
>
> The only German that I have on my list . . . is the young Baron Overbeck. You will remember that I sent his letters to you in New York; that he claims to be a brilliant musician; well up in Literature—German, English, Italian and French. . . . [H. R. D. Wood] impressed me most favorably as to his intelligence, agreeableness and conversational capacity—the best in these respects of all I have seen but unfortunately he is flat-footed to an extent that makes him almost hobble along, turning out his toes markedly. . . . [Foggo] rides well . . . as to his capacity to gut a magazine or book satisfactorily I am much in doubt. [As for George Home, he] would drink nothing but diluted wine, and he didn't appear to care much for the pleasures of the table. He is undoubtedly a man of ability and cultivation, but he is not what you would call festive, and has an anxious, worried look. . . . He doesn't dress very well and has something of a slouchy gait, with very high shoulders. His temperament, possibly, has been affected by overwork when he was at the University.[24]

By the time Pulitzer moved on for a stay at Etretat in July, several candidates had been nominated by Tuohy and were running for election, visiting Pulitzer for the final vote. Lindsay Bashford was elected, to stay in office for more than a year before deciding that life contained easier careers. Tuohy was now looking for a London house for the master, who expressed a preference for St. John's Wood. This, Tuohy wrote, was impossible because the new Great Central Railway ran through the district:

> I don't think there is any part of St. John's Wood proper where you would be secure from the noise of trains at night. That remark applies to all the Western side of Regent's Park. On the Eastern side there is the Albany Street Barracks, where bugling, which you found so annoying at Maitland House, would have to be endured.[25]

Tuohy scoured the Lancaster Gate area, finding it unsatisfactory because of Underground noises. The Carlton, he said, was out of the question, being on a busy thoroughfare and having throngs of diners. So too with the Savoy and Cecil, where Pulitzer would hear every stroke of Big Ben as well as boats whistling on the Thames. The Hyde Park Hotel had excellent possibilities except that traction engines were repairing the street in front and there was a question whether they would be finished when he arrived. When Pulitzer, after a short stay in St. Moritz, reached London early in September, Tuohy had settled on a house at 21 Kensington Palace Gardens, far enough from the palace itself so that the royal peacocks should not intrude. What was more, Tuohy had another candidate for him.

This was 31-year-old Norman G. Thwaites, son of a canon, educated in Germany, a soldier in the Boer War, sometime barrister and actor who had known Oscar Wilde, familiar with drama and books, a good rider, accomplished at shorthand, possessor of a pleasant voice, a noiseless eater—in short, a paragon unless hidden flaws emerged, as they so often did. After his original examination by the Tuohys, Thwaites now went through another by Butes, followed by the last and crucial one by Andes himself. He began the inquiry, as he always did, by asking, "What's in the papers?" and there ensued a long cross-examination on books, plays and politics. ". . . He took me to the window and peered into my face," Thwaites recalled, "running his long tapering fingers over my features. I was then requested to describe myself to him! Every member of his staff was afterwards asked to describe [me], down to the last detail; height, figure, colour of eyes . . . and type of character, as indicated by the outward appearance." [26] Thwaites was hired on a trial basis that would extend for Pulitzer's lifetime.

IV. MAYOR McCLELLAN'S SHOCKER

Pulitzer remained in London that fall while his papers supported Mayor Low, an honest if not thoroughly efficient executive, against Tammany's handsome George B. McClellan. McClellan won by 62,000 votes. A machine-bred politician, brought up under Croker's wing and a firm believer in Tammany, he was honest and honorable within these severe limitations, and the World was not far from the mark in calling him "this young protégé of the bosses, who has always 'done as he was told' and never showed a sign of political or personal independence . . ." [27] Years later a McClellan accusation came to light which, so far as is known, no one else ever made. He charged that Pulitzer, immediately after the election, proposed a sly political bargain in order to get a tax reduction.

The Croker–Van Wyck administration had taken revenge on him by boosting his real and personal property taxes sky-high. Personal property taxes were then largely overlooked. It was a Tammany trick to gain support from wealthy residents by levying heavy taxes on them which went uncollected as a "favor" to them. As John T. Hettrick, a World City Hall reporter, recalled it, "It was a custom for the millionaires of New York to send down a clerk and they would swear off the personal taxes. . . . Pulitzer would not allow anyone to swear off his personal taxes. Year after year he'd pay the highest personal tax of any one of the wealthy men of New York. More taxes than Carnegie, Morgan and any of the other millionaires who were residents of New York." [28] He knew of course that to request a reduction would give Tammany a hold on him. Yet McClellan said he was visited on this very errand by Harry Macdona, once a World man but now an aide to Thomas Fortune Ryan. McClellan's account follows:

> After a while McDona [*sic*] introduced the subject of the New York press and from that turned to the New York *World* and its owner, Joseph Pulitzer. For the life of me I could not understand what he was driving at. Presently it developed that, while Pulitzer had bitterly opposed me, he really held me in the most profound esteem. [I said,] "Harry, you didn't come here to tell me of Pulitzer's secret love for me. What is it all about and what is it that you want?" For another half hour McDona talked of the excessive taxes that Pulitzer was paying . . . and said that he had been sent by Pulitzer to say that he would very much like to support my administration. A great light dawned on me and I turned to McDona and said, "I gather that what you are driving at is this: Pulitzer offers me his support in return for a reduction of his taxes . . . Am I right?" McDona replied, "George, you have put the matter very crudely, but quite correctly." I stood up and said, "Harry, I am ashamed of you. What Pulitzer is offering me is a corrupt bargain, his support in return for a dishonest reduction of his taxes." McDona seemed greatly hurt. "George," he said, "I am surprised that you take the proposition in this spirit. I thought that you were more a man of the world." I bowed him out and never saw him again. I realized, however, that I had won the uncompromising enmity of Pulitzer at the very beginning of my administration. [29]

To think that Pulitzer would barter away his cherished editorial independence to the Almighty Himself, much less the Tammany mayor, is preposterous. McClellan, as a former newspaperman and a shrewd politician, must have known it was preposterous and that if such a proposition was offered it would never have been fulfilled, since Pulitzer's whole policy was founded on his freedom to praise an official on one issue and criticize him on another. McClellan does not make clear for how long a time the World's "support" was offered, or on what issues. Although it seems strange that Pulitzer had not requested a tax reduction from the administration of Mayor Low, whom he had helped elect, it is not impossible that he had won a reduction from Low and wished a further one. It is not necessary to believe the honorable McClellan a liar in this instance to regard his story as too shadowy to be accepted without further light. One must at least hear the other side—the Pulitzer-Macdona side—before passing judgment. But the other side will never be heard, since McClellan's account remained unpublished until 1956, 45 years after Pulitzer's death.

McClellan's ambitions were high, reaching to the White House. His story was written in bitterness over the ruin of his political career. He held a lifelong hatred for Pulitzer, who he declared later told a shipboard companion, "I helped to make McClellan; now I am going to smash him." [30] He was scarcely an unprejudiced observer.

Could his antipathy toward Pulitzer have added nonexistent overtones to what was actually an ethical request? Could Macdona have been sent not by Pulitzer himself but by some World official asked by the chief to request a tax reduction—some executive not averse to exerting a bit of pressure? Could Macdona himself have exceeded instructions, injecting an unauthorized hint or the wink of an eye? Could Macdona, as an aide to the millionaire Ryan, who often had the World on his back, have had some ax of his own to grind? These and other questions would have to be answered before giving serious attention to McClellan's little shocker.

V. *THE RAT FIGHT*

Pulitzer's propensity for secrecy caused the use of code even when not strictly necessary. When Dr. Hosmer cabled the World, "Keep degenerate confidential," he was not shielding depravity but asking that profits be kept sub rosa. When Dumont Clarke wired, ". . . Balance labial ludicious lettuce," it informed the chief that he had $202,000 left in his bank. When Butes telegraphed Pulitzer, ". . . Yesterday and todays senior hopping, yesterdays junior hydropsy, last seniority gross hypocrite hands crew hydrant," [31] he knew instantly that the World had sold 295,000, the Evening World 430,000 and the Sunday World 400,000.

"Under present necessities," Pulitzer wrote, "Mr. Seitz must concentrate primarily . . . on potash. I say potash deliberately, meaning more than Rat. *Rat* of course is the Burning Question. . . . During the course of the *Rat* fight Mr. Seitz is not to bother about office routine." [32]

The Rat fight went on for several years. "Rat" was a combine of department stores including Macy's, Straus's and Bloomingdale's which spent millions annually in Potash (advertising), wielded enormous power and knew it. Rat was nibbling for lower Potash rates, even threatening to boycott one newspaper at a time, which could be fatal. Naturally the newspapers tried to present a united front of their own, and there had been negotiations between the World and Hearst people. Seitz visited Hearst's handsome home at Lexington Avenue and 28th Street, picking his way among armor, statuary and an Egyptian mummy with a gold-plated face he thought resembled that of Boss Charles F. Murphy, Croker's successor. He found Hearst agreeable about concerted action against Rat and amiable in every way.

"Of course we have had a pretty fierce encounter in the past," Hearst said of the World-Journal battle. "Coming in new, I naturally had to make my way the best I knew how, while you naturally resisted, just as I would now if some other fellow started to come in. . . . I recognise that the World is here to stay and I feel pretty well established myself. . . . I'm for anything that's mutually to the good. I don't care if Mr. Pulitzer makes $600,000 to my $500,000. Let's take all we can make." [33]

In Carlsbad Pulitzer ran into another competitor almost a foot shorter than Hearst, little Adolph Ochs, who had revitalized the dying Times from a circulation of 9,000 to well over 100,000 in eight years and had recently opened the new building on 42nd Street that was even taller than Pulitzer's. Undoubtedly the two discussed Rat. "[Pulitzer] is a remarkable man," Ochs wrote later, "a man of great strength and great intellectual power, and of education and culture. His success has not been accidental. He is a man among thousands. He is positive, well informed on current topics, truly a philosopher. It is a great and tragic misfortune that he is virtually blind. If he had not that affliction he would be a tremendous figure in national affairs. . . . He is so nervous that he objected to the scraping of the brakes of the carriage wheels." [34]

A bit later, from Aix, Pulitzer wrote Ochs to invite him to Chatwold, adding, "You may not know that I have The Times sent to me abroad when The World is forbidden, and that most of my news I really receive from your paper." [35] He had a tendency to say such pleasant things even if not strictly true. At the same time he was writing a third competitor, Whitelaw Reid, probably discussing Rat and going on, "I am reading the Tribune here with pleasure. I prefer its political news to that of all other papers. I always like to see the other side." [36]

In May he hired German-born Dr. Friedrich Mann, an accomplished pianist also well versed in European literature, whose duty would be to read to him in German and to soothe him with Beethoven, Wagner or Brahms. By summer he was back at Chatwold, where a letter to Butes from the chief housekeeper there, Elizabeth Harper, showed that troubles arose at all levels:

> The appearance of the Pink Drawing Room is at this hour a disgrace to a first class housekeeper. So I walked through and to the housekeeper forbidden ground, namely the Dining Room and Butlers Pantry to find the 2d Footman—who it was agreed between the butler and myself should daily care for the Pink Drawing Room (while the 3rd Footman cleans the Yellow Drawing Room and Main Hall and stairs)—I find . . . the family butler engaged in the Dining Room but, the third footman who ought to be cleaning or at least tidying the Pink Drawing Room set to *sweeping* the Dining Room for our lazy family butler. The First footman cleaning silver and the third washing and wiping dishes. This arrangment in order that the five men hurry through the Dining Room work to allow two to do nothing for a couple of hours before luncheon is served—in my censure I do not include Mr. Pulitzer's butler who must have free time—but the incapacity of the family butler and the stolid indifference of one of the footmen. It is impossible for me to send either of the chambermaids into the Drawing Room during the forenoon—and I neither can nor will do a parlor maids work properly apportioned to a footman that he may lie down in his chambers and smoke cigars in the middle of the day. . . .[37]

Unaware of this crisis, Pulitzer had a discussion of drinking with Seitz and Billing, scoffing at tales of vast liquor consumption. When Billing remarked that it was not unusual for English gentlemen to drink a quart of champagne without visible effect, Pulitzer snorted, "Impossible!" Billing suggested that he could do it himself.

"Good," Pulitzer said, "we will test it now. Mark [his butler], bring a quart of Mumm and place it before Mr. Billing. Seitz, you shall umpire and see that he drinks it to the last drop. Make sure that there is no shirking!"

Billing downed the quart within 15 minutes with no sign of intoxication, a feat that astonished the host.[38] Another visitor was the martinet Charles Chapin (Pinch), still city editor of the Evening World, one of the most fabulous of newspapermen. It was of Pinch that Irvin S. Cobb, who worked under him, made the remark on hearing he was ill, "Let's hope it's nothing trivial." Chapin's granduncle was Russell Sage, the millionaire so miserly that he wore no socks, ate one apple for lunch, used his stockholder's pass to save a nickel on the elevated railroad and allowed his wife one new dress a year. Chapin expected to inherit a fortune from Sage, was performing many friendly services for him on that theory, and would later be affronted when the skinflint left him not a sou. On his $125 weekly salary he plunged so successfully into stocks that he lived with his wife (whom he was later to murder) at the Plaza and owned fast horses and a yacht. His admiration for Pulitzer was boundless.

"And how shockingly that blind man could swear!" he observed. "With him profanity was more of an art than a vice." When Chapin read to him from the World, one article so angered him that he uttered a succession of expletives. A few minutes later, nine-year-old Herbert Pulitzer, arguing with his tutor in the next room, was heard to use similar language. Pulitzer frowned, saying, "I wonder where that boy learned to swear." [39]

Yet he prized courtesy as a mark of civilization and an aid to human relations and business. He wrote Ralph:

> Moral for my son Ralph, who needs it badly . . . be polite to everybody . . . The cheapest capital in the world is politeness. . . . In reading the life of Brahms I came across the following lines:—
>
> "For, habitually, Brahms possessed in a high degree that princely courtesy which consists not only in *never being too late,* but also in not leaving the *slightest attention* unacknowledged."
>
> I wish you would oblige me by pasting this on your desk.[40]

If this seemed odd coming from such a connoisseur of profanity, he often exempted himself from rules applying to others and in any case his swearing was less incessant now, reserved for emotional explosions, and he could use fastidiously correct language even when flaying an editor for some folly. When Arthur Clarke, a younger World editor, served a temporary stint as his secretary at Bar Harbor, he invited Clarke to take dinner with the family and a group of guests. Clarke protested that he had brought no evening clothes, but the master insisted, there was no escape, and when Clarke joined the party he discovered that Pulitzer himself wore a business suit—a graceful gesture to make Clarke feel at ease in the otherwise formal gathering.[41]

Chapter 4

The Fever of 1904

I. TWO MILLIONS FOR COLUMBIA

A factor adding to the Pulitzer legend was his refusal to allow his ailments to impair his appearance. Although he still battled insomnia with daily massages and was subject to fierce headaches, asthma, rheumatism, dyspepsia, diabetes, catarrh and other ills as well as fulminating nerves, he did not look like an invalid. Strangers expected to meet a bowed, shrunken, shaking hulk. Instead they found a man tall, erect, well-muscled and energetic, distinguished in every line and movement. He ate heavily and with gusto. He allowed himself three cigars a day, one after each meal. He dressed impeccably, favoring pristine white linens in warm climates, and his beard was perfectly trimmed, his nails meticulous. Blindness, which usually slackens facial muscles to blankness, had not done so to him, for his face was so mobile and expressive that it was easy to forget his dim vision. But he wanted it understood that he was an invalid working against great odds. He expected his family and friends to accord him all the sympathies and prerogatives of invalidism even though he personally declined to succumb to it. He became irked if secretaries reported that he was well or improved. It was not surprising that some of his executives believed mistakenly that he was as sound as a dollar except for his nerves and vision.

Now he pushed his second effort to coax Columbia University to accept $2,000,000 for a journalism school—one gift to scholarship not accepted with instant alacrity. His opinions on education were as decided as those he held on politics. This martinet who spent so much time and money on education was not free from a suspicion that college sometimes encouraged laziness, and his scorn for any man who regarded an academic degree as a sure entrée to success was devastating. Mental and physical labor was the first requirement. His simple recipe for achievement was, "to work and work, to think and think and think." He once said, "The best college is the college of the world . . . the university of actual experience," although he conceded that "a college education [is] valuable, but it is not indispensable." [1]

Learning, however, if combined with character and industry, was unexceptionable. One feels that he would have approved of higher education without reservation had he had time to supervise it personally and weed out the loafers. As a firm believer in competition, he insisted that the many young men whom he subsidized at college every year must first prove their industry and character and then compete for the prize. He received regular reports on their academic grades and on their careers after graduation, being gratified when they achieved distinction. He expected his own sons to get the best in education, but it must be practical, with no time wasted on Latin or Greek and with emphasis on such useful subjects as history, economics and public speaking. Yet the heart of education lay in their own absorption, use and constant expansion of it. They might pass their courses brilliantly and still be utter failures unless they cultivated thought, industry and ideals. The fear that his children were wasting their time on trivialities so haunted him that he wrote hundreds of letters bearing on their education and intellectual life. He implored them to cudgel their brains daily and to write him of any ideas they had beyond the commonplace. He frequently wrote Joseph's tutors to urge on them the high dedication he expected in his editors, once writing, "It is part of [a tutor's] duties to arouse the boy's energies, to develop his intelligence, to imbue him with the ideas of honor and right living." [2] He was fond of quoting Goethe's axiom, "Everything has been thought of before, but the difficulty is to think of it again."

Women he set apart, regarding their primary functions as home management, motherhood, decoration, intellectual companionship and inspiration. He was skeptical of college training for them because it gave them foolish ideas of careers of their own. The thought of women in the professions or in politics—even in the voting booth—aroused his disapproval. His own daughters never went to public school but were educated by private tutors until the time of their debuts, given sound academic instruction along with the training in music, dancing, elocution and art that would enable them to converse and entertain with brilliance. But social gloss was not the ultimate aim, for he wrote of Edith, "I want her to be a good rather than a society woman, with high ideals and intellectual tastes and inclined to interest herself in the serious things of life."

No school of journalism then existed—a neglect he deplored, since he saw the press as the most potent force (for good or evil) in civilization. Almost more than any other man, he knew the ambivalence of journalism, its conflict of counting-room and ideals, the terrible pressure for circulation and success which so often eroded its honesty. Although he decidedly did not say so, one of the things he wished to prevent was the excess caused by the kind of struggle he had had with Hearst. "One of the chief difficulties with journalism," he wrote delicately, "is to keep the news instinct from running rampant over the restraints of accuracy and conscience." That was Junior's Charles Chapin to the life. "My idea," he added, "is to raise the character of the profession to a higher level." [3] He wanted no mere trade school. He wished to elevate the newspaperman to an enlightenment, responsibility and prestige equaling or exceeding that of the lawyer or physician.

His similar proposal to Columbia in 1892 had been rejected, and now President Nicholas Murray Butler and the trustees again considered it warily. Journalism still hardly qualified as a respectable profession, the World's aggressive liberalism did not endear it to academicians, and there were fears that the university's dignity might suffer. The collegiate training of newspapermen was almost as unheard of as advanced study for salesmen or sea captains. There was the possibility that the project would arouse public derision. Although Pulitzer specified that once the gift was made, neither he nor the World would have any connection with the school and it would be wholly under university supervision, it was not impossible that there would be suspicions of World "influence" in its operation. Even Kate was skeptical of the idea's practicality, writing her husband, "Your [proposal] is splendid I think it very able & very good, but I still doubt the necessity for a School of Journalism." [4]

Yet he composed such an eloquent and convincing argument for its need that the trustees ultimately accepted. He insisted, however, on naming an advisory board which would organize the school and initiate its operation. He labored by mail for weeks to round up a group combining academic and journalistic eminence including President Charles W. Eliot of Harvard, Whitelaw Reid, President Andrew D. White of Cornell and Victor Lawson of the Chicago Daily News. Here developed a snag, for President Butler, disinclined to have representatives of Harvard and Cornell on the board, was disposed to argue the point. The donor waxed wroth. He cabled Seitz from St. Moritz:

> Further cables about Butler forbidden. Everything must wait my return. Inform Butler verbatim unless he really welcomes greatest advisors, Eliot, White, my confidence in him and trust committed to his charge lost. I will stop promptly and assume [in their] sense of honor, pride, trustees will return endowment allowing transfer where advisors, gift and giver more appreciated. Hope he realizes his responsibility. Again: All disagreeable cables forbidden.[5]

At length he waived the disputed point. He deposited the first million with Columbia but postponed the actual organization of the school until full agreement could be reached—an interval that dragged out until the end of his life. Meanwhile he became even more eager to engage in philanthropy, writing Dumont Clarke, "I want to save more money than ever for public institutions and purposes." [6]

II. DISCOVERING FRANK COBB

Ralph Pulitzer (Cybira), whom his father felt lacking in initiative, had been elevated to membership in the five-man editorial-writing staff under William H. Merrill—the biggest such group in the country—specializing in lighter commentaries for which he developed a graceful touch. Like so many others, he also served as his father's part-time eyes, sending him occasional reports on the activities and abilities of World men. In 1904 Pulitzer took steps forecasting the enforced retirement of Merrill. Cantabo was now 64 and so wary of the boss's temper that he would seldom take any clear editorial stand without direct word from on high, leaving the page feeble when no such word was available. Pulitzer felt that the page needed new blood, a vigorous outsider who would stir things up. This involved a search and a weighing of talents even more exhaustive than the hunt for white mice. He privately sent the World writer Samuel Williams on a cross-country tour with orders to study editorials in big-city newspapers and find likely men.

Williams, knowing the celestial specifications, had no luck until he reached Detroit. There he read the editorials in the Free Press and saw exceptional skill in the writer, 34-year-old Frank I. Cobb, who in 13 years had worked for four Michigan newspapers as reporter, city editor, political writer and now chief editorialist for the Free Press. After careful inquiries seemed to attest his character and abilities, Williams wired Pulitzer about him and received a characteristic reply:

> What has Cobb read in American History, Rhodes, McMaster, Trevelyan, Parkman? What works on the constitution and constitutional law? Has he read Buckle's History of Civilization? Where did he stand during Bryan's Free Silver campaigns? What about the state of his health? How tall is he? Is his voice harsh or agreeable? My ears are very sensitive. Take him to dinner and note his table manners. Is his disposition cheerful? Sound out his ambitions—whether satisfied or looking to a larger field. Be very careful to give no intimation I am interested. Describe minutely his appearance, color of eyes, shape of forehead, mannerisms, how he dresses. Search his brain for everything there is in it.[7]

Williams dined with Cobb, a handsome, vital, forthright man who revealed himself freely. His only visible flaw was his admiration for President Roosevelt, but even this was mitigated by two Cobb editorials sharply critical of Roosevelt. Williams again reported to the chief, who authorized him to disclose his purpose. A few weeks later Cobb traveled to Jekyll Island to see Pulitzer and to undergo the most searching examination of his life, ranging from delicate political problems to the silent consumption of soup and toast. He performed so well that Andes was convinced.

"Cobb will do," he said to Williams. ". . . He knows American history better than any man I have found. He has the damnable Roosevelt obsession; he must learn to be brief. But I think we can make a real editor of him, in time." [8]

So Cobb, who became Grammarite, was given an office in the Dome, not yet aware that his examination had only begun. Pulitzer gave Cantabo instructions in running his staff and training the new man:

> . . . I spoke to you about increasing age and declining vigor, emphasizing the need on your part of overseeing and suggestion, of thought, study, revision, editing, reading, *directing*, and *far less,* mere writing. . . . You must try to write as little as possible, just as I did, but you must try to *think* just as I did, to *suggest* as hard as I did, to edit copy as I used to do, and to feel satisfied in proportion, as you furnish to the other writers, not only thoughts and topics that would occur to *them,* but thoughts and topics that would *not* occur to *them.*
>
> . . . You must get more work out of the others; you must keep them spurred to the largest possible suggestiveness, impulse, courage; develop independent thought and fearless comment; get ideas beyond the commonplace for them, and yet keep judgment, decision and responsibility in your own hands. . . . And don't forget that *leader.* I will forgive dullness in all other articles, if you will only manage to have one leader strong, striking and respect-commanding. After a while people will be educated to look for that leader, and therefore the man who writes it should touch no other thing the same day. Indeed, I will give him forty-eight hours, making him re-write it sixteen times. . . .[9]

Cobb became the object of a close Andean scrutiny. A subsequent Pulitzer-to-Merrill letter read in part:

> My dear Old Man: I hope Cobb will improve with age, but I must tell you that the first two editorials you sent as excellent specimens of irony, (one on Cortelyou's selection as chairman of the Nat. Committee; the other on Rockefeller's wife going to church) were to my mind or taste, very poor.
>
> Flippancy, dear old fellow, triviality, frivolity, are not irony—please underscore these few words and put them in Cobb's brain.
>
> Irony requires a delicacy of touch which triviality does not supply—indeed destroys.[10]

This was only the first of a series. Cobb, an independent man, was in for a period of baiting that presaged an explosion as the World swung into the 1904 presidential campaign.

III. GUSH, GUILDER AND GLUTINOUS

Pulitzer's most careful political thought, now and for the remainder of his life, was devoted to coping with three remarkable phenomena, Hearst, Bryan and Roosevelt. Hearst's hat was in the ring for the Democratic nomination for President. Pulitzer had such deep reservations about his judgment and sincerity that he would lock the White House door to him if he could. As for Bryan, he had long since appraised the Commoner as the Democratic party's albatross and did his best to dump him. Of them all Roosevelt was the power and the puzzle, a shining knight one day and a villain the next.

Andes' microscope had had Roosevelt on the slide for 21 years as assemblyman, mayoral candidate, Civil Service Commissioner, police commissioner, Assistant Secretary of the Navy, warrior in Cuba, governor of New York, vice president and now President. He had been fascinated by the Rough Rider's career, generally opposed to his Republican policies, sometimes profanely angry, but occasionally impelled to grudging or even hearty admiration. In fact, the two men were much alike—energetic to the point of "pure act," imaginative, impulsive, reformist, belligerent, dictatorial, courageous, formidable in attack, both swinging big sticks, both endowed with a rare aspect of greatness, a willingness to essay "impossibilities" and more often than not succeed at them. At times Pulitzer obviously had a wistful regret that Roosevelt was not a Democrat. There was a dash and romance about him entirely lacking in the stolid Cleveland. A vast annoyance to Pulitzer was Roosevelt's open stealing for the Republicans of the thunder of the one great reform move that should rightly have belonged to the Democrats. For years Pulitzer had urged Cleveland and Olney to enforce the Sherman anti-trust act and they had failed. McKinley of course had forgotten that such a law existed. Then along had come the young man of the incisors, to do precisely what Pulitzer had begged of Cleveland and had been denied.

It was not only what Roosevelt had done, but the flair with which he had executed it. With stunning intrepidity he had attacked not some backwoods trust but the huge Northern Securities railroad merger fashioned by J. P. Morgan, the national symbol of the money power. He had brought out the rusty Sherman popgun, somehow managed to cram it with buckshot, and had hit Morgan squarely between the eyes. He had inspired such fear and indignation among the grandees of his own party that they were not sure they wanted him as President again. But that one well-aimed shot had brought him what Cleveland had never been able to achieve, public acclaim. The crash of Morgan's fall echoed all over the country, causing cheers from coast to coast, and Glutinous was easily the most popular President within memory. Pulitzer himself was moved to the generous praise of a political opponent so emblematic of his stature:

People will love him for the enemies he has made. Mr. Cleveland lost popularity among the Democratic masses by not enforcing this [Sherman] law. Mr. Roosevelt will gain by enforcing it. It cannot now be said that the Republican party is owned by the trusts. It cannot now be said that Mr. Roosevelt is owned by them.[11]

The President was pleased. George Harvey, now president of Harper's, returned from a Washington visit to encounter Ralph Pulitzer and to steer him into the Waldorf bar. "While [Harvey] was consuming a monstrous Scotch and soda," Ralph reported to his father at Jekyll Island, "& I a modest glass of sherry, he told me that . . . Roosevelt had said he was very anxious to meet you and had asked Harvey to ask you if you would not come to see him at any time to suit your convenience, either lunch or dinner. Harvey said Roosevelt spoke in terms of the highest admiration of you." [12] Pulitzer replied by wire:

Tell Harvey impossible for me to answer Roosevelt's invitation received in such a roundabout casual accidental way. My health forbids Washington as you know.[13]

He and the World cooled rapidly toward Roosevelt when his aggressiveness against the trusts relaxed as he gave thought to the 1904 election and his need of support from the very monopolists he had attacked. Pulitzer fumed. Kate's quadrennial warnings that he must spare himself his usual ruinous concern with the election were stronger than ever since this one involved all three of his bugbears, Roosevelt, Hearst and Bryan. Though Bryan, the two-time loser, knew he could not be a candidate this year, he was still a power, and what would happen if he should throw his influence to Hearst, who had supported him loyally in two campaigns? Pulitzer ordered Samuel Williams to sound out Boss Murphy and to let Murphy understand that Pulitzer had not suggested the interview. Murphy, no Hearst man, assured Williams that he was not aware of a Hearst-Bryan entente. In behalf of his chief Williams also called on Bryan, who dodged any discussion of Hearst but delivered his opinion of Pulitzer:

Tell Mr. Pulitzer that the trouble with him is that he has too much money. He does not believe in silver because he thinks that it would be too heavy to carry around so much. But if he will come out to Omaha and turn farmer like the rest of us he will not be troubled with the weight of money. He used to be a socialist when he was poor but now that he has acquired wealth he is just like the rest of the capitalists. . . . Don't tell me that the World is a Democratic paper.[14]

Pulitzer's heart was set on making Judge Alton B. Parker of New York the Democratic nominee and the President. Parker was so aware of the World's importance in his campaign that—certainly at Pulitzer's suggestion—he took the World political reporter William McMurtrie Speer as his secretary. Kate's anxiety for her husband's well-being caused further wifely admonitions that he flee the country lest he explode in excitement. He sincerely tried to take the advice. He sailed April 20 after instructing Bradford Merrill to keep his reports down to one page and to go lightly on politics: "I am going away really to escape thought. I can have no rest if my mind is to be disturbed." By the time he reached Queenstown he was more disturbed over what he might be missing and what tricks Hearst might be staging in his drive for the nomination. "Mail Geranium's political editorials daily and Sunday," he cabled Merrill.[15]

As he went on to Aix he was alarmed by Hearst's progress in getting delegates, and the do-nothing policy of Judge Parker. He cabled:

> FOR BRAD SEND CREELMAN TO GREGORY [Parker] TO REKINDLE ENTHUSIASM PREVENT DEFEAT ABSOLUTELY NECESSARY GREGORY SHOULD SAY SOME MANLY RINGING WORDS ON SUCH PARAMOUNT ISSUES AS TRUSTS PHILIPPINES TARIFF REFORM SHOCKING EXTRAVAGANCE IN WASHINGTON USURPATION LEGISLATIVE POWERS BY EXECUTIVE ABDICATION BY CONGRESS ET CETERA. . . . SILENCE NOT ALWAYS GOLD SOMETIMES GIVES CONSENT.[16]

Kate was writing him weekly, once in response to a cable that he felt wretched:

> I wish there was more sunshine in your life—worry & wearisome work are dull companions. If you could only take pleasure in things outside your work it would be a God send. . . . I have not heard a word from you save brief and discouraging telegrams, I think some one of your secretaries might find time to send me a few lines even if not at your dictation. . . . I thought of the 21st anniversary of the paper! Twenty-one long years of slavery for you and—we will pass over what it has been to me,—and my heart was so full of the conflicting elements of pride & pain that I could not speak of it—[17]

Since she was competing with a presidential election she continued to get only brief cables, although he wrote Joseph inquiring about the large sum spent for beer, Joseph replying that he drank very moderately but his friends consumed it wholesale. From Carlsbad he messaged Merrill again, surrendering to himself: "As I find it impossible to suppress my foolish weakness for politics you must write me once a week at least on the political situation only . . ."[18] Capitulating still more, he summoned Williams to Carlsbad to get his detailed report on developments in both parties. Williams was also sizing up S. S. Fontaine of the World staff as a possible Pulitzer secretary, writing, "I regret as yet I have had no opportunity to 'eat soup' with him."[19]

Hearst, who now owned eight newspapers, was using them shamelessly as his own political organs. He had whipped the National Association of Democratic Clubs into a powerful nationwide Hearst organization, supervised by his own men. The Pulitzerian excitement was intense. Would Bryan swing the nomination for Gush?

Temporary relief came when, at the Democratic convention in St. Louis, Bryan failed to back Hearst and Parker was nominated. The sound-money Parker then sent his famous telegram warning the convention that he could accept the nomination only on a gold-standard basis. The message fell explosively among the assembled Democrats, who had gingerly evaded the hot coinage issue in their platform in the hope of presenting a united front. The united front dissolved as the convention, after a fierce battle with the Bryan forces, accepted Parker nevertheless. The judge has rightfully been praised for his courage in sending the telegram, but the evidence is clear that it was inspired by none other than Pulitzer, through the World man Speer, who was Parker's secretary and pressed the judge until he sent it.[20]

After causing this uproar, Parker receded into quietness when his only hope lay in slashing attack. Pulitzer's worry now progressed to the question of whether his nominee would be elected. He had already written Samuel E. Moffett, a World editorialist, to compose an article treating Roosevelt with "absolute fairness":

> Put together all that can possibly be said about the wonderfully interesting career of the young man, who less than ten years ago held only a little local office—noted for his teeth. Do him full justice for whatever he has done, whatever ability he has shown . . . the Northern merger decision, &c, &c. Then, having done him full justice, unroll the indictment. . . . My idea is that his real weakness and vulnerability lie in his jingoism, blatant militarism, unconstitutionalism, in the personal Government he has substituted for that of *law*. . . . [21]

Before he sailed homeward to put his own shoulder to the Parker wheel, Kate wrote him from Chatwold in a vein suggesting the difficulties of being married to a human torpedo: "The sea comes in, rolls slowly out with that old soothing swish you know so well. . . . Tomorrow will be our 26th anniversary[,] over a quarter of a century married, I feel that I should take to goggles & a cane, a hacking cough & a rasping voice. Oh! me [,] 26 years is a long time. Now old boy remember we will all be 'en fete' to welcome you home so you must be in a very good humor, very tender, in fact the man of 26 years ago. This letter is to wish you bon voyage." [22]

But it was hard for him to be tender and cheerful when he joined his family. He not only suffered rheumatic twinges but was utterly impatient at Parker's failure to utter the "manly, ringing words" so necessary. He wrote Parker personally to urge more fire. With the Hearst press sour toward Parker and exerting itself chiefly to reelecting its owner to Congress, only the World injected life into this dullest of all campaigns. Pulitzer had solid information from Daniel Lamont that enormous sums had been contributed to the Roosevelt campaign by the very corporations he had vowed to control. He was incensed by Roosevelt's selection of his recent Secretary of Commerce and Labor, George B. Cortelyou, as chairman of the Republican National Committee with authority over fund-raising—certainly a questionable appointment because as Secretary he had been in charge of the Bureau of Corporations and might have information that corporation owners would prefer kept under the rose. On October 1 the World published one of those famous Pulitzer-signed editorials, eight columns long and addressed as an open-letter challenge to the President. It gave chapter and verse for Roosevelt's relaxation of his war against monopolists, the love for him now shown by moguls formerly fearful of him, and asked whether Cortelyou's appointment did not mean that the corporations "that are now pouring money into your campaign chests assume that they are buying protection?"

Kate, now in France, wrote him again in warning: "I see your handiwork in the paper for which I am both glad and sorry, glad, because of my pride in you & your work . . . and sorry because I fear the effect on you. . . . I will not have you wear your nerves and my patience out . . . I don't wish you to be cross & snappy & irritable when I see you. On the contrary I expect you to be as mild & balmy as a Summer's morning. . . ."[23]

His patience was worn out by the unaggressive Parker. Pulitzer had handed him an issue whose validity would later be paraded before the public in another World exposure. Roosevelt had indeed been given huge contributions by the monopolists—$125,000 from J. P. Morgan, $50,000 from E. H. Harriman, $125,000 from Standard Oil, a total of some $1,500,000 from corporations. Despite repeated Pulitzer urgings, Parker made no use of it until the final days of the campaign, and then with unwise strategy. He was buried in a Roosevelt landslide.

The World wished the President well. But by this time the peripatetic publisher, after lingering briefly at Chatwold, had fled to London to escape the tension of being in the United States as returns were coming in. He was riding in Hyde Park with Thwaites as his companion when Thwaites's horse, frightened when a small boy threw his cap in front of it, bolted. "Pulitzer was in the midst of a disquisition on great painters," Thwaites recalled. "I careered madly to the end of the Row and pulled up only at the powder magazine . . . Pulitzer had reached the respective qualities of Sargent as compared with the French portrait painters by the time I got back. He turned to me for my opinion as I drew alongside him, rather breathless. 'I quite agree,' I gasped. Then I mentioned what had happened. 'I thought you were rather silent,' he remarked."[24]

Chapter 5

Insurance Scandal

I. $644,000 FAILURE

Early in 1904 the Pulitzers (except for the absent master) had moved into the new 73rd Street mansion which, with the land, cost him $644,000 and cost McKim, Mead & White considerable vexation. One or another of the architects had traveled several times to Bar Harbor and Europe to consult with him about complaints and changes in plans. They had furnished him with a plaster model of the facade which he could appraise by touch and make sure it was free from the excessive ornamentation he loathed. They had labored to achieve absolute silence in his own bedroom apartment. Indeed Ledlie, Butes and Billing had all tested that suite, giving it the ultimate trial by shouting like savages outside it, pounding on floors and finding almost no penetration of sound. But by the time he gave it the test of his own presence, a sump pump had been installed to divert spring water in the cellar. The heating system carried the throb of the pump efficiently to his room, and this, along with the faint noise of an elevator door in the hall and the minute creaks of shrinking woodwork, drove him frantic. The house, he wrote his cousin Politzer in Vienna, was a "wretched failure."

Professor Wallace Sabine, the Harvard authority on acoustics, was called in consultation. The pump was moved under the sidewalk, the elevator door silenced and cork floors installed. But by this time Pulitzer gave up on it and ordered the construction of a separate annex for himself at the rear, which became known by the secretaries as the Vault. Its double walls were filled with insulation, its windows triple-glazed, and there were three doors in the short passage to the main house, the passage floor being rested on ball bearings to prevent vibration.

Yet he swore he heard whistles and trolley bells. The leak was found in the ventilating fireplace chimney. Thousands of silk threads were hung across its interior to absorb the vibrations, and at last he found the nullity of sound that satisfied him.[1]

He had given Cantabo instructions to let his younger editorialists "take charge" of the page for a few days at a time to determine their mettle, and had found Cobb to measure up well as a successor. Yet, since he was not Pulitzer, he received a stream of critical appraisal from the chief that made him breathe hard. In the spring of 1905 he was offered a stock interest in the Detroit Free Press if he would return. Since he was under contract, he wrote Pulitzer saying that both of them would be happy if he were released. Andes, much upset, called Seitz to 73rd Street and took him for a carriage ride in Central Park to discuss the problem. Seitz, though he admired Cobb's abilities, felt it useless to "drive an unwilling horse" and that there was little to do but release him.

"I liked that young man," Pulitzer said. "I liked the way he swore."

Then, after some meditation, his face went pink and he uttered a succession of his bluest interjections.

"Go back to the office," he shouted furiously, "and tell that —— young fool I will *not* let him resign, —— him!"

Seitz gave the message to Cobb, who was called to the Vault next day to find Andes at his charming best. "My dear boy," he said, tweaking Cobb's ear, "don't you know you quite spoiled my Easter?"[2] The crisis was over, although there would be others. Cobb became head of the page as Cantabo retired on a pension, which he soon ended by becoming editor of the Boston Herald.

In Park Row there was some argument as to whether it was worse to work for Pulitzer or for Hearst, who generally left good men alone but occasionally fired batches of executives by telegram. One Journal editor, returning from lunch, spied bright yellow envelopes on several of his colleagues' desks, quickened his pace nervously and found one on his own. When he opened it and uttered a joyous exclamation, his secretary commented that he must have received good news. "Yes," he said happily, "my father is dead!"

II. A BALL AT SHERRY'S

Although all World executives reported to him about their colleagues, Pulitzer could not be certain that they might not get their heads together in a plan to deceive him and deceive Ralph too. Doubtless this underlay his strategy when he occasionally sent Alfred Butes to work at the World for a few weeks at a time and report to him. Butes was on the job in 1905 when a World reporter, David Ferguson, quietly began an investigation of corruption among insurance companies that would swell into a master stroke of journalistic public service.

It began with a ball at Sherry's new building on Fifth Avenue given by a brilliant eccentric, the towering, 29-year-old James Hazen Hyde, vice president of the Equitable Life Assurance Society. He was an honor graduate of Harvard, the son of the firm's founder, Henry Baldwin Hyde, who had been a Pulitzer friend in New York and Jekyll Island before he died in 1899. Young Hyde had inherited an estate of several millions including 51 percent of Equitable's stock, left him in trust but to become his sole property when he reached 30. A lover of French culture, he maintained a home in Paris, dressed grandly with fresh boutonnieres twice daily and patent leather shoes with red heels, and reputedly said, "I have wealth, beauty and intellect: what more could I wish!" He was involved in a secret corporate struggle with a group led by Equitable's $130,000-a-year president, James W. Alexander. These men, nervous because in another year he would control the company, were working diligently to ease him out and seize control themselves.

Hyde's costume ball, given in honor of his debutante niece, saw Sherry's decorated to resemble the gardens at Versailles and was quite proper despite all reports to the contrary. In the midst of it, footmen carried in a sedan chair bearing Madame Gabrielle Réjane, the vivacious French actress famous for her portrayal of Catherine in Sardou's *Madame Sans-Gêne*. The applause hushed as she mounted a chair and recited a poem stressing the happy relations between France and America.

Rumor exaggerated the incident and almost every newspaper, the World included, ran front-page stories describing the affair as decadent as well as extravagant. It was said that Mme. Réjane had not only recited indecencies but had leaped upon the table and executed a can-can. The cost of the party was given as $100,000 (Hyde said $20,000). Insurance companies had long been regarded as conservative institutions devoted to the public good, and business leaders joined preachers in denouncing such debauchery.

To most of the newspapers it was a two-day sensation. Only the World's Ferguson kept digging into Equitable's corporate affairs. On February 12 the World scored a clean beat with a revelation of the struggle between Alexander and Hyde and of Alexander's charges of "misconduct, incompetence and misuse of funds." Equitable officially denied the story, warning of lawsuits. The World replied with another story giving the full text of a document in which Alexander and 25 other Equitable officials threatened to resign unless Hyde quit as vice-president. These exposures caused a hurried effort among the company's hierarchy to muffle their family troubles and stop the unfavorable publicity; but by now the World was after them in full cry with charges of reckless management and speculation with policyholders' money. The World began an almost daily series of editorials, all headed "Equitable Corruption," starting with "No. 1" and going on into the dozens. It suggested that things were no better in the other two of the Big Three of insurance, New York Life and Mutual Life, causing threats of lawsuits by these companies as well. The World, finally joined by other newspapers, demanded that Governor Frank Higgins launch a legislative investigation of the whole insurance business. Instead, Higgins asked for a report from Insurance Superintendent Francis Hendricks, who made an inquiry and then, backed by the governor, refused to make the testimony public.

Pulitzer, in Carlsbad and about ten days behind events, made one of his rare misjudgments in news value. The World at the same time was publicizing Charles Evans Hughes's probe of the gas trust, and he felt the paper was overloaded with complicated corporate details boring to the reader. Gas and insurance, gas and insurance! But he praised the fifth editorial on "Equitable Corruption":

> Excellent, admirable in every respect. Flawless, which is saying a good deal. Particularly struck by the strength coming from moderation of language and real knowledge. But again—following so long, and so very serious an article, comes immediately a dissertation on the tariff. . . . After the Equitable article should have come something lighter in touch and topics. . . .
>
> The breath is not yet out of me, dictating the above, when I hear about "A Blow at Dingleyism," as the leader of the next day, May 18th. It is simply terrible! I must go out of the room to draw fresh breath before reading it. . . . I feel the heart ache when I have to read these damned things in succession. I presume the average reader is happier because he doesn't have to read them [at] all. There are a hundred other subjects. Try to think of them. The country is not going to the devil. No country is more happy, more prosperous, more growing. . . . Hold up your hand and swear that at least for one month you will not write a single word about railroad rates, free trade, tariff or any other dry as dust political matter.[3]

From London he cabled to "concentrate on Equitable Corruption without exaggeration, also to avoid superlatives, like: monstrous, traitor, anarchist, etc., as rather juvenile, feeble."[4] This last was one of his recurrent orders, entertaining to the staff because his own language, both verbal and in his letters, bristled with such superlatives.

While in London he sat for John Singer Sargent at his Tite Street studio. Wanting to look his best, he rode in Hyde Park with Thwaites before each sitting, but he told Sargent, "I want to be remembered just as I really am, with all my strain and suffering there." Sargent replied, "I paint what I see. Sometimes it makes a good portrait; so much the better for the sitter. Sometimes it does not; so much the worse for both of us. But I don't dig beneath the surface for things that don't appear before my eyes."[5]

He smoked Egyptian cigarettes, and Pulitzer, who never allowed his secretaries to smoke cigarettes of any kind in his presence, behaved with such sweetness that Sargent, who had heard of his irascibility, said to Thwaites, "What a delightful man Mr. Pulitzer is." But the sitter flew into a temper when a London acquaintance whom he had marked down as a bore called on him at the studio. He refused to see him and, as Thwaites noted, "A look of fury and impatience entirely changed the face of the subject, and Sargent contemplated the scene with keen interest . . ."[6] The completed canvas was a remarkable portrait of duality, showing the character, intellect and intensity blended subtly with a touch of the Mephistophelian.

Sailing homeward, he reviewed a later batch of Worlds and decided it was going hog-wild in attack and might destroy public confidence in insurance companies. On shipboard he dictated nearly 100 pages of minute criticism, ordering a more measured approach and the dropping of the Equitable Corruption series. Meanwhile there was vast curiosity about Insurance Superintendent Hendricks' report, locked in his safe in Albany. The governor said he had not seen it, District Attorney Jerome could not get a copy, and the newspapers were exerting immense effort to learn its contents. It was a World political reporter, Louis Seibold, who had the necessary official friend in Albany, a man who slipped him the report long enough to copy it. When it was published in the World July 11, there was amazement that it could secure a document unavailable even to public officials—a surprise shared by the governor and insurance commissioner.

But the greatest surprise was in its revelations, proving all that had been charged and more. It demonstrated that insurance company officials had carried on improper but highly profitable speculation with policy-holders' money, and showed numerous links between them and powerful politicians. The Republican state administration obviously had been loath to disclose the report because of immense political pressure from above.

Pulitzer, reaching New York a few days later, was unable to adjust himself immediately to the new situation. He had worked steadily during the crossing to establish a more moderate World policy, and he flew into a rage when he discovered that all his work had been nullified, that Cobb had gone ahead on his own, that Seibold had intrigued in Albany. Although this kind of intrigue would normally have won his praise, he was for the moment quite unreasonable. He suspended Cobb for three weeks—an order that was ignored, unknown to him. He summoned to the Vault the 37-year-old Seibold, a reporter of extraordinary ability to whom he had given several presents, a roving newspaperman of the old school who had worked for a dozen papers ranging from San Francisco to Denver to Washington before settling on the World.

"My God, Seibold, you made a lot of trouble for me," he said. "I spend four days on shipboard writing an editorial and you go and do something that makes me look foolish. You deserve to be punished, Seibold; and, Great God! you shall be punished." [7] The reporter was dismissed, though he was given a $1,000 check in appreciation of past services. (He soon returned to the World fold after the Old Man had recovered from his pet, and in 1920 would win the Pulitzer Prize for reporting for his interview with Woodrow Wilson.)

By the time he reached Bar Harbor, Pulitzer had absorbed information demonstrating that the World had turned up something of superlative importance, and he reversed his field. Many men who had dined at his table were directors of the insurance companies involved, among them Levi P. Morton, Colonel John Jacob Astor, A. J. Cassatt and, closest of all, Chauncey Depew, now a United States senator. "Keep up the headline of Equitable Corruption," he ordered. ". . . We may get to 200 before we land someone in prison. Mistake to drop 'Equitable Corruption.'" [8] He did not add that it was his own mistake, which it was. Later he wired the World:

> Print following editorial to-morrow double-leaded under head Equitable Corruption dash the State is guilty number blank dash the State of New York is guilty paragraph the State inactive complacent acquiescent to corruption cynical towards vice indifferent to most vital interests of the public dash the State is guilty paragraph Superintendent Hendricks represents the State and the State represents his guilt. . . .[9]

Yes, yes, he agreed, the insurance scandal was a whopper and must be pushed to the limit, but the staff must realize that readers tired of endless columns of corporate data. Condense, condense! Already 385 columns had been devoted to insurance, and it really could have been done as effectively in 185, leaving 200 columns for colorful human interest. Take the Nan Patterson case for example. Who was the simpleton who minimized that on the theory that it was beneath the World's dignity?

Nan, a simply fetching member of the sextette in a *Florodora* road show, had been riding with her wealthy married lover, Caesar Young, in a hansom cab down West Broadway when Young was shot dead. She tearfully insisted that Young had shot himself, which seemed odd since he had just bought a new hat, was about to abandon her and sail for Europe, and medical evidence said the wound could have been self-inflicted only if he were a contortionist. Juicy details of their affair had splashed the front pages of Hearst's American and every other paper including Ochs's Times, and it was believed that Nan's beauty was a factor in the state's failure to convict her.

It was an egregious blunder for the World to give her such grudging attention, he insisted. "When a woman, no matter what her character or morality may be, does something that attracts thousands of people to her in the street, that is an event of extraordinary interest." [10] This, however, was not to suggest that every draggletail must be featured simply because she shot someone—not at all. It was a question of news judgment.

III. DON'T BE UNNECESSARILY CRUEL

The furor over the World-publicized Hendricks report forced the reluctant Governor Higgins to appoint a committee to investigate the insurance companies, and it was Don Seitz of the World who suggested Charles Evans Hughes as counsel. Hughes, who had gone to Switzerland with his family after the successful ending of his gas probe, returned to launch immediately into a far greater one that would make him famous. His grasp of corporate matters was masterly, his treatment of squirming insurance dignitaries polite but deadly. To one who protested "Those relations are confidential," he replied, "There is nothing confidential about the insurance business now," and proceeded with his questions. To the elegant President Richard A. McCurdy of Mutual, who described his company as "a great beneficent missionary institution," he replied, "Well . . . . The question comes back to the salaries of the missionaries." [11] McCurdy's phrase was ill-advised, for he was thenceforth tagged by the World as Missionary McCurdy. Part of his beneficence was showered on his son Robert, who had received more than $1,700,000 from Mutual in 16 years, and a son-in-law, who received $145,687 in one year. The World, pointing out that the McCurdy mission began at home, estimated that the clan had drawn about $15,000,000 from Mutual over the years.[12]

Hughes (who would have been shocked to learn that his World code name was Rake) was just getting his teeth into the investigation when certain groups and individuals with varying motives made an effort to sidetrack him by urging his nomination for mayor. Among those involved in the negotiations were William Randolph Hearst; Ervin Wardman, editor of the Republican New York Press; Pulitzer; and Benjamin B. Odell, the Republican state boss. On October 4 Hearst had been nominated for mayor by the Municipal Ownership League and evidently was of two minds about it. He was gunning for the governorship in 1906 as a step to the presidency, and the mayoralty did not fit in with that plan. Yet he had been nominated with great enthusiasm by reform groups, he dearly wanted to lay Boss Murphy of Tammany by the heels, and he debated the idea. On October 6 Florence D. White at the World sent Pulitzer at Bar Harbor the following telegram:

> Los [Carvalho, still with Hearst] for Gush asks me to wire as follows: If Andes will give Gush moderate support Gush will accept Municipal nomination and make fight against Gammon [Boss Murphy] working to induce republicans to put up cleanest strongest man period Girondist [the New

York Press] favors plan but Gush will not run without Andes moderate support considering race big personal sacrifice. . . .

White again wired Pulitzer a few hours later: "Los subsequently telephoned that Odell says he will try for consent of any republican Andes will name today." [13]

Here indeed was a paradox—Hearst dickering with the Republicans and also with his greatest journalistic rival; Boss Odell of the Republicans offering to let the Democrat Pulitzer name his candidate for mayor. An Italianate touch is not impossible to imagine. Pulitzer's admiration for the Republican Hughes was evident in every issue of the World, which had already urged him as the Republican candidate. Hughes was pressing his insurance investigation entirely too forcefully, and if he kept it up some eminent Republicans would not only be embarrassed but possibly jailed. It would be a splendid escape if Pulitzer would help elect him mayor—get him out of the investigation, to be replaced by some accommodating hack who would let the probe quietly dwindle.

Pulitzer's reply cannot be found. However, he was opposed to Hearst's socialistic theories and it seems likely that he refused to commit the World to even moderate support. His sensitive nose certainly sniffed the Republican undermotive in seeking to sidetrack Hughes, and yet he could do even greater work as mayor and the World would see to it that the insurance probe was not dropped. Andes was firmly behind Rake.

Indeed, so was Hearst a day or two later. Through Wardman of the Press he urged Hughes to accept the Republican nomination, saying he would not only support him but would even run himself on a third ticket to split Mayor McClellan's vote and make Hughes's election certain.[14] This apparently self-abnegating gesture becomes clearer in view of Hearst's aim for the governorship in 1906, his knowledge that Hughes might be a very powerful candidate against him, and that putting Hughes in City Hall would eliminate that threat.

But Hughes foiled them all when he was waited upon by a group of Republican leaders, some with motives not above suspicion. He declined, saying, "Were I with the best of intention to accept the nomination, it is my conviction that the work of the [insurance] investigation would be largely discredited. . . ." [15]

Pulitzer was so upset by Hughes's refusal that he swore he did not sleep a wink that night. Yet the World approved: "This action is a good measure of the quality of the man." Did Hearst interpret the move as a sign that Hughes also was shooting for the governorship and might well win it? One does not know, but he thought the matter over for three days more before deciding October 10 to accept the Municipal Ownership League nomination tendered him six days earlier, and to win if he could.

So Pulitzer, badly though he wanted to beat McClellan and Tammany, felt unable to support either of his opponents, Hearst or the Republican candidate, William M. Ivins. By his instructions the World publicized Hearst's campaign without prejudice, and he saw his "partyless" rival gain greatly in political stature as he assailed Boss Murphy, fought favored Tammany against impossible odds and yet came within a hairline 3,500 votes of winning.

Hughes meanwhile proceeded with devastating thoroughness, finding in a few months flimflammery that had escaped Superintendent Hendricks in six years. Among hundreds of facts he brought out about the practices of the leading insurance companies, these were a few:

While their profits and those of their officials had soared, dividends to policyholders had shrunk.

It was a common practice among executives of several companies to invest policyholders' money at great profit to themselves, using subsidiary firms as a screen for their speculations.

Mutual Life's "legal expenses" in 1904 were $364,254. Most of this was paid to its chief Albany lobbyist, Andrew C. Fields, for suppressing bills unfavorable to the company and encouraging favorable bills. No records were kept of Field's disbursements and it could not be proved that he had bribed legislators, but it was shown that he maintained a mansion in Albany called the House of Mirth where he entertained lawmakers with bed, board and poker games which they never failed to win. Fields had skipped town and could not be found.

President John A. McCall of New York Life admitted that he had paid out $1,167,697 in ten years without any accounting to *his* chief Albany lobbyist, Andrew Hamilton, most of it charged as "legal expenses." Hamilton had hurriedly departed for Paris for health reasons.

Equitable had also employed both Hamilton and Fields plus a third lobbyist, Thomas D. Jordan, who had also left the state with scarcely time to pack a bag. An examiner in the state insurance department had been appointed on requests from Fields and a state senator living at the House of Mirth.

The insurance Big Three had divided the nation into four districts, with Equitable lobbyists charged to kill unfavorable laws in one, New York Life in another and Mutual in a third, the fourth being open territory. They had also corrupted the press wherever possible, paying a dollar a line for insurance-company puffs disguised as news.

The intimate relations between insurance companies and financial houses gave individuals in each splendid opportunities to profit in "syndicate" speculation with policyholders' money. George W. Perkins, for example, was a Morgan partner and was also vice president of New York Life, and Jacob Schiff of Kuhn, Loeb was a director of Equitable.

When Hughes discovered that New York Life also had an office at the Hanover Bank and demanded the books of that bank to explain a $48,000 payment, Republican Boss Odell protested privately that this was inadvisable, that the evidence "might actually lead to the door of the White House." George Perkins drew Hughes aside and said, "Mr. Hughes, you're handling dynamite. That $48,000 was a contribution to President Roosevelt's campaign fund. You want to think very carefully before you put that in evidence." [16] The inexorable Hughes did not have to think carefully at all. He asked the question and put the answer in evidence.

The World's charges a year earlier of large corporate payments to the Roosevelt fund were further borne out by testimony that Mutual and Equitable had each paid $40,000 to the fund. Insurance company money had also helped elect Republican congressmen and legislators.

Both of New York's United States senators had shared in the insurance cornucopia. Senator Thomas C. Platt, the former Easy Boss who had been replaced by Odell, admitted that he had received $10,000 "from time to time" from Missionary McCurdy of Mutual. Senator Chauncey Depew testified with evident shame that he drew a $20,000 annual retainer from Equitable, of which he was a director. Boss Odell himself sweated on the stand as he tried to explain (to the man he had sought to nominate for mayor) a transaction that had paid him $75,000 from a bank allied with Equitable, insisting that he had never threatened to discommode the bank by promoting an "unfavorable" law in Albany.

The World had indeed started something. It could also claim instrumentality in launching the political career of Hughes, whose ambitions had been bent solely toward the law. Great political pressure aided many squirming witnesses, and nobody went to jail, but the inquiry resulted in wholesale reforms.

McCall arranged to repay New York Life $235,000 improperly spent, resigned and died a few weeks later. President Alexander of Equitable, already ousted, was in a sanitarium and soon died. The McCurdy family restored $815,000 to Mutual, while McCurdy himself left for Europe and died abroad. James Hazen Hyde, who could blame it all on Mme. Réjane, had sold his Equitable stock and later went to Paris to spend the remainder of his long life there. George Perkins resigned from New York Life and restored the $48,000 (with interest) that had helped elect Roosevelt. He was arrested for larceny in that transaction and suffered much embarrassment in a long legal battle, but was never convicted despite the World's steady insistence that he belonged behind bars. Insurance Superintendent Hendricks quite properly resigned. But the lasting public benefit came from a series of new state laws, recommended by Hughes and passed by the legislature, that put insurance companies under rigid controls and cleansed an institution that had long soiled itself in corruption.[17]

When Frank Cobb received a large bonus check for his good work, and protested that he was already paid well for doing his duty, the great moneybags replied, "No, no, no to your letter. . . . Remember that there is plenty more if you will please me. And you could not possibly please me more than by swearing to accept my criticism in the future without feeling hurt, even if it should seem to you very wrong. Will you remember this? Swear!" [18]

The charming, witty Depew had been a Pulitzer friend, guest and correspondent for 20 years. "What a spectacle," Andes wrote the World. "A Senator of the United States!" But he was moved enough by sentiment to make one of his rare retreats from merciless objectivity. "Apropos of Depew," he added later, "I don't want to stifle the paper in its duty, don't want favoritism and am suggesting no suppression. But I don't think it necessary to kick him too hard. When a man is down we may show a little charity—especially toward an old man of seventy-two, who has some good qualities and perhaps I ought to add, who has been polite. Don't misunderstand me. I have not a word to say in criticism of the hard criticism of him. But don't be unnecessarily cruel." [19]

Chapter 6

Nerves in Tatters

1. THE PULITZER-VANDERBILT ENTENTE

Since the Pulitzer children were expected not to make important decisions without their father's advice, it followed that their courtship and marriage required close consultation with him. Although Ralph was now 26, Pulitzer's control over him was almost as firm and tyrannical as when he was a boy. To his father he reported his daily activities in a diary. From his father he received his orders along with praise or blame. From his father he received his salary plus a personal allowance. He knew that he was a disappointment because of his rather retiring nature, and his letters reveal the effort of an intelligent and sensitive young man to placate the fiercely critical overlord.

Ralph had been embarrassed in his friendship with Mary Harriman because the World was heaping insult on her railroad-mogul father. He risked similar difficulties when he gave his heart to Frederica Vanderbilt Webb, great-granddaughter of the immortal Commodore and granddaughter of William Henry Vanderbilt. It was the latter whom the World had assailed for his vulgarity, his mythical 350-ton ingot of gold, his ruthless manipulation of New York Central rates and his evasion of taxes. Yet the World had praised his children for marrying "plain Americans." Frederica Webb was the daughter of William Henry's fourth daughter Eliza and of Dr. William Seward Webb. The Vanderbilt inheritance, despite its splitting in a large family, amounted to $10,000,000 for the Webbs. Dr. Webb, who no longer practiced medicine, was a Vanderbilt railroad director, president of the Wagner Palace Car Company and founder of a brokerage firm, but he preferred "elegance to affairs." The Webbs lived on Fifth Avenue, spent their winters at Palm Beach and their summers at their 3,500-acre estate, Shelburne Farms, near Burlington, Vermont.

Ralph's announcement of his intentions interrupted his father's routine and propelled him into a crisis. Kate sent him a list of jewelry he might buy for Frederica in Paris costing 150,000, 315,000, 460,000 and 740,000 francs, though she admitted that the last was perhaps too expensive. Although he was pleased at the acceptance of his son by a family as famous and socially prominent as the Vanderbilts and Webbs, he could not look on the contemplated marriage simply as a social event. The earlier Vanderbilts, whatever their sins, had been workers and builders, but now he felt that the family had largely become mere heirs and cotillion-hoppers. Ralph's wife must not only be socially acceptable but equipped with character, force and ideals that would spur him to greater energy and ambition. He was torn by doubt that Miss Webb would make the kind of consort who would improve Ralph as an editor and coming executive of the World. He was annoyed when Ralph went to his mother for money, writing him from Carlsbad:

> . . . It was a great mistake to take shelter behind your mother and I beg you not to do it again because we have practically no communication whatever except when she wants money and if she interferes on your behalf would only prejudice your case & cause a reaction. [But he was eager to learn every detail of Ralph's plans, adding:] My imagination is in flames & my thirst for news covets even the smallest trifle [1]

When Miss Webb met her prospective father-in-law on his return from Europe, she was under an examination as searching as those given to World editors. Since she was only a dim blur in his vision, his sole avenue of acquaintance was through conversation, which of course meant endless questions probing her mind and abilities. Although fashionable young ladies of the time did not perspire, the charming Frederica underwent an ordeal that shook her. The blind inquisitor was satisfied enough to be resigned to the marriage but determined that she must not lead Ralph into frivolity. He wrote Ralph, "I dare say I think more constantly about your plans & yours & her future than you do yourself. *What will she do with you?* Ask her please—I mean outside of four-in-hands & shooting and the usual aristocratic sports." He wanted to see her again, continuing:

> Is there any possibility of her coming to Bar Harbor in July or August. I need hardly tell you how deeply interested I am in the young lady & how very glad I should be to see her & to have a talk with her—not frightening her as I did the last time. [He added warm words:] Give her my real sincere love.[2]

In August Ralph took Frederica to Chatwold where she underwent another cross-examination designed to test her seriousness of mind and purpose. Pulitzer's code name for her was Destiny, signifying something that might be pleasant or not but which in any case could not be averted. Destiny survived the interview but never quite got over her fear of the inquisitor. She later wrote him in placatory vein: "Thank you again many times for your kindness, and hoping that someday I may prove myself less frivolous and unambitious than you now think me!" [3]

Pulitzer sent her a copy of *Famous Women* to spur her ambition. He transferred a substantial amount to his son's account for gifts and other expenses incidental to the wedding, which would take place at Shelburne. Ralph was irked enough by the fatherly demands to let it show when Pulitzer reproached him for deserting the office and making a trip to Shelburne: "I think I ought to answer your question in your telegram by saying that I 'was stupid' enough to go to Shelburne because my presence there was necessary to obtain a license, and a license, though perhaps frivolous, is an indispensable adjunct to a wedding in Vermont." [4]

The wedding was held at the Episcopal church at Shelburne on October 14—an event as significant in its way as would have been the union of the late Winnie Davis and Alfred Wilkinson, a joining of Republican and Democrat, of fashion and reform, of society beauty and social critic. Scores of telegrams had been sent by Ralph and Dr. Webb to make sure that Pulitzer would reach the scene by the best private car and that the car would not be left among noisy locomotives while changing lines at Albany. Kate and the rest of the family were there, Edith being a bridesmaid and Joseph Jr. best man, mingling with shoals of Vanderbilts, Twomblys, Shepards and Sloanes. For Pulitzer, sitting unseeing in a pew in a strange church without his cordon of secretaries to shield him, it was an ordeal, a shattering strain on the nerves which he could not end by leaving at the close of the first act. The gifts were perhaps a trifle plutocratic for a World man, emphasizing gems and silver valued at $500,000. An orchestra and a military band provided music following the ceremony. Pulitzer left before the reception, having given Ralph $5,000 for a honeymoon beginning in the Adirondacks (where he assured his father he read the World daily) and continuing with a tour of England, France and Italy. He wired Ralph:

> I wish for nothing more than that by some divine inspiration and imagination both you and Destiny could really feel in your hearts how much I have thought of you and am thinking of you.
>
> Not to speak of the tears that were in my eyes during the ceremony; when I came very near breaking down. God bless you both.[5]

The old dragon seldom allowed such sentiment to emerge from his scales. Ralph wired him his love, "and wish I could give you some of my happiness," adding later, "I looked at you as we walked down the aisle, in fact yours was the only face I saw, and I felt a lot of things that I probably would not have been able to express to you . . . After the reception & the breakfast we bolted on board the yacht amid the damnedest bombardment of rice. . . ."[6] The Sunday World gave the wedding almost a full column under the headline, "MISS WEBB BRIDE OF RALPH PULITZER," but the story was on page 6 and there were no pictures, nor was there any mention of Pulitzer's presence, as if he preferred not to stress overmuch his family alliance with plutocracy.[7]

Ralph's World salary was now $500 a month plus an allowance which still lacked the opulence to permit a married man to live on the Pulitzer-Vanderbilt scale. His father settled that by making him a vice president at an increased salary and by raising the allowance to $2,000 a month. And when Ralph and Destiny returned from their honeymoon they received a surprise gift from Pulitzer—an $89,000 house at 17 East 73rd Street, *next door* to his own. Ralph could neither enter his house nor look out his window without being reminded of his dependence on the father he could never satisfy.

II. SUSPICION AND DESPAIR

At Christmas Pulitzer distributed the usual largesse at the World and Post-Dispatch, sent cigars to Carl Schurz, gave a $93 collection of hats to his editorialist Samuel Moffett, sent $100 to Booker T. Washington (who arrived to dine at Chatwold at his invitation, greatly upsetting the Southern-oriented Kate) and donated $5,000 for the relief of sufferers in the Russian pogroms. In his gifts to his own personal staff he showed his fondness for Alfred Butes, who received $380 to Hosmer's $160 and Dunningham's $100. He was overjoyed to find a new secretary who qualified—Harold Stanley Pollard, an honors graduate of Harvard well versed in music and art who had briefly been a Times reporter.

When he sailed for Europe after the wedding, he was in a more than usually nervous condition. He began a search for a yacht that would take him out to sea away from the telegrams and letters that so upset him. The splendid Vanderbilt yacht *Valiant* was for sale, and Ledlie was sent to Marseille to look her over while Tuohy inspected another one at Cowes. At last Pulitzer decided to build his own, to be designed by G. L. Watson & Sons of Glasgow and constructed by Ramage & Ferguson at Leith, but he chartered the comfortable yacht *Honor* in the meantime. Arthur Billing left his post at the World to spend much of his time in Scotland for more than a year watching the construction of the new yacht.

Pulitzer took the waters at Carlsbad, where John Wanamaker also happened to be sojourning. He had met Pulitzer only once, in 1884, at a Philadelphia luncheon with George Childs (now dead 12 years), and had been impressed by what he called "the furnaces of his intellect." When Wanamaker in 1889 became Postmaster General under Harrison, and the World attacked him savagely for his spoilsmanship, the furnace heat became uncomfortable. But he was a kindly man. Now as he walked alone through the woods near Carlsbad, he saw four men riding toward him, the central figure being Pulitzer. He shouted, "Mr. Pulitzer of the New York World, halt!"

To his astonishment, the blind man who had met him only once, 22 years earlier, replied instantly, "Wanamaker of Philadelphia, is that you?" As Wanamaker put it, Pulitzer had "sight in his ears," and after this meeting they had several pleasant chats,[8] although Pulitzer was in depression deeper than he had suffered in a year or more.

He had visited Dr. Pagenstecher, who had earlier given him some hope that an operation might restore partial vision, and had been told it was impossible. Kate wrote him, ". . . I had so absolutely counted upon an operation that his failure to perform it was a shock to me. My poor dear, I wish I could do something for you. If the knowledge that you have my tenderest sympathy and constant thought helps you at all you may be assured of that. . . . Take hold of your courage in both hands, dear."[9]

Resurgent diabetes had forced his observance of a loathsome diet. Probably Ralph's marriage had added to his upset, along with other worries such as the pitiable state of the Democratic party, Kate's expenditures and young Joseph's irresponsibilities. In such a mood, the failure of any member of his family to write him weekly and at great length, expressing elaborate sympathy, could throw him into despair or rage. He was capable of suspecting that his family was deceiving him behind his back and that his old friends had all deserted him. He was not free from occasional suicidal inclinations.

He was convinced that Sargent, who had painted Kate's portrait the previous summer, was infatuated with her. Kate wrote him, innocently adding to the suspicion, "I took tea with Sargent in London. He seemed really delighted to see me, was very complimentary & said in quite a pained voice, 'I did not do you at all justice in your portrait [;] you are much better looking than I painted you.' He spoke very nicely of you . . ."[10]

Young Joseph, in his father's view, had been positively impossible. After his unsatisfactory record at St. Mark's, he had worked briefly at the World, then had begged to be permitted to take special tutoring for entrance at Harvard. This had been granted in 1904 on the strict condition that he live within his allowance, do brilliant work and send his father a weekly diary of his activities and thoughts. On the contrary, his letters had frequently been devoted to appeals for more money, he had often failed to send the diary, and had staggered through the 1904–1905 year with barely passable grades. Now in 1905–1906 he had been cutting classes and doing so poorly that a Harvard dean had written Pulitzer a letter of warning. In April the ax had fallen. Joe had been expelled, which to his father was nothing short of disgrace.

Yet he was brimming with talents that would have overjoyed any other parent. Except for Edith, he was the only one of the children blessed with excellent health and an emphatic intrepidity of spirit. He had a superior mind, exceptional writing ability, great energy and a genuine zest for journalism. He had delighted in working as a reporter, had groaned and lost interest when he was shifted to the business department, but had shown a swiftness of decision and a fertility in ideas which at the moment could take second place to the merriments of a 21-year-old.

When Pulitzer returned briefly in the spring, his words to Joseph could not have been gentle, but he put the young man to work as a reporter on the Evening World under Chapin, the redoubtable Pinch. "Treat him exactly as you would any other beginner . . ." he warned Pinch. "There is to be no partiality shown because he is my son. . . . Promise me you will do as I ask."

Chapin promised. Joe was an hour late his third day, explaining that the butler had forgotten to wake him. Chapin observed that most members of the staff made do without butlers by utilizing alarm clocks, and warned him sternly a week later when he missed an entire day. The young man walked the line for a fortnight or more, then missed another day and, as Chapin recorded, "When he did come in I fired him." [11] Joe went to Bar Harbor to sail his yacht, and one can imagine the furious roasting he received when his father reached Chatwold.

He sent Joe to St. Louis to work on the Post-Dispatch at $20 a week plus an additional weekly allowance of $70—a double-entry system Pulitzer always followed with his sons, evidently so that their known newspaper salaries would not anger other members of the staff. Joe was required to send a daily report of his newspaper and social activities and also an account of his expenses. One of the things he had to explain was the purchase of an excessive number of underdrawers. Why was that? "Apropos of the large number of drawers I ordered," the son reported, "I must say it mystifies me as much as it did you. All I know is that my drawers disappeared one by one, and after all, you know, one does need drawers!" [12]

The inspector-general Pulitzer was in no mood for humor. Another upsetting circumstance was Ralph's violent seizure with asthma, causing him to faint dead away one morning and requiring him to take an extended vacation at Shelburne. Pulitzer had told Ralph very plainly that his diabetes tormented him and that his physical and nervous condition was worse than it had ever been—so bad that at times he feared he might do something reckless. He charged Ralph to relay this information to Joseph and to let him know that he was doing the condition no good. This caused Joseph to write his father one of those contrite and placatory letters at which the brothers were expert but which they resented writing.[13]

However real and terrible Pulitzer's occasional suicidal tendencies might have been, it was unfair of him to use them as a weapon in bolstering his authority and gaining sympathy, unless the use of them was simply another uncontrollable facet of his illness. Ralph himself, fearful about his father, wrote him to suggest that in circumstances other than Pulitzer's health there was room for actual optimism. The World had outdistanced Hearst's morning American and the combined morning-evening World circulation was about 700,000. It took diplomacy to hint that some of his father's worries were irrational, but Ralph was equal to the task:

> . . . Anyone else would consider [conditions] more favorable than they have been for 20 years. When the papers you created can earn a million dollars a year, and far more important, have re-earned the respect of the community; when your sons are at least doing their best to fit themselves for preserving what you created; when your family is ready to obey your largest wish or humor your slightest whim. Of course dear father, no one realizes more keenly than I do that all these things do not restore to you your sight, do not heal your nerves, do not cure that damnable disease [diabetes]. Please don't think I do not fully realize & deeply grieve for the misery of your personal condition. But these other things that I have mentioned ought to serve as mitigations, and not as aggravations of it. Now I hope that all this will not offend you. I only write it because I was so deeply & painfully impressed by your situation during this last visit . . .[14]

His periods of depression, rather than disabling him, often inspired greater activity as an escape, an even greater flow of directives to the World. The paper was pushing a favorite crusade against the law's distinction between the rich and the poor, upbraiding District Attorney William Travers Jerome as a terror against small-time madams and two-bit criminals but easy on wealthy offenders such as George Perkins, who was still very much at large. The angry Jerome reached back into his memory and pulled out the Gumbo-Ryan incident. In a public speech he lampooned a newspaper where "the walls [were] decorated with large printed placards 'Accuracy, Terseness, Accuracy!' while the city editor and others were going short of Metropolitan Street Railway." Stung, Pulitzer wrote Jerome to admit that the World attacks were perhaps too strong at times but insisting, "If you can point to a single editor or reporter, writer or manager of the *World* who has been guilty of any venality . . . that person will be instantly dismissed . . . I hope I know you well enough, as I knew your father before you, to believe that you surely will not hesitate to make proper amends for a reckless and unfounded attack upon editors whose reputation and integrity are their sole professional assets."[15]

In May, Carl Schurz died at 77 after long work on his interesting three volumes of memoirs, in which not even minor mention was made of Pulitzer although lesser individuals by the score received attention. Evidently Schurz had been disillusioned by his former protégé's wayward journalism during the war. While Pulitzer on his part thought Schurz's politics often unsound, he always honored the older man's unshakable integrity. Kate, who attended the memorial service, wrote him a careful description of it, adding, "It was a meeting that must do mens souls good to feel that a man's upright life even more than his splendid mind commanded such respect. You would have been proud of your chief." [16]

News of a different sort broke June 25 when the stocky, perfectly groomed Stanford White (a Pulitzer friend whose wife had been at Ralph's wedding) strolled into the canopied roof of the Madison Square Garden he had designed 16 years earlier. A theatrical meringue called *Mamzelle Champagne* was being viewed by a throng including the millionaire Pittsburgh psychopath Harry Thaw and his wife, the fetching showgirl Evelyn Nesbit, who was said to have "eyes like blue-brown pansies." On the stage, chorus girls in pink tights waved foils at each other and sang:

I challenge you,
I challenge you
To a duel, to a du-el.

At that moment Thaw walked over to White's table and shot him three times, killing him instantly. Some of the audience thought it a part of the show and waited for White to get up, while others shrieked and ran for the exits. Albert Payson Terhune, covering the entertainment for the Evening World, telephoned news of the murder instead. Thereafter, for almost two years, Genuine and all other New York papers would cover two trials featuring the bizarre sadism of Thaw, the startling conduct of Evelyn with Thaw, John Barrymore and other men, and the straight-faced charge that White "ruined" her despite evidence of her accessibility. It was shortly after this that Bradford Merrill informed Terhune that he was a candidate for the honor of becoming a Pulitzer secretary, that he would be interviewed by Mr. Butes and that a pleasant voice was one essential. Terhune had heard enough of the secretarial horrors so that when Butes arrived, as he put it, "I talked to him through my nose and at the top of my lungs . . ." He was relieved to be rejected.[17]

III. THE MANNERS OF A HORSE

Being uncertain of the motives of President Roosevelt, Pulitzer sought to examine his brain as he would that of an editor. Frank Cobb occasionally went to Washington to talk with the President, and in May Samuel

Williams visited the White House for two off-the-record interviews which he reported in detail to the chief. Williams was instructed not to commit Pulitzer in the slightest degree, and his remarks to the President were replete with, "I understood Mr. Pulitzer to say . . ." and "It seems to me that Mr. Pulitzer believes . . ." Roosevelt repeated emphatically his refusal to seek a third term and went on with complimentary words:

> The *World* and I stand on the same ground. Your paper is magnificent and strong. It is ably edited, it is courageous in its views and its editorial page is the finest in the country. The *World* is not afraid to express its principles. . . . You are against fakirs; so am I. Your showing up of [District Attorney] Jerome, for example, was magnificent. . . . Then there are your attacks on the big fellows, the men of wealth and power, the class of predatory wealth. The way you went after them was magnificent. . . . That is a magnificent phrase of Mr. Pulitzer's—"Predatory wealth and predatory poverty." I have used in the past Predatory Wealth, but I wish I had thought of its complement, "predatory poverty." I am going to use it in my next public letter.[18]

It was indeed a "magnificent" phrase, one Pulitzer had occasionally used in editorials and would use again, expressing a conviction that grew with his age and conservatism that capitalism was not alone in seeking unfair advantage.

To Cobb, Roosevelt was most friendly, saying with great good humor, ". . . I have sometimes detected a hiatus in [Pulitzer's] support of the administration, and it has seemed at times that he had his Roosevelt enthusiasm under excellent control." [19]

This was truer than he knew. Although Pulitzer applauded such presidential acts as his part in the Russo-Japanese peace negotiations, he was deeply suspicious of Roosevelt, fearful of what he regarded as his irresponsible exercise of power. At times Andes, who insisted that his editors maintain cool objectivity toward politicians, erupted in almost irrational bitterness against Roosevelt in letters to Cobb. To his logical reasons for criticism it is not impossible that he added a subconscious motivation of envy for the vibrant presidential health that reminded him so keenly of his own infirmities. He even complained frequently that Roosevelt lacked the dignity indispensable to a President, writing Cobb, ". . . His manners are bad, worse than the manners of a horse." [20]

Now, however, he faced the perennial problem of the ambitions of Hearst, who was reaching for the governorship of New York through his new party, the Independence League. He reacted strongly to a World statement that Hearst had no more chance of being endorsed by the Republicans than by the Democrats. On the surface this seemed the safest of assumptions, since Hearst had always put dollar signs on the Republicans and for more than a year had left few epithets unused in his attacks on Boss Murphy of Tammany and Boss Patrick McCarren of Brooklyn. Pulitzer, who always looked beneath the surface, telegraphed the World that this was a "great mistake," going on:

> Mr. Hearst's chances to obtain the Democratic nomination excellent, almost probable as far as any one can see to-day . . . no sign of an opposition whatever; Hearst's getting things by default; Democratic machine rotten to the core interior of State; no leader has raised his voice yet, no activity organization against him; ceaseless energy and work in his favor by his agents day and night all over State . . . unprincipled persons like Murphy and McCarren will control at least half the memberships of the convention . . . Whether Mr. Hearst is sincere or not in his professions is no more the question than whether Mr. Murphy is sincere in his alleged Democratic principles. The main question is who teaches more independence in voting, who awakens more indignation against corruption and misgovernment, who comes nearer presenting the real truth, who is more against party humbug, who against fooling the people. We sincerely hope Mr. Hearst will receive a very large vote. . . . The idea is to approve his candidacy without approving his principles and character . . . An able, independent man.[21]

He was right as usual. Hearst performed the rare political feat of eating his cake and having it too. He had stigmatized Murphy as "The Colossus of Graft," "The Black Hand" and "Bill Sykes"; his Journal had cartooned Murphy in prison stripes; he had denounced him as "as evil a specimen of a criminal boss as we have had since the days of Tweed," and had rung endless changes on the theme of Murphy's infamy. A month before the Democratic state convention he said, "I repeat now that I am absolutely and unalterably opposed to the Murphys and the McCarrens, and also to the . . . McClellans and to the kind of politics they all represent." But it was noted that this last was so much softer as to be by comparison an accolade. Murphy needed Hearst, the only man with a chance for a Democratic victory, and Hearst needed Murphy. The boss swallowed his pride, and at the Buffalo convention, by dint of some ruthless work with delegates, Tammany swung the nomination of Hearst.

The journalistic outcry in New York gave a false impression that Gush had not a friend in the metropolis. The Tribune, Times, Herald, Sun, Post, Telegram, Mail, World and others vibrated with scornful belly laughs and variations on "Waltz Me Around Again, Willie." Edmund Wetmore versified the Hearst-Murphy turnabout:

So I lashed him and I thrashed him in my hot reforming zeal,
Then I clasped him to my bosom in a most artistic deal.

Bennett's Herald, indeed, carried over such venom from the previous year's mayoralty race that Hearst achieved an ingenious revenge. For years the otherwise well-edited Herald had run "personals" columns so replete with prostitutes' cunningly worded appeals for assignations that newsmen called it "The Whores' Daily Guide and Handy Compendium." This feature not only brought in Mustard revenue but was so titillating that it boosted circulation, many readers buying the Herald solely to pore over those agate-type euphemisms. A Hearst reporter tracked down enough of the female advertisers to give evidence that resulted in Bennett's conviction for sending obscene matter through the mails. Bennett paid a $25,000 fine, and the already slumping Herald, once the most profitable paper in the country, suffered a blow in prestige and circulation from which it never recovered.

Hearst's opponent was the man he had failed to sidetrack the year before, Hughes, for whose candidacy Pulitzer was in some part responsible. Reluctant to run, Hughes asked Bradford Merrill for Pulitzer's advice. "He wants to know," Merrill wrote the chief, "if you think there is any real public call for him. Mr. Hughes said frankly that the attitude of the World added very greatly to his perplexity, because it always seemed to speak from principle and conviction, never from personal motive." [22]

Rake *must* run, Pulitzer replied, and Rake did. Pulitzer gave Frank Cobb careful instructions to support Hughes on his record, which Cobb followed so enthusiastically that the master of Chatwold complained, "Please don't call Hughes a political and intellectual giant. It is an exaggeration and hurts him and the paper. He is an honest, able man. That, the people will believe and that is enough. . . . Accuracy, Accuracy, Accuracy." [23]

In the midst of it all he became the grandfather of Ralph Pulitzer Jr. on August 28. He grew so excited that he had to let off steam, which he did with one of his boat rides, sailing to Southampton, making the briefest of stays in London and sailing directly home. He telegraphed the World:

> Treat Hearst without a particle of feeling of prejudice, if this is possible . . . while as a matter of conviction [I] sincerely detest most of his professions, principles, purposes and party, the same conviction compels an expression of respect for his courage in accepting a candidacy which cannot lead to his election and must appear as devotion to his principles. . . . Irony of fate, humor of situation that Hearst denounces Tammany's boss, owes his popularity to this denunciation . . . that now Hearst [receives] Murphy's support. . . . Try to raise a sense of humor for Monday.[24]

In believing that Hearst had no chance, his political judgment for once was wrong. The World treated Hearst with less spleen than its contemporaries, but it lampooned the Murphy deal and it threw more heart-and-soul support to Hughes than it had for any candidate since Cleveland. As other papers, particularly the vengeful Herald, showered Hearst with abuse including thinly veiled charges that he was an utter debauchee, he retaliated with abuse of his own. In a Brooklyn speech he swung out at a dozen of them, specifically calling Pulitzer "a coward, a traitor and a sycophant."[25] Pulitzer's nerves became so unbearable that he sailed again before election day, taking Kate and 11-year-old Herbert with him, going on with Herbert to Wiesbaden while Kate and Miss Macarow took the cure at Divonne les Bains. He had been upset for several years about what he regarded as Herbert's inadequate education and had made strenuous efforts to get him the best tutors in English and French. Now he canvassed the area around Wiesbaden for a German tutor, having his secretaries interview dozens before one was selected. He wrote Kate:

> He is the brightest of your children—by far the brightest & [most] promising of all. He ought to be a public man of great distinction if properly educated and trained.
>
> I see no reason why he might not be President of the United States. But nobody can learn a language after he has grown up in America. [He complained of terrible headaches, and went on with a deep revelation of self:] I want the child about me as an idea or feeling, with sense, or sentiment [,] not as a reality (because I scarcely ever see him), but he is the only thing I love about me & my nature is so constituted & always has been, that I must have someone to love about me.
>
> It is not that he loves me, but he is useful to me because I can love him. That is why I have carried him around like a woman who wears a crucifix or talisman & that is why it is a great sacrifice to me to feel that he is away.[26]

Back home, with the aid of a devastating last-hour speech by Elihu Root, delivered by authority of President Roosevelt and fairly flaying Hearst, Hughes won by 58,000 votes. The closeness of the race would have left Hearst with some prestige but for the fact that all his Democrat-Independent running mates won. Thousands of voters had split their ballots against him. It was the end of his astonishing rise, the knell of his hopes for the presidency, although he would remain a powerful political factor for decades. Pulitzer sent a cable of warm praise to his staff, predicting that Hughes would be the state's ablest governor since Tilden. Herbert, not without some fatherly coaching, composed a speech reading in part:

> Now my frends and countrymen, please lesen to me. Why do you not try to crush this lier, this trient, this decetful wrech called Murphy, why do you not crush him under the iron heel of the majority the same as you have done with Hurst . . . ?[27]

Evidently Herbert needed tutoring in spelling as well as German. Meanwhile Hearst headed for Mexico with his family and party in his private car, stopping in St. Louis with Mrs. Hearst to dispatch a message through the Associated Press correspondent. It happened that the AP office was in the Post-Dispatch building. Twenty-one-year-old Joseph Pulitzer Jr. walked over to the big man, introduced himself pleasantly, then asked if he had meant what he said about Joe's father during the campaign.

"I usually mean what I say," Hearst replied.

Joe swung, hitting him in the midriff. Hearst backed away, tossed off his overcoat and advanced with his fists upraised. By this time the lovely Mrs. Hearst dashed between them and bystanders restored peace.[28] Certainly that one punch raised Joseph in his father's estimation and repaid much of the worry he had caused.

IV. UTTERLY UNREASONABLE

While Kate sailed home for Christmas, Pulitzer went with Herbert to Cap Martin. His stomach tormented him, his headaches were frequent, he felt likely to die at any moment, his villa was impossibly small, there was a $1,500,000 addition to the Pulitzer Building to worry about, and he was upset because Dr. Hosmer had been forced to go home because of illness. Perhaps the most stunning blow of all was that Bradford Merrill after ten years had taken that most traitorous of steps and gone over to Hearst. For several years Pulitzer had shaken things up by shifting his three top men, Seitz, Merrill and White, back and forth, from business side to editorial side, from Senior to Junior, so that none of them knew precisely where he stood, knowing only that he was never quite satisfactory. The chief seemed to take it as a point of pride that he knew just how hard to push without alienating a man, but now he had missed. The loss of the valued Merrill, the keenest political analyst of the trio, shook him and automatically raised his estimation of Seitz and White even though Seitz still forgetfully crunched his toast at times and White's voice was not as mellifluous as it might be. Both received Pulitzer Christmas presents perhaps a trifle more lavish than might otherwise have been the case, White's being a pin glittering with large emeralds. Yet his gifts were seldom wholly expedient. Dumont Clarke and Frederick Judson, his St. Louis attorney, received cuff links costing $1,100 and $900 respectively, while lesser members of the World and Post-Dispatch staffs were not forgotten.

His standing order for independence in treating the news was honored as usual when a jealous husband shot his estranged wife dead in a department store restaurant, causing some panic. The store's management threatened to cancel its heavy schedule of advertising unless the World avoided mentioning where the murder had occurred. Seitz strode into the city room and said, "Listen, I want the name of that dam' store stuck into the first line of the first sentence of the first paragraph of this shooting story. I want the store's name repeated throughout the story whenever the use of it is warranted and maybe, for good measure, a few times when it isn't warranted. . . . We're going to teach certain busybodies that when they buy space in this paper they don't buy the paper along with it."[29]

Pulitzer was in physical and mental misery as he sailed with Herbert in the *Honor* for Taormina, Athens and Alexandria. Although he still had Butes, Thwaites, Pollard (a great success) and the German reader-pianist Friedrich Mann, in addition to one or two recent acquisitions, the temporary absence of Hosmer unmanned him and he sent out wild pleas for additional secretaries. Tuohy, Ledlie and Stephen McKenna, the World Paris head, were all on the qui vive in Europe. Kate was advertising in New York for candidates, writing him, "a great number of impossible people applied—such as valets, masseurs & even gardeners."[30] She asked Nicholas Murray Butler, Baron Hengelmuller and other friends to help find suitable secretaries, Ralph was also doing his best, and the search for companions again took on a color of international emergency.

Pulitzer was suspicious, impossible to please, utterly unreasonable. Whether or not there was real danger that he might lose his sanity or "do something desperate," the family could not discount the possibility. Although he wanted news about everything, he could take no pleasure in Kate's careful report that she had given a dinner for 70, including Vanderbilts, Fishes, Choates and Hengelmullers, had fed her guests terrapin and canvasback duck for only eight dollars a head and entertained them with a short Russian play enacted by Madame Alla Nazimova. Although Kate had pleaded for permission to rejoin him in Europe with Edith and Constance, and he refused, he suggested that he had been abandoned by his family.

"You refused to let me or me & the children join you," she protested. ". . . You then cable that it is a reflection on the family that they are not with you, all this worries me greatly & makes me extremely anxious as to your nervous, as well as physical condition, please have your doctor write me as to how you are. If you knew how miserable I feel about you, how many wakeful nights I spend thinking of you, you would give me more definite information & more frequent." To which she added later, "You would be so much happier my dear Joseph if you would only believe in the friendly intentions & good feeling of the people about you."[31] It was her own forthright nature to do this, and the strain of accommodating her life to his, of interceding for the children and of worrying about his condition was severe.

Ever since his exile and "retirement" from his newspapers he had delighted in publicly projecting his personality into them on special occasions as if to show that the old admiral was still running the ship. Now, as his 60th birthday approached, he suggested (i.e., ordered) birthday banquets in New York and St. Louis, each to be attended by 60 staff members of the World and Post-Dispatch, with himself as host even though he was far away. He took the opportunity to "retire" once more with one of those ringing messages intended for publication in both papers. Joseph was one of the speakers at the St. Louis banquet at the Planters' Hotel on April 10, while Ralph was one of those addressing the New York gathering at Delmonico's. Ralph, happy over a promotion and a salary increase, was careful to stress the loyalty and praise the Old Man enjoyed, as he announced that he had been appointed acting head of the World and president of the Post-Dispatch.

"If this were . . . the case," he told the 60 guests, "this would not be a celebration, but a wake, for I think you all know as well as I do, so long as Joseph Pulitzer has the breath of life in him, who the acting head of this paper is, and who its thinking head is, and who its planning and directing head is, and who it's going to be, God willing, for a great many years to come." He was also careful to write his father a very long and detailed description of the banquet, telling of the "storm of applause" that broke out when his cabled retirement message was read and adding, "Everyone was talking about it for the rest of the evening, saying it was the finest thing you had ever written beating both your salutatory and your cornerstone cable. And I think they are right." [32]

The retirement announcement was duly published in the Post-Dispatch, but not in the World because the practical-minded Frank Cobb thought that Pulitzer, like Patti and Bernhardt, was retiring too often and did not really mean to retire anyway. Although Andes was annoyed by the omission, Cobb got away with it and it would have an odd sequel the following year.

Returning from his unhappy Mediterranean cruise and settling at Menton, Pulitzer arranged through his secretaries and his Paris man, McKenna, to have Auguste Rodin execute a bronze and a marble bust, the fee being 35,000 francs. The 67-year-old sculptor journeyed to Menton to find Pulitzer in an unruly mood. Rodin asked him to bare his shoulders to reveal the posture of the head and neck. He refused. He had an almost girlish shyness about exposing any part of his person except his head, which itself was largely covered by his bushy black mane of hair and the reddish beard now flecked with gray. Not until Rodin said he must give up the commission and return to Paris did the subject relent, stipulating that only Rodin and his assistant be permitted to see his undraped shoulders. So the sittings progressed in surly silence, with Pulitzer so petulant that he refused to speak to the sculptor. The finished bronze showed only the head and neck, but in the marble, showing also the shoulders and upper chest, Rodin had his innings. He applied a lacy ripple across the chest strongly suggesting the neckline of a chemise.[33]

Meanwhile Pulitzer was corresponding through Alfred Butes with Nicholas Murray Butler about the proposed journalism school at Columbia. He moved on to Carlsbad in May for another of his endless cures, then returned for a short stay at Jekyll Island. Here he was a guest at a dinner honoring Andrew Carnegie and attended by an assembly of moguls who, almost to a man, had been roughly handled by the World, among them J. P. Morgan, Cornelius Vanderbilt, Nelson Aldrich, Edward S. Harkness, George F. Baker and William Rockefeller. His eccentricities were a subject of comment on the island, among them his offer to the captain of a dredging boat: "If you will not blow your whistle as you pass my cottage, I will pay you $100 a day for the time that you are dredging the river." Dr. Hosmer had rejoined him, and a friend, knowing of Hosmer's extreme anticlericalism, was amazed to see him enter the island chapel. He asked Butes if Hosmer had embraced the church. "No," Butes replied. "Each Sunday morning Dr. Hosmer goes to chapel and remains until the offertory is taken up, when he places a new $5 bill on the plate and decorously retires. Mr. Pulitzer has then attended church." [34]

The next stop was Chatwold, where a crushing blow befell him. The incomparable Alfred Butes, after 13 years in his service, succumbed to the inevitable shell shock and resigned to become secretary to Lord Northcliffe in London. The affection Pulitzer bore for Butes, the gifts he had lavished on him (among the many being a Butes family tour of Europe) could not forever repay the tensions, the explosions, the irrationalities. Pulitzer had regarded Butes as an aide and companion for life. In his will he had named the young man a trustee of his estate as well as leaving him a handsome legacy—stipulations he now erased. Butes's defection almost prostrated him. He was unable to continue his negotiations with Butler Blaming Northcliffe (who called Butes "the best secretary God ever made"), he sent him a bitter cable that ended their friendship.[35]

As Norman Thwaites recalled it, "It was my unfortunate lot to try to console Pulitzer when Butes finally decided to leave his service. I rode out with him through the woods at Bar Harbour. I sought to keep his mind engaged by bits of news from the day's papers. He responded not at all, and gradually I sank into silence. 'Well, why don't you talk? Is there no news in the papers? Dammit, man, talk, talk!' and he swung at me with his riding-crop and belaboured me heartily. 'I have been talking steadily for an hour,' I retorted. He relented at once and, after apologising, he bade me tell him why he was treated so cruelly." [36]

Chapter 7

Artificial World

I. MY LONG LONGED FOR FRIEND

In 1907 Pulitzer summoned Frank Cobb to the Vault and said, "Boy, I am, as you probably know, a large owner of stocks. Some of them are bound to be affected by public action. I am not sure of myself when I see my interests in danger. I might give way some day to such a feeling and send you an order that would mean a change in the paper's policy. I want you to make me a promise. If I ever do such a thing swear you will ignore my wishes." [1]

He never did such a thing, although in a lesser man some deterioration in ideals might have been excused by such foul health and nerves. His World was rather hard on President Roosevelt, William Jennings Bryan and District Attorney Jerome. Jerome, once a flaming reformer dear to Pulitzer's heart, had suffered the decline almost inevitable in his estimation as he weighed the public official against the candidate—a decline only Governor Hughes seemed to escape—and it had to be admitted that Jerome had gone rather soft in his prosecution of George Perkins and others accused in the insurance scandal. A World photographer snapped a picture of a weary Jerome asleep in his swivel chair with his feet on the desk, and now and again the picture reappeared in the World with the suggestion that Jerome did too much dozing while misdoers got away. One of Pulitzer's basic convictions was that wealthy transgressors escaped punishment while impecunious ones did not, and the World never stopped urging that the imprisonment of even one monopolist or Wall Street charlatan would have a salutary effect.

He was enthusiastic about Roosevelt's pursuit of the Standard Oil trust that resulted in the famous $29,000,000 fine (that was never collected), but condemned his dispatch of the battle fleet around the world as jingoistic and possibly third-termish. As for Bryan—that plague again, that quadrennial disease of the Democratic party! Would he again infest the campaign in 1908—? Were the Democrats so poor that they could not find a man big enough to head him off?

Why not Woodrow Wilson? Why not John A. Johnson, Minnesota's great governor? He wrote Cobb:

> If there is a new thought—a new tone that you could bear in mind that I should like, it is the sense of the ridiculous—a sense of the utterly preposterous—a sense of the comic (if I may use synonyms) as applied to the Democratic politicians and thinkers if they nominate Bryan. I can hardly blame Bryan . . . if the fools are going to give him the nomination, but why should the politicians be such asses? . . . I have a headache and must not talk. [He went on talking.] As a P.S. consider a subhead of "16 to 1" without a solitary word of elucidation. Say sixteen names that might be considered. There is Fuller, White and Peckham, whose father was an illustrious judge. There is Gray, there is Woodrow Wilson, there is Douglas, of Mass., who was elected Governor at the very hour when Roosevelt swept the State. A shoemaker. There is Tom Johnson, if a Socialist is wanted. There is John Johnson, a blacksmith, who could not carry his State in a Presidential year, son of a washerwoman—a good man. We need washwomen and blacksmiths. There is Folk, Governor of Missouri and a Southern man who prosecuted the thieves. There is Governor Higgins of Rhode Island. There is Gaynor, if the party wants a radical Socialist of the most pronounced type. There is Francis. I don't believe in him, but he is an ex-Governor [of Missouri]. There is Governor Hoke Smith. All Democrats. Now pick out four from the South. I give you that inestimable privilege. [He had already picked one and now went ahead to pick three more.] There is Culberson, Daniel of Virginia and Bacon of Georgia.
>
> Now these are sixteen Democrats who might be considered [for the Presidential nomination]. . . . Every Democrat should have a free and unlimited deliberative convention, unpledged, uninstructed and unrestricted to select the best man at the time they meet. Now don't put this list of sixteen as if we were committed to support any of them. There are many that I would not support.[2]

He wrote Cobb about Governor Hughes:

> I am simply crazy about Hughes, so vitally important do I regard his work. . . . Support Hughes with all the fire and force you possess. But be independent even about him. I would not go through thick and thin for anybody—not even myself. Your friends must be criticized when they are mistaken, like other people.[3]

A judicial decision forbidding Sunday entertainments brought out the anti-puritan in him and made him lay out the entire plan of an article to be written by John L. Heaton of the editorial page:

For Sunday you ought to have a liberally [*sic*], able, thorough article on Sunday amusements—on the beautiful, refining, elevating music shut out—the desirable amusements absolutely cut off, but the saloons open, compelling the people who work the whole week to find a substitute. Go over the whole subject of Sunday Laws. They are obsolete—part of the dark ages—behind the times, against enlightenment and the progressive spirit of the age.

Particularly so in this city, which is more European and continental in spirit than puritanical. . . .

Let [Heaton] make a list of all the dead laws here and in Massachusetts and demand their enforcement simply to create a realization of the absurdity of the thing. Go back to the despotism of the sumptuary laws of Rome, or of the French Revolution, when in the name of Liberty, Fraternity and Equality they actually ordained . . . that no child should know its father, but that all children should be educated by the State—and eat, drink and dress and be exactly alike. . . .

. . . But do not denounce the decision of the judge, which is probably based upon the strict letter of the law, and as a law-abiding newspaper we must respect it. But I have a distinct notion that dead letter laws might be left dead. Let Speer [William McMurtrie Speer of Parker's "gold" telegram, now a World editorialist], as he is a lawyer, go to work and dig out every single law on the statute book not executed.

Try to make this the piece de resistance; at the same time give some statistics in tabloid form showing the population of New York. How many of the four and one half millions of people are really, in so far as race and national habit and custom are concerned, descendants of this puritan stock, and how many otherwise. This alone would make it striking. Also, and this is very important, how many laws are there that should be enforced and are entirely ignored?

I feel personally aggrieved because I like to go to the Sunday concerts at Carnegie Hall. I have no other amusement and now I am deprived of them. I feel like writing a letter to the great editor.[4]

These are samplings of the thousands of orders and suggestions that poured from the blind invalid who combined the most profound grasp of political and social history with the most intense desire to bring it to bear on current events of any editor who ever lived—a man always fleeing his nerves. He sailed for Europe in the fall, still in miserable health, still mourning Butes. A secretarial candidate nominated by Ralph had been tried and rejected, as had one proposed by Baron Hengelmuller. John McNaught of the World staff was with him for weeks in Europe, only to be found wanting.

Starved for affection, he yearned for someone who could supply the warmth and intimacy denied him in his separation from his family, the love which he could not help repulsing in tormented moments. Endlessly he sought a friend and confidant to lighten the terrible loneliness that hounded him despite his circle of secretaries. It was impossible, since the requirements demanded a saint rather than a mortal. His later note to

McNaught revealed the unattainable hope as well as the princely status he perhaps unconsciously assumed:

> I do hope you enjoy yourself and wish you could realize how much I learnt . . . to esteem and like you,—how much I would give if I could only deceive myself with the thought that my anxiety to attach you to me as my long lost and longed for friend is not entirely unappreciated.[5]

II. KICKING HOMER

The world's champion sightless reader was later said to have "read" a book every day—an exaggeration, although his own incomplete records show that his secretaries read him an average of about a hundred books a year for 21 years. Since only about one third of his reading time was devoted to books, the rest to newspapers, magazines, letters and reports, one gets an approximation of the countless millions of words that came to him by voice and a better understanding of his insistence that the voice be pleasant and the mind guiding it be keen. The reader was required to know the book in advance so that he could summarize windy passages and get to the point—always get to the point. Dr. Hosmer was still the best reader he ever had, good at fiction or fact. Pollard read to him novels and plays in English and French. Mann, in addition to his piano-playing, read to him in German and often had the ticklish duty of reading him to sleep at night. Thwaites did little reading, having taken over Butes's duty of handling correspondence, but other secretaries came and went, some of them World men on temporary duty, and most of them spent much of their time reading to him.

He constantly received tips on interesting reading from his friends, secretaries and World executives, Frank Cobb often sending suggestions. Occasional bundles of new books from Scribner's store reached him wherever he happened to be. Although he had long since absorbed many of the ancient classics—Plutarch, Thucydides, Herodotus, Plato, Aristotle, Tacitus—he reread stirring passages at intervals. Avoiding pure science, he enjoyed such leaders in contemporary thought as Spencer, Darwin and Huxley. He had little use for poetry, with notable exceptions such as Shakespeare and Goethe. Reading far more fiction than fact, he was familiar with scores of classics, among them the novels of Fielding, Thackeray, Sienkiewicz, the Brontës and Meredith, as well as with minor writers from Maarten Maartens to Walter Besant. Yet his fiction reading was largely for relaxation or cultivation, and most of his favorite books were factual. It was perhaps significant that he read many biographies of Napoleon (of whom he owned three portraits) and many accounts of the French Revolution, admiring Acton's and condemning Carlyle's. He much enjoyed Boswell's *Johnson,* Lord Hervey's memoirs, Montaigne and the memoirs of Madame Roland. In the middle of President Polk's diary he uttered an oath, pronounced Polk stupid and quit him. Since perhaps his most abiding interest was the study of greatness, and as an old orator he loved a stirring style, one of his top favorites was Macaulay's *Essays,* some of which he reread many times and could quote verbatim. He owned a portrait of Macaulay.

Vanity of course was strong in him, coupled with the conviction that his illnesses had robbed him of public greatness which would otherwise have been his, and he could not resist the substitute triumph of savoring and sometimes proving his superior knowledge of literature and the arts. Reading, which illumined his whole life, was so important to him that he judged his editors and secretaries to some extent by the books they had read. When a book impressed him he would send copies of it to his editors and friends—Morley's *Gladstone,* Acton's *French Revolution,* Dasent's life of John Delane, and above all Macaulay's *Essays* and Trevelyan's life of Macaulay, which he once sent to 39 people. To have failed to read a great book was to him sinful, and one of his gloomiest convictions was that most people, including his own children, were too lazy or uninterested to enlarge their talents by broad reading. He requested frequent reports from his children on what they were reading, and often sent them books, stressing works on music and art for Edith and Constance, although Constance, at least, also got the inevitable Macaulay. He enjoyed having his profitable annual *World Almanac* specially bound in sumptuous leather and giving it to a score of friends with the recipient's name lettered in gold. He once ordered scores of sets of the Encyclopedia Britannica to be sent to his editors and his children.

He had saved up the reading of the *Odyssey* for his later years, looking forward particularly to enjoying the Trojan horse episode. When he found it described in seven fairly commonplace lines he said, "I was so damned mad that I could have kicked Homer!" [6]

III. COMPLETE CONTROL

On December 5, Pulitzer's yacht slid down the ways at Leith, christened with the best champagne by Jane Tuohy, the small daughter of the World's London chief. Measuring 269 feet with a 35-foot beam, she was one of the biggest private yachts ever built, 65 feet longer than J. P. Morgan's second *Corsair* and only a few feet shorter than *Corsair III,* and costing about $1,500,000—twice as expensive as James Gordon Bennett's luxurious *Lysistrata.* Pulitzer named her *Liberty,* a word expressing his conception of the greatest good humanity could achieve and also recalling the World's rescue of the harbor Goddess. She was a beauty, all white but for masts and funnel. Commissioned early in January, she had every imaginable comfort for a blind man sensitive to noise—smooth teak decks with no bolts or projections, a huge cabin for Pulitzer sealed by thick carpeting, double bulkheads, double doors, double portholes and, in the big bathroom, a high washstand at which he could wash without stooping. His immense four-poster bed bristled with bell cords of different lengths so that he could call the major-domo, captain, head butler, chief steward or physician. Doors near his stateroom were lettered "This door is not to be opened when Mr. Pulitzer is asleep." The yacht had a crew of 60 men, plus his own personal staff, and had a coal capacity for 6,000 miles. Wireless equipment was purposely omitted so that he could escape the messages that excited him.

She steamed to Nice, where Pulitzer had been joined by Kate and Herbert. Tuohy had come up with another British secretary, Randall Davies, F.S.A., the son of a curate and the author of *The History of English Art*. He had also produced a tutor for Herbert, William Gray Elmslie, an Oxonian who would also serve on occasion as a Pulitzer secretary and who would ultimately marry Constance Pulitzer. While Kate went on to Aix, Pulitzer took a few trial cruises in the *Liberty*, one of them to Naples and Syracuse. He was much pleased with the craft—although, as a matter of policy, he complained of her inadequacies in a letter to Kate. "My dear Joseph," Kate wrote, "You have been as impossible to locate as a criminal hiding from justice." She met a friend who had seen his marble bust at a Paris exhibition: "I think she felt inclined to rush out & buy a mackintosh to cover your naked shoulders. She said it was a fine work . . . particularly because it showed great force & a dominating character—thank God it does, for I think this is high praise." [7]

Kate had also sent a panegyric about how splendid his portrait by Sargent appeared, lighted, in the hall at home. Laudation of one kind or another often appeared in family letters to him because it tickled his vanity, made him feel better, indeed because he rather expected it. It had become a family policy, somewhat like encomiums heaped on an ailing child, and Ralph joined in it with the rest. Ralph perhaps could not be said to be truly fond of his father. Though he had great sympathy for him and high regard for his abilities, he resented his tyranny and the absolute necessity to bow to this tyranny. His father was the cross the family had to bear with stiff upper lip. Pulitzer, the apostle of independence, had shorn Ralph most of all of independence, placing him somewhat in the position of a receiver of patronage who was expected to be grateful for it. Yet he felt forced to cater to the tyrant in many ways, among them by giving him the praise he so enjoyed. He wrote his father:

> I wish you could have been hidden in this room the other day when Cobb was speaking to me about you. He said that this anti Bryan campaign you had mapped out was the greatest intellectual achievement that he could remember of a man not actively in politics . . . that he would give anything to have you back here as there were such opportunities as only you could rise to, that you talked about your declining powers but

that he was convinced that your political genius was . . . far stronger than it ever had been before. And every word he said I would swear he honestly believed.[8]

On his 61st birthday Pulitzer distributed gifts again, one of them $10,000 for Ralph to buy art for his home. He had become a confirmed automobilist, enjoying tours of the invisible countryside, relishing the sensation of speed for its own sake, often dictating letters as he rode. One of them began, "Memo dictated in the automobile making 80 kilos per hour," another, "I have one leg out of the automobile getting off, horses waiting," and going on with long instructions. Now he moved to Aix for his cure and ordered a new 35-horsepower Renault for 31,500 francs, specifying that it must be "carefully tested and regulated to render it as *noiseless* as possible . . ." [9] Arranging for its September delivery at Wiesbaden, he returned to his yacht at Nice. She had been equipped with a reference library of 500 volumes that was growing fast, an assemblage of pharmaceuticals, a store of fine wines and other comforts, and in mid-June she set out across the Atlantic.

The *Liberty* was the last link in Pulitzer's elaborate artificial world, the best possible realization of it since in this luxurious craft he was uncontaminated by influences, regulations or persons beyond his jurisdiction and command, out of reach of church bells, trolleys and drill sergeants, surrounded only by things he desired and by some 75 employees, every one of them trained to cater to his whims. The yacht represented the logical end toward which the eccentric despot, so concerned with democracy, had been working for decades. It gave him *complete control.* It was an absolute monarchy, he was king, and the 75 employees were his subjects. He took great pride in his very own seagoing vessel and in the thought that she emancipated him from his dependence on White Star to get him across the ocean. (Even J. P. Morgan preferred not to risk the deep in his *Corsair,* always deadheading her across and joining her on the Mediterranean.)

The king, with his hundred ailments, was never afflicted with seasickness, even on the rough north Atlantic. Not all his subjects were so lucky. Stout Friedrich Mann groaned, "Always der cold gray sky, always der cold gray sea."

Pulitzer gave deep thought to the Democratic national convention coming up in July. He praised a Frank Cobb editorial, writing him, "By Acclamation! Your article clever—very clever. Thanks! Thanks particularly for brevity. Brevity is really beauty. . . . Take a drink!" [10] But the World espionage system was working, for he wrote Cobb later to enunciate a rule he seldom observed himself:

Private gossip, private belief, private conviction even, can never be permitted to be the basis of editorial action influencing cold, responsible and presumably provable and conscious type and print. I am more and more alarmed by the way you talk about public persons in private and perhaps allow this talk to influence your action, which should be judicious, calm, as well as conscientious—instead of personal and passionate.[11]

The *Liberty* sailed directly to Bar Harbor—a complete surprise to Kate and one not entirely pleasing since she had to alter her own plans and accommodate many extra guests without preparation. Pulitzer had warned Ralph not to attend the Democratic convention at Denver, because "they might want to know what the World will do after the nomination, perhaps be influenced by it and ask you questions which might commit you or me or the paper. Even silence can be misunderstood." [12] When the Democrats failed to perceive his "sense of the preposterous" and the perpetual candidate was nominated at Denver, Pulitzer decided after all that there was nothing to do but give him limited support. He wrote Cobb:

Guilder [Bryan] is as dead as a door nail. A vote for Guilder is not a practical living vote but a protest; a protest against the tendencies of the party in power; a check and rebuke to stop these tendencies; an exceedingly important rebuke and check if the vote is large enough to keep the party in power after the election on the anxious seat. Without such emphatic popular protest the successful party, instead of being checked and restrained, would be encouraged to carry these tendencies further than ever. A strong protest would also mean a strong opposition party, while the absence of such a protest would mean an impotent opposition without vitality or effect. . . . Guilder is not one one-hundredth, not one-thousandth part as dangerous or bad to-day as he was in 1896.

Again looking ahead, always looking ahead beyond November, Guilder absolutely beaten, new lines drawn, new men coming to the front, new ideas—Genuine will have ten times more influence, if it does not now antagonize Gosling [the Democratic party]. . . . there is no question that while we don't belong to the party as such we have always stood on the Democratic side and our honest sympathy and affiliations, not allegiance, are with that side. . . .[13]

He discovered that Cobb was so fed up with Bryan that he intended to vote for Taft. He would never ask—indeed never permit—his editor to write editorials against his conscience. Cobb was therefore excluded from editorializing on the presidential campaign and Ralph was given more responsibility for this, aided by other members of the staff including Horatio Seymour, recently brought in from the Post-Dispatch.

A Chatwold visitor was his old friend Charles H. Taylor of the Boston Globe who, although he described Pulitzer as "the greatest journalist this country has known," sometimes found his passion for minutiae tiring, as when he asked, "Taylor, do you know how many want ads we had in the *World* this morning?" [14] Taylor neither knew nor cared. In July the

Liberty took the Mustard-counter to New York, where he visited Ralph at Manhasset, communed with his executives in the Vault, and made news by visiting the Pulitzer Building on Sunday, July 26. The remarkable Esdaile Cohen was still there, now and then startling his colleagues by saying distinctly such things as, "God damn *The World.* God damn all editors. God damn Mr. Pulitzer. God damn everybody," and then going out for a drink.[15]

Pulitzer had been in the building only twice, very briefly, since its completion 18 years earlier. Now the occasion was to "see" the new addition. George Carteret, the telegraph news editor, was more than an hour late that morning after a convivial Saturday night. Arriving at 11, he rushed into the news room and shouted to Arthur Clarke, the news editor, "Arthur, Joseph Pulitzer is in the reception room! . . . Seitz, Lyman, Arthur Billing, and a swarm of secretaries are with him."

They heard the master's sharp voice in the corridor. "I'll go to Van Hamm's office if you say so, but I won't go in any damned roundabout way." He came in, wearing a business suit and dark glasses. A secretary pushed him gently to keep him from colliding with a telephone booth. "Clumsy!" he snapped. Shepherded by Seitz, Night Editor Robert H. Lyman and the secretaries, he entered the office of Managing Editor Caleb Van Hamm, who was home after a long night's work, then went into Lyman's office.

"How far is this room from the copy desk?" he asked.

"About fifty feet."

"That's damned foolish! Whose idea was it to put Lyman's room so far from the copy desk? Idiotic! Why not put it over in City Hall Park? The night editor must be near the copy desk. No nonsense about it. Swear you will change it!"

They swore it would be done, but it never was. He was introduced to Carteret, whom he had never met personally, and complimented him on good reports he had received of his work. He asked permission to feel Carteret's head, and in view of the telegraph editor's Saturday night there was suppressed laughter when he exclaimed, "My God! You have a big head, Mr. Carteret." Since Monday was usually a light news day, with a corresponding slump in circulation, Pulitzer had always demanded special effort to find rousing ideas for the Monday issue. ". . . What is in that big head for tomorrow's paper?"

Carteret, who had not yet read the day's news and had little in his head but an ache, attempted some evasion that was unsuccessful against this keen prosecutor. He finally admitted, "I regret it, Mr. Pulitzer, but you see—well, the fact is that I was a little late this morning."

The blind man frowned. There was an exchange of worried glances among Seitz, Lyman and the rest. "When I was on Park Row," Andes said, "I had all the papers read before eight o'clock. . . . Mr. Carteret, you have spoiled my morning!"

Carteret's morning had also become dolorous. But Pulitzer relented a trifle, saying he would invite him to Chatwold. "And for God's sake, when you come, please be prepared. I swear I shall ask you many questions. You must not mind that. It will be for your own good." (He later sent Carteret tickets to a Damrosch concert.) He spoke kindly with Clarke, who *had* read the news and in response to questions reeled off a summary of his plans for the Monday World. Pulitzer put his hand on Clarke's head. "That is where your Monday morning feature should be. You must cudgel your brain all week for it." As he left with his troupe, he said:

"I know you will have a good paper tomorrow, Mr. Clarke." [16]

It was his last visit to the Pulitzer Building.

IV. UNPRESIDENTIAL GLUTINOUS CONDUCT

After leaving pleas with his family and friends to find him more secretaries, Pulitzer sailed for Plymouth from New London in the *Liberty* in August. He was fleeing the intimate involvement in the presidential election which he could not resist if he stayed in America. He had snatched Arthur Billing away from the World to aid him for a season. A terrible crisis loomed, for this was the last voyage of Dr. Hosmer, who was about to retire in his 80th year, and Tuohy had been alerted to find a British physician of exemplary endowments. Tuohy was in for trouble, for no one could replace Hosmer. He boarded the yacht at Cowes with a candidate. At dinner the new doctor made the error of cutting an apple so that his knife clattered repeatedly against the plate. "We watched the storm rising on Pulitzer's face," Thwaites recalled. "To relieve the tension I remarked to the . . . offender: 'If you cannot break that plate with your knife, I will send for the ship's axe.' It had the desired effect and the great man laughed."

What was his favorite novel, Pulitzer demanded of the candidate, who had little knowledge of books and was at a loss. One of the secretaries, intending to help, slipped him a note with *The Ordeal of Richard Feverel* scribbled on it—an error, for now Pulitzer pressed him with questions about the characters and situations in the novel. The physician stumbled hopelessly until at last the prosecutor said with quiet bitterness, "I suppose you *can* read?" The doctor made his farewell after dinner, muttering, "I would not accept the job at ten thousand a year." [17]

Several other candidates failed, one because he wore perfume, which Andes could not abide. Tuohy would spend many more months canvassing Harley Street and all of London. The party sailed on to Amsterdam and entrained for Wiesbaden, where they were joined by young Herbert, who had come to Europe with his mother, now taking the cure at Divonne. From Wiesbaden Pulitzer cabled Cobb to support Hughes for reelection as governor but to favor the Democrats on the rest of the ticket. A report that the corporation attorney William Nelson Cromwell had given $50,000 to the Taft campaign fund drew his attention:

> Who is he? What great devotion to public purity and public morality has he contributed? Examine his record, especially his Panama record and his relations with corporations and trusts. Is it true he gave $50,000 to the campaign fund? If so, why? [18]

He ordered broadsides against Rough-Riderism and Republican corruption. About Hearst, who had entered the campaign with his own Independent party with little-known candidates for President and some state offices, he changed his mind. He had first felt Hearst entitled to respect for forming a national third party. Now he wrote:

> The Republican party only means to defeat the Democratic, but the Hearst, Debs, Watson parties mean to destroy it and to build upon its ruins a new party. . . . Question: Would it be best for the country if the Democratic party were destroyed by a new party, led by Hearst and Debs? Would it not be *infinitely worse* however many faults the Democratic party may have? [19]

Although racked by acute dyspepsia, headaches, and insomnia, he gave more thought to the education of Herbert, lavishing on him a love that was heightened by his growing belief that the boy had abilities enough to repay him for his disappointments in Ralph and Joseph, and might some day take over the dynasty. It was the old story—his affection for the child and his impatience with the adult—but it was more than that. It was an evidence of his loneliness, his great need to pour love on someone, particularly someone who was still totally dependent on him, someone not yet guilty of mature ideas that countered his own. He advertised for a German tutor for Herbert. Sixty candidates were interviewed before one satisfied him, as he let Kate know in petulant letters:

> I have done everything I could with the utmost care and pains as to the uttermost details. I can't repeat myself as I have even a worse headache than yesterday. I am sure that no man in my condition would have taken such infinite pains even as to trifles and his diet as I have done,—I think really at the expense of sleepless nights. . . .
>
> I also arranged that a German riding teacher should accompany Herbert who must only talk German when he rides. . . .
>
> Nobody will ever know how often I collapsed in cross-examining these candidates. If Herbert will ever give me credit for anything which he will not do any more than you, it ought to be about the trouble and acute mental suffering I have passed through trying to find a tutor for him—trying to

correct the terrible initial mistake in . . . depriving him of both German and French at the right time.[20]

Although Herbert had his mother's sunny nature, the knowledge that he was regarded as precocious and was being prepared for greatness was not inclined to develop humility in a 13-year-old. His diet was supervised, his hours scheduled, his activities regulated, his playmates carefully screened—the prince in training for the throne, with the king keeping a fond eye on him. By the clock he studied, wrote papers in German, rode in the park, played tennis, dressed for dinner and attended the Wiesbaden opera, hearing, among others, Caruso in *Rigoletto*. It was Pulitzer's intention to sail October 6 on a leisurely cruise that would get him home just before election time, and to leave Herbert at Wiesbaden to continue his studies. He and his entourage traveled to Amsterdam, where the *Liberty* awaited them, and where he found he could not bear being separated from Herbert, who was summoned to meet the yacht with his tutor and governess at Cherbourg.

"Herbert going with me," Pulitzer wired Kate, "was miserable without him, almost prostrated. Have good German tutor. . . ."

The *Liberty* tarried at Madeira, where he wrote Kate, "I still sleep badly and this morning my old enemy the stomach catarrh knocked me out despite two bolstering drinks of brandy." [21] Dr. Hosmer, with blessed retirement now in sight, had his troubles with the invalid on the long ocean voyage, and several of the secretaries were seasick. Reaching New York by November 1, Pulitzer telegraphed Cobb in a tone lacking that calm dispassion he urged on his editors:

> Closing days make memorable dropping timidity for hot shot against Glutinous crooks corruption[,] you concentrating forging bullets sharp pithy bullseye paragraphs scattered in news columns daily[,] including Junior [,] Gamma [Seymour] concentrating on editorials summing up campaign showing unprincipled undignified unpresidential Glutinous conduct. . . .[22]

He established himself in the Vault and on election day gave Cobb a careful definition of the World's post-election policy. Rotund's (Taft's) election would be due to Guilder's weakness rather than Rotund's strength. Rotund had failings galore (he listed many) including some inherited from Glutinous' "Reign of Terror," which it was to be hoped Rotund would end.

> Lastly and Firstly, of course, you will say whatever can be said in appreciation of Taft emphatically pledging the support of the *World* wherever he shows that judicial, magisterial, independent spirit in administering law and government according to reason and justice, which the country peculiarly needs in the successor of Rough-riderism. [He included ideas for headlines and editorial slants.] All this is respectfully submitted

with the repeated injunction that it is only submitted subject to your free will in accordance with the figures.

This is dictated exactly at seventeen minutes before three P.M., before a single poll has been counted, but after a very thick headache, and the Lord only knows what surprises the figures may contain.

. . . I honestly declare that I want you to say nothing that your conscience, carefully examined, does not approve as really true. Impartiality, entire dismissal of prejudice [or] personal dislike alone can discover the real truth. I know this is difficult, especially to a gentleman of your ardent temperament, but I pay you the compliment of supposing that you at least try. I pay you another compliment, which possibly I may regret, as I have not read your damned page for over a month, and that is that you have labored under very trying circumstances, which I appreciate.[23]

He went to bed at ten as usual, refusing to await the returns. Taft was elected by a popular plurality of 1,269,906 over Bryan, a bit less than half of Roosevelt's plurality in 1904, showing some Democratic resurgence. Pulitzer was annoyed to discover that Seitz and other World executives had become interested enough in Bryan to vote for him. "I didn't mean that they should do that," he said. "I hope no one had such a thought. I did not want to influence them at all." He warned Cobb to stress the rebuilding of the Democratic party, to make it plain that the World had not supported Bryan personally but as a protest. His verdict on Bryan was penetrating:

He . . . will remain an important factor and force on the Democratic side although he never can, never will be elected President. He is an agitator, not an administrator. So far he has only been of great service to the Republican party, having done more to keep it in power than a thousand Republican speakers. Let us hope he will realize the final verdict of the people, drop the Presidential bee and devote himself to real Democratic ideas.[24]

Despite his conviction that Roosevelt was "entirely unfitted" for the Presidency, Pulitzer felt that he, and every ex-President, "ought to have a liberal pension of $25,000 a year, and a seat in the Senate." The announcement that after retiring Roosevelt would become an editor of *Outlook* drew a caustic comment:

. . . With all respect for journalism, whose noble ideas we appreciate far more than Mr. Roosevelt, the [pension] plan would prevent the purchase for cash of an ex-President of the United States . . . four months before he actually leaves the White House [he] is already used as an advertisement all over the world, just like a new and attractive liver pill or skin soap.[25]

Frederick Duneka had suggested to him a candidate for sailing companion, 40-year-old James Barnes, who went through two long grillings at the hands of Dr. Hosmer, noting, "One might have thought that I was an applicant for an honorary degree to judge from the examination to which the doctor submitted me." [26] The sociable son of a New York railroad mogul, Barnes had had a colorful career as foreign correspondent, globe-trotter, clubman, magazine editor and writer. Passing muster, he was invited to dine with Pulitzer and the staff at 73rd Street, and was a member of the entourage (Pollard being the only other American) when the *Liberty* set sail for Havana later in November. Before leaving, Pulitzer had given Ralph permission for a fortnight's hunting in New Brunswick—an excursion that would have astonishing consequences.

V. *A BIG DRINK OF WHISKEY*

The specialist in self-torment found much of it in his anxiety over the competence of his sons to carry on his newspaper dynasty. In the Vanderbilt family he saw the tendency of great energy and enterprise to dwindle in succeeding generations to mere fashionable wealth. He had greater respect for robber barons than for coupon-clippers and wastrels. John W. Garrett, he noted, had built the Baltimore & Ohio into a mighty system, and his son had destroyed it. Jay Gould was long gone ("Ten thousand ruined men will curse the dead man's memory," the World had said), and see how his sons had dissipated his holdings!

Pulitzer employed methods not always free from cruelty to prevent the same decline in his own progeny. He insisted that Ralph and Joseph be fit not only to manage the World and Post-Dispatch as successful business enterprises but also as powerful and beneficent public institutions, and he was eternally dissatisfied with them both.

Joseph was under somewhat less pressure, being younger and being in St. Louis, where the management was instructed by his father, "He is to be treated . . . exactly as if his name were Joe Smith or Joe Brown." [27] Once, when Pulitzer suggested that he return to New York, he replied carefully that he felt he was improving himself on the Post-Dispatch and that he did not trust himself among the temptations of New York, where "the very air is full of amusement, frivolity & dissipation." [28] Possibly also he preferred his comparative remoteness from the parental scrutiny. There was plenty of this as it was, Pulitzer once sending him a long Pollard-written copy of one of Lord Chesterfield's letters to his son including the admonition, "You ought, for your own sake, to attend to and follow my advice. If, by the application which I recommend to you, you acquire great knowledge, you alone are the gainer; I pay for it." [29]

Ralph at the World, however, was under endless Andean supervision. He had dutifully written his father, "You don't know how hard I shall try to take some of that burden off you . . . ." [30] but there was some question whether his father *wanted* to relinquish the burden. He had raised Ralph's salary and suggested that he would soon be in line for the presidency, to which Ralph had replied in an access of joy, "I am sure you would be pleased if you could know how a word of praise from you makes me feel for the rest of the day as though I had just had a big drink of whiskey—so happy and exhilarated, and as if I could surmount any obstacle or perform any task." [31] But praise was rarer than censure, and Kate felt impelled to write her husband that he should be proud of Ralph, adding, "In the future should Ralph not come up to your expectations in some things or dissatisfy you in others, remember that you cannot make a man to please yourself, but let the man make himself even though his way might not be your way." She returned to the theme in another letter:

> Ralph goes to the office early & stays late. I wish you at all realized how entirely his heart is in the paper & its success. I wish you could realize your want of realization of his ambition & hopes for the future, particularly since his marriage. . . . He is very proud & very sensitive & very shy & I think timid about expressing these things to you.[32]

Pulitzer had trained Ralph for eight years, with the inevitable disappointment because he was not superhuman. At 29 he was over six feet tall, weighed under 140 pounds and had to be careful about his health. He was long on brain, a careful executive and a polished writer, but he had no more than average aggressiveness, the quality his father demanded in his own Pulitzerian superabundance. Pulitzer had often taxed him about this, thrust him into duties calculated to stimulate his ardor, ordered him to join civic clubs and enter into public affairs, and once had wired him, ". . . Try make personal acquaintances have self confidence don't be too modest." Ralph had heard the whip cracking over him even more than had Seitz or White. The insistence that he report in lavish detail was constant, one fatherly message reading in part, "important write write and also write." [33] His salary had once been stopped for a month because Pulitzer felt him laggard in this respect. The martinet tone of some of the chieftain's orders to him is indicated by an earlier letter:

> Please read this note every day for at least one week until every word has engraved itself upon your mind & observe my wishes strictly.
>
> If you are well enough spend at least 5 hours a day at the office *concentrating* your entire mind on the study of management, managers, editors, talking to everybody of importance on anything of interest but particularly to the 3 principal managers. You are to comprehend what I want as I have expressed myself on this point 100 times or more with the utmost detail.
>
> 2nd. While doing this during my absence stop writing editorials as it would divert your mind from the supreme effort of concentration on management which is your great need and which I desire.
>
> 3rd. In doing this fix upon your mind the idea that I am dead & that you are president of the company in my place with supreme powers—an hypothesis most natural & presumably not remote.

4th. Keep a diary of your observations & make entries every evening—ready to send when I telegraph. Don't neglect this a single day.

5th. Wake up.

Affectionately, Father [34]

It is likely that Pulitzer never quite recovered from the loss of Butes, and his overexcitement about the election had taken its toll. When he had ordered Ralph to assume much of the political responsibility for the World because of Cobb's preference for Taft, his words were not far from contemptuous:

> I do not think you are any more fit for this opportunity than Thwaites. I ought to leave the paper in charge of a man. . . . Although you are not fit for it I would rather put you in charge of that political sub-division. It is a choice of evils. I have at least some hope that you understand my views.[35]

Undoubtedly there were times when Ralph asked himself, asked his wife, asked his mother whether he could longer pocket such treatment without protest. If so, he realized that while Andes would accept measured protest from his other executives, he would brook none from his own children, and there was at any rate the blessing that he was never at the Dome looking over one's shoulder. He was not a normal individual and had to be accorded the concessions given to abnormality. If he was a monster at times, there were also those occasions (when he felt like it) when he could be warmly generous and affectionate. His kindnesses, however, seemed to be dwindling and his unreasonableness increasing, since for two years his health and temper had usually been bad. Father was the family problem, childish, demanding, mercurial, outrageous, autocratic, obsessed—but all-powerful. He was the despot before whom all the Pulitzers genuflected because he insisted on genuflection. All of them (except for Kate's limited essays at financial freedom) catered to him with implicit obedience, obeisant letters of sympathy, and praise for his achievements. Behind it all was the strong familial attachment that had been more and more superseded by fear of his power and probably by fear for his sanity.

Ralph left for Canada November 8, reached a remote camp in New Brunswick and for a week was cut off by snows so heavy that a messenger entrusted to deliver his mail failed to get through. As a result he did not get back to the Dome until December 4. Meanwhile Pulitzer tried to reach him, evidently from Havana, and found him still absent. To him a fortnight was a fortnight, and nothing infuriated him more than a relaxed attitude toward office attendance.

When Ralph entered his office he was visited by a worried J. Angus Shaw, the World treasurer for many years. Shaw showed him a cable from Pulitzer. It instructed Shaw to cut off Ralph's December salary and to ask his resignation as vice president of the World.

Pulitzer, who believed that a man's true mettle was shown best by his reaction to crisis, occasionally tested his staff by supplying the crisis. One might suspect that this was such a test except that Ralph, who knew his father's methods intimately, did not so interpret it.

Pulitzer's order was cruel and irrational. Ralph's shock and humiliation were increased by the dispatch of the order through Shaw, letting him relay the news as if to a subaltern rather than dealing directly with Ralph and keeping it in the family. Ralph immediately cabled his resignation of the vice-presidency. Probably he had little doubt that he still retained an executive post. But his ousting from the vice-presidency would become a minor but embarrassing family scandal, with gossip flying not only in the journalistic fraternity but also in his own wealthy social circle. He would have been scarcely human had he not yearned at this mortifying moment to emancipate himself with one crisp, sharp letter to his father, perhaps saying that he would take a position with Hearst or with the Tribune.

But on realistic examination this was impossible on several counts. Worse yet, Ralph knew that his father knew that *he* knew it was impossible. This was another of those situations where Pulitzer had clear mastery—the complete financial and moral control he always sought. Ralph was now drawing at least $50,000 annually from the World (i.e., from his father) in salary, allowance and gifts. He had lived up to it to the hilt, enforcing his own dependence on his father's largesse. He had lost his independence. He had in fact never had any; his father had never allowed him any. For all his abilities, with his indifferent health any other position he might have secured would have paid him much less, placing him in financial straits that would have humiliated him socially and in his relations with his wife's wealthy family. He simply could not afford to strike out for his own liberty, nor could he have forgotten that to do so would also be to renounce an inheritance of millions that otherwise would eventually be his. Moreover, he was to the core a Pulitzer, a World man. One powerful consideration was Joseph Pulitzer, a great and famous personage who might be trembling on the verge of nervous collapse and who might, unless this were handled carefully, slip into the abyss. Word had come that he was in terrible shape, and the cable to Shaw confirmed it.

Ralph was as imprisoned by his responsibility for his father's health and sanity as he was by his own financial requirements. "Handling it carefully" meant dutiful submission. Few scions of wealth must drink such a bitter draft as that handed to Ralph in the form of a few curt words from Cuba.

He composed a 13-page letter to his father with more care than he ever put into a World editorial, employing the tone of Oriental reverence that was expected but nicely balancing the concession that his father had a right to be angry with the argument that his decision was unjust and unwise:

My dear Father, On going to the office yesterday on my return from the woods, Shaw showed me your cable instructing him to cut off my December pay and to request my resignation of the Vice Presidency. With this request I immediately complied as I cabled you. On the night previously I had been distressed to read, in your cable to Mother, in what wretched condition and situation you were; yesterday I was deeply grieved to see the proof of that condition in your cable to Shaw, for I should not like to believe that you would normally have sent such a message.

I can appreciate perfectly how you could have been displeased at my lengthened absence, without any explanation to you, how you had a perfect right to expect such an explanation and (if such explanation were not satisfactory) to inflict punishment. That you did not await the explanation before inflicting the punishment, (a course of common justice which you would ordinarily not have denied the humblest groom in your stable) distresses me greatly. I do sincerely hope that the week's cruise of which you cabled Mother has in the meantime greatly improved your health and spirits, and that when you now read the following explanation you will agree that I was not so much to blame as you originally considered me.

He explained that his "fortnight's" outing meant a fortnight actually in Canada, with travel time added, as in the past, though he apologized for not making this clear. He told of the snow that had further delayed him. He mentioned the illnesses he had suffered—some of them inherited from his father—and the agreement of four physicians that he must take time off for "roughing it" to preserve his health. "Dr. James put the proportion at 3 months out of every year—as much as that I do not ask, but I do need and must take approximately one month every fall and one month every spring. You yourself have been always the first to agree with this theory, and have been kind and considerate in yourself suggesting my going off on these trips as you did this very fall. . . ."

Now as to cutting off my December pay—there too I concede your perfectly just right to do so in the capacity of my *employer* . . . But in this case I wish to appeal to you not in the capacity of my *employer,* but as my *father.* For I cannot think that you would wish to deprive your son of the means of supporting himself and his family; yet that is the condition in which I am placed by my pay being stopped. For you know, my dear Father, that I have no income save that which you give me and have no means of creating an income while I work on the paper without pay.

He and Frederica, he went on, had economized by reducing the number of their horses and in other ways, but what with the baby and the cost of maintaining the town house and their summer place at Manhasset they had no reserve. "I am sure you will see therefore that if my pay is stopped even for one month, I have either to leave my bills unpaid and run into permanent debt which I cannot do, or I am obliged to let Frederica ask her parents to increase her allowance, and this latter I am sure you will agree with me is the last thing in the wide world I should or would do." He apologized for so long a letter. "But the present circumstances seem to make a clear understanding of the whole question absolutely necessary . . ." He asked for a cabled reply to relieve his suspense.[36]

It took the letter some days to reach his father, and of course had to be read to him by a secretary. Certainly he weighed every word of it. Diplomatic and well-reasoned it was, but lacking in the "force and fire" he worshiped and perhaps adding to his disappointment in his son, though the son scarcely could have written otherwise. Joseph Pulitzer himself would never have written such a letter. But while he had the breath of life in him he would not permit Vanderbilt money to support his son. He restored Ralph's salary without restoring the vice-presidency—a sign of his opinion that the young man did not measure up to the job. Indeed he suggested that Ralph sound out John M. Bowers of the law firm of Bowers & Sands, who had long been a World attorney, for the post. Bowers declined because it would conflict with his legal duties and added a cogent reason:

> It would be bad for Andes because I know him . . . well enough to know that my holding the vice presidency would lead to a permanent rupture of all our relations within a year. For Andes is by nature excessively suspicious. It arises I suppose partly from his blindness, and partly from the treatment he has received from men he trusted in the past . . .[37]

The worry about it all was perhaps a factor in Ralph's recurrence of ill health. Within a fortnight, at the suggestion of the suddenly remorseful Andes, he left for Paris with his wife and then went on to Pau to recover his strength.

Chapter 8

Roosevelt vs. Pulitzer

1. INTRIGUE OVER PANAMA

When Pulitzer complained of Roosevelt's "reign of terror" he meant his impulsive and autocratic manner of government. Now, although the Rough Rider had only a few months left in office, a Roosevelt reign of terror of a more specific sort was brewing, with Pulitzer himself as the target.

It had its beginnings in the President's roughshod policy in 1903 when he sent warships to Panama just in time to aid a revolution which succeeded in establishing the independence of Panama, formerly a province of Colombia. The revolution had come with delightful timeliness for the United States, since Colombia had objected to the plan to cut a canal through the isthmus whereas the new republic of Panama instantly agreed to everything. It was evident that this was more than happy chance and that some furtive arrangement had preceded the revolution. Strangely, no one—not even the World—inquired very deeply into the affair at the time, and it took years to uncover a melodrama of international flimflammery and multimillion-dollar legerdemain that has no parallel. Pulitzer showed his usual prescience in asking why William Nelson Cromwell gave $50,000 to the 1908 Republican war chest, for the lawyer-promoter Cromwell was the leading actor in the tropical extravaganza, with a company of thousands. To understand how Pulitzer came to be cast as the villain of the piece, branded an enemy of the country and threatened with imprisonment, one must go back over the facts.

The old French company formed by Ferdinand de Lesseps had raised $260,000,000 and had begun work on the Panama Canal, but much of the money was dissipated corruptly and the project sank into bankruptcy and scandal in 1889. Shrewd Philippe Bunau-Varilla, who at 26 had become chief engineer of construction, returned to his native Paris to raise more money. In 1894 the New Panama Canal Company was formed, taking over the assets of the original syndicate, including the Panama railroad. But since 600,000 French peasants had lost their savings in the De Lesseps disaster, it was impossible to raise capital in Europe. Soon Bunau-Varilla and the new French company gave up any idea of completing the canal and their sole object became to sell their rights to the United States for as much as the traffic would bear. The handsome, persuasive Cromwell, senior member of the New York firm of Sullivan & Cromwell, was retained to aid them. In 1899 he began four years of energetic lobbying, political manipulation and campaign donation that would make him in a very real sense the father of the Panama Canal.

The United States had long determined to build a canal, but there was strong sentiment favoring Nicaragua as the site rather than Panama. The Nicaragua idea was abhorrent to Cromwell and Bunau-Varilla, since it would leave their company out in the cold. Cromwell gave $60,000 to the Republican campaign fund in 1900, and possibly this had some bearing on a change in the party platform, which originally had favored "a Nicaraguan Canal" but came out instead for "an Isthmian Canal." [1] Thereafter both Cromwell and Bunau-Varilla and their press agents spent much of their time in Washington, stressing the great advantages of the Panama route. Bunau-Varilla saw the powerful Senator Hanna, won him over to the Panama idea, and even had a talk with President McKinley, who began to speak favorably of Panama. Meanwhile Cromwell organized an American syndicate about which very little was known but whose purpose was to buy up the assets of the French company and finish the canal in Panama. Backers of this syndicate were said to include J. P. Morgan, August Belmont, Levi P. Morton and others.

But in December 1901 McKinley's Isthmian Canal Commission reported in favor of Nicaragua, with compelling reasons. The French company was asking $109,000,000 for its assets, which would raise the cost of a Panama canal far above that for one in Nicaragua. The French rights in Panama, the commission insisted, were worth no more than $40,000,000. Bunau-Varilla hurried to Paris, where he persuaded the French group to lower their price to that exact $40,000,000. Roosevelt, now President, favored Panama as a result and persuaded the commission to switch its recommendation to Panama. But Nicaragua still had many supporters and the commission's report stipulated that that route should be used if Panama proved unavailable. In fact, the House in 1902 passed a bill for a Nicaraguan canal, and with the decision up to the Senate in May, Cromwell and Bunau-Varilla faced the ruin of all their hopes unless enough senators could be made to see the light.

Bunau-Varilla returned on the fastest steamer to join Cromwell in Washington. These two used every kind of influence they could exert,

Bunau-Varilla conceiving the idea that the Nicaraguan route was dangerous because of active volcanoes. Why build a canal that would be destroyed by stone and lava? He must have been overjoyed when on May 6 Mt. Pelée erupted, destroying St. Pierre and bringing home the idea to thoughtful senators. His luck was even better eight days later, just before the final Senate debate, when Mt. Monotombo in Nicaragua erupted. It happened that Nicaragua had an engraving of a volcano on its stamps. Bunau-Varilla sent Nicaraguan stamps to every senator, stressing the volcanoes along with propaganda showing the superiorities of the Panama route. The Senate thereupon voted in favor of Panama, to which the House quickly agreed. The bill authorized President Roosevelt to buy the property and rights of the New Panama Canal Company for not more than $40,000,000; and to get from Colombia on terms he felt reasonable a strip of land not less than six miles wide for the canal. If satisfactory terms could not be made, he was authorized to negotiate for a Nicaraguan canal.

Secretary of State John Hay began parleying with General José Concha, the Colombian envoy in Washington. But Concha felt that Colombia should get some payment from the New Panama Canal Company as well as from the United States, and he was also angered by Senate changes in the proposal which he said imperiled Colombian sovereignty. In November 1902 Concha returned to Colombia because of failing health.

Hay resumed negotiations with Concha's chargé, Dr. Tomás Herran, who gradually came around after Hay frightened the Colombian government by warning that the Nicaraguan route would be substituted. On January 22, 1903, he signed the Hay-Herran treaty which proposed to give Colombia $10,000,000 in gold and an annual rental of $250,000 for permission to build the canal and control the adjacent zone.

A point to bear in mind is that the treaty protected Cromwell's interests by stipulating that Colombia could not dicker independently with the New Panama Canal Company—that is, ask a share of the $40,000,000 the United States would pay that company—which would seem to show that Cromwell's influence had been successful. But despite Herran's signing of the treaty for his government, there was immediate resentment in Colombia. Although the United States Senate quickly ratified the treaty, it appeared that Colombia would not, and Roosevelt was furious at the "contemptible little creatures in Bogota." [2] Hay took the surprising step of warning Colombia that delay or rejection of the treaty might impair the friendly understanding between the two countries. Bunau-Varilla warned Colombia's envoys that Panama would secede unless the canal project were authorized. Both Cromwell and Bunau-Varilla were active in Washington, with ready access to lawmakers and Cabinet members, and Cromwell had at least one talk with the President. It was at this time that the World published an oddly prophetic Washington dispatch saying that the President was determined to have the Panama route, that Cromwell had had "a long conversation with the President," and that "Panama stands ready to secede . . . and enter into a canal treaty with the United States."[3] The reason for its clairvoyance was that the information came from a Cromwell press agent seeking to intimidate Colombia into approving the treaty.

On August 12 the Colombian Senate confounded them all by rejecting the treaty unanimously. It wanted a $10,000,000 payment from the New Panama Canal Company and it preferred not to relinquish all sovereignty in the canal zone.

One can imagine the despair of Cromwell and Bunau-Varilla, for now the United States Senate, irked by the delay, could ask for negotiations with volcanic Nicaragua. The President, however, had his back up and would not submit to Colombian "blackmail." He had talks with both Cromwell and Bunau-Varilla. To friends he said confidentially that it would be convenient if Panama were an independent state. In a draft of his message to Congress he urged that the United States take possession of the isthmus "without any further parley with Colombia"—a suggestion that was removed in a later draft.

Cromwell and Bunau-Varilla now set out to free Panama from the Colombian yoke. They were aided by the fact that the Panama Railroad Company was owned by the New Panama Canal Company and had many agents in Panama City and Colón who could be useful in starting a rebellion. Bunau-Varilla set up headquarters at the Waldorf-Astoria in New York, where he was visited by Dr. Manuel Amador, the revolutionist physician for the railroad company. Bunau-Varilla laid out the plan: He would supply $100,000 for advance expenses for the revolution, to be staged November 3; he supplied also a draft of a new Panama constitution and even a message to be sent when Panama was free. This last was a deft touch, for the message was an appeal to Bunau-Varilla (though a French citizen) to become the first Panamanian minister to the United States. Meanwhile Madame Bunau-Varilla, as liberty-loving as her husband, was stitching away at a Panamanian flag she had designed, with red and yellow stripes flanked by two suns.

Dr. Amador, of course, knew that the $10,000,000 offered to Colombia would instead go to the Panama republic. He returned to Panama, where General Esteban Huertas, commander of the Colombian garrison, was reportedly bribed with $25,000 to become commander of the rebels, and other bribes were distributed. The opéra-bouffe revolution occurred on November 4, only a day late. Its success was assured by the arrival of the United States warships *Nashville* and *Dixie,* sent by the President under his own astonishing definition of an old treaty guaranteeing "free transit" on the Panama Railroad. His determination to maintain free transit was underlined by the subsequent arrival of five more United States naval vessels. The only failure of the Cromwell-Bunau-Varilla New Panama Canal Company interests was in the selection of a flag, for the revolutionists rejected Madame Bunau-Varilla's creation and on November 6 raised one of their own design, proclaiming the new Republic of Panama, with Dr. Amador as provisional president.

Scarcely an hour later Secretary of State Hay recognized the new Amador government.[4]

Not yet was Bunau-Varilla quite at ease, for the Amador government might demand a piece of the $40,000,000 the United States was to pay the canal company. He hurried to Washington, where he was recognized as minister from Panama and where he signed, with Hay, the treaty for the canal. The new republic made Cromwell its general counsel. The United States paid the $40,000,000 to the New Panama Canal Company, and the $10,000,000 to the Panama Republic. The whole shabby affair reflected the United States government's extreme care to safeguard the private financial interests of the New Panama Canal Company and a cynical disregard for the rights of Colombia, whose sense of outrage lingered for decades. Roosevelt's feelings thereafter were divided between great pride in his successful inaugural of the canal and some unhappiness at the methods used, and he was as sensitive on the subject as a dowager about a past indiscretion.[5]

All this was not well understood at the time, although the World was so critical of Bunau-Varilla's activities that he threatened suit. In 1908 the whole affair came to the surface in the oddest of ways, to cause war between Pulitzer and the President. Even then, Cromwell, who had sent a bill to the canal company for $800,000 for his services (and had listed himself in *Who's Who* as "instrumental in securing passage of Panama bill in Congress"), was still being bothered by various Panamanians who felt they had not been paid adequately for their part in the revolution and demanded more. Cromwell called this blackmail. On the night of October 2 he sent one of his press agents, Jonas Whitley, to the World's managing editor, Caleb Van Hamm, to warn him not to print falsities about Cromwell. Whitley said that a Cromwell partner, William J. Curtis, had complained to District Attorney Jerome that the Panama blackmailers were even threatening to make political use of their charges in the 1908 campaign. Cromwell evidently was uneasy, seeking to spike a campaign against him and the Republicans before it got started. The World published a story authorized by Cromwell and checked word for word by Whitley, reading in part:

> In brief, Mr. Curtis told Mr. Jerome it had been represented to Mr. Cromwell that the Democratic National Convention was considering the advisability of making public a statement that William Nelson Cromwell, in connection with M. Bunau-Varilla, a French speculator, had formed a

> syndicate at the time when it was quite evident that the United States would take over the rights of the French bond-holders in the . . . Canal, and that this syndicate included among others Charles P. Taft, brother of William H. Taft, and Douglas Robinson, brother-in-law of President Roosevelt. Other men more prominent in the New York world of finance were also mentioned.
>
> According to the story unfolded by Mr. Curtis, it was said that the men making this charge against Mr. Cromwell had averred that the syndicate thus organized in connection with Bunau-Varilla had gone into the French market and purchased for about $3,500,000 the stocks and bonds of the defunct de Lesseps company, and of the newer concern which had taken over the old company . . .
>
> These financiers invested their money because of a full knowledge of the intention of the Government to acquire the French property at a price of about $40,000,000, and thus—because of their alleged information from high Government sources—were enabled to reap a rich harvest.[6]

Along with this the World published a Cromwell statement denying all the charges. Nevertheless, the charges received as much publicity as the denial, and Cromwell's move must have been inspired by real apprehension. Van Hamm was guilty of imprudence in bringing in the names of Taft and Robinson without first interviewing the two. Taft later denied any connection with the Panama syndicate, while Robinson refused to make any statement. The complaint to District Attorney Jerome came to nothing, and before election day the World published five articles critical of the canal deal.

The story was then picked up by the prosperous Indianapolis News, which was universally believed to be owned by Delavan Smith although the actual owner was Vice President Charles W. Fairbanks. Fairbanks was incensed because he had been sidetracked when Roosevelt forced the nomination of Taft. On November 2, the day before the election, the News published an editorial asking embarrassing questions about the Panama enterprise:

> The campaign is over and the people will have to vote tomorrow without any official knowledge concerning the Panama Canal deal. It has been charged that the United States bought from American citizens for $40,000,000 property that cost those citizens only $12,000,000 [*sic*]. Mr. Taft was Secretary of War at the time the negotiation was closed. There is no doubt that the government paid $40,000,000 for the property. But who got the money? We are not to know. The administration and Mr. Taft do not think it right that the people should know. The President's brother-in-law is involved in the scandal, but he has nothing to say. The candidate's brother has been charged with being a member of the syndicate. He has, it is true, denied it. But he refuses to appeal to the evidence, all of which is

in the possession of the administration, and wholly inaccessible to outsiders. For weeks this scandal has been before the people. The records are in Washington, and they are public records. But the people are not to see them—till after the election, if then.

Here was the first clear newspaper charge of a scandal, based on the original World account from Cromwell. But the News was on its own in its dangerous and unverified suggestion of misdoing on the part of Robinson and Taft. The President took his time about replying, and meanwhile Pulitzer, unaware of the brewing storm, was sailing homeward from Havana.

11. MY GOD! NO PROOF!

The new secretary-companion James Barnes noted that although Pulitzer could be unreasonable, he exerted a "distinct fascination" and was so agreeable to Barnes that "I actually looked forward with eagerness to the companionship of his mind." [7] The *Liberty* put in at Charleston on December 7. On that same day Roosevelt's reply to the Indianapolis News charges was published in all the morning papers. Don Seitz and Joseph Pulitzer Jr., meeting the yacht at Charleston, brought aboard the local News & Courier, which was read to Pulitzer. The President called Delavan Smith of the News "infamous," and in answer to the specific charges said in part:

> The fact has been officially published again and again that the Government paid $40,000,000 . . . direct to the French Government . . . The United States Government has not the slightest knowledge as to the particular individuals among whom the French Government distributed the sum. That was the business of the French Government. The mere supposition that any American received from the French Government a "rake-off" is too absurd to be discussed. It is an abominable falsehood, and it is a slander, not against the American Government, but against the French Government. [The President denounced the implication that his brother-in-law and Charles Taft were involved in any scandal, saying there *was* no scandal except in the conduct of Delavan Smith, and going on:] So far as I know there was no syndicate: there certainly was no syndicate in the United States that to my knowledge had any dealings with the Government directly or indirectly. . . .

Along with the story was an interview with Delavan Smith in which he said his editorial statements about the Panama deal were based on an account in "a prominent New York newspaper."

"What New York paper does Smith mean?" Pulitzer inquired.

"The *World*," Seitz replied.

"I knew damned well it must be. If there is any trouble you fellows are sure to be in it." [8]

He did not know half of the trouble the World was courting. As the *Liberty* sailed for New York with Seitz and the younger Pulitzer aboard, William McMurtrie Speer of the editorial page was composing a leader hurling defiance at the President and calling him a liar. Speer, an attorney and a seasoned student of politics, strongly opposed to Roosevelt, had long been suspicious of the Panama transaction. In Roosevelt's assault on Smith he found evasions and/or errors. His 1,600-word editorial, done under Cobb's nominal supervision, was headed, "THE PANAMA SCANDAL—LET CONGRESS INVESTIGATE," and began:

"In view of President Roosevelt's deliberate misstatements of fact in his scandalous personal attack upon Mr. Delavan Smith, editor of the Indianapolis *News,* The World calls upon the Congress of the United States to make immediately a full and impartial investigation of the entire Panama Canal scandal."

The World listed four Roosevelt statements: (1) that the United States did not pay a cent of the $40,000,000 to any American citizen; (2) that the money was paid direct to the French government; (3) that the United States government had no idea as to the individuals among whom the money was distributed; and (4) that "There certainly was no syndicate in the United States that to my knowledge had any dealings with the Government, directly or indirectly." The editorial said:

"To the best of The World's knowledge and belief, each and all of these statements made by Mr. Roosevelt and quoted above are untrue, and Mr. Roosevelt must have known they were untrue when he made them."

"WHO GOT THE MONEY?" the World demanded in capitals. It asserted that the United States had paid the $40,000,000 for the canal properties, and the $10,000,000 for the manufactured Panama republic, not to the French government but to J. P. Morgan & Company—a group of American citizens.

It told of Cromwell's persistent influence in the whole deal, and of his close relations with the President and other officials. It emphasized that Cromwell himself, in testimony before a Senate committee, had told of an American syndicate through which he was empowered to deal with the French canal group. "This company," said the World, "was incorporated in New Jersey with dummy directors." It described the Cromwell-inspired Panama revolution. It suggested that in reality the United States had not dealt with the French government at all but with Cromwell and his American colleagues, all of whom profited richly. It declared that Cromwell had been made general counsel for the Panama republic, that he and J. P. Morgan had become the "fiscal commission" for the republic, and that they still held three-quarters of the $10,000,000 which had been paid to them instead of to Panama. It said, "The inquiry was originally

The World's and The World accepts Mr. Roosevelt's challenge." The editorial ended:

> Whether Douglas Robinson, who is Mr. Roosevelt's brother-in-law, or any of Mr. Taft's brothers associated himself with Mr. Cromwell in Panama exploitation or shared in these profits is incidental to the main issue of letting in the light.
>
> Whether they did or not, whether all the profits went into William Nelson Cromwell's hands, or whatever became of them, the fact that Theodore Roosevelt as President of the United States issues a public statement about such an important matter full of flagrant untruths, reeking with misstatements, challenging line by line the testimony of his associate Cromwell and the official record, makes it imperative that full publicity come at once through the authority and by the action of Congress.[9]

Seldom has such denunciation been heaped on a President. Roosevelt's reaction was swift. He wrote next day to Henry L. Stimson, United States Attorney for New York, "I do not know anything about the law of criminal libel, but I should dearly like to have it invoked against Pulitzer, of the *World*. . . . Would you have his various utterances for the last three or four months . . . looked up?" [10] By the time the *Liberty* reached New York the editorial had raised a nationwide sensation and the President had made overtures to have District Attorney Jerome prosecute Pulitzer under the state libel law. Pulitzer, much upset, summoned Van Hamm to the Vault and asked, "What proof have you that Douglas Robinson and Charles P. Taft are involved in this matter?"

"None at all," Van Hamm admitted.

"My God! No proof? You print such stories without proof?" [11]

Van Hamm, whose code name was Gyrate, was spinning downward in the chief's estimation. He explained that it was Cromwell who had named the pair. But this did not absolve the World, and what with Speer's blistering editorial Pulitzer foresaw deep trouble from Roosevelt and Jerome. Strenuous efforts were made by the World staff to learn if Jerome was taking action against him. On December 15 the President took the remarkable step of giving Congress a special message on the libels. He quite lost his head in his anger, saying in part:

> Mr. [Delavan] Smith shelters himself behind the excuse that he merely accepted the statements which appeared in a paper published in New York, the World, owned by Mr. Joseph Pulitzer. It is idle to say that the known character of Mr. Pulitzer and his newspaper are such that the statements in that paper will be believed by nobody; unfortunately, thousands of persons are ill informed in this respect and believe the statements they see in print, even though they appear in a newspaper published by Mr. Pulitzer. . . .
>
> Now, these stories as a matter of fact need no investigation whatever. They consist simply of a string of infamous libels. In form they are in part libels upon individuals, upon Mr. Taft and Mr. Robinson, for instance. But

> they are in fact wholly, and in form partly, a libel upon the United States Government. I do not believe we should concern ourselves with these particular individuals who wrote the lying and libelous articles . . . The real offender is Mr. Joseph Pulitzer, editor and proprietor of the World. While the criminal offense of which Mr. Pulitzer has been guilty is in form a libel upon individuals, the great injury done is in blackening the good name of the American people. It should not be left to a private citizen to sue Mr. Pulitzer for libel. He should be prosecuted for that by the governmental authorities. . . . It is . . . a high national duty to bring to justice this vilifier of American people, this man who wantonly and wickedly and without one shadow of justification seeks to blacken the character of reputable private citizens and to convict the Government of his own country in the eyes of the civilized world of wrongdoing, of the basest and foulest kind . . . The Attorney General has under consideration the form in which the proceedings against Mr. Pulitzer shall be brought.[12]

So the President intended to use the full force of the government in an effort to put Pulitzer in prison. Norman Thwaites, in some trepidation as he read Roosevelt's statement to the chief in the Vault, noted:

> Instead of an explosion, Pulitzer said quietly: "Go on," and I proceeded to read other news items. Suddenly he arose from the couch . . . and smote the coverlet with clenched fist. "*The World* Cannot be Muzzled! *The World* cannot be muzzled! That's the headline," he said, and then proceeded a stream of words which . . . I had difficulty in getting down.[13]

The editorial appeared next morning:

> Mr. Roosevelt is mistaken. He cannot muzzle The World.
>
> While no amount of billingsgate on his part can alter our determination to treat him with judicial impartiality and scrupulous fairness, we repeat what we have already said—that the Congress of the United States should make a thorough investigation of the whole Panama transaction, that the full truth may be known to the American people.
>
> It is a most extraordinary circumstance that Mr. Roosevelt himself did not demand such an inquiry. . . .
>
> The World fully appreciates the compliment paid to it by Mr. Roosevelt in making it the subject of a special message to the Congress of the United States. In the whole history of American Government no other President has ever paid such a tribute to the power and influence of a fearless, independent newspaper. . . .
>
> If The World has libeled anybody we hope it will be punished, but we do not intend to be intimidated by Mr. Roosevelt's threats, or by Mr. Roosevelt's denunciation, or by Mr. Roosevelt's power. . . .
>
> So far as The World is concerned, its proprietor may go to jail . . . but even in jail The World will not cease to be a fearless champion of free speech, a free press and a free people.
>
> It cannot be muzzled.[14]

III. THE BIG MAN OF ALL NEWSPAPERS

His competitors noted that Pulitzer did not fail to wring all possible publicity even out of a presidential denunciation and threatened lawsuit. It can be said without reservation that the World was right (though rash), that Roosevelt had made misstatements, that the Panama affair richly needed investigation. It was also true that Pulitzer had known little of the original libels and had no responsibility for the fiery Speer editorial other than as proprietor. Yet he backed up his men with a fine courage that concealed frantic misgivings. He was worried about the unwise references to Robinson and Taft, and by Speer's insults. Even a millionaire publisher could not view with equanimity the prospect of defending himself against the awesome might of the government, with an angry Rough Rider at its head. He said only half-jokingly to Cobb that it was his fault—that if Cobb had announced Pulitzer's retirement in 1907 as ordered, he would have had a perfect alibi. Thinking of his nerves, feeling that the case might well kill him, he even pondered the idea of proving his own remoteness from the World and his ignorance of the libels. Cobb, as head of the editorial page, of course shared responsibility for Speer's blast. He was taken aboard the *Liberty* for a short cruise during which he argued so heatedly over tactics that Pulitzer summoned the skipper and said, "Put into Atlantic Highlands and throw this man off the yacht." The captain pointed out that it was late and Mr. Cobb might have trouble getting back to New York. "I don't care how much trouble he has getting back to New York. The more trouble he has the better I'll be pleased." Cobb was put off—one of a World editor's vicissitudes.[15] He received a later memo from the chief reading in part:

> Show how the machinery of justice is prostituted. For years we have asked Roosevelt to send somebody to jail; so he begins on the editors of the *World*. We pitched into Jerome because he did not do anything about wealthy lawbreakers; now he turns against the *World*. Say frankly that neither he nor Roosevelt can muzzle the *World*, nor anybody. But make it dignified.[16]

Jerome, not forgetting those World photographs of him asleep at his desk, detested Pulitzer. Since he also detested Roosevelt, he was in the pleasant position of being able to harass them both. For days he gave out ambiguous statements but did nothing. Pulitzer's suspense rose, and at last more urgent steps were taken to divine Jerome's intentions. Irvin S. Cobb (not related to Frank Cobb) of the Evening World, who knew the district attorney well, was summoned to the Dome, where Seitz and White anxiously inquired whether he might be able to learn Jerome's plans—something other World agents had tried to do and failed. Cobb had never met Pulitzer, but had a vivid mental picture of him and his ways, describing him as "a giant intelligence eternally condemned to the darkest of dungeons, a caged eagle furiously belaboring the bars. Not one in twenty of his employees, and these few all veterans, had ever laid eyes on him, although most there, from the straw-bosses in the private sanctums down to the most callow seminarians of the lower grades, had felt the weight of his heavy displeasure . . . or, by roundabout, had praise and perhaps a cash bonus or a quick promotion or both, for a job done smartly and to his autocratic standards." [17]

"A grave emergency exists," Seitz said. "Mr. Pulitzer is in a very depressed, very harassed state. The possible consequences to his health are dangerous . . ."

Cobb agreed to do his best. It was felt that the chore might take much time and effort. He was told that his work was most confidential and his expense account would be unlimited. He took a nickel trolley to Jerome's office on Center Street, had lunch with him at Pontin's and asked him point-blank what he intended to do about Pulitzer. The district attorney replied, as Cobb recalled it:

"I don't like a hair of that man's head. He has attacked me viciously, violently and, as I see it, without due provocation. . . . [The World] has had their crepe-heeled flunkeys dogging my steps and shadowing my people . . . Whereas, if any properly accredited reporter from the *World* had come to me . . . I'd have told him . . . So, because of all that and for nothing else, I've let King Pulitzer—and his gang of sycophants—stew in their own juice." He then said he had no intention of prosecuting Pulitzer.

Cobb was back at the Dome within two hours to give the news to an astonished Seitz. He was put on the wire with Thwaites at the Vault, who said joyfully, "Cobb, Mr. Pulitzer is sitting here beside me. He has just asked me to express his deep appreciation for the service you have rendered. . . . Mr. Pulitzer is desirous of knowing how this most gratifying result was accomplished so speedily."

"I got on a surface car," Cobb said, "and went up to the Criminal Courts and I sent in word to Mr. Jerome that a reporter from the *World* wanted to see him and when he came out . . . I asked him—and he told me."

Over the wire Cobb heard Pulitzer's voice for the first and only time in his life: "Well, I wish I might be God-damned!" Cobb's expenses were ten cents in carfare. Thereafter, he noted, "my name would go up on the bulletin board as the recipient of a cash award—usually on the strength of some commonplace story." [18]

Since the President could not strike at Pulitzer through Jerome, the next question was, how would he strike? Andes took his usual cure for nerves, boarding the *Liberty* and again making for Havana. In January the presidential secretary Archie Butt recorded a conversation between Roosevelt and his brother-in-law Robinson, writing: "They discussed the Panama libel suit, and both the President and Mr. Robinson think they will put —— in prison for criminal libel." [19] The dash of course stood for Pulitzer.

On February 17, 1909, a District of Columbia grand jury indicted Joseph Pulitzer, Caleb Van Hamm and Robert Hunt Lyman of the World, as well as the Press Publishing Company (the corporate name of the World) on five counts charging criminal libel of Theodore Roosevelt, J. P. Morgan, Douglas Robinson, Charles P. Taft, Elihu Root and William Nelson Cromwell. Delavan Smith and Charles R. Williams of the Indianapolis News were indicted on seven counts. The World replied in a Frank Cobb editorial characterizing the indictments as "a political proceeding" and defining the status of the World in a manner dear to the owner's heart:

> Mr. Roosevelt is an episode. The World is an institution. Long after Mr. Roosevelt is dead, long after Mr. Pulitzer is dead, long after all the present editors of this paper are dead, The World will still go on as a great independent newspaper, unmuzzled, undaunted and unterrorized.[20]

John M. Bowers, who was Pulitzer's trustee and personal attorney as well as attorney for the World, announced (possibly with relief) that he was counsel for Douglas Robinson in large real estate matters and would not be able to defend Pulitzer or the World. As trustee, he retained De Lancey Nicoll to handle the defense—the same Nicoll whom Pulitzer had supported so ardently in 1887 for district attorney. He was now a lawyer of great prestige and ability, but in the meantime he had represented Tammany Hall and various capitalists of whom Pulitzer disapproved. When the latter learned some time afterward of Bowers' move, he was so angry that he dismissed him both as his trustee and counsel, but Nicoll had already taken up the case and was allowed to proceed.

While Andes was unmuzzled, he was not as unterrorized as he made out. If Roosevelt was an episode, he knew the measure of this episode's wrath and strength, and he was anxious for Glutinous to be succeeded by Rotund in March. His health suffered as he contemplated the distinct possibility that he might go to jail. He even had his staff inquire into the location and accommodations of the prison in which he might be immured. All that winter his yacht skulked like a smuggler beyond the three-mile limit, cruising between Montauk Point and Florida as he directed operations. The case was a violent shock to him, destroying his precious travel routine, for normally he would be on the Mediterranean at this time. Ralph cabled him dutifully from Pau: "Many thanks greatly appreciate present hope presidential persecution not greatly troubling you love." [21] Since the *Liberty* had no wireless, he occasionally put into a

United States port to get news and send instructions, apprehensive that a federal marshal might be waiting on the pier. World men in Washington were snooping for information, and the government conducted its own espionage. "The Administration placed an extraordinary number of secret agents upon the *World's* trail," observed Seitz, not usually one for exaggeration; "Its mail was opened in the postoffice; the portfolios of its messengers between New York and Washington were examined and the Pulitzer Building itself filled with spies." [22] Perhaps with more justice than usual, Pulitzer enjoined the utmost secrecy in communication. He devised a special code for use in messages about the prosecution in which Roosevelt became "Styx," Robinson "Strutter," Cromwell "Battalion" and J. P. Morgan & Company "Nobility." He wrote Cobb:

> *Lèse-majesté* seems worse in America than Europe. There you have it limited to the sacred person of the ruler. . . . In America Roosevelt is developing *lèse-majesté* to the extent of protecting his brother-in-law (by the way, an estimable and admirable gentleman). To terrifying and bulldozing the House of Representatives and the Senate, abusing and blackguarding judges, he now adds threatening the Press and freedom of speech. . . . Treat the thing ironically, sarcastically and yet in a serious vein. He is drunk with success, drunk with power, drunk with popularity. . . .
>
> The question is: Who got the money?
>
> . . . Roosevelt did not do anything until the *World* printed a certain editorial charging him with inveracity—an editorial, perhaps too strong, let us frankly admit—still, is it not cowardly for a trustee for the nation to use the whole machinery of Government for revenge? [23]

Since Jerome had backed down, and the Washington indictments were of no use unless the defendants should take the unlikely course of going to the capital to invite arrest, the government made its third attempt. Hearings were held before a New York grand jury at which United States Attorney Stimson and Deputy Attorney General Stuart MacNamara fired questions at witnesses including Frank Cobb, who gave interesting testimony:

> MACNAMARA: When you go to see Mr. Pulitzer, what do you talk about?
>
> COBB: Mostly about politics, in which he is very deeply interested. But chiefly we discuss the policy of *The World*. Mr. Pulitzer conducts a school of journalism in regard to me. He often says he expects that I shall be able to carry on the principles of *The World* for the next twenty years.
>
> MACNAMARA: When you receive instructions from Mr. Pulitzer do you carry them out?
>
> COBB: Not necessarily. It depends upon the nature of the suggestions and the circumstances.
>
> MACNAMARA: You would feel free to disregard something Mr. Pulitzer told you to do?

COBB: I would.

A GRAND JUROR: You look upon Mr. Pulitzer as your employer, do you not?

COBB: I do not. The first time I ever saw Mr. Pulitzer he told me I must never assume that any such relations existed between us.

JUROR: If Mr. Pulitzer wished to discharge you, however—he could do so?

COBB: I infer that if Mr. Pulitzer wanted me discharged, he would find some way to get rid of me.

JUROR: You regard Mr. Pulitzer as the Big Man of *The World?*

COBB: I regard Mr. Pulitzer as the Big Man of all American newspapers.[24]

The now retired Dr. Hosmer was among the many witnesses called. His listeners were incredulous when he testified that Pulitzer almost never entered his own building. He wrote Pulitzer, "I responded that in the course of eighteen years I had accompanied you to the *World* office on two occasions and they, I believed, were the only occasions on which you had visited the office. This appeared to be incredible and had to be gone over several times." [25]

On March 4, 1909—Roosevelt's last day as President—Stimson secured a federal indictment of the World in New York on the ground that 29 copies of the offending issues had been circulated at the military reservation at West Point. Other copies had been sent routinely to the inspectors in the New York post office for their examination as prescribed by law. This indictment was secured by a remarkable interpretation of an 1825 statute "to Protect the Harbor Defense from Malicious Injury, and for other purposes"—a law never before invoked for libel. According to Stimson, the appearance of the World at each or any federal reservation "would constitute a separate offense." Since there were 2,809 government reservations in the United States, and many more beyond its boundaries, this meant that a newspaper could be prosecuted repeatedly all over the nation and in other parts of the world. In this proceeding, however, Pulitzer himself was not named, only two indictments being returned, one against Van Hamm and one against the World itself. Pulitzer wrote Cobb:

> Make a list of names and places of Government forts, islands, possessions, reservations absolutely belonging to the United States, like Fort Slocum, Governors Island, West Point, Annapolis, Hawaii, Porto Rico. I presume there are thousands. If this precedent is established . . . [it] would apply to Yellowstone Park or to the twelve hundred islands in the Philippines, compelling editors to go to these places, if need be, to defend themselves. The mere threat of such a thing would stop any liberty of the press. . . . Make a map in the news columns, indicating the number of these possessions, but don't be too funny; give the two sides of the globe. Make this the feature tomorrow, with perfect good humor. In your edi-

torial you must be serious and brave, and you must appeal to every serious man; you can't do that if you crack jokes, but it is possible to combine seriousness and a mock vein of severity.[26]

On March 8 the schoolmaster in him emerged:

> Another lesson I want to impress upon you all is that we shall not increase the power of the Executive any further; if this is to be a government of the people, for the people, by the people, it is a crime to put into the hands of the President such powers as no Monarch, no King, or Emperor ever possessed. He has too much power already, and . . . Congress is largely responsible for it. We must have an independent Congress, just as much as an independent President. Congress has given this man too much power. I would rather have corruption than the power of one man. . . . I want you to express this. . . .[27]

On March 14 the *Liberty* put in at Hampton Roads, where Barnes got permission to return to New York and rejoin her there. Pollard went to a local hotel to telephone Pulitzer's instructions to Seitz—an interminable conversation which the uneasy operator interrupted occasionally to let them know the toll was mounting. It finally came to $104. Next day the yacht set out for a leisurely cruise to New York, when Pulitzer asked the captain, Hiram Dixon, the direction of the course.

"Due east, sir," Dixon said.

"If we keep on 'due east,' where will we fetch up?"

"Lisbon, sir."

"Keep on, due east."[28]

Thus were the plans of all those aboard summarily altered. Hardly had they set out for Lisbon than Pulitzer changed his mind and the yacht turned northward, slipping through Long Island Sound and anchoring March 23 at Greenwich. Dunningham relayed his master's warning that no one on board was to mention the unexpected stop at Greenwich. Pulitzer's "will lawyer," William B. Hornblower, was summoned, and with Frank Cobb (also called from New York) and the secretary Randall Davies as witnesses, he executed a codicil to his 1904 will showing the ascendancy of Herbert in his estimation and the decline of Ralph and Joseph. He stipulated that after his death the income from the newspaper trust was to be divided on a basis of three-fifths for Herbert, one-fifth for Ralph and one-tenth for Joseph, the remaining tenth to go to the editors and managers of the newspapers whom the trustees felt most deserving. Another astonishing item was the omission of Ralph alone among the brothers as a trustee and executor.

This done, they set out once more for Lisbon. The yacht careened in rolls of up to 40 degrees in her stormiest crossing, there was much seasickness, and Pulitzer himself fell prey to a strange bronchial ailment. They reached Lisbon in exhaustion. It happened that one of the many Pulitzer family physicians, Dr. Frank Kinnicut, was vacationing at Pau. He was summoned to Lisbon, to find that Pulitzer had whooping cough—a disease far from trivial in older patients. As he took treatment, the entourage was joined by a new secretary recently secured by Tuohy, an encyclopedic young Scotchman named William Romaine Paterson. Paterson had been instructed to study all the Velásquezes and Murillos at the Prado and be ready to describe them. Along with his art lore he evidently had picked up some germs. They sailed with Paterson, who promptly came down with smallpox. They put in at Gibraltar, where they waited while Paterson received attention, the yacht was fumigated and everybody on board including the protesting owner was vaccinated before they went on to Marseille. Barnes, left behind in New York, was requested by cable to join the party in Europe.

IV. WHO GOT THE MONEY?

Meanwhile the unintimidated World said goodbye to President Roosevelt—off to hunt in Africa with nine pairs of glasses—with a full-page editorial, "Seven Years of Demagogy and Denunciation." The new President Taft's Attorney General George W. Wickersham continued the libel prosecution—one so enormously expensive that it would have ruined a publisher of ordinary means. The World not only retained Nicoll's firm in New York but Coudert Brothers in Paris to aid in the French investigation. Since the government refused to pay travel expenses of its own counsel, the World bore the expense of sending United States Attorney Henry Wise and Deputy Attorney General MacNamara to Paris, as well as another federal attorney to Panama. Seitz and other World officials were sent to Paris from time to time in efforts to clear up the canal transactions. Earl Harding, Gus Roeder, Henry N. Hall and other World newsmen were sent to Panama and Colombia in search of evidence.

Who got the money? Although on December 10, 1908, Roosevelt had written, "Mr. Cromwell has sent on to me the complete list of the stockholders of the Panama Canal Companies,"[29] the list was never made public nor has it been found at the Library of Congress. Although both Roosevelt and Cromwell had said that "all records" were available at the Paris offices of the canal company, they were not. In Paris the World attorneys met only frustration. The records had been sealed in the vault of the Crédit Lyonnais, one of the backers of the canal enterprise. Under French law, the records of a corporation retired from business were sealed for 20 years and then destroyed, and no persuasion could win so much as a glance at those momentous papers.

As the case dragged on, Pulitzer sought to recover from whooping cough at Carlsbad, where he was joined by Herbert and his current tutor. He sent $15,000 to the New York Association for the Blind and ordered a bonus of an extra week's pay to the entire Evening World staff on that paper's attainment of 400,000 circulation. He celebrated the 25th anniversary of J. Angus Shaw's employment by arranging by cable a dinner for Shaw at the University Club in New York, where Florence White and young Joseph Pulitzer were speakers, a congratulatory cable from Pulitzer was read, and Shaw (long complimented by the code name Solid) was presented with a mink-lined overcoat. Pulitzer had taken a keen interest in the work of Booker T. Washington and was paying the expenses of several Negro students at Tuskegee Institute. Now he was irate at President Taft's announcement that no Negro would be appointed in the South against the wishes of the whites. Calling it a "nullification of the XV amendment," he added, "we cannot agree in drawing such a skin color or race line," and ordered an editorial hot-shot against it. He was unhappy when he found the editorial too bland: " 'Dropping the Negro' is wonderfully timid. I really admire the amazing moderation and toning down to the uttermost minimum of my convictions—life-long convictions, if you please." [30]

After making do with several medical successors to Dr. Hosmer, none of them satisfactory, he was now trying out a young Briton, Dr. O.E. Wrench, an opera-lover and author of *The Grammar of Music*. Though valuable for his musical knowledge, Wrench was temperamental and caused difficulties because he "developed an extreme affection for Herbert which brought him into continuous conflict with Milligan," [31] the boy's tutor. Pulitzer was further harassed by his own compulsion to control every detail of his ménage. He had ordered another new Renault, which was being driven from Paris to Carlsbad by a chauffeur, Georges Trochon. Trochon was required to telegraph Pulitzer daily about his four-day progress, on the last day wiring, "I proceed on my way and I will do my possible [*sic*] to be in Karlsbad this evening."

Hardly had the car arrived than the master left for a summer cruise into the North Sea. Although pleased by Paterson, who could quote Burke, Voltaire or Goethe from memory, he was worried about Dr. Wrench, for whom Tuohy, Ledlie and others were seeking a replacement. "Mr. Pulitzer was a sick man, at times a pitiable object," Barnes noted. As they lay in a lovely Norwegian fjord, Barnes failed utterly in an attempt to describe the scenery for him. "But where are we?" Pulitzer broke in. "What is it like? Where are the shores? Where are these hills you talk about? How far away are they? What are the points of the compass?" Then he subsided, saying, "Forgive a poor, blind man." Ten minutes later he was dictating a message to Cobb about the coming city elections.[32]

They steamed to North Cape, where they exchanged greetings with the Kaiser's yacht *Hohenzollern*, then back to Christiania for a three-day stop for coal and an interval on solid ground. A crowd of Norwegians gathered to see the blind American millionaire, no longer "pitiable," tall and erect, clad in a wide-brimmed brigand hat, a blue cape with silver buckles and the usual dark glasses. ". . . He looked more than distinguished—he was overpowering," Barnes observed. After renting most of a small hotel on the outskirts, Barnes took Pulitzer for a carriage ride. They entered a long paved drive marked with Norwegian signs unintelligible to Barnes, skirted by fields where men were cutting hay. "How fresh it is, how fragrant!" Pulitzer exclaimed, his nostrils wide. Later at the hotel they learned that they had been in the grounds of Dr. Sundstrom's private insane asylum—a discovery that made Pulitzer laugh heartily. "A lunatic asylum!" he said. "Oh, my God! Why didn't you leave me there?" [33]

After visiting North Germany and Denmark, they put in at Leith to get cables and letters, then set out, it was rumored, for Reykjavik. The secretaries boned up hastily on Icelandic lore, since Pulitzer would expect to be meticulously informed. North of the Orkneys he changed his mind and they sailed for Dunkirk, making the Icelandic studies valueless except in the Baconian sense.

Barnes was seeing Pulitzer in his most broken condition, his battered health still the worse for whooping cough, his nerves on edge over the libel suit and his worries over his children. He had been studying the enigma, trying to understand how a man could be so suspicious, so menacing and yet so fascinating. "Depending so much on others," he wrote, "[Pulitzer] had at his beck the arts of flattery and cajolery; but also, in reverse . . . a positive and, perhaps, ugly method of expression that ranged from sarcasm to downright invective. . . . But no man could be so bitter against himself as he was, in respect to what he called his own 'constant and manifold failures.' He could pity himself in more varied terms of speech than anyone I ever knew." The New Yorker felt that the government prosecution preyed on his mind. He noted that aboard the yacht Pulitzer was mentioned much like the Deity—"the owner was always referred to as 'He.' " Barnes was warned by the regular secretaries that "He" preferred not to have the subject of Jews brought up, but, "One evening I spoke of the great Jewish leaders in England and the great Jewish philanthropist, Sir Moses Montefiore. Instead of the disquietude that might have been expected, Mr. Pulitzer joined in most naturally." Barnes found the study of his mental processes "interesting to the point of enchantment," and added, 'insistent and dominant though he was, he could be intimate, kindly and—I use the word advisedly—affection compelling."[34]

Evidently it was at Dunkirk that they took aboard Herbert and the tutor Milligan, after which they circled Spain and anchored at Tangier, Gibraltar, Cartagena and several other ports. At this point Barnes began to tire of his job, for one reason because although the *Liberty* sometimes remained in harbor for 24 hours, no one but the officers and Dunningham were allowed to go ashore, the explanation given being that they might sail at any time. Barnes felt that "the suddenly imposed restrictions did not conform to the name of the vessel." He was also annoyed by Herbert, an untrammeled lad whom Milligan was unable to handle and who Barnes thought should be in boarding school. At Cannes he resigned, offering to rejoin the entourage later as a guest rather than an employee.

"I am King Lear robbed of my children," Pulitzer sighed. He urged Barnes to look for other secretarial candidates for him, then went on to Aix, becoming immersed in the New York mayoralty campaign, fond of the unstable but independent Judge Gaynor. He cabled Cobb:

> Urge vigorously Gaynor's nomination by the Democrats. Admitting his defects he is an able man; nobody's pocket judge. Urge nomination of equally strong Fusion candidate, mentioning President [Nicholas Murray] Butler type, insuring good Mayor, whoever wins. This is true independence. After both candidates are nominated and their qualities examined, will decide which to support.[35]

Chapter 9

Pulitzer—and the Press —Victorious

I. NO USE, MY DEAR BOY

During the year 1909 Pulitzer did not make even a short visit to the United States. From afar he directed one of those World shake-ups that threw the Dome into ferment. He had lost confidence in Van Hamm and Speer for their costly incaution, and both were dropped on generous terms at the expiration of their contracts. He had also suffered disappointment in Frank Cobb (of whom he was very fond) for approving the Speer editorial. He presented Cobb with a fine Panama hat as a subtle reminder. Horatio Seymour was elevated to a position of vague equality with Cobb—a situation that guaranteed bloodletting between the two. Now four men were nominated to compete for Van Hamm's managing editorship—Robert Hunt Lyman, Charles M. Lincoln and J. J. Spurgeon of the World, and O. K. Bovard of the Post-Dispatch—with Seymour and Ralph Pulitzer ordered to watch them all closely and find the best man. "Don't be too severe," the severely hypercritical Pulitzer warned Seymour. "Don't be hypercritical. . . . Do praise just as much as you can . . ."[1]

In September he took an apartment near the Tiergarten in Berlin, one first altered—although he was there only a month—under Ledlie's watchful eye with soft rugs, heavy drapes, triple windows and special care in the bathroom, "sharp edges in construction to be carefully avoided and the whole to be carried out with the direction and approval of Mr. Pulitzer's agent." Having at last shaken off the effects of his whooping cough, he enjoyed himself at concerts, the theater and the opera. Here he was shocked to learn of the suicide of his brother Albert in Vienna on October 3.

Of late years Albert's insomnia and mental derangement had increased. He lived as a virtual recluse at the Hotel Bristol, employing a secretary and also a woman aide who read newspapers and books to him daily. The latter had read him an item about a man troubled by insomnia who had killed himself, at which he said, "*Wenn ich nur Muth dazu hätte*"—"If only I had the courage." Later he sought to buy prussic acid from a chemist who, noting his look of desperation, gave him harmless almond extract instead. Evidently Albert drank the contents of the vial, discovered the deception, then shot himself in the head.

One can imagine Pulitzer's gloomy review of his brother's symptoms, so like his own even if more severe. Although he had shut Albert out of his life for a quarter-century, he gave Thwaites 3,000 marks and sent him to Vienna to investigate and make sure that Albert had a decent burial. Thwaites learned that both Catholic and Jewish groups had made inquiries about the deceased man, but he had trouble finding the body, which he finally located at the Jewish cemetery. "Covered with a white cloth and lying in an open box of the cheapest kind," he observed, "the unfortunate remains lay in the mortuary. No money having been found, the millionaire was about to be buried as a pauper." [2] Thwaites supplied money for a better burial and was chief mourner at the Jewish services next day. The World's obituary, very brief, made no mention of Albert's relationship to Joseph, though other New York newspapers commented that the brothers had been estranged for many years.

A few days later Pulitzer got better news from Indianapolis, where Federal Judge Albert B. Anderson dismissed the government's case against the News with a few trenchant observations: "There are many very peculiar circumstances about the history of this Panama Canal . . . business. . . . There were a number of people who thought there was something not just exactly right about that transaction, and I will say for myself that I have a curiosity to know what the real truth was. . . . If the history of liberty means anything—if constitutional guarantees are worth anything—this proceeding must fail. . . ." [3]

Roosevelt later reacted to Judge Anderson's decision by calling him "a jackass and a crook." In the World's own case, still pending, it was decided to challenge the government's jurisdiction rather than to accept jurisdiction and fight the charges. Behind this strategy was Pulitzer's conviction that the freedom of the press was more vital than the exposure of plunderers. If the World could prove that the government's claim of jurisdiction under the old act was unfounded, a precedent would be established freeing every newspaper henceforth from such ruinous harassment. If the World should lose its bid, then the privilege of the press to criticize public officials—a right treasured since the foundation of the republic—was virtually abolished and the Fourth Estate was in a sorry way indeed. The freedom of the press, that ideal so often importuned in paltry causes, was here threatened in its foundations. Pulitzer's fat purse was defending not only himself but every journalistic contemporary as well as generations to come, the wealthy as well as the backwoods editor who could not afford a ten-dollar lawyer. One can only marvel at the action of Roosevelt, whose own position in the Panama affair was scarcely above reproach, in starting such an ungallant, vengeful and mad-brained prosecution.

The case dragged on. Gaynor was elected with the World's support. Roosevelt was still in Africa, shooting game, becoming ever more irked by moves of his hand-picked successor, Taft. Pulitzer, feeling that he was slowly dying, unhappy about Dr. Wrench, left Berlin in October to take a Mediterranean cruise, then settled at the Villa Arethusa at Cap Martin. It was a lovely spot, commanding a sweeping view of blue water by day, the lights of Monte Carlo visible across the bay by night. He saw none of it, for his blindness was now almost absolute. One night aboard the yacht, Pollard was so entranced by the Mediterranean moon that he took the chief to the rail, faced him in the right direction and begged him to try to see it. After peering in vain, he said, "It's no use, my dear boy, I cannot even get a glimmer of its light." [4]

His splendid head, proud carriage and meticulous grooming gave him a distinction that made strangers stare in some awe. Time, battle and pain were etched on the face, the instantly mobile face now showing clearly the duality Sargent had painted. As one secretary noted, "the face moved between a lively, genial animation, a cruel and wolf-like scowl, and a heavy and hopeless dejection. No face was capable of showing greater tenderness; none could assume a more forbidding expression of anger and contempt." [5] In his mealtime conversational jousts with his secretaries he showed his impressive command of every political experiment from the democracy of the Greeks to the struggles of the American colonists. He enjoyed discussions of style and of the differences in languages, often saying that Hamlet's "To be or not to be" soliloquy had greater meaning and drama in German: *"Sein oder Nichtsein, das ist hier die Frage."* [6] With what must have been a strong effort of will he had cured himself of his swearing, possibly deciding that it detracted from his dignity. Now he used only "damn" and "My God!", the latter incessantly. His enjoyment of subtleties in no wise impaired his delight in gossip, to which Tuohy catered in a long letter from London telling of Ponsonby, of Labouchere, of H. G. Wells's shocking sexual exploits, and adding, "It is also a subject of general report that Winston Churchill has been found impossible by his Wife, and that she has left him twice already . . ." [7]

To Seitz, visiting him at Cap Martin, he said that his heart was running down: "We will not have many more rows." Seitz replied gallantly that he hoped this pleasure would not be denied the staff. "No, I am serious," Pulitzer said. "I am not going to live long. I have had warnings. Besides I am no longer equal to thinking or deciding. You will have to get along without me more and more from now on and see less and less of me." [8]

Although some World executives felt that underneath his ailments he was as strong as a horse and would live to be 90, they were quite willing to have him at a distance. Throughout the Dome and the city room, where he was called "J.P." or "the Old Man," he was regarded with a peculiar veneration as the most cantankerous and brilliant individualist ever to own a newspaper, and there was a definite sense of pride in possessing the qualifications to remain in his employ. At 62 he had become an institution and a legend. He seemed to have run the World forever. His earlier exploits—his Civil War service, his amazing rise in St. Louis, his election of Cleveland, his feud with Dana, his truncated term as congressman—seemed more like passages from an old saga than the record of a living man. No one now could compare with him. Hearst was admittedly a power, a great fighter, but ruined as a newspaperman by his itch for office. Reid was an apologist for privilege who married a fortune and let his tired Tribune decline. Bennett was a gray ghost of the past, his Herald dwindling every year. Ochs, however—there was a bright young man in the counting room, a fine purveyor of news whose Times was gaining steadily, but cautious, with no taste for battle. Indeed, "battle" was a synonym for the tall bundle of nerves whose picture hung in the Dome, whose passion for conflict made life interesting and often painful for editors and reporters.

Still, those in the Dome could breathe more easily when he was at a good long distance, and the paper *was* running largely without him. As the poetic Seitz put it, "The *World* establishment . . . was always like a great steamship, going over a regular route, streaming with lights, quivering with motion . . ." [9]

The Old Man kept tinkering with his will (which he had started in 1892), anxious that his millions be left in testamentary perfection to protect the World, safeguard his family, reward his most loyal men and effect the most public good. Summoning an attorney from Paris, on January 17, 1910, he executed a second codicil aboard his yacht. It appointed Governor Hughes as executor-trustee with a fee of $100,000; Frederick N. Judson, Pulitzer's long-time St. Louis attorney, as executor until Joseph Jr. reached 30; and J. Angus Shaw, now president of the World, as executor until Herbert reached 21, both Judson and Shaw to receive $50,000 fees.

A week later, on January 25, when at long last the government's case against the World came up before Judge Charles M. Hough in New York, Pulitzer and the American press won a resounding victory and the Rough Rider took the defeat he deserved. Judge Hough quashed the indictment, saying in part, "I am of the opinion that the construction of this act claimed by the prosecution is opposed to the spirit and tenor of legislation for many years . . ." [10]

Pulitzer was still dissatisfied. He wanted the principle established beyond question in the highest court in the land, and since only the government as losing plaintiff could appeal the verdict, the World kept needling, insisting on an appeal. At the same time, the chief, in bed for a fortnight at Cap Martin with a bronchial cold, had Thwaites write another request to Tuohy for a new personal physician, saying in part:

> You will see that it is quite different from anything he has asked for before in that it distinctly eliminates the point of intellectual companionship, and asks merely for a first-rate doctor. Mr. Pulitzer says he may stutter, or be a hunchback, but, of course, not preferably so. This ought to make the search much easier. Mr. Pulitzer has really been very ill and ought not to go off [on a Mediterranean cruise] without a serious-minded, capable physician in whom he and Mrs. Pulitzer can have some confidence.[11]

Late in March he was able to sail for Italy and Greece. Kate, who at times had been unclear as to his whereabouts, now turned the tables on him. At Syracuse he received telegrams from her making it uncertain whether she was at Cap Martin, Paris or Aix. He wired her at all three addresses: "Your telegrams most confusing. Where are you. Telegraph Syracuse immediately . . ." [12] Reaching Athens, the whole party went ashore to see the Acropolis. Pulitzer, planning to go with them, at the last moment decided to stay on the yacht with Dunningham, and this was one of the few times when his blindness and his self-pity brought him such despair that he gave way to tears.

11. THE RED THREAD

Having warned his men to treat President Taft with utmost fairness, he felt that the World had become a purring tabby and exploded in a Mediterranean memo:

> I have never known the *World* to come so near to being muzzled, afraid of saying anything about Taft. . . . Now Taft has the very highest place in the country, and has made a lot of mistakes perfectly obvious to everybody, and yet the *World* remained silent—studiously silent. Please—Why?—Frankly! And don't think that my desire to treat Taft with *sympathy* and *fairness* has changed for a moment. Taft as a tariff reformer is one thing. Taft as the defender of the extreme protectionists is another character. . . .
>
> Now do ignore, without hesitation, some of my suggestions coming from far, far away with complete ignorance of conditions on the spot, or when

the conditions are entirely changed by time . . . I do not wish to kill initiative, courage, discretion in the gentleman who is in charge of the [editorial] page.[13]

He feared that Roosevelt, who would soon return after his safari and his visits with European royalty, was thinking of the Presidency in 1912. "As much silence as possible for Roosevelt during his holiday glorifications," he warned the World. "There is time enough afterwards."[14]

Back at Cap Martin, he made a third codicil on May 11, doubling the trust fund for his daughters Edith and Constance from $250,000 to $500,000 and increasing Kate's trust fund from $2,000,000 to $2,250,000, the extra quarter-million to be divided on her death between the two daughters. Referring to his gifts to his secretaries, to World men and to philanthropies, he wrote:

> If any of my children think excessive such gifts of mine outside of my family, I ask them to remember not only the merit of the causes and the corresponding usefulness of the gifts but also the dominating ideals of my life. They should never forget the dangers which unfortunately attend the inheritance of large fortunes, even though the money come from the painstaking affections of a father.
>
> I beg them to remember that such danger lies not only in the obvious temptations to enervating luxury, but in the inducement . . . to withdraw from the wholesome duty of vigorous, serious, useful work. In my opinion a life not largely dedicated to such work cannot be happy and honorable. And to such it is my earnest hope—and will be to my death—that my children shall, so far as their strength permits, be steadfastly devoted.[15]

To Cap Martin came Charles Lincoln (Mohican), one of the four candidates for the managing editorship, all expenses paid, to endure a Pulitzerian search of soul. The inquisitor later cabled White at the World, "Scrutinize Mohican's expenses sharply as he had no right to bring wife." Mohican passed the test, however, for a day later the chief cabled Cobb:

> Continue Mohican assistant Gruesome making Gushless Gruesome during Glorify's vacation . . .[16]

Gruesome meant "managing editor," while Gushless was Bovard and Glorify, Spurgeon. After a cure at Aix, Pulitzer reached New York on the *Cedric* June 19, one day after Roosevelt landed to receive a tremendous public ovation. Andes shunned New York, being met at quarantine by the *Liberty,* which took him up the Sound and loafed off Greenwich for a week while he conferred with World executives and watched the activities of the ex-President he cordially hated. Roosevelt's reception was so triumphant that it seemed to establish him as the first citizen in the hearts of the people and to relegate President Taft to subaltern status. The elephant hunter said he was "ready and eager" to help solve national problems. Did this mean an intention to return to public life—perhaps a break with Taft? Pulitzer was convinced of the former, at any rate. He sailed up to Chatwold, where he settled the Lincoln-Lyman-Bovard-Spurgeon contest for Gruesome. Lincoln should have the job, with Bovard as assistant. He summoned Lincoln to Bar Harbor to tell him of his responsibility, and Bovard also made the trip to be told of the importance and promise of the second post.

The 38-year-old Oliver K. Bovard was a flinty character who, on his earlier elevation to the city editorship of the Post-Dispatch, had coldly informed his former reportorial cronies that he was no longer to be called "O. K." but was to be addressed as *Mr.* Bovard. Now, for six straight hours, he had small opportunity to reply while the chief gave him rapid-fire journalistic instruction, one of his observations being, "I am a terrible critic and fault-finder. Above all I am crazy to improve the paper It is the only thought I have. After all I am not running the paper for an income . . ." [17]

He was astonished when Bovard rejected the offer. He refused to work under Lincoln, he said, because he was a better man than Lincoln. The master's complexion grew very pink. Was Mr. Bovard impugning his judgment? Bovard replied that Pulitzer, not having seen either of them work, was not in a position to judge. When Pulitzer ordered him to take the post or return to St. Louis, he said that he preferred the Post-Dispatch and made his farewell. Pulitzer's outrage was quickly succeeded by esteem for a fighting spirit which he would never brook in his own sons. Calling Bovard back, he said, "I differ with your judgment, but I admire your character." During the next fortnight he directed Ralph to urge Bovard to stay with the World, writing him, "I am well disposed to appreciate him, educate him." [18] But the bulldog returned—at an increase in salary—to the Post-Dispatch, where he would later carve out fame of his own as managing editor under Joseph Pulitzer Jr.

James Barnes was a guest at Chatwold, taking a week's cruise with Pulitzer, enjoying "long walks up and down the deck, dissertations that rambled from the political situation to Shakespeare's plays—and he could quote Shakespeare by the page . . ." [19] He renewed his request that Barnes find another secretary or two for him. He sent Cobb careful instructions:

> Watch Roosevelt in connection with Governorship and Senatorship. Republicans may nominate him for Governor with intention of making him Senator. When he was elected Senator that would make the machine Lieutenant Governor the Governor, and give the bosses exactly what they wanted. Roosevelt could play that game beautifully and is capable of playing it.
>
> Have a strong endorsement of Woodrow Wilson as Democratic candi-

date for Governor [of New Jersey]. Force his nomination. Great thing for party, not only in New Jersey but all over the country. . . . Help the Democrats everywhere, especially in Ohio, but support insurgents like Bristow, Cummins and Dolliver warmly, and insurgent movements in States where Democrats have no chance. . . .

As to the editorial page in general:

It lacks persistence and continuing force. Instead of striking once it should strike a dozen times; hammer its ideas into the people's heads. It lacks the red thread of continuous policy, which should run through it like a Wagnerian motif. . . .

To this he added his exalted conception of his newspaper's power and obligations:

I want the *World's* Democratic sympathies plain and unmistakable, while retaining full measure of honest independence. The *World* should be more powerful than the President. He is fettered by partisanship and politics and has only a four-years term. The paper goes on year after year and is absolutely free to tell the truth and perform every service that should be performed in the public interest. You have the utmost liberty and freedom, only do not slop over and do not be inaccurate. Be fair. If Roosevelt, for example, should come out in favor of a great reform like tariff revision, I'd praise him for that one thing and support him on that one thing, without altering a word of criticism as to his follies.

Don't be content with making the best editorial page in town, because there is no other editorial page, and when you have made the best you are taking only a small part of your opportunity. . . .[20]

III. A COURSE IN JOURNALISM

The new managing editor, Lincoln, was slated for a free course in journalism at the hands of the schoolmaster, who defined news and World policy and adjured the pupil never to forget the lesson:

1st. What is original, distinctive, dramatic, romantic, thrilling, unique, curious, quaint, humorous, odd, apt to be talked about, without shocking good taste or lowering the general tone, good tone, and above all without impairing the confidence of the people in the truth of the stories or the character of the paper for reliability and scrupulous cleanness.

2nd. What is the one distinctive feature, fight, crusade, public service or big exclusive? No paper can be great, in my opinion, if it depends simply upon the hand-to-mouth idea, news coming in anyhow. One big distinctive feature every day at least. One striking feature each issue should contain, prepared before, not left to chance.

3rd. Generally speaking, always remember the difference between a paper made for the million, for the masses, and a paper made for the classes. In using the word masses I do not exclude anybody. I should make a paper that the judges of the Supreme Court of the United States would read with enjoyment, everybody, but I would not make a paper that only the judges of the Supreme Court and their class would read. I would make this paper without lowering the tone in the slightest degree.

4th. Accuracy, accuracy, accuracy. Also terseness, intelligent, not stupid, condensation. No picture or illustration unless it is first class both in idea and execution. . . .[21]

In August the *Liberty* took him again to Greenwich, where he had final conferences with his editors before she sailed for Plymouth August 13. He went on to Wiesbaden, continuing his education of Lincoln:

The man who wrote the enclosed story on "Why Tennessee will Elect a Republican Governor" certainly ought to be discharged and the copy reader and the man who passed it. Who is Hooper? Banker, cow puncher, astronomer or what? The story does not say . . . Somebody ought to be ashamed of himself.

Apropos of the sketch of Stimson [the same Henry L. Stimson who had prosecuted the World, now Roosevelt's candidate for governor of New York] in the paper . . . what is ordinary height? Would it not have been just as easy to have said, "The man is five feet six, or seven, or eight?" Just ask any number of men "What is ordinary height?" and see whether you can get two men to agree.

Again, "A sizeable nose!" Who edited that copy? Who was the reporter? Who was the editor in charge? Is this the result of over twenty-seven years of teaching the importance of personal description . . . ? I want to know every man who had anything to do with this description. . . .

Again, "His hands do not hide themselves because of nervousness." Who said they did? Did anybody make that charge? . . . Pretty bad workmanship. . . .

Apropos of the destruction by explosion of the Los Angeles *Times,* what is the matter with twenty people killed? The story is put on the thirteenth page . . . I wonder it was not put on the eighty-seventh page. Has there been any story like this for years? Did it not happen on Saturday morning? That would be four o'clock New York time. Kindly explain. It was worth first page position, more than that it was a dreadful story. The P-D printed it Saturday afternoon and a hundred times better. Whose fault? Whose judgment? [22]

At Wiesbaden he was seized by one of his intermittent urges to consult with doctors. Several famous European specialists arrived one by one, to charge substantial fees despite their failure to find a cure. One can imagine the surprise of the noted Dr. Carl H. Von Noorden, who traveled from Vienna only to be informed that Mr. Pulitzer was "too ill" to see him. But there was nothing humorous about the devilish despair that he fought alone in darkness—an inner battle implicit in his message to Kate:

Sincerely hope you have pleasant trip am dreadfully despondent sick at heart but will try hard much love.[23]

He had the World support the uninspired Democrat John A. Dix for governor on the ground that the defeat of Roosevelt's candidate Stimson would also defeat Roosevelt's hopes for a third term as President. Dix won by 67,000 votes, the first Democrat given the governorship in 16 years—a victory the World hailed as a repudiation of Roosevelt and his certain elimination for consideration by the Republicans in 1912. Pulitzer was as happy over the victory of Woodrow Wilson in New Jersey, a man he had watched for four years. Indeed, Wilson propelled him into the President-making fever that always erupted at mid-term election time. He was soon corresponding with George Harvey of Harper's, Wilson's most fervent drum-beater, laying plans. From his World friend John McNaught came a jocular rumor about Harvey's motives:

> . . . The talk of the clubs is that Woodrow Wilson's boom as a Presidential candidate was started by the Harper publications, to sell his books. The story goes that the Harpers were confronted by the probability of a big loss in the publication of Wilson's five volumes; so they set Editor Harvey . . . to the task of getting Wilson talked of to the end that his books, like those of Roosevelt, should have the vogue of best sellers . . .[24]

Pulitzer scorned such talk. To George Johns of the Post-Dispatch he wrote:

> I think that [Wilson] is an abler man than Tilden was; and I admired Tilden. I think he is ten times more intellectual than Cleveland and I knew both Tilden and Cleveland personally. Tilden had intellect beyond question. Cleveland had little, but his great force was *moral courage*.[25]

But he was appalled when the secretary Randall Davies was inconsiderate enough to leave his employ in order to marry, and he wrote Barnes to request his further attention to the matter of more secretaries. The hard-working Tuohy in London furnished one replacement, George Craven, formerly with the British civil service in Rajputana. A new physician, Dr. Guthman, had replaced the long-suffering Dr. Wrench. Still, there were only five secretaries and Tuohy was looking for more. In November Pulitzer settled at Cap Martin, where he leased the Villa Cynthia, sent a stream of journalistic instruction to Lincoln and other World men, maintained an affectionate correspondence with Dr. Hosmer, now living on a Pulitzer pension in Summit, New Jersey, and presented Hosmer with a fur coat. Hosmer, as well as Kate and Ralph, had vainly urged him to write his autobiography. Now he wrote Hosmer of his surprise on learning that the doctor was essaying a biography:

> I never dreamt of your even attempting anything like a sketch of a life . . . a story of misery and decrepitude, to be sure, but still, a story of unceasing work and worry. You are the only man living who can speak from actual knowledge about my connection with the editorial page. That feeble, invalidish activity was my only thought. As Mary Stuart said about

her heart being left in France as she sailed for Scotland, my heart was and still is in the editorial page. . . .[26]

Nothing could have been truer than this. Over the years the World in a sense had been and still was a display window cunningly devised to lure readers inside to the editorial page, where the schoolmaster would instruct them, lecture them on the issues and how to meet them, lecturing also public officials from the President down to aldermen, prison wardens and policemen on the beat. Unfailingly it had reflected the thoughtfulness, experience, constructiveness and sense of justice (and occasionally the spleen) of the nation's most gifted political professor. The assistant professors who wrote the editorials had been selected by standards as rigid as those applying to the papacy. The master had instructed *them* like so many schoolboys. Who could tell how many thousands, how many millions, had joined this largest and longest of all classes—had learned their political lore from this page appearing 365 times a year in the 27 years since the professor had opened his New York academy? Who could weigh every ounce of its influence, or assay the credit it surely deserved in the instruction of the public, the gradual betterment of American politics, the elevation of aims, the slow retreat of the robber-baron ideology and the advance of a sense of social responsibility to all the people?

One of the minds in which the seed of reform was planted so well as to grow a flourishing crop was that of the young Fiorello LaGuardia, who later wrote, ". . . I would carefully read every word of the *World's* fight against the corrupt Tammany machine. . . . I could not understand how the people of the greatest city in the country could put up with the vice and crime that existed there."

No other newspaper had offered a tenth of such red-thread tutelage. If the professor had a few sins to answer for, he had a right to be proud of his page. In fact, he was so proud of it that he urged John L. Heaton of Cobb's staff to write a history of it—a quaint idea that would eventually emerge as a book, *The Story of a Page*.

Hearing that Lloyd George was vacationing at Monte Carlo, Pulitzer found a way to show his delight at the Welshman's victory over the House of Lords in pushing through his social insurance plan. He wired Mrs. Tuohy, who was also in Monte Carlo:

> Please accept my automobile for three weeks but if you feel like it for first week place it at disposal of Lloyd George with my compliments and appreciation of his splendid ability.[27]

He arranged for the presentation of hundreds of Christmas gifts for employees of the World and Post-Dispatch, among them several gramophones costing Leprosy ($300). To Lincoln he wrote:

> I want to thank you for your notes during the summer and your effective efforts. You certainly cannot complain about my having interfered or

being disagreeable. I am in a very appreciative mood, although disappointed about Curate. If you don't know the word, ask Seitz. It is either a dreadful word or a very fortunate one. You should always have it on your mind.

Later he was less appreciative in commenting on the World's "wretched" reporting of public banquets:

This mystery I beg you to explain. It is not new. . . . It was very bad last year, but it is just as bad today. I dare not read the paper. If any big meeting takes place, I am sure to be made sick by reading of it.[28]

On January 3, 1911, the cable brought him news that he read not with sickness but with triumph. The Supreme Court ended two years of litigation by deciding in favor of the World, which commented:

The unanimous decision handed down by the United States Supreme Court yesterday in the Roosevelt-Panama libel case against The World is the most sweeping victory won for freedom of speech and of the press since the American people destroyed the Federalist party more than a century ago for enacting the infamous Sedition law.

. . . The Supreme Court upholds every contention advanced by The World since the outset of this prosecution. . . . The decision . . . is so sweeping that no other President will be tempted to follow in the footsteps of Theodore Roosevelt, no matter how greedy he may be for power, no matter how resentful of opposition. . . .[29]

If Pulitzer had done nothing else in his life, he would have been entitled to national gratitude for this courageous and expensive battle.

Who got the money?

That has remained one of history's best-kept secrets, and probably will remain so forever.

Chapter 10

The Last Election

I. I'VE SEEN IT ALL

To the Monte Carlo hotel of the notoriously tardy Henry Watterson, the minute-watching Pulitzer wired: "Yes auto will call 12:30 and hope you will be punctual."[1] And so to Cap Martin came that bulky bundle of protest and charm, that lover of good wine, good music and a good fight, the editor of the Courier-Journal. As they met in the Riviera sunshine, he and Pulitzer must have experienced a sense of gathering isolation, a realization that time had removed their spiritual contemporaries and placed them alone, the last famous exemplars of independent, personal journalism whose own political exploits went back to Reconstruction days. Watterson was 70, Pulitzer 63, but the Kentuckian could still read fine print and execute a waltz and would outlive his host by ten years.

They sailed in the *Liberty* to Corsica. Not always had they agreed over the years, but in most important issues they had been as one. When Roosevelt secured the World's indictment, Watterson had exploded in indignant editorials, saying of the Panama affair, "A more palpable confidence game, a greater robbery, was never perpetrated upon a people's treasure house." He was more orotund, more openly sentimental, more promiscuously sociable than Pulitzer; a bon vivant, clubman and dinner speaker who numbered his friends among the hundreds. He could not equal Pulitzer's vast learning and incisive intellect but he was immeasurably the superior now in expansive health that permitted the enjoyment of living. Pulitzer was excited about Wilson for 1912. Watterson was not excited at all, thinking Wilson too much the pedagogue.

Pulitzer detested misty reminiscences as a sign of the senility he fought. Look forward, not back! Yet these two could hardly have refrained from reliving memories they alone shared, of '72 and later, of Grant, Greeley,

Tilden, Schurz and a whole gallery of political ghosts. The *Liberty* put in at Ajaccio, where Pulitzer stayed aboard to "read" the World while Watterson went ashore to visit Napoleon's birthplace and to sample the vintage. When he returned a few hours later he was unmanned by both. He flung his arms around Pulitzer's neck and dampened his shoulder with a flood of tears.

"Oh, Joe," he blubbered, "I've seen it all—his cradle, the room where he was born, the streets on which he walked, the school where he learned his letters . . . and O, Joe, it all came over me. Paris, Vienna, Victory, Waterloo! O, Joe, what does it all mean?" [2]

No one since Rodin had so invaded Pulitzer's sacred person. He was much embarrassed until Watterson was disengaged and led to his cabin.

Another visitor that winter was Ralph Pulitzer, who brought his wife Frederica and joined the entourage for a cruise to Athens. Ralph, long accustomed to his father's disappointment in him, played his difficult role with tact. He carried more prestige among his colleagues than his father perhaps realized, and was part of an office plot to shield the Old Man from news that might bedevil him. Thwaites wrote Seitz from Naples:

> I have not brought to Mr. Andes' attention the letters from Villard and MacBride nor the pamphlet you send which was apparently gotten out by Greyhound [Tammany]. Ralph agrees that at this time it would serve no good purpose.[3]

As the *Liberty* steamed eastward, the kind of melodrama that seemed part and parcel of Pulitzer's life touched him again in the tragic fate of David Graham Phillips. Phillips, enormously successful with his muck-raking magazine articles and problem novels, received threatening letters from an utter stranger, Fitzhugh Goldsborough. Goldsborough, who was mentally unstable, believed that his sister had been caricatured in a Phillips novel. On January 23, 1911, as the 44-year-old Phillips walked from his 19th Street apartment to Gramercy Park, Goldsborough followed and shot him fatally.

Cruise or no cruise, Andes was sending his usual torrent of memoranda to Seitz, White, Cobb, Seymour and especially the student Lincoln. Let Woodrow Wilson be watched closely and handled with sympathy. The publication of the 1910 census figures inspired him to suggest a story on America's amazing growth. A London Times item mentioning that there were 185 homicides in New York in 1910 impelled his request for a Sunday feature on the more interesting cases, with tables of motives, nationality, social rank, and comparisons with London and Paris. He authorized the payment of up to $500 for unusual Sunday articles:

> Try hard to get General Sickles to write reminiscences for the *World*. It ought to make a splendid series with pictures. Of course, you know per-

fectly well what a life he has led. Murdered Key. He was a Tammany man half a century ago. . . .

. . . Try old [John] Bigelow. Of course he would be much more dull . . . but interviewed by a very clever writer, a lot of pictures and the charm of the first person singular conversational talk would make a good series. . . . New York of fifty, sixty or even seventy years ago in the case of Bigelow would [be] . . . quaint, curious, odd. What a change! What a wonder! The thought grows on me. Make up a list of a dozen old people conspicuous in name, of position, intelligent, with memory. Include Frank Work, father of Mrs. Burke-Roche, who is now ninety-two years old. Take a year for all these if necessary. Don't spoil it by dashing it off like the usual slap-dash article.[4]

On the *Liberty*'s return, a different sort of visitor was 40-year-old Alleyne Ireland, who had been forced by illness to drop a distinguished career in the British civil service and had read an interesting "companion wanted" advertisement in the Times. He was interviewed in London first by Tuohy and then by Ledlie, passing muster very well except for his admission that he was unfamiliar with Milton's *Comus.* Next he was interviewed at the Cafe Royal by Ralph, on his way home. Next he wrote a 2,000-word account of his life for Pulitzer to read. Then he cooled his heels for several weeks before Tuohy gave him a ticket to Menton and money for incidental expenses. He had heard much of the eccentric millionaire who had been painted by Sargent and modeled by Rodin. Demanding though he was, to be one of Pulitzer's half-dozen secretaries seemed not unbearable, with probably only a couple of hours of work a day, caviar and champagne and luxurious cruises in the Mediterranean. Reaching Menton, he boarded the yacht, where the secretaries lived, and met some of the officers.

"I was a good deal puzzled . . ." Ireland recalled, "by something peculiar but very elusive in their attitude toward me . . . With their courtesy was mingled a certain flavor of curiosity tinged with amusement, which . . . gave me a vague sense of uneasiness. In fact the whole atmosphere of the yacht was one of restlessness and suspense."[5]

II. DON'T PAINT THE DEVIL AS BLACK AS HE IS

By now, Pulitzer's years of torment and of imprisonment within his artificial world had made him a monumental abnormality. Encompassed in his lonely frame were aspects of the grand and the sinister, the kindly and the venomous, the attractive and the dangerous—of maturest wisdom that could sink instantly to childishness, of courage mingled with self-pity.

His brain and spirit still burned with a fierce heat that his physique and nerves could not stand, and though he was aware of this, he was unable to turn off the heat. It is not surprising that some of this pent-up energy found expression in occasional sadism, a trait common enough among invalids but uncommon as practiced by him.

Pulitzer's car carried Ireland up the hill to the villa, where he dressed for dinner and met the master, escorted by Dunningham, in the drawing room. "My first swift impression was of a very tall man with broad shoulders, the rest of the body tapering away to thinness, with a noble head, bushy reddish beard streaked with gray, black hair, swept back from the forehead and lightly touched here and there with silvery white. One eye was dull and half-closed, the other was of a deep, brilliant blue which, so far from suggesting blindness, created the instant effect of a searching, eagle-like glance."

He shook Ireland's hand and said, "Well, here you see before you the miserable wreck who is to be your host; you must make the best you can of him. Give me your arm in to dinner." [6]

They entered the dining room, where the new man felt himself appraised by the veterans—Thwaites, Pollard, Paterson, Mann and Craven. "Gentlemen," Pulitzer said, "this is Mr. Alleyne Ireland; you will be able to inform him later of my fads and crotchets; well, don't be ungenerous with me, don't paint the devil as black as he is."

Questioned immediately by Pulitzer about his reading, Ireland mentioned a number of books including Townsend's *Asia and Europe*. "Well, tell me something about *Asia and Europe*," the host said. Ireland recounted the life of Mohammed, the traits of the Arabs, the charm of Asia. When he was beginning to run out he was interrupted: "My God! You don't mean to tell me that anyone is interested in that sort of rubbish. Everybody knows about Mohammed, and about the bravery of the Arabs, and, for God's sake, why shouldn't Asia be attractive to the Asiatics! Try something else. Do you remember any plays?"

Ireland named a few, including Shaw's *Caesar and Cleopatra*. "Go on, try and tell me about that." The candidate, whose dinner was now cold, knew the play well. He was able to give a good summation and quoted almost the exact words in the comical scene in which Caesar, in reply to Britannus' protest against the recognition of Cleopatra's marriage to her brother, Ptolemy, says, "Pardon him, Theodotus; he is a barbarian, and thinks that the customs of his tribe are the laws of nature." Pulitzer shook with laughter but raised his hands and cried, "Stop! Stop! For God's sake! You're hurting me."

Ireland later learned that too hearty laughter was actually painful to him and gave him a headache. Pulitzer now asked if he had a good memory—one of the most rigid of the secretarial requirements. Ireland replied cautiously that he thought he had a fairly good one.

"Oh! That's just an affectation; as a matter of fact you think you've got a splendid memory, don't you? Now, be frank about it; I love people to be frank with me."

Ireland remarked that a "wise friend" had observed that the invention of printing had made memory less important, leaving thought as the paramount function of the mind.

"Your wise friend was a damned fool!" Pulitzer cried. "If you will give the matter a moment's thought you'll see that memory is the highest faculty of the human mind. What becomes of all your reading, all your observation, your experience, study, investigations, discussions, if you have no memory?"

Ireland tried to make light answer: "I might reply by asking what use it is to lumber up your mind with a mass of information of which you are only going to make an occasional use when you can have it filed away in encyclopedias and other works of reference, and in card indexes, instantly available when you want it." [7]

Pulitzer, obviously annoyed, dropped him and turned to Paterson with a query about Bismarck. Except for the voices, the meal had an eerie silence about it. There were no utensil noises, the secretaries evidently eating without touching silver to their plates. A footman, moving silently on rubber soles, had warmed Ireland's dinner and at any rate he was able to eat. He noted that Pulitzer delighted in finding a flaw in any discourse and exposing it with delicate or sometimes ferocious irony. Although his food was cut up for him in advance, he ate without other aid, finding the morsels by skillful search with knife and fork. At the dinner's end the butler lighted his cigar for him and he left on Paterson's arm, the door closing silently behind him. Another secretary then drew a heavy velvet curtain across the door to further muffle sound, and the group was able to talk. They complimented Ireland on his performance, warning him that Pulitzer was deliberately hard on a new man, seeking to discover at once whether he was worth further trial.

Pulitzer had asked him to come to the villa at 11 next morning, which he did. He arrived to find his employer waiting in his car in a fury, insisting that he had said 10:30. But he subsided as they drove up the Corniche road.

"You'll find this business of being a candidate a very trying and disagreeable one," he said; "well, it's damned disagreeable to me, too. What I need is rest, repose, quiet, routine, understanding, sympathy, friendship, yes, my God! the friendship of those around me. Mr. Ireland, I can do much, I can do everything for a man who will be my friend. . . . But how am I to do this? I am blind, I'm an invalid; how am I to know whom I can trust? I don't mean in money matters; money's nothing to me; it can do nothing for me; I mean morally, intellectually. I've had scores of people pass through my hands in the last fifteen years . . . men from a dozen universities, self-taught men, young men, old men, and, my God! what have I found? Arrogance, stupidity, ingratitude, loose thinking, conceit, ignorance, laziness, indifference; absence of tact, discretion, courtesy, manners, consideration, sympathy, devotion; no knowledge, no wisdom, no intelligence, no observation, no memory, no understanding. My God! I can hardly believe my own experience when I think of it."

He spoke with excited gestures. "Mind! I'm not making any criticism of my present staff; you may consider yourself very lucky if I find you to have a quarter of the good qualities which any one of them has; and let me tell you that while you are with me you will do well to observe these gentlemen and to try to model yourself on them."

He asked Ireland to describe the scenery. "Remember that I am blind, and try to make me get a mental picture of everything—everything, you understand; never think that anything is too small or insignificant to be of interest to me; you can't tell what may interest me; always describe everything with the greatest minuteness, every cloud in the sky, every shadow on the hillside, every tree, every house, every dress, every wrinkle on a face, everything, everything!"

As they drove homeward he seemed taken by sheer madness. Although he had already inferred that Ireland was on trial as a secretary, he now denied that this was the case, insisted that somebody had blundered, that what he wanted was a competent man to go to the Philippines and write a series of articles about American policies there. Ireland had been in the Philippines and had done articles for the Times of London, but that was not good enough for him and he doubted that Ireland was qualified. The candidate's head was still spinning by dinner time, when Pulitzer interrogated him with inquisitorial insistence. He inquired into his knowledge of country after country, down through the centuries, switching to politics, music, art, literature and the drama. Whenever he found a hole in Ireland's knowledge he pounced on it joyfully, filled him in and passed on. When he found him well-versed on any topic he would immediately shelve it and find something more difficult. Again, Ireland had time only for hasty mouthfuls. Now and then, when Pulitzer took time to attack his fish, one of the other secretaries would try to take the pressure off the newcomer by bringing up another subject. This worked very well near the end of the dinner, when mention of the British death duties was made. Ireland, who had carefully read a news story giving a list of estates on which heavy taxes had been paid, was able to reel off some of the figures.

"Stop!" Pulitzer commanded. "Are you reading those figures?"

"No. I read them over last night in the *Daily Telegraph*."

"My God! Are you giving them from memory? Haven't you got a note of them in your hand? Hasn't he? Hasn't he?" He appealed to the others.

Reassured, he told Ireland to proceed. When he had finished, Pulitzer sent Craven for the Telegraph. "Now, Mr. Ireland, go over those figures again; and you, Mr. Craven, check them off and see if they're correct. Now, play fair, no tricks!"

He nodded on learning that Ireland had made two errors. "Well, you see, you haven't got them right after all. But that's not so bad. With a memory like that you might have known something by now if you'd only had the diligence to read." [8]

III. WALKING THE TIGHTROPE

Pulitzer was never alone for a moment except when asleep. He took breakfast with only one secretary, usually Pollard—so clearly his favorite that the others made jokes about The Importance of Being Pollard. During the meal Pollard read him articles from such magazines as the *Fortnightly Review* or the *Revue des Deux Mondes,* selected in advance for special interest and skillfully condensed so that a piece taking 15 minutes to read in full was given in no more than four minutes. Then Pulitzer closeted himself in his cabin with that model of tact, Dunningham, the man most of all in his confidence. To him he laid out his plans for the day and dictated letters he felt too private to entrust to other members of the staff. Thereafter, another secretary read him the papers—not only the World and Herald and others from New York but highlights from several London and Paris newspapers. This was an exacting chore, and since it was not always known which secretary would be charged with it, all of them often had to prepare in advance. Copies of the World arrived with the name of the writer of each article noted in pencil so that he would know whom to praise or blame. He expected secretarial mastery of political situations, speeches, murders, fires, strikes and all important events—expected also to be informed of any difference in accounts of the same event as reported in the World and other New York papers. It was a good idea first to read him a few light human interest items to put him in good humor.

This done, he called in Thwaites to dictate to him those long, detailed criticisms and suggestions that eventually reached the various editors of the World and Post-Dispatch. Then he was off for a ride or drive with one or more of the secretaries, who had to produce stimulating conversation to keep him from dejection or anger. All of them read copiously and kept notebooks filled with unusual or diverting items to have ready for such occasions.

Before lunch he took a 20-minute stroll with a secretary who was expected to "gut" a half-dozen magazine articles for him during that time—a brief biographical note of the author, then a hammer-blow précis of the facts without an unnecessary word. Since he always took the secretary's right arm, and the latter had also to guide him away from obstacles, this required intense memorization. Ireland would spend three hours or more preparing for that short crisis. In his left-hand pocket he carried cards containing notes to which he referred as they strode along, glancing at the notes and simultaneously steering their course.

The master had lunch with the full group, then took a siesta, being read to sleep by one of the secretaries—and woe to him if he coughed or was guilty of a mispronunciation. Arising, Pulitzer resumed his newspaper-reading and dictating of letters, then dressed for dinner. This was the hardest meal of the day, for by now he was apt to be tired and crotchety, and Dunningham, who knew his every mood, might warn the group to keep the conversation light and amusing.

After dinner he might attend a concert at Monte Carlo, taking a box with two secretaries to preserve his privacy. Otherwise he would repair to the library, where a secretary would read to him from a novel or play while Dr. Mann played Wagner, Liszt or Brahms on the piano only a dozen feet away, always finishing off with the "Liebestod" from *Tristan and Isolde*. This was one of Andes' devices for wringing more out of every fleeting moment of life. It was especially difficult for the reader since he was expected not only to condense adroitly but to keep his voice at that exact level of volume (without shouting) so that it could be heard above the music, which itself could change from pianissimo to fortissimo. Any misplay by Mann—a B instead of a B flat—drew the master's instant rebuke. At 10 he went to bed, with Mann reading him to sleep in German. Mann was required to watch him closely, note his breathing, and lower his voice by degrees as slumber approached. Otherwise Pulitzer would murmur, *"Leise, ganz leise"*—"Softly, quite softly"—and the reader's voice sank to a whisper for a time until he was certain the master was asleep.[9] Mann would then sneak out softly, quite softly, on rubber-soled shoes. Often Pulitzer would awaken during the night and would arouse a secretary to read to him until sleep came again.

Thus passed a typical day at the Villa Cynthia, or, with minor modifications, aboard the *Liberty*. Ireland found himself working 12 hours a day, much of it in anxious mental preparation for his meetings with the chief, who bore down on him pitilessly. To test his men, he often had two secretaries read separately from the same group of newspapers, thus discovering and scolding omissions by each. At dinner he could be hard on any of them, as one learned when he unwisely said that he had reread all of Shakespeare's plays. Pulitzer pounced. For an hour and a half the victim was required to outline clearly each of the historical plays, tragedies and comedies, name the principal characters, describe the outstanding scenes and quote vivid passages. Perspiring, he got through it with the aid of notes passed to him by his sympathetic colleagues, whereupon Pulitzer said, "Well, go on, go on, didn't you read the sonnets?" This extravagance brought a ripple of laughter from the group in which he at length joined.

Always he probed minds and memories until he found the flaw that established his own superiority. When another secretary professed some knowledge of a play, Pulitzer said, "Good! Now begin at the second scene of the third act, where the curtain rises on the two conspirators in the courtyard of the hotel; just carry it along from there." He carried it along, but the blind expert soon found an error. He permitted disagreement with him if the other's argument was logical and convincing; if not, his contempt was crushing. Occasionally, when feeling well at the table, he would launch into an hour's discourse on Athenian government or a British parliamentary crisis in which his scholarship was so deep, his language so well-ordered and his points made with such vivid emphasis that the group listened with utter admiration and pleasure.

Any change from his life of insulation upset him. He was of course well known in Menton, and while walking with a secretary on the plage he would occasionally be addressed by name by some stranger. He would stamp his foot and cry, "My God! What's this? Tell him to go away. I won't tolerate this intrusion. Tell him I'll have him arrested."

His changes of mind were notorious. The whole entourage would be alerted to board the *Liberty* for a cruise, wagonloads of baggage would be carted from the villa to the yacht, the crew would be in readiness with steam up, and at the last moment he would decide to stay ashore after all and the work was undone. On a cruise to Naples and Syracuse, he sent his men ashore to bring him descriptions of the streets, the statuary, the art. At Naples, Ireland visited the National Museum and scrutinized the main gallery without time for taking notes. When he described the pictures to Pulitzer, he discovered that they had been described to him many times before and that he knew them better than the secretary. Ireland described five paintings in minutest detail, with Pulitzer criticizing some lapses and saying, "Go on." He still said "Go on" after 15 descriptions were given, when Ireland finally had to admit defeat. As Ireland put it, "he knew practically everything, but specially he knew the thing you had forgotten." [10]

He took such delight in a good description of a face, famous or infamous, that the secretaries regularly studied illustrated catalogs of the National Portrait Gallery and Royal Academy exhibitions as well as newspaper likenesses of politicians, embezzlers or murderers. If one secretary's word-picture disagreed with another's, there was a reproof and a demand for the truth. He often had several things on his mind, and once, as Ireland read him a newspaper account of a railroad accident, he broke into laughter. Ireland stopped, whereupon Pulitzer patted his arm and said, "Go on, boy, go on, don't mind me. I wasn't laughing at you. I was thinking of something else. What was it? Oh, a railroad wreck, well, don't stop, go on reading."

He had always lived in battle, and now the battle was one of wits and words between the blind invalid and his six young, vigorous secretaries. He had always specialized in attack, and his attacks now, when gripped by a headache or by dyspepsia, could at times be unreasonable and savage. Yet he wanted no companion who would not stand up and return fire at a given point. He learned the length to which he could push each one of them, and seldom did he go beyond, though he sometimes rather liked to hover around the margin. If he was cruel, he would often apologize later with what for him was humility. During a walk when he was bitter with Ireland, he suddenly touched the younger man's shoulder and said, "What do you feel when I am unreasonable with you? Do you feel angry? Do you bear malice?" Ireland replied, "Not at all. I suppose my feeling is like that of a nurse for a patient. I realize that you are suffering and that you are not to be held responsible for what you do at such times."

"I thank you for that, Mr. Ireland," he said. "You never said anything which pleased me more. Never forget that I am blind, and that I am in pain most of the time." [11]

The six secretaries probably comprised the most remarkable blend of intelligence, experience, education, talent, cultivation (and patience) to be found anywhere in the world. They understood the illness and pain. Doubtless also they understood that the invalid's lifelong dream of leadership of men had been and still remained so powerful that he had never recovered from its loss, that he had taken the only escape that would preserve his life and his sanity by creating his own small private world in which he was acknowledged master. They submitted to his authority in this mad microcosm not for money alone. They regarded him with an admiration not untinged with affection. They would have understood perfectly Duneka's line to Pulitzer on leaving his employ: "I thank you for the privilege of knowing you." For all the bitterness, they never quite forgot the advantage of being exposed to a mind unique in its scope, keenness, excitement, urgency and menace. Each day was a challenge to their own intelligence, resourcefulness and nerve. Each day they experienced the fear and the triumph of the man who walks the high wire, knowing that any misstep means disaster, and reaches the end in safety.

Each of the secretaries who left any record mentioned his admiration as well as his despair. Dr. Hosmer, the "victim" of longest standing, was frank about the difficulties and equally certain of the greatness of the association. Pollard, who remained with Pulitzer six years, later spoke of their almost father-son relationship.[12] Barnes, a man of means who could not quite stomach being an employee, was yet so fascinated that he returned twice as a guest.

Thwaites, who would stay until he had eight service stripes on his sleeve (plus a mourning band), wrote, "My early fear of him was replaced by affection and immense admiration, not only for his amazing talents but for his idealism and his desire for public service through journalism. . . . Yet few have been more misunderstood and misjudged. The abuse hurled at Pulitzer has made me very reluctant to believe ill-natured gossip of public men . . ."

Ireland, whose service was measured in months rather than years, called it "an adventure with a genius," which indeed was the title of the little masterpiece he produced about it, and wrote:

> When I recall the capaciousness of his understanding, the breadth of his experience, the range of his information, and set them side by side with the cruel limitations imposed upon him by his blindness and by his shattered constitution, I forget the severity of his discipline, I marvel only that his self-control should have served him so well in the tedious business of breaking a new man to his service.[13]

IV. LIBERTY—HA!

The secretaries had long since rechristened the yacht the *Liberty Ha! Ha!* While each man was given a fortnight's paid vacation a year, and Pulitzer was generous in cases of trouble or illness, he felt uneasy unless all of the six were on call night or day, and their hours of leave were few. After a month, however, Ireland's severest test had been passed and he was elevated to full membership in the retinue despite a slight harshness of voice that grated on Pulitzer's ear. But there was still the question of whether he was of suitable character to mingle with Mrs. Pulitzer and the daughters, and an elaborate investigation of his earlier social life was being conducted by Tuohy.

He was on dangerous ground when he admitted to Pulitzer that during an earlier stay in New York he had read only the editorial page of the World, never the news pages because he felt them too devoted to crime and disaster. "Go on," the martinet said; "your views are not of any importance, but they're entertaining." Ireland had clipped from an old copy of *Life* rhymed characterizations of the various New York newspapers, and he was daring enough to read aloud the one about the World:

A dual personality is this,
Part yellow dog, part patriot and sage;
When't comes to facts the rule is hit or miss,
While none can beat its editorial page.
Wise counsel here, wild yarns the other side,
Page six its Jekyll and page one its Hyde;
At the same time conservative and rash,
The World *supplies us good advice and trash.*

"That's clever," Pulitzer admitted, "but it's absolute nonsense, except about the editorial page. . . . Now, I'm going to give you a lecture about newspapers, because I want you to understand my point of view. It does not matter whether you agree with it or not, but you have got to understand it if you are to be of any use to me." Ireland listened to a dissertation which perhaps contained a few rationalizations and which made no mention of Pulitzer's passion for wealth and power but which otherwise expressed the essence of his journalistic philosophy:

"I do not say that *The World* never makes a mistake in its news columns; I wish I could say it. What I say is that there are not half a dozen papers in the United States which tamper with the news, which publish what they know to be false. But if I thought that I had done no better than that I would be ashamed to own a paper. It is not enough to refrain from publishing fake news, it is not enough to take ordinary care to avoid . . . mistakes . . . you have got to do much more than that; you have got to make everyone connected with the paper—your editors, your reporters, your correspondents, your rewrite men, your proofreaders—believe that accuracy is to a newspaper what virtue is to a woman. . . .

"I do not say that *The World* is the only paper which takes extraordinary pains to be accurate; on the contrary, I think that almost every paper in America tries to be accurate. I will go further than that. There is not a paper of any importance published in French, German or English, whether it is printed in Europe or America, which I have not studied for weeks or months, and some of them I have read steadily for a quarter of a century. . . . [A]lthough there are in Europe a few newspapers, and they are chiefly English, which are as accurate as the best newspapers in America, there are *no* newspapers in America which are so habitually, so criminally stuffed with fake news as the worst of the European papers. . . .

"Now about this matter of sensationalism: a newspaper should be scrupulously accurate, it should be clean, it should avoid everything salacious or suggestive, everything that could offend good taste or lower the moral tone of its readers; but within these limits it is the duty of a newspaper to print the news. When I speak of good taste and of good moral tone I do not mean the kind of good taste which . . . refuses to recognize the existence of immorality—that type of moral hypocrite has done more to check the moral progress of humanity than all the immoral people put together—what I mean is the kind of good taste which demands that frankness should be linked with decency, the kind of moral tone which is braced and not relaxed when it is brought face to face with vice. . . .

"We are a democracy, and there is only one way to get a democracy on its feet in the matter of its individual, its social, its municipal, its State, its National conduct, and that is by keeping the public informed about what is going on. There is not a crime, there is not a dodge, there is not a trick, there is not a swindle, there is not a vice which does not live by secrecy. Get these things out in the open, describe them, attack them, ridicule them in the press, and sooner or later public opinion will sweep them away.

"Publicity may not be the only thing that is needed, but it is the one thing without which all other agencies will fail. If a newspaper is to be of real service to the public it must have a big circulation, first because its news and its comment must reach the largest number of people, second, because circulation means advertising, and advertising means money, and money means independence. If I caught any man on *The World* suppressing news because one of our advertisers objected to having it printed I would dismiss him immediately; I wouldn't care who he was. . . ." [14]

In the spring, vast preparations were made to go to Wiesbaden via Genoa and Milan. The *Liberty* would take them to Genoa, so that the critical part of the journey was from that point on. Paterson went to Milan in advance, inspected the six best hotels and selected the quietest of them. He chose a suite of rooms, bearing in mind that they must not be near the elevator, the hotel orchestra, a street carrying heavy traffic or a courtyard where dogs barked or rugs were beaten. He tested the floors to make sure that they did not creak. He eliminated the possibility of noisy neighbors by engaging rooms all around, above and below. He rode several times between the hotel and the railroad station to find the quietest and smoothest route, one not adjacent to trolleys. All this was not for an overnight stay but for five hours during the day, so that Pulitzer could have lunch and his afternoon siesta. The party then took a private railroad car from Milan to Frankfort and on to Wiesbaden, where Ledlie had engaged a villa in advance.

At the spa, Pulitzer was so eager for new experience that he dined several times at the *Kurhaus* restaurant, despite noise that at times made him wince. The town was agog over the presence of the martially mustachioed Kaiser Wilhelm II, arrived to review troops, and was alive with dashing officers and their women. Pulitzer would ask a secretary to look around, pick out the most interesting man or woman, and give a careful description. Or: "There are some gabbling women over there. Describe them to me. How are they dressed, are they painted, are they wearing jewels, how old are they?"

He continued his interminable instructions to the World, cautioning one editorial writer on style: "Thiers compares a perfect style to glass through which we look without being conscious of its presence between the object and the eye." He interviewed several candidates for positions at the World—men whose superior work he had noted in other newspapers and who were given a delightful trip to Europe marred only by this dreadful interrogation, from which each emerged shaken. He attended concerts—one night even motored to Frankfort to hear the brand-new *Der Rosenkavalier* about which everybody was talking. The revolutionizer of the press gagged at Strauss's revolution in music and left after the second act, saying, "My God! I can't stand any more of this."[15]

Ireland's admission to the circle was marked by a handsome gift of money from Pulitzer, who then sent him to London to take voice lessons to eliminate the harshness, and also to visit the art galleries and prepare careful descriptions of scores of paintings. Paterson, on vacation, was in London with instructions to visit the same galleries and bring descriptions of different paintings. Paterson would remain for a time and join the group in America. Ireland, his voice improved but his eyes rather sore from fixed examination of dusty canvases, went on to Liverpool to meet Pulitzer and the entourage, now joined by Kate and the stunning young Edith Pulitzer. They sailed on the *Cedric,* to be met at quarantine by the *Liberty,* which had crossed directly from Marseille. They all transferred to the yacht and next day were at Chatwold.

V. MOST PEOPLE THINK I'M DEAD

It was Pulitzer's last summer at Bar Harbor—his last on earth. Perhaps there was a presentiment that the man who had believed himself near death for a decade now really felt the soft brush of the wings, for there was more "family" than usual at Chatwold. Kate was mistress of the household as always, a vision of charm at 58, a woman who had exerted singular patience and a modicum of independence for 35 years to make a success of marriage to the world's outstanding eccentric, and who perhaps could have written a book about her experiences that no one but her children, Dr. Hosmer and some few others would have believed. The vivacious Edith, the more retiring and fragile Constance, Ralph and his wife and small son, Joseph and his recent bride, the former Elinor Wickham of St. Louis, the irrepressible Herbert—all were there for stays long or short to catch brief glimpses of the busy invalid at mealtime and to be catechized by him as they were always catechized. He demanded incessant descriptions of his five-year-old grandson Ralph, and also of Herbert, now a student at St. Mark's.

His great pride in his children, his fear that they were not developing all of their talents, so exercised his nerves that he had to keep his meetings with them short or suffer insomnia. Ralph and Joseph, however, he met on a business as well as paternal plane and he questioned them unmercifully about every phase of their respective newspapers. As Ireland observed, "[I]t was an easier task to be one of Mr. Pulitzer's secretaries than to be one of his sons. I have never seen men put to a more severe test of industry, concentration, and memory than were Mr. Ralph and Mr. Joseph, Jr., while they were at Bar Harbor or on the yacht."

The telephone to the World was a constant temptation, but even though he always spoke through a third person, these conversations left him unstrung. For relaxation he took short excursions on the launch, or longer ones in the yacht. To get him over the gangplank from the yacht to the launch on anything but limpid water was an ordeal. The faithful Dunningham went over first, backward, with Pulitzer following, one hand on Dunningham's shoulder, the other on the rail, an officer and a secretary behind him to help him if he slipped. The climax was the step from the gangplank to the bobbing launch. Dunningham would await the moment when the drop was short, then say, "Now, step, please, Mr. Pulitzer." But the cantankerous monster would hesitate, the launch would sink several feet and then he would step into nothing, to be seized by his aides.

"My God!" he would cry. "What's the matter? You told me to step." And there would be arguments and explanations, quite exasperating, but all who partook of them later missed them. Life without Pulitzer lacked the magic element of suspense always present in life with Pulitzer.

He fluctuated between intense energy and such weariness that he rested almost his full weight on Dunningham when walking only a short distance. The major-domo, who had been his closest companion for 15 years, had seen him fail visibly since 1908 and laid his decline most of all to the worries connected with the Panama prosecution. Ireland by now had won enough of his confidence so that he told the new secretary something of the history of his illness and blindness.

"From the day on which I first consulted the oculist," he said, "up to the present time, about twenty-four years, I have only been three times in *The World* building. Most people think I'm dead, or living in Europe in complete retirement. Now, go on and give me the morning's news." [16]

Although the Old Man preferred to look ahead, he could review more than four thundering decades of newspapering during which his achievements dwarfed those of any other American journalist. Never losing sight of his ten-point 1883 World platform for public service, he had pursued it with the "red thread" and had seen much of it come to pass. Yet, for all the importance of these specific issues, his greatest contribution was a totally new attitude of mind and heart along with a genius at communicating it. The most vicious evil he had found was the middle- and upper-class complacency of the eighties, unmoved by manifest injustice. No one had so punctured complacency as he had, nor had anyone won such abuse from the stand-patters. But editors all over the country had read the World and discovered not only that the masses had some rights but that it might be profitable as well as decent to tell them so. In New York Hearst frankly copied and overblew him, accomplishing much good along with the harm in a string of journals that spread across the land and were themselves copied. Blowing his own personal gale, Pulitzer had whipped up ripples in the stagnant expanse of national selfishness—

ripples that grew to a wave of reform that still rolled and would continue to roll.

The true greatness of his sometimes noisy World was in its inspiration, its infectious spirit of optimism, of confidence that reform was possible, that America could realize its promise by work, by vigilance, by electing men of intelligence and vision. Somehow he had escaped that bane of the press, that disease among journalists, that barricade against all progress, cynicism. Now in his enfeeblement he was as hopeful and excited about the future as he had been while working as a cub for the Westliche Post.

Once again his family and secretaries saw him gripped by that recurrent distemper, *electionitis Pulitzerium.* Although the symptoms were the same, they were less violent and his motives were perhaps more innocent and unselfish than they had ever been. The firehorse could not help responding to the bell. He wanted to elect a President, but the lust for personal power that had driven him when the years ahead stretched long had waned now with his shrunken future, and his deliberations seemed disinterested, benevolent, devoted to the good of the party and the country. Despite 15 years of failure—the pestilence of Bryan, the Dewey comedy, the Parker fiasco—eagerness and hope plucked at his brittle nerves. The Democratic party, which in 1908 he had feared would die, seemed to him resurgent in Woodrow Wilson, who was acclaimed by the World code name of Melon. Wilson was the man who, given proper guidance and support, could rescue the country in 1912. Pulitzer had studied Wilson's speeches minutely and had been delighted. He had been coaching Frank Cobb to give Melon the Pulitzerian instruction he needed in cautionary editorials in the World, the peril being that he might adopt some of the Bryan folly. Pulitzer wrote the World:

> I would like very much anything Woodrow Wilson has said on Standard Oil, Tobacco and Union Pacific–Southern Pacific decisions. Should prefer essence to verbosity. Ditto Bryan's opinions in essence on same subjects. Ditto reciprocity by both gentlemen. But brevity, brevity! [17]

He sailed to New York to give Cobb and others personal instructions and to spend many hours with the attorney Hornblower in revising his will. He sailed back to Bar Harbor. What with the excitement of family gatherings, legal discussions and his fear that Wilson might make some foolish error, he was so exhausted that he set out again on September 3 on a slow coastal cruise for sheer survival, not knowing where he was going.

The great white *Liberty,* a leviathan of seagoing luxury, poked along without destination at the whim of the most miserable man alive. The escape he sought was impossible since he could not escape himself, his nerves, his compulsion to communicate, to govern. To Kate he wired, "Hold all mail forward nothing [,] just off don't know where [,] much love." He touched at Heron Island, at Marblehead, at New London, at each place picking up newspapers and dispatching a flock of the telegrams to which he was helplessly addicted. Most of them were tender and approving, as if he felt that he had little time remaining to express tenderness and approval. He sent his compliments to Ralph and particularly to Frederica, knowing that she was soon to bear her second child, a prospect that both excited and unnerved him. He sent a pleasant greeting to young Mrs. Joseph Jr., and to Joseph he wired that he and his wife must take a fortnight's holiday together, adding:

> My movements still uncertain but wish extremely your mother would permit Herbert to [remain out of school and] go with me for fortnight into Southern warm climate. . . . I am hungry for him or somebody. I am dreadfully tired and unfit. Miss you. Love to all.

At once pathetic and indomitable, he simultaneously fled responsibilities and pursued them, sought rest and demanded action, one lobe of his tired brain longing for peace, another lobe rejecting it. Even the luxuries he depended on trapped him in the planning that compounded his weariness, for he cabled Tuohy in London: "Hope Paterson will enjoy fortnight's study of National Portrait Gallery [,] British Museum [,] Tower and sail around September twentieth." He was looking forward to Paterson's description of paintings and crown jewels. To Billing at the World: ". . . Send file Worlds [,] Evening Post other papers . . ." To Cobb:

> I wish you knew how much pleasure Friday and Saturday's [editorial] pages gave me. Compliments. Better get a hundred first class cigars but don't smoke more than three daily for your health.

To J. Angus Shaw, president of the World:

> Give Ketten one week's extra pay with my special compliments for yesterday's cartoon.

To Ralph he wired instructions and added, "Hoping all well especially Frederica." To Kate again: "How are you [,] Herbert. Hope well. . . ." [18]

There were many others. On September 18 he reached Greenwich, where in response to his telegrams Ralph and other World executives arrived by train to board the launch that would take them out to the *Liberty* for their lessons. At last, late in September, he reached New York for a short stay at his "wretched" 73rd Street residence, where the swimming pool was never used because the water bill was so high.

Here he took his meals in a small soundproof inner room with a glass dome from which light filtered over slim columns of Irish marble. Although Cobb had received frequent and explicit instructions from him all summer, he sent further thoughts in a 600-word memorandum, the last written lecture of the great professor, the very last of countless thousands of messages of instruction to John Cockerill, John Dillon, Ballard Smith, George Harvey, Charles Jones, Don Seitz, Bradford Merrill, Florence

White—to Cantabo, Grinding, Glitter, Pinch, Gumbo and a hundred others, some of them long dead. He counseled measured praise for a Taft speech. The main thing in his mind, however, was the Red Thread. Despite all the trust prosecutions by Roosevelt and Taft, not a single offender had gone to jail. He wrote in part:

> . . . You ought to have somewhere at the end (perhaps the very end), a reaffirmation and reassertion of our shibboleth that half a dozen men, nay, one man (say Mr. Morgan) or Swift or Armour, particularly the Beef Trust fellows, in prison for twenty-four hours, would do more to help the law and make it respected than all the monopolies dissolved and a hundred prosecutions by Mr. Wickersham . . . It would save further prosecutions. A telegram sent you last Sunday a week ago on this point was not well treated. Read it over again. . . . There is a chance for a very neat bit of serious, ironical and sarcastic writing. That is, not that Mr. Morgan is behind the bars, but that the public welfare would be more affected by the example of his being in jail for twenty-four hours, than by one thousand speeches by the most illustrious demagogues in the land . . .[19]

A procession of Democratic leaders called at the Vault, their heels sinking silently into thick rugs, looking to 1912 and paying obeisance not only to the most powerful Democratic newspaper but also to the most sagacious political mind extant. Advised by Ralph and Seitz, he authorized the purchase of the De Grasse paper mill at Pyrites, New York, so that the World would have its own newsprint supply. On October 5, Frederica bore his second grandson, who also happened, by an alchemy possible only in America, to be a great-great-grandson of Commodore Vanderbilt. Again his blindness barred him from the joy of seeing his new descendant. But the imaginative Pulitzer, the lover of children, worn out at 64, feeling himself near death, could not have failed to discover in the event the eternal continuity that obsessed him—the continuity he had labored to implant in his sons and editors, the continuity Cobb had expressed so well:

> Mr. Roosevelt is an episode. The World is an institution. Long after Mr. Roosevelt is dead, long after Mr. Pulitzer is dead, long after all the present editors of this paper are dead, The World will still go on as a great independent newspaper, unmuzzled, undaunted and unterrorized.

He relaxed by listening to music from the fine organ which he had once ordered *not* to be built into his home. The hit song of the year was "Alexander's Rag-time Band," by the young Irving Berlin, but he preferred Wagner or Bach. In this he differed from many contemporaries including Henry Clay Frick, whose mansion, just around the corner on Fifth Avenue, also had a church organ. Frick would settle back in deep contentment as the pipes pealed out his favorite tune:

Dearie, my dearie, nothing's worth while but dreams of you,
And you can make ev'ry dream come true; dearie, my dearie! [20]

Pulitzer was so wearied by the incessant nearness of business and politics at 73rd Street that by mid-October he was ready for the usual cure, a cruise. Unhappily, Paterson had not yet arrived to describe all those pictures. Craven had left his service, and he felt naked with only four secretaries. Through Dunningham he wrote James Barnes, asking him so importunately to go along that Barnes, though his father was ill, agreed. The *Liberty* sailed for Jekyll Island October 18, with Herbert and his tutor-governess, Elizabeth Keelan, in the company along with Barnes, Thwaites, Pollard, Ireland, Mann, Dunningham and Dr. Guthman.

Ireland, appointed official humorist to amuse the tired monarch, read to him from Mr. Dooley, Artemas Ward, and George Horace Lorimer's *Letters of a Self-Made Merchant to His Son.* He also had a collection of humorous stories culled from *Puck, Judge, Life* and *Answers.* Once or twice he tried jokes in which the point was not instantly visible. When he came to the end there would be that awkward pause and Andes would say, "Well, go on, go on, come to the point. For God's sake, isn't there any end to this story?"

Barnes found him talkative enough, discussing his plans for the school of journalism at Columbia, his intention to make further changes in his will, his concern for the freedom of the press. "What is to be feared in this country," he said, "is the combination of destructive, radical opinion arrayed against freedom and constitutional liberty." Yet he agreed that the Constitution might be to some extent outgrown, and that it would be the Democrats who would strike out in the direction of revision. "The Republicans will always be the conservatives," he said. "You may live to see all this come to an issue; I will not." [21]

On October 24 the yacht put in to Charleston to pick up letters and newspapers, something to which he looked forward as a hungry man awaits a meal. Since there were warnings of an imminent West Indian hurricane, it was decided to stay in port until the blow was over. Next day, when he was seized by stomach pains, Dr. Guthman (well knowing he was not fully trusted) called in Dr. Robert Wilson of Charleston, who diagnosed the trouble as indigestion and administered veronal. Soon Andes seemed himself again, and on Friday, October 27, he had Robert Lathan, editor of the Charleston News & Courier, on board for luncheon and an animated discussion of Wilson and of Democratic chances in 1912. Lathan cited a political argument made by Edmund Burke, whereupon Pulitzer, remarking that he had not read Burke in 20 years, "instantly quoted verbatim from one of Burke's later speeches in which he had expressed a directly contrary view to that suggested."

On Saturday morning he was ill again—not surprising in his life of infirmity. Thwaites merely followed orders in telegraphing Mrs. Pulitzer, who had received many such messages over the years. Now, however, she had a premonition. Her husband had looked more fatigued than usual. She took the next train from New York, riding a private car as usual.

If Monday was usually a lean news day for the World, the chief was to provide a front-page sensation for this coming Monday. At three o'clock Sunday morning, Dunningham aroused Ireland in his cabin, saying, "Mr. Pulitzer wishes you to come and read to him."

Ireland donned a robe, snatched up books and hurried to the bedside to read to him steadily for two hours, finishing off with Macaulay's essay on Hallam. Pulitzer, obviously in pain, twitched from side to side and for a time got out of bed and sat in an easy chair. But he listened attentively, interrupting Ireland occasionally to ask him to repeat a passage. At length he sent for Dr. Guthman. "Good-bye, I'm much obliged to you," he said to Ireland. ". . . Go, now, and have a good rest, and forget all about me."

The *Liberty* heaved almost imperceptibly as dawn illumined the harbor, the ruin of Fort Sumter, and touched the handsome spire of St. Michael's. The secretaries knew Andes as the kind who could be expected to spring from his bed of pain and demand the world's news engraved on the head of a pin. They had breakfast and studied the newspapers with traditional attention.

Toward noon Friedrich Mann read to Pulitzer in German from a life of Louis XI, once being interrupted when the master asked, "Is there any new political development today?" The eleventh Louis interested him, although in his own monarchical status he might have found something disturbing in Louis' unfilial intrigues against his father while dauphin, and his dismissal of his late father's most trusted advisers when he became king.

Around one o'clock he murmured quiet final words, for one whose life had driven steadily into the tempest: "*Leise, ganz leise.*"

Mann dropped his voice and continued reading. Kate Pulitzer arrived at 1:20, winning the race by some 15 minutes. She entered the cabin with Herbert to find him unconscious, to see him die so gently that his passing was invisible. Thwaites, Pollard and Ireland were dawdling over their luncheon coffee when the head butler opened the door to the dining saloon and announced with the dignity characteristic of the establishment, "Mr. Pulitzer is dead." [22]

Afterword

Decline and Fall

Thwaites immediately telephoned the World about Pulitzer's death. The news went to the Associated Press from the Charleston News & Courier, resulting in "a perfect swarm of telegrams from newspapers all over the country desiring full particulars." The body was embalmed at a local undertaker's and returned to Pulitzer's spacious cabin in the *Liberty,* where the 60 crewmen passed by the open coffin in single file. "So peaceful was his face," said the News & Courier, "that one would have said that he slept."

The Monday World, under Lincoln but certainly with advice from Seitz and White, gave the event the importance it represented to the paper—the importance Andes would have expected. The story of his life and death covered the front page in toto, with the fine Sargent portrait given four columns at top center. His passing also made front-page news in virtually every daily in the country, drawing comment as well in newspapers in every European capital. Starting penniless as he did, his career, except for the absence of a log-cabin birthplace, seemed to fulfill the external aspects of the great American success story. The aura of mystery that had surrounded his later years added to his greatness and flaws as a journalist in testing the interpretive abilities of newswriters and editorialists the world over. None disputed his greatness, but not all passed over the flaws.

While there were elements of puritanism and perhaps envy in some of the criticism, there was also honest perplexity. Which was the real man—the front-page sensationalist or the schoolmaster-idealist of the editorial page? Could one really reconcile the millionaire capitalist, the palace-dweller, the man of yachts and private cars, with the Pulitzer who attacked capitalists and trusts? The most moving and generous laudation, without a particle of fault-finding, came in the sturdy prose of William

Randolph Hearst, who had learned much of his journalism from Pulitzer. It began:

> A towering figure in National and international journalism has passed away; a mighty democratic force in the life of the Nation and in the activity of the world has ceased; a great power uniformly exerted in behalf of popular rights and human progress is ended. Joseph Pulitzer is dead.

Lord Northcliffe forgot the unpleasantness over his kidnaping of Alfred Butes and wrote a two-column tribute in his Daily Mail, mentioning among many other things Pulitzer's "rare faculty of viewing things exactly as they are" and stressing his absolute courage in backing unpopular causes, as when he threw his weight against war with England over Venezuela, a stand that "brought upon him abuse, a temporary loss of subscribers . . . and the violence of a general public attack . . ."

Although there was emphasis on his illness, blindness and nervousness, no one touched on the real nature of his malady or mentioned his 22-year battle against the demons of depression and mental anguish in which he had, by methods uniquely his own, won his greatest victory even though he would have called the victory a Pyrrhic one. Henry Watterson noted the difficulties experts were having in determining the value of Pulitzer's newspapers to make an appraisal of the estate because (as one of the appraisers, Melville Stone, admitted) Pulitzer's own contribution to their value was priceless, impossible to estimate. And Watterson let himself go in words that were typically extravagant but true: "His life reads like a story out of the books of giants, goblins and fairies."

From a standpoint of sheer publicity, the publicist Pulitzer would have approved. His death was the subject of far more newspaper coverage than that given any other journalistic titan.

His body rode north on a crepe-hung express car on an Atlantic Coast Line train carrying also relatives and staff members. At Manhattan Transfer it was discovered that the express car was of a new type two inches too high to enter the tunnel under the Hudson. Had this not have been noticed, the car would have been wrecked. The express car was detached and the coffin rode under the river and into Pennsylvania Station on the open platform of a Pullman car.

The funeral was held November 1, a sunlit fall day, at the ultra-fashionable St. Thomas Episcopal Church at Fifth Avenue and 53rd Street, which it was believed Pulitzer had never entered before. Edith Pulitzer, who was in France at the time of his death, and Constance, in Colorado Springs, were unable to reach New York in time for the services. Among the honorary pallbearers were Pulitzer's long-time physician Dr. James W. McLane, J. Angus Shaw, George Harvey, Seth Low and Nicholas Murray Butler. Hundreds of "Pulitzer scholars"—lawyers, doctors, educators and men in other walks of life who had been aided by his grants since 1893 in completing their educations—were represented by a deputation. Three hundred employees of the World and Post-Dispatch were present, as were those aides who knew him best of all: Dr. Hosmer, Arthur Billing, Norman Thwaites, Harold Pollard, Friedrich Mann and Jabez Dunningham. Three sightless men represented the Blind Men's Club. Many of the 2,000 mourners could not be accommodated, and a huge crowd blocked traffic on Fifth Avenue. Notable among the floral offerings was a wreath of roses bearing the card, "Republic of Colombia, to Her Friend." The service was read by the Rev. Dr. Ernest M. Stires, who had officiated at Ralph's wedding.

"For five minutes at the beginning of the service," said the World, "not a wheel turned nor a word was spoken in the offices of The World and of the Post-Dispatch in St. Louis. The presses were brought to a standstill, the electric lights extinguished . . . The telephone and telegraph systems were disconnected, so that . . . the two offices were cut off from the outside world."

Among the many silk-hatted officials present was state Supreme Court Justice Leonard A. Geigerich, who perhaps had not read that morning's World, which charged that he had paid $9,000 for his nomination.

Pulitzer was buried that afternoon at Woodlawn Cemetery next to the grave of Lucille Irma. There was much speculation about the size of his estate, estimates running from thirty to eighty millions. Surprise was general when it was appraised at a comparatively modest $18,525,116. Those who felt that the morning, Evening and Sunday Worlds must have returned a million-dollar annual profit were also surprised to learn that the average net profit (or Nelson) for the years 1908 to 1911 was $536,-580, the flourishing Post-Dispatch in St. Louis being not far behind in showing an annual average of $408,456 for the same period. The estate would of course have been larger but for the family's luxurious mode of life. The cost of maintaining the *Liberty* was estimated at nearly $200,000 a year, while the bill for the homes in New York, Bar Harbor, Jekyll Island and the best villa at Cap Martin came to around $350,000 annually. No one estimated the amount Pulitzer had paid to physicians for himself and his often ailing family, and for scores of stays at European spas, but that total alone would obviously have represented a sizable fortune.

He left $100,000 to Jabez Dunningham, $20,000 to Dr. Hosmer and $100,000 to be divided among his secretary-companions and his leading recruiter, James M. Tuohy. His earlier bequest of $50,000 to Alfred Butes had been canceled when Butes left him. He left $50,000 for the fountain which now ornaments the Plaza at 59th Street, and $25,000 for a statue of Jefferson, a Democratic father whom he felt was neglected in the nation's largest Democratic city. Another $1,000,000 went to Columbia University for its school of journalism, not yet begun; and a fund of $250,000 to provide scholarships and annual prizes for outstanding journalistic, historical, musical and dramatic work. A half-million was given the Metropolitan Museum of Art, and a like sum to the Philharmonic Society, the donor urging that its programs be not too severely classical and that they be "open to the public at reduced rates, and will also receive my favorite composers, Beethoven, Wagner and Liszt."

Kate Pulitzer was given the income of a fund of $2,500,000, the two daughters that of $1,500,000, and the residuary estate was left in trust for the grandchildren. The wife of Joseph Pulitzer Jr., the former Elinor Wickham, received $250,000, perhaps being favored because she would come into no such family inheritance as would Ralph's wife. The stipulations that startled observers were those relating to the sons and to the newspapers. The will read:

> I particularly enjoin upon my sons and my descendants the duty of preserving, perfecting and perpetuating The World newspaper, to the maintenance and publishing of which I have sacrificed my health and strength, in the same spirit in which I have striven to create and conduct it as a public institution, from motives higher than mere gain . . .

His partiality for Herbert made a flurry of news headlines. The capital stock of the New York and St. Louis newspapers was left in trust for the sons, Herbert being given six-tenths, Ralph two-tenths and Joseph one-tenth, the remaining tenth to be sold later at "liberal terms" to "the principal editors or managers" felt by the trustees to be most deserving. However, none of the sons was given actual control of the newspapers, this being left in the hands of four trustees—J. Angus Shaw, the St. Louis attorney Frederick N. Judson, Judge Harrington Putnam of Brooklyn, and the New York attorney George L. Rives, president of the Board of Trustees of Columbia University. Charles Evans Hughes had declined his $100,000 trusteeship because in 1910 he had become a justice of the Supreme Court. Judson would serve as trustee for three years, when Joseph Jr. would become 30 and would replace him. Shaw would serve for six years, when Herbert Pulitzer would become 21 and take his place. Ralph, now 32, was the only one of the brothers not given a trusteeship then or at any time in the future.

Why the proportion of six-tenths to Herbert, who of course as yet knew nothing of journalism—three times that of Ralph and six times that of Joseph, both of whom had made their mark? Why had Pulitzer felt that Herbert would become competent for trusteeship at 21, whereas Joseph had to wait until he was 30? And why, if Ralph received twice the share of Joseph, was he omitted entirely as a trustee?

Ralph, obviously deeply embarrassed, made a public statement noting that the omission might mistakenly suggest "a lack of confidence in me on [my father's] part." He was supported by a letter from Attorney Hornblower making it appear that Pulitzer had indeed intended that Ralph be a trustee. Hornblower pointed out that Ralph had been given trusteeship in the will of 1904 and that his omission in the codicil of 1909 must have been unintentional, a secretarial error. In fact, in Pulitzer's last will of 1911, which he had framed with Hornblower but which never became controlling because he died with it unfinished and unexecuted, Ralph *was* named as a trustee.

The difficulty was repaired by two steps. J. Angus Shaw withdrew as president of the World to resume his former post as treasurer, and Ralph was elected president by the trustees; and Judge Putnam resigned as a trustee, Ralph being elected in his place.

In December, six weeks after her father's death, Edith Pulitzer married William Scoville Moore, grandson of Clement Moore, the scholar and poet who wrote "A Visit from St. Nicholas." The wedding took place quietly at the 73rd Street house because of the mourning, Constance Pulitzer being her sister's only attendant. In September, 1913, Constance married William Gray Elmslie at Lake Tahoe, California. Elmslie, son of a British judge, had been a tutor of Herbert Pulitzer before going into business in Winnipeg.

The widowed Kate Pulitzer spent much of her latter years in France, making her home variously at Deauville, Cap Martin and the impressive Château de la Garoupe at Nice, which she leased, a Riviera showplace famous for its flower garden. She died suddenly at 74 on July 29, 1927, at the Villa Romaine at Deauville, with Herbert at her bedside, and was buried beside her late husband at Woodlawn.

Meanwhile the Post-Dispatch under Joseph Jr., with O. K. Bovard as managing editor, had become one of the nation's best, most influential and profitable newspapers. But the World, though still an interesting and independent journal, was surrounded by vigorous competitors and was in trouble. In 1920 Ralph had made the brilliant Herbert Bayard Swope editor and the World had shifted from its old aim at the masses, now catering to a middle-road readership and in some respects to intellectuals. It had abandoned Pulitzer's aversion for bylines and carried a galaxy of stars including Heywood Broun, Walter Lippmann, Franklin P. Adams and Alexander Woollcott.

Doubtless the shift was made in part because the surging morning tabloids had almost preempted the sensational field, but the move was unsuccessful. Advertising dwindled. Some World men felt a lack of aggressive leadership. The personal guidance of the Old Man was gone—his flaming ability to stimulate enthusiasm, his sense of urgency, his insistence that the World must improve every day. The esprit de corps of a newspaper staff is intangible but priceless. "The Pulitzer Building was a haunted house," Adams wrote, containing the "ghost of Joseph Pulitzer." There was high respect for the industrious Ralph, but, as FPA put it, "It seemed to me many times that it took too long for him to decide, and that there were too few of us in the office who knew him." The command that had once been so personal had become impersonal. The death of Frank Cobb in 1923 removed the fighter dearest to Pulitzer's heart, a dynamic personality who had radiated some of the Old Man's infectious excitement. His replacement by the calm, scholarly Lippmann—a man of unexcelled attainments for intellectual readers—was another sign of the World's withdrawal from the aggressiveness and excitement Pulitzer had demanded.

In 1924 Ralph had been divorced in Paris from Frederica Vanderbilt Webb, who soon remarried. In 1928 he married Margaret Kernochan Leech, the novelist who would later become a distinguished biographer. Herbert, after his graduation from Harvard, worked briefly as a reporter and later did some European correspondence for the World. But he had never drunk at the fount as his brothers had and did not understand journalism as they did, nor was he vitally interested. A likable personality, he traveled widely and had a shooting lodge in Scotland. In 1926 he married Mrs. Gladys Mildred Munn Amory. There could be only one JP, and just as his newspaper interests were divided unequally at his death, so were the talents inherited from him, but in reverse order. Joseph Jr., who received the smallest share, was the best newspaperman of the three, a leader of great abilities, character and intelligence who gave the Post-Dispatch what the World lacked—a sense of driving force from the top.

The annual profits of the World trio sank from $500,000 in 1922 to half that in 1925. It could hardly have been gratifying to the two hard-working brothers that Herbert, who contributed little effort, drew by far the largest share of profit. In 1924, Herbert paid an income tax of $198,000, while Ralph paid $83,000. In 1925, the morning World raised its price to three cents although its competitors held at two cents. It was a disastrous move. Until then, Senior had still held top morning circulation with 404,000. By 1926 it was down to 285,000. In 1927 the price was dropped to two cents again, but the recovery of circulation was small.

Certainly there were worried conferences among the brothers. Early in 1928 Herbert took an office in the Dome with the intention of devoting himself to the papers. The move was disquieting because he was an aloof executive known to few members of the staff and it was felt that he was not really a newspaperman and that he was there for financial rather than editorial reasons. Some of the World's good reporters and writers were leaving and, as City Editor James W. Barrett put it, "we reached the absolutely low ebb of morale . . ." Swope, evidently seeing the handwriting, resigned in October. Only a few of the men who had known Andes were still there, among them John Tennant, now editor of the Evening World, and Florence D. White, who had started with the Post-Dispatch as a youngster in 1881 and now was general manager of the World newspapers.

The papers thereafter lost money, showing a deficit in 1928 of $97,000, in 1929 of $737,000 and in 1930 (the first depression year) of $1,677,625. In February, 1930, Ralph resigned as president because of "ill health" and Herbert was elected to the post. There had been rumors, all denied, that the papers were to be sold. In December, 1930, Herbert offered to dicker with Roy Howard of the Scripps-Howard chain, who owned the New York Evening Telegram and was anxious to expand. There were parleys also with Hearst, Adolph Ochs, Paul Block and others. Some of the discussions were held at the Plaza Hotel overlooking the Pulitzer Memorial Fountain.

The World's circulation early in 1931 was 313,000, but it had been outstripped by the Times, with 417,000, and by the tabloid Daily News, and Daily Mirror. The Evening World's 276,000 was less than that of Hearst's Journal and the revived evening Sun. The Sunday World's 492,000 trailed the Sunday Times and Hearst's Sunday American as well as the tabloids. The Pulitzers were unwilling to risk further heavy losses. They felt that the middle group solicited by the World was shrinking—that the Times, Herald Tribune and Sun were drawing away conservative readers, while the growing tabloids were winning the sensation-lovers.

The factors contributing to the decay of a newspaper are many and complex. Pulitzer himself, had he been living, might have had trouble in the changing newspaper scene. But observers felt that in the twenties the World had begun to scatter its shots and to lose its remarkably forceful character, the Red Thread. Yet Andes was not without blame in the debacle. The unhappy error in his will excluding Ralph as a trustee had been technically corrected, but of course some doubt had persisted as to whether it really was an error and the sensitive Ralph had begun his leadership under a cloud. His own morale could hardly have been improved by the will's stipulation that gave Herbert an interest far greater than Ralph's or Joseph's. Joseph, by far the most forceful of the brothers, not at all neurotic, was able to surmount this implied lack of fatherly confidence. One feels that Ralph never quite removed his late father's critical shadow, and indeed there was little he could do but give up the battle when the less experienced Herbert with his 60 percent interest took an office in the Pulitzer Building.

Ultimately the three Worlds were sold to the Scripps-Howard bidders for $5,000,000. This meant only the diluted perpetuation of the Evening World in the new World-Telegram. The Sunday World was dead. *The* World, the mighty Senior, the heart and soul of Joseph Pulitzer, was dead. Its last front page, dated Friday, February 27, 1931, still displayed the Goddess of Liberty between the two faces of the globe on its nameplate, but below it was a statement signed by Ralph, Joseph and Herbert as trustees pointing to "inexorable" economic conditions and ending:

> The trustees cannot pretend that it is anything but a painful duty to pass the World newspapers into other hands. But there is a fortunate mitigation in the spirit of the new ownership which is thoroughly hospitable to

the World tradition. May it carry on that tradition with the fullest measure of public service and success.

The World had outlived Joseph Pulitzer by 19 years and four months. The Post-Dispatch, which he had several times tried to sell and to which he devoted much less attention, survived—and still does—as a vigorous leader among afternoon papers, perpetuating also the famous name of its founder in its present owner, the third Joseph Pulitzer.

The Pulitzer Building, no longer housing a newspaper, continued rather forlornly as an office building. As one former Evening World man, Emmet Crozier, described it, "It resembled a once beautiful and vivacious woman who had lost her interest in life." It was razed in 1955 to gain space for a new approach to the Brooklyn Bridge.

Author's Note and Acknowledgments

The enormous scope of Joseph Pulitzer's efforts in journalism, politics, social reform, philanthropy, education and self-preservation would make a definitive biography assume encyclopedic proportions. This book has a more modest aim—to show the man himself as clearly as possible within moderate space, and to illustrate his methods and achievements only in some of their more outstanding instances.

One portion of *Pulitzer* necessarily covers, from the opposite side of the battlefield, the journalistic struggle narrated in my earlier *Citizen Hearst*. New information throws more light on Pulitzer's strategy in the contest, and it is hoped that readers familiar with the previous book will forgive a few inescapable repetitions.

As in earlier books, my wife, Dorothy Green Swanberg, a researcher of infinite talents, was my collaborator in studying and compiling the Pulitzer data—a partnership useful not only in the division of labor but in the coffee-time discussion of doubtful points often resulting in better understanding. Her reading of the manuscript and her questioning of unsatisfactory passages suggested many improvements.

My debt to Professor Julian S. Rammelkamp is likewise incalculable. As I was embarking on a study of Pulitzer's St. Louis Post-Dispatch for the years 1878–83, I learned that Dr. Rammelkamp had just completed his excellent book *Pulitzer's Post-Dispatch*, covering that same ground in the most scholarly and engrossing detail. He kindly let me read his manuscript and permitted me to use his full-length work as the basis of my brief account of those five important years of St. Louis journalism. I gratefully acknowledge my use of his material and his generosity as an accessory in the theft.

For other researches into Pulitzer's St. Louis career I relied on John D. Heyl, a graduate student at Washington University in that city and a thorough investigator, at home in German. He translated passages from the Westliche Post and explored other local newspapers of that era. Much of his work was done at the Missouri Historical Society, where thanks are due to the archivist, Mrs. Frances H. Stadler.

Members of the Pulitzer family rendered the kind of help that only relatives can give. I am grateful to Mrs. William Scoville Moore of New York, daughter of

Joseph Pulitzer, for telling me her recollections of her father and her family; to Mrs. Ralph Pulitzer of New York (a biographer of consummate endowments) for her own recollections, for permission to quote from her late husband's letters, and for her generous help in locating fine family pictures; to Mrs. Joseph Pulitzer of New York, widow of the son of the subject of this book, for permission to quote from her husband's letters; to Herbert Pulitzer Jr. of Palm Beach for kind cooperation; to Joseph Pulitzer Jr. of St. Louis, grandson of the subject, for permission to quote from papers under his authority; and to Mrs. William C. Weir of Cleveland and Sydney J. Freedberg of Cambridge, Mass., for providing valuable family pictures.

Roland Baughman, head of Special Collections at Columbia University's Butler Library, and Kenneth A. Lohf, Assistant Librarian, were most helpful in making available the Pulitzer papers there. At the Library of Congress, Dr. David C. Mearns, Chief of the Manuscript Division, extended his expert aid as always, and the researcher Robert Weinstock explored the archives with real interest of his own.

To Professor Irving Dilliard of Princeton University, formerly a staff member at the Post-Dispatch, I render special thanks for his extreme kindness in directing me to fruitful sources of information.

Dr. Henry Wexler, the New Haven psychiatrist, is as wary of the couch school of biography as I am. He discussed Pulitzer with me, as he has done with previous subjects I have undertaken, always with the proviso that judgments of a man long dead must be made with caution. Illumination came as much from his keen understanding of human nature as from his purely professional skills. Any conclusions drawn here, of course, are my own.

For discriminating appraisal and correction of the manuscript, I thank my accomplished literary agent, Patricia Schartle, and Burroughs Mitchell of Scribner's, with both of whom I have enjoyed a long and thoroughly pleasant publishing relationship. Mrs. Renni Browne's copy-reading of the manuscript showed rare sensitivity and perception.

The kind assistance of the following was valuable in a variety of ways: Mrs. Livingston L. Biddle of Bryn Mawr, Penn.; James Boylan, editor of the *Columbia Journalism Review;* Dorothy W. Bridgwater, assistant head, Reference Department, Yale University Library; Professor William N. Chambers, chairman, Department of History, Washington University, St. Louis; The Charleston Library Society; George A. Cornish of New York; Emmet Crozier of New Haven; Roy A. Grisham Jr. of Princeton, N.J.; Mrs. Carter Hayward of Naugatuck, Conn.; James Henle of New York; Robert W. Hill, Keeper of Manuscripts, New York Public Library; Frank L. Johnson of Newtown, Conn.; Mrs. E. A. Lindberg of Minneapolis; Tom Mahoney of New York; Miss Gertrude McDonald of St. Louis; Thomas L. McLane of New Canaan, Conn.; the Princeton University Press; Mattie Russell, Curator of Manuscripts, Duke University Library; Charles Scribner Jr.; Judith Schiff, head, Historical Manuscripts Department, Yale University Library; R. H. Shinn of Philadelphia; Dr. Louis M. Starr of Columbia University; Dr. Howard C. Taylor Jr. of New York; Nicholas B. Wainwright, Director, The Historical Society of Pennsylvania; and Juliet Wolohan, Senior Librarian, New York State Historical Library.

Notes

Abbreviations used below are: "CU" for the Joseph Pulitzer Papers at Columbia University; "LC" for the Joseph Pulitzer Papers at the Library of Congress, unless otherwise indicated; "Yale" for the several collections at Yale University; "*MHR*" for the *Missouri Historical Review;* "NYPL" for the New York Public Library; and "NYSHL" for the New York State Historical Library at Albany.

PART I

Chapter 1

1. Don. C. Seitz, *Joseph Pulitzer,* p. 47.
2. St. Louis Post-Dispatch, Dec. 28, 1924. Among the dozens of newspaper and other accounts of JP's search for work and journey to St. Louis, there is variation in details but agreement in basic facts.
3. N. Y. Evening Post, Oct. 30, 1911.
4. Cleon Forbes, "The St. Louis School of Thought," *MHR,* XXV, No. 4 (July, 1931).
5. Alleyne Ireland, *Adventure with a Genius,* pp. 171–72.
6. Missouri Republican, Aug. 21, 1866.
7. William Hepworth Dixon, *New America,* pp. 11–12.
8. Seitz, *op. cit.,* p. 55.
9. George S. Johns, "Joseph Pulitzer in St. Louis," *MHR,* XXV, No. 2 (Jan. 1931).
10. N. Y. Tribune, Dec. 20, 1885.
11. Cleon Forbes, *op. cit.*
12. George S. Johns, *op. cit.*
13. "Loud applause," etc.: Westliche Post, Dec. 15, 1869. "We suppose," etc., quoted in Westliche Post, Dec. 18, 1869.

Chapter 2

1. Westliche Post, Jan. 27, 1870.
2. The accounts in the St. Louis Dispatch and Missouri Democrat are quoted in Seitz, *op. cit.,* pp. 65–67.

3. Westliche Post, Jan. 30, 1870.
4. Thomas S. Barclay, "The Liberal Republican Movement in Missouri," *MHR*, XXI, No. 1 (Oct. 1926).
5. N. Y. Sun, Aug. 24, 1871, cited in Candace Stone, *Dana and the Sun*, p. 53.

Chapter 3

1. L. U. Reavis, *St. Louis, the Future Great City of the World*, p. 37.
2. *MHR*, XXI, No. 2 (Jan. 1927), pp. 271–72.
3. N. Y. Tribune, May 1, 1872.
4. Henry Watterson, *Marse Henry*, I, pp. 255–56.
5. *Reminiscences of Carl Schurz*, II, p. 376.
6. *Editor and Publisher*, Nov. 4, 1911.
7. W. F. Switzler, *Switzler's Illustrated History of Missouri*, p. 473.
8. Seitz, *op. cit.*, pp. 2–3.
9. John McDonald, *Secrets of the Great Whiskey Ring*, pp. 70, 338.
10. Watterson, *Marse Henry*, I, p. 211.
11. Jim Allee Hart, *A History of the St. Louis Globe-Democrat*, p. 113; Walter B. Stevens, "The New Journalism in Missouri," *MHR*, XVII, No. 3 (April 1923), p. 327.
12. John McDonald, *op. cit.*, p. 93.
13. JP to Schurz, June 3, 1874; Schurz Prs., LC.
14. Three JP letters to Davidson, July 1874, all in the Davidson Prs., Yale.
15. Johns, *op. cit.*, *MHR*, XXV, No. 3 (April 1931), p. 418.
16. Quoted in Seitz, *op. cit.*, pp. 80–82.
17. McDonald, *op. cit.*, p. 102; also, Allan Nevins, *Hamilton Fish*, p. 763.
18. Walter B. Stevens, "The Political Turmoil of 1874 in Missouri," *MHR*, XXXI, No. 1 (Oct. 1936), pp. 5–6.

Chapter 4

1. Stevens, "The New Journalism in Missouri," *MHR*, XIX, No. 2 (Jan. 1925), p. 330.
2. Seitz, *op. cit.*, p. 85.
3. N. Y. Tribune, June 27, 1876.
4. St. Louis Times, Sep. 4, 1876.
5. Seitz, *op. cit.*, pp. 88–89.
6. Edward P. Mitchell, *Memoirs of an Editor*, p. 264.
7. N. Y. Sun, Feb. 15, 1877.
8. N.Y. Times and N.Y. Herald, both April 12, 1877.
9. Seitz, *op. cit.*, pp. 91–92.
10. N.Y. World, Nov. 9, 1885.
11. Seitz, *op. cit.*, pp. 93–94.
12. *Ibid.*, pp. 94–95.
13. George Johns, *op. cit.*, MHR, XXVI, No. 1 (Oct. 1931), p. 67.
14. Kate to JP, Oct. 2, 1904 (CU).
15. N.Y. Sun, Oct. 6, 1878.
16. N.Y. Sun, Oct. 20, 1878.
17. Julian Rammelkamp, *Pulitzer's Post-Dispatch*, pp. 1–4, 13–19.

PART II

Chapter 1

1. Post-Dispatch, Dec. 12, 1878.
2. Post-Dispatch, Jan. 10, 1879, cited in Rammelkamp, *Pulitzer's Post-Dispatch,* p. 47.
3. Post-Dispatch, Feb. 15, 1879 (in Rammelkamp, *op. cit.*, p. 52).
4. Post-Dispatch, Feb. 14, 1879 (in Rammelkamp, p. 58).
5. O. O. Stealey, *130 Pen Pictures of Live Men,* p. 345.
6. Post-Dispatch, Dec. 5, 1879 ff. (in Rammelkamp, p. 72).
7. Post-Dispatch, May 18, 1882.
8. For a full JP dissertation on sensationalism, see Alleyne Ireland, *Adventure with a Genius,* pp. 107–116.
9. Mrs. William Scoville Moore told Swanberg Mar. 10, 1965.
10. Homer W. King, *Pulitzer's Prize Editor,* pp. 92–94.
11. O. O. Stealey, *op. cit.*, p. 348.
12. Post-Dispatch, Jan. 17, 1880 (in Rammelkamp, p. 98).

Chapter 2

1. Quoted in Joseph Pulitzer Jr. to JP, Mar. 10, 1903 (CU).
2. Post-Dispatch, Feb. 12, 1879 (in Rammelkamp, p. 129).
3. Post-Dispatch, Mar. 2, 1880.
4. Post-Dispatch, April 28, 1880 (in Rammelkamp, p. 131).
5. O. O. Stealey, *op. cit.*, p. 347.
6. Post-Dispatch, Sep. 22, 1880.
7. Post-Dispatch, Dec. 22, 1880 (in Rammelkamp, p. 155).
8. Orrick Johns, *Time of Our Lives,* p. 67.
9. John L. Heaton, *The Story of a Page,* p. 312.
10. Post-Dispatch, Jan. 3, 1881 (in Rammelkamp, p. 251).
11. Stealey, *op. cit.*, p. 349.
12. Rammelkamp, *op. cit.*, chap. VIII.
13. Post-Dispatch, Sep. 8 and Sep. 15, 1881 (in Rammelkamp, p. 175).
14. Rammelkamp, *op. cit.*, p. 179.
15. *Ibid.*, p. 199.
16. Wickham Steed, *Through Thirty Years,* Vol. I, p. 75.
17. James Morgan, *Charles H. Taylor,* p. 114.

Chapter 3

1. Post-Dispatch, Oct. 13, 1882.
2. Augustus Thomas, *The Print of My Remembrance,* pp. 135–37.
3. Post-Dispatch, Oct. 18, 1882 (in Rammelkamp, p. 291). Years later, Slayback's daughter Suzanne became society editor for the Post-Dispatch.
4. In Cockerill's obituary, N. Y. Times, April 11, 1896.
5. Quoted in Post-Dispatch, Nov. 4, 1882 (in Rammelkamp, p. 290).
6. N. Y. Tribune, May 17, 1883, and Dec. 20, 1885.

7. Seitz, *op. cit.*, p. 131.
8. Melville Stone, *Fifty Years a Journalist*, p. 122.
9. Henry Watterson, *Marse Henry*, Vol. I, pp. 207–208.
10. Burton J. Hendrick, *The Training of an American*, pp. 155, 158.

PART III

Chapter 1

1. James Creelman, "Joseph Pulitzer—Master Journalist," *Pearson's Magazine*, Mar. 1909.
2. N.Y. World, May 11, 1883.
3. N.Y. Times, Nov. 5, 1911.
4. World, May 17, 1883.
5. Gibson to JP, May 14, 1883 (CU).
6. JP to F. D. White, Feb. 26, 1905 (CU).
7. Mark D. Hirsch, *William C. Whitney*, p. 227 fn.
8. "A good round oath:" World, Oct. 23, 1883; "another Cleveland:" World, June 6, 1883.
9. Holmes to JP, N.D. (CU).
10. N.Y. Sun, May 15, 1883.
11. World, May 16, 1883.
12. World, Sep. 26, 1883.
13. World, Dec. 7, 1883.
14. Belmont to JP, Dec. 26, 1883 (CU).
15. Dillon to JP, Sep. 5, 1884 (CU).
16. Crawford to JP, Jan. 29, 1884 (CU).
17. World, Sep. 22, 1884.
18. *The Works of Theodore Roosevelt*, Vol. XXIII, p. 43.
19. World, Aug. 26, 1884.

Chapter 2

1. Candace Stone, *Dana and the Sun*, p. 157; Edward P. Mitchell, *Memoirs of an Editor*, pp. 328–29.
2. Gibson to JP, Oct. 10, 1884 (CU).
3. George Cary Eggleston, *Recollections of a Varied Life*, p. 335.
4. World, June 5, 1883.
5. N.Y. Tribune, Aug. 1, 1884.
6. N.Y. Herald, Aug. 1, 1884.
7. The three quotations from the Sun are from the issues of Sep. 30, 1882; Aug. 7, 1884; Oct. 19, 1884.
8. Walt McDougall, *This Is the Life!*, pp. 96–97.
9. World, Aug. 12, 1884.
10. *The Journalist*, July 26, 1884.
11. World, Sep. 15, 1884.
12. N.Y. Tribune, Sep. 16, 1884.
13. World, Oct. 30, 1884.
14. Conkling to JP, Nov. 29, 1884 (CU).
15. *The Journalist*, Nov. 8, 1884.

Chapter 3

1. World, Oct. 2, 1886.
2. World, Mar. 14, 1885.
3. World, Jan. 9, 1885.
4. World, June 23, 1883 (quoted in George Juergens, *Joseph Pulitzer and the New York World,* p. 269).
5. World, Oct. 29, 1883.
6. The three quotations in order are from the World, Nov. 16, 1883; Jan. 13, 1884; Jan. 28, 1885.
7. World, Jan. 13, 1885.
8. World, May 27, 1884.
9. World, Oct. 13, 1883.
10. Conroy to JP, Nov. 15, 1884 (CU).
11. Keevil to JP, Nov. 17, 1885 (CU).
12. Eads to JP, Jan. 19, 1885 (CU).
13. Gibson to JP, Dec. 14, 1884 (CU).
14. Belmont to JP, Mar. 9, 1885 (CU).
15. W. M. Clarke to JP, April 11, 1885 (CU).
16. *The Journalist,* Jan. 24, 1885.
17. James Morgan, *Charles H. Taylor,* p. 114.
18. Childs to JP, Mar. 9, 1885 (CU).
19. Undated draft, unsigned (CU).
20. World, Mar. 5, 1885.
21. World, Mar. 16, 1885.
22. McDougall, *This Is the Life!,* p. 164.
23. Childs to JP, Mar. 27, 1885 (CU).
24. Reavis to JP, June 16, 1885 (CU).
25. From three Cockerill letters to JP, June 17, June 23 and June 30, 1885 (CU).
26. Dillon to JP, July 8, 1885 (CU).
27. Louisville Courier-Journal, Aug. 7, 1900 (CU).
28. Allen Churchill, *Park Row,* p. 151. See also Richard O'Connor, *The Scandalous Mr. Bennett,* pp. 137–44.
29. Quoted in George W. Childs to JP, June 27, 1887 (CU).
30. Charles Edward Russell, *These Shifting Scenes,* p. 77.
31. Cockerill to Whitney, June 22, 1885 (Whitney Prs., LC).
32. Quoted in Heaton, *The Story of a Page,* p. 34.
33. World, Sep. 12, 1885.
34. World, Sep. 10, 1885.
35. Hill to JP, Sep. 18, 1884 (CU).
36. Chauncey Depew, *My Memories of Eighty Years,* pp. 391–92.

Chapter 4

1. JP to Mother Mary Clare, Feb. 9, 1887 (CU).
2. McDougall, *This Is the Life!,* p. 103.
3. Sutton to JP, Nov. 6, 1886 (CU).
4. McDougall, *op. cit.,* p. 102.
5. Orrick Johns, *Time of Our Lives,* p. 61.
6. Dated "New Years, 1886" (CU).

7. Diary fragment dated Oct. 16 [1885] (CU).
8. Two Crawford letters to JP, Nov. 21 and Nov. 27, 1885 (CU).
9. McDougall, *op. cit.*, p. 106.
10. Miss Goff to JP, Mar. 29, 1886 (CU).
11. H. A. Brachvogel to JP, Nov. 27, 1886 (CU).
12. JP to Cleveland, June 7, 1903 (Cleveland Prs., LC).
13. JP to Crawford, Feb. 11, 1886 (CU).
14. Crawford to JP, Nov. 18, 1885 (CU).
15. Crawford to JP, Mar. 22, 1886 (CU).
16. *Ibid.*, April 13, 1886 (CU).
17. Conkling to JP, N.D. (CU).
18. E. J. Kahn Jr., *The Merry Partners,* p. 98.
19. Shafer to JP, Mar. 23, 1887 (CU).
20. Shafer to the World, May 16, [1887] (CU).
21. JP to Hill, April 14, 1886 (George S. Bixby Prs., NYSHL).
22. Biographical material in the Davidson Prs. (Yale).
23. Quotations from the World, Mar. 20, 1885, and June 2, 1886.
24. Merrill to JP, July 28, 1886 (CU).
25. Quotations from two Davidson-to-JP letters, Aug. 15 and Sep. 24, 1886 (CU).
26. JP to Davidson, Sep. 24, 1886 (Yale).
27. Pallen to JP, Oct. 23, 1886 (CU).
28. World, Aug. 5, 1884.
29. Two Depew-to-JP letters, Dec. 6 and Dec. 14, 1886 (CU).
30. Davidson to JP, Oct. 7, 1886 (CU).
31. Pallen to Mrs. Pulitzer, Nov. 3, 1886 (CU).

Chapter 5

1. World, Sep. 9, 1883.
2. Banquet quotations from N.Y. Tribune and World, both Nov. 24, 1886.
3. Jerome to JP, April 1, 1887 (CU).
4. JP to Crawford, Mar. 28, 1887 (CU).
5. Conner to JP, Oct. 18, 1886 (CU).
6. N.Y. Sun, Oct. 29, 1887.
7. World, Nov. 9, 1885.
8. Quoted in Heaton, *The Story of a Page,* p. 45.
9. Quotations in order from the World, Nov. 3, Nov. 5 and Nov. 4, 1886.
10. World, Oct. 1, 1886.
11. World, Oct. 30, 1886.
12. N.Y. Tribune, Mar. 12, 1886.
13. Newspaper clipping, N.D. (CU).
14. Childs to Mrs. Pulitzer, Nov. 27, 1886 (CU).
15. May to JP, Mar. 9 [1887?] (CU).
16. Marble to JP, Feb. 4, 1887 (CU).
17. Pallen to JP, Mar. 16, 1887 (CU).
18. Davidson to JP, Dec. 28, 1886 (CU).
19. McDougall, *op. cit.*, p. 116.
20. N.Y. Herald, Feb. 9, 1887.
21. Tiffany to JP, June 27, 1887 (CU).
22. From two Childs-to-JP letters, July 5 and July 15, 1887 (CU).
23. Crawford to JP, Aug. 13, 1887 (CU).

24. World, July 10, 1887.
25. Four Smith-to-JP letters, Aug. 6 and 25, and Sep. 7 and 10, 1887 (CU).

Chapter 6

1. N.Y. Sun, June 9, 1887.
2. Eggleston, *Recollections of a Varied Life*, p. 305.
3. N.Y. Sun, Oct. 28, 1887.
4. N.Y. Sun, Oct. 18, 1887.
5. World, Oct. 19, 1887.
6. N.Y. Sun, quoted in James W. Barrett, *Joseph Pulitzer and His World*, p. 105.
7. World, Oct. 29, 1887.
8. N.Y. Evening World, Oct. 30, 1911.
9. N.Y. Sun, Nov. 8, 1887.
10. N.Y. Sun, Nov. 9, 1887.
11. World, Nov. 10, 1887.

PART IV

Chapter 1

1. Alleyne Ireland, *op. cit.*, p. 220.
2. Whitney to Mrs. Pulitzer, Dec. 22, 1887 (CU).
3. JP to Whitney, draft, Dec. 26, 1887 (CU).
4. Marble to JP, Jan. 14, 1888 (CU).
5. N.Y. Tribune, Jan. 13, 1888.
6. Marshall Gates to JP, Feb. 27, 1888; Dr. McLane to JP, Feb. 13, 1888; and George Turner to JP, Feb. 25, 1888 (all CU).
7. Greaves to JP, Mar. 31, 1888 (CU).
8. Dr. McLane to JP, Mar. 14, 1888; and Conkling to JP, Mar. 16, 1888 (both CU).
9. N.Y. Tribune, April 11, 1888. See also Matthew P. Breen, *Thirty Years of New York Politics*, p. 767.
10. Barlow to JP, April 10, 1888 (CU).
11. World, April 11, 1888.
12. Charles H. Dennis, *Victor Lawson, His Time and Work*, p. 117.
13. George B. McClellan Jr., *The Gentleman and the Tiger*, edited by Harold C. Syrett, pp. 67–68.
14. World, Nov. 4, 1888.
15. World, Nov. 1, 2 and 3, 1888.
16. Julius Chambers, *News Hunting on Three Continents*, p. 307.
17. Ponsonby to Kate, June 21, 1889 (CU).
18. Quotations from Chambers, *op. cit.*, pp. 332–34; and Frank Wilson Nye, *Bill Nye*, p. 249.
19. JP to Kate, June 11, 1889 (CU).
20. Ponsonby to Kate, June 21, 1889 (CU).
21. Ralph D. Blumenfeld, *In the Days of Bicycles and Bustles*, p. 33.
22. World, Oct. 10, 1889.

23. Hudson Strode, *Jefferson Davis,* Vol. III, p. 510.
24. Eggleston, *op. cit.,* p. 320.

Chapter 2

1. Quoted in Seitz, *Joseph Pulitzer,* pp. 174–76.
2. Norman Thwaites, *Velvet and Vinegar,* pp. 53–54.
3. Barrett, *Joseph Pulitzer and His World,* p. 137.
4. *Ibid.,* pp. 137–38.
5. Julius Chambers, *op. cit.,* p. 331.
6. About Standard Oil: World, May 18, 1887; about Rockefeller, World, Feb. 28, 1888.
7. World, Oct. 16, 1890.
8. Mrs. William Scoville Moore told Swanberg, Mar. 10, 1965.
9. World, Dec. 10, 1890.
10. Letter Dec. 17 [1891] (CU).
11. James Barrett, *op. cit.,* p. 142.
12. *Ibid.,* p. 143.
13. *Ibid.,* p. 144.
14. JP to World, Aug. 10, 1891 (CU).
15. Charles E. Chapin, *Charles Chapin's Story,* p. 156.
16. Quotations from Julius Chambers, *op. cit.,* p. 330; from Russell, *These Shifting Scenes,* pp. 78 and 276; and from McDougall, *op. cit.,* p. 107.
17. Quotations from Russell, *op. cit.,* 273; McDougall, *op. cit.,* pp. 138 and 197; Eggleston, *op. cit.,* pp. 311–12; Cockerill, *Cosmopolitan* XIII (Oct. 1892) and Stealey, *op. cit.,* p. 344.

Chapter 3

1. Quoted in Heaton, *The Story of a Page,* p. 81.
2. JP to Smith, Feb. 17 [1892?] (CU).
3. Quoted in Willis Fletcher Johnson, *George Harvey,* p. 41.
4. Carvalho to (?), N.D. (CU).
5. World, July 3, 1892. From June 29 to July 11 the World favored the workers.
6. Johnson, *George Harvey,* pp. 41–42.
7. JP to Harvey, Aug. 6 and Aug. 22, 1892, both in Johnson, *op. cit.,* pp. 42–43.
8. Pagenstecher to Kate, 1892, date unclear (CU).
9. Miss Beere to JP, undated 1892 (CU).
10. Seitz, *op. cit.,* p. 190.
11. JP to Harvey, after Aug. 27, 1892, in Johnson, *op. cit.,* p. 44.
12. *Ibid.,* Sep. 6, 1892, in Johnson, p. 45.
13. JP to Cleveland, Nov. 9, 1892 (Cleveland Prs., LC).
14. Barrett, *Joseph Pulitzer,* p. 149.
15. Seitz, *op. cit.,* p. 192.
16. Blumenfeld, *op. cit.,* p. 53.
17. Isaac Marcosson, *David Graham Phillips,* p. 142.
18. Quoted in Heaton, *The Story of a Page,* pp. 95–96.
19. Johnson, *George Harvey,* p. 53.

20. Quoted in Barrett, *Joseph Pulitzer,* pp. 152–53.
21. Silas Bent, *Ballyhoo,* p. 77.

Chapter 4

1. Walter B. Stevens, "The New Journalism in Missouri," *MHR,* XIX, No. 4 (July 1925), p. 679.
2. Johnson, *George Harvey,* p. 57.
3. Marcosson, *David Graham Phillips,* pp. 165–66.
4. JP to Harvey, Dec. 12, 1893 and Jan. 24, 1894, both in Johnson, *op. cit.,* pp. 58–59.
5. Brisbane to Harvey, Jan. 24, 1894, in Johnson, p. 59.
6. Two Hosmer letters to Kate, Jan. 7 and Mar. 9, 1894 (CU).
7. JP to Depew, May 17, 1894 (Depew Prs., Yale).
8. Two quotations from N.Y. Times, Aug. 26 and Sep. 12, 1894.
9. World, July 4, 1894.
10. World, July 9, 1894.
11. McClellan, *The Gentleman and the Tiger,* pp. 99–100.
12. Stevens, as cited in Note 1 above, pp. 678–684.

Chapter 5

1. World code book (CU).
2. Marcosson, *op. cit.,* p. 135.
3. Joseph and E. R. Pennell, *The Whistler Journal,* p. 226.
4. JP to John McNaught, July 16, 1908 (CU).
5. JP to Davidson, June 30, 1895 (Davidson Prs., Yale).
6. World, May 17, 1895.
7. TR to Henry Cabot Lodge, quoted in Henry F. Pringle, *Theodore Roosevelt,* p. 143.
8. Quoted in Heaton, *op. cit.,* p. 108.
9. World, Sep. 26, 1895.
10. N.Y. Times, Mar. 19, 1896.
11. Samuel Flagg Bemis (ed.), *The American Secretaries of State and Their Diplomacy,* Vol. VIII, p. 306.
12. Henry James, *Richard Olney,* pp. 119–20.
13. Quotations from Sun and Tribune are from Heaton, *op. cit.,* pp. 113–14; TR letter from E. E. Morison (ed.), *The Letters of Theodore Roosevelt,* Vol. I, p. 501; and N.Y. Times, Dec. 20, 1895.
14. First quotation is from World, Dec. 21, 1895; second from Sunday World, Dec. 22, 1895.
15. Heaton, *The Story of a Page,* p. 122.
16. *Ibid.,* pp. 122–23.
17. E. E. Morison, *op. cit.,* Vol. I, p. 504.
18. Arbitration, with U.S. good offices, established the border eight years later.
19. Eggleston, *Recollections of a Varied Life,* pp. 329–30.
20. World, Jan. 3, 1896.
21. Seitz, *op. cit.,* p. 209.

PART V

Chapter 1

1. Frank Nye, *Bill Nye,* p. 396.
2. Seitz, *op. cit.*, p. 214.
3. Blumenfeld, *In the Days of Bicycles and Bustles,* pp. 66–67.
4. Wickham Steed, *Through Thirty Years,* Vol. I, pp. 75–76.
5. Watterson, *Marse Henry,* Vol I, p. 209.
6. Heaton *op. cit.*, p. 129.

Chapter 2

1. Eggleston, *op. cit.*, p. 320.
2. All directives from JP to the World, fall 1896 (LC).
3. McClellan, *op. cit.*, p. 116.
4. Willis Abbot, *Watching the World Go By,* p. 147.
5. N.Y. Journal, Nov. 8, 1896.
6. JP to Norris, Dec. 11, 1896 (CU).
7. Beatrice Fairfax, *Ladies Now and Then,* p. 21.
8. Butes to Kate, Jan. 3 [1897], (CU).
9. JP to Kate, Jan. 14, 1897 (CU).
10. Seitz, *op. cit.*, p. 233.
11. Kate to Butes, draft, June 8, 1897 (CU).
12. Jim Allee Hart, *A History of the St. Louis Globe-Democrat,* p. 168.
13. JP to Davidson, Oct. 13 and Dec. 8, 1897 (Davidson Prs., Yale).
14. The entire list of JP directives, all 1897, is from the Pulitzer Prs., LC.
15. Fitts to Davidson, Jan. 1, 1898 (Davidson Prs., Yale).
16. JP to Seitz, Feb. 3, 1898 (Pulitzer Prs., LC).

Chapter 3

1. Bradford Merrill to JP, N.D. (CU).
2. World, Mar. 19, 1895.
3. Three quotations from the World, Jan. 18, Jan. 26 and Feb. 27, 1896.
4. N.Y. Sunday Journal, Feb. 23, 1896.
5. World, May 17, 1896.
6. World, May 19, June 4, June 10, June 12, June 25 and June 28, 1896.
7. World, May 29, 1896.
8. World, Jan. 2, 1896.
9. N.Y. Herald and N.Y. World, both Oct. 13, 1896.
10. George Bronson Rea, *Facts and Fakes About Cuba,* 212–15.
11. James Creelman, *On the Great Highway,* p. 160.
12. N.Y. Journal, Mar. 29, 1897.
13. JP to Norris, Dec. 8, 1897 (Pulitzer Prs., LC).
14. JP to Seitz and Norris (in order), Dec. 23, May 21, Aug. 25, Nov. 9, Aug. 21 and Jan. 25, all 1897 (Pulitzer Prs., LC).
15. Rea, *op. cit.*, p. 200; and Ralph D. Paine, *Roads of Adventure,* pp. 62–63.
16. N.Y. Journal, Feb. 12, 1897.
17. Willis Abbot, *op. cit.*, pp. 213–14.

18. Quotations in this paragraph (in order) from the World, Jan. 12, Jan. 8, Feb. 7, and Feb. 11, 1897.
19. Journal, Feb. 20, and World, Feb. 21, 1897.
20. World, Feb. 23, 1897.
21. World, Mar. 10, 1897.

Chapter 4

1. Creelman, *On the Great Highway,* pp. 179–80.
2. N.Y. Journal, Aug. 18 and Aug. 22, 1897.
3. World, Aug. 21, 1897.
4. Rea, *op. cit.,* p. 233; also World, Sep. 9, 1897.
5. A fuller account of the "rescue" is in W. A. Swanberg's *Citizen Hearst,* pp. 119–129.
6. Creelman, *op. cit.,* pp. 185–86.
7. N.Y. Sunday Journal, Oct. 10, 1897.
8. Two JP-to-Seitz letters, Dec. 23 and Dec. 3, 1897 (Pulitzer Prs., LC).
9. To Norris, Dec. 4 and Dec. 8, 1897 (LC).
10. Stone, *Fifty Years a Journalist,* pp. 227–28; also N.Y. Times, Nov. 22, 1912.
11. JP to Seitz, May 23, 1897 (LC).
12. JP to Norris, Nov. 27, 1897 (LC).
13. N.Y. Herald, Times and Tribune, Jan. 1, 1898.
14. Norris to Chamberlin, May 1, 1897 (Seitz Prs., NYPL).
15. Ledlie to JP, Feb. 17, 1898 (CU).
16. Long list of JP directives, dated 1896, 1897 and 1898, all in the Pulitzer Prs., LC.
17. JP to Seitz, Dec. 8, 1897 (LC).

Chapter 5

1. Capt. Charles D. Sigsbee, *The Maine,* p. 76.
2. World, Feb. 16, 1898.
3. N.Y. Evening Post, Mar. 17, 1898.
4. World, Mar. 2, 1898.
5. Barrett, *op. cit.,* pp. 176–77; also, Chapin, *Charles Chapin's Story,* pp. 173–74.
6. JP to Seitz, Mar. 14, 1898 (LC).
7. JP to Seitz, Mar. 21, 1898 (LC).
8. Ledlie to Kate, April 8, 1898 (CU).
9. N.Y. Times, July 7, 1898.
10. JP to Seitz, June 3, 1898 (LC).
11. Swanberg, *Citizen Hearst,* pp. 148–49.
12. N.Y. Journal, July 20, 1898.
13. To Seitz, Sep. 10, 1898 (LC).
14. World memorandum dated Nov. 28, 1898 (LC).

PART VI

Chapter 1

1. JP to Kate, Mar. 20, 1899 (CU).
2. *Ibid.,* June 20, 1899 (CU).

3. Times clipping, N.D. 1899 (CU).
4. Leyman to JP, Oct. 9, 1899 (CU).
5. To Phillips Aug. 17, 1899, in Seitz, *op. cit.*, p. 248.
6. To Kate, Oct. 22, 1899 (CU).
7. From Davidson, Oct. 30, 1899 (CU).
8. Frederick Palmer, *With My Own Eyes,* p. 122.
9. Clarke to JP, Nov. 1, 1899 (CU).
10. JP to Kate, Nov. 2, 1899 (CU).
11. Seitz, *op. cit.*, p. 250.
12. Marcosson, *David Graham Phillips,* p. 198.
13. World, April 4, 1900; also, Mark Sullivan, *Our Times,* Vol. I, p. 310 fn.
14. N.Y. Tribune, April 5, 1900.
15. World, April 6, 1900.
16. The same.

Chapter 2

1. N.Y. Times, Jan. 10, 1900.
2. Marcosson, *op. cit.,* p. 200.
3. Whitney to JP, Mar. 2, 1900 (CU).
4. Norris to JP, April 2, 1900 (CU).
5. Duneka to JP, Feb. 5, 1900 (CU).
6. JP to Seitz, Nov. 9, 1899 (CU).
7. Mrs. Gouley to JP, April 27, 1900 (CU).
8. To St. Mark's School, draft, N.D. 1900 (CU).
9. To Seitz, N.D. 1900 (CU).
10. Two Seitz-to-JP messages, Oct. 26 and Nov. 22, 1900 (both CU).
11. Clarke to JP, Nov. 3, 1900 (CU).
12. Adam Politzer to JP, Oct. 19, 1900 (CU).
13. Kate to JP, Sep. 15, 1904 (CU).
14. Ralph to JP, N.D. (CU).
15. Tuohy to Butes, Mar. 27, 1900 (CU).
16. Kate to JP, N.D. (CU).
17. Harmsworth to JP, June 11, 1900 (CU).
18. Kate to JP, July 22, 1900 (CU).
19. H. Botsford to Matier, Aug. 31, 1900 (CU).
20. Hosmer to Kate, Oct. 15, 1900 (CU).
21. Nevill to Jerningham, Oct. 23, 1900 (CU).
22. S. M. Williams to JP, Nov. 7, 1900 (CU).
23. Leitner to JP, Dec. 2, 1900 (CU).
24. JP to Kate, Nov. 20, 1900 (CU).
25. Two Seitz messages, Oct. 22 and Oct. 26, 1900; Merrill to JP, Oct. 30, 1900 (all CU).
26. Leitner to JP, Dec. 12, 1900 (CU).
27. Letter dated Jan. 2, 1901 (CU).
28. Seitz to JP, Jan. 5, 1901 (CU).
29. Bradford Merrill to JP, Aug. 10, 1900 (CU).
30. Seitz to JP, Dec. 11, 1900 (CU).
31. Two Seitz messages, Jan. 9, 1901, and Dec. 27, 1900 (CU).
32. Brad Merrill to JP, July 28, 1902 (CU).
33. JP to White, N.D. 1905 (CU).
34. Stanford White to JP, Nov. 27, 1900 (CU).

35. JP to McKim, Mead & White, April 16 (1900?) (CU).
36. N.Y. Evening Journal, April 10, 1901.
37. N.Y. Journal, Feb. 4, 1900.
38. James W. Gerard, *My First 83 Years in America,* pp. 62, 66.
39. World, Oct. 17, 1901.
40. M. R. Werner, *Tammany Hall,* p. 340.
41. Hosmer to JP, Sep. 13, 1901 (CU).
42. JP to Seitz, Sep. 30, 1901 (CU).
43. Seitz message Sep. 17, Burton message Sep. 10, 1901 (CU).
44. Chapin to JP, April 10, 1903 (CU).
45. World, Oct. 20, 1901.
46. JP to Clarke, N.D. (CU).
47. Clarke to JP, Aug. 14, 1901 (CU).
48. To JP, Nov. 27, 1901 (CU).
49. Van Benthuysen to JP, Nov. 28, 1901 (CU).
50. Ledlie to JP, Sep. 10, 1901 (CU).
51. W. H. Merrill to JP, Feb. 16, 1902.

Chapter 3

1. Hosmer notes, N.D., CU, with punctuation added.
2. JP to Joseph Jr., N.D. (CU).
3. JP to Ralph, N.D. (CU).
4. JP to Edith, N.D. (CU).
5. Two letters from Joseph Jr., Dec. 17, 1904, and Feb. 29, 1904 (CU).
6. JP to Kate, N.D. (CU).
7. Kate to JP, Oct. 2, 1904 (CU).
8. Two messages from Kate, Oct. 29, 1904, and April 6, 1905 (CU).
9. JP to Miss Macarow, May 20, 1905 (CU).
10. Kate to JP, Mar. 24, 1905 (CU).
11. Phillips, *The Great God Success, passim.*
12. In Marcosson, *op. cit.,* p. 211.
13. Seitz, *op. cit.,* p. 432.
14. JP personal account, 1902 (CU).
15 and 16. Seitz, *op. cit.,* pp. 22–23.
17. Mar. 22, 1901 (CU).
18. JP to Clarke, Mar. 18, 1903 (CU).
19. From Tennant, Mar. 16, 1903 (CU).
20. Quoted in Bradford Merrill to JP, April 11, 1903 (CU).
21. Merlo J. Pusey, *Charles Evans Hughes,* Vol. I, p. 115.
22. May 9, 1903 (CU).
23. JP to Brad Merrill, May 30, 1903, with punctuation added (CU).
24. Excerpts from three Tuohy letters, June 21, July 7 and July 8, 1903 (CU).
25. Tuohy to JP, Sep. 3, 1903 (CU).
26. Norman Thwaites, *Velvet and Vinegar,* p. 53.
27. Quoted in Heaton, *The Story of a Page,* p. 195.
28. Hettrick account in Oral History Department, CU.
29. McClellan, *The Gentleman and the Tiger,* pp. 186–87.
30. The same, p. 217.
31. Butes to JP, Feb. 19, 1904 (CU).
32. JP to Seitz, May 14, 1901 (CU).
33. Seitz to JP, Aug. 22 (1904?) (CU).

34. Quoted in Meyer Berger, *The Story of the New York Times,* p. 153.
35. The same, p. 154.
36. Royal Cortissoz, *The Life of Whitelaw Reid,* Vol. II, p. 294.
37. To Butes, dated "Oct. 20" (CU).
38. Seitz, *op. cit.,* pp. 19–20.
39. Chapin, *Charles Chapin's Story,* pp. 218–19.
40. JP to Ralph, N.D. (CU).
41. George Cornish told Swanberg, Jan. 1, 1967.

Chapter 4

1. N.Y. Mail & Express, Nov. 26, 1887 (CU).
2. N.D., CU.
3. JP wrote an article in the *North American Review,* May 1904 issue, urging the need for a school of journalism. This is quoted here, as is a JP letter to Bradford Merrill, from Seitz, *op. cit.,* p. 452.
4. Kate to JP, May 4, 1904 (CU).
5. Aug. 17, 1903, in Seitz, *op. cit.,* p. 460.
6. JP to Dumont Clarke, N.D. (CU).
7. Allen Churchill, *Park Row,* pp. 268–69.
8. John L. Heaton, *Cobb of "The World,"* p. xv.
9. In Seitz, *op. cit.,* pp. 257–58.
10. The same, pp. 258–59, dated July 5, 1904.
11. World, Mar. 15, 1904. There had been earlier World praise of TR.
12. Ralph to JP, Jan. (?), 1904 (CU).
13. JP reply, Jan. 25, 1904 (CU).
14. Williams to JP, Feb. 27 (Murphy interview) and Feb. 25, 1904 (Bryan statement), CU.
15. Two JP-to-Merrill messages, April 19 and 27, 1904 (CU).
16. Cable May 23, 1904 (CU).
17. Excerpts from two Kate-to-JP letters, May 4 and May 13, 1904 (CU).
18. To Merrill, May 24, 1904 (CU).
19. Williams to JP, Aug. 25, 1904 (CU).
20. See Henry L. Stoddard, *As I Knew Them,* pp. 56–57. Jan. 18, 1908, Frank Cobb wrote JP (CU) of seeing Congressman John Sharp Williams, adding, "[Williams] began by lecturing me on the inherent wickedness of the *World* in stirring up Democratic strife. Then he referred to the gold telegram which you forced Parker to send, and said it split the party wide open during the campaign."
21. June 15, 1904, in Seitz, *op. cit.,* pp. 260–61.
22. Kate to JP, June 18, 1904 (CU).
23. Kate to JP, Oct. 2, 1904 (CU).
24. Thwaites, *Velvet and Vinegar,* pp. 54–55.

Chapter 5

1. Ireland, *An Adventure with a Genius,* p. 229.
2. Seitz, *op. cit.,* pp. 265–66.
3. The same, p. 271.
4. The same, p. 273.
5. Charles Merrill Mount, *John Singer Sargent,* p. 264.
6. Thwaites, *op. cit.,* p. 56.

7. Barrett, *op. cit.*, pp. 201–202.
8. Seitz, *op. cit.*, p. 275.
9. The same, pp. 276–77.
10. JP to the World, Aug. 9, 1905 (CU).
11. Pusey, *Charles Evans Hughes*, Vol. I, pp. 146, 152.
12. World, Oct. 15, 1905.
13. Two White telegrams both dated Oct. 6, 1905 (CU).
14. Pusey, *op. cit.*, Vol. I, p. 150.
15. The same, p. 150.
16. John A. Garraty, *Right-Hand Man*, p. 182.
17. See Marquis James, *The Metropolitan Life*, Chap. 9.
18. Seitz, *op. cit.*, p. 280.
19. The same, p. 275.

Chapter 6

1. Draft, June 11 [1905] CU.
2. The same.
3. Aug. 26, 1905 (CU).
4. Oct. 7, 1905 (CU).
5. JP to Ralph, Oct. 16, 1905 (CU).
6. Two messages from Ralph, Oct. 14 and 16, 1905 (CU).
7. World, Oct. 15, 1905.
8. Herbert Adams Gibbons, *John Wanamaker*, Vol. I, pp. 271–72, and Vol. II, pp. 164–66.
9. Kate to JP, N.D. (CU).
10. Kate letter, May 7, 1906 (CU).
11. Chapin, *op. cit.*, pp. 225, 228.
12. Joseph Jr. to JP, Oct. 13, 1906 (CU).
13. The same, Mar. 26, 1906 (CU).
14. Ralph to JP, Aug. 9 [1906], CU.
15. Jerome speech in N.Y. Times, Mar. 24, 1906; JP to Jerome, April 20, 1906 (CU).
16. Dated Nov. 24, 1906 (CU).
17. Albert Payson Terhune, *To the Best of My Memory*, p. 220.
18. Williams to JP, May 24, 1906 (CU).
19. Cobb to JP, after May 24, 1906 (CU).
20. See William Robinson Reynolds, *Joseph Pulitzer* (unpublished thesis, CU), pp. 637 ff.
21. Seitz, *op. cit.*, pp. 281–82.
22. Bradford Merrill to JP, N.D. (CU).
23. To Cobb, Aug. 18, 1906 (CU).
24. Seitz, *op. cit.*, pp. 287–88, dated Oct. 11, 1906.
25. N.Y. Tribune, Oct. 28, 1906.
26. JP to Kate, draft, Sep. 27 (1906?), CU.
27. Dated Dec. 1, 1906 (CU).
28. Unidentified clipping, CU.
29. Irvin S. Cobb, *Exit Laughing*, p. 132.
30. Kate to JP, Mar. 4, 1907 (CU).
31. Two Kate-to-JP letters, Feb. 13, 1907, and April 17, 1908 (CU).
32. Ralph to JP, N.D., 1907 (CU).
33. Reynolds, *op. cit.*, p. 561; Seitz, *op. cit.*, p. 38.
34. Seitz, *op. cit.*, p. 19.

35. Hamilton Fyfe, *Northcliffe*, p. 161.
36. Thwaites, *op. cit.*, pp. 61–62.

Chapter 7

1. Seitz, *op. cit.*, p. 36.
2. The same, pp. 327–28.
3. The same, p. 309.
4. The same, pp. 282–83.
5. To McNaught, July 16, 1908 (CU).
6. Seitz, *op. cit.*, p. 31. See also Reynolds, *op. cit.*, pp. 232–38.
7. Two Kate-to-JP letters, May 4 and April 16, 1908 (CU).
8. Ralph to JP, Feb. 11, 1908 (CU).
9. Three JP letters in order: N.D. 1908 (LC); Nov. 20, 1910 (LC); and June 1, 1908, to William S. Hogan (CU).
10. Seitz, *op. cit.*, p. 330.
11. The same, pp. 325–26.
12. To Ralph, N.D. (spring, 1908), LC.
13. July 6, 1908 (CU).
14. James Morgan, *Charles H. Taylor*, p. 155.
15. Donald Henderson Clarke, *Man of the World*, p. 82.
16. Barrett, *Joseph Pulitzer*, pp. 210–14.
17. Thwaites, *op. cit.*, p. 59.
18. Seitz, *op. cit.*, p. 343.
19. The same, p. 343–44, dated Oct. 2, 1908.
20. Portions of three JP-to-Kate messages, Oct. 1, Oct. 3 and Oct. 17, 1908 (all CU).
21. To Kate, Oct. 10 and Oct. 17, 1908 (CU).
22. Nov. 1, [1908], CU.
23. In Seitz, *op. cit.*, pp. 346–48.
24. The same, p. 350.
25. The same, p. 351.
26. James Barnes, *From Then Till Now*, p. 364.
27. June 12, 1909 (CU).
28. Joseph Jr. to JP, Feb. 15, 1907 (CU).
29. N.D., CU.
30. Ralph to JP, Nov. 25 [1905], CU.
31. Undated 1907, CU.
32. Two Kate-to-JP letters, one N.D., the other Jan. 9, 1906 (CU).
33. Two JP-to-Ralph messages, N.D. (CU).
34. Draft, Jan. 25 (1904?), with punctuation added (CU).
35. To Ralph, Aug. 13, 1908 (CU).
36. Ralph to JP, Dec. 6 [1908], CU.
37. Bowers note included in Ralph to JP, N.D. (CU).

Chapter 8

1. Pringle, *Theodore Roosevelt*, p. 304.
2. The same, p. 311.
3. World, June 14, 1903.
4. E. Taylor Parks, *Columbia and the United States*, pp. 395–402.
5. The Panama affair is discussed in Pringle, *op. cit.*, pp. 301–333; George E.

Mowry, *The Era of Theodore Roosevelt,* pp. 150–55; Joseph Bucklin Bishop, *Theodore Roosevelt and His Time,* Vol. I, Chaps. 24–25; Tyler Dennett, *John Hay,* pp. 370–76. Under President Wilson in 1914 there was a movement, postponed by war, to proffer Columbia an apology and $25,000,000. The payment was finally made in 1921, under Harding, but without the apology.

6. World, Oct. 3, 1908.
7. Barnes, *From Then Till Now,* pp. 365–66.
8. Seitz, *op. cit.,* p. 356.
9. World, Dec. 8, 1908.
10. Pringle, *op. cit.,* p. 336.
11. Barrett, *op. cit.,* p. 233.
12. World, Dec. 16, 1908.
13. Thwaites, *op. cit.,* pp. 57–58.
14. World, Dec. 16, 1908.
15. Barrett, *op. cit.,* pp. 187–88.
16. Dec. 23, 1908, in Seitz, *op. cit.,* p. 369.
17. Irvin S. Cobb, *Exit Laughing,* p. 131.
18. The same, pp. 156–59.
19. Lawrence Abbott (ed.), *The Letters of Archie Butt,* p. 314.
20. World, Feb. 18, 1909.
21. Ralph to JP, Feb. 9, 1909 (CU).
22. Seitz, *op. cit.,* p. 373.
23. N.D., the same, pp. 371–72.
24. Barrett, *op. cit.,* p. 240.
25. Hosmer to JP, April 13, 1909 (CU).
26. N.D., Seitz, *op. cit.,* pp. 372–73.
27. The same, pp. 374–75.
28. The same, p. 376.
29. To Philander Knox, in Pringle, *op. cit.,* p. 332.
30. JP to Cobb, Mar. 29, 1909 (LC).
31. Pollard to Tuohy, May 25, 1909 (CU).
32. Barnes, *op. cit.,* p. 371.
33. Barnes, pp. 374, 376.
34. The same, pp. 366, 368–69.
35. To Cobb, Sep. 10, 1909 (LC).

Chapter 9

1. To Seymour, Mar. 11, 1909 (CU).
2. Thwaites, *op. cit.,* pp. 64–65.
3. World, Oct. 13, 1909.
4. Seitz, *op. cit.,* p. 392.
5. Ireland, *An Adventure with a Genius,* p. 41.
6. The same, p. 203.
7. Tuohy to JP, Nov. 22, 1909 (CU).
8. Seitz, *op. cit.,* pp. 392–93.
9. The same, p. 4.
10. Heaton, *The Story of a Page,* p. 279.
11. In Seitz, *op. cit.,* p. 395, dated Mar. 9, 1910.
12. April 19 [1910], CU.
13. In Seitz, pp. 401–402.
14. The same, p. 403.

15. N.Y. Times, Nov. 14, 1911.
16. To White June 7, to Cobb June 8, 1910 (CU).
17. Notes dated July 14, [1910], CU.
18. To Ralph Aug. 12, 1910 (LC). See also James W. Markham, *Bovard of the Post Dispatch,* p. 88.
19. Barnes, *op. cit.,* p. 382.
20. JP to Cobb, Aug. 6, 1910 (LC).
21. In Seitz, *op. cit.,* pp. 416–17.
22. The same, pp. 418–19.
23. JP to Kate, Oct. 28 [1910], CU.
24. McNaught to JP, Dec. 28, 1910 (CU).
25. JP to Johns, Dec. 5, 1910 (LC).
26. Dec. 22, 1910, in Seitz, pp. viii, ix.
27. To Mrs. Tuohy, Dec. 31, 1910 (CU).
28. Two JP-to-Lincoln letters, in Seitz, pp. 420–21.
29. World, Jan. 4, 1911.

Chapter 10

1. To Watterson, Feb. 25, 1911 (CU).
2. Seitz, *op. cit.,* p. 408.
3. Jan. 30, 1911, Seitz Prs., NYPL.
4. Feb. 3, 1911, in Seitz, *Joseph Pulitzer,* pp. 424–25.
5. Ireland, *An Adventure with a Genius,* p. 37.
6. Ireland, "A Modern Superman," *American Magazine,* Vol. 73, No. 6 (April 1912), p. 660.
7. Ireland, *An Adventure with a Genius,* pp. 46, 48, 49–50, 52, 53.
8. The same, pp. 62–66, 82–83.
9. World, Oct. 30, 1911.
10. Ireland, *Adventure,* pp. 135, 80, 93, 139.
11. The same, pp. 47, 159.
12. Reynolds, *Joseph Pulitzer,* p. 245.
13. Quotations from Barnes, *op. cit.,* p. 366; Thwaites, *op. cit.,* p. 60; and Ireland, *Adventure,* p. 141.
14. Ireland, *Adventure,* 106–116.
15. The same, pp. 181, 202, 184.
16. The same, pp. 215, 225–26, 221.
17. July 4, 1911, in Seitz, *op. cit.,* p. 410.
18. In order: to Kate, Sep. 4, 1911; to Joseph Jr., Sep. 7; to Tuohy, Sep. 4; to Billing, Sep. 7; to Cobb, Sep. 7; to Shaw, Sep. 29; to Ralph, Sep. 17; to Kate, Sep. 17, 1911 (all CU).
19. JP to Cobb, Oct. 2, 1911, in Seitz, *op. cit.,* pp. 411–13.
20. Mark Sullivan, *Our Times,* Vol. III, Chap. 10.
21. Barnes, *op. cit.,* p. 396.
22. JP's last hours are described in the Charleston News & Courier and the Charleston Evening Post, Oct. 30, 1911, as well as the N.Y. World and virtually every other daily newspaper. Ireland, *Adventure,* pp. 234–36, gives the impressions of one present.

Bibliography

The largest group of Pulitzer papers is in the Special Collections at Butler Library, Columbia University. Comprising some 25,000 pieces, the collection has been arranged in rough chronological order but not yet catalogued. A few of the personal letters are charred, some almost illegible, perhaps as a result of the 1900 fire that gutted the Pulitzer home and which may have destroyed some letters entirely. The Pulitzer Collection at the Library of Congress is less than half as large but still sizable. Other places in which Pulitzer letters were found are listed below.

The most thoroughgoing study is the unpublished doctoral dissertation *Joseph Pulitzer,* by William Robinson Reynolds. Among published works, Don C. Seitz's *Joseph Pulitzer—His Life and Letters* is a valuable all-around portrait, with the insights of a World executive who knew his employer well. James W. Barrett's *Joseph Pulitzer and His World* tells of Pulitzer's life and continues the story to include the last years of the World. Alleyne Ireland's *An Adventure with a Genius* is a splendid personal account of the man by one of his last secretary-companions. The *Missouri Historical Review* was a source of information about Pulitzer's St. Louis years. Newspapers consulted are cited in the Notes.

Two excellent special studies have recently been published by the Princeton University Press: Julian Rammelkamp's *Pulitzer's Post-Dispatch,* which closes a great gap with its careful and perceptive examination of his journalistic and political career in St. Louis; and George Juergens' *Joseph Pulitzer and the New York World,* a skillful investigation of his journalistic techniques during his first years in New York.

Unpublished Collections

George S. Bixby Papers, New York State Historical Library.
Grover Cleveland Papers, Library of Congress.
Thomas Davidson Papers, Yale University.
Chauncey Depew Papers, Yale University.
Hemphill Family Papers, Duke University.
John T. Hettrick Narrative, Oral History Project, Columbia University.
John J. Jennings Papers, Yale University.
Joseph Pulitzer Papers, Columbia University.
Joseph Pulitzer Papers, Library of Congress.

Carl Schurz Papers, Library of Congress.
Don C. Seitz Papers, New York Public Library.
Henry Watterson Papers, Library of Congress.
William C. Whitney Papers, Library of Congress.

Books

Abbot, Willis J. *Watching the World Go By,* Boston, 1933.
Abbott, Lawrence (ed.), *The Letters of Archie Butt,* New York, 1924.
Abels, Jules. *The Rockefeller Billions,* New York, 1965.
Alexander, DeAlva S. *Four Famous New Yorkers* (Cleveland, Platt, Hill and Roosevelt), New York, 1923.
Allen, Frederick Lewis. *The Great Pierpont Morgan,* New York, 1956.
Amory, Cleveland. *The Last Resorts,* New York, 1948.
Andrews, Wayne. *The Vanderbilt Legend,* New York, 1941.
Ayer, Mary Hubbard, and Isabella Taves. *The Three Lives of Harriet Hubbard Ayer,* Philadelphia, 1957.
Baehr, Harry W. *The New York Tribune Since the Civil War,* New York, 1936.
Baldwin, Charles C. *Stanford White,* New York, 1931.
Barnes, James. *From Then Till Now,* New York, 1934.
Barrett, James Wyman. *Joseph Pulitzer and His World,* New York, 1941.
———. *The World, The Flesh and Messrs. Pulitzer,* New York, 1931.
Barrett, James Wyman (ed.). *The End of The World,* New York, 1931.
Barry, David S. *Forty Years in Washington,* Boston, 1924.
Bass, Herbert J. "I AM A DEMOCRAT": *The Political Career of David Bennett Hill,* Syracuse, 1961.
Beard, Charles A. and Mary R. *The Rise of American Civilization,* 2 vols., New York, 1927.
Beebe, Lucius. *The Big Spenders,* New York, 1966.
Beer, Thomas. *The Mauve Decade,* New York, 1926.
———. *Hanna,* New York, 1929.
Bemis, Samuel Flagg (ed.). *The American Secretaries of State and Their Diplomacy,* New York, 1928.
Benson, E. F. *As We Were,* London, 1930.
———. *King Edward VII,* London, 1934.
Bent, Silas. *Ballyhoo,* New York, 1927.
———. *Newspaper Crusaders,* New York, 1927.
Berger, Meyer. *The Story of the New York Times, 1851–1951,* New York, 1951.
Bigelow, Poultney. *Seventy Summers,* 2 vols., London, 1925.
Bishop, Joseph Bucklin. *Theodore Roosevelt and His Time,* 2 vols., New York, 1926.
Bleyer, Willard G. *Main Currents in the History of American Journalism,* Boston, 1927.
Blumenfeld, Ralph D. *In the Days of Bicycles and Bustles: The Diary of R. D. Blumenfeld 1883–1914,* New York, 1930.
———. *The Press in My Time,* London, 1933.
Bly, Nellie (pseud. for Elizabeth Cochrane). *Nellie Bly's Book,* New York, 1890.
Breen, Matthew P. *Thirty Years of New York Politics,* New York, 1899.
Britt, George. *Forty Years, Forty Millions,* a biography of Frank Munsey, New York, 1935.
Brown, Henry Collins. *In the Golden Nineties,* Hastings-on-Hudson, N.Y., 1928.
Butler, Nicholas Murray. *Across the Busy Years,* 2 vols., New York, 1935–39.
Campbell's Gazetteer of Missouri. Anonymous, St. Louis, 1875.

Carlson, Oliver. *Brisbane,* New York, 1937.
Chambers, Julius. *News Hunting on Three Continents,* New York, 1921.
Chambers, Walter. *Samuel Seabury—A Challenge,* New York, 1932.
Chapin, Charles E. *Charles Chapin's Story: Written in Sing Sing Prison,* New York, 1920.
Chidsey, Donald Barr. *The Gentleman from New York,* a biography of Roscoe Conkling, New Haven, 1935.
Churchill, Allen. *Park Row,* New York, 1958.
Clark, Champ. *My Quarter Century of American Politics,* 2 vols., New York, 1920.
Clarke, Donald Henderson. *Man of The World,* New York, 1950.
Clarke, Joseph I. C. *My Life and Memories,* New York, 1925.
Cleveland, Grover. *Letters of Grover Cleveland* (Allan Nevins, ed.), Boston, 1933.
Cobb, Irvin S. *Exit Laughing,* Indianapolis, 1941.
Commercial and Architectural St. Louis. Anonymous, St. Louis, 1888.
Corey, Lewis. *The House of Morgan,* New York, 1930.
Cortissoz, Royal. *The Life of Whitelaw Reid,* 2 vols., London, 1921.
Cox, James. *Old and New St. Louis,* St. Louis, 1894.
Creelman, James. *On the Great Highway,* Boston, 1901.
Croly, Herbert. *Marcus Alonzo Hanna,* New York, 1912.
———. *The Promise of American Life,* New York, 1909.
Dacus, J. A., and James W. Buel. *A Tour of St. Louis,* St. Louis, 1878.
Dark, Sidney. *The Life of Sir Arthur Pearson,* London, 1922.
Davis, Oscar King. *Released for Publication,* Boston, 1925.
Dennett, Tyler. *John Hay: From Poetry to Politics,* New York, 1933.
Dennis, Charles H. *Victor Lawson, His Time and Work,* Chicago, 1935.
Depew, Chauncey M. *My Memories of Eighty Years,* New York, 1922.
Dixon, William Hepworth. *New America,* Philadelphia, 1869.
Dorsey, Florence. *Road to the Sea: The Story of James B. Eads,* New York, 1947.
Downey, Fairfax. *Portrait of an Era, As Drawn by C. D. Gibson,* New York, 1936.
———. *Richard Harding Davis: His Day,* New York, 1933.
Eggleston, George Cary. *Recollections of a Varied Life,* New York, 1910.
Ellis, Elmer. *Mr. Dooley's America,* New York, 1941.
Fairfax, Beatrice (pseud. for Marie Manning). *Ladies Now and Then,* New York, 1944.
Faulkner, Harold. *Politics, Reform and Expansion, 1890–1900,* New York, 1959.
Filler, Louis. *Crusaders for American Liberalism,* Yellow Springs, O., 1961.
Fiske, Stephen. *Off-Hand Portraits of Prominent New Yorkers,* New York, 1884.
Flick, Alexander C. *Samuel J. Tilden,* New York, 1939.
Ford, Edwin H., and Edwin Emery (eds.). *Highlights in the History of the American Press,* Minneapolis, 1954.
Fuess, Claude Moore. *Carl Schurz, Reformer,* New York, 1932.
Fyfe, Hamilton. *Northcliffe: An Intimate Biography,* New York, 1930.
Gardiner, A. G. *Pillars of Society,* New York, 1914.
Gardner, Gilson. *Lusty Scripps,* New York, 1932.
Garraty, John A. *Right-Hand Man: The Life of George W. Perkins,* New York, 1957.
Gerard, James W. *My First 83 Years in America,* New York, 1951.
Golding, Louis T. *Memories of Old Park Row* (pamphlet), New York, 1946.
Gosnell, Harold F. *Boss Platt and His New York Machine,* Chicago, 1924.
Gregory, Horace. *The World of James McNeill Whistler,* New York, 1959.
Hale, William Harlan. *Horace Greeley, Voice of the People,* New York, 1950.
Hapgood, Norman. *The Changing Years,* New York, 1930.
———. *The Stage in America,* New York, 1901.
Hart, Jim Allee. *A History of the St. Louis Globe-Democrat,* Columbia, Mo., 1961.

Harvey, George. *Henry Clay Frick,* New York, 1928.
Heaton, John L. *Cobb of "The World,"* New York, 1924.
———. *The Story of a Page,* New York, 1913.
Hendrick, Burton J. *The Training of an American,* Boston, 1928.
Hibben, Paxton. *The Peerless Leader,* New York, 1929.
Hicks, John D. *The Populist Revolt,* Minneapolis, 1931.
Hirsch, Mark D. *William C. Whitney, Modern Warwick,* New York, 1948.
Hofstadter, Richard. *The Age of Reform,* New York, 1955.
———. *The American Political Tradition,* New York, 1951.
Hohenberg, John. *The Pulitzer Prize Story,* New York, 1959.
How, Louis. *James B. Eads,* Boston, 1900.
Hudson, William C. *Random Recollections of an Old Political Reporter,* New York, 1911.
Huneker, James Gibbons. *Steeplejack,* 2 vols., New York, 1920.
Ireland, Alleyne. *An Adventure with a Genius,* New York, 1920.
Irwin, Will. *The Making of a Reporter,* New York, 1942.
———. *Propaganda and the News,* New York, 1936.
James, Henry. *Richard Olney and His Public Service,* Boston, 1923.
James, Marquis. *The Metropolitan Life,* New York, 1947.
Jenkins, Roy. *Victorian Scandal,* New York, 1965.
Jessup, Philip G. *Elihu Root,* 2 vols., New York, 1938.
Johns, Orrick. *Time of Our Lives,* New York, 1927.
Johnson, Gerald W. *An Honorable Titan,* New York, 1946.
Johnson, Willis Fletcher. *George Harvey, A Passionate Patriot, Boston,* 1929.
Jordan, Elizabeth. *Three Rousing Cheers,* New York, 1938.
Josephson, Matthew. *The Politicos,* New York, 1938.
———. *The Robber Barons,* New York, 1934.
Juergens, George. *Joseph Pulitzer and the New York World,* Princeton, 1966.
Kahn, E. J. Jr. *The Merry Partners: The Age and Stage of Harrigan & Hart,* New York, 1955.
———. *The World of Swope,* New York, 1965.
Kennedy, A. L. *Salisbury: Portrait of a Statesman,* London, 1953.
King, Homer W. *Pulitzer's Prize Editor,* Durham, N.C., 1965.
Kohlsaat, H. H. *From McKinley to Harding,* New York, 1923.
Krock, Arthur (ed.). *The Editorials of Henry Watterson,* New York, 1923.
Laver, James. *Edwardian Promenade,* Boston, 1958.
Leech, Margaret. *In the Days of McKinley,* New York, 1959.
Leslie, Anita. *The Remarkable Mr. Jerome,* New York, 1954.
Loeb, Isidor, and Floyd C. Shoemaker. *Journal, Missouri Constitutional Convention of 1875,* 2 vols., Columbia, Mo., 1920.
Long, J. C. *Bryan, the Great Commoner,* New York, 1928.
Longford, Elizabeth. *Victoria R.I.* London, 1964.
Lyon, Peter. *Success Story: The Life and Times of S. S. McClure,* New York, 1963.
McAllister, Ward. *Society as I Have Found It,* New York, 1890.
McClellan, George Brinton Jr. *The Gentleman and the Tiger* (autobiography, edited by Harold C. Syrett), Philadelphia, 1956.
McDonald, John. *Secrets of the Great Whiskey Ring,* St. Louis, 1880.
McDougall, Walt. *This Is the Life!,* New York, 1926.
McElroy, Robert. *Jefferson Davis,* 2 vols., New York, 1937.
———. *Levi Parsons Morton,* New York, 1930.
Marcosson, Isaac F. *David Graham Phillips and His Times,* New York, 1932.
———. *"Marse Henry": A Biography of Henry Watterson,* New York, 1951.
Markham, James W. *Bovard of the Post-Dispatch,* Baton Rouge, 1954.

Martin, Frederick Townsend. *Things I Remember,* New York, 1913.
Merriam, George S. *The Life and Times of Samuel Bowles,* 2 vols., New York, 1885.
Millis, Walter. *The Martial Spirit,* Boston, 1931.
Missouri: A Guide to the "Show Me" State, New York, 1941.
Missouri State Gazetteer, 1885–86, Detroit, 1885.
Mitchell, Edward P. *Memoirs of an Editor,* New York, 1924.
Morell, Parker. *Lillian Russell,* New York, 1940.
Morgan, James. *Charles H. Taylor: Builder of the Boston Globe,* Boston, 1923.
Morris, Clara. *Life on the Stage,* London, 1902.
Mott, Frank Luther. *American Journalism: A History of Newspapers in the United States through 250 Years,* New York, 1941.
Mount, Charles Merrill. *John Singer Sargent,* New York, 1955.
Mowry, George E. *The Era of Theodore Roosevelt,* New York, 1958.
Muzzey, David S. *James G. Blaine,* New York, 1934.
Nevill, Ralph. *London Clubs,* London, 1911.
Nevins, Allan. *Abram S. Hewitt,* New York, 1935.
———. *The Evening Post,* New York, 1922.
———. *Grover Cleveland: A Study in Courage,* New York, 1932.
———. *Hamilton Fish: The Inner History of the Grant Administration,* New York, 1937.
———. *John D. Rockefeller,* 2 vols., New York, 1940.
Noble, Iris. *Nellie Bly,* New York, 1956.
Noyes, Alexander Dana. *Forty Years of American Finance,* New York, 1909.
Nye, Frank Wilson. *Bill Nye—His Own Life Story,* New York, 1926.
O'Brien, Frank M. *The Story of the Sun,* New York, 1928.
O'Connor, Richard. *Courtroom Warrior: The Combative Career of William Travers Jerome,* Boston, 1963.
———. *Gould's Millions,* New York, 1962.
———. *The Scandalous Mr. Bennett,* New York, 1962.
Palmer, Frederick. *With My Own Eyes,* Indianapolis, 1933.
Parks, E. Taylor. *Colombia and the United States, 1765–1934,* Durham, N.C., 1935.
Peacock, Virginia Tatnall. *Famous American Belles of the 19th Century,* Philadelphia, 1901.
Pauli, Hertha, and E. B. Ashton. *I Lift My Lamp,* New York, 1948.
Pearson, Hesketh. *Labby,* London, 1937.
Peck, Harry Thurston. *Twenty Years of the Republic,* New York, 1913.
Pennell, Joseph and E. R. *The Whistler Journal,* Philadelphia, 1921.
Phillips, David Graham (pseud. "John Graham"). *The Great God Success,* New York, 1901.
Pink, Louis Heaton. *Gaynor,* New York, 1931.
Pollard, James E. *The Presidents and the Press,* New York, 1947.
Pringle, Henry F. *Theodore Roosevelt,* New York, 1931.
Pulitzer, Ralph. *New York Society on Parade,* New York, 1910.
Pusey, Merlo J. *Charles Evans Hughes,* 2 vols., New York, 1952.
Rainsford, W. S. *The Story of a Varied Life,* New York, 1922.
Rammelkamp, Julian S. *Pulitzer's Post-Dispatch,* Princeton, 1967.
Ratner, Sidney (ed.). *New Light on the History of Great American Fortunes,* New York, 1953.
Rea, George Bronson. *Facts and Fakes About Cuba,* New York, 1897.
Reavis, L. U. *St. Louis, the Future Great City of the World,* St. Louis, 1871.
Reynolds, William Robinson. *Joseph Pulitzer,* unpublished dissertation, Columbia University, New York.
Rhodes, James Ford. *The McKinley and Roosevelt Administrations,* New York, 1922.

Richter, Werner. *Bismarck,* London, 1964.
Riis, Jacob A. *How the Other Half Lives,* New York, 1890.
Roosevelt, Theodore (E. E. Morison, ed.). *The Letters of Theodore Roosevelt,* Cambridge, Mass., 1951.
———. *An Autobiography,* New York, 1925.
Rosebault, Charles J. *When Dana Was the Sun,* New York, 1931.
Roseboom, Eugene A. *A History of Presidential Elections,* New York, 1957.
Rosewater, Victor. *History of Cooperative Newsgathering in the United States,* New York, 1930.
Ross, Earle D. *The Liberal Republican Movement,* New York, 1919.
Ross, Ishbel. *First Lady of the South,* New York, 1958.
———. *Ladies of the Press,* New York, 1936.
Russell, Charles Edward. *Bare Hands and Stone Walls,* New York, 1933.
———. *These Shifting Scenes,* New York, 1914.
———. *Blaine of Maine,* New York, 1931.
St. Louis Illustrated, anonymous, St. Louis, 1876.
Schlesinger, Arthur Meier. *The Rise of the City, 1878–1898,* New York, 1933.
Schurz, Carl. *Reminiscences of Carl Schurz,* 3 vols., New York, 1908.
Seitz, Don C. *The James Gordon Bennetts,* Indianapolis, 1928.
———. *Joseph Pulitzer: His Life and Letters,* New York, 1924.
Sigsbee, Captain Charles D. *The Maine,* New York, 1899.
Simonis, H. *The Street of Ink,* London, 1917.
Smith, William Ernest. *The Francis Preston Blair Family in Politics,* 2 vols., New York, 1933.
Stealey, O. O. *Twenty Years in the Press Gallery,* New York, 1906.
———. *130 Pen Pictures of Live Men,* New York, 1910.
Steed, Henry Wickham. *Through Thirty Years,* 2 vols., London, 1924.
Steffens, Lincoln. *The Shame of the Cities,* New York, 1904.
Steiner, Edward A. *From Alien to Citizen,* New York, 1914.
Stoddard, Henry L. *As I Knew Them,* New York, 1927.
Stoddard, Lothrop. *Master of Manhattan: The Life of Richard Croker,* New York, 1931.
Stone, Candace. *Dana and the Sun,* New York, 1938.
Stone, Melville E. *Fifty Years a Journalist,* New York, 1921.
Strode, Hudson. *Jefferson Davis,* 3 vols., New York, 1964.
Sullivan, Mark. *Our Times,* New York, 1926 ff.
Swanberg, W. A. *Citizen Hearst,* New York, 1961.
Switzler, W. F. *Switzler's Illustrated History of Missouri,* St. Louis, 1881.
Terhune, Albert Payson. *To The Best of My Memory,* New York, 1930.
Thomas, Augustus. *The Print of My Remembrance,* New York, 1922.
Thwaites, Norman. *Velvet and Vinegar,* London, 1932.
Tuchman, Barbara. *The Proud Tower,* New York, 1966.
Van Wyck, Frederick. *Recollections of an Old New Yorker,* New York, 1932.
Villard, Oswald Garrison. *Fighting Years,* New York, 1939.
———. *Some Newspapers and Newspapermen,* New York, 1923.
Violette, Eugene M. *A History of Missouri,* New York, 1918.
Walker, James Blaine. *Fifty Years of Rapid Transit,* New York, 1918.
Wall, E. Berry. *Neither Pest Nor Puritan,* New York, 1940.
Watterson, Henry. *Marse Henry, An Autobiography,* 2 vols., New York, 1919.
Wecter, Dixon. *The Saga of American Society,* New York, 1937.
Weitenkamp, Frank, and Allan Nevins. *A Century of Political Cartoons,* New York, 1944.
Werner, M. R. *It Happened in New York,* New York, 1957.

———. *Tammany Hall,* New York, 1928.
Wheeler, Everett P. *Sixty Years of American Life,* New York, 1917.
White, Horace. *The Life of Lyman Trumbull,* Boston, 1913.
Who's Who on the World, anonymous, N.D., after 1920 (pamphlet published by the World).
Wilkerson, M. A. *Public Opinion and the Spanish-American War,* Baton Rouge, 1932.
Winkler, John K. *Hearst: An American Phenomenon,* New York, 1928.
Winter, William. *The American Stage of Today,* New York, 1909.
Winwar, Frances. *Oscar Wilde and the Yellow Nineties,* New York, 1958.
Wisan, Joseph E. *The Cuban Crisis as Reflected in the New York Press,* New York, 1934.
Young, John Russell. *Men and Memories,* New York, 1901.

Articles

Barclay, Thomas S. "The Liberal Republican Movement in Missouri," *Missouri Historical Review,* Vols. XX and XXI (Oct. 1925, Jan. 1926, April 1926, July 1926 and Oct. 1926).
Brisbane, Arthur. "Joseph Pulitzer," *Cosmopolitan,* May, 1902.
Cockerill, John A. "Some Phases of Contemporary Journalism," *Cosmopolitan,* Oct. 1892.
Creelman, James. "Joseph Pulitzer—Master Journalist," *Pearson's Magazine,* XXI (Mar. 1909).
———. "The Dramatic Intensity of Joseph Pulitzer," *Current Literature,* XLVI (April 1909).
Forbes, Cleon. "The St. Louis School of Thought," *Missouri Historical Review,* XXV (Oct. 1930, Jan. 1931, April 1931, July 1931).
Hapgood, Hutchins, and Arthur Bartlett Maurice. "The Great Newspapers of the United States," *Bookman,* XV (Mar. 1902).
Hettrick, John T. Unpublished account, Oral History Project, Columbia University Library.
Hyde, William. "Newspapers and Newspaper People of Three Decades," *Missouri Historical Society Collections,* I, No. 12, 1896.
Inglis, William. "An Intimate View of Joseph Pulitzer," *Harper's Weekly,* LV (Nov. 11, 1911).
Ireland, Alleyne. "A Modern Superman," *American Magazine,* LXXIII (April 1912).
Johns, George S. "Joseph Pulitzer in St. Louis," *Missouri Historical Review,* XXV and XXVI (Jan. 1931, April 1931, July 1931, Oct. 1931).
Judson, Frederick N. "The Administration of Governor B. Gratz Brown," *Missouri Historical Society Collections,* II, No. 2 (April 1903).
McDougall, Walt. "Old Days on *The World,*" *American Mercury,* IV (Jan. 1925).
Pulitzer, Joseph. "The College of Journalism," *North American Review,* May, 1904.
Stevens, Walter B. "Joseph B. McCullagh," *Missouri Historical Review,* XXV to XXVIII, in every issue from Oct. 1930 to April 1934 inclusive.
———. "The New Journalism in Missouri," *MHR,* XVIII to XIX, in every issue from April 1923 to July 1925 inclusive.
———. "The Political Turmoil of 1874 in Missouri," *MHR,* XXXI (Oct. 1936).

Index

Books by W. A. Swanberg

THE RECTOR AND THE ROGUE

PULITZER

DREISER

CITIZEN HEARST

JIM FISK:
The Career of an Improbable Rascal

FIRST BLOOD:
The Story of Fort Sumter

SICKLES THE INCREDIBLE